HAVANA
HANDBOOK

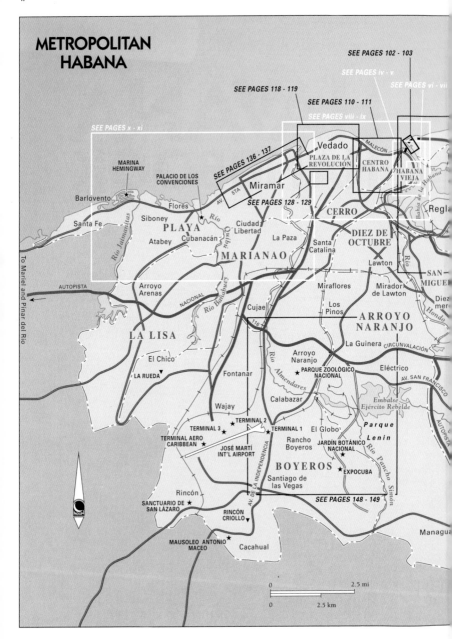

METROPOLITAN HABANA

SEE PAGES 102 - 103

SEE PAGES iv - v

SEE PAGES vi - vii

SEE PAGES 118 - 119

SEE PAGES 110 - 111

SEE PAGES viii - ix

SEE PAGES x - xi

SEE PAGES 136 - 137

Vedado

MALECÓN

MARINA HEMINGWAY

PALACIO DE LOS CONVENCIONES

PLAZA DE LA REVOLUCIÓN

CENTRO HABANA

HABANA VIEJA

Barlovento

Florés

Miramar

SEE PAGES 128 - 129

AV. 5TA.

Bahía de la Habana

Regl

Santa Fe

Siboney

PLAYA

Río Quibú

Ciudad Libertad

La Paza

CERRO

Río Jaimanitas

Cubanacán

Santa Catalina

DIEZ DE OCTUBRE

Atabey

MARIANAO

SAN-MIGUEL

Lawton

Río

To Mariel and Pinar del Rio

AUTOPISTA

Arroyo Arenas

NACIONAL

Miraflores

Mirador de Lawton

Diez mer Hondo

Río Bubuhey

Cujae

Los Pinos

ARROYO NARANJO

LA LISA

116

La Guinera

CIRCUNVALACIÓN

El Chico

Río Almendares

Arroyo Naranjo

Eléctrico

LA RUEDA

Fontanar

PARQUE ZOOLÓGICO NACIONAL

AV. SAN FRANCISCO

Wajay

Calabazar

Embalse Ejército Rebelde

AUTOPISTA

TERMINAL 3

TERMINAL 2

TERMINAL 1

El Globo

Parque Lenin

TERMINAL AERO CARIBBEAN

JOSÉ MARTÍ INT'L AIRPORT

Rancho Boyeros

JARDÍN BOTÁNICO NACIONAL

Río Pancho Simón

AV. DE LA INDEPENDENCIA

BOYEROS

EXPOCUBA

Rincón

Santiago de las Vegas

SEE PAGES 148 - 149

SANCTUARIO DE SAN LÁZARO

RINCÓN CRIOLLO

Managua

MAUSOLEO ANTONIO MACEO

Cacahual

MOON

0   2.5 mi

0   2.5 km

STRAITS OF FLORIDA

SEE PAGES 154 - 155

Camilo Cienfuegos

Cojimar

Alamar

VIA BLANCA

TORREON DE BACURANAO

Celimar

SEE PAGES 164 - 165

Tarará

Playas del Este

Antonio Guiteras

REGLA

Río Cojimar

Guanabacoa

Presa la Ceiba

Santa Fe

Río Bacuranao

MARTI

Río Tarará

Santa María del Este

Boca Ciega

Guanabo

Río Itabo

Río Guanabo

Río Peñas Altas

To Matanzas and Varadero

Presa las Monjas

MONUMENTAL

AUTOPISTA

DEL PADRÓN

Presa el Pitirre

Presa las Palmas

Presa Bacuranao

Minas

HABANAS DEL ESTE

MARTI

Campo Florida

San Francisco de Paula

VIA

GUANABACOA

NACIONAL

Santa María del Rosario

Presa la Zarza

Río

Presa la Coca

Cotorro

CARRETERA CENTRAL

COTORRO

100

Río Almendares

101

HABANA

Cuatro Caminos

MELENA

MAP SYMBOLS

Divided Highway
Primary Road
Secondary Road
Pedestrian
Footpath
Tunnel
Ferry
Railroad
District Boundary

★ Point of Interest
• Accommodation
▾ Restaurant/Bar
▪ Other Location
　 Park
　 Plaza
　 Moat or Fountain

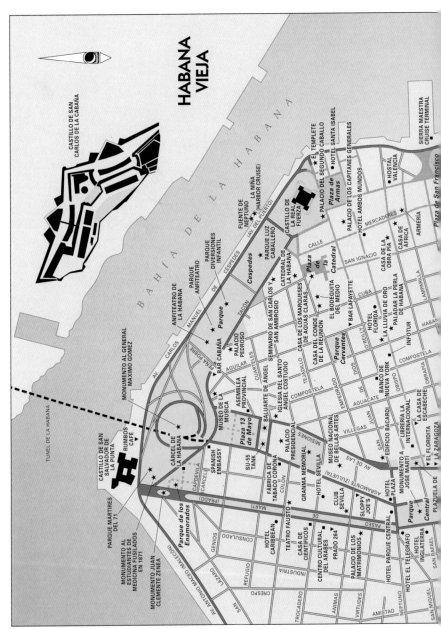

HABANA VIEJA

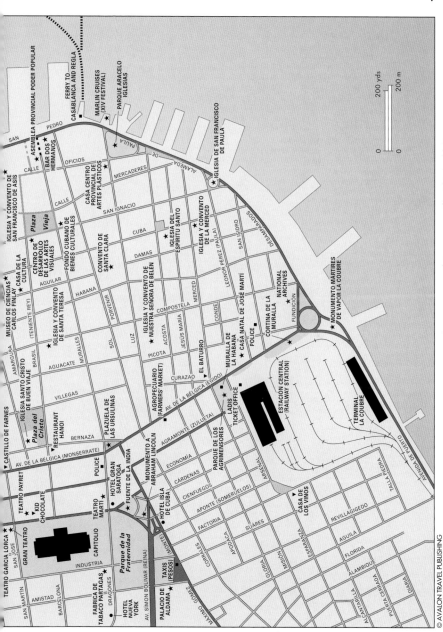

FERRY TO CASABLANCA AND REGLA
MARLIN CRUISES (XIV FESTIVAL)
PARQUE ARACELO IGLESIAS
SAN PEDRO
SAN
ASEMBLEA PROVINCIAL PODER POPULAR
BAR DOS HERMANOS
CALLE OFICIOS
IGLESIA DE SAN FRANCISCO DE PAULA
IGLESIA Y CONVENTO DE SAN FRANCISCO DE ASIS
CALLE MERCADERES
Plaza Vieja
CASA CENTRO PROVINCIAL DE ARTES PLÁSTICAS
SAN IGNACIO
CENTRO DE DESARROLLO DE LAS ARTES VISUALES
CASA DE LA CULTURA
CUBA
FONDO CUBANO DE BIENES CULTURALES
IGLESIA DEL ESPIRITU SANTO
MUSEO DE CIENCIAS CARLOS FINLAY
CONVENTO DE SANTA CLARA
DAMAS
IGLESIA Y CONVENTO DE LA MERCED
AGUILAR
LEONOR PÉREZ (PAULA)
SAN ISIDRO
HABANA
IGLESIA Y CONVENTO DE SANTA TERESA
(TENIENTE REY)
IGLESIA Y CONVENTO DE NUESTRA SEÑORA DE BELÉN
COMPOSTELA
MERCED
NATIONAL ARCHIVES
MONUMENTO MARTIRES DE VAPOR LA COUBRE
AMARGURA
IGLESIA SANTO CRISTO DE BUEN VIAJE
Plaza del Cristo
BRASIL
MURALLES
SOL
LUZ
ACOSTA
JESUS MARIA
CONDE
CASA NATAL DE JOSÉ MARTÍ
CORTINA DE LA MURALLA
CASTILLO DE FARNES
VILLEGAS
AGUACATE
PORVENIR
PICOTA
CURAZAO
EL BATURRO
MURALLA DE LA HABANA
POLICE
FUNDICIÓN
RESTAURANT HANOI
BERNAZA
PLAZUELA DE LAS URSULINAS
AGROPECUARIO (FARMERS' MARKET)
AV. DE LA BÉLGICA (EGIDO)
ESTACIÓN CENTRAL (RAILWAY STATION)
AV. DE LA BÉLGICA (MONSERRATE)
AGRAMONTE (ZULUETA)
LADIS TICKET OFFICE
TERMINAL LA COUBRE
TEATRO PAYRET
POLICE
HOTEL GRAN SARATOGA
MONUMENTO A ABRAHAM LINCOLN
PARQUE DE LOS AGRIMENSORES
ARSENAL
TALLA PIEDRA
KID CHOCOLATE
FUENTE DE LA INDIA
ECONOMÍA
AVENIDA DE PUERTO
TEATRO GARCÍA LORCA
SAN JOSÉ
TEATRO MARTÍ
HOTEL ISLA DE CUBA
CÁRDENAS
CIENFUEGOS
CASA DE LOS VINOS
GRAN TEATRO
CAPITOLIO
Parque de la Fraternidad
APONTE (SOMERUELOS)
REVILLAGIGEDO
SAN MARTÍN
INDUSTRIA
TAXIS (PESOS) MONTE)
FACTORIA
SUÁRES
AGUILA
AMISTAD
FÁBRICA DE TABACO PARTAGAS
DRAGONES
PALACIO DE ALDAMA
AV. SIMON BOLIVAR (REINA)
APODACA
GLORIA
MISIÓN
ESPARANZA
FLORIDA
BARCELONA
HOTEL NUEVA YORK
CORRALES
ALAMBIQUE
SAN NICOLAS
MÁXIMO GOMEZ
PUERTA CERRADA
ACANTARILLA
DIARIA

0   200 yds
0   200 m

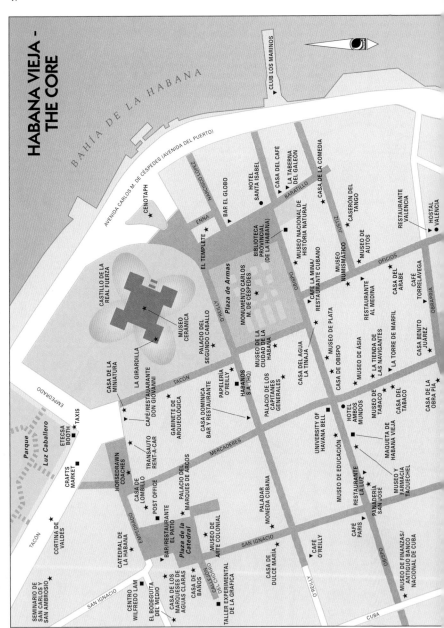

CRUISE TERMINAL

CUSTOMS

BAR DOS HERMANOS

CASA DEL CONDE DE LA MONTERA

SAN PEDRO

CARPINETTI

LA LONJA DEL COMERCIO

EL MERCURIO

Plaza de San Francisco

FUENTE DE LOS LEONES

MUSEO DE ARTE RELIGIOSO/IGLESIA DE SAN FRANCISCO DE ASÍS

ASAMBLEA PROVINCIAL

PARQUE HUMBOLDT

OFICIOS

SOL

CADECA (MONEY EXCHANGE)

POST OFFICE

AGENCIA DE VIAJES SAN CRISTÓBAL

CAFÉ DEL ORIENTE

BENETTON

GALERÍA CARMEN MONTILLA

GALERÍA LOS OFICIOS

BANCO FINANCIERO INTERNACIONAL

CAFÉ LA MARINA

BRASIL (TENIENTE REY)

MURALLA

Plaza de Bolívar

ARMERÍA 9 DE ABRIL

PARQUE RUMIÑAHUI

CASA SIMÓN BOLÍVAR

HOSTAL DE HABANA/ CASA DEL CONDE DE VILLANUEVA

CAFÉ HABANA

MERCADERES

TABERNA BENY MORÉ

FOTOTECA DE CUBA/ SALÓN NACIONAL DE FOTOGRAFÍA

PALACIO CUETO

INQUISIDOR

CASA DE ÁFRICA

APARTHOTEL (IN CONSTRUCTION)

POLICE

Plaza

FOUNTAIN

Vieja

FONDO CUBANO DE BIENES CULTURALES/ CASA DE LOS CONDES DE JARUCO

SAN IGNACIO

CASA DE LAS HERMANAS CÁRDENAS/ CENTRO DE DESARROLLO DE LAS ARTES VISUALES

ARTESANÍAS PARA TURISMO TALLER/ CASA DEL CONDE DE SAN ESTEBAN DE CANONGO

CASA DEL CONDE DE CASA LOMBILLO

LA CASONA JOYERÍA

MURALLA

COMUNIDAD PROVISORIA DE PLAZA VIEJA

OBRAPÍA

LAMPARILLA

AMARGURA

MUSEO HISTÓRICO DE LAS CIENCIES CARLOS J. FINLAY

CUBA

IGLESIA Y CONVENTO DE SAN FRANCISCO EL NUEVO

ANTIGUA ACADEMIA DE CIENCIAS MÉDICAS FÍSICAS, Y NATURALES

CASA DE CULTURA MUNICIPAL

BRASIL (TENIENTE REY)

AGUILAR

50 yds

50 m

0

0

© AVALON TRAVEL PUBLISHING

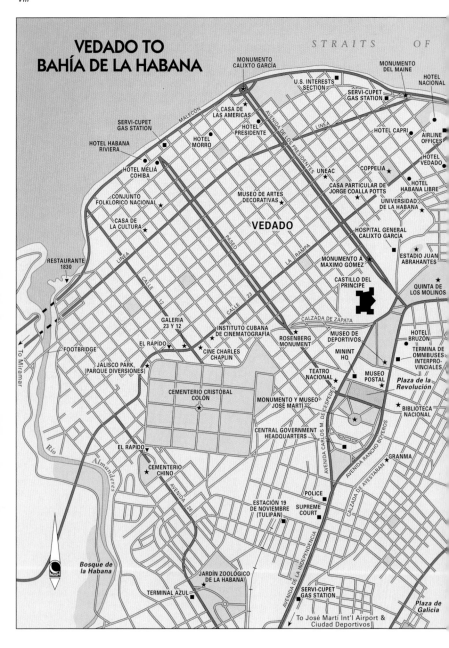

VEDADO TO BAHÍA DE LA HABANA

STRAITS OF

MONUMENTO CALIXTO GARCÍA

U.S. INTERESTS SECTION

MONUMENTO DEL MAINE

HOTEL NACIONAL

SERVI-CUPET GAS STATION

MALECÓN

CASA DE LAS AMERICAS

AVENIDA DE LOS PRESIDENTES

LINEA

HOTEL CAPRI

AIRLINE OFFICES

SERVI-CUPET GAS STATION

HOTEL PRESIDENTE

HOTEL HABANA RIVIERA

HOTEL MORRO

HOTEL VEDADO

HOTEL MELIÁ COHIBA

UNEAC

COPPELIA

HOTEL HABANA LIBRE

CASA PARTICULAR DE JORGE COALLA POTTS

CONJUNTO FOLKLORICO NACIONAL

MUSEO DE ARTES DECORATIVAS

UNIVERSIDAD DE LA HABANA

CASA DE LA CULTURA

VEDADO

PASEO

HOSPITAL GENERAL CALIXTO GARCÍA

RESTAURANTE 1830

LINEA

LA RAMPA

MONUMENTO A MAXIMO GÓMEZ

ESTADIO JUAN ABRAHANTES

CALLE 12

CALLE 23

CASTILLO DEL PRINCIPE

QUINTA DE LOS MOLINOS

GALERIA 23 Y 12

CALZADA DE ZAPATA

EL RÁPIDO

INSTITUTO CUBANA DE CINEMATOGRAFÍA

MUSEO DE DEPORTIVOS

HOTEL BRUZÓN

FOOTBRIDGE

CINE CHARLES CHAPLIN

ROSENBERG MONUMENT

MININT HQ

TERMINA DE OMNIBUSES INTERPROVINCIALES

To Miramar

JALISCO PARK (PARQUE DIVERSIONES)

TEATRO NACIONAL

MUSEO POSTAL

Plaza de la Revolución

CEMENTERIO CRISTÓBAL COLÓN

MONUMENTO Y MUSEO JOSÉ MARTÍ

BIBLIOTECA NACIONAL

AVENIDA CARLOS M. DE CÉSPEDES

CENTRAL GOVERNMENT HEADQUARTERS

Río Almendares

EL RAPIDO

AVENIDA RANCHO BOYEROS

GRANMA

CEMENTERIO CHINO

AVENIDA 26

CALZADA DE AYESTARÁN

POLICE

ESTACIÓN 19 DE NOVIEMBRE (TULIPAN)

SUPREME COURT

AVENIDA DE LA INDEPENDENCIA

Bosque de la Habana

JARDÍN ZOOLÓGICO DE LA HABANA

TERMINAL AZUL

SERVI-CUPET GAS STATION

Plaza de Galicia

To José Martí Int'l Airport & Ciudad Deportivos

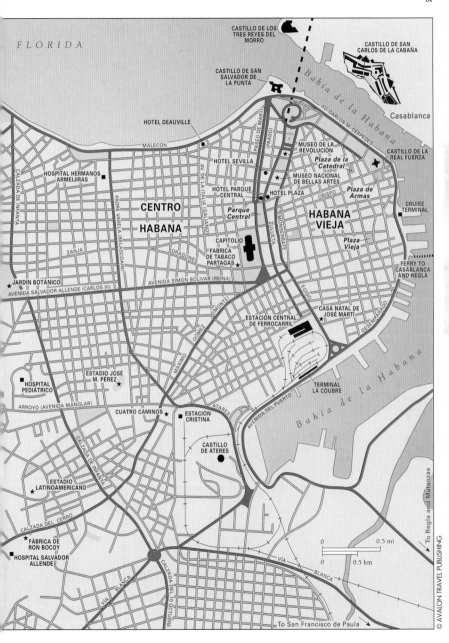

FLORIDA

CASTILLO DE LOS
TRES REYES DEL
MORRO

CASTILLO DE SAN
CARLOS DE LA CABAÑA

CASTILLO DE SAN
SALVADOR DE
LA PUNTA

Bahía de la Habana

Casablanca

HOTEL DEAUVILLE

AV CARLOS M CESPEDES

MALECÓN

MUSEO DE LA
REVOLUCIÓN

CASTILLO DE LA
REAL FUERZA

HOTEL SEVILLA

*Plaza de la
Catedral*

HOSPITAL HERMANOS
ARMEIJIRAS

MUSEO NACIONAL
DE BELLAS ARTES

HOTEL PARQUE
CENTRAL

OBISPO

*Plaza de
Armas*

HOTEL PLAZA

CRUISE
TERMINAL

**CENTRO
HABANA**

*Parque
Central*

**HABANA
VIEJA**

ZANJA

CAPITOLIO

*Plaza
Vieja*

DRAGONES

FÁBRICA
DE TABACO
PARTAGAS

FERRY TO
CASABLANCA
AND REGLA

★ JARDÍN BOTÁNICO

Avenida SIMÓN BOLÍVAR (REINA)

AVENIDA SALVADOR ALLENDE (CARLOS III)

ESTACIÓN CENTRAL
DE FERROCARRIL

CASA NATAL DE
JOSÉ MARTÍ

★ HOSPITAL
PEDIÁTRICO

ESTADIO JOSÉ
M. PÉREZ

Bahía de la Habana

ARROYO (AVENIDA MANGLAR)

TERMINAL
LA COUBRE

CUATRO CAMINOS

ESTACIÓN
CRISTINA

AVENIDA DEL PUERTO

ESTADIO
LATINOAMERICANO

CASTILLO
DE ATERES

To Regla and Matanzas

CALZADA DEL CERRO

★ FÁBRICA DE
RON BOCOY

HOSPITAL SALVADOR
ALLENDE

0   0.5 mi

0   0.5 km

VÍA
BLANCA

To San Francisco de Paula

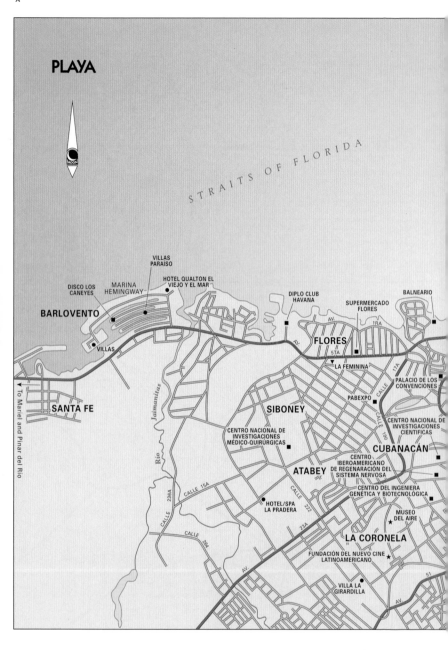

PLAYA

STRAITS OF FLORIDA

VILLAS PARAISO

HOTEL QUALTON EL VIEJO Y EL MAR

DISCO LOS CANEYES

MARINA HEMINGWAY

DIPLO CLUB HAVANA

SUPERMERCADO FLORES

BALNEARIO

BARLOVENTO

AV. 1RA

FLORES

AV.

5TA

VILLAS

LA FEMININA

PALACIO DE LOS CONVENCIONES

▼ To Mariel and Pinar del Río

SANTA FE

Río Jaimanitas

PABEXPO

CALLE 17A

SIBONEY

CALLE 190

CENTRO NACIONAL DE INVESTIGACIONES CIENTIFICAS

CENTRO NACIONAL DE INVESTIGACIONES MÉDICO-QUIRÚRGICAS

CENTRO IBEROAMERICANO DE REGENARACIÓN DEL SISTEMA NERVOSA

CUBANACÁN

ATABEY

Río

CALLE 236A

CALLE 15A

CALLE 222

CENTRO DEL INGENIERA GENÉTICA Y BIOTECNOLÓGICA

HOTEL/SPA LA PRADERA

MUSEO DEL AIRE ★

CALLE 264

CALLE 23A

LA CORONELA

FUNDACIÓN DEL NUEVO CINE LATINOAMERICANO ★

AV.

AV.

51

VILLA LA GIRARDILLA

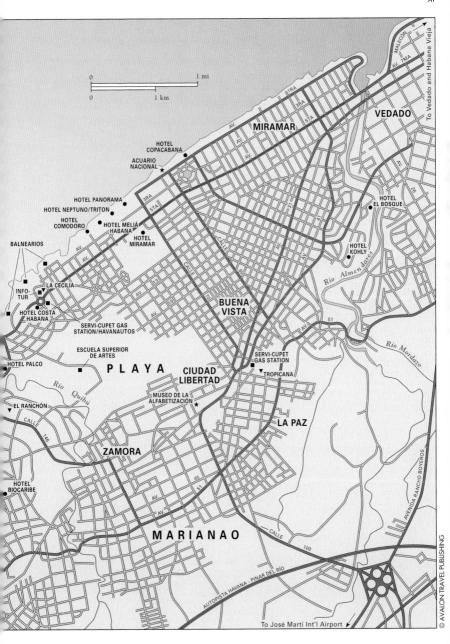

To Vedado and Habana Vieja

MALECON

AV. 7MA.

VEDADO

1RA.

3RA.

5TA.

MIRAMAR

AV.

AV.

AV.

HOTEL COPACABANA

ACUARIO NACIONAL ★

3RA.

5TA.

HOTEL PANORAMA

HOTEL NEPTUNO/TRITON

HOTEL COMODORO

HOTEL MELIÁ HABANA

HOTEL MIRAMAR

BALNEARIOS

INFO-TUR

LA CECILIA

HOTEL COSTA HABANA

SERVI-CUPET GAS STATION/HAVANAUTOS

ESCUELA SUPERIOR DE ARTES

HOTEL PALCO

PLAYA

CIUDAD LIBERTAD

MUSEO DE LA ALFABETIZACIÓN ★

EL RANCHÓN

CALLE 146

ZAMORA

HOTEL BIOCARIBE

AV.

AV.

FAV.

45

51

Río Quibú

CALLE

AV.

31

41

CALLE

CALLE 70

AV.

AV. 13

AV. 19

BUENA VISTA

HOTEL EL BOSQUE

26

HOTEL KOHLY

Río Almendares

51

SERVI-CUPET GAS STATION

TROPICANA

LA PAZ

Río Mordazo

AV.

AVENIDA RANCHO BOYEROS

MARIANAO

CALLE

100

AUTOPISTA HAVANA - PINAR DEL RÍO

To José Martí Int'l Airport

0   1 mi

0   1 km

© AVALON TRAVEL PUBLISHING

HAVANA
HANDBOOK
FIRST EDITION

CHRISTOPHER P. BAKER

MOON
T R A V E L
HANDBOOKS

HAVANA HANDBOOK
FIRST EDITION

Published by
Avalon Travel Publishing
5855 Beaudry St.
Emeryville, CA 94608, USA

Printed by
Colorcraft, Ltd.

Please send all comments, corrections,
additions, amendments, and critiques to:

**HAVANA HANDBOOK
C/O MOON TRAVEL HANDBOOKS
AVALON TRAVEL PUBLISHING
5855 BEAUDRY ST.
EMERYVILLE, CA 94608, USA
e-mail: travel@moon.com
www.moon.com**

Printing History
1st edition—April 2000
5 4 3 2 1 0

ISBN: 1-56691-182-6
Library of Congress Cataloging-In-Publication-Data has been applied for.

Editors: Gregor Johnson Krause, Marion Harmon
Production & Design: Carey Wilson
Cartography: Mike Morgenfeld, Chris Alvarez
Index: Sondra Nation

Front cover photo: Dancer in Traditional Costume © 2000 by Nik Wheeler

All photos by Christopher P. Baker unless otherwise noted.
All illustrations by Bob Race unless otherwise noted.

Distributed in the United States and Canada by Publishers Group West

Printed in China

CONTENTS

SPECIAL TOPICS

ENTERTAINMENT, RECREATION, AND SHOPPING . . 168~217

Festivals and Events; Folk Music and Dance; Cabarets (*Espectáculos*);
Discotheques and Dancing; Tango and Flamenco; Jazz Venues; Bars;
Cinema; Theater and Classical Performances; Museums and Galleries;
Other Entertainment

Sports and Recreation 193
Participatory Activities; Spectator Sports; For the Kids

Shopping 201
Antiques; Arts and Crafts; Books; Clothing; Department Stores and
Diplotiendas; Music and Musical Instruments; Posters; Rum and Liquors;
For Children

Cuban Cigars 210
A Bit of History; The Production Process; Visiting Havana's Cigar
Factories; Shopping and Buying; Further Reading

SPECIAL TOPICS

ACCOMMODATIONS . . . . 218~238

Habana Vieja; Centro Habana; Vedado and Plaza de la Revolución;
Playa (Miramar and Beyond); Suburban Havana; Habana del Este

SPECIAL TOPIC

MAP LIST

BLACK AND WHITE MAP SYMBOLS

═══	Superhighway	★	Point of Interest
══	Primary Road	•	Accommodation
──	Secondary Road	▼	Restaurant/Bar
- - - -	Tunnel	■	Other Location
··········	Ferry	⌡	Golf Course
┼─┼─┼	Railroad		
── ·· ──	Province Boundary		

ACKNOWLEDGMENTS

Heartfelt thanks are due to those individuals who in sundry ways assisted my research for this book.

I especially appreciate the support of Raúl Durruthy Rodríguez and Juan Carlos Aguilar Cabello, for ongoing permission to photograph the Tropicana; Michael Douglas of Cuba Travel, in Mexico, for miscellaneous introductions and contacts; Manuel Estefanía Seoane, vice president of Gran Caribe, for facilitating VIP status to the Tropicana; Emilio Falcón, Maria del Carmen Hernández, and Ana Delia Pérez of the Golden Tulip Parque Central, for assistance with accommodation; Christopher Howard, author of *Living and Investing in the New Cuba;* Jim Krantz, for inviting me to write the text for *Havana,* his haunting collection of photo illustrations; Michael Larrow of Bahatours in Nassau, and Alicia Pérez Casanova of Horizontes, for assistance with transportation; Ralph Martell, for the gift of his books and for being a much-admired friend; Tom Miller, for permission to quote from his *Trading with the Enemy;* Lourdes Mulen Duarte, of the Consultória Jurídica Internacional; Mirabel Riquenes Pérez of the Convención de Turismo; Nancy Stout, for showing me aspects of Havana I might otherwise have missed; Robert Walz and Tony Carey of Last Frontier Expeditions; and all others who through my forgetfulness have not been acknowledged.

Special words of appreciation and affection go to Damaris Bencomo Nay, of the Cuban national handball team; Jorge Coalla Potts, his wife Marisol, and their daughter Jessica; and Yamilka García, of the Cabaret Parisien, all of whom added to the warmth of Havana in springtime.

Special acknowledgement must also go to the Biblioteca Nacional Jose Martí, Archivo del Museo de la Ciudad de la Havana, and Publimerc S.A., for their indelible historical images.

Last, and above all, I offer my deepest affection, gratitude, and a lifelong *abrazo* to Daisy Frómeta Bartólome, whose gaiety, love, and affection filled my time in Havana with boundless sunshine. Cuba will never be the same without her.

HELP US MAKE THIS A BETTER BOOK

Inevitably, a book of this size and scope is a long time in the making. While every effort has been made to keep abreast of the rapid pace of change and development in Cuba, some information may already be out-of-date by the time you read this book. A few inaccuracies are also inevitable. You—the reader—are a valuable resource in ensuring that future editions contain the most up-to-date and accurate information. Please let us know about any price changes, new accommodations or restaurants, map errors, travel tips, etc.

To assist future travelers, feel free to photocopy maps in this book: while sightseeing, mark the exact locations of new hotels and other travel facilities, and cross off those that may have closed down. Mail your revised map, along with any information you wish to provide (including, if possible, a business card, brochure, and rate card for hotels) to:

Havana Handbook
c/o Avalon Travel Publishing
5855 Beaudry Street
Emeryville, CA 94608
USA
e-mail travel@moon.com

CALLING CUBA FROM OUTSIDE

Outside Cuba, all telephone and fax numbers need to be preceded by 53 (the code for Cuba) and 7 (the code for Havana).

INTRODUCTION

Winston Churchill, approaching Havana by sea in 1895, wrote that he felt "delirious yet tumultuous. . . . I felt as if I sailed with Long John Silver and first gazed on Treasure Island. Here was a place where anything might happen. Here was a place where something would certainly happen. Here I might leave my bones."

Countless writers have commented on the exhilarating sensation that engulfs visitors to this most beautiful and beguiling of Caribbean cities. The potency of Havana's appeal is owed to a quality that "runs deeper than the stuff of which travel brochures are made. It is irresistible and intangible," wrote Juliet Barclay—as if, adds Arnold Samuelson, recalling his first visit to Havana, in 1934, "everything you have seen before is forgotten, everything you see and hear then being so strange you feel . . . as if you had died and come to life in a different world." The city's ethereal mood, little changed today, is so pronounced that it finds its way into novels. "I wake up feeling different, like something inside me is changing, something chemical and irreversible. There's a magic here working its way through my veins," observes Pilar, a Cuban-American character

from New York who returns to Havana in Cristina García's novel *Dreaming in Cuban*.

Set foot one time in Havana, and you can only flee or succumb to its enigmatic allure. It is impossible to resist the city's mysteries and contradictions.

Walking the city's streets you sense you are living inside a romantic thriller. You don't want to sleep for fear of missing a vital experience. Before the Revolution, Havana had a reputation as a place of intrigue and tawdry romance. The whiff of conspiracy, the intimation of liaison, is still in the air.

Your first reaction is of being caught in an eerie colonial-cum-1950s time warp. Fading signs advertising Hotpoint and Singer appliances evoke the decadent decades when Cuba was a virtual colony of the United States. High-finned, chrome-spangled dowagers from the heyday of Detroit are everywhere, conjuring images of dark-eyed temptresses and men in Panama hats and white linen suits. Havana, now Communist but still carnal, is peopled in fact as in fiction by characters from the novels of Ernest Hemingway and Graham Greene. All the glamor of an abandoned stage set is here, patinated by age. For foreign visitors, it is heady stuff.

Havana Redux

In the 1950s, Cuba was North America's premier playground. Tens of thousands of *yanquis* flocked to Havana each year, lured by tourist brochures selling gambling and "glamorous, lissome Latin lasses, black-eyed señoritas, langorously, enticingly swaying." North Americans arrived by plane or aboard the *City of Havana* ferry from Key West to indulge in a few days of sun and sin. They went home happy, unaware of General Batista's reign of terror or that behind the scenes revolutionary forces were at work.

On New Year's Eve 1958, Castro & Co. triumphed and the tourist business succumbed, says Rosalie Schwartz, "to uncertainty, inconvenience, and unpleasantness."

Eager to reassure tourists, in October 1959 Fidel Castro spoke to the American Society of Travel Agents (ASTA) convention, held that year in Havana's old Blanquita (now the Karl Marx) Theater. "We have sea," said Castro. "We have bays, we have beautiful beaches, we have medicinal waters in our hotels, we have mountains, we have game and we have fish in the sea and the rivers, and we have sun. Our people are noble, hospitable, and, most important, they hate no one. They love visitors—so much in fact that our visitors feel completely at home."

Normal relations with the United States still existed back then, and US ambassador Philip Bonsai also lauded Cuban tourism at the ASTA convention: "Cuba is one of the most admirable countries in the world from the point of view of North American tourism and from many other points of view."

Despite good intentions, the convention proved a last hurrah. Even as the delegates departed, five major steamship companies eliminated their stops in Havana. Shortly afterward, Cuba spun off into the Soviet orbit and the doors slammed shut to tourists. Lack of revenue doomed the city's hotels, restaurants, and bars, and the city sank into decay.

But time has a way of coming full circle. Castro's view of tourism has shifted profoundly since the demise of the Soviet Union. Four decades after they were essentially made obsolete, he is putting a polish on Havana's old tourist haunts and extending his hand to the rest of the world. Castro's 40th anniversary in power sees his country enjoying cult status again, exerting a powerful pull on trendy tourists.

About 1.7 million foreign visitors arrived in Cuba in 1998, including more than 100,000 US citizens, many of whom traveled legally to worship at the shrine of fifties kitsch and savor a frisson of the forbidden. The rest circumvented US travel restrictions by entering Cuba through Canada, Mexico, or the Bahamas, which is remarkably easy to do. Cubans play their part by abstaining from stamping passports, so Uncle Sam need never know. (Most *yanquis* harbor the misimpression that it's illegal for US citizens to travel to Cuba. It's not; it's merely illegal to spend dollars there. In any event, no US tourist has ever been prosecuted merely for visiting Cuba.) Cuba has set itself a long-term goal of 10 million tourists annually by 2010. The goal is ambitious but will likely be met.

Cuba's hip, happenin' capital may well be the destination of the millennium. Havana, the most exhilarating and exasperating city between Miami and Montevideo, is in the midst of a tourist boom.

Havana's Lures

One of the great historical cities of the New World, Havana (pop. 2.2 million—one-fifth the total population of Cuba) is made for tropical tourism. Gilded castles; rococo churches; cobbled plazas still haunted by Hemingway's ghost; flirty *mulattas* tendering whispered promises of perfumed romance; bars drowsy with the proletarian fusion of dialectics, cigars, and rum; the magnesium light gleaming on the chrome of old Yankee *cacharros* (wrecks). There is nowhere else like it.

Havana has a flavor all its own; a surreal and sensual amalgam of colonialism, capitalism, and communism merged into one. The city is a far cry from the Caribbean backwaters that call themselves capitals elsewhere in the Antilles. It is obvious, as you walk tree-lined boulevards and eerily Neapolitan streets as tranquil and unthreatening as any in Latin America, that Havana was wealthy to a degree that most South American and Caribbean cities were not—and not too long ago. Havana is a city, notes architect Jorge Rigau, "upholstered in columns, cushioned by colonnaded arcades."

*bathers on
the Malecón*

The Spanish colonial buildings hard up against the Atlantic are handsome indeed. They come in a spectacular amalgam of styles—from the academic classicism of aristocratic homes and baroque palaces to the bold modernism of art deco and art nouveau public buildings.

At the heart of the city is enchanting Habana Vieja (Old Havana), a living museum inhabited by 60,000 people that contains the finest collection of Spanish colonial buildings in all the Americas. Baroque churches, convents, and castles that could have been transposed from Madrid or Cádiz still reign majestically over squares embraced by the former palaces of Cuba's ruling gentry. Ernest Hemingway's house, Finca Vigía, is one of dozens of museums dedicated to the memory of great men and women. And although many of the older monuments—those of politically incorrect heroes—were pulled down, they were at least replaced by numerous monuments to those on the correct side of history.

Street names may have been changed, but balmy city streets with walls in faded tropical pastels still smolder gold in the waxing sun. Sunlight still filters through stained-glass *mediopuntos* to dance on the cool marble floors. And time cannot erase the sound of the "jalousies above the colonnades creaking in the small wind from the sea," in the words of Graham Greene. Havana's is an incomparable mood—and an utterly compelling moment.

Havana's greatest, most enigmatic appeal is that you sense you are living inside an unfolding

drama. It awakens your senses completely. Everything is tinged faintly with the slightly shady air of "a Latin woman, beautiful but exhausted, dancing through the perfumed night with a gun in her hand," thought novelist Bob Shacochis. The city is still intoxicating, still laced with the sharp edges and sinister shadows that made Spanish poet Federico García Lorca write to his parents, "If I get lost look for me in Cuba," and that made Hemingway want "to stay here forever."

Still, an open-minded visitor is torn two ways: Havana is both disheartening and uplifting. You'll most probably fall in love with the city, while being thankful you don't have to live in it.

Forty years of negative media reports have led many visitors to expect the worst—a fossilized shell of a city with a population cowed and sullen, their lips glued shut in fear. Those who see only the negatives—the overwhelming decay and dishevelment, the inept bureaucracy, the shortages and suffocating restraints that make life for locals a *lucha* (fight)—fail to see the smiling children or healthy, educated youth eager to challenge you to a game of chess or discuss Voltaire. Havana is inhabited by a cultured and civilized people. Alive and vivacious, they impress and astonish.

The Habaneros (residents of Havana) are perhaps the most remarkable part of this remarkable city. The rest of the world could do much worse than see them as role models. It is not simply the noble way they demonstrate how to squeeze pleasure out of adversity. Cubans are so unstintingly generous, so gracious, so full of decent, considerate behavior that they exemplify a more elegantly human way of being. This "New Man" is the very essence of the Revolution. In a sense, he—or she—is what the Cuban Revolution is all about: the creation of a society in which a person's social conscience prevails over selfish material interest, living to serve his or her community, preferring a virtuous existence over indulgent ways. Havana is full of such people.

Habaneros you have met only moments ago will invite you into their homes, where rum and beer are passed around and you are lured to dance by narcotic rhythms. How much they have to give and we to receive if only, in the words of photographer David Garten, we can "Houdini out of the straightjacket" of our own culture. It is hard to believe that the US government's Trading with the Enemy Act is directed at these compellingly warm-hearted people. How often have I teared up and cried, laughing, flirting, dancing, as it were, with the enemy?

It is a rare visitor to Cuba who, exploring beyond the tourist circuit, does not at some time break down in tears. Everyone, everything, touches your heart. It is the way the Cubans embrace you with global innocence, how their disarming charm and irrepressible gaiety amid the heartrending pathos of their situation moves you to examine the meaning of life.

There is nothing depressing about the Habaneros, only the situation in which they are forced to live their lives.

Faded Glory

It has been fashionable among foreign journalists of late to portray Havana as a slum, a crumbling city of sagging walls and peeling paint. A city shadowed by somnolent remorse. True enough, Havana aches with pathos and penury, combining all the sultry sadness and sun-washed spontaneity of Naples and New Orleans.

Havana has been "a city in lamentable decline" for more than a century, but policies since the Revolution have only hastened its tragic decay. Even Esteban Lazo, the mayor of Havana, has admitted that "the Revolution has been hard on the city." The sultry seductress of prerevolutionary days needs a million gallons of paint (political humorist P.J. O'Rourke has

written that "[h]alf an hour in Havana is enough to cure you of a taste for that distressed look so popular in Crate & Barrel stores"). But at least the best of the buildings are still standing and haven't been swept away by a gaudy wave of tourist hotels, shopping malls, and marinas—although that *is* beginning to happen.

Soon after Castro took power, his government announced a policy emphasizing rural development over urban improvement. The countryside had long been neglected, and a significant portion of the rural population lived in abject poverty. But the triumphs of the Revolution in the countryside could not stem migration to the cities, particularly Havana, which suffered ongoing neglect and impoverishment. Little new construction has taken place in the past 40 years (except in the suburbs, where melancholic "internationalist" apartment housing and other Communist carbuncles reflect Cuba's gravitation into the Soviet orbit). "The unhealthy shanty towns, which had disappeared during the early years of the Revolution, have reappeared," Castro declared in 1989, speaking of the *ciudadelos,* the decrepit tenements "where families live in one or two little rooms, with very little space." Castro estimated that 300,000 people in Havana live in slum conditions and that only 50% of inhabitants have proper sewage.

In certain areas, conditions are now truly depressing. Many Habaneros cling tenaciously to family life behind crumbling facades festooned with makeshift wiring and inside tottering buildings that should have faced the bulldozer blade long ago. Many buildings have fallen masonry and piles of plaster on the floor, unpainted walls mildewed by the tropical climate, and stairs so dilapidated one is afraid to step onto them. Once-pleasant strolls in Cerro and Habana Vieja have become obstacle courses over piles of rubble and beneath wooden braces propping up one building after another.

But Havana has an efficient street-cleaning operation, at least by Caribbean standards. Although when it rains the streets fill with puddles, they are thankfully free of the pestilent aromas that pervade so many other cities elsewhere in the tropics.

The decade since the collapse of Cuba's Soviet benefactor—"pompously baptized," says Humbert Werneck, "as a 'Special Period in Time of Peace' "—has been desperate (Cuba lived on largesse for four decades, while its own economy stagnated). Fortunately, Havana has begun to return to some semblance of normality. The notorious *apagones* (power outages) that plagued the city nightly in the early 1990s have now become occasional and brief inconveniences. Gasoline is again plentiful, and reports of Havana's transport system having come to a virtual standstill are now outdated (although the bus service is a Third World ordeal).

Habana Vieja, with its vast reservoir of attractions, is in the midst of a dramatic, decade-old restoration. Scores of mansions in Vedado and Miramar are being restored to haughty grandeur and turned into posh boutiques, restaurants, and offices for Cuban and foreign corporations. Most Habaneros insist that the "new" Havana is a Potemkin village, a kind of Disneyland with a false frontage. The improvements don't as yet extend beyond the tourist zones, so they continue to struggle with the hardships of their daily lives. Today, as dollars generated by tourism have begun to filter down to the local populace, Habaneros look better fed and clothed than a few years ago. But the domestic economy is in shambles, and the state has been able to provide less and less for its citizenry. Most Habaneros have become dependent on the scramble for dollars to survive.

A Future Reality

Travelers visiting Havana today do so at a fascinating historic moment, as Cuba is emerging from its Marxist cocoon. Cuba is coming up for sale and in the quest for survival has been forced to turn back to the entrepreneurial spirit it once eschewed. A new Cuba is taking shape based on a homespun paradigm of socialism-cum-free-market economy (a "market dictatorship," dubbed *capitalismo frío*, or cold capitalism) that relies on tourism to restore economic growth while avoiding social and political upheaval. Havana today drifts somewhere between communism and capitalism, and is already showing signs of becoming a Caribbean Hong Kong (even deluxe condominiums are going up, with prices beginning at US$67,000—but not for Cubans).

The biggest challenge now facing the city is whether it can save its substance without losing its soul. The tourism boom has the hallmarks of a Faustian bargain. In the 1960s, the Castro government scorned tourism for its attendant bourgeois decadence—the gambling, prostitution, live sex acts, and drugs. Things are now coming full circle as the inequity between the dollar and the peso has created an inverted economy in which bellhops and *jiniteras* (prostitutes) make far more money than professors and surgeons. An economic elite of *masetas* (rich Cubans) is once again becoming visible. Prostitution has returned stronger than ever. Drugs and corruption are once again evident, as are beggars. The current crisis is severely testing Cubans' faith in human cooperation.

The mood on the streets is now one of frustration and restlessness. Support for the Revolution is at an all-time low and highly tenuous. Support for Castro remains strong in the countryside, but the majority of Habaneros long ago lost faith in *El Jefe*. While his hold on power seems as strong as ever, his hold on hearts and minds has faded. James Michener wrote of Havana, "Only the kindness of the climate prevents the smoldering of revolt that might accompany the same conditions in a cold and relentless climate."

It doesn't take great imagination to envision how Havana could again become, in Somerset Maugham's piquant phrase, "a sunny place for shady people." The city's demimonde continues to bubble beneath the surface, just waiting for someone to marshal it. What makes Havana so fascinating won't last forever. As the foreign influence spreads, the more Havana may be "spoiled," changing the face of the Malecón and creating a Havana skyline as hazy as Cuba's future.

But no matter what, there'll still be impassioned poetry, *santería,* salsa, and sunny days on diamond-dust beaches trolled by sultry Habaneras in tiny *tanguitas*. Whatever the temperature, there'll be a fresh breeze blowing, carrying the city's aroma—a combination of sea air, tobacco, mildew, and mimosa—through cobbled colonial plazas. There'll be *mojitos* to enjoy in the Bar Dos Hermanos and the world's finest cigars to smoke fresh from the factory as you rumble down the narrow streets in a chrome-spangled 1955 Cadillac to the rhythm of the rumba on the radio.

Hemingway, who loved Cuba and lived there for the better part of 20 years, once warned novice writer Arnold Samuelson against "a tendency to condemn before you completely understand. You aren't God, and you never judge a man," advised Hemingway. "You present him as he is and you let the reader judge." My job, as I've seen it, is to tell the truth. The admirable and the harsh realities in equal measure.

Like Hemingway, who when asked what he worried about in his sleep replied, "My house in Cuba," Havana for me is a special place. It satisfies my soul. When I return home, I feel homesick.

HISTORY

THE EARLY COLONIAL ERA

The Spanish Arrival

On the evening of 27 October 1492, Genoese explorer Christopher Columbus first set eyes on the hazy mass of Cuba, at the time inhabited by peaceable Taino Indians. The explorer voyaged along the north coast for four weeks, touching land at various points and finally dropping anchor on 27 November in a perfectly protected harbor near today's Gibara, in eastern Cuba.

In 1509, King Ferdinand gave Christopher Columbus's son, Diego, the title of Governor of the Indies with the duty to organize an expedition to further explore Cuba. In 1511, four ships from Spain arrived carrying 300 settlers under Diego Columbus and his beautiful wife, María de Toledo (grandniece of King Ferdinand). Also on board was the new governor of Cuba—a tall, portly, blond soldier named Diego Velásquez de Cuellar, looking very dashing in a great plumed hat and a short velvet cloak tufted with gold (a young Hernán Cortés was also on board; he would later set sail from Havana for Mexico to subdue the Aztecs).

Velásquez founded the first town at Baracoa in 1512, followed within the next few years by six other crude *villas* whose mud streets would eventually be paved with cobblestones shipped from Europe as ballast aboard the armada of vessels now bound for the Americas. Humble little San Cristóbal de la Habana began life in July 1515 as the westernmost of Velásquez's seven cities, founded by one of Velásquez's deputies, Pánfilo de Narváez.

Foundation of a City

Fledgling Havana was first located on the south coast, where Batabanó stands today, and the name, unusually, came from the Indians, who named this western part of the island for their local chief, Habaguanex. The site for this rough-hewn settlement was an unmitigated disaster. Within four years, the settlers had moved to the north coast, where they erected rough huts at the mouth of the Río Chorrera (now Almendares). The swampy site was also ill-chosen, and the occupants were tormented by plagues. A few years earlier, the expeditionary Sebastian de Ocampo had discovered a more promising site—Puerto de Carenas, so named because the site was ideal for careening ships—a few km farther east, and on 25 November 1519, the date of the second founding of San Cristóbal de la Habana, the settlers moved to the shore of this flask-shaped, deep-water bay surrounded by rolling hills and hidden within a cliff-hung narrow channel.

The first houses stood facing the sea in a row between the present sites of the Plaza de Armas and the Plaza de San Francisco. Initially, life was extremely spartan, and for several decades the town was composed entirely of shacks. But Puerto de Carenas' proximity to the deep channel between Cuba and the shallow seas of the Bahamas was highly advantageous, and the township grew quickly.

The Spaniards were not on a holy mission. Medieval Spain was a greedy and cruel civilization that foreshortened its cultural lessons with the sword and musket ball. The Spaniards had set out in quest of spices, gold, and rich civilizations. Thus, the once-happy indigenous island cultures—considered by the Spaniards to be a backward, godless race—were subjected to the Spaniards' ruthless and mostly fruitless quest for silver and gold.

Although the Spanish found little silver and gold in Cuba, they had greater luck in Central and South America, whose indigenous cultures flaunted vast quantities of precious metals and jewels (when Mexico and Peru were conquered, the quantities rose to astronomical heights).

Cuba was set to become a vital stopover and the hub of trade and shipping for Spanish galleons and traders carrying the wealth of the Americas back to Europe.

The Key to the New World

Throughout the 16th century, an ever-increasing number of ships called in Havana's port as the New World began to yield up its riches. In 1526, a royal decree declared that ships had to travel in convoy to Spain (the Crown had a vested interest; it received one-fifth of the treasure), and Havana's sheltered harbor, at the gateway to the Gulf of Mexico, was the logical gathering point. Havana gained such prominence that in July 1553 the governor of Cuba, Gonzalo Pérez de Angulo, moved the capital (and his residence) there from Santiago de Cuba in the east of the island. The port city of Havana earned the title "key to the New World."

Havana's fortunes were further bolstered in 1564 when a Spanish expedition reached the Philippines. The next year, it discovered the northern Pacific trade winds that for the next 250 years propelled ships laden with Oriental treasures to Acapulco, from where the booty was carried overland to Veracruz, on the Gulf of Mexico, and loaded onto ships bound for Havana, where a great armada was assembled for the dangerous passage to Europe. Every spring and summer, all the ships returning from the Americas crowded into Havana's harbor before setting off for Spain in an armed convoy. Perfumes, pearls, silks, and ivories passed through the city. To these shipments were added silver from Bolivia, alpaca from Peru, and rare woods from central America, plus Cuban tobacco, leather, fruit, meats, hides, and precious hardwoods. The forests surrounding the city were felled for the needs of the shipbuilding industry (the city was renowned for building the best galleons in the Indies) and also for the raising of cattle and planting of tobacco—and later, sugar—for sale in Europe. The fleet of 1583 had to leave one million pesos behind because there was no more room in the ships' holds. Havana could never have imagined such wealth.

To provision the treasure fleet, an aqueduct was built to bring water down to the harbor, fruit and vegetables came from smallholdings outside Havana, and the citizens made soup and *tasajo* (salted meat) from the vast quantities of crabs and tortoises that overran the city, whose air reeked. The city overflowed with drunken sailors, packs of wild dogs, cutthroats, and whores—at night, few citizens dared venture out unless heavily armed.

At the end of the century, Havana—which had already assumed what historian Hugh Thomas called its "semi-criminal, maritime, and cosmopoli-

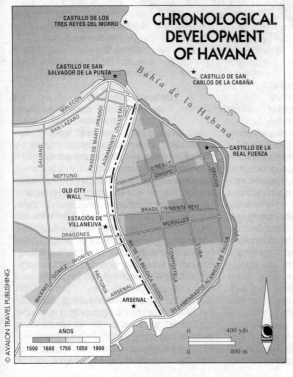

CHRONOLOGICAL DEVELOPMENT OF HAVANA

© AVALON TRAVEL PUBLISHING

tan character"—was still a small town of about 3,500 permanent residents, mostly poor and uncouth. The town was dirty and smelly (today's Calle O'Reilly was then known as Sumidero, or sewer; and Calle Teniente Rey was Basurero, or rubbish dump). When it rained, the streets ran with mud. During heat waves, epidemics of yellow fever decimated the population.

Black Gold and Piracy

Cuba's indigenous Taino culture was quickly choked by the stern hand of Spanish rule—condemned so that Jehovah and Mammon might triumph over the local idols—and the 16th century witnessed the extinction of the Taino race. Those Taino not put to the sword or worked to death in mines and plantations fell victim to exotic diseases. Within 100 years of Columbus's landfall, virtually the entire indigenous Cuban population (and those of neighboring islands) had perished. Spain turned to West Africa to supply its labor. By the end of the 16th century, an incredibly lucrative slave trade had developed. Treasure ships bound for Europe returned to Cuba with their holds full of "black gold." Havana was the major conduit and the New World's unrivaled emporium of human flesh. After being herded into ships, slaves were shackled below and endured the most deplorable conditions at sea. They arrived in Havana diseased and half-starved, and after being sold were shipped to Cuban plantations or other colonies of the Americas to be worked as beasts of burden, blasting and pummeling stone for gold and cutting sugarcane beneath the searing sun.

Havana—Pearl of the Antilles—grew inordinately rich on the proceeds. The wealth from sugar and slavery grew exponentially, as did that from the Spanish treasure fleets, which continued to multiply in Havana harbor year by year. Landowners, slave traders, and merchants were in their heyday. So, too, were smugglers. The Spanish Crown heavily taxed exports and prohibited *cri-*

Sir Francis Drake

ollos (Cuban-born) from trading with anyone but Spain (in 1717, Spain monopolized tobacco trading, resulting in a rebellion by tobacco growers that Spanish troops brutally crushed; in 1740, it formalized the monopoly on trade between Cuba and Spain by creating the Real Compañia, which bought Cuban products cheaply and sold necessities from Europe at inflated prices). Understandably, Havana was a center for contraband on a remarkable scale. The goods of the hinterlands, especially precious leathers and timber, flowed out from the harbor, while the black gold of slaves and the fineries of Europe flowed in. The Spaniards tried to regulate both smuggling and illegal slaving, but these activities were so profitable and official corruption so great that they resisted control.

The city rose to such prominence that in 1607 it officially became the island's capital. It was a treasure chest without a lid.

Defending the City

Cuba was a plump plum ripe for plucking. Lured by the island's vast wealth, pirates followed in the Spaniards' wake. French corsairs and English pirates preyed mercilessly on smaller cities and plantations across the island. In 1537, Havana itself was raided when two shiploads of French pirates came ashore and torched part of the town until the Habaneros counted out 600 ducados (three Spanish ships that arrived after the pirates had left were cajoled into giving chase; alas, they lost their nerve and when they encountered the French, turned tail. They were in turn pursued by the pirates, who called once again on the city and, not content with the fat ransom offered, looted the town for 15 days). One year later, French pirate Jacques de Sores arrived and demanded a ransom. When a bid by the Spaniards to retake the city faltered, de Sores put its inhabitants to the sword before razing the city. News traveled fast, and as the surviving Habaneros struggled to rebuild their city, other pirates arrived to cart off whatever de Sores had been unable to carry. Again the city was burned.

Military engineers were sent from Spain, and in 1558, work began on a fortress—the Castillo de la Real Fuerza—to protect the harbor (even the city's free slaves and mulattoes had their freedom revoked; they were ordered to abandon all other work and aid in construction). Work was so slow, however, that in 1561 a pirate ship sailed into the harbor in pursuit of a galleon groaning under the weight of a hold full of silver (to save his ship, the captain threw his cargo of 100,000 ducados overboard). The fortress was completed in 1582, and the governor of Cuba set up residence within (the island's governors lived here until 1762).

The fortress had arisen to no avail. Daring foreigners—most notably the English privateer John Hawkins and his nephew, Francis Drake—were perpetual thorns in the sides of the Spanish, whose galleons they seized at random. Drake's reputation preceded him, and when he arrived off Havana with a fleet of 14 ships on May 29, 1586, intent on testing the fortress' mettle, the entire town was seized by fear. While the citizens "shook like rabbits frozen before the approach of a stoat," Drake got cold feet and, after firing a few desultory shots, departed. The citizens wisely chose to add another castle on the *morro* (headland) across the harbor mouth, and work began in 1589 on this and another fortress—Castillo de la Punta—that could catch any enemy ship in a withering crossfire. As added defense, a massive chain could now be drawn across the harbor channel at night. Additional small fortresses were built along the coast, at the mouth of the Río Chorrera and at Cojímar, to the east.

As the 17th century progressed, the pirates became highly organized, able to muster small armies. Grand fortresses meant little as pirates devised devious plans to capture Spain's cities in the Americas. They organized into powerful groups that were soon encouraged and eventually licensed by the governments of France, Holland, and England to prey upon Spanish shipping and ports as a prelude to challenging Spanish dominance in the Americas.

In 1587, King Philip of Spain determined to end the growing sea power of England and amassed a great armada to invade her. This proved a fateful error, for Drake, Hawkins, and Sir Walter Raleigh assembled a fleet and destroyed the armada in the English channel, breaking the power of Spain in the Old World. The humbling defeat left Spain impotent, but Havana's new defenses served their purpose and kept all but a handful of miscreant pirates away: in 1634, a royal decree proclaimed that Havana was "the key to the New World and bulwark of the West Indies." A new coat of arms for the city was bestowed in 1665 showing the three castles. In 1662, however, Havana's defenses had been proved hollow when Henry Morgan, a stocky Welshman and leader of the Buccaneers (a motley yet disciplined group of pirates operating under British license from Port Royal in Jamaica), ransacked Havana, pilfered the cathedral bells, and left with a taunt that the Spanish weren't equal to the stone walls that Spain had built: "I could have defended Morro Castle with a dog and a gun."

Building for Posterity

While the British went out to their colonies to grow rich and return, the Spanish went to grow rich and stay. They brought a permanence of design and planning to their New World cities that other colonial powers never achieved. "The Spanish built cities where they settled, but the English just let cities grow. The poorest street of Havana had dignity compared to the shanty towns of Kingston," wrote Graham Greene.

By the 17th century, gone were the days of mud and palm thatch. Havana was an immensely prosperous city on a par with European counterparts and became even more so as the tobacco industry prospered from European noses, which reverberated with satisfied sneezes induced by Cuban snuff. All this wealth found its outlet in stone. Spanish ships unloaded builders and craftsmen, hired to help citizens display their earnings—legitimate and ill-gotten alike—in an outpouring of architectural sophistication. These Andalusian craftsmen brought with them a Moorish aesthetic, which they translated into a unique "tropical synthesis of column, courtyard, and chiaroscuro," wrote Juliet Barclay.

Life was lived ostentatiously by those with the means. Wealthy merchants and plantation owners erected beautiful mansions graced with baroque stonework painted in every conceivable combination of pastel colors, "all shimmering

SLAVE SOCIETY

The majority of slaves that were shipped to Cuba came from highly developed West African tribes such as the Fulani, Hausa, and Yoruba (they came mostly from Senegal, Gambia, and Guinea at first, and later from Nigeria and the Congo). Unlike in North America, distinct ethnic groups were kept together; as a result, their traditions, religions, and languages have been retained and passed down.

After being rounded up and herded to African ports, slaves were loaded onto ships, where they were scientifically packed like sardines. Space meant profit. Chained together body to body in the airless, dark, rancid hold, they wallowed in their own excrement and vomit on the nightmare voyage across the Atlantic. Dozens died from sickness and starvation.

Once ashore, the Africans were herded into *barracoons* to be stored until sold to plantation owners or to work in Havana's grand mansions or on civic construction projects. To avoid the expense of advertising, the Havana *barracoons* were located near the governor's summer palace at the western end of Paseo (now Avenida Salvador Allende), where citizens out for a stroll could view the merchandise like zoo-goers. No attention was paid to family relationships. Parents, children, and siblings were torn asunder forever.

House slaves, while treated poorly, experienced better conditions than slaves in the country, where plantation life was exceedingly cruel. Even so, urban slaves were not spared harsh punishment, which was carried out in public by trained experts. Agonized screams emanated at all times of day from the designated whipping place near Havana's Punta.

Understandably, rebellion was always around the corner. Slaves were considered dangerous barbarians (Victor Patricio Landaluze's representations of 19th-century life, which hang in Havana's Palacio de Bellas Artes, vividly portray how Africans were regarded at the time, as do the series of 19th-century cigarette labels on display in Havana's national library). The first slave revolt occurred in 1532 in Oriente. A few years later, Havana was sacked by slaves in the wake of an attack by French pirates.

Other slaves chose to run away and flee to the mountains. While runaways on other islands developed fiercely independent communities, such as the Maroons of Jamaica, Cuba's *cimarrones* tended to be independent; runaways often captured and sold other runaways. To track down runaways, the authorities used posses of *ranchadores,* cruel white peasants with specially trained hunting dogs. When a slave was caught, it was standard procedure to cut off one ear as a warning to other slaves.

Nonetheless, slaves had the legal right to buy their own and their relatives' freedom. Once free, they could even own and sell property. Many free blacks set up small businesses or worked as artisans, while women hired out as domestics. Some rose to positions of wealth and prominence. All in all,

slaves fared better in Cuba than on neighboring islands. Anthony Trollope, comparing Cuba to Jamaica, wrote that "a present healthy condition is cared for, but long life is not regarded." The estates in Cuba were "on a much larger scale, in much better order, overlooked by a larger proportion of white men, with a greater amount of skilled labour. The evidences of capital were very plain in Cuba; whereas, the want of it was frequently equally plain in our own island."

It was common for white men to take a black mistress, and their offspring usually received their freedom. Havana's free mulattas soon found their way to Europe and North America, where their combination of African exoticism and grace and Spanish hauteur found favor with discerning males. Occasionally, a black mistress would be particularly favored and treated well, although there were limits to their upward mobility. Any mulatta who had ideas of rising above her station usually ended up caught short, as with Cecilia Valdés, the beautiful heroine of the marvelous, tragic, and eponymous novel by Cirilo Villaverde about a mulatta who cherishes the idea of rising to become accepted by Havana's upper social stratum, but whose ambition ends in a violent denouement.

and quivering in the hot, glowing air." Inside, they were fitted with every luxury in European style. Most households in Havana were also maintained by slaves—often in great numbers, for the slave trade through Havana had multiplied astronomically as sugar began to dominate the slave-based agricultural economy, contributing even vaster sums to Havana's coffers. As may as 2,000 slaving ships a year called into Havana annually during the 1830s, for example. In 1817, at Britain's behest, Spain had agreed to end its slave trade, but slaving continued throughout the century (slavery was ended in Cuba in 1888, but only because of the collapse of the domestic sugar industry following the rise of European beet production). Slavery was too profitable to quell, with Habaneros from the governor down to the harbormaster profiting immensely from bribes. The British sent representatives to Havana to ensure that Spain complied with its agreement, but, says Juliet Barclay, "they might as well have tried to catch mercury in a sieve." Slaving ships operated under the noses of the British, and Spanish authorities claimed ignorance. To outwit the British navy, the slave traders merely adopted foreign flags; others simply unshackled their cargo and tossed the incriminating evidence overboard.

Many Havana homes still have rings in the walls where recalcitrant slaves were chained. Other slaves were sent to a special whipping place near the Punta, where trained experts meted out any punishment that the slave owner found too onerous to personally give, and the streets outside the punishment building echoed to the screams within.

Havana's slaves drew on their spiritual resources to resist the oppression of their Spanish masters. For example, they organized into *cabildos,* social groups defined according to tribal origin, and members held meetings at which they played music and performed religious rites drawn from their African heritage and from which contemporary *santería* is derived. The Spanish authorities even granted slaves their own celebration, the sacred *Día de los Reyes.* On 6 January, a colorful ceremonial procession was permitted to take to the streets, ending in Plaza de Armas, where the slaves engaged in a pandemonium of singing and dancing before the governor and his entourage.

Havana's upper social stratum lived grandly. Notes Rachel Carey: "The grand Havana house plan was the perfect expression of the heirarchy of privilege accorded to members of an upper-class Habanero household." A private enclosed gateway, or *zaguán,* big enough for carriages opened directly from the street. Arrayed around the ground floor courtyard were warehouses, offices, and other rooms devoted to the family business, with stables and servants' quarters to the rear, while the private family quarters were sequestered above around the galleried second story reached by a stately inner stairway. The design was unique to Havana houses. Another design unique among Cuban cities (borrowed from Jerez and Cádiz) was the *entresuelo,* a kind of mezzanine of half-story proportions tucked between the two stories and used to house servants and slaves (and sometimes rented out).

By the late 1600s, Spanish baroque had reached Havana (many of the elaborate stone doorways of mansions such as the Casa de la Obra Pía were crafted in Spain and shipped to Havana) and reached its zenith in the late 1700s, when it had largely displayed the Mudéjar style, with floors of marble, panels of porcelain tiles, rails of iron, lofty ceilings with open rafters, and massive windows grated like dungeons. Havana was, in contrast with today's time-worn, paint-starved city, gaily colored, with the incandescent light of the tropics dancing on walls and shining through stained-glass *ventrales* of prussian blue, hansa yellow, and blood red.

The 17th and 18th centuries also saw a surge of pious energy and ecclesiastical construction as the ever-powerful bishops brought their influence to bear in statuary and stone. Most notable of the "builder-bishops" was Diego Evelino de Compostela, a vigorous ecclesiastic who arrived from Spain in November 1687. In short order, he initiated the Convento de Belén, Convento de Santa Clara de Asís, Iglesia Santa Teresa de Jesús, and Iglesia del Santo Ángel Custodio. He was so revered by the citizens of Havana that when he died in 1704, a guard had to be mounted to stop them from taking pieces of his clothing and body. Compostela's work was continued by an equally dynamic bishop, Gerónimo Valdés, who founded the University of Havana. The wealth of the Americas helped fill the churches and convents with silver and gold.

Meanwhile, Havana's city walls went up, beginning in 1674 under Captain General Don Francisco Orejón y Gastón. The walls replaced weak wooden barricades. They took a century to build, measuring 10 meters high and 1.4 meters thick, with sentry boxes and nine entry gates. They ran along the edge of the bay and on the landward side along today's Calles Egido, Monserrate, and Zulueta. Havana's streets had evolved in an orderly grid pattern, with plazas and plazuelas between them.

Life coursed through Havana's plazas like a storm of sweetpeas: peasants leading mules bearing baskets of fruit and vegetables, farmers adding to the great crush as they drove cattle and pigs to market, acrobats and clowns doing tricks for handouts, musicians serenad-

ing, lottery-ticket sellers bearing down on anyone who looked as if they deserved some good luck that day, water vendors hawking foul-smelling water, and goats being milked door-to-door. *Volantas* (carriages—as many as 3,000 plied the streets of Havana), with light bodies suspended as if in midair between enormous wheels, raced around the streets, each pulled by a well-groomed horse ridden by a Negro *calesero* (postilion) in resplendent livery. The *volante* was usually kept in the hall of the house and entered by the home's vast arched doorway. The rank and wealth of Havana nobility was displayed by the horses' distance from the body of the carriage. The higher the rank, the longer the shafts, so that those with the most prodigious length had great difficulty negotiating tight corners. Two carriages traveling in opposite directions found it impossible to pass and was "the occasion of much hard swearing," recorded Samuel Hazard. Thus, Habana Vieja's system of one-way streets dates to this period. Many of the street signs embedded in the walls of Habana Vieja still bear a hand in a frilly cuff pointing the way for passing *caleseros* (coach drivers).

The city must have resembled a grand operatic production—especially at night, with the harbor, crosshatched by masts and spars, shining under the glint of soft moonlight. It also must have been a sight to watch the coquettish maidens wearing white ballgowns and necklaces of giant *coculios* (fireflies) gathering on Sunday for the brilliant masked balls. These occasions were eagerly anticipated by Habaneras, who were "passionately fond of dancing, and tax the endurance of the gentlemen in their heroic worship of Terpsichore," wrote traveler Maturin Ballou. Adds Juliet Barclay in her marvelous book, *Havana: Portrait of a City:* "The *Criollo* stalked about, exchanging stately salutations and lifting an eyebrow at the parvenu, who, with one eye on his own wife and the other on everyone else's, sought introductions."

By day, the female citizenry—at least the well-to-do—spent most of their time indoors (to walk the streets was considered a social solecism). Here, eligible maidens stared through the *rejas* (wooden grills), looking out wistfully upon life itself passing by and, presumably, exuding flirtatious naughtiness at handsome men. Occasionally they went shopping, hidden from view in *volantas* to which the goods were brought for inspection. Havana's cloistered beauties could receive visitors, however, when formalities were as starched as the collars of the gentlemen who came to visit.

While Habaneras wiled away their days indoors, wealthy menfolk spent most of their days in idle splendor: gambling, dallying with their mistresses, enjoying the thrill of a bullfight or the Valla de Gallos, where cockerels were tormented into a frenzy, then released to fight to the death (gambling was dear to citizenry, who often "went wild, roaring, howling, and shrieking 'Mata! Mata!,' 'Kill! Kill,' " records Juliet Barclay). The gentry also frequented brothels, of which Havana had several hundred, concentrated along Calles Teniente Rey and Habana. Like the chaste virgins, prostitutes by law were resigned to life behind bars. While husbands philandered, many of their wives found solace in religion, although, claims Barclay, "not necessarily in the traditional sense," for "many of them were visited by Holy Fathers, who went ostensibly to hear confession but frequently gave further cause for it."

Amid the splendor, Havana had its sordid side. It was a "villainously odiferous" city, and many fastidious Northerners, who flocked there for the winter sun and a taste of exoticism, commented on the offensive olfactory cocktail. The cacophony of noises also preyed upon their fragile sensibilities (even late at night, when the arguing, partying mobs were sound asleep, the bells in the churches and castles rang the quarter hours, while the stomping boots and stentorian cries of *serenos* (street watchmen) caused insomniacs to contemplate murder with their nocturnal cries of "All serene!" Life was indeed hard for many citizens, and to survive, the desperate and cut-throat evolved entrepreneurial skills worthy of Sweeney Todd (during the 19th century, a gang of sausage manufacturers grew wealthy kidnapping plump Negroes for the mincer; their sausages, sold as prime meat, were highly popular until their deeds were eventually discovered). Indeed, Regla, the little town across the harbor, had developed into a rendezvous for smugglers and remained a center for cut-throats and pirates into the 20th century.

The British Take Over

By the turn of the 18th century, Havana, which by then numbered about 40,000 inhabitants, was the third-largest city in the New World (after Mexico City and Lima). It was also heavily fortified, so its citizens must have felt few qualms for the future when, on 4 January 1762, George III of England declared war on Spain. Some years before, the British governor of Jamaica, Charles Knowles, had been hosted on an official visit to Havana, where he spent much of his time reconnoitering the city's defenses. Knowles was consulted by England's military leaders, and a plan was drawn up for an attack on Havana. It was an audacious scheme that would shake Havana, and Cuba, to the core.

Though the city was heavily defended, its Achilles' heel was the Cabaña, a long ridge overlooking Morro Castle and Havana's harbor. On 6 June, a British fleet of 28 warships and 145 transport ships carrying 11,000 troops arrived off Cojímar, a small cove about 12 miles east of the city. The next day, the troops put ashore and Havana erupted in panic—various governors and the citizenry had been resting on their laurels for decades, had grown lazy, and were ill-prepared to repel a well-organized attack. Every fit man in Havana was summoned to fight, and 9,000 foreign seamen in harbor were coerced to the city's defense. The Spanish—encumbered by what Juliet Barclay terms "Governor de Prado's bovine serenity"—scuttled three ships in the harbor mouth, ineptly trapping their own warships inside the harbor, while the governor's order to evacuate all women and children managed to block all the streets to troop movement. That night, when Spanish guards atop the Cabaña began firing at British scouts, the Spanish warships began blasting the ridge, causing their own troops to flee and thereby permitting British troops to take the ridge and begin preparations for a siege of Havana. The castle governor, Captain Luis de Velasco, knowing that his position was hopeless, sent an emissary to the city requesting instructions from the Capitán General as to whether he should surrender. The vague reply left him no choice but to fulfill his military honor and hold out until the last man.

Meanwhile, the British entrenched, and a six-week bombardment of the Castillo de Morro ensued. On 29 July, British sappers blew an enormous hole in the seaward side of the Morro, which was swiftly captured (Velasco was seriously wounded in the assault and could do little to organize the defense as British troops rushed in), and the flag of St. George was raised over the castle. The British commander, George Keppel, Count of Albermarle, remarked that "Spanish sloth and stupidity is unaccountable," although Keppel was a person with more influence at court than military prowess. The British had not had it all their own way. They lost thousands of troops to heat and sickness, and had to call on reserves from North America. Still, Havana held out, though the British had dammed the Zanja, the aqueduct that supplied the city with water. On 3 August, after the governor had refused to surrender, British cannonballs began to rain down on the city. At two o'clock on 13 August 1762, the surrender flag fluttered over Havana. British Admiral Sir George Pocock permitted the Spanish troops to depart, then took over the city (Pocock received a reward of £122,697 for taking Havana).

The Spanish Crown had treated Cuba as a colonial cash cow to milk dry as it pleased. The British, it appeared, were more enlightened, and immediately lifted trade restrictions and opened the island up to free trade to foreign vessels (including unrestricted trade in slaves). Foreign merchants flocked, and Cuba witnessed surging prosperity as a trading frenzy ensued. Overnight, Havana became what Abbé Guillaume Raynal called the "boulevard of the New World." To his discredit, however, Keppel seemed equally bent on milking Havana dry. He imposed usurious levies upon the citizens and especially upon the Catholic church (after the British commandeered Iglesia San Francisco de Asís for Protestant worship, the church was never again used for service by Havana's citizens), creating a bitter loathing for the British.

The Habaneros were relieved of further indignation on 10 February 1763, when England and Spain signed the Treaty of Paris, ending the war and allowing England to exchange Cuba for Florida (sugar planters in Jamaica had pressured England to cede back to Spain what would otherwise become a formidable rival for the British sugar market). On 6 July, the last British troops departed Havana.

The Spanish lost no time in rebuilding their forts, and between 1764 and 1774 constructed an enormous fortress—San Carlos de la Cabaña, the largest fortress in the Americas—atop the Cabaña ridge. The British invasion ensured that Havana fortunes and fortifications would never again be neglected by Spain.

THE LATE COLONIAL ERA

Havana Comes of Age

Meanwhile, Spain had acquired a more enlightened king, Charles III. The boom continued, encouraged a decade later when the newly independent United States began trading directly with Cuba. The North Americans' collective sweet tooth fostered the rapid expansion of sugar plantations in Cuba. Vast fortunes were being made in sugar—and therefore also in slaves. Wealthy Cuban and US slave merchants funded planting of new lands in sugar by granting loans for capital improvements, all meant to foster an increasing need for slaves. Land planted in sugar multiplied more than tenfold by the turn of the 18th century. For the first time, sugar outstripped tobacco in importance. Havana reaped the benefits as wealth continued to pour into the city. (The planters themselves, however, weren't as a rule wealthy men. Their estates were deeply mortgaged to various port merchants, who were normally Spaniards, Americans, or Europeans, but rarely Cubans. "The slave-owners are but go-betweens, who secure the profits of the slave-trade for the merchants," wrote Anthony Trollope.)

Cuba's slave population had been slow to develop compared to that of neighboring Caribbean islands. The short tenure of British rule in 1765, however, sent the slave trade soaring. British slave traders established themselves in Havana and remained thereafter to profit in the booming trade alongside Habaneros. Between 1791 and 1810, more than 100,000 slaves arrived (and countless more undocumented slaves were brought in illegally). A royal decree in 1818 opened Cuba's ports to free trade; the sudden explosion in the sugar trade and production saw more than 500,000 slaves imported in the ensuing decade. By 1840, slaves constituted 45% of the population.

Havana grew more elegant and sophisticated every year. By 1760, it was already larger than New York or Boston. The first university had been established in 1728. The first newspaper appeared in 1763, and the postal service in 1764.

Cuba's citizenry was growing vastly wealthy on trade with North America, with the difference that now much of the prosperity flowed back to Cuba, changing the face of Havana.

Late colonial Havana benefited from repeated urban renewal plans intended to lend a powerful public face to Spain's cherished island. Following the return of Cuba to Spain in 1763, the new Spanish governor, the Marqués de la Torre, initiated a public works program. Havana attained a new focus and rigorous architectural harmony, with a more comprehensive approach to urban planning following a grid pattern dictated by the New Laws of the Indies. Elegant Paseo de Extramuros (later renamed the Paseo del Prado) was laid as the first boulevard outside the city walls, great warehouses went up along the harborfront, and most of the streets—which had by now been given the names they possess today—were cobbled. The first gas lighting arrived in 1768, along with a workable system of aqueducts. Until 1790, when night fell, darkness kept most Cubans off the streets, except those who were up to no good. That year, street lamps went up throughout the city.

Havana's oldest plaza—the Plaza de Armas—was reconstructed, with a fine park and a grandiose governor's residence (the Palacio de los Capitanes Generales) and other grand *palacios* lining each side. The Plaza de Viejas, dating back to 1584, emerged afresh as a fashionable quarter with galleried palaces. And a baroque cathedral and ornate merchant's palaces were erected in the Plaza de Cienaga (today's Plaza de la Catedrál), formerly a swampy area that earlier in the century had functioned as a fish market. The elaborately contoured facade of the Havana Cathedral, completed around 1777, epitomized the peak of Spanish baroque. (On 15 January 1796, the *San Lorenzo* sailed into Havana harbor, bringing what were thought to be the ashes of Christopher Columbus from Santo Domingo, after the island had passed into the hands of France. The coffin, swathed in black velvet, was laid to rest in the new cathedral and remained there until 1899, when it was returned to Spain.)

Havana owes much of its modern face to Governor Miguel Tacón y Rosique, an ultra-conservative monarchist named governor in 1843. He conceived an integrated urban expansion plan and initiated a brisk program of redesign in which old facades were realigned and "set to the rhythmic cadence of columned *portales* running for blocks at a time," according to Rachel Carey. Tacón ordered the streets cleaned, drove out criminals, and whipped the idle and unemployed into action. He built fountains and a great theater (a precursor to today's Gran Teatro), paved the streets and erected street signs, and created a fire brigade and Havana's first police force. Tacón also supported the first railroad in the Spanish colonies, linking Havana with Bejucal in 1837 (Havana's first railroad station opened that year). The Prado Militar—today known as Avenida Salvador Allende—was laid out, knifing east-west to permit rapid troop deployment into the city from the Castillo del Príncipe in the event of revolt.

Tacón also commissioned a governor's country house—the Quinta de los Molinos—midway along the length of the Prado Militar, which became a ceremonial avenue popular for fashionable perambulation by the social elite. The ancient, uncovered aqueduct that carried water from the Río Almendares to the city center was covered, increasing the water purity (later, 400 springs nine miles south of Havana were enclosed, and an aqueduct and storage facility increased the water supply). Fortunately for latter-day tourists, Tacón had a rival: the Conde de Villanueva, the *criollo* administrator of the royal estates.

The elitist *peninsulares* (native Spaniards) ran Cuba as a fiefdom, and *criollos* were allowed no say in administration of the island. Unquenchable animosity had arisen between them, firing the wars of independence that were to tear Cuba asunder during much of the ensuing century, but also fueling a contest to erect public and rival edifices as expressions of Spanish and disaffected *criollo* pride. We owe the Templete, the neobaroque Gran Teatro on Parque Central, and the contemporary face of the Prado to this feud.

The City Bursts its Seams

Havana was by now a densely populated city. But its 55,000 citizens were trapped *intramuros* (within the city walls). New buildings were going up, and the city was bursting with uncontainable energy. Soon not a square centimeter was left for building within the city walls, and affluent families had begun moving to the city outskirts in search of healthier surroundings. A rapid expansion of

ARCHIVO DEL MUSEO DE LA CUIDAD DE LA HAVANA

Governor Miguel Tacón y Rosique

residential districts *extramuros* (beyond the city walls) began with El Cerro, a cool, hilly region immediately southwest of the old city.

In 1863, the city walls came tumbling down—less than a century after their completion. Urban green spaces were introduced in Vedado, a new upscale district laid out in 1859 behind the shore west of Habana Vieja. It became the first city quarter with strips of planted greenery between sidewalk and street. The city's eternal nemesis, an inadequate water supply, was resolved by a Cuban engineer, Don Francisco de Albear, who in 1856 began work on an aqueduct to take water from the fast-flowing Vento springs on the left bank of the Río Almendares. Graceful boulevards pushed westward—part of a planned redesign of the city (aided by the city's first formal building codes, passed in 1861)—into the surrounding hills and countryside, lined with a parade of *quintas* (country houses) fronted by classical columns. The baroque bowed out, as architects harked back further to the heyday of Greece, utilizing neoclassicism in their public edifices to convey a sense of cultural achievement and dignity (the period saw a surfeit of marble, imposing colonnades, and pediments).

The upper classes abandoned their inner-city *palacios,* many of which gradually deteriorated into slums called *cuarterías.* By mid-century, the early colonial quarter contained many crowded, low-class rental buildings called *solares.* Richard Henry Dana Jr. recorded: "The drive, by way of Calzada de Jesús del Monte, takes one through a wretched portion, I hope the most wretched portion, of Havana, by long lines of one-story wood and mud hovels, hardly habitable even for Negroes."

War!

Spain continued to rule Cuba badly. Spain's colonial policy, applied throughout its empire, was based on exploitation, with power centralized in Madrid and politics practiced only for the spoils of office and to the benefit of *peninsulares.* Spain's monopoly laws encouraged the migration to Cuba of a kind of Spanish carpetbagger. Native *criollos* resented the corrupt *peninsulares,* who denied them self-determination. No Cuban could occupy a public post, set up an industry or business, bring legal action against a Spaniard, or travel without military permission. By the early 19th century, a new generation of young Cuban intellectuals and patriots began to make their voices heard. Nationalist feelings ran high. On 10 October 1868, a lawyer, poet, and planter named Carlos Manuel de Céspedes freed the slaves on his plantation at La Demajagua, near Manzanillo, in Oriente province. He raised the *Grito de Yara* (Shout of Yara), a cry of liberty that resounded around the island. The wars of independence erupted.

Havana's intellectual elite were *criollo* nationalists whose illicit writings and speeches for the cause of independence brought a wave of repression to the city streets. Spanish volunteers were recruited as a militia, and once arrived, they quickly slipped beyond control of authorities, terrorizing the people of Havana. Spanish authorities in Havana meted out harsh sentences against anyone who declared himself against Spain. La Cabaña became a jail, and many famous nationalist figures, including José Martí, a young *criollo* writer and thinker born in 1854 on Calle Leonor Pérez who would later lead the independence movement, were imprisoned here. The walls of the Foso de los Laureles, the moat of La Cabaña, resounded to the crack of the firing squad as scores of *criollos* were shot for treason.

Meanwhile, Cuba's commercial development had broadened and a large middle class had developed. While Havana matured, the surrounding countryside was being laid waste by war, and many wealthy land-owning Habaneros were forced to sell their crippled estates to US citizens.

Spain clung to its colony with despairing strength and the support of many wealthy *criollos* (concentrated in western Cuba), who feared that abolitionist sentiments in Europe would lead to the abolition of slavery in Cuba. They looked to the United States, where slavery thrived, for support. Public sentiment in the United States favored the Mambí—the independence fighters. The US public hungered for information about the war, feeding sales of newspapers. The *New York World* and *New York Journal* (owned, respectively, by Joseph Pulitzer and William Randolph Hearst) started a race to see which newspaper could first reach one million subscribers. The press took on the job of inflaming Yankee patriotism and fanning war fever based on fabrication and lies. While Hearst's hacks made up stories from Cuba, the magnate himself worked behind the scenes to orchestrate dramatic events. He sent artist Frederic Remington to Cuba in anticipation of the US entering the war. At one point, Remington wired Hearst: "There will be no war. I wish to return." Hearst hastily replied: "Please remain. You furnish the pictures and I'll furnish the war."

Remember the *Maine!*

Responding to public pressure, President McKinley had sent the USS *Maine* to Havana, ostensibly to protect US citizens living there. The US government had long coveted Cuba and found its pretext when the warship mysteriously exploded in Havana harbor on 5 February 1898, killing 258 people. No one knows whether this was an accident or the work of the Spanish, Cuban nationalists, or, as is more likely, merely an accident, but Hearst had his coup and rushed the news out in huge red headlines, beating the *World* to one million sales. He blamed the Spanish, and so did the public. His *New York Journal* coined the phrase "Remember the Maine, to hell with Spain." The paper belabored the jingoistic phrase day after day. The reaction in the US was furious; it was taken for granted that Spain was responsible. (The hulk of the *Maine* lay in the harbor until 1912, when the rusting symbol of *norteamericano* interference in Cuban affairs was raised, hauled far out to sea, and sunk.)

Other North Americans were eager to test their mettle, too, especially the army and navy, which hadn't seen action in more than three decades and had modern equipment to put to the test. Theodore Roosevelt, then Assistant Secretary of the Navy, also fanned the flames, seeing the venture as "good for the navy."

Thus, on 25 April 1898, Congress declared war against Spain (US forces also invaded Puerto Rico, Guam, and the Philippines, which they captured in one day). On 17 July, Spain surren-

the US battleship Maine explodes in Havana Harbor

dered. The Spanish flag was lowered and the Stars and Stripes raised, ending one of the most foolishly run empires in the world. In an act of gross arrogance, US military leaders refused to invite the Mambí (the Cuban freedom fighters) to the victory ceremony and parade. The Cuban people have never forgotten the slight.

The US military occupation formally began on 1 January 1899, when 15 infantry regiments, one of engineers and four of artillery, arrived to "pacify" Cuba. For the first, but not the last time, US troops occupied Havana. Officers who spoke no Spanish, had never lived in a hot country, and had no notion of Spanish or Cuban history and ideals found themselves in charge of a tired, starving people and a devastated land wrecked by war. US intentions were at least partly honorable: "It would have been a poor boon to Cuba to drive the Spaniards out and leave her to care for herself, with two-thirds of her people unable to read and write, and wholly ignorant of the art of self-government," stated Secretary of War Elihu Root. Although the US military administration swiftly initiated far-reaching reforms—including setting up schools, starting a postal system, establishing a judiciary and civil service, and eradicating the yellow-fever epidemics then common in Havana—Cuba ended the century as it had begun—under foreign rule.

THE REPUBLICAN ERA (1898-1959)

Into the 20th Century

On Ascencion Day (20 May) 1902, the Stars and Stripes was lowered and the lone-star flag of Cuba rose into the sunny sky of Havana. The city broke up in a three-day spree of rejoicing. But Washington "granted" Cuba "independence"—at the end of a short leash. Even the Cuban Constitution was written by Washington, in 1901, ushering in a period known as the Pseudo-Republic. "It's not the republic we dreamed of," said black general and war hero Máximo Gómez.

The opening years of the Cuban republic were a time of great opportunity. The economy was in shambles and everything was up for grabs. Cuba witnessed a great influx of capital as US companies invested in every major industry—tobacco, railroads, utilities, mining, and, above all, sugar. Several thousand US citizens settled

there, bringing their North American style and sensibilities to the city. Cuba became a giant Monopoly board controlled by Uncle Sam (politically, Washington called the shots), but the economy blossomed. Havana witnessed a postwar boom and expanded markedly during the early 1900s, when Cuba received a surge of immigrants from the West Indies, the United States, and Europe, including 200,000 Spaniards who continued to dominate the city's mercantile trade (Cuba almost tripled its population 1900-30). Cuba's postwar boom and rising land values fostered a frenzied real estate boom, setting the stage for the development of Havana's periphery.

Havana's residential expansion had hitherto moved outward from the ancient core along routes that had originally followed its topography. Housing occupied ridges and hills, avoiding flood-prone valleys. By the mid-19th century, Chinese immigrants had occupied the marshy lowlands, which they drained and planted with market gardens to supply the Habaneros. As the city expanded, land values rose and the Chinese were squeezed out. A massive public works initiated in 1907 moved millions of tons of earth into the valleys, which were raised for residential development. Surveyors laid out the roads that would link Habana Vieja with the rapidly expanding areas of Vedado, Cerro, Vista Alegre, and other suburbs beyond the Río Almendares, where the middle classes were building dwellings in eclectic, neo-classical, and revivalist styles.

As early as the mid-19th century, wealthy Spanish officials and sugar planters had built fine summer homes in Marianao, about eight miles west of the city center, laying down streets on the breeze-swept land that rose inland of the shore. A railroad had been laid in 1863, and a paved road in 1864. General Fitzhugh Lee, the region's US military governor during the occupation, also found Marianao to his liking. He had established his headquarters here in a Spanish nobleman's abandoned home, with views across luxuriant gardens and, beyond, a bucolic landscape edging down to the sea. Lee set up Camp Columbia atop Marianao's heights as headquarters of the occupation troops, fueling a new prosperity for the region. Electricity and new water supplies were extended westward, local merchants soon followed, and Marianao experienced a rapid expansion (its population doubled from 18,156 to 37,464 between 1907 and 1919).

Most of the investors were local, led by Carlos Miguel de Céspedes and his partners, José Manuel Cortina and Carlos Manuel de la Cruz (the "Three C's"). With an eye to forging a tourism boom, their Compañia Urbanizadora Playa de Marianao developed residential lots in Marianao and pushed for the legalization of gambling. Céspedes and his Cuban buddies had a vested interest: they were partners in a tourism-related gambling concession. Marianao was set to become Havana's tourist mecca. At the time, it was already a nontourist amusement center that at night resounded to the heartbeart and songbeat of Africa "from rows of café hovels" and "smoky, low-roofed dance halls" where the poor of Havana went for entertainment after dark. The middle-class blacks had their own sophisticated cultural organizations, such as Club Atenas. No rumbas here, however. In the Cuba of the time, "only the poor and déclassé, the sporting elements, and gentlemen on a spree danced the rumba," recalls Frederic Remington.

The desire to foster tourism proved good for the city. By 1900, water pipes had been laid throughout the city to supply water tanks that had been built under most buildings, and Havana could boast a clean water supply throughout the city (the aqueduct begun by Don Francisco de Albear in 1856 had taken four decades to complete, but proved outstanding enough to win a gold medal at the Paris Exhibition; today it still brings water into the city center). But only one-eighth of the city had sewers (most houses were served by cell-pools, which were occasionally drained and the contents dumped into the harbor). Although fresh water flowed from hotel faucets, passengers aboard ships arriving in Havana harbor were greeted by the gut-wrenching smell of sewage flowing directly from the long-neglected sewers. Disease was rife— and bad for tourism. In 1907, therefore, the Cuban government initiated far-reaching public works that included new highways and sewers. By 1920, $55 million had been spent on public works, and more than 265 miles of sewer pipes and storm drains had been built, with a pumping station that bilged human waste into the sea at Cojímar, several miles east of the city.

All this fine public work, of course, benefited government officials and their civilian cronies immensely, but many of them ploughed their money back into tourism. The crowded narrow streets and tight, shade-giving colonial quarters of older sections gave way to broad sidewalks and shaded porches facing onto broad lawns. The city began to spread out, its perimeter enlarged by grid extensions (*ensanches*) incorporating parks, boulevards, and civic spaces. By 1910, uncrowded neighborhoods lined the city's western edge, including seaside communities beyond the Río Almendares. "Havana's physical reaching out from cramped quarters to openness symbolized the optimism of a generation," wrote Rosalie Schwartz. The capital city—jewel of the Caribbean—wore a new luster, and "a healthful and pleasurable city unfolded before the tourists' eyes."

Meanwhile, many colonial mansions disappeared, leveled by the wrecking ball and replaced by commercial establishments such as banks. Many other once-grand colonial homes were subdivided and rented to less affluent Habaneros who could not afford the upkeep, while the real estate boom sponsored further spatial fragmentation, turning homes that once belonged to single families into beehives. The communities of *solares* expanded, the humble, unsanitary dwellings crowded within patios and back lots of buildings and hidden from the street. Some *solares* were in *ciudadelas*, small cities—virtual rabbit warrens—within the city, in independent buildings erected inside the enclosed grounds of a large urban unit. One such configuration was the Arco building in Vedado, looking like a fortress, with three structures of six stories appropriately detached from the city by a moat. Havana's population explosion also fostered speculative housing developments for the poorer classes, built by low-paid bricklayers working without architectural designs; the tenement houses that sprang up throughout Havana were called *casa de vecindad.*

Discontent among the poorer classes found its outlet in frequent violent demonstrations that prompted US intervention. When an August 1906 uprising in Pinar del Río province spread to Havana, President Estrada asked for US marines to help quash it. US troops occupied Cuba for 28 months, during which time US Secretary of State William Taft ran the island as governor of a provisional government before turning the country over to an appointee of President Theodore Roosevelt. In 1912, US troops were again rushed to Havana when an outlawed Afro-Cuban party demonstrated against injustice toward blacks; the US response was to arrest and execute the party's leaders. Marines again poured into Havana in 1917 when workers called a general strike (this time the troops remained until 1923).

The Roaring Twenties

Following the end of World War I, materials and labor were again available, and Cuba experienced a renewed building boom fed by a rush from high sugar prices. The peak of the sugar boom—the "dance of the millions"—lasted from 1915 to 1920, when the price of sugar climbed to 22.5 cents a pound. Sugar money paid for the plush mansions then blossoming in Havana's Vedado district as the older residential areas settled into a period of decay. Thus, the capital city entered a new era.

Havana received electric lights, and electric trams reached into the surburbs. The Malecón was laid out. In the older city, the Presidential Palace (now the Museum of the Revolution) went up in 1920, melding vaguely classical allusions with Spanish colonial overtones, its interior appointments by the New York firm of Tiffany. Stylistically, architects stuck with the classical canon well into the republican period, though by the late 19th century, the Beaux Arts style was popular, and North American influences were now obvious (General Leonard Woods had reorganized the school of architecture along US lines). In the early 20th century, many of the financial buildings that went up in Habana Vieja took on the look of Wall Street. The art deco style then prevalent in Miami influenced other buildings, utilizing the geometrical terra-cotta motifs and vertical setbacks popular in North American skyscrapers.

Although sugar profits crashed in 1921 (and again in 1929), the building boom didn't end, as desperate suppliers of construction materials extended credit, and real estate bargain hunters took advantage to build on land they had purchased. Apartment blocks went up all over Havana, with cafés and corner stores at ground level. Many of the once-fashionable houses along the Prado and in Habana Vieja were converted for commercial use (many cherished old buildings were demolished because their ground space increased in value beyond that of the standing structure).

Céspedes was now President Machado's Public Works Secretary and the Cuban official most responsible for boosting Cuba's tourism industry. Hand in hand with wealthy Cuban investors, he promoted the expansion of the Miramar area west of the Río Almendares. They built streets and highways, and financed homes within reach of both the downtown area and the socialites' clubs and tourist facilities—such as the new Marianao country club. These facilities were farther west, in the fashionable new residential districts accessible by a lovely landscaped boulevard called La Quinta (Fifth Avenue). Wealthy *yanquis* and *Cubanos* built their posh mansions side by side in these western suburbs, where Havana's Oriental Park racetrack opened in 1915. (In 1919, and much to the chagrin of the US Congress, the Cuban congress passed a bill legalizing casinos. The politically connected Three C's managed to get another bill passed the same evening committing the

President Gerardo Machado

Cuban government to build a bridge that would link Vedado with Marianao.) Marianao and the adjacent area called Country Club—now called Cubanacán—were significant for evolving in a "garden-city" tradition, with winding tree-lined streets and enormous parklike lots. Wealthy businessfolk (17,000 foreign merchants, bankers, and the like lived in Havana) flocked to play golf at the Havana Country Club and gamble at Marianao's Oriental Park racetrack and Grand Nacional Casino. The Club became the place to be, and Country Club Park became the most exclusive address in town—Havana's Beverly Hills. Here were built the architecturally distinctive homes of the Cuban elite, who danced the *danzón* and Charleston at afternoon teas on the country club terrace.

Private clubs proliferated during the Republican era. The Lyceum Lawn Tennis Club and Vedado Tennis Club dated from the pre-WWI years, followed by the Havana Yacht Club (founded in 1888, though the clubhouse dates from 1924) and similar clubs west of the Río Almendares. Predominantly utilized by the Cuban upper crust, architecturally they combined a North American Beaux Arts style with a conservative expression of tradition quite aristocratic in scope.

President Gerardo Machado (1925-33) and Céspedes envisioned Havana as a model modern city on the grand European theme using a city beautification plan based on Jean-Claude Nicolas Forestier's Beaux Arts scheme. Forestier, an internationally acclaimed landscape designer who had reshaped Paris, led an interdisciplinary team of Cuban designers who would pay homage to Havana's history while reshaping the city. They created landscaped malls, tree-lined avenues, parterres, and a gigantic park at the heart of a new metropolitan center. In 1926, Machado signed off on a master enlargement plan for the capital, financed by new real estate and luxury taxes, and bonds issued by Chase Manhattan Bank in New York. It was the most ambitious plan since that of colonial governor Miguel Tacón in the 1830s.

Machado's fall from power in 1933 left much of the plan unfulfilled, but not without leaving behind some notable achievements. These included giving the Paseo de Prado its modern face, with a double aisle of laurel trees; remodeling and extending the Malecón west to the Almendares River and east to the docks along the newly constructed Avenida del Puerto; conceiving an acropolis-like structure and classically inspired tiered staircase for the University of Havana; and planning new hotels for Vedado. Also, in 1929 a Central Post Office had been added, and that same year, the ribbon was cut on the statuesque Capitolio, a symmetrically massed structure some 692 feet long that is perhaps Havana's greatest symbol of classical ceremony, an appropriate place for the legislature to take its seats. The Capitolio was begun in 1912 under President Mario Menocal (1912-20) on the site of a partially built presidential palace. Redesigned during the Machado years and completed only after the initial dome had been blown off with dynamite, it soaked up 25 percent of the US$50 million national budget.

Cuba of the 1920s was far and away the richest tropical country anywhere, with a per capita income equivalent to that of Ireland, two-thirds that of Britain, and half that of the United States. Most of the wealth was concentrated in Havana. The city truly was the Pearl of the Antilles and soon vied with Florida for the title of America's Riviera.

Yankee Doodle Comes to Town

The US Congress gave Cuban tourism a major boost on 1 July 1919 when it enacted Prohibition. Within months of the US going dry, John Bowman, New York hotelier and father of the Biltmore hotel chain, purchased Havana's Hotel Sevilla (built in 1908). He pumped half a million dollars into the hotel and reopened it in 1920 as the most lavish hotel in Havana.

Cuba beckoned from tourist posters and brochures, and US magazines outdid themselves in purple prose full of sultry mahogany-colored maidens and sensuous men. In a 1923 issue of *Travel* magazine, Sir Basil Thompson wrote of tourists strolling the Malecón, whose lights "shone like a diamond necklace about the throat of a dusky Aphrodite." Tourism promoters also began to boost Cuba's African heritage, and Regla, the working-class *barrio* across the harbor, received gawkers seeking out the sight of near-naked, dark-skinned Cubans dancing to rhythms "more savage than the beat of tom-toms." As Prohibition and a wave of morality swept through the United States, Yankees flocked to Havana, where those who chose could wallow up to their noses in cocaine and sex. At least 20 steamships arrived in Havana's commodious harbor weekly from US ports (so lucrative was the New York-Havana route that P&O ordered a 700-passenger steamer for the passage to compete with Cunard and the Ward Line). Passengers escaping the snows of New York for Havana's winter sunshine paid as little as $40 one-way, first-class, with meals.

In ensuing decades, Havana attracted the good and the bad in about equal measure. Prostitution was rampant (it had always been present in Cuba's major port city), and the 1928 edition of *Terry's Guide to Cuba* told readers how to find houses where voyeurs could witness live sex or, in Havana's officially nonexistent "indecorous quarter," procure "teenagers who ranged in color from peach to coal" roaming the streets alongside ebony antiques. Guidebooks even lured tourists with accounts of tong wars and murky opium dens in Havana's Chinese quarter, where narcotics were sold openly on Dragones Street. Nightclub revues enhanced Havana's reputation for often salacious sensuality. "Nights of HOLLYWOOD" were "nights of pleasure," proclaimed Club Hollywood, which touted a "gorgeous revue" of "15 GIRLS." The Rex Dancing Club had 200 girls. Open-air restaurants on Miramar's boulevards offered their own floor shows alfresco as desserts after dining.

Havana, wrote Juliet Barclay, filled with "milkshakes and mafiosi, hot dogs and whores. Yanqui Doodle had come to town and was having martini-drinking competitions in the Sevilla Bar." When US naval vessels entered Havana harbor, the narrow harbor mouth beneath Morro Castle was "jammed with rowboats full of clamoring prostitutes," recalls one sailor.

By the mid-1920s, when Havana's population reached about 250,000, some 80,000 tourists called on Cuba each year to realize their dreams of romance and adventure. When Havana's first scheduled airline service began in 1931, socialites and the working class alike hopped a plane for Havana to sidestep propriety and class barriers. They hoped to find youthful self-expression and nourish their human frailties with swarthy gigolos and dusky maidens at a time when "scandalizing one's parents and

pastors became the thing to do" and sex appeal "signaled a willingness . . . to pluck a new personality from under the apron or the pinstriped suit," suggests Rosalie Schwartz. Hollywood, too, helped bolster the image of a Latin mystique. Who could resist Rudolf Valentino's smoldering eyes or the come-hither look of Marlene Dietrich personifying the "sexual danger" of a cabaret dancer. Havana offered new frontiers at a time when old ones had been tamed.

The city's hotels jammed with curious sightseers who scattered their dollars throughout the city, filling the cash boxes of nightclubs and casinos. (More than US$400 million flowed in from US tourists in 1926.) Tourism revenues sifted through the economy, multiplying in effect as dollars turned over many times in the local economy, through restaurants, taxi services, souvenir sellers, and, not least, prostitution. Tourists called the shots. Havana's traditional carnival was even changed to meet their expectations, moving the Mardi Gras Lenten season forward, increasing the number of days to enhance the tourist season, and adding imported theatrical pageantry to the sensuous music and dance of Afro-Cuban *comparsas* (the two traditional *comparsas* of the 1930s expanded to 10 companies in the 1950s). Unlike other Caribbean countries, where carnival is traditionally celebrated in spring, Havana's carnival was held, devoid of Christian significance, in late July (after the Revolution, it neatly coincided with the anniversary of Castro's attack on the Moncada barracks on 26 July 1952).

While Havana was developing a reputation for libertine pleasures, it was also a cultured city with rapidly expanding middle and upper classes. They found new pleasure in golf at Bowman's Biltmore Yacht and Country Club, completed in 1928 behind a fine beach on the shorefront of Cubanacán, its 2,000-acre lot stretching along five miles of shore and offering fine views of the Straits of Florida. Billed as the "world's grandest resort," it boasted its own casino and seafront hotel and marina blasted from the coral foreshore. To serve the middle classes, a bathing pavilion with 1,000 cabanas was also added at La Playa, the public beach on the Cubanacán shore. The poorer classes found their pleasures along the Malecón, where square baths called the Elysian Fields had been carved into the shoreline rocks. It was "delicious to while away hot afternoons under the striped awnings . . . wriggling one's toes in the white sand and shells, and splashing in the gentle swirl of the waves," wrote Juliet Barclay. "Visitors to the city were fond of what the Habaneros considered the lunatic pursuit of sea bathing all year round."

Big Trouble in Havana

Cuban society has been triple-tiered in social color terms. At the base are the pure-blooded blacks. In the middle, the mixed bloods. At the top, the whites and near-whites. But these lines have never been as tightly drawn as in the other Caribbean islands. "The British islands are the worst in this respect. The Latin Islands are more careless concerning racial matters," observed Langston Hughes, who also thought Havana's color lines to be "much more flexible than that of the United States, and much more subtle. There are no Jim Crow cars in Cuba, and at official state gatherings and less official carnivals and celebrations, citizens of all colors meet and mingle." Nonetheless, a separate culture had developed, and Havana had its own black social clubs and fine restaurants for the black middle classes.

Unfortunately, Americans brought Southern racial prejudice to their winter playground. To court the approval of racially bigoted yankees, hotels that were formerly lax in their application of color lines began to discourage even mulatto Cubans. The Biltmore club, which had taken over the city's only wide, clean stretch of beach, now charged a dollar for the privilege of its use (no small sum in those days) and introduced a color bar as well, although mulatto plutocrats and policemen still mingled there. Later, in the 1950s, even President Batista would be blackballed by the Havana Yacht Club because he was mulatto. Havana society of the time, wrote Hugh Thomas, was "one in which relations between black and white were of an extreme, if tolerant complexity, endogamy combined with joint preoccupation with Afro-Cuban cults as well as left wing politics. The prejudices which kept blacks from the new luxury hotels of the late 1950s were still things of the future."

Despite Washington's better intentions, Cuban politics had swiftly sunk into a spiral of corruption and graft. Following the War of Independence, Washington had firmly wanted to establish a stable, democratic government in the US tradi-

tion. Alas, Uncle Sam—who, in writing the Cuban Constitution, had copied the US Constitution almost verbatim—chose an Anglo-Saxon system unsuited to the Cuban mentality; the centuries of corruption and graft could not be eradicated overnight. Cubans sought political office by which to get rich—an idea heartily endorsed by powerful US business interests, which also profited—and the US government was constantly influenced to support this or that Cuban who had given, or would give, opportunities to US investors or who had borrowed from North American banks. Year by year, Cuba became more corrupt.

Each Cuban president forged new frauds of his own, handing out sinecures (which the Cubans called *botellas*—milk bottles given to babies) to cronies. Through successive administrations, Cuban politics sank deeper into iniquity. Despite its hopes for a better system, Washington discouraged any changes in the status quo where the country's efforts at political and economic reform threatened North American investors. "Dollar diplomacy" it was called (a term coined by President Howard Taft). When US economic interests were threatened, Uncle Sam sent in troops. Dollar diplomacy was blind to the corruption, state violence, and poverty plaguing the country. The sordid system would last six decades, until a bearded young rebel came down from the mountains to oust the ancien régime.

Like his predecessors, Machado and his cronies were corrupt men susceptible to *la mordida* (literally, the bite—bribes). Although he sponsored Cuba's economic development and was responsible for magnificent enhancements to Havana, he gradually became a tropical Mussolini: at the end of his democratic four-year term (Machado had manipulated the phony 1928 election, triggering a wave of opposition), he announced that the demands of government called for a six-year term, and he himself would fill it. The dictator was unwilling to accommodate opposition. However, it blossomed during the Great Depression, which coincided with the collapse of Cuba's one-crop sugar economy and wrought misery throughout the country. Poverty stalked the streets of Havana.

Machado responded to mounting antigovernment demonstrations with an iron fist. Thousands of Cubans were imprisoned, tortured, and executed as Machado's sense of self-importance mounted. Labor leaders were murdered, as were students. When fellow students protested, he closed the universities. Havana was mired in deep unrest and violence, including assassinations and random bombings. Carleton Beals, a journalist who visited Havana in 1932 against a backdrop of chaos, wrote: "Beneath the tropical opulence of Cuba, hidden in the tangled jungle of her present cruel political tyranny, are the fangs of bitter discontent. . . . Outwardly Havana was a tomb. In reality it was a boiling cauldron." Beals blamed Machado and an American policy toward Cuba that "helped drive her to despair and ruin." Machado in fact remained in power because he was supported by powerful US economic interests. Walker Evans was assigned to shoot the photographs to complement Beals' text, published in *The Crime of Cuba.*

In July 1933, a Havana radio falsely announced that Machado had resigned, and delighted citizens took to the streets by the thousands with the rallying cry, "Long live free Cuba!" Machado's police taught them the truth by mowing them down, killing 20 people. Finally, in the summer of 1933, a general strike brought the whole country to a halt. On 11 August, Machado fled the country carrying a suitcase full of gold.

Yet tourism was barely affected: free-spending foreigners staying at the newly opened Hotel Nacional above the Malecón saw only a prosperous and exotic city with modern amenities, and went home to spread the good news.

The Post-Machado Years

The post-Machado era witnessed a series of ineffectual presidents in rapid succession. Only the army could reestablish control. A few weeks after Machado fled, a 32-year old sergeant named Fulgencio Batista y Zaldívar effected a *golpe* (coup) called the Sergeant's Revolt. Havana's university students signed on, and one of their own professors—Ramón Grau—became president. Grau's leftist leanings, however, proved untenable for Washington, which persuaded Batista to force him aside. Supported by the US, the upstart sergeant wielded control behind a veil of stooge presidents whom he selected and deposed in quick succession.

President Roosevelt advised the Cubans to expand tourism, but to forsake gambling and cabarets in favor of more culturally uplifting at-

President Ramón Grau

tractions. "In Roosevelt's view," wrote Rosalie Schwartz, "a country concerned with its well-being had to attract responsible persons, using entertainment compatible with human dignity." A new breed of civic-minded businessmen had similar thoughts and put its shoulder into constructing and enhancing cultural facilities throughout the capital, substituting museums for Monte Carlo. A vast new park—Bosque de la Habana—was even laid out. Although sporadic violence broke out in 1935 as Batista consolidated his authority, tourists responded to Havana's many allures. Despite Roosevelt's admonition, the casinos gained a new vigor.

The outbreak of World War II burst Havana's tourist bubble, but Habaneros had again arrived at a relative calm. In 1940, a new constitution reflected more enlightened attitudes toward civil liberties, workers' rights, and public welfare. That year, Batista put away his marionettes and ran for the presidency on a progressive platform. Cuban voters gave him a four-year term (1940-44) in what was perhaps the nation's first clean election. In 1944, following a benign term, Batista retired to Florida, leaving his country in the hands of men who permitted their administrations to again sink into chaos and corruption. Street demonstrations, assassinations, and bombings were once more daily events on the streets of Havana.

As the end of World War II approached, the United States became concerned that cutbacks in US production would coincide with the return of hundreds of thousands of GIs to the civilian labor force. It therefore sponsored tourism as an economic development strategy, and Havana—what the *Washington Times* called a "prodigious pastel Paradise"—was a beneficiary.

War-ravaged Europe would be unable to absorb the outpouring of US production. Washington needed to promote rapid market expansion and looked to Latin America. Tourism, it figured, would put dollars in the hands of Latin Americans, who would then buy US goods. High-volume, low-coast air travel would be facilitated by the entry into the commercial market of thousands of wartime aircraft. Backed by Roosevelt, a bullish Pan American World Airways, as the major airline, founded the Intercontinental Hotel Corporation—the "hotel chain with wings."

GENERAL FULGENCIO BATISTA

Fulgencio (he was christened Rubén) Batista y Zaldívar was born out of wedlock and into dire poverty in 1901 at Veguitas, near Banes, a backyard region of Oriente. His father was a sugarfield worker (and the son of an indentured Chinese laborer), his mother black. He enlisted and became a professional soldier and, after learning stenography, was promoted to sergeant.

Batista, an insecure, "fiery little bantam of a fella," rose to the top during a *golpe* in 1933, when Fidel Castro was only seven. He became chief of staff of the army and, as such, took over the government. The general brutally suppressed the opposition and began a 25-year tenure as the most powerful man in Cuba. He ruled through a series of puppet presidents before winning the 1940 presidential election himself (Batista was himself a puppet, whose puppeteers lived in Washington).

Batista, who ruled during a period of prosperity, was at first popular with the masses, perhaps because of his lowly origins but also because he enacted progressive social reforms and a new, liberal constitution that favored labor. He also began massive civic construction works that enhanced the face of Havana. Despite this, he was blackballed by the social elite for being *mulatto* and gradually became despised by the masses because his government was immensely corrupt.

In 1944, Batista retired to Florida, having accumulated US$20 million during his 11-year tenure. He missed the limelight, however, and after working out a deal with the Mafia, returned to Cuba, venal and gluttonous. In March 1952, he pulled off his second coup. Batista oversaw an economic boom for Cuba that included major civic works for Havana.

But the general had come back to power to commit grand larceny hand in hand with the mob. Corruption and terror on the streets rose to new heights during his time in office.

At midnight on New Year's Eve 1958, Batista fled Cuba with a group of followers. He eventually settled in Spain, where he lived a princely life until his death in 1973. The poor cane cutter died as one of the world's wealthiest men—he had milked Cuba of almost US$300 million.

PUBLIMERC S.A.

Havana, however, faced new competition from Mexico, the Bahamas, and other destinations with exotic treats—primarily beaches—that the city couldn't offer. Havana's hotels also were looking a bit tattered, but hotel developers feared Cuba's newly empowered and militant labor unions, and therefore shunned Cuba. In the immediate postwar years, Cubans spent more money abroad than tourists brought in.

Desperate to lure tourists, in 1948, newly elected president Francisco Prío opened the doors to gambling. At the time, only the Tropicana, Jockey Club, and Casino Nacional had gaming licenses, but the Sans Soucí and Montmartre cabarets soon added casinos. The ploy worked. Cuban developers rushed to put up new hotels in anticipation of a rush of Yankee vacationers (it wasn't until the mid-1950s that an infusion of foreign capital built Havana's Las Vegas-style hotel-casino with which prerevolutionary Havana will always be associated). By 1950, reformist zeal had swept through the government, which briefly closed the casinos and cracked down on houses of prostitution, but hoteliers and nightclub owners convincingly argued that their financial success relied on the casinos, forcing the government to relent. In the eyes of tourists, Havana was the "coolest place because it was the hottest."

By 1958, 80 flights a week served Havana from Miami alone in high season. Everything that tourists had enjoyed in the 1920s emerged afresh with new vigor: a greater variety of restaurants—from the kosher menu at Moishe Pipik's and the Russian food at Boris's to the pedestrian fare at Woolworth's food counter—livelier bars, and racier nightclubs such as the Tropicana, which had opened in 1939 as Havana's most spectacular show with the most lavishly costumed, most statuesque Cuban showgirls. An open-air theater in the gardens of a mansion that had once housed the US ambassador, the Tropicana quickly eclipsed all other nightclubs and drew international stars such as Josephine Baker, Carmen Miranda, and Nat "King" Cole, putting on elaborate productions with spectacular theatrical settings. The Tropicana was so lavish—it needed to pull in US$5,000 nightly to break even—and popular that a "Tropicana Special" flew nightly from Miami for an evening of entertainment that ended in the nightclub's casino.

By the late 1950s, more than three-quarters of total investment in Cuban construction was earmarked for Havana. The city was overcrowded, and dozens of new neighborhoods sprang up, aided by the 1952 Law of Horizontal Property that encouraged investment in apartment projects and rental houses on tiny lots measuring only four meters across and 30 meters deep (on the eve of the Revolution, about 75 percent of Havana's housing units were rentals). Needless to say, the boom led to deteriorating construction standards. Much of Havana's modern face is a legacy of this era, including La Rampa, the sloping boulevard that rises from the Malecón to the heart of Vedado.

Batista Take Two

In 1952, Batista—presumably bored by retirement—again put himself up as a presidential candidate in the forthcoming elections. When it became clear that he wouldn't win, he upended the process with a bloodless *golpe*. One of the candidates for congress whose political ambitions were thwarted by Batista's coup was a dashing young lawyer with a predilection for stylish suits and baseball. His name was Fidel Castro, a 25-year-old who had risen to great prominence as the most outspoken critic of corrupt government and was being hailed as an incorruptible future president.

Batista had lingered too long in Miami with *mafiosi* and returned spoiled with ambition and greed. Mobsters began to take over the hotels and casinos with Batista's blessing (for a cut of the proceeds, of course), and Cuba sank into a new round of corruption: "From the very beginning, every public works contract, of which there were many, brought its 30% commission to various secretaries and assistants of the President and thence to Batista's bank account," wrote Hugh Thomas. But Cuba's military leader also accomplished fine deeds. Batista initiated plans for the nation's economic welfare and attempted to reconfigure Havana's public profile with a modernist plan for redevelopment. One of his first acts was to appoint a National Planning Board, which commissioned a modernist plan by Cuban architect José Luís Sert that owed its inspiration to Frenchman Le Corbusier and envisioned a Havana of "superblocks" intersected by green corridors. The plan was conceived with touristic expansion at heart.

The government issued $350 million in bonds to finance public works programs, including construction of a long-awaited tunnel beneath Havana harbor. Batista fixed up the roads, expanded the airport at Rancho Boyeros, enforced sanitation codes for restaurants, and set up a special police force to protect against tourist abuse. A fine arts museum was established. Havana acquired skyscrapers such as the 35-story FOCSA building, a minimalist design typical of the postwar era (it boasted its own garage, power plant, school, and restaurant, epitomizing a trend toward luxury that the 1959 revolution cut short). Government ministries were moved to a new center of construction, the Plaza de la República (today the Plaza de la Revolución), completed in 1959 inland from Vedado. The Palace of Justice, National Library, and National Theater all lay at the heart of the trapezoidal plaza, which is almost one km in length. Spanning the entire square is a monument to José Martí, a 450-foot modernist edifice built 1938-1959 that includes a star-shaped base bearing a more traditional granite statue of the national hero.

Although the benefits may have been lopsided, Batista's government undoubtedly spurred economic growth and fueled a period of renewed prosperity in a society frustrated by long years of economic stagnation (due mostly to Cuba's ties to a dormant sugar economy). Havana of the late 1950s was a wealthy and modern city on a par with Buenos Aires and Montevideo. The overwhelming majority of homes in Miramar and Marianao were owned by wealthy Cubans, and the membership of the Biltmore Country Club consisted primarily of wealthy Habaneros. By the late 1950s, Cubans had regained majority control of the island's vast sugar industry for the first time in decades. Meanwhile, the city's vast and financially comfortable middle class had likewise developed a taste for American TV and cars, went to Coney Island and the newly developed beach resorts on weekends, and enjoyed the same restaurants, bars, and cabarets as tourists. "The future looks fabulous for Havana," said Wilbur Clarke, the croupier who operated the Hotel Nacional casino, little knowing what the course of history had in store.

The Heyday of Sin

Havana will always be primarily associated with sin—the Babylon of the Caribbean—and the pre-Fidel mobsters who seared the city into our consciousness. In truth, the period of mobsters and sin was very short-lived, spanning the few years immediately prior to the Revolution. "A few years of profitable frivolity ensured [Havana's] lasting reputation as the premier pleasure island of the time and the rallying cry and a focal point for antigovernment rebels," wrote Schwartz.

The line between legitimate business and organized crime began to blur in the early-1950s as Batista actively promoted Havana's latest tourism boom. He launched a frenetic era of hotel construction hand in hand with mobster-genius Meyer Lansky, whom he appointed as his gambling supervisor. Economically, building a new breed of casino-hotels made sense. Cuba's share of Caribbean tourism had fallen (from 43% in 1949 to 31% in 1951), and with new competition from neighboring islands, the country needed to put a polish on its attractions. Casino-hotels had built Las Vegas and could do so for Cuba, too. Batista promised to issue a casino license for investors willing to put up one million dollars for hotel construction, with a portion of the casino proceeds to be designated for charity. A hotel boom followed (room capacity doubled 1955-58).

Lansky, a bootlegger and a Batista friend from the days of Prohibition, had bought an early interest in the Montmartre casino (displaced American mobsters became partners in four of Havana's five casinos). Lansky had long since mastered the art of professional casino operation and, with maximum profits in mind, shared Batista's desire to ensure that foreign tourists had a good time. He set up a school for casino employees and ensured that the casinos ran an honest game. Batista regulated the casinos to make certain that tourists weren't being cheated; the tourist commissioner even sent troops into the casinos to put an end to crooked games. Lansky also headed an investor group of Prohibition-era friends and built the sumptuous Havana Riviera on the Miramar seafront under the watchful eye of the Banco Desarrollo Económico y Social (Bandes), a public financial institution that the Cuban government set up in 1955 to fund economic development and oversee foreign investment. The

THE MOB IN HAVANA

For three decades, the Mafia had dealings in Cuba, and though it never had the run of the house as claimed, prerevolutionary Havana will forever be remembered for its presence.

During Prohibition (1920-33), mobsters such as Al Capone had contracted with Cuban refineries to supply molasses for their illicit rum factories. When Prohibition ended, the Mob turned to gambling. The Mafia's interests were represented by Meyer Lansky, the Jewish mobster (as a Jew he could never be a full member of the Mafia) from Miami who arrived in 1939 and struck a deal with Fulgencio Batista, Cuba's strongman president (Lansky described Batista to national crime syndicate boss Salvatore "Lucky" Luciano as "the best thing that ever happened to us"). Lansky, acting as lieutenant for Luciano, took over the Oriental Park racetrack and the casino at Havana's Casino Nacional, where he ran a straight game that attracted high rollers. The Cuban state was so crooked, the Mob didn't even need to break the law (Lansky had brilliant business acumen and was as skilled in making money disappear without a trace as he was in bringing it in).

World War II effectively put an end to the Mob's business, which was relatively small scale at the time. Lansky returned to Florida, followed by Batista in 1944, when he lost to Ramón Grau in the national election.

After the US deported Luciano to Italy in 1946, he immediately moved to Cuba, where he intended to establish a gambling and narcotics operation and regain his status as head of the US mob. He called a summit in Havana's Hotel Nacional. The meeting—the biggest since Chicago in 1932—was immortalized in *The Godfather,* and the official cover, records Alan Ryan, "was that it was meant to honor a nice Italian boy from Hoboken called Frank Sinatra," who went down to Havana to say thanks. The US, however, pressured Grau to deport Luciano back to Italy. Before leaving, Luciano named Lansky head of operations in Cuba.

Lansky's aboveboard operation had withered in the mob's absence, replaced by rigged casinos. Havana's gambling scene had developed a bad reputation: Cuban casinos rented space to Cuban entrepreneurs who, says Stephen Williams, ran "wildly crooked games with the only limit to their profit being the extent of their daring."

When Florida voters declined to legalize gambling, the state's casinos were closed down. This was followed by a federal campaign to suppress national crime syndicates. Mobsters decided Cuba was the place to be. A new summit was called at Batista's house in Daytona Beach, attended by Cuban politicians and military brass. A deal was struck: Batista would return to Cuba, regain power, and open the doors to large-scale gambling. In return, he and his crooked pals would receive a piece of the take.

A gift of US$250,000 (personally delivered by Lansky) helped convince President Grau to step aside, and on 10 March 1952, Batista again occupied the Presidential Palace.

New laws were quickly enacted to attract investment in hotels and casinos, and banks were set up as fronts to channel money into the hands of Cuban politi-

Meyer Lansky

cos. In the United States, the Mafia faced certain limitations. In Cuba, anything was permissible: gambling, pornography, drugs. Corruption and self-enrichment occurred on a colossal scale. Organized crime became one of the three real power groups in Cuba (the others being Batista's military regime and American business), although there was never any doubt that Batista was in control, and he kept the mob on a tight chain.

Four "families" ruled the roost. The first, headed by Cuban-Italian Amleto Batistti, controlled the heroin and cocaine routes to the United States and an emporium of illegal gambling from Batistti's base at the Hotel Sevilla. The "family" of Amadeo Barletta organized the "Black Shirts" in Havana. The third family, headed by Tampa's Mafia boss, Santo Trafficante Jr., operated the Sans Souci casino-nightclub, plus the casinos in the Capri, Comodoro, Deauville, and Sevilla-Biltmore Hotels. Watching over them all was Lansky, who ran the Montmartre Club and the Internacional Club of the Hotel Nacional.

Lansky again cleaned up the gambling to attract high-stakes gamblers from the States. No frivolities were allowed. Games were regulated, and cardsharps and cheats were sent packing. Casinos were extensively renovated, and cocaine and prostitutes were supplied to high rollers.

The tourists flocked. Lansky's last act was to build the ritziest hotel and casino in Cuba—the US$14 million Hotel Riviera and Gold Leaf Casino, which opened on 10 December 1958. Within three weeks, on New Year's Eve, the sold-out floor show at the Riviera's Copa Room nightclub had 200 no-shows. Batista and his crooked henchmen had fled the country.

Ironically, Trafficante and the mob had considered Castro "a joke" but were hedging their bets for all eventualities by secretly funding the rebels as well as Batista. To no avail. Once Castro took power, the casinos were closed down (only after they had paid their employees), and, in June 1959, Lansky, Trafficante, and other "undesirable aliens" were kicked out of Cuba. Said Lansky: "I crapped out."

For the scoop on the Mafia's involvement in Havana, read *The Mob*, an autobiography by mob lawyer Frank Ragano.

---

government, which permitted 24-hour gambling and no limit on wagers, got more than its fair share of the proceeds; a gambling license cost US$25,000, but US$250,000 was expected under the table (Batista's wife got 10 percent of the proceeds from Trafficante's five casinos; she would roll up to casinos in her sleek black limousine and sit in the back while the bagman collected her weekly take).

The Riviera opened in December 1957 to general fanfare, with the casino at the core of operations (it pulled in three dollars for every two spent on hotel rooms, restaurants, shops, and cabaret). That month, the 250-room Hotel Caprí also opened with its own casino and fancy nightclub, as well as a rooftop swimming pool, where guests could watch an underwater show through specially constructed windows. The Hotel Nacional also gained a Las Vegas-type casino and cabaret. Casinos opened at the old Sevilla-Biltmore Hotel and the new Hotel Comodoro, in Miramar. Several smaller hotels also popped up in Vedado, where a US$32 million Bandes loan helped finance construction of the 32-story Hotel Habana Libre, built by Hilton but owned by the culinary workers' union's pension fund with a casino franchise leased to the Mob (for one million dollars a year). Hilton's neon-lit name emblazoned across the skyline of Havana imparted new stature to Cuba's capital city.

Cuba's capital city had everything. It had opera. It had baseball and ballroom dancing. Havana's many museums and theaters hosted major cultural productions: a symphony orchestra and an internationally acclaimed ballet company had been formed, and the ultra-modern, air-conditioned Blanquita Theater was added in 1949 to accommodate 7,000 patrons, with a parking lot for more than 1,000 cars (the stage could also be lowered to form a skating rink). Tens of thousands of tourists—probably the majority—were family types who visited Havana for its cultural attributes, perhaps finding titillation along the way, much as latter-day tourists do when they visit Amsterdam's Rosse Buurt or New Orleans' Bourbon Street.

What really made the city so popular was that it also had sex. "The first thing every secretary, schoolteacher, and nurse wants to see when they come here is *la exhibición*," recorded mobster lawyer Frank Ragano. *Los Exhibiciones*—live sex shows. John F. Kennedy occasionally popped down to Havana for sexual excitement. In 1957, Mob boss Santo Trafficante claims to have set Kennedy up with a private party, supplying three gorgeous prostitutes in a special suite in the Hotel Comodoro (which Trafficante owned) in the hope that it would put Kennedy in his debt. Unbeknownst to the young senator from Massachusetts, the room had a two-way mirror, and Trafficante and casino owner Evaristo Garcia watched the antics—but neglected to film them.

Visitors flocked to carouse with "glamorous, lissome Latin lasses, black-eyed señoritas, langorously, enticingly swaying" in the words of one vintage tourist brochure selling "night-time in Havana." North Americans arrived by plane or aboard the *City of Havana* ferry from Key West to indulge in a few days of sun and sin, with 10,000 prostitutes in the city to service their needs. "In the transitional era between the clumsy groping of the drive-in movie and the boastful sexuality of the hot tub, Cuba offered tourists an acceptable way to succumb to temptation without scandalizing the neighbors," wrote Schwartz. They went home happy, unaware that behind the scenes, chaos and corruption were rife.

Cuba's tourism boom worked in Batista's favor, bringing in millions of dollars that spread throughout the economy and creating thousands of jobs across the spectrum, from hotel maids to urban migrants peddling souvenirs from streetside stalls ("fully ninety percent of Havana's lighted storefronts had signs in English," claims Tom Miller). And the Mob-run syndicates invested their profits in banking, hotels, restaurants, real estate, and scores of other legitimate businesses, employing tens of thousands of Habaneros directly or indirectly. By 1957, when "tourism appeared to have fulfilled its economic promise," suggests Schwartz, "Cuban rebels escalated their challenge to Fulgencio Batista's government and began to hurl the island's Las Vegas image like a grenade at the leaders who had fashioned it." Fidel Castro and other rebels effectively propagandized the underworld connections in a moralistic, nationalist call to arms.

The Gathering Storm

While tourism pumped millions of dollars into the Cuban economy, rebels charged that it had corrupted the country, while gambling, they claimed, soaked up precious dollars that should be used for socially beneficial programs. Casinos became the rallying call of the rebels, eager to mobilize popular discontent. The US media picked up the scent and published a series of accusatory articles linking Mob ties to Havana's casinos. The stories were prompted by the murder of New York mobster Albert Anastasia in 1957. Although ties with Cuba were never proved, Havana was tarred and feathered with speculative accusations that bore the precedent of history and would be difficult to remove.

History has exaggerated the scale of the problem. As Schwartz points out: "Foreign gamblers introduced neither gangsterism nor vice to the island, nor did they necessarily corrupt righteous islanders." Nor did the Mob move in and take over. Batista might have brought big-time casinos to Cuba, but Cubans still ran the show. When it came to extortion rackets and payoffs, the Mob was playing ball with seasoned veterans, not second-stringers. Havana's policemen, for example, made daily rounds of the brothels and gambling houses, where they collected a "tax" (Cubans called it *el forrajeo*), and the payments climbed up the chain of command. The deadly rivalries and rampant corruption of the times—*gangsterismo* (a term for the assassinations and street violence that marked the politics of the period)—had brutalized Cuban politics long before the Mob arrived. Castro and his generation of student rebels became radicalized during the mid-1940s and early 1950s, when student and political activities settled their ideological differences with guns (there were 64 political assassinations on the streets of Havana during Grau's 1944-48 administration). Castro himself was accused of assassination and went into hiding. "The machine gun in the big car became the symbol not only of settling scores but of an approaching change of government," wrote Hugh Thomas.

The urban terrorism was mostly the work of José Antonio Echevarría's Revolutionary Directorate—the militant arm of the University of Havana's student federation—which targeted Havana, while Castro's Twenty-Sixth of July Movement fomented rebellion in Oriente (the two groups had signed a pact that gave free rein to the other), but both groups planted phosphorus bombs in hotels, movie houses, nightclubs, and other prominent public places, claims Schwartz. Exploding bombs occasionally rocked the hubbub of Havana's streets. Political terrorists were at work, bent on undermining the tourism boom. Says Schwartz: "Cuba became a holiday paradise in the midst of a political hell."

As radical opposition to Batista found its violent outlet on the streets, he struck back. In the escalating conflict, the police and military became increasingly heavy-handed. General opposition to Batista's authoritarian rule was mounting. His rule became so widely hated that it united the Cuban people. He got himself *elected* president in November 1954. But it made no difference. He maintained his empire with a brutal police force.

Neither Washington nor Batista understood the revolutionary forces at work.

Almost immediately following Batista's *golpe*, Castro had begun to plot the dictator's denouement. The rebel possessed a vision of his place in Cuba's future that seemed preordained. He was also ruthlessly focused. He organized the Movement (later known as MR-26-7, for *Movimiento Revolucionario 26 Julio*) and ran it with military discipline. Soon the Movement was an army in training. Castro launched his revolution on 26 July 1953 with an attack on the Moncada barracks in Santiago de Cuba. It collapsed in a hail of bullets, and Castro was sentenced to 15 years in jail. In May 1955, Batista bowed to mounting public pressure and freed Castro.

When the train carrying Castro reached Havana, he was hoisted aloft by a huge crowd and carried through the streets. He immediately launched his anti-Batista campaign. Castro was banned from making public addresses, and newspapers that printed his articles were shut down. But the public was with him. When police brutally beat students who took their demonstration onto the baseball field at Havana stadium, the scene (broadcast on national television) helped turn the tide in Castro's favor. A year later, Havana's pro-Batista mayor was booed out of the stadium by a crowd chanting "Viva Fidel!"

On 7 July 1955, Castro boarded a flight to Mexico to prepare a guerrilla army to invade Cuba. On 2 December 1956, Castro and 81 men came ashore. While his Rebel Army nibbled away at Batista's troops in the Sierra Maestra mountains, a war of attrition spread throughout the countryside and cities. In Havana, Batista's henchmen were assassinated; army posts, police stations, and public utilities were destroyed; and a terror campaign was enacted to scare away tourists.

On 13 March 1957, an attack on the presidential palace in Havana by almost 100 members of the Student's Revolutionary Directorate—acting independently of Castro—failed (35 students died in the attack). Batista met the increasing storm with increasingly brutal violence. In Havana, Batista's secret police tortured suspected opposition members and hung them from trees (the leader of the opposition Ortodoxo Party, for example, was murdered and his body dumped on the grounds of the Havana Country Club). In the countryside, night fell with a blackness made more menacing by the awareness of mysterious forces at work.

Tourists also became targets as rebels competed for media attention. In February 1957, Cuba had initiated the Cuban Gran Premio, and 30 of the world's leading auto racers, including England's Stirling Moss and the four-time world champion Argentinian driver, Juan Manual Fangio, roared down the Malecón in their Ferraris and Maseratis. (The Batista government spent $150,000 to promote the race and enacted strict press censorship to ensure that the more than 20 bombs that exploded on the streets of Havana in the three weeks preceding the race went unreported.) On 23 February 1958, on the eve of the second Cuban Gran Premio, Fangio was kidnapped by members of Castro's Twenty-Sixth of July Movement in the lobby of the Hotel Lincoln. The news was trumpeted around the world.

After the race, Fangio showed up safe and sound, and proclaimed that the rebels might have saved his life: the world champion was referring to a terrible accident during the race that had killed four people and injured more than 50, but his appreciative words were taken out of context and provided a major public relations coup for Castro's rebels. Little media attention was paid to the fact that Castro had called for a boycott of the race and, to get the point across, had thrown phosphorus bombs into the Radio Centro Theater alongside warnings for Habaneros to stay at home. Suddenly the international media was paying attention to Havana's turmoil, especially after a US tourist got in the way of a bullet during a gun battle on the streets of Habana Vieja. Although a general strike called by Castro failed—even when more than 100 Cubans were killed by police on the streets, most workers stayed on the job—he was winning the media battle.

As bombings of buses, major shopping districts, and theaters escalated, Cubans thought it wise to stay home. So did foreigners. "Castro's bombs were frightening away the tourists," wrote Graham Greene in *Our Man in Havana*.

Prompted by the mounting crisis and foreign pressure, Batista set a date for new elections in 1959. Buoyed by Cuba's economic prosperity, Batista also opened a peace offensive, restoring constitutional guarantees and encouraging political parties to organize for the coming elections. But it was too late. "The President's regime was creaking dangerously towards its end," wrote Greene. For Castro, the scent of victory was in the air. His rebel armies were closing in on Havana.

At midnight on New Year's Eve 1958, Batista and his closest supporters boarded a plane for the Dominican Republic (Batista intended to leave Captain Ventura, his evil police chief, behind, but Ventura arrived at the airfield and held Batista at gun point, forcing him to remove some of his baggage to make room for him). Two days later, the Rebel Armies of Camilo Cienfuegos and Che Guevara entered Havana.

While jubilant citizens celebrated Batista's ouster, scores of others went on a rampage of looting and general destruction that swept through Havana. Few, of course, understood what it meant. Castro had been careful to understate his intentions (he himself kept repeating that he had no political ambitions).

THE REVOLUTIONARY ERA

On 3 January 1959, the triumphant guerrilla army began a five-day Romanesque victory march to Havana, with crowds cheering Castro atop a tank, all of it televised to the nation. Castro, ever the grand showman, arrived in Havana on 9 January—the city had settled down—to a tumultuous welcome. That night, Castro bathed in spotlights while delivering his victory speech before the nation. Two white doves suddenly appeared, and one miraculously flew down to rest on his shoulders—a stupefying event that fulfilled an Afro-Cuban superstition (doves in *santería* mythology represent life) and granted Castro the protection of the gods. It was "one of those rare, magical moments when cynics are transformed into romantics and romantics into fanatics," wrote photojournalist Lee Lockwood.

Castro—now the "Maximum Leader"—set up his headquarters in the recently opened Havana Hilton, while croupiers worked the first floor and a puppet "democratic" government under President Manuel Urrutia ostensibly ruled from the Presidential Palace (Castro moved cautiously but vigorously to solidify his power under the guise of establishing a pluralist democracy). He was intent from day one on turning the old social order upside down. In retail shops, new signs spelled the future: "The Customer Is Always Right Except When He Attacks the Revolution."

In 1959, Havana was a highly developed city—one of the most developed in Latin America—with a large wealthy and a prospering middle class, and a vigorous culture. The island's per capita rankings for automobiles, literacy, and infant mortality (32 per 1,000 live births) suggest that it was comparatively advanced in socioeconomic terms (in 1958, Cuba ranked fourth among the 20 Latin American nations on a per capita basis). It had a mature market economy and banking sector, more cars per capita than Italy, and shops full of produce cheap enough for mass consumption. About one-fifth of Cuba's 6.5 million population lived in Havana, where most of Cuba's wealth and facilities were concentrated. (Havana was six times larger than Santiago de Cuba, the island's second city). But tens of thousands of Habaneros also lived without light, water, or sewage. Poverty was endemic, and thousands of citizens lived by begging and prostitution.

One of the first acts of the government was to close the strip clubs, casinos, and brothels. It was a highly unpopular move. Thousands of Cuban workers faced unemployment if the casinos were closed down. They joined hands with vested interests and demanded—successfully—that the casinos be reopened. Castro soon saw the light: Casinos helped pay off the negotiated loans that the inexperienced new government had inherited. Says Rosalie Schwartz: "The contribution of American tourists, projected to reach six billion dollars a year by 1964, appeared as economic redemption to revolutionaries in need." A new tourism commission—the Instituto Nacional de Industriales Turísticas—was founded with experienced staff at its head, and a commitment of US$200 million made to a four-year development program. Havana even hosted the annual convention of the American Society of Travel Agents (ASTA) in October 1959, and Oriental Park—Havana's racetrack—opened its horse-racing season with a big media splash.

Wholesale change was already being felt in the city as the revolutionary government set itself to redressing social needs that had long been neglected. On 6 March 1959, all rents in Cuba were reduced by 50%. Electricity, gas, and public transport fees were dramatically lowered, as were other fees. Price controls were instituted on goods sold on the free market. The government poured money into health care. Castro set up special schools for the indigent; the blind, deaf, and mute; and ex-prostitutes.

Castro was everywhere in Havana, speaking before huge crowds in an ingenious exercise he called "direct democracy," by which he utilized his incredibly manipulative powers to gauge and shape the public mood. Havana's new government was wherever Castro happened to be at the time. On 13 July 1959, President Urrutia denounced the growing communist trend. Castro resigned as prime minister, then played a typically brilliant gambit. He understood that the key to the Revolution was Cuban sentiment. At the time of Urrutia's resignation, Castro had arranged for peasants to be brought to Havana to celebrate the attack on Moncada. Castro then appeared on TV and denounced Urrutia, selling the Revolution direct to the masses. The streets of Havana erupted in calls for the President's resignation and pleas for Castro's return. He had carried out the world's first coup d'état by TV. On 1 May 1960, Castro reneged on his promise to hold elections within one year: the "people," he proclaimed, had declared them unnecessary, rationalizing the suspension of the Constitution and refusal to seek a popular mandate.

On 4 March 1960, *Le Coubre,* a French freighter carrying Belgian armaments for Cuba, exploded in Havana harbor, killing more than 80 Cubans. Castro blamed the CIA. If true, the CIA had managed to rally the Cuban people around Castro at a time when he was facing increasing domestic opposition. During the funeral ceremonies, Castro responded with a new battle cry: *"¡Patria o Muerte!"*—Fatherland or Death! Recalls Nobel Laureate Gabriel García Márquez: "The level of social saturation was so great that there was not a place or a moment when you did not come across that rallying cry of anger, written on everything from the cloth shades on the sugar mills to the bottom margins of official documents. And it was repeated endlessly for days and months on radio and television stations until it was incorporated into the very essence of Cuban life."

The Revolution was turning ugly. Gun-toting street thugs and unemployed youngsters had joined Castro's urban militia. Angry blacks and *guajiros* (peasants) shouting revolutionary slogans roamed the streets. *Prensa Libre* and other independent publications disappeared from the streets. Repression was making itself felt. The atmosphere was tense. Counter-revolutionary groups also became active. Bombs once more exploded on the streets of Havana in protest at creeping communism within the revolutionary government.

Political denunciations had created a climate of fear as accusations by loyal *fidelistas* led to arrests in the middle of the night. Fusillades rang out once again in the Foso de los Laureles as revolutionary firing squads headed by Che Guevara—the "supreme prosecutor"—shot hundreds of Batista supporters. The summary justice recalled the worst excesses of the French Revolution—scores of innocent people, fingered by *chavatos* (informers) were shot; Guevara dismissed the flippant murder of innocents as "a revolutionary process of justice at the service of future justice." No exact figures are known of how many were executed in the wave of revolutionary retribution.

Castro's fiery speeches had turned distinctly anti-American. Tourists got the message, dooming Havana's hotels, restaurants, and other businesses to bankruptcy. Visitation declined from more than 270,000 in 1957 to a scant 12,000 in 1974. Havana's former hot spots gathered dust. Apart from a handful of Russians, the beaches belonged to the Cubans throughout the 1960s and '70s, when tourism contributed virtually nothing to the nation's coffers.

In the Wake of the Bay of Pigs

In the predawn hours of 15 April 1961, residents of western Havana were awakened by the frightening noise of diving airplanes and exploding bombs. Cuban exiles trained by the CIA were bombing Campamento Libertad airfield in Cubanacán as a prelude to the Bay of Pigs invasion. The strike destroyed most of Cuba's tiny air force. Next day, standing at the corner of Avenida 23 and Calle 12, Castro gave a fiery funeral speech in honor of those Cubans killed and claimed that the attack happened because the United States couldn't forgive Cuba for having created a "socialist revolution" under its nose. It was the first time that Castro had uttered the dreaded word.

(continues on page 38)

FIDEL CASTRO

Whatever you think of his politics, Fidel Castro is unquestionably one of the most remarkable and enigmatic figures of this century, thriving on contradiction and paradox like a romantic character from the fiction of his Colombian novelist friend Gabriel García Márquez.

Fidel Castro Ruz, child prodigy, was born on 13 August 1926 at Manacas *finca* near Birán in northern Oriente, the fifth of nine children of Ángel Castro y Argiz. Fidel's mother was the family housemaid, Lina Ruz González, whom Ángel married after divorcing his wife. (Fidel's father immigrated to Cuba from Galicia in Spain as a destitute 13-year-old. In Cuba, Ángel gradually rose to become a modestly wealthy landowner who employed 300 workers on a 26,000-acre domain; he owned 1,920 acres and leased the rest from the United Fruit Company, to whom he sold cane.) Fidel weighed 10 pounds at birth—the first hint that he would always be larger than life. The early records of his family are sketchy, and Castro, who seems to have had a happy childhood, likes to keep it that way—much as he attempts to suppress the notion that he comes from a bourgeois family.

As a boy he was extremely assertive, rebellious, and combative. He was a natural athlete and grew especially accomplished at track events and baseball. He was no sportsman, however; if his team was losing, he would often leave the field and go home (Gabriel García Márquez has said, "I do not think anyone in this world could be a worse loser"). It became a matter of principle to excel—and win—at everything. His Jesuit teachers identified what Richard Nixon later saw in Castro: "that indefinable quality which, for good or evil, makes a leader of men." His school yearbook recorded that he was *excelencia* and predicted that "he will fill with brilliant pages the book of his life."

Star Rising

Fidel enrolled in Havana University's law school in October 1945, where he immediately plunged into politics and gained the limelight as a student leader. Castro earned his first front-page newspaper appearance following his first public speech, denouncing President Grau, on 27 November 1946. In 1947, when the foremost political opposition figure, Edward Chibás, formed the *Ortodoxo* party, Castro, at the age of 21, was sufficiently well known to be invited to help organize it. He stopped attending law school and rose rapidly to prominence as the most outspoken critic of the Grau government, including as head of his own revolutionary group, Orthodox Radical Action.

The period was exceedingly violent: armed gangs roamed the campus, and Fidel never went anywhere without a gun. As organizer of the street demonstrations calling for Grau's ouster, Castro was soon on the police hit list, and several attempts were made on his life. In February 1949, Fidel was accused of assassinating a political rival, Manolo Castro (no relation). After being arrested and subsequently released on "conditional liberty," he went into hiding.

He remained determined to stay in the limelight, however. In March, he flew to Bogotá to attend the Ninth Inter-American Conference, where foreign ministers were destined to sign the charter of the Organization of American States. Soon enough, Castro was in the thick of student demonstrations opposing the organization as a scheme for US domination of the hemisphere. One week later, while he was on his way to meet Jorge Eliécer Gaitán (the popular leader of the opposition Progressive Liberal Party), Gaitán was assassinated. Bogotá erupted in spontaneous riots—the *Bogotázo*. Castro was irresistibly drawn in and, arming himself with a tear-gas shotgun and police uniform stolen from a police station, found himself at the vanguard of the revolution—with a police detachment under his command. Inevitably, Castro again made headline news.

On 12 October 1949, Castro married a pretty philosophy student named Mirta Díaz-Balart, and they honeymooned for several weeks in the United States. (The couple divorced in 1954; she left for the

USA, then Spain.) Back home, Castro was once again in the thick of political violence. Gangsterism had soared under President Prío. In November, Fidel gave a suicidal speech in which he denounced the gangster process, admitted his past associations with gangsterism, then named all the gangsters, politicians, and student leaders profiting from the "gangs' pact." Again in fear for his life, Fidel left Cuba for the United States.

He returned four months later to cram for a multiple degree. In September 1950, Castro graduated with the titles of Doctor of Law, Doctor of Social Sciences, and Doctor of Diplomatic Law (in the press, Fidel is often referred to as Dr. Castro). He then launched into a law practice, concentrating on "lost causes" on behalf of the poor (most of his legal work was offered pro bono publico—free).

Congressional Candidate

By 1951, Castro was preparing for national office. Fulgencio Batista, who had returned from retirement in Florida to run for president, even asked to receive Castro to get the measure of the young man who in January 1952 shook Cuba's political foundation by releasing a detailed indictment of President Prío. Castro's campaign was far ahead of his time. The dizzyingly imaginative 25-year-old utilized mass mailings and stump speeches with a foresight and veracity theretofore unknown. His personal magnetism, brilliant speeches, and unquestioned honesty aroused the crowds, who cheered him deliriously. He had championed the cause of the urban poor and had no problem earning their loyalty.

Castro was certain to be elected to the Chamber of Deputies. It was also clear that Batista was going to be trounced in the presidential contest. Batista couldn't stomach defeat, so, at dawn on 10 March 1952, he effected a *golpe* (military coup) and, next day, moved back into the presidential palace he had vacated eight years before.

Says Tad Szulc: "Many Cubans think that without a coup, Castro would have served as a congressman for four years until 1956, then run for the Senate, and made his pitch for the presidency in 1960 or 1964. Given the fact that Cuba was wholly bereft of serious political leadership and given Castro's rising popularity . . . it would appear that he was fated to govern Cuba—no matter how he arrived at the top job."

The rest, as they say, is history.

A Communist *Caudillo*?

At 30 years old, Castro was fighting in the Sierra Maestra, a disgruntled lawyer turned revolutionary who craved Batista's job. At 32, he had it. He was determined not to let go. When he came down from the mountains, he was considered a "younger, bearded version of Magwitch: a tall outlaw emerging from the fog of history to make Pips of us all," wrote Guillermo Cabrera Infante, a brilliant novelist who, like thousands, supported Castro but later soured on him. "The outlaw became a law unto himself." Many have made the same claim: that Fidel used the Revolution to carry out a personal *caudillista* coup (a *caudillo* is a Spanish strongman leader). "Communist or not, what was being built in Cuba was an old-fashioned personality cult," wrote John Anderson.

Castro has since led Cuba through four decades of dizzying experience. He has outlasted nine US presidents, each of whom predicted his imminent demise and plotted to hasten it by fair means or foul. He shows no sign of relinquishing power and has said he will never do so while Washington remains hostile—a condition he thrives on and is determined to maintain regardless of appearances otherwise (Graham Greene determined that Castro was "an empirical Marxist, who plays Communism by ear and not by book").

Castro is consummately Machiavellian (masking truth to reach and maintain power) and rules Cuba with a firm thumb. His obsession for complete control is such that he makes decisions about the minutest aspects of government (it was he, for example, who decided that nurses should wear trousers, not skirts, because a nurse in skirt leaning over a patient, he suggested impishly, might cause a man lying in a bed behind her to have a heart attack). Even minor decisions are delayed until they have received Castro's blessing.

He is not the saint his ardent admirers portray; nor is he the evil oppressor described by Washington. He deserves full credit for the extraordinary gifts of social justice, dignity, and advances in health and education that the Revolution has bestowed upon Cuba and wishes to share with the underprivileged world. Castro—who knew he could never carry out his revolution in an elective system—believes disease, malnutrition, illiteracy, economic inadequacy, and dependence on the West are criminal shames and that a better social order can be created through the perfection of good values. Despite the

(continued on next page)

FIDEL CASTRO
(continued)

turn of events, Castro clings to the thread of his dream: "I have no choice but to continue being a communist, like the early Christians remained Christian . . . If I'm told 98% of the people no longer believe in the Revolution, I'll continue to fight. If I'm told I'm the only one who believes in it, I'll continue."

A Hatred of Uncle Sam

Castro turned to Communism mostly for strategic, not ideological, reasons, but his bitterness toward the United States undoubtedly also shaped his decision. He has been less committed to Marxism than to anti-imperialism, in which he is unwavering. He has cast himself in the role of David vs. Goliath, in the tradition of José Martí, who wrote "my sling is the sling of David." Castro sees himself as Martí's heir, representing the same combination of New World nationalism, Spanish romanticism, and philosophical radicalism. His trump card is Cuban nationalist sentiment.

His boyhood impressions of destitution in Holguín province under the thumb of the United Fruit Company and, later, the 1954 overthrow of the reformist Arbenz government in Guatemala by a military force organized by the CIA and underwritten by United Fruit, had a profound impact on Castro's thinking. Ever since, Castro has viewed world politics through the prism of anti-Americanism. During the war in the Sierra Maestra, Castro stated, "When this war has ended, a much bigger and greater war will start for me, a war I shall launch against them. I realize this will be my true destiny."

He brilliantly used the Cold War to enlist the Soviet Union to move Cuba out of the US orbit, and was thus able—with Soviet funds—to bolster his stature as a nationalist redeemer by guaranteeing the Cuban masses substantial social and economic gains.

Castro, however, has no animosities toward North Americans. His many close personal contacts range from media maverick Ted Turner to actor Jack Lemmon and even the Rockefeller clan.

Many Talents

Castro has a gargantuan hunger for information, a huge trove of knowledge (he is an avid speed-reader), and an equally prodigious memory (he never forgets facts and figures, a remarkable asset he nourished at law school, where he forced himself to depend on his memory by destroying the materials he had learned by heart).

There is a sense of perfection in everything Castro does, applied through a superbly methodical mind and laser-clear focus. He has astounding political instincts, notably an uncanny ability to predict the future moves of his adversaries (he is a masterly chess player). His "rarest virtue," says his intimate friend Gabriel García Márquez, "is the ability to foresee the evolution of an event to its farthest-reaching consequences."

Castro is also a gambler of unsurpassed self-confidence. Says Infante, "Castro's real genius lies in the arts of deception and while the world plays bridge by the book, he plays poker, bluffing and holding his cards close to his olive-green chest." His daring and chutzpah are attributed by some observers to his Galician temperament—that of an anarchist and born *guerrillero* (guerrilla fighter). He has stood at the threshold of death several times and loves to court danger. For example, in 1981, he chose to run to the Mexican port of Cozumel in a high-speed launch just to see whether the US Navy—then patrolling the Gulf of Mexico to stop Cuban arms shipments to Nicaragua—could catch him.

Castro's vanity is monumental (he never laughs at himself unless he makes the joke). He wears glasses but dislikes being seen in public in them, considering them a sign of weakness. His beard is also more than a trademark; he likes to hide his double chin.

He nurtures his image with exquisite care, feigning modesty to hide his immense ego. "I am not here because I assigned myself to this job . . . I am here because this job has been thrust upon me," Castro told journalist Ann Louise Bordach in 1994. He also claims that his place in history does not bother him: "All the glory in the world can fit into a kernel of corn." Yet in the same breath he likens himself to Jesus Christ, one of his favorite allusions.

Castro's revolutionary concept has been built on communicating with the masses, whom he sees and treats as his "children," and he conducts much of his domestic government through his frequent public speeches, usually televised in entirety. He understood at an early stage that he and television were made for each other. Castro—"one of the best television actors in the world"—is masterfully persuasive, an amazingly gifted and hypnotic speaker who holds Cubans spellbound with his oratory.

His early speeches often lasted for hours; today he is more succinct. (Castro's loquaciousness is legendary. When he and brother Raúl were imprisoned together on the Isle of Pines in 1954, Raúl complained that his elder brother "didn't let me sleep for weeks . . . he just talked day and night, day and night.") He is not, however, a man of small talk; he is deadly serious whenever he opens his mouth. He also listens intently when the subject interests him; he is a great questioner, immediately homing in on the heart of the matter.

Adored or Hated?

A large segment of Cubans see Castro as a ruthless dictator who cynically betrayed the democratic ideals that he used to rally millions to his banner, and his support—which is mostly rural-based—today seems pencil-thin in Havana. To Miami exiles especially, *El Líder* is just a common tyrant. Nonetheless, Castro's longevity and success are due in great measure to the admiration of a large portion of the Cuban people, to whom he was and remains a hero. There persists an adulation for *El Máximo,* also know as *El Caballo* (the horse—an allusion to the Chinese belief that dreams represent numbers to place bets on, and that the horse is number one).

Castro has consistently proven his concern for honesty and social justice in a nation mired for five centuries in corruption and inequality. Traveling through Cuba, you'll come across countless families who keep a framed photograph of him. You'll even hear of women offering themselves to Castro, "drawn by his power, his unfathomable eyes."

Cubans' bawdy street wisdom says that Castro has various domiciles—a sane precaution in view of the CIA's numerous attempts on his life—so that he can attend to his lovers. Certainly, many highly intelligent and beautiful women have dedicated themselves to Castro and his cause, but he saves his most ardent passions for the Revolution. Nonetheless, he is a "dilettante extraordinaire" in esoteric pursuits, notably gourmet dining (but not cigars; he

quit smoking in 1985). His second love is deep-sea fishing. He is also a good diver and often flies down to spear-fish at his tiny retreat on Cayo Piedra, where he dines on an offshore barge and sleeps in a rustic old caretaker's home while guests relax more luxuriously in a modern guesthouse.

El Jefe retains the loyalty of millions of Cubans, but he is only loyal to those who are loyal to him. He feels that to survive he must be "absolutely and undeviatingly uncompromising." In 1996, his biographer Tad Szulc wrote, "He is determined not to tolerate any challenge to his authority, whatever the consequences." You are either for the Revolution or against it. Castro does not forget, nor pardon; his heart is made of both gold and steel. Thus, while he has always shown solicitude for those who have served him or the Revolution, his capacity for fury is renowned, and it is said that no official in his right mind dares criticize him. (Paradoxically, he can be extremely gentle and courteous, especially toward women, in whose company he is slightly abashed.) Cubans fear the consequences of saying anything against him, discreetly stroking their chins—an allusion to his beard—rather than uttering his name. He is *El Tío, El Papá,* and *El quien tu sabes* (Uncle, Big Daddy, and You Know Who).

Castro denies that a personality cult exists. Yet he lives, suggests Szulc, "bathed in the absolute adulation orchestrated by the propaganda organs of the regime." The first page of newspapers and the lead item on the evening television news are usually devoted to Castro's public acts or speeches. And, although there are no streets or public edifices named for him, on May Day and other special holidays, posters and billboards are adorned with his face.

Given his innate conviction of destiny and unquenchable thirst to lead, the indefatigable Cuban leader, who turned 73 in 1999 and has outlasted all other world leaders of his time, could be around for many years. His hair and beard have grayed and his skin is dotted with sunspots, but in 1999 I found him looking in good health. Says writer Guy Talese: "His facial skin is florid and unsagging, his dark eyes dart around the room with ever-alert intensity, and he has a full head of lustrous gray hair not thinning at the crown." Rumors persist of ill-health, but doctors say Castro maintains a mostly vegetarian diet and works out every day on an exercise bicycle.

The Bay of Pigs fiasco consolidated support for Castro and solidified his regime, enhanced by the unanimous distaste among Cubans for the all-encompassing US trade embargo that since 1961 has hung like an ax over Cuba. But the sordid CIA debacle also provoked a wave of repression. Castro ordered the arrest of anyone considered disloyal to the revolution. Havana's bohemian middle-class sectors were suddenly sealed off. Armed with lists, the revolutionary police swept the city, arresting, in the words of Carlos Franquí, "homosexuals, vagrants, suspicious types, intellectuals, artists, Catholics, Protestants, practitioners of voodoo . . . prostitutes and pimps." Detainees were made to wear uniforms stitched with a large P on the back, much like Jews had been branded in prewar Nazi Germany.

In September 1961, Castro created the Committees to Defend the Revolution (CDRs). The inhabitants of every block in Havana (and the rest of Cuba) formed a committee to ensure the implementation of revolutionary decrees and perform the grassroots vigilante work of the State Security apparatus. For more on this, see the special topic The Cuban Government in the Sightseeing chapter.

In October 1962, Havana's ports were sealed off and a curfew enacted as Soviet missiles were brought into Cuba. They were a public secret that everyone knew, including Cuban exiles leaving for Florida. Their discovery by a U-2 spy plane triggered the Cuban Missile Crisis, which Cubans refer to as the Caribbean Crisis. The population of Havana went on combat alert, prepared to face down the atomic bomb with rifles. "A New York telephone operator, at that time, told a Cuban colleague that people in the United States were quite alarmed over what might happen," recalls Márquez. "We, on the other hand, are quite calm," replied the Cuban operator. "After all, the atomic bomb doesn't hurt." In *Return to Havana,* Maurice Halperin recalls living in Havana in October 1962: "Unbelievably, the popular mood was defiance. *'¡Patria o Muerte!'* Castro shouted, and the masses seemed almost eager to take on the Yankees. There was an air of celebration in the city . . . Havana was throbbing."

Jean-Paul Sartre and Simone de Beauvoir reported that "Havana has changed; no more nightclubs, no more gambling, and no more American tourists; in the half-empty Nacional Hotel, some very young members of the militia, boys and girls, were holding a conference. On every side, in the streets, the militia was drilling. . . . [There was] less gaiety, less freedom, but much progress on certain fronts." The elimination of individualism lay at the heart of the revolution. A personality cult was being built in its place.

A Tragic Progression

As time unveiled the communist nature of the Castro regime, a mass exodus of the wealthy and the middle class began, inexorably changing the face of Havana. Miami received a flood of unhappy exiles. At first, these were composed of corrupt elements escaping prosecution—pimps, politicos, thugs, assassins, henchmen, political hacks and their accomplices, mafiosi, and the thousands of underlings that support a corrupt regime. Then the reforms extended to affect the middle classes. An Urban Reform Law was passed, canceling existing leases and mortgages, and reducing rents to 10% of tenants' incomes, payable now to the state. The rental revenues that had been a prime source of revenue for Havana's middle classes were choked off; tens of thousands of families with their income tied up in real estate lost it all. Although rent payments could now be amortized toward the nontransferable purchase of a house, few buildings passed into private ownership. Says Rachel Carey: "Thousands of tenants did not keep up with rent payments. . . . [C]ourts did not evict, and occupants were reluctant to sign agreements authorizing title to property confiscated by the State." Thus, Castro's government became Havana's chief landlord, despite an initial intent not to do so. The State made a lousy landlord. It took the cash and divested itself of further responsibility: tenants were made responsible for the upkeep of properties.

Inevitably, the trickle of emigrés turned into a flood. About 250,000 Cubans left by 1963, most of them white, urban professional—doctors, teachers, engineers, technicians, businesspeople, architects, and others with entrepreneurial skills—ensuring Havana's inevitable decay as entrepreneurship and know-how were replaced by socialist ineptitude and turmoil. As Castro's Revolution turned blatantly communist, many of his revolutionary cohorts also began to desert him. Later, intellectuals and homosexuals were persecuted, and they, too, joined the flood.

Those who were forced to leave Cuba had to leave their possessions behind. Their houses were confiscated—"donated to the Revolution" is the official verbiage—and divvied up to citizens in need of housing (formerly whites-only neighborhoods rapidly became mixed). Havana faced a tremendous housing shortage. Festering slums and shanty towns marred the suburbs, and the new government ordered them razed. Concrete high-rise apartment blocks were erected on the city's outskirts, especially in Habanas del Este.

Unfortunately, about 90 percent of Cuba's architects had already fled Cuba. While a few creative individuals found room to express their creativity in stone, the move to centralized industrial planning under the Ministry of Construction soon eclipsed the independent mind. It was replaced with a utilitarian doctrine that defaced the Havana landscape with mass-produced, prefabricated concrete modules: the Soviet *gran panel* (involving in-place casting) was introduced to Cuba in 1963, joining the Yugoslavian IMS, which relied on precast columns and slabs, post-tensioned during installation. Good intentions failed to encourage good design. Everyone agrees that these trial-and-error prototypes were failures, but they continued being used until the Soviet Union itself collapsed. Meanwhile, the Presidential Palace and Capitolio—ultimate symbols of the "sordid era"—were turned into museums, while the new government moved into new ministry buildings surrounding the Plaza de la Revolución.

That accomplished, the Revolution turned its back on the city and gave its attention instead to the countryside. Marxist-Leninist ideology dictated an equalization in the rural-urban equation. Resources were diverted away from Havana. Left to deteriorate, thousands of older homes collapsed (almost 100 important colonial houses a year collapse by one estimate), forcing their occupants into temporary jerry-built shelters that eventually became permanent, while "pragmatism invaded tall rooms," says Nancy Stout, "forcing them to yield their height to additional sleeping quarters popularly labeled *baracoas*." The city was relayered horizontally as tens of thousands of migrants poured into Havana. Some estimates suggest that as many as 400,000 *palestinos,* immigrants from Santiago

and the eastern provinces, live in Havana. (The "Palestinians" are not liked by a large segment of Habaneros.)

Havana's aged housing and infrastructure, much of it already decayed, have ever since suffered benign neglect. The acres and acres of high-rises once lauded as exemplars of Cuba's socialist achievements are now little more than vast slums.

Mismanaging the Economy

The Cuban Revolution attempted to make equality in every sphere the basic operating principle of society. Cuban capitalism and Catholic power were crushed, and a host of redistributive policies were initiated that have helped make Cuba one of the most egalitarian societies in the world. Nonetheless, the honeymoon was over. Cuba's infant socialism was living off the fat accumulated by Cuban capitalism. Castro and Guevara, the new Minster of Finance and Industry, may have been great revolutionaries, but they didn't have the sharply different set of skills and understanding necessary to run an efficient economy, which they had swiftly nationalized.

There were few coherent economic plans in the 1960s—just grandiose schemes that almost always ended in near ruin. The revolutionaries had zero experience in marketing, financing, and other mercantilist skills—Guevara was intent on doing away with money altogether. Worse, they tried to buck the law of supply and demand. They replaced monetary work incentives with "moral" incentives, set artificially low prices, and got diminishing supplies in return. The awesome brain drain, a lack of foreign exchange, CIA sabotage, bad administration, lack of economic incentives, and naive policy all conspired to reduce production. Soon the economy was in appalling shape. In 1962, rationing was introduced. The black market began to blossom.

By 1968, the Cuban economy was coming apart at the seams. To make matters worse, that year Castro nationalized the entire retail trade still in private hands. More than 58,000 businesses—from corner cafés and ice cream vendors to auto mechanics—were eliminated in the "Great Revolutionary Offensive," part of the plan to create the "New Man." As a result, even the most basic items disappeared from Havana's shelves. Socialism had nationalized wealth but, says Guillermo Cabrera Infante, in a "Hegelian capriole" it "socialized poverty," too. Havana's population was learning to do without. Even Santa Claus had disappeared from Havana's streets at Christmas.

In an attempt to alleviate the difficulties Cuba was facing, in 1974 Castro created the system of *poder popular* (popular power) based on elected local assemblies designed to improve public administration through limited decentralized power. The organs of poder popular, still in use today, also serve as forums for citizens' grievances and deal with problems such as garbage collection and the operation of day-care centers. They are not autonomous bodies, however, and the Communist Party closely monitors their performance.

A brief attempt to abandon a sugar-based economy and to industrialize failed, so Castro switched tack and mobilized the entire workforce to achieve a record 10-million-ton sugar harvest by 1970. To achieve the goal, tens of thousands of inexperienced "voluntary" workers left their jobs in Havana and headed to the countryside. Holidays were abolished. Every inch of arable land was turned over to sugar. Nonetheless, the effort was a failure, leaving the economy in chaos; production everywhere had been severely disrupted and output declined.

Cuba was kept afloat by massive amounts of Soviet aid. With the Soviet Union as benefactor, "the Cubans got the luxury of running their economy along the lines of a Berkeley commune, and like California hippies wheedling their parents for cash, someone else paid the tab," notes P.J. O'Rourke. In the wake of the Yankees came the Russians, or *bolos* (balls), as the Cubans called them. Rough-hewn and poorly dressed, to the Cubans they acted like peasants. "The women were fat and wore long peasant dresses and headscarves, and the men, ill-fitting suits of poorquality cloth. They sweated heavily in Cuba's heat, but used no deodorant, and to the finicky Cubans, the Russians smelled bad," reports John Anderson. (Alas, by now the Cubans themselves had to make do without deodorant.)

Beneath the triumphalist rhetoric, severe shortages were being felt on the streets. Rising discontent found an outlet in 1980 when 12 Cubans walked through the gates of the Peruvian embassy in Havana and asked for asylum. When the Peruvians refused to hand them over, Castro removed the embassy guards. Within 72 hours, 11,000 Cubans had sought shelter in the embassy. When the foreign press gave the case prominence, Castro decided to allow them to leave. He also seized the opportunity to empty his prisons of dissidents, hardened criminals, homosexuals, and other "antisocial elements." Many were coerced to leave. The Cuban government called them *escoria* (scum), much as Joseph Goebbels called Jews *Ungeziefer* (vermin). Thus, Castro disposed of more than 120,000 critics in what is known as the Mariel Boatlift, after the port 45 km west of Havana.

In 1985, Mikhail Gorbachev became leader of the Soviet Union and initiated fateful reforms—just as Castro turned more sharply toward communist orthodoxy. Castro's program of Rectification of Errors and Struggles Against Negative Tendencies was initiated in 1986 in response to Cuba's faltering economy. The decision resulted in the closure of the highly successful free farmers' markets, which had blossomed on the streets of Havana and had led to an increase in the food supply, placing unobtainable items, such as garlic, back on kitchen tables. It was Castro's first warnings that *glasnost* and *perestroika,* Gorbachev's "heresies," would not be tolerated in Cuba. To get the point across, thuggish "Rapid Response Brigades" were introduced, called out for supposedly spontaneous "repudiations" (with fists and stones) of dissidents.

In 1989, the Berlin Wall collapsed, and the communist dominoes came tumbling down. With the collapse of Eastern Europe, goods began to disappear from Havana's shelves. When East German powdered milk ceased to arrive, Cuba eliminated butter; when Czechoslovakian malt no longer arrived, Cuban beer disappeared. Soaps, detergents, deodorants, toilet paper, clothing—everything vanished.

The city had been honored in 1977 when the Cuban government named Old Havana a national monument and formalized a restoration plan endorsed in 1982 by UNESCO's Inter-Governmental Committee for World Cultural and Natural Protection, which named Habana Vieja a "World Heritage Site" worthy of international protection. The revolutionary government established a preservation program for Habana Vieja, creating the Centro Nacional de Conservación, Restauración y Museologia to inventory

Havana's historic sites and implement a restoration program that would return much of the ancient city to pristine splendor without displacing the residents. But the rest of Havana—once the Pearl of the Antilles—was going to the dogs.

The Special Period

In January 1990, Castro declared that Cuba had entered a "Special Period in a Time of Peace." He also announced a draconian, warlike austerity plan. A new slogan appeared on Havana's walls: ¡Socialismo o muerte! (Socialism or death!). Tensions simmered until political discontent boiled over, on 21 April 1991, when clashes erupted in Havana between roqueros (rock-music fans) and police—the first act of spontaneous rebellion since 1959.

Then, on 18 August 1991, on the last day of the highly successful Pan-American Games in Havana (which Cuba won with 140 gold medals), the Soviet Union began its dizzying unraveling. Boris Yeltsin—an economic reformer who had infuriated Castro by meeting with right-wing Cuban exiles—took power. Subsidies and supplies to Cuba virtually ceased. The same year, General Manuel Noriega was ousted in Panama—Cuba's main source for Western goods. Cuba was cast adrift, a lone socialist island in a capitalist sea.

With the umbilical cords severed, Cuba's economy slipped into a coma. The lights went out on the Revolution—literally. After the last Soviet tanker departed, in June 1992, the government began electricity blackouts. There was no air-conditioning, fans, refrigeration, or lights. There was no fuel for transportation. Buses and taxis gave way to coches—homemade, horse-drawn carts. Everywhere, human and animal labor replaced oil-consuming machinery.

Without oil or electricity to run machines, or raw materials to process, or spare parts to repair machinery, factories closed down. State bureaucracies began transferring laid-off workers to jobs in the countryside. By the end of 1994, half of Havana's industrial factories had shut down. Lunch breaks were eliminated so that office workers could leave early to save on electricity. Power outages further disrupted industrial production (between 1990 and 1994, the economy shrank 34%, according to the Cuban government; it was surely far higher). Once-full nightclubs, restaurants, and hotels all closed. Gaiety

on the streets was replaced with a forlorn melancholy. Traffic ground to a halt, and gas (petrol) rationing was introduced, although as Nancy Stout points out, "Havana women still wear high heels even knowing that they may have to walk home."

Without their fans or air-conditioners, people couldn't sleep. The apagones (blackouts) could last for hours, and ugly and previously unknown incidents began to occur. Crime rose swiftly, and envy and anomie filled the vacuum left by the collapse of the egalitarian promise. Holdups became common. In the rough-and-tumble suburb of Cerro, so many bodegas (bars) were robbed that the authorities rigged the area to avoid apagones.

Harvests simply rotted in the fields for want of distribution, undermining one of Castro's bedrock promises—that all Cubans would have enough to eat. People accustomed to a government-subsidized food basket guaranteeing every person at least two high-protein, high-calorie meals a day were stunned to suddenly be confronting shortages in almost every staple. The scarcities were manifest in long lines for rationed goods, a phenomenon that had nearly disappeared by the mid-1980s. A kind of line organizers' mafia evolved, selling turnos (places) in la cola (the queue). Habaneros spent their days standing and waiting.

Havana went from down to destitute. Even cigarettes were rationed—to three packs a month. First toiletries, then meats and other staples disappeared. Cubans had to resort to simulating hamburger meat from banana peels and steaks from grapefruit rinds. Many Habaneros began rearing chickens, pigs, and even jutías (ratlike native rodents), while the most desperate resorted to eating rats. Black marketeers were said to be melting condoms and passing the rubber off as cheese on pizzas. Havana's population faced malnutrition on a massive scale. Beggars and buzos—people who live off garbage bins—resurfaced. (Begging was banned following the Revolution. Most of its practitioners were put to work and rehabilitated, while others were placed in psychiatric wards. But a handful of well-known exceptions were permitted to continue their trade; notably a crazy yet harmless, long-haired chap called the Caballero de Paris, who died in 1985 in a psychiatric ward but who had been permitted to walk the streets of Ha-

vana picking up garbage as he went.) Poverty had returned to Havana.

When state-owned restaurants closed, unauthorized restaurants in private homes—*paladares*—began offering a black-market supply of meals cooked from food "borrowed" by staffers at tourist hotels or purchased from enterprising farmers who sold surplus produce.

Cuba's No. 1 priority was to increase food production. Ground zero in the battle was the fertile agricultural land around Havana, where large tracts of land were switched from export crops to food crops. Vacant land, such as that along roadsides, was cultivated. Vegetable gardens—previously a rare sight—sprouted in the urban centers. (In early 1992, the government claimed that there were 30,000 such gardens in Havana, and nearly one million across the country; this is surely an exaggeration.) Legions of "volunteers" and laid-off workers were shipped from Havana to the countryside to help boost production. However, the massive mobilization of cityfolk to farmlands did not solve the problem. The "national food self-sufficiency program" failed to meet basic needs, especially for vegetables and fruits. Tensions in Havana ran high.

Riots erupted on the streets of Havana, invoking a new wave of repression. While dissidents were being rounded up and jailed, the growing reformist movement found an unexpected ally in Raúl Castro, Fidel's younger brother, who argued for deregulating key sectors of the economy. Market-savvy reformers were elevated to positions of power and scrambled to nail together a long-term economic recovery plan led by tourism. The Revolution's ideological principles were turned on their head. In 1993, possession of the dollar was legalized. Private enterprise was also permitted, and enterprising *bizneros* popped up everywhere, mending shoes, punctures, and cigarette lighters. The legal availability of dollars eased life for those Cubans who had access to greenbacks, and farmers' markets eased life for those without. And although the Special Period precluded any major building projects, Cuba finally abandoned the construction of high-rise prefabricated apartment blocks in favor of a more humanistic and manageable approach to housing. A new microbrigade effort was launched to renovate existing buildings, providing experts to guide inhabitants in the rehabilitation of their own units, beginning in the Cayo Hueso neighborhood of Havana (different government ministries each adopted a street).

Throughout all of this, the exigencies of the Special Period drove the government to revive Cuba's moribund tourism industry, with Old Havana as the natural focus.

Trouble All Over Again

On 5 August 1994, crowds gathered along the Malecón in response to a rumor that a major exodus was to be permitted and that a flotilla of boats was en route from Florida. When police attempted to clear the boulevard, a riot ensued. Passions were running dangerously high, and two police officers were killed and 35 people injured. Castro saw a chance to defuse a dangerous situation and benefit at the same time. He declared that Cuba would no longer police the US borders: if the US would not honor its agreement to allow people to migrate legally, then Cuba would no longer try to prevent anyone from going illegally. The US was hoisted on its own petard as thousands of *balseros* fled Cuba on makeshift rafts. (More than 500,000 Habaneros have left the capital city and Cuba for the United States since the Revolution.)

During the three weeks following Castro's declaration, at least 20,300 Cubans were rescued at sea and shipped to Guantánamo naval base in eastern Cuba. President Clinton's major goal, at almost all costs, was to avoid a replay of the 1980 Mariel Boatlift. The US was forced to negotiate an immigration accord with Cuba. Henceforth, the Coast Guard would intercept Cubans heading for the US and return them to Cuba.

Meanwhile, a Miami-based volunteer group led by José Basulto called Brothers to the Rescue had been operating rescue missions. When the flood of *balseros* stopped, pilots of the organization began buzzing Havana and dropping "leaflets of a subversive nature." On 24 February 1996, three Brothers to the Rescue Cessnas took off from Opa-Locka airfield near Miami. The civilian-paramilitary planes, led by Basulto, were cleared to fly to the Bahamas. Once airborne, they diverted to Cuba. Cuban jet fighters shot two Cessnas down, killing both pilots and resulting in a wave of anti-Castro sentiment in Miami and Washington that permitted Sen. Jesse Helms to steer a piece of draconian anti-Cuban legislation—the Helms-Burton Bill—into law. Castro, who craftily works to keep the anti-American flame alive, may have planned the whole affair. In May 1999, US federal agencies had finally pieced together the events leading to the shooting down of the two Brothers to the Rescue planes in 1996. US Attorney General Janet Reno issued indictments against 14 Cuban agents, including several spies rounded up in Miami plus "MX," the code name for the head of Havana's Directorate of Intelligence, and charged them with actively working to provoke the incident in a plot called Operación Escorpión.

On the domestic front, Havana again felt the pinch as Cubans poured into the city from else-where in Cuba (annually, an estimated 25,000 arrived). Lacking the resources to build new housing—and with water, electricity, and transportation services stretched to the limit—a law was passed in May 1997 banning such migration. Meanwhile, in mid-1997, four free-trade zones were opened on the outskirts of Havana (including the 600-acre Havana City Free Trade Zone, at Berroa) to lure foreign companies eager to take advantage of a 12-year tax holiday and low wage rates.

About the same time, a series of bombs planted by right-wing-sponsored exiles exploded in Havana's tourist zones with the aim of scaring off a new wave of tourists. The campaign primarily targeted leading hotels, claiming the life of an Italian businessman when a bomb exploded in September 1997 at the Chateau Miramar (another bomb exploded at the El Bodeguita del Medio bar the same night). The Cubans arrested the culprits: two Salvadoreans reputedly working on behalf of the Cuban-American National Foundation, a leading anti-Castro organization in the United States. The Salvadoreans received the death sentence.

In January 1998, Pope John Paul II made a highly publicized four-day visit to Cuba and delivered a sermon to half a million Cubans in the Plaza de la Revolución. For the occasion, Castro declared Christmas an official holiday, and festive lights went up in the streets for the first time in decades. Castro had invited the Pope in the hope that a papal embrace magnified by television exposure might diffuse much of the internal opposition and give the regime new legitimacy. According to a joke making the rounds at the time, the reason Castro didn't object to picture of Jesus next to him is because he thought it was another picture of himself. The pontiff denounced the US embargo as immoral but also appealed for greater political and economic liberty in Cuba, raising cheers from the crowd that were drowned out by piped-in music. The most vociferous dissidents were surrounded by plain-clothes police and "disappeared." Some 4,000 journalists descended on Havana to cover the event, including the major US media, who promptly turned heel and fled when the Monica Lewinsky scandal broke as the Pope touched Cuban soil. More jokes made the rounds in Havana. Question: "What do the Vatican and a Cuban have in common?" Answer: "They've both had only four *papas* (the Spanish word for popes and potatoes) in 40 years."

Paranoia about a US invasion is such that recent years have seen construction of miles of tunnels beneath the city's streets. Most are hidden, although you can see a few concrete-lined entrances in exposed limestone cliffs throughout the city. But the enemy lies within. The intrinsic sense of dignity, egalitarianism, and moral rectitude fostered by the Revolution is wearing thin. Serious crime such as muggings, which the Revolution had virtually eradicated, returned to the streets of Havana. An armored van was even robbed by armed youths in Guanabacoa (an unprecedented occurrence), and two Italians tourists were killed in September 1998 during an armed robbery. Havana developed a significant drug problem, with cocaine and crack sold openly on the street and at discos. Thousands of young Cuban women also turned to quasi-prostitution as *jiniteras*, spawned by the city's overt sexuality and a boomlet of tourists in search of something just a little bit dirty with Havana's slim and pouty teenage hookers. Low-level corruption among police and government officials was becoming obvious, and a local mafioso was beginning to develop.

The government sensed that it was losing control. When two Cuban *jiniteras* died of cocaine overdoses in December 1998, Havana's discos and bars were closed down, and thousands of young men and women were arrested on the streets, accused of prostitution and pimping.

Latest Developments

On 1 January 1999, Cubans celebrated the 40th anniversary of the Cuban Revolution. Commented *The Economist:* "There does not seem much to celebrate. The economy is a mess. Corruption is rife. Prostitution is rampant. Despite police or neighborhood watchdogs on every street corner, crime is rising. . . . The grand promises of the past 40 years are in tatters. In some ways, Cuba seems worse off in 1999 than it was in 1959."

In January, President Clinton announced that he was easing the trade embargo, permitting more cash to be sent to Cuban individuals and nongovernment organizations. Castro called the move a "fraud" and later that month announced

the Law for the Protection of Cuba's National Independence and Economy. This draconian bit of legislation was admirably aimed at cleaning up Havana and even met with initial success, but it was also a repressive tool that created a counterrevolutionary felony: "supporting" hostile US policies. Anyone providing information to foreigners could face a 30-year sentence. Outlawed are the "supply, search, or gathering of information" for and the "collaboration" with foreign media. To get the point across, in March 1999, four prominent dissidents—the Group of Four—were labeled "counterrevolutionary criminals" and received harsh sentences for sedition. The sentence signaled a harsh crackdown throughout Havana and resulted in the United Nations Commission on Human Rights condemning Cuba as a "significant violator."

Meanwhile, in January 1999, several thousand black-bereted police from an elite National Brigade were deployed on street corners throughout the city to round up prostitutes and petty hustlers. Hundreds of *jiniteras* were arrested (many were interned in "rehabilitation camps"), as were scores of other hustlers. at least 10 convicted criminals were executed, and, in June 1999, dozens of high officials within the tourism and business sectors were fired and arrested for corruption.

The police remain on the streets 24 hours a day, checking IDs at random and questioning Habaneros seen talking with foreigners. The policy is officially "a battle against that which means disorder, crime, disrespect for authority, illegal business, and lack of social control." Drug traffickers now face the firing squad (drugs have gone underground but are still available; some areas, notably the Sitio area of Centro, south of Salvador Allende, are said to be trafficking centers), and prostitutes face a 24-year jail term.

But Castro, in an echo of King Canute, may have also decided to chill relations between Cubans and foreigners, pulling back after realizing that his modest economic reforms could undermine the government's political control. Some savvy taxi drivers and *jiniteras* had accumulated small fortunes, at least by Cuban standards (most *bizneros* had already been squeezed out of business by taxation; stall holders at artisans' markets pay taxes of US$250 a month for one square meter of display space), a modest economic success that posed a threat to the regime. Getting on well outside the state-controlled economy, thousands of Cubans had discovered they no longer needed the state to get by.

Castro got a break in March 1999 when the Baltimore Orioles came to Havana and beat the Cuban Sugar Kings, the national baseball team, 3-2 in the first meeting of a US professional club and a Cuban squad since March 1959 (the 50,000-seat stadium was filled with loyal fans of Castro; only party members were invited to attend the game). On 3 May, the Cubans got their revenge in Oriole Park, trouncing the Baltimore team 12-6 in a game that had all Havana glued to the TV. The streets were deserted.

THE HABANEROS

The population of Havana is approximately 2.2 million, or 19.9% of Cuba's population, according to the last census, in 1993. The people of Havana are called Habaneros (Habaneras for women).

Their lives are so surreal that Cuban society is not easy to fathom. Attempts to analyze Cuba through the North American value system are bound to be wide of the mark. Habaneros "adore mystery and continually do their damnedest to render everything more intriguing. Conventional rules do not apply," notes author Juliet Barclay. Adds author Pico Iyer: "When it came to ambiguity, Cuba was the leader of the pack. An ironist can have a field day."

It is worth taking time to understand the complexities that shape the Cuban psyche and determine contemporary life in Havana.

THE ETHNIC MIX

The 1993 census reported that, officially, about 66% of the population are "white," mainly of Spanish origin. About 12% are black, and 22% are mulattoes of mixed ethnicity. In reality, the percentage of mulattoes is far greater. Chinese constitute about 0.1%.

Havana's population has grown markedly darker since the Revolution. More than two million Cubans have left the island since 1959. The vast majority were urban and white (98% of Miami's Cuban-exile community is white), and the vacuum drew in thousands of blacks from the countryside. Black culture enriches the city's daily life.

Race Relations

Slavery has burdened many countries of the Americas with racial and social problems still unresolved today. But Cuba has gone further than any other to untangle the Gordian knot. Cuban society is more intermixed than any other on earth., and racial harmony is evident everywhere on the streets of Havana.

Despite slavery, by Caribbean norms Cuba has been a "white" society, whose numbers were constantly fed by a steady inpouring of immigrants from Spain. After emancipation in 1888, the island was spared the brutal segregation of the American South. There was significant mobility and opportunity. To be sure, a color code prevailed, with the whites at the top and the pure-blooded blacks at the bottom. But the caste system was much more subtle and flexible than that of the United States and other Caribbean islands, such that citizens of all colors mingled freely and a significant black middle class evolved, with its own social clubs, restaurants, and literature. However, many blacks in Havana lived as described by Ernest Hemingway in *Islands in the Stream*: "The lean-to was built at a steep slant and there was barely room for two people to lie down in it. The couple who lived in it were sitting in the entrance cooking coffee in a tin can. They were Negroes, filthy, scaly with age and dirt, wearing clothing made from old sugar sacks."

Jim Crow came to Cuba with the boom in Yankee tourism in the 1920s and '30s, and legal racial segregation gradually became the norm in Washington's Caribbean protectorate. Capitalist Cuba eventually boasted "whites only" clubs, restaurants, schools, hotels, beaches, recreation centers, and housing areas, as well as discrimination in job hiring. By the 1940s, racism had become so endemic among the elite that when dictator Fulgencio Batista—who was a mixture of white, black, and Chinese—arrived at the exclusive Havana Yacht Club, they turned the lights out to let him know that although he was president, as a mulatto he was not welcome.

Then, in the late 1950s, Cuba's revolutionary government swiftly outlawed institutionalized discrimination and vigorously enforced laws to bring about racial equality. Castro said: "We can't leave the promotion of women, Blacks, and mestizos to chance. It has to be the work of the party: we have to straighten out what history has twisted."

There is no doubt that the Cuban government has achieved marvelous things. By replacing the social structures that allowed racism to exist, the Revolution has made it virtually impossible for any group to be relegated forever to racial servitude. Afro-Cubans are far healthier, better educated, and more skilled and confident than blacks in Brazil, Colombia, Panama, Jamaica, Haiti, or the urban underclass of the US. They enjoy the lowest rate of infant mortality in Latin America and the Caribbean—one vastly superior, it should be added, on average, to that of blacks in the United States. Hence, blacks are, on the whole, more loyal to Castro than whites.

The social advantages that opened up after the Revolution have resulted in the abolition of lily-white scenes. Mixed marriages no longer raise eyebrows. Everyone shares a Cubanness. Black novelist Alice Walker, who knows Cuba well, has written, "Unlike black Americans, who have never felt at ease with being American, black Cubans raised in the Revolution take no special pride in being black. They take great pride in being Cuban. Nor do they appear able to feel, viscerally, what racism is." (A negative perspective is offered by Carlos Moore, an Afro-Cuban writer who left Cuba in 1963, in his *Castro, the Blacks, and Africa,* Center for Afro-American Studies, University of California, Los Angeles, 1988, available through www.cubabooks.com.)

Behind the Veil

Cubans feel proud of the racially liberating Revolution that has achieved what appears to be a truly color-blind, multiracial society. Yet there are still cultural barriers and discrimination. Some social venues attract an almost exclusively white crowd, while others are virtually all-black affairs (blacks still retain their religion, their bonds, their worldview). Most Cuban blacks still work at menial jobs and earn, on average, less than whites. The most marginal Havana neighborhoods still have a heavy preponderance of blacks. And blacks are notoriously absent from the upper echelons of government (an exception is Esteban Lazo, the tall, girt black First Secretary of the Communist Party of Havana, a position equivalent to City Mayor).

Nor has the Revolution totally overcome stereotypical racial thinking and prejudice. Black youths, for example, claim to be disproportionately harassed by police. Racist comments can still be heard, and many Cuban mulattoes prefer to define their racial identity with whites rather than with blacks (prior to the Revolution, it was common for mulattoes with lighter skin to be referred to as *mas adelantados*—more advanced).

CHARACTER, CONDUCT, AND CUSTOMS

Cubans are somewhat schizoid. In the four decades since the Revolution, most Habaneros have learned to live double lives. One side is spirited, inventive, irrepressibly argumentative and critical, inclined to keep private shrines at home to both Christian saints and African gods, and profits however possible from the failings and inefficiencies of the state. The other side commits to being a good revolutionary and to cling to the state and the man who runs it. Hence, Havana is a divided society populated by two sets of people: revolutionary stalwarts and those who long for the return of their individual liberty. Both groups, however, hold an innate Cubanness in common, and in many regards the distinctions are blurred.

The Cubans' value context, their philosophical approach to life differs markedly from North American or northern European values. Thus, attempts to analyze Cuba through the North American value system is bound to be wide of the mark. For example, most North Americans don't understand what the "Revolution" means. When Cubans speak of the Revolution, they don't mean the toppling of Batista's regime, Castro's seizure of power, or even his and the country's conversion to communism. They mean the ongoing process of building a society where everyone benefits and the individual lives motivated by concern for fellow beings before himself. Their philosophical framework is different. Most Cubans, regardless of their feelings for Castro, take great pride in the achievements of the Revolution, and, at least until the onset of the Special Period, many (perhaps a majority) of Habaneros were happy to accept the sacrifice of individual liberties for the sake of improving equality. Those who did not were jailed, or chose exile or sullen silence.

Most Habaneros hold a broad view of "democracy," based on a commitment to social justice and equality. The idea that democracy includes every person's right to culture and guaranteed health care and education—the twin jewels in the revolutionary crown—is deeply ingrained in their consciousness. This has less to do with an innate Cuban characteristic than with *Fidelismo,* whose tenets—an antithesis of decades of greed and corruption—call for puritanism and morality, which after four decades have seeped into the masses.

As such, most Habaneros are not concerned with the accumulation of material wealth, although this is changing. Unlike North Americans, they are not individual "consumpto-units." Most Cubans are more interested in sharing something with you than getting something from you. (Cubans call each other *compañero* or *compañera,* which has a cozy sound of companionship.) They are unmoved by talk of your material accomplishments. It is more important that everyone has more than the basic minimum—more important, too, to live life. Four decades of socialism has not changed Cubans' hedonistic culture.

Although it puts certain restrictions on individual liberty, Castro's government has attempted to maximize its human potential, and despite several obvious failings, its education system is justifiably a source of national pride. It is a joy to hear throughout the city the intelligent voices of an educated and evocatively philosophical people. In general, Habaneros are highly knowledgeable, often displaying an astonishing level of intellectual development and erudition. Their conversations are spiced with literary allusions and historical references. On the downside, the hyper-educated population is hard pressed to find books, and panorama is severely circumscribed: only politically acceptable works are allowed, proving, as the Brazilian economist Roberto Campos noted, that statistics are like bikinis—they show what's important but hide what's essential.

Cuban women are astute and self-assured, and Cuban men are very sentimental. The struggles of the past four decades have fostered a remarkable sense of confidence and maturity. As such, there's no reserve, no emotional distance, no holding back. Habaneros engage you in a very intimate way. They're not afraid of physical contact; they touch a lot. They also look you in the eye; they don't blink or flinch but are direct and assured. They're alive and full of emotional intensity. You sense that Habaneros are so chock-full of verve and chutzpah that though regimes may come and go, Cuba will surely remain the same.

The economic crisis and demise of socialism elsewhere in the world, however, has fostered an identity crisis; even the most dedicated communists admit their fears about the future, particularly that a loss of values, morals, and solidarity is eroding the principles of the New Man. The *jineteras,* the petty thieves on the streets, the children who are now taught to beg: all these things are the result of Cuba's poverty. The New Man—one of the Revolution's greatest gifts—is slowly dying. "The world is poorer for the loss of that intangible, optimistic, altruistic spirit," says Saul Landau. Indeed it is.

Social Divisions and Family Life

The Revolution destroyed the social stratification inherited from Spanish colonial rule. Distinct delineations among the classes withered away. Not that prerevolutionary Cuba was entirely rigid—it was unusual in Latin America for its high degree of "social mobility." For example, Castro's father was a poor farm laborer when he emigrated from Spain but rose to become a wealthy landowner in Cuba. Havana boasted a huge middle class, although it has been argued that there was no characteristically middle-class way of life—no conscious middle-class ideal. As an agrarian-populist movement pitted against Havana-based "bourgeois" interests, *Fidelismo* warred against the middle class and destroyed it; the foreign tourist, suggests Humberto Werneck, is a "kind of floating bourgeoisie in a country that has chased its own away." (The old privileged class has been replaced by a *nueva clase* of senior Communist Party members who enjoy benefits unavailable to other Cubans; the old underclass has been replaced by a class of outcasts who do not support the revolutionary government and have therefore been deprived of social benefits.)

Habaneros lack the social caste system that makes so many Europeans walk on eggshells. There is absolutely no deference, no subservience. Habaneros accept people at face value and are slow to judge others negatively. They are instantly at ease, and greet each other with hearty handshakes or kisses. Women meeting for the first time will embrace like sisters. A complete stranger is sure to give you a warm *abrazo* (hug). Even the most fleeting acquaintances will offer you a meal or go out of their way to help you. As a foreigner, you'll meet with the warmest courtesies wherever you go, although this is nothing new: last century, Anthony Trollope reported that "they welcome you with easy courtesy; offer you coffee or beer; assure you at parting that their whole house is at your disposal; and then load you—at least they so loaded me—with cigars."

Habaneros are uncommonly generous, extremely courteous and gracious, and self-sacrificing to a fault. They can't understand why foreigners are always saying, "Thank you!" Doing things for others is the expected norm. Cubans rarely say "thank you" when they receive gifts—which you, the wealthy foreigner, are expected to provide.

The city's social life revolves around the family and, to a lesser degree, friends and neighbors. Cubans are a gregarious people, and foreigners are often amazed by the degree to which Cubans exist in the public eye, carrying on their everyday lives behind wide-open windows visible to the streets as if no one were looking. To Cuban passersby, this is nothing remarkable, but foreigners can't resist satisfying their curiosity and taking a gander at what might be happening inside.

Cuban Curiosity

A sense of isolation and a high level of cultural development have filled Habaneros with intense curiosity. One reason why so many Cubans ask foreigners *"¿Qué hora es?"* is to strike up a conversation (another reason is that they really do need to know the time in a country where time stopped years ago). They will guess at your nationality and quiz you about the most prosaic matters of Western life, as well as the most profound. Issues of income and costs are areas of deep interest, and you may be questioned in intimate detail. Sexual relations arouse equally keen interest (Cubans discuss sex forthrightly), and Cubans of both genders are often eager to volunteer their services to help guide Cupid's arrow.

If you tell them you are a *yanqui,* most Cubans light up. They are genuinely fond of US citizens and keen to discuss international affairs and philosophies (although the minority who remain ardent revolutionaries still harbor suspicions). Habaneros want to know about the outside world and resent being kept in the dark by their gov-

ernment. They watch Hollywood movies and often converse with a surprising mix of wordly wise erudition and naiveté. They often will pepper you with questions.

Although Habaneros thrive on debate, they hesitate to discuss politics openly, except behind closed doors, when the vitriol felt for the system and you-know-who comes pouring out. Although *his* name is never used, the silent reference is usually communicated by the gesture of a hand stroking a beard. Only rarely will someone open up to you publicly with sometimes unexpected frankness—in which case you should be cautious!

Humor

Despite their hardships, Cubans have not lost the ability to laugh. Their renowned humor is called the "yeast for their buoyant optimism about the future." Stand-up comedy is a tradition in Havana's nightclubs, and *chistes* (jokes) race around the city.

Habaneros turn everything into a *chiste,* most of which are aimed at themselves. Their penetrating black humor spares no one—the insufferable bureaucrat, *jiniteras,* the Special Period. There are no sacred cows. Not even Castro (perhaps *especially* not *El Jefe*) is spared the barbs. Other favorite targets of scorn are Russian-made Lada cars and Hungarian buses, which every Cuban agrees are all lemons and which the Hungarian government stopped making after selling the fleet to Cuba—hence, no spare parts.

Like the British, Cubans also boast a great wit. They lace their conversations with double entendres and often risqué innuendo. Even the Spanish-speaking foreigner is often left behind by subtle inflections and Cuban idioms.

Many Habaneros are alternately sad and high-spirited. Conditions are often heartbreaking, yet most Cubans don't get beaten down. They never seem to lose their sense of humor, reminding me of a statement by the 18th-century Englishman Oliver Edwards: "I have tried in my time to be a philosopher, but I don't know how, cheerfulness was always breaking in."

The Nationalist Spirit

Cubans are an intensely passionate and patriotic people united by nationalist spirit and love of country. They are by culture and tradition politically conscious. The revolutionary government has tapped into this and has engaged in consciousness raising on a national scale. Cubans are nationalists before they are socialists or even incipient capitalists. They had not expected socialism from the Revolution, but those who were not forced into exile or otherwise devastated could accept it, at least during the 1960s, not simply because so many benefitted from the Revolution but because, as Maurice Halperin suggests, "it came with nationalism, that is, an assertion of economic and political independence from the United States, the goal of Cuban patriots for a half century." This reality provides Cubans with a different perspective and viewpoint on history.

Cubans—in fact, all Latin Americans—also resent the way North Americans take to themselves the word America. "We, too, are Americans," they'll remind you.

Labor and the Work Ethic

Cubans are distinct from all their Caribbean neighbors in one important respect. They combine their southern joy of living with a northern work ethic and an intellectual ability that makes them unique achievers. Through the centuries, Havana has received a constant infusion of the most energetic Spanish people in the Caribbean, what author James Michener calls "a unique group, one of the strongest cultural stocks in the New World": the wealthier, better-educated, and most motivated colonizers fleeing rebellion and invasion on Haiti, Santo Domingo, and Jamaica. The entrepreneurial spirit isn't dead, as evidenced by the way in which Cuba's new profit-oriented corporations are getting with the capitalistic 21st century, the success of *paladares* (private restaurants), and the brief flourishing in the mid-1990s of self-employed, makeshift entrepreneurs. Those entrepreneurs have since virtually disappeared, driven out of business by crippling taxation and state harassment; Castro is not about to let individual Habaneros accumulate wealth.

The vast majority of Habaneros work for the state, which, with few exceptions, dictates where an individual will work. At some stage, most citizens must participate in "volunteer" brigades, in which urban workers, university students, and even schoolchildren are shipped to the country-side to toil in the fields. Few Habaneros sign up these days out of a sense of duty. Most do so out of fear of recrimination or because volunteer workers get an *estimulo* (reward), such as priority listing for scarce housing. There are moral as well as material rewards—perhaps a week at Varadero, or the right to buy a refrigerator—for other workers. Wages are given according to a salary scale of 22 levels, with the top level getting six times that of the lowest. Though paid slightly more, doctors, engineers, and lawyers are not a separate "class" as they are in the US, Europe, or even the rest of the Caribbean. Life is little different for those who earn 350 pesos a month and those who earn 850. Highly trained professionals share the same struggles as unskilled workers.

The degree of anomie is great. Many Habaneros ask their doctor friends to issue *certificados* (medical excuses) so that they can escape the boredom of employment that offers little financial reward and little hope of promotion. *Socio* is the buddy network that shields citizens from the demands of the state. *Pinche* and *mayimbe* are their high-level contacts, those who help them get around the bureaucracy, such as the doctor who writes a false note to relieve someone of "voluntary" work in the countryside.

Simple Pleasures

Havana has no *fiesta* tradition. The populace is too industrious for that—too busy playing volleyball or baseball or making love while the other half whiles away the long, hot afternoons at the cinema or eating ice cream at Coppelia park or playing dominoes in the cool shade of arcaded balconies.

Havana's nocturnal pleasures are simple: movies, *trovas* (musical soirees), discos, cheap rum, and sex. For the vast majority of Habaneros, those without money, life is reduced to making do and making out, with the frequent highlight of a *cumbancha,* the Cuban equivalent of a party that might go on all night, with plenty of saucy rumba and saucier females to dance the hip-shaking rumba with. Habaneros move sinuously to Latin rhythms under bare light bulbs that cast shadows on garishly painted cinder block walls, while others gather around the TV to watch *Te Odio, Mi Amo*—an immensely popular Brazilian *telenova* (soap opera) dubbed into Spanish—and state-

a domino match in Habana Vieja

prescribed programs. (In the early 1990s, Habaneros rigged their roofs with *parábolas*—improvised parabolic antennas of aluminum, wire netting, or an empty sunflower oil can—that pointed at the Hotel Habana Libre, which was linked to a satellite and distributed US television signals to other hotels. The government tolerated the *parábolas* briefly during the hardest years of the Special Period, when tensions were running high. As conditions improved, the dishes were ordered removed. For good measure, the government coded the signals.)

Elsewhere, life on the dimly lit streets disappears except for the occasional courting couple murmuring in darkened doorways while shirtless neighbors rock on their porches or sit on their doorsteps into the wee hours, waiting for something to happen.

SEX AND GENDER

Sexual Mores

Cuba is a sexually permissive society. As journalist Jacobo Timerman wrote, "Eros is amply gratified in Cuba and needs no stimulation." Habaneros—men and women alike—emanate a joyous eroticism that transcends the hang-ups of essentially puritanical Europe or North America. They are sensualists of the first degree. Judging by the ease with which couples neck openly, wink seductively at strangers, and spontaneously slip into bed, the dictatorship of the proletariat that

transformed Eastern Europe into a perpetual Sunday school has made little headway in Cuba.

"'We [Cubans],'" noted one Habanera, "have been able to elevate eroticism into national genius." The Cuban revolution counted on this genius to lend its social experiment a unique flavor. "It would be, said Guevara, 'a revolution with *buchango* [pizzazz],' " wrote Lois Smith and Alfred Padula in *Sex and Revolution: Women in Socialist Cuba*.

Their mature attitude, unfettered by shame or guilt, is a direct result of state policy that has brought serious sex education to the masses, challenging many traditional taboos and myths. Though in regard to sexual freedom, the party argued that this "does not imply licentiousness, which degrades the beauty of relations between men and women." The state may promote the family, but Habaneros have a notoriously indulgent attitude toward casual sex that has defied the efforts of the regime to control it. Seduction is a national pastime pursued by both sexes—the free expression of a high-spirited people confined in an authoritarian world. After all, Cubans joke, sex is the only thing Castro can't ration.

In *Chronicles of the City of Havana*, Uruguayan journalist Eduardo Galeano tells the following story:

One day at noon, guagua [bus] 68 screeched to a halt at an intersection. There were cries of protest at the tremendous jolt until the passengers saw why the bus driver had jammed on the brakes: a magnificent woman had just crossed the street.

"You'll have to forgive me, gentlemen," said the driver of guagua 68, and he got out. All the passengers applauded and wished him luck.

The bus driver swaggered along, in no hurry, and the passengers watched him approach the saucy female, who stood on the corner, leaning against the wall, licking an ice cream cone. From guagua 68, the passengers followed the darting motion of her tongue as it kissed the ice cream while the driver talked on and on with no apparent result, until all at once she laughed and glanced up at him. The driver gave the thumbs-up sign and the passengers burst into a hearty ovation.

Promiscuity is rampant. So are extramarital affairs. Love is not associated with sex. And both genders are unusually bold. Men and women let their eyes run slowly over strangers they find attractive. *Ojitos* (long glances), often accompanied by uninhibited comments, betray envisioned improprieties. Even the women murmur *piropos* (courtly overtures) and sometimes comic declarations of love. "Dark-eyed Stellas light their feller's panatelas," Irving Berlin once wrote of Cuba. And how!

Male and female, old and young alike insist that promiscuity is a natural attribute. "Cubans like sex," says the director of Baracoa's family planning clinic. "It's part of our daily meal. Here you have girls who at 13 are already experts in sex."

SPANISH SURNAMES

Spanish surnames are combinations of the first surname of the person's father, which comes first, and the mother's first surname, which comes second. Thus, the son of Ángel Castro Argiz and Lina Ruz González is called Fidel Castro Ruz.

After marriage, women do not take their husbands' surnames; they retain their maiden names.

Teenagers become sexually active at an early age: girls at 13 on average, boys at 15, according to Cuba's National Center for Sex Education, which dispenses sex counseling to youths, along with condoms and birth control pills (considered to be tools of liberation for women). More than 160,000 abortions are performed free of charge each year, one-third on teenagers; in 1989, 61% of births were out of wedlock.

Women and Machismo

Castro set an ambitious and ambiguous goal of "full sexual equality." Today, according to Saul Landau, Cuba is the only "unisex" country in the world. A United Nations survey ranks Cuba among the top 20 nations in which women have the highest participation in politics and business. Women make up 50% of university students and 60% of doctors (a review of the University of Havana yearbooks shows that women were also well represented *before* the Revolution), although they are still poorly represented in the upper echelons of government.

Cuba's solid achievements in the past four decades reflect Castro's own faith in the equal abilities of women, and the belief that the Revolution cannot be called complete until women share full opportunities. Equality of the sexes is also given legal guarantees through the Cuban **Family Code,** which even stipulates that the male must share household duties.

The Spanish heritage is patriarchal—under the Spanish Civil Code, which was extended into the Cuban Republic, a husband had exclusive rights to property, finances, and, legally, the obedience of his wife and children. The Revolution has broken down the strict Spanish pattern, but it still colors family life. Prejudices and stereotypical behaviors still exist. Male machismo continues, and pretty women walking down the street are often bombarded with comments ranging from *piropos* to forthright invitations to sex. Although the sexes may have been equalized, the Revolution has not been able to get the Cubanness out of Habaneras who, regardless of age, still adore coquetry.

Few Habaneras simply put on a dress and go out. Instead, they make a great show of expressing their bodily beauty. "Cuban women don't walk, they sway," Naty Revuelta, one of Castro's former mistresses (and the mother of his daughter), has said. "When they walk, everything is in motion, from the ankle to the shoulder. The soldiers had a terrible time in the beginning, trying to teach them to march in the militia. They just couldn't get the sway out of them." Even the most ardent revolutionaries still paint their faces and attempt a toilette to heighten the femme fatale effect, as in their preference for minimalist and tight-fitting clothing. Women still routinely shorten and take in their uniforms to show their legs, outline their backsides, and generally be noticed.

Overt appreciation of the female form may seem sexist to politically correct North Americans, but in Cuba, rear ends have a value and meaning much more significant than in other cultures. Cuban literature overflows with references to *las nalgas cubanas* (the Cuban ass), usually plump and belonging to a well-rounded *mulatta*. Tom Miller synthesizes the long-standing fascination with *el culo* (the butt) in his marvelous travelogue, *Trading with the Enemy.* "I found enough material to keep a culophile busy for months."

The *mulatta* is particularly revered among Cuban males for her perceived sexuality. White Cubans have always had an appreciation for black beauty and have never been shy about saying so. Most Cuban love songs have always had a risqué quality, with lyrics praising the charms of *mi negra* (my black girl), *mi morena* (my dark girl), my chocolate sweetie, or my mulatto beauty, plainly described as such in racial terms. Interracial sexuality is the central theme, for example, of Cuba's most famous novel, Cirilo Villaverde's *Cecilia Valdés.* Today no less than in the past, the married white Habanero is likely to maintain a *mulatta* mistress, who is probably married herself (even José Martí abandoned his wife and was consoled by a mistress).

Of course, these stereotypes belie the ongoing debate within Cuba about the "correct" role of women, led by the **Cuban Federation of Women** (Federación de Mujeres Cubanas), Paseo #250, Havana, tel. (30) 6043, headed by Vilma Espín, former wife of Raúl Castro and known as the First Lady of Cuba. The Federation was founded to rouse women to be good revolutionaries but in recent years has devoted more effort to women's issues and rights, particularly the fight against a rising tide of teenage pregnancy (the *average* Cuban girl begins sexual activity at 13 and has her first baby at 18). Likewise, a nongovernmental organization called **Association of Women Communicators,** MAGIN, Calle 11 #160 e/ K y L, Vedado, Havana, tel. (32) 3322, fax (33) 3079, organizes workshops designed to build self-esteem and develop a greater understanding of the concepts of gender and feminism.

The Cubans themselves have yet to produce a book-length analysis of women's status in post-revolutionary Cuba. For that, refer to the excellent *Sex and Revolution: Women in Socialist Cuba,* by Lois Smith and Alfred Padula (Oxford University Press, 1996, www.cuba-books.com).

Homosexuality

Cuban gays must find it ironic that the heart of the homosexual world is Castro St. in San Francisco. It is assuredly not named in *El Jefe's* honor, as gays—called "queens," *maricónes,* or *locas* in the Cuban vernacular—were persecuted following the Revolution. Castro (who denies the comment) supposedly told journalist Lee Lockwood that a homosexual could never "embody the conditions and requirements of . . . a true revolutionary."

Castro says that such prejudices were a product not of the Revolution but of the existing social milieu. "We inherited male chauvinism—and many other bad habits—from the conquistadores," he told Tomás Borge in *Face to Face with Fidel Castro* (Ocean Press, 1992). "That historical legacy . . . influenced our attitude toward homosexuality." It is also true that at the onset of the Revolution, the gay rights movement had not yet been born in the United States, and the same prejudices that the revolutionaries inherited about homosexuals were prevalent elsewhere in the world. Thus, gays and lesbians met with "homophobic repression and rejection" in Cuba, just as they did in the US. In Cuba, however, it was more systematic and brutal.

The pogrom began in earnest in 1965; homosexuals were arrested and sent to agricultural work and reeducation camps called UMAP (Units for Military Help to Agricultural Production). Echoing Auschwitz, over the gate of one such camp in Camagüey was the admonition: "Work Makes You Men." Many brilliant intellectuals lost their jobs because they were gay, or accused of being gay through anonymous denunciation. Homosexuality was also considered an aberration of nature that could weaken the family structure. Hence homosexuals were not allowed to teach, become doctors, or occupy positions from which they could "pervert" Cuban youth.

Although UMAP camps closed in 1968, periodic purges occurred throughout the 1970s and early '80s. Many homosexuals left—or were forced to leave—on the Mariel Boatlift. However, by the mid-1980s, Cuba began to respond to the gay rights movement that had already gained momentum worldwide. Officially, the new position was that homosexuality and bisexuality are no less natural or healthy than heterosexuality. In 1987, a directive was issued to police to stop harassment. The 1994 Oscar-nominated *Fresa y Chocolat,* which deals with the persecution of gays in Cuba and the government's use of informers, was officially approved by Cuba's Film Institute (headed by Alfredo Guevara, a homosexual and close confidante of Castro), offering proof that the government was exorcising the ghost of a shameful past.

Nonetheless, deep prejudice still exists throughout Cuban society, and there is still a restriction on gays joining the party.

LIFE IN HAVANA

Havana's physical destitution and the miscellaneous hardships are so obvious that one of the first things almost every visitor to Havana asks is, "How on earth do the Habaneros get by?"

On the eve of the Revolution, Havana was a highly developed city with more millionaires than anywhere south of Texas. It had a rapidly evolving capitalist infrastructure and an urban labor force that had achieved "the eight-hour day, double pay for overtime, one month's paid vacation, nine days sick leave, and the right to strike." On the other hand, Habaneros who drove Cadillacs and otherwise lived a well-to-do middle-class life were as remote culturally as they were economically from the mass of their countrymen. In 1950, a World Bank study team reported that 40% of urban dwellers and 60% of rural dwellers were undernourished. More than 40% of Cuban

people had never gone to school; only 60% had regular full-time employment. The city orphanage in Havana even had a drop chute with flaps to facilitate the abandonment of babies by mothers who couldn't afford to bring them up.

The Revolution immeasurably improved the material and spiritual condition of millions of Cubans, eliminating poverty and gross disparities, albeit at the cost of destroying the middle and wealthy urban classes, emasculating individualism, and imposing a general paucity. But at least everyone had the essentials. The government provided five crates of beer as a wedding present, and birthday cakes for kids under 10. Everyone enjoyed two two-week vacations a year at the beach. But things changed for the worse overnight when the beneficence of the Soviet Union ended following the latter's collapse (the Soviets had propped up the moribund Cuban economy with subsidies of US$3 billion annually; on the eve of the collapse, 84% of Cuba's trade was with the Soviet Union and Eastern Europe).

The 1990s have been devastating for a population accustomed to a much higher standard of living. In 1991, when Castro told his people that they were entering a "special period," he was warning them that their society was about to experience a special kind of collapse, and they were about to feel a special kind of pain. Now, the Cuban economy is finally beginning to bounce back from disastrous collapse, much thanks to tourism, but the average Habanero still feels the pain.

Habaneros will tell you that life is a *lucha* (fight). Today, Havana's citizens are focused on issues of everyday survival. Every morning, people prepare to cobble together some kind of normalcy out of whatever the situation allows them. Cubans are masters at making the best of a bad situation. *Resolver* (to resolve, to overcome obstacles with ingenuity, spontaneity, and humor) is one of the most commonly used verbs on the island. For many of the city's people, the socialist dream has turned into a nightmare. Socialist equality can begin to look dismal as you contemplate the aged and destitute walking around inconsolably as if they'd been castrated—*jaca* is the local term—and at a loss over their lives, ruminating over what has gone terribly wrong with a Revolution that held greater promise.

The Bare Essentials

Row upon row of citrus trees grow just 30 miles from Havana, but it is nearly impossible to find an orange for sale. Vast acres of state farms and co-operatives go unfarmed, while cultivated land is poorly tended. What happens to the food produced is a mystery. Hospitals, schools, and works canteens get priority, but almost nothing reaches the state groceries (almost 40% of produce is stolen as it passes through the dysfunctional distribution system known as *acopio*). The *campesinos* (farm workers) do okay. But many Habaneros go without. The *libreta*—the ration book meant to supply every Cuban citizen with the essentials—cannot provide.

A certain amount of staples is allowed per person from the state grocery store per month—six pounds of rice, 11 pounds of beans, four ounces of coffee, four ounces of lard—but only when available. Candles, kerosene, and matches all appear in the *libreta* but are hardly ever in stock. Nor are cooking oil, household detergent, or soap—the items most direly felt. (Habaneros are notoriously toilet-conscious. Even the poorest Habanero manages to keep fastidiously clean. It has been said that "to take away their soap would be Castro's greatest folly. Almost anything else can be tolerated, but take away their soap and the regime would fall!") The *libreta* also gives them the theoretical right to 20 liters of gasoline monthly, but only 60 liters per car was distributed in the whole of 1997. Conversations are laced with an obsession for items that many Habaneros haven't seen in years.

Much of the food supplied by the state you wouldn't feed to your cat. (Not that there are many of those anyway; cats are only now making a comeback on the streets of Havana, most of their forebears having ended up in the cooking pot during the early 1990s. Dogs fared better, although hundreds were put out on the street to fend for themselves because their owners could no longer feed them.) For example, *picadillo* is second-grade ground meat mixed with soybean, hailed by bureaucrats as a "meatsome mass." Worse than that, says Humberto Werneck, is the *pasta de oca*, a "culinary enigma which is bought to contain the viscera of geese, none of them noble like the liver from which the famous paté is made."

The US embargo worsens the situation, to be sure, by denying the export of US-made goods to Cuba; one of Uncle Sam's most shameful and sordid acts, in 1993, a year that Castro called "so hard, so difficult, so terrible," when malnutrition haunted Cuba, was to tighten the loophole that permitted food sales to Cuba. But today there's no shortage of US products in Havana, from Marlboro cigarettes to Nikes and Coca-Cola, imported through Mexico or other countries. The US embargo is seen by Cubans for what it is: an attempt to starve them into bringing Castro down. Thus, Castro is able to make Uncle Sam the scapegoat for the country's woes, which are assuredly due to the overriding faults of the system. In response to a Gallup poll in 1994—the first-ever independent poll held in Cuba—the largest group, 31%, answered that the US embargo was the most serious problem facing Cuba.

To make matters worse, Cubans are paid in pesos but anything worth buying today is sold (by Cuban state enterprises) for US dollars. The average monthly wage is about 350 pesos—about US$17 at black market exchange rates—yet meat in the *mercados agropecuarios* (the independent farmers' market created in 1993 to resolve the food crisis) can cost 25 pesos a pound, and black beans nine pesos. Fortunately, rent and utilities are so heavily subsidized that they are virtually free.

A few years ago, a peso income had some value. Today it is virtually worthless. Life has become organized around a mad scramble for dollars. The lucky ones have access to family cash, known as *fulla*, sent from Miami (social obligations dictate that if you make money, you are expected to support family members) or donated by a foreign lover and benefactor.

Much of the cash coming from Florida is smuggled in by *caballos* ("horses"), often in creative schemes that come a cropper, such as the one conceived by an unfortunate Cuban in Miami who answered his brother's plea for *fulla*. As told by Humberto Werneck, the latter was disappointed to receive only a pair of shoes—and one size too small at that. He sold them to a stranger and then almost went mad when he later discovered that his clever brother had hidden $1,000 in each shoe.

Cuban economists reckon that only about 25% of the population has regular access to dollars.

The rest, including the professionals (doctors, engineers, architects, white-collar workers), are experiencing downward mobility, replaced by a new breed of upper class—black marketeers, part-time prostitutes, waiters, criminal entrepreneurs, and anyone else with access to a significant amount of dollars. Without access to US dollars, Cubans must rely on their wits and faith (Cubans joke about getting by on *fe,* Spanish for faith, but today an acronym for *familia extranjera*—family abroad). The majority of Cubans must simply *buscar la forma* (find a way).

Habaneros have always survived by *resolviendo*—the Cuban art of barter, the cut corner, the gray market where much of Cuba's economy operates.

The Black Market and *Resolviendo*

Most Habaneros rely on *los bisneros* (the underground economy), doing business illegally. The black market, known as the *bolsa* (exchange), resolves the failings of the state-controlled economy. For four decades, it has touched all walks of life. Gas station attendants sell gasoline "stretched" with kerosene (the good stuff is siphoned off and sold on the black market), while store managers routinely set aside part of the state-supplied stock to sell on the *bolsa.*

Habaneros are maestros at inventing to get around shortages. Barter is common. So are time payments, verbal contracts for future delivery, and a hundred variations on the theme. Those with a few dollars might buy scarce products and then barter them to other Cubans with no link to the dollar economy. One neighbor might bring another canned goods in exchange for fish. A third may get his car engine fixed in exchange for peanut butter. And many Cubans live off swindles, or *trampas.*

Habaneros are also the world's best recyclers. The *libreta,* for example, provides only four cigars and six packets of cigarettes monthly. Hence even cigar and cigarette butts are recycled to make *tupamaros,* hand-crafted cigarettes rolled in a rustic oversized roller. To save energy, crafty Habaneros have rigged their bicycles with engines taken from chain saws and even fumigators.

Many front and backyards, rooftop *azuelas,* and even household quarters have been turned into chicken coops and pig sties. Havana households often share living quarters with a pig, as depicted in the movie *Fresa y Chocolate,* in which a pig is seen being pushed up the stairs of a tenement. Raising a pig inside remains illegal, so many of the urban pigs are mute—they've had their vocal chords slit (a practice so common that it, too, was mentioned on celluloid, in *Adorable Lies*).

Cubans have learned to laugh about their hardships. Nonetheless, having sacrificed for the Revolution for four decades, many Cubans are exhausted. Frustrations have set in. It's a remarkable testament to the enduring spirit of the people that they have been able to withstand the upheavals without grave social and political consequences.

Housing Conditions

Until the Revolution, government expenditures were concentrated mostly in and around Havana. The provinces were neglected, rural housing was basic, and many towns had few sewers, electricity, plumbing, or paved roads. Since the Revolution, the government has concentrated its energies on developing the countryside and replacing urban shantytowns with apartment housing.

Today, virtually every house in Havana has electricity, although a large percentage do not have hot water. (Households are metered separately for use of electricity. Payments for this are made directly to state authorities.) By law, no renter can pay more than 10% of his or her salary in rent. However, almost 80% of Cubans own their own homes. "Mrs. Thatcher's vision of a homeowners' society come true in communist Cuba," Martha Gellhorn notes, wryly. "Rents pile up like down payments year after year, until the sale price of the flat is reached, whereupon bingo, you become an old-fashioned capitalist owner." Those who owned houses before the Revolution have been allowed to keep them; those who fled Cuba forfeited their property to the state. Cubans can swap their houses without state approval but cannot sell them. But as with everything in Cuba, they find a way by posing the transaction as barter. Not surprisingly, a new breed of real estate broker—a "barter agent"—has emerged. Houses located in areas with few or no *apagones,* such as those close to hotels or hospitals, are most highly priced.

Conditions vary markedly. Although much of Havana prerevolutionary housing has deteriorated to a point of dilapidation, there *are* also many fine, well-kept houses. Half of Havana's housing is rated "poor" to "bad," and the housing shortage is so critical that many Habaneros live in a *barbacoa,* a partitioned room, often divided into several tiny cubicles for individual family members. In many cases, the high-ceilinged rooms of many old colonial buildings have been turned into two stories by adding new ceilings and wooden staircases.

Interiors often belie the dour impression received on the street. Rooms everywhere are kept spick-and-span and furnished with typically Cuban decor: family photos, kitschy ceramic animals, plastic flowers, and other effusive knick-knackery—and frequently a photo of Castro, Guevara, or Camilo Cienfuegos. Always there is a large refrigerator (Russian or prerevolutionary Yankee) and at least one TV.

Most housing built since the Revolution (in both town and country) is concrete apartment block units of a standard Bulgarian design—the ugly Bauhaus vision of uniform, starkly functional workers' housing, which had the advantage of being cheap to build and, in theory, easy and cheap to maintain. Most have not been maintained. And do they ever need it! Most were jerry-built by unskilled volunteer labor, adding salt to the wound of the aesthetic shortfall.

Why is there no paint? Because the centralized planning process has always been intent on meeting production quotas, not on allocating scarce resources for maintenance and repair. Spare parts aren't ordered to maintain sewers or electrical boxes, so, over time, everything is jerry-rigged. Until 1993, it was illegal for Cubans to freelance as electricians, plumbers, or construction workers, so everyone relied on the state, which gave home and public utility repair low priority (freelancer entrepreneurs have since been squeezed out by a control-obsessed Communist bureaucracy). For four decades, Habaneros have also been denied access to pots of paint, whitewash, and chemical treatments to prevent molds and mildews, so that the latter abound. When walking the streets of Habana Vieja, it is common to pass an open doorway that delivers a lungful of mildew, quite horrible to breathe.

Since the Special Period, Havana has become littered with half-finished structures looking like dinosaur skeletons. Materials are simply no longer available to finish the jobs. Today, in a deteriorating situation, as many as half a million Habaneros are "ill-housed." Squatting is common, and homelessness has begun to appear.

CHILDREN AND YOUTH

One of the simplest pleasures for the foreign traveler is to see smiling children (Cuban children are always smiling) in school uniforms so colorful that they reminded novelist James Michener of "a meadow of flowers. Well nourished, well shod and clothed, they were the permanent face of the land." And well behaved, too.

Parents dote on their children. They save money from the day a girl is born to do her right on her 15th birthday with a memorable *fiesta de quince* marking her coming of age and, though a direct legacy of a more conservative Spanish heritage, marking the day on which the *quinceañera* may openly begin her sexual life without family recrimination. Getting ready for the *fiesta* may involve a whole arsenal, from the hairdresser and dressmaker (a special dress resembling a wedding gown or a knock 'em dead Scarlett O'Hara outfit is de rigeur) to the photographer and chauffeur in the classic American car to take the young woman and her friends to her party.

Children also are treated with great indulgence by the state. The government has made magnificent strides to improve the lot of poor children. Once, when asked about the sister who turned her back on the Revolution, Castro told TV interviewer Barbara Walters, "We have the same mother and father, but different ideas. I am a committed socialist. She is an enemy of socialism and that is why she says [bad] things about me. But let me tell you. I have five million brothers and sisters, and between us we have millions of children. We love these children." There is no doubt he is sincere.

About 35% of Havana's population is below 16 years of age. Throughout Havana, you'll come across bright-eyed children laden with satchels, making their way to and from school in pin-neat uniforms colored according to their grades.

people-watching from the balustrade

Younger ones wear short-sleeved white shirts, light-blue neckerchiefs, and maroon shorts or miniskirts; up to the 12th grade, secondary school children wear white shirts, red neckerchiefs, and ocher-yellow long pants or miniskirts. The neckerchiefs show that they are Pioneers, similar to Cub and Boy Scouts.

There's a school in Havana every few blocks, usually indicated by a small bust of José Martí in the forecourt. Today, the literacy rate is about 98.5%. According to UNICEF statistics, nine out of 10 Cuban children complete four years of primary schooling—the minimum required for a child to have a chance of being literate and numerate (the US average is 9.6; Costa Rica 8.4; Chile 7.5; Haiti 1.2). School is compulsory to age 15 (ninth grade). Children may then choose to continue three years pre-university study or at technical schools. Anyone who has ever visited a Cuban classroom will remark on the enthusiasm displayed by willing, lively pupils.

Occasionally, Havana's secondary schoolchildren ship out to spend time working in the countryside, where they live in boarding schools attached to 1,250-acre plots of arable land and fulfill José Martí's dictum: "In the morning, the pen—but in the afternoon, the plow." Half of all intermediate-level children also attend a rural boarding school for at least some of their education. Here, time is divided equally between study and labor, the latter most often in citrus plantations, where the kids bring in the harvest. Here, too, unintended by the state, children learn

to be lovers. Promiscuity is a staple in the fields.

Cuban youth have grown up in a mature Revolution—more than 60% of the Cuban population was born after the Revolution (every child is sworn in at the age of six to become a communist pioneer). The older generation has attempted to make the Revolution, has faced down the threat of US invasion, has witnessed astounding social achievements—all through collective endeavor. Although there is respectful communication between generations, clashes are becoming more common. Where their parents use "we," Havana's youth use "I"—I want to do so and so. The majority are bored by the constant calls for greater sacrifice and tired of being treated as if they were stupid. They want to enjoy life.

Havana's youth are in a confusing limbo where neither the socialist role model nor its complete rejection is appropriate to the current circumstances. Young people growing up in the current era of hardship and economic opening are not necessarily abandoning revolutionary principles (although the war in Angola—Cuba's Vietnam—was a misadventure that left many of the young angry and disaffected). But the methods and ideas many are adopting alarm the authorities. As the quest for US dollars tightens its grip, an increasing number of Cuban youth are asking, "What's the point in studying?" They are more concerned with their own future than with the party's. Many realize they can get further through their own work and initiative, and are going into business for themselves as *jiniteros* and *cuenta propistas* (freelancers), making a buck doing anything from driving taxis to repairing tire punctures.

The government worries that the increased association with foreign tourists helps foster nonconformism, such as the growing number of long-haired youths—*roqueros* and *frikis*—who sport ripped jeans and would look at home at a Metallica concert.

Cuban youth are expressing their individuality—they want to be themselves, which today means showing a marked preference for anything North American, especially clothing. They wouldn't be caught dead in a *guayabera,* the traditional tropical shirt favored by older men; instead, young women dress in the latest fashion—halter tops, Lycra bodysuits, diaphanous blouses, miniskirts, tight jeans, flared pants, and platform shoes. Young men follow suit, though more conservatively, and as well as their budgets allow. Egotism is flourishing. Consumerism is capturing the imagination of Havana's youth, spawned by the notion that the only way to advance is by making money. Teenagers are becoming sexually promiscuous at an earlier age, and their casual attitude toward sex is fueling a rapid rise in prostitution.

More and more, youth feel there is no future in Cuba. "We can't wait forever," they say. Many still look up to Castro as a hero, but the vast majority of youth today see him as a dour father figure who can't get with the times.

Cuban youth are served by their own state newspapers, such as *Pioniero* and *Juventud Rebelde (Rebel Youth).*

For study tours to explore Cuban youth culture, contact **Global Exchange,** 2017 Mission St. #303, San Francisco, CA 94110, tel. (415) 255-7296, fax (415) 255-7498, e-mail: globalexch@igc.org, website: www.globalexchange.com. Also look for a copy of *Cuba Va!,* a splendid hour-long documentary released in 1993 in which Cuban youth express their fears and hopes; US$95; Cuba Va Video Project, 12 Liberty St., San Francisco, CA 94110, tel. (415) 282-1812, fax (415) 282-1798.

RELIGION

Cuba is officially an atheist country, and proselytizing is illegal. Nonetheless, a recent government survey found that more than half of all Cubans are *creyentos,* believers of one sort or another.

Christianity

Habaneros have always been lukewarm about Christianity, mostly because the Catholic Church sided with the Spanish against the patriots during the colonial era. After independence, the constitution therefore provided for separation of church and state, depriving the former of its political influence and state support. Later, the Catholic Church had a quid pro quo with the corrupt Machado, Grau, and Batista regimes—"you keep out of our business and we'll keep out of yours." When the Revolution triumphed, many of the clergy left for Miami along with the rich to whom they had ministered.

The Catholic Church has since been a focus of opposition. Hence, although the Castro regime has never banned the practice of religion, the church was allowed to engage in only marginal social activities. Church attendance came to be considered antisocial. Religious education was eliminated from the school curriculum. Practicing Catholics were banned from the Communist Party. Consequently, religious believers declined from more than 70% of the population to less than 30%, and church attendance plummeted. The Cuban Conference on Bishops estimates that only about one percent of the population goes to church at least twice a year. Churches had to close down due to disrepair, and many priests resorted to holding services in private homes.

In 1986, Castro performed an about face: religion was no longer the opiate of the masses. In 1990, he admitted that believers had been unjustly treated. That year, for only the second time in more than 30 years, radio and television stations began transmitting religious music and songs. The following year, the Communist Party opened its doors to believers, and security agents disappeared from churches. It was a timely move, co-opting the shifting mood. The collapse of the Soviet Union proved the adage that "when the earth moves under the people's feet, they naturally look up to the sky." The collapse left a spiritual vacuum that has fed church attendance, while the number of seminarians has also skyrocketed. The trendiest piece of jewelry these days is a gold cross.

Pope John Paul II's emotionally charged visit to Cuba in January 1998 was an extraordinary event that boosted the influence of the Catholic church in Cuba and reignited an expression of faith among the Cuban people. But a huge percentage of Habaneros—perhaps the majority—remain atheistic, or at least agnostic, and bring to their dialectic an unusually rigid investigative rationale by which to reach their conclusions.

A far larger percentage, however, are superstitious and believe to lesser or greater degree in *santería.*

Santería

It's said that if you scratch a Cuban, Catholic or non, you'll find a *santería* believer underneath. Even Castro, a highly superstitious person, is said to be a believer.

Santería, or saint worship, has been deeply entrenched in Cuban culture for 300 years. Then, as now, its "headquarters" have been in the Regla and Guanabacoa districts, across Havana harbor. The cult is a fusion of Catholicism with the *Lucumí* religion of the African Yoruba tribes. Since slave masters had banned African religious practice, the slaves cloaked their gods in Catholic garb and continued to pray to them to preserve a shred of their souls and strengthen them against indignities.

Thus, in *santería,* Catholic figures of virtue are avatars of the hedonistic Yoruban *orishas.* These divine beings of African animism are worshipped in secretive and complex rituals that may feature animal sacrifices along with chanting, dancing, and music. Gods change their sex at midnight: by day, adherents may pray in front of a figure of Santa Barbara and at night worship the same figure as Changó. As sociologist Nelson Valdés notes, Cubans live comfortably with this paradox. There are several hundred gods in the pantheon, but only about 20 are honored in daily life. Almost every home in Havana has a statue of a *santería* god and a glass of water and other miscellany to appease the spirits of the dead. And walking Havana's streets, you'll see believers clad all in white, having just gone through their initiation rites.

It is thought that the *orishas* control an individual's life (a string of bad luck will be blamed on an *orisha*) and must therefore be placated. The gods are believed to perform all kinds of miracles on a person's behalf and are thus consulted and besought. They're too supreme for mere mortals to communicate with directly. Hence, *santeros* or *babalaos* (priests) act as go-betweens to honor the saints and interpret their commands.

Santería is a sensuous religion. It lacks the arbitrary moral prescriptions of Catholicism—the *orishas* let adherents have a good time. The gods themselves are fallible and hedonistic philanderers, such as the much feared and respected Changó, god of war, fire, thunder, and lightning. Changó's many mistresses include Oyá (patroness of justice) and Ochún, the sensuous black goddess of pleasure who loves to dance and make love, whom many Cuban women identify as the *orisha* of love in an erroneous syncretism with Venus. This fits well with the sensualist Cuban psyche.

Followers of Changó wear collars decorated with red and white plastic beads; followers of Ochún wear yellow and white beads. Each saint has his or her own dance, as well as an "altar," such as the ceiba tree in the corner of Havana's Plaza de Armas, where good charms and bad (fruits, rum-soaked cakes, pastries, and coins) are strewn near its trunk, the stirred earth near its sacred roots bulging with buried offerings. At other altars, caged pigeons await their fate at the end of a knife.

Organized Tours: The government has set up *diplosanterías* where foreign visitors can consult with *santería* priests for dollars. **Rumbos** offers an excursion to witness *santería* in Regla, at Santuario #13, tel. (90) 0812. Reservations can be made through any Infotur office (US$22). **Havanatur,** Calle 2 #17 e/ 1 y 3, Miramar, Havana, tel. (33) 2273 or (33) 2161, fax (33) 2877, offers a weeklong tour ("Rendezvous with the Orishas"), which includes visits to Regla, Guanabacoa, and Santa María del Rosarío.

HOW HABANEROS FEEL ABOUT THE REVOLUTION

The fall of the Berlin Wall and the disintegration of the Soviet Bloc brought expectations of a Ceausescu-like ending for Castro. Why, then, have Cuba's internal and external crises not produced Castro's downfall? The US State Department and right-wing Cuban-Americans sow the field with stories of a "one-party monopoly," "40 years of brainwashing," and the "grip of fear" imposed on Cubans by "the police state." While there is truth in all these assessments, they don't take into account the unifying power of national pride, the very real achievements of the Revolution, and perhaps above all, Castro's unique charisma and the Machiavellian way he is able to shape Habaneros' minds, like a hypnotist.

Many of the same Cubans who complain about harrowing privation in almost the same breath profess loyalty to Castro. A 1992 report by the US Army War College concluded that in spite of the current crisis, Castro still retains a substantial base of popular support among the Cuban public. Those with a hate-hate relationship are resigned to sullen silence, prison, or exile. Most Cubans, however, have a love-hate relationship with *El Máximo,* although they hesitate to express their negative feelings too openly. Feelings expressed are schizophrenic. On one side, the average Cubans hate Castro for the turmoil and hardship he has wrought in their lives. On the other, they respect him for what he has brought in national dignity.

After five centuries of humiliation, Castro was, and remains, a symbol of Cuban pride. Unlike Eastern Europe, Cuba's revolution was homegrown, not imposed by Soviet troops. It came from the Cubans themselves. Just as Yankees take pride in the men of 1776, Cubans take pride in *their* revolutionary heroes: they are the nation's embodiment of independence from Spain and the United States. Castro is Cuba's George Washington.

Tangible Gains

Most Cubans who support the Revolution do so not from reading Karl Marx but because they know they are better off than many residents of neighboring countries. While it is easy to compare themselves—and to be compared by Westerners—to North America, Cubans prefer to compare Cuba to Mexico, Jamaica, Haiti, and the Dominican Republic—countries beset by true poverty. Cuba has invested 40 years of resources to become one of the few underdeveloped nations with a system that protects all members of society from illiteracy and ill health. Conditions in Cuba are hard, but virtually nowhere do you find, as you do in many Latin American and Caribbean countries, hordes of child beggars in squalid slums. Instead, uniformed schoolchildren attend day-care centers and schools, which do experience shortages of books and pencils. Everyone still eats—even if not well—and medical care is free and available to all, although doctors and hospitals are hardpressed to dispense aspirin or antibiotics (unless patients have dollars). The Cubans are acutely aware of all this.

The tremendous advances in racial and sexual equality, the guarantees offered workers and their families against any eventual risk or contingency, the fact that Cuba's vital culture is nourished and protected—all this and other tangible benefits have produced mammoth goodwill among the Cuban populace, especially in the countryside, where support for the Revolution is strongest.

Rising Discontent

Since the onset of the Special Period, however, Cuba has found it impossible to sustain its cradle-to-grave benefits. "Our real problem," said Ricardo Alarcón, head of the National Assembly, "is comparing ourselves with ourselves five years ago," referring to the "golden years" of the 1980s. The social gains of the Revolution were achieved two decades ago and were taken for granted. Today, a majority of Cubans—especially Habaneros—are tired of the inefficiencies, the endless hardships, and the growing inequalities. How, for example, can the government explain the US$250,000 charcoal-gray Lamborghini Diablo parked outside Havana's five-star Melia Cohiba hotel?

Castro's spell over his people, his ability to manipulate the mood, has been such that Cubans, to an astonishing degree, have separated their discontent with the situation from the man in charge. Even the disaffected have tended not to speak with hatred, as East Germans did of Erich Honecker. They usually spoke of Castro with a combination of the respect and anger a son feels for an overbearing father who can't get with the times. His heart is in the right place, they said, but his head isn't.

Today the mood on Havana's streets is very different. Cuba's economic crisis has created palpable discontent. They are sick of deprivation. Habaneros are increasingly anxious for a return to the market economy and a chance to improve their own lives. They are tired of being answerable to the state for their every move (anyone criticizing the state of affairs or trying to express their individuality to get ahead economically is likely to suffer severe consequences). They feel like they are on a yo-yo; any brief liberalization is always followed by a yank on the string. Habaneros are forced to break the law constantly to survive. They live under enormous stress of being caught for the slightest transgression and are tired of having to look over their shoulder for the secret police in the shadows. Even buying and selling produce such as bread and eggs illegally can result in huge fines and a stain on their record. It is disconcerting to see police harassment of pedestrians on the street, noticeably of black youths, who can expect to be stopped at random for ID checks; dozens are arrested daily this way quite literally for being in the wrong place at the wrong time, or for being unable to account for a few extra loaves of bread.

Habaneros are a paranoid people, never sure who might be a *chivato*, a finger-man for the CDR or MININT, the much-loathed Ministry of the Interior. In this regard, Havana doesn't seem to have changed much since the 1930s, when Hemingway told Arnold Samuelson, "Don't trust anybody. That fellow might have been a government spy trying to get you in bad. You can never tell who they are."

"What Alternative Do We Have?"

Habaneros increasingly are less inclined to accept the lie—the propagandist facade that Cubans call "the mantle"—and are more inclined to point the finger toward the top. Most Habaneros say that things cannot go on as they are: "We must have change!" But when you ask them how change will come, most roll their eyes and shrug. Politically, the majority of the city's population—those not firmly committed to the political apparatus—are weighed down with passivity. Silence, congruity, and complicity—pretending to be satisfied and happy with the system—are cultural reflexes that have been called indicative of cultural decay. Jacobo Timerman's *Cuba: A Journey* provides a baneful look at this passivity.

Even Habaneros who do not actively support Castro are hard-pressed to name a viable alternative; as they struggle to improve, these people feel that they are on familiar ground with Castro. And *El Jefe* makes sure that no one else grows so popular or powerful that he might be seen as a rival who can lead Cubans out of their misery. There is no opposition in Cuba, and mistrust of those who have fled to the US runs high. "We will never accept a government dictated by Miami," says leading Cuban dissident Elizardo Sánchez. The majority of Cubans want change, but they do not want to open their door to a type of interference that has taught some bitter lessons in the past.

SIGHTSEEING

Outside Cuba, all phone and fax numbers given here need to be preceded by 53-7, the codes for Cuba and Havana respectively.

GEOGRAPHY

Havana lies 150 km (93 miles) due south of Florida, on the northwest coast of Cuba, the largest of the Caribbean islands at 114,524 square km (44,218 square miles). Havana lies just south of the Tropic of Cancer and looks out upon the Straits of Florida at the eastern perimeter of the Gulf of Mexico.

La Ciudad de la Habana (the City of Havana) is built on the west side of a sweeping bay with a narrow funnel entrance—Bahía de la Habana—but extends for miles to the west and south of the bay. The city slopes gradually inland from the shore. The core is divided into three regions of tourist interest: Habana Vieja, Centro Habana (Central Havana), and Vedado and Plaza de la Revolución. The suburbs extend for a radius of about 20 km from the center.

East of Havana, a chain of hills runs parallel to the shore inland of the rocky coast. The coast is indented with coves. About 15 km east of the city, a series of long, white sand beaches—the Playas del Este—prove tempting on hot summer days. The shore west of the city is less appealing, mostly rocky with a few beaches of modest appeal.

Municipios and Districts

The metropolitan area of Havana—a sprawling city—covers 740 square km (286 square miles) and incorporates 15 *municipios* (municipalities), subdivided into distinct districts. The urban center mostly lies west and south of the harbor, and encompasses almost 15,000 *manzanas* (blocks). Like all fine cities, Havana is a collection of neighborhoods, each with its own distinct character that owes much to the date that each developed.

The *municipio* of **La Habana Vieja** (the oldest part of the city) lies immediately west of the harbor, and with neighboring **Regla** across the harbor, dates from the 16th and 17th centuries, though most structures are of the 17th and 18th centuries.

Centro Habana, west of Habana Vieja, and Casablanca, the fishing village facing Havana to the north (and part of the *municipio* of Regla) date from the 18th century. They were the first residential areas outside the ancient city walls.

Residential Vedado, the modern heart of the city, and Nuevo Vedado to the south, form the *municipio* of **Plaza de la Revolución,** blending neighborhoods of the 19th and 20th centuries. Plaza de la Revolución extends west from Centro to the Río Almanderes.

The now-decrepit residential districts of **Cerro** and **Diez de Octubre,** which includes La Vibora district, lie south of Plaza de la Revolución and Centro Habana, respectively, and date from the 19th century.

Playa extends west of the Río Almanderes and includes, in order, the districts of Miramar and (to its south) Buena Vista, with once glamorous Cubanacán, and Flores, Siboney, Atabey, and Santa Fe beyond. These areas date from the late 19th and early 20th centuries.

The suburban, residential *municipios* of **La Lisa** and **Marianao** lie south of Playa and offer little of touristic interest.

Encircling the core are the expansive and mostly rural outrider *municipios* of **Boyeros, Arroyo Naranjo, Cotorro,** and **Guanabacoa,** pinned by the 17th-century eponymous village.

HAVANA HIGHLIGHTS

You could spend two or three days strolling the streets of Habana Vieja (Old Havana) and be mesmerized at every turn. It's a given that you'll visit **La Bodeguita del Medio** and **El Floridita** to pay homage to Papa (Ernest Hemingway) with a *mojito* in one hand and a daiquiri in the other. Then what? Here's my list of top *must-sees and -dos:*

Capitolio: Habana Vieja. Cuba's former congressional building is a stunner both inside and out.

Castillo de la Cabaña: Habana Vieja. Largest fortress in the Americas, superbly restored with cannons in situ, a fabulous historical armaments museum, and marvelous views over the city. Every night, soldiers in 18th-century period costume reenact the *canoñazo,* when a cannon is fired to commemorate the signal to close the city gates.

Coppelia: Vedado. Enjoying an ice-cream sundae on a hot day in Coppelia park is one of the sublime experiences of Havana, but be sure to forsake the dollars-only section and do it the Cuban way—by standing in line and savoring your *helado* alfresco at communal tables, paying in pesos and filling up for a pittance.

Fábrica de Tabaco Partagas: Habana Vieja. A visit to a cigar factory is a must for the heady aromas, a sense for a uniquely enchanting socialist workplace, and an appreciation of how the world's finest cigars are made.

Plaza de la Catedral: Habana Vieja. The heart and soul of old Havana, this compact plaza will steal your heart. Visit by both day and night.

Monumento y Museo Martí: The towering marble and granite statue dominates Plaza de la Revolución. Enjoy all-around views of Havana from the

mirador. The splendid museum honors Cuba's National Hero.

Museo Hemingway: San Francisco de Paula. Finca Vigía, Hemingway's home for 20 years, on a hill southeast of Havana, is preserved as it was the day he died. His sportfishing boat, the *Pilar,* stands on the grounds.

Museo de la Revolución: Habana Vieja. This former presidential palace now tells the tale of the Revolution. It includes the ***Granma* Memorial,** featuring the vessel that brought Fidel Castro, Che Guevara, and fellow revolutionaries from exile to initiate the Revolution. For the complete tale on events leading up to and during the Revolution, this is the place. Compulsory education.

Playas del Este: When the sun beats down on a weekend, half of Havana heads to the beach—ideally, the wide, white, diamond-dust sands of Playas del Este, where you can watch the locals tanning and flirting. You, of course, get to do the same. Do it the Cuban way: rent a Yankee *cacharro* and be chauffeured, rolling along on under-inflated tires to the rhythm of the rumba on the radio.

Tropicana Nightclub: Marianao. Perhaps the world's most spectacular cabaret, with more than 200 singers and dancers—predominantly stupendous mulattas in fantastical costumes—performing beneath the stars.

Maqueta de la Habana: This detailed 1:1,000 scale model of Havana provides a bird's-eye perspective of the entire city.

Cojímar: This is the old fishing village where Hemingway berthed the *Pilar.* A memorial to Hemingway and the Las Terrazas bar and restaurant recall his presence.

ADDRESSES

Addresses are normally given as locations. Thus, the Havanatur office is at Calle 6 e/ 1ra y 3ra, Miramar, Havana, meaning it is on Calle 6 between (e/ stands for *entre,* between) First and Third Avenue (Avenida 1ra y 3ra).

Street numbers are occasionally used. Thus, the Hotel Inglaterra is at Prado #416 esq. San Rafael, Habana Vieja; at the corner (*esq.* stands for *esquina,* or corner) of Prado and Calle San Rafael, in Old Havana (Habana Vieja).

Piso refers to the floor level (thus, an office on *Piso 3ra* is on the third floor).

Much of Havana is laid out on a grid pattern with parallel streets *(calles)* running perpendicular to avenues *(avenidas).* Some areas, such as Vedado and Miramar, however, have even-numbered *calles* (north-south) running perpendicular to odd-numbered *calles* (usually east-west), with the main boulevards called *avenidas.*

Note that many streets have at least two names: one predating the Revolution (and usually the most commonly used colloquially) and the other a postrevolutionary name. For example, the Prado is the old (and preferred) term for the Paseo de Martí. On maps, the modern name takes precedence, with the old name often shown in parentheses.

These municipios combine historic villages, such as Santiago de las Vegas and San Francisco de Paula, with more modern industrial enclaves.

La Habana del Este extends east from the harbor for some 30 miles along the shore as far as the beaches of the Playas del Este—a playground for Habaneros and, increasingly, tourists.

Between the city and Playas del Este are the postrevolutionary urban enclaves of Ciudad Panamericano, Ciudad Camilo Cienfuegos, Alamar, and Celimar, and the 18th-century fishing village of Cojimar.

Sightseeing Tips

Since the main sights are so spread out, it is best to explore Havana in sections, beginning with Habana Vieja, where the vast majority of historical sites are located and the narrow streets lend themselves to pleasure-filled perambulation. All touristed areas are patrolled by police, which in early 1999 stood on virtually every other corner on a 24-hour basis.

A guided city tour provides a good way of getting your bearings. The best option is to hop aboard the **Vaivén Bus Turístico,** which circles Havana on a continual basis, taking in most sites of tourist appeal. A US$4 ticket is good all day for as many stops and times as you wish.

Tour & Travel, Avenida 5 #8409, e/ 84 y 86, Miramar, Havana, tel. (24) 9200 or (24) 9199, fax (24) 1547, and La Rampa and Calle M, Vedado, tel. (24) 7541, fax (24) 2074, offer guided city tours by minibus daily (US$15). **Agencia Viajes San Cristóbal,** Calle Oficio 110, tel. (33) 8693, offers guided walking tours of Habana Vieja.

I recommend you call in first at the **Maqueta de la Habana** in Miramar to peruse the 1:1,000-scale model of Havana that will give you an idea of the city's layout. Next, visit the **José Martí Memorial** in Vedado to take the elevator to the top of the *mirador* (lookout), where you gain a bird's-eye view of the entire city. For views over Vedado, head to **La Torre** bar or restaurant at the top of the FOCSA building, or the *azotea* (rooftop) bars of the Hotel Capri or the Hotel Habana Libre Tryp.

HABANA VIEJA~THE OLD CITY

Evocative Habana Vieja (4.5 square km; pop. 105,000) is colloquially defined by the limits of the early colonial settlement that lay within fortified walls. Today, the legal boundary of Habana Vieja includes the Paseo de Martí (Prado) and everything east of it. The vast majority of sites of interest are concentrated here. Don't underestimate how much there is to see in Habana Vieja.

At least two days are required, and one week isn't too much.

The original city developed along a polynuclear axis that extended roughly north-south from Castillo de la Real Fuerza to Plaza Vieja. Here are the major sites of interest, centered on two plazas of great stature: the Plaza de Armas and the smaller but more imposing Plaza

HAVANA'S MUSEUMS

You can purchase a one-day ticket for US$9 good for all the museums in Habana Vieja; it's available from the Museo de la Ciudad, in the Palacio de los Capitanes Generales.

The following are the major museums:

Museo y Archivo de la Música: (Music Archives and Museum) Calle Capdevilla #1, e/ Aguiar y Habana, Centro Habana, tel. (80) 6810. Exhibits trace the evolution of Cuban musical styles.

Museo Antropológico Montane: (Anthropological Museum) Universidad de La Habana, Calle L y San Lázaro, Vedado, tel. (79) 3488. Contains exhibits on pre-Columbian culture.

Museo de Arte Colonial: (Museum of Colonial Art) Casa del Conde de Bayone, Plaza de la Catedral, Habana Vieja, tel. (62) 6440. This fine museum contains stunning period furniture and decorations from the colonial era.

Museo de Artes Decorativas: (Museum of the Decorative Arts) Calle 17 #502, Vedado, tel. (32) 0924. A splendid mansion displaying colonial-period furniture and decorations.

Museo Casa Abel Santamaría: (House of Abel Santamaría) Calle 25 #154, Vedado, tel. (70) 0417. The house where the martyred revolutionary hero lived, and also headquarters for Fidel Castro's nascent MR-26-7 movement.

Museo Casa Natal de José Martí: (Birthplace of José Martí) Calle Leon Peréz, Habana Vieja, tel. (61) 3778. The birthplace of national hero José

Martí records his contributions to the cause of independence.

Museo de la Ciudad de Habana: (City Museum of Havana) Calle Tacón #1, Habana Vieja, tel. (61) 2876. This museum traces the development of the city from its earliest colonial days. Many fine exhibits from the Spanish period. A must-see.

Museo de la Educación: (Museum of Literacy) Calle Obispo esq. Mercaderes, tel. (61) 5468. This museum traces Cuba's achievements in the Great Literacy Campaign to eradicate illiteracy.

Museo de la Perfumeria: (Perfume Museum) Calle Oficios e/ Obispos y Obrapía, Habana Vieja. This aptly named museum is replete with antique jars and perfume bottles.

Museo Ernest Hemingway: San Francisco de Paula, tel. (91) 0809 or (55) 8015. The Nobel-winning author's former home, Finca Vigía, has been left as it was when Hemingway died in 1961. A must-see.

Museo Histórico de las Ciencias Carlos Finlay: (Carlos Finlay Historical Museum of Sciences) Calle Cuba #460, Habana Vieja, tel. (63) 4824. Honors the achievements of Cuban medical scientist Carlos Finlay and other noted Cubans in the field of science.

Museo de História Naturales Felipe Poey: (Felipe Poey Museum of Natural History) Universidad de La Habana, Calle L y San Lázaro, Vedado, tel. (32) 9000. Contains stuffed and pickled exhibits of Cuba's flora and fauna, and traces aspects of pre-Columbian culture.

---

de la Catedral. The old squares concentrate the past into an essence that is so rich, suggests Juliet Barclay, "that it is indigestible unless taken in small sips": each square has its own unique flavor, which seems to change with the hours and light—melancholic in the rain, bustling and alive in the sun, "voluptuous when a hot midnight is illuminated by lamps and vibrates with guitar music and the muffled heartbeat of an African drum." The plazas and surrounding streets shine after a complete restoration, their structures newly painted and seeming like confections in stone.

The much deteriorated southern half of Habana Vieja is given short shrift by most visitors. The restoration has yet to reach the area, although a fistful of gems are worth a peek, and several now gleam after being restored. The area east of Avenida de Bélgica and southwest of Plaza Vieja, between Calles Brasil and Merced, was the great ecclesiastical center of colonial Havana and is replete with churches and convents. The area around Calle Belén was also the site of the first community of Sephardic Jews in Cuba following their expulsion from Castile and Aragon in 1492. A Jewish community became well established, and this century, many Polish and Lithuanian Jews settled here after fleeing Nazi persecution. The Cuban government proposes to reconstruct the Jewish settlement, having made a start by rehabilitating the regional synagogue.

Museo de Máximo Gómez: Avenida Salvador Allende, Centro Habana, tel. (79) 8850. Intended to honor the hero-general of the Wars of Independence, it suffers from a pitiful and motley collection.

Museo Municipal de Guanabacoa: (Municipal Museum of Guanabacoa) Calle Martí #108, Guanabacoa, tel. (97) 9117. This small museum of *santería* profiles the influence of slavery and African cultures on the evolution of Cuban culture and the syncretic Afro-Cuban cults.

Museo Municipal de Regla: (Municipal Museum of Regla) Calle Martí #158 e/ Facciolo y La Piedra, Regla, tel. (97) 6989. Similar to the Guanabacoa museum and equally tiny, with a strong emphasis on *santería*.

Museo Nacional del Aire: (National Air Museum) Avenida 212 y La Coronela, Cubanacán. A splendid array of military and civilian aircraft (mostly Soviet-made), plus models and exhibits recording notable moments in Cuban aviation history.

Museo Nacional de Bellas Artes: (National Fine Arts Museum) Calle Animas e/ Agramonte y Monserrate, Habana Vieja, tel. (63) 9042. Cuban paintings and sculptures, plus important works representing Impressionist and other major styles, as well as Latin America's largest collection of Greek, Roman, and Egyptian treasures. A must-see.

Museo Nacional de Cerámica: Castillo de la Real Fuerza, Plaza de Armas, Habana Vieja, tel. (61) 6130. A good collection of ceramicware from the colonial to contemporary eras.

Museo Nacional de Música: (National Music Museum) Calle Capdevila #1, Habana Vieja, tel. (61) 9846. Instruments and scores spanning several centuries trace the evolution of Cuban music and the contributions of its finest composers and performers.

Museo Napoleónico: (Napoleonic Museum) Calle San Miguel #1159, Vedado, tel. (79) 1412. This splendid mansion houses personal possessions of Napoleon Bonaparte and other memorabilia relating to the French Emperor.

Museo Numismático: (Numismatic Museum) Calle Oficios #8 e/ Obispo y Obrapía, Habana Vieja, tel. (61) 5857. Coins of the realm dating back centuries are displayed.

Museo Postal Cubano: (Postal/Philatelic Museum) Avenida Rancho Boyeros, Plaza de la Revolución, tel. (70) 5581. Displays a superb collection of Cuban and international stamps.

Museo del Pueblo Combatiente: (Museum of the Fighting People) Avenida 5ta #7201, Miramar, tel. (29) 1497. Tells the Cuban government's version of the counter-revolutionary struggles, including the CIA's Operation Mongoose and the mass exodus from Cuba in the wake of the Revolution.

Museo de la Revolución: (Museum of the Revolution) Calle Refugio #1, Habana Vieja, tel. (62) 4091. Housed in the former Presidential Palace, this is Cuba's most complete exhibition on the Revolution, with maps, weaponry, personal articles, photographs, the *Granma*, tanks, and warplanes. A must-see.

Parque Histórico Militar El Morro-La Cabaña: (El Morro-La Cabaña Historical Military Park) Carratera de la Cabaña, Habanas del Este, tel. (62) 0607. The Morro Castle and La Cabaña fortress are testaments to Havana's military history. A must-see.

Habana Vieja is a living museum (as many as 60,000 people live within the confines of the old city wall) and suffers from inevitable ruination brought on by the tropical climate, hastened since the Revolution by years of neglect. The grime of centuries has been soldered by tropical heat into the chipped cement and faded pastels. Beyond the restored areas, Habana Vieja is a quarter of sagging, mildewed walls and half-collapsed balconies festooned with laundry seemingly held aloft by the grace of God and by telegraph cords and electrical wires strung across streets in a complex spiderweb. The narrow streets reverberate with the honking of horns, as well as salsas, rumbas, and "feeling" songs emanating from open windows, inside which eerie neon lights glimmer, illuminating ceramic figurines and velveteen pictures of cats.

You'll frequently find humble and haughty side by side, since for most of the colonial period, areas were socially mixed. Slaves lived in separate quarters or their masters' mansions. Merchants lived above their warehouses, where the slaves also lived. The best stores in colonial days were along Calles Obispo and O'Reilly, seething Oriental bazaars that were once covered in colorful awnings that softened the sun's glare. They were Aladdin's caves of European fineries, incense, crystal and china, muslin and ribbons, and *piña* cloth, a silky gauze made of pineapple fiber and dyed in radiant colors. Obispo is still the lifeline connecting Centro Habana with Habana Vieja.

RESTORING OLD HAVANA

Old Havana has been called the "finest urban ensemble in the Americas." The fortress colonial town that burst its walls when Washington, D.C., was still a swamp is a 350-acre repository of antique buildings. More than 900 of Habana Vieja's 3,157 structures are of historic importance. Of these, only 101 were built in the 20th century. Almost 500 are from the 19th; 200 are from the 18th; and 144 are from the 16th and 17th. But only one in six buildings is in good condition. Many are crumbling into ruins around the people who occupy them.

In 1977, the Cuban government named Habana Vieja a National Monument. The following year, it formalized a plan to rescue the city from centuries of neglect under the guidance of Eusebio Leal Spengler, the charismatic city historian. Thanks to his efforts, Havana was proclaimed a UNESCO World Heritage Site in 1982. (Leal is considered a potential future leader; many Habaneros make the claim that he is positioning himself for succession.)

The ambitious plan stretches beyond the year 2000 and concentrates on five squares: Plaza de Armas, Plaza de la Catedral, Plaza Vieja, Plaza de San Francisco, and Plaza del Cristo. The most important buildings have received major renovations; others are being given facelifts—symbols of triumph over horrendous shortages of materials and money. Nonetheless, the project has been seriously jeopardized by the current economic crisis. Hence, the Cuban government is seeking foreign investors to help salvage the collapsing buildings.

To satisfy a mix of needs, structures are ranked into one of four levels according to historical and physical value. The top level is reserved for museums; the second level for hotels, restaurants, offices, and schools; and the bottom levels for housing. Priority is given to edifices with income-generating tourist value, usually the oldest buildings, so that many of the stupendous art nouveau structures are, as Nancy Stout points out, "quietly sinking into ruin." Havana contains as many splendid art deco buildings as Miami (perhaps even more), plus countless art nouveau houses.

A government-run company, **Habaguanex,** Calle Oficios #110, Plaza de San Francisco, tel. (33) 8693, fax (33) 8697, website: habaguanex.cubaweb. cu/habaguanex.html, has responsibility for restoring and opening hotels, restaurants, cafés, shops, etc., in Habana Vieja. Leal selects sites for renovation, supervises the construction teams, and chooses the hotels and restaurants that will occupy the restored buildings. Habaguanex caters primarily to the tourist trade. The profits (US$70 million, 1993-98) help finance infrastructural improvements throughout Habana Vieja and elsewhere in the city; in 1998, 33 percent of revenues was devoted to social projects.

Leal—who is easily identified by his trademark gray cotton suit—has been criticized for prettifying Habana Vieja with little concern for its inhabitants. He took the criticism to heart and, determined to avoid making the old city merely a quaint stage set for tourists, has added a sociologist to the restoration teams to work with those people who have been moved from their homes. Explains Nancy Stout: "Leal still wants people to be able to hang out their laundry. He doesn't want to be criticized for gilding rotten lilies." Where do the relocated residents go? Well, Leal has set up a little community—**Comunidad Provisoria Plaza Vieja**—of plastic houses (imported from Canada) on a *plazuela* on Calle Muralla, half a block southwest of Plaza Vieja, to temporarily house displaced residents.

It's an awesome task. In southern Habana Vieja, where there are relatively few structures of touristic interest, far more houses are collapsing than are being restored. The inflow of tourist dollars is but a trickle in a desert of need.

Florida-based Cuban-Americans, including architects and art historians, have formed **The Bridge for Historic Preservation,** 1625 Colony Ave., Kissimmee, FL 34744, tel. (407) 847-7892, fax (407) 847-2986, to assist in Havana's restoration efforts. It requests donations. Other Cuban-Americans have formed the Miami-based **Cuban National Heritage** as a trust-in-exile that sponsors symposiums with Cuba's architectural historians (but not state agencies) and is developing zoning codes to help fend off powerful southern Florida developers who are hungrily eyeing the island and are likely to bulldoze historic areas.

The maze of narrow one-way streets is pur-gatory for anyone with a motor vehicle, so *walk*. In any event, the main plazas and the streets between them are barred to traffic by huge ar-tillery shells in the ground.

Many important street names in Habana Vieja betray a feature of historical note. For example, the ecclesiastics who strolled down Calle Obispo gave it its name: Bishop Street. Similarly, Calle In-quisidor was named for the member of the Span-ish Inquisition who lived here; and Calle Mer-caderes is named for the merchants who lived here. Empedrado means "cobbled," and is so named because it was the first paved street in the city; Lamparilla means "small lamp," as the first street lamps in the city went up along here; like-wise, Calle Tejadillo is named for the tiles that graced its facades, another first in Havana.

Orientation

Habana Vieja is roughly shaped like a diamond, with the Castillo de la Punta its northerly point. Its western boundary, Paseo de Martí (colloquially called the Prado) runs south at a gradual gradi-ent from the Castillo de la Punta to Parque Cen-tral and, beyond, Parque de la Fraternidad, from where Avenida de la Bélgica runs southeast, tracing the old city wall to the harborfront at the west end of Desamparados. East of Castillo de la Punta, Avenida Carlos Manuel de Céspedes (Avenida del Puerto) runs along the harbor chan-nel and curls south to Desamparados.

PARQUE CENTRAL AND VICINITY

For travelers and Cubans alike, spacious **Parque Central** is ground zero, the social epicenter of Habana Vieja, and an appropriate point from which to begin your perambulation. Buses ar-rive and depart from the busy square, a center for Havana's social life, as it was during the city's heyday from the late 19th century onward.

The park—bounded by the Prado (Paseo de Martí), Neptuno, Agramonte, and San Martín—is presided over by stately royal palms, poin-ciana, and almond trees shading a **statue of José Martí**, poet, lawyer, writer, revolutionary fighter, and Cuba's foremost national hero, killed in combat in 1895. Inaugurated in 1905, this was the first such monument built in his honor in

---

RECOMMENDED WALKING TOUR 1

B egin your tour at **Parque Central**, taking in the **statue of José Martí** at its center and the **Hotel Inglaterra** and **Gran Teatro** on its western side.

Head south to the **Capitolo**, taking time to explore inside.

Continue south to **Parque de la Fraternidad**, passing the **Fuente de la India** and **bust of Abraham Lincoln**, and on its south side the scores of old yankee cars serving as taxis.

From here, head west 200 meters along Dragones past the **Dragon Gate** to **Barrio Chino**.

Retrace your steps along Dragones, timing your arrival at the **Fábrica de Tabaco Partagas** for a tour of the cigar factory.

Return to Parque Central and walk north, tak-ing in the length of the **Prado**, calling in at the **Hotel Sevilla**. Past the **Parque de los Már-tires**, cross the Avenida Carlos M. Céspedes (be careful crossing this awkward junction) for the view along the **Malecón** toward Vedado. Browse the **Castillo de la Punta**.

Return to the Parque de los Mártires, and visit the **Monumento de Máximo Gómez**. Walk the central median of **Plaza 13 de Mayo** to the **Presidencial Palacio**, where you should visit the **Museo de la Revolución** and **Granma Memorial**.

Follow Agramonte (Zulueta) south one block to the **Museo de Bellas Artes**. Return to Parque Central via Agramonte.

Cuba and was made of Carrrara marble by the Cuban sculptor José Vilalta de Saavedra. Base-ball fanatics gather near the Martí statue at a point called *esquina caliente* (hot corner) to dis-cuss and argue the intricacies of the sport.

Its position is pivotal. From here, the Prado spills north to the harbor channel and the Malecón, and south past the Capitolio to Parque de la Fraternidad. Calle Obispo slopes one km east to Plaza Armas and the heart of the old city.

Much of the action happens in front of the **Hotel Inglaterra,** which opened as a café on the west side of the square in 1843, before the hotel existed. The boulevard in front of the hotel, known as the Acera del Louvre, was always a

THE ROYAL PALM

The indisputable symbol of Cuba is the ubiquitous *Rostonea regia*, the majestic royal palm (*palma royal* in Spanish), which grows singly or in great elegant clumps and graces the Cuban capital at every turn. Its smooth gray trunk, which can tower 25 meters, resembles a great marble column with a curious bulge near the top. Long leaves droop sinuously from the explosive top, blossoming afresh with each new moon.

Even found on the national emblem and protected by law, the royal palm is as useful as it is stately. Its fronds *(pencas)* make good thatch, and the thick green base—the *yagua*—of the *penca,* being waterproof, also makes an excellent roof or siding material. The trunk itself makes excellent timber. Bees favor palm honey; and pigs seem to like the seeds, which are used for pig feed. Humans devour the delicious, succulent palm-heart *(palmito)* from the center of the trunk. And birds love its black fruit and carry the seeds *(palmiche)* all over the country.

gathering point for the youth of Cuba and a focal point for rebellion against Spanish rule. A plaque outside the hotel entrance honors the "lads of the Louvre sidewalk" who died for Cuban independence. General Antonio Maceo—the Bronze Titan, and perhaps the only soldier of any war to have survived 24 bullet wounds—recruited here between the two wars of independence. Today, its café beneath the shady *portal* provides a splendid vantage point for watching the toing and froing.

The old **Hotel Telegrafo,** due to reopen in 2000 after a complete restoration, adjoins the Inglaterra to the north. Another imposing hotel, the ocher-colored **Hotel Plaza,** built as a triangle in 1909, sits on the northeast face of the square, while the facade of the recently constructed **Hotel Parque Central,** due north of the park, blends historic components into a contemporary guise (with questionable success).

Immediately south of the Inglaterra is the exquisitely detailed **Gran Teatro de la Habana,** tel. (62) 9473, built in 1837 as a social club for the large Galician community. Its exorbitantly baroque facade drips with caryatids, and it has four towers, each tipped by an angel of white marble reaching gracefully for heaven. It still functions as a theater for the National Ballet and Opera, and patrons still settle into the plush velvet seats of the two theaters within: the Teatro García Lorca and the Teatro Tacón, in its time considered by some to be the finest theater in the world, and by all to be one of the three finest theaters in the world. Operatic luminaries such as Enrico Caruso and Sarah Bernhardt performed at the theater in its heyday. Entrance costs US$2 with guide.

Another, less imposing theater, the **Teatro Payret** (built in 1878), faces the square from the south. Today it functions as a cinema.

On the southeast side of the square, the building with a tower at each of its corners is the **Centro Asturiano,** erected in 1885 and until recently housing the postrevolutionary People's Supreme Court, where a questionable version of justice was dispensed. The **Museo Nacional de Bellas Artes** (Fine Arts Museum) moved here in 1999.

The **Teatro Martí** (dating from 1884), two blocks south of Parque Central, on Dragones at Agramonte, was in virtual ruins in early 1999, when a full restoration was underway.

PASEO DE MARTÍ (PRADO)

Paseo de Martí, colloquially known as the Prado, is a kilometer-long tree-lined boulevard that slopes northward downhill from Parque Central to the harbor mouth and Castillo de San Salvador de la Punta. The Prado is a smaller but no less courtly version of the Champs-Elysées and a splendid place to linger and watch Havana's life unfold.

The beautiful boulevard lay *extramura*, outside the old walled city of San Cristóbal de la Habana, and was initiated by the Marquis de la Torre in 1772 and completed in 1852. Until the end of the last century, it was Havana's most notable thoroughfare, what Anthony Trollope called "the public drive and fashionable lounge of the town—its Hyde Park, the Boise de Boulogne, the Cascine, the Corso, the Alaméda." The mansions of aristocratic families rose on each side, with spacious portals for carriages, and it was a sign of distinction to live on Prado Promenade. In time, the Prado lost its luster as the rich moved into exclusive new neighborhoods. During the "sordid era," the Prado and the area immediately west of it—the infamous Colón borough of Centro Habana—became famous for sleazy shows and gambling houses such as La Central, where President Prío held "his infamous nights of white powder and tall showgirls."

Two bronze lions guard the Prado's upper, southern end. Its central median is an elevated walkway. An ornate wall borders the path, with alcoves inset into each side containing marble benches carved with scroll motifs. At night it is lit by old brass gas lamps with big globes atop dark green wrought-iron lampposts in the shape of griffins. Schoolchildren sit beneath the shade trees, listening attentively to history or literature lessons presented alfresco. Midway down the Prado, between Calle Colón and Refugio, the laurel trees provide a shady gathering place for those seeking apartments or homes for swap or rent, because the state prohibits the buying and selling of real estate. Pinned to the trees and trestled noticeboards are announcements for *Se Permuta* (For Exchange).

One block north, at Prado #207, between Colón and Trocadero, is the **Academía Gimnástico,** where budding gymnasts train for potential Olympic careers. Visitors are occasionally welcomed inside this converted old mansion to see preteens practicing on the ropes and vaulting horses, surrounded by fluted columns and a baroque stucco ceiling. It's open Mon.-Fri. 8:30 a.m.-5:30 p.m. and Saturday 8 a.m.-noon.

Up and down the Prado you'll see tiled mosaics reflecting the Moorish style that has influenced Havana's architecture through the centuries. Observe, for example, the mosaic mural of a Nubian beauty on the upper wall of the **Centro Cultural de Árabe** (between Refugio and Trocadero). Note, too, the facade of the former Hotel Regis on the corner of Refugio, combining art nouveau and arabesque flourishes. The most stunning example, however, is the lobby of the **Hotel Sevilla** (at Calle Trocadero), which is like entering a Moroccan medina. No wonder, for it was inspired by the Patio of the Lions at the Alhambra in Granada, Spain. The Sevilla was the setting for the comical intrigues of Wormold in Graham Greene's *Our Man in Havana.* The hotel opened in 1908 with the novelty of telephones and private baths in every room. It became a place of repose and merriment for fashionable society, as reflected in the gallery, where the walls are festooned with black-and-white photos of famous figures who have stayed here, from singer Josephine Baker (who was refused at the Hotel Nacional because she was black) and boxer Joe Louis to Al Capone, who took the entire sixth floor for himself and his bodyguards (Capone occupied Room 615).

Another resplendent building worth a browse is the **Casa de los Científicos,** on the west side of the Prado at Trocadero, now a budget hostel that offers the benefit of superlative if albeit slightly chipped architectural surrounds. Also note the **Ciné Fausto,** a simple yet powerful rectangular modernist building with an ornamental band on its upper facade harking back to art deco. At #306, on the corner of Animas, is Habana Vieja's **Palacio de Matrimonia,** where wedding ceremonies are performed.

The bronze statue at the base of the Prado is that of Juan Clemente-Zenea, a patriotic poet shot for treason in 1871. Others who suffered at the hands of the Spanish colonialists are honored immediately to the right in the Martyr's Park and Park of the Lovers.

Parque de Martires
and Parque de los Enamorados

The parkland at the base of the Prado occupies the ground of the former Tacón prison, built in 1838, where horrible mutilations were performed on common criminals and Cuban nationalists charged with conspiracy and treason. Nationalist hero José Martí was imprisoned here between 1969-70, never recovering from the hard labor he was forced to perform. The prison was designed to hold 2,000 people, with separate divisions according to sex, race, and social status. It was demolished in 1939, and the park dedicated in memory of all those who suffered for their ideals. Preserved for posterity, however, were two of the punishment cells and the chapel used by condemned prisoners before being marched to the firing wall.

The park is divided in two by **Avenida de los Estudiantes,** with the Park of the Lovers to the south and Martyr's Park to the north. The most important monument here is the **Monumento de Estudiantes de Medicina,** a small Grecian-style temple shading the remains of a wall used by Spanish colonial firing squads. Here on 27 November 1871, eight medical students met their deaths after being falsely accused of desecrating the tomb of a prominent loyalist, Gonzalo Castañón. A trial found them innocent, but enraged loyalist troops—the Spanish Volunteers—held their own trial and shot the students. The monument stands at the juncture of the Prado and the Avenida del Puerto, facing the Castillo de San Salvador de la Punta.

Castillo de San Salvador de la Punta

This charming fortress guards the entrance to Havana's harbor channel. Small and low-slung, it sits at the base of the Prado, with the Avenida Manuel de Céspedes running east along the harbor channel and the Malecón leading west to Vedado. The fortress was initiated in 1589 directly across from Morro Castle so that the two fortresses might catch invaders in a crossfire. Between them, a great chain was slung each night to secure Havana harbor in colonial days; you can still see the cannons embedded in the reefs and to which the chain was attached. Originally, the fortress stood upon an outcrop that jutted out into the harbor channel. Its site remains pivotal, and from the plaza overlooking the channel (a favorite spot for trysting lovers at night), you may revel in the sweeping vista westward along the Malecón toward the statuesque facade of the Vedado district. A restoration of the fort was nearing completion at press time, promising to elevate the recently morose site into a gem.

PARQUE DE LA FRATERNIDAD
AND VICINITY

This large, bustling, tree-shaded square 200 meters south of Parque Central was laid out in 1892 on an old military drill square, the Campo de Marte, to commemorate the fourth centennial of Columbus's discovery of America. In olden times, a bull ring also stood here, and the plaza was a setting for the city's festivities. By the mid-1850s, it was the site of the city's railway station, terminating the railway that ran along today's Zanja and Dragones. The current layout dates from 1928, with a redesign to celebrate the sixth Pan-American Conference, held in Havana that year. The streets around the park are a major start and drop-off point for urban buses and peso taxis, which congregate in vast numbers, forming a veritable auto museum of Americana.

The most important site in the park is the **Árbol de la Fraternidad Americana** (the Friendship Tree), planted at its center in 1928 to cement goodwill between the nations of the Americas. Each delegate to the conference brought soil from his or her home country. Busts of outstanding American leaders such as Simón Bolívar as well as a **statue of Abraham Lincoln** look out over the comings and goings.

Another monument of interest is the **Fuente de la India Noble Habana,** in the middle of the Prado, 100 meters south of Parque Central. The fountain, erected in 1837, is surmounted by a Carrara marble statue of La Noble Havana, the legendary Indian queen after whom the province is named. She is coyly clad in fringed drapes, a feather headdress, and palm leaves. In one hand she bears a cornucopia, in the other a shield with the arms of Havana. Four great fishes lie at her feet and spout water when the tap is turned on.

Worth checking out, too, is the **Palacio de Aldama,** a grandiose mansion considered one of Havana's finest; it's on the park's far southwest corner, on Avenida de Bolívar. It was built in neoclassical style in 1844 for a wealthy Basque, Don Domingo Aldama y Arrechaga, with a facade lined by Ionic columns and an interior of colored marbles and murals of scenes from Pompeii. Unfortunately, it was ransacked and the interior defaced in 1868 by the archly promonarchist Spanish Volunteers militia when the owner's nationalist feelings became known. Today, duly restored, it houses the **Instituto de la Historia de la Ciudad,** also known more pompously as the Institute of the History of the Communist Movement and the Socialist Revolution. Hardcore lefties might get a thrill.

Capitolio

This fabulous building, on the north side of Parque de la Fraternidad and one block south of Parque Central, dominates Havana's skyline. It was built between 1926 and 1929 as Cuba's Chamber of Representatives and Senate and was obsequiously designed after Washington's own Congress building, reflecting the United States' expanding influence in the early 1900s. The 692-foot-long edifice is supported by flanking colonnades of Doric columns, with semicircular pavilions at each end of the building. The lofty stone cupola rises 61.75 meters, topped by a replica of 16th-century Florentine sculptor Giambologna's famous bronze Mercury in the Palazzo de Bargello. The dome—inspired by the Parisian Pantheon—sits not in the center of the structure, but forward near the front portico.

A massive stairway—flanked by neoclassical figures in bronze representing Labor and Virtue—leads steeply up to a 40-meter-wide entrance portico with three tall bronze doors. The doors are sculpted with 30 bas-reliefs that depict important events of Cuban history up to the Capitolio's inauguration in 1929. (You can have your photo taken at the base of the stairs by any of several official photographers whose antique cameras sit atop wooden tripods.)

The pristine, recently restored building is constructed of local Capellania limestone, hinting at the overwhelming opulence and beauty within. The stunning Great Hall of the Lost Steps is made almost entirely of marble, with bronze bas-reliefs all around and massive lamps on tall carved pedestals of glittering copper. Facing the door is the **Statue of the Republic,** a massive

bronze sculpture of Cuba's Indian maiden resembling the Statue of Liberty and representing the Cuban Republic. At 17.54 meters tall, she is the world's third-largest indoor statue. Weighing 49 tons, her voluptuous figure gleams sensuously after a recent cleaning. In the center of the floor is a 24-carat diamond that marks km 0—the starting point from Havana for the country's highways. The diamond, alas, is a replica (rumor has it that the original is kept securely in Fidel's office). Above your head is the dome with its gilt-covered, barrel-vaulted ceiling carved in refulgent relief.

Two long lateral galleries lead from this entrance vestibule. The semicircular Senate chamber and the former Chamber of Representatives at each end are quite stunning.

The Capitolio is open Mon.-Sat. 9 a.m.-5 p.m. Entrance is US$3. A breeze-swept veranda café serves sandwiches and refreshments and offers grand views down over the Prado.

In 1960, the Capitolio became the headquarters of the **Academy of Sciences.** The library—the **Biblioteca Nacional de Ciencias y Naturales**—is still here (open Mon.-Sat. 8 a.m.-5 p.m.), on the ground floor on the Capitolio's south side; but the science and natural history museums recently moved to Plaza de Armas.

Fábrica de Tabaco Partagás

A highlight of your time in Havana will undoubtedly be a visit to the Partagas Cigar Factory (officially named Fábrica Francisco Pérez Germán), behind the Capitolio at Industria #502, tel. (33) 8060. Here you may see Cuba's premium cigars being hand-rolled for export. The exterior of this four-story structure is fabulous, built in a classical Spanish style with cream walls and chocolate brown detailing, capped by a *remate superior,* a roofline of baroque curves topped by lions and bearing in large block letters the words "1845 PARTAGAS REAL FÁBRICA DE TABACOS," proudly testifying that it has been making cigars here for more than 150 years. Within is an interior patio surrounded by colored glass windows.

The factory specializes in full-bodied cigars such as the spicy, strongly aromatic La Gloria Cubana, Ramón Allones, the Montecristo, and, of course, the Partagas, one of the oldest of the Havana brands, started in 1843 by Don Jaime

Partagas. The three-story structure was built in 1845 to house the Vilar y Vilar Cigar Factory, one of the main cigar factories of the 19th century, when the Partagas cigar firm first occupied the site. Partagas turns out five million cigars a year, among them no fewer than 40 types of Partagas brand (many machine-made and of inferior quality). The factory's classy showroom displays a cigar measuring 50 inches!

The humidor to the right of the entrance—the most visited cigar store in Cuba—serves as an information booth and salesroom, and cigar aficionados might pop into the "secret" air-conditioned lounge, replete with plump leather lounge chairs, TV, coffee bar, and its own humidor.

Guided tours of the cigar factory are offered daily at 10 a.m. and 2 p.m. (US$10).

CALLE AGRAMONTE (ZULUETA)

Calle Agramonte, more commonly referred to by its colonial name of Zulueta, slopes gently from the northeast side of Parque Central to the Monumento de Máximo Gómez and the harbor channel. Agramonte parallels the Prado, and traffic runs one-way uphill.

One block north of Parque Central, at the corner of Agramonte and Animas, a mosaic on the paving (on the west side of the street) announces your arrival at **Sloppy Joe's**, "a high-ceilinged, bottle-encrusted, tile-floored oasis" commemorated as Freddy's Bar in Hemingway's *To Have and Have Not.* (Former owner Joe Russell served as the model for Freddy, the character later immortalized on-screen by Humphrey Bogart.) The bar, formerly La Victoria, became an institution among partying tourists during Prohibition after an inebriated journalist sought a $50 loan, was rebuffed by the owner, and wrote a vengeful editorial accusing the owner of running an unsanitary place, claiming it should be called "Sloppy Joe's." There's no such thing as bad publicity, and the crafty owner changed the name. Dedicated drinkers flocked and continued to do so through the decades. As of spring 1999, the near-derelict building was still shuttered, its interior a dusty shambles awaiting the restoration now sweeping Habana Vieja. It is slated to be restored as a bar and (possibly) a hotel.

Across the way is the diminutive and quaint **Museo de Bomberos,** in the old Cuartel de Bomberos fire station. The museum, which opened in late 1999, exhibits turn-of-the-century firefighters' uniforms plus three vintage fire engines, including a 1901 horse-drawn machine made by Shand, Mason & Co., London. In 1999, the museum moved from its former location at Calle Oficios and Lamparilla, where it was housed on the site of the worst day in Havana's firefighting history and the cause of the largest funeral of the 19th century. On 17 May 1890, a devastating fire broke out in that building, and 28 firefighters (and numerous bystanders) were killed when an enormous explosion took place; the owner had defied a ban on storing explosives within the ancient city and had failed to notify the fire department. A mausoleum to the firefighters can be seen in the Cementerio de Colón in Vedado.

Cuba's most important art museum, the **Museo Nacional de Bellas Artes,** is housed in the ugly concrete Palacio de Bellas Artes, on Trocadero between Zulueta and Monserrate, tel. (63) 9042 or (61) 2332. From the atrium garden, ramps lead up to two dim floors. On the second floor, the museum contains a fabulous collection of Cuban paintings, and on the ground floor, European collections that include works by Goya, Murillo, Rubens, and Velásquez, as well as various impressionists. English painters such as Reynolds, Gainsborough, and Turner are represented. The museum also boasts Latin America's richest trove of classical antiquities, including Roman, Greek, and Egyptian statuary and artworks. Rotating exhibits display the works of Cuba's leading contemporary artists.

The museum was closed for restoration at press time. A three-year reorganization of the museum was planned, and the works will likely be dispersed, with some slated to move to the Centro Asturiano.

Fifty meters north of the museum is the three-story green facade of the **Fábrica de Tabaco La Corona**, dating from 1888, when this cigar factory, at Agramonte #106, e/ Refugio y Colón, tel./fax (62) 6173, was built by the American Tobacco Company. Today it is officially called the Miguel Fernandez Roig, but colloquially as La Corona. A favorite on the tourist circuit, it provides a splendid background of the intricacies of cigar manufacture, as well as a heady experience thanks to the cigar aromas. It's open to the public Mon.-Sat. 7 a.m.-5 p.m.

Fronting the former Presidential Palace, on Refugio, is a **SAU-100 Stalin tank**, illuminated at

RUNNING AGROUND IN THE NAME OF REVOLUTION

Shortly after midnight on 25 November 1956, Castro and his revolutionaries set out from Tuxpán, Mexico, sailing without lights for Cuba. The 1,235-mile crossing was hellish. Their vessel, the *Granma,* had been designed to carry 25 passengers. Battered by heavy seas and with a burden of 82 heavily armed men and supplies, the vessel lurched laboriously toward Cuba, which Castro had planned to reach in five days. Batista's army and navy were on alert. Castro figured they would not patrol far from shore, hence he planned a route 170 miles offshore, beyond reach of Cuban surveillance.

In the violent seas, the men, packed in like sardines, became seasick. The boat rose and dropped beneath them. In the open, the drizzle began to turn into a cold, penetrating rain. Castro smelled victory, but to the men on the slippery decks the smell in the air was vomit. Then one engine failed and the boat slowed, falling two days behind schedule. Castro ordered rationing: for the last two days there was neither water nor food—which may have been just as well.

At dawn on 2 December, the ship ran aground at low tide, two km south of the planned landing site, at Playa Las Coloradas. Two hours later, just after dawn, Castro stood on *terra firma* alongside 81 men, with minimal equipment, no food, and no contact with the Movement ashore. "This wasn't a landing," Che Guevara later recalled. "It was a shipwreck."

The motley group set out toward the safety of the Sierra Maestra none too soon. Within two hours of landing, *Granma* had been sighted and a bombardment of the mangroves began. Batista's military commander foolishly announced to the press that the rebels had been ambushed and captured or killed, "annihilating 40 members of the supreme command of the revolutionary 26th of July Movement—among them its chief, Fidel Castro." The United Press bureau sent the news around the world. Meanwhile, the exhausted, half-starved rebels moved unseen and unscathed.

On 5 December, however, the rebels were betrayed by their guide and ambushed by Batista's troops. Only 16 of the survivors eventually managed to meet up, including Fidel and Raúl Castro, and Che Guevara.

Thinking that the danger was over, Batista canceled his search-and-destroy missions and withdrew his forces. On 13 December, Castro's meager force finally made contact with a peasant member of the 26th of July Movement, and with that, word was out that Castro had survived. That day, 20 peasants joined the rebel army. Aided by an efficient communications network and intense loyalty from the Sierra peasants, the rebel unit was passed from homestead to homestead as they moved deeper into the mountains, and safety.

night on its lofty pedestal. It was supposedly used by Fidel Castro himself at the Bay of Pigs. To the north is a wide-open park, **Plaza 13 de Mayo,** leading down to Calle Carcél and, beyond, the General Máximo Gómez monument. The ornate building at the base of Agramonte, on the west side of Carcél, is the **Spanish Embassy.** Wealthy businessman Dionisio Velasco was the former owner of the mansion—one of the most flamboyant of Havana's structures in Art Nouveau style.

Palacio Presidencial

This ornate palace, at Refugio e/ Agramonte y Monserrate, was initiated in 1913 to house the provincial government. Before it could be finished, it was earmarked as the Presidential Palace, and Tiffany's of New York was entrusted with its interior decoration. It was from here that a string of corrupt presidents, ending with Fulgencio Batista, spun their webs of dissolution.

Following the Revolution, the three-story palace was converted into the **Museo de la Revolución,** tel. (62) 4091; open Tuesday 10 a.m.-6 p.m. and Wed.-Sun. 10 a.m.-5 p.m.; entrance US$3 (cameras US$5 extra). The marble staircase in the foyer leads upstairs to a massive lobby with a fabulous muraled ceiling. Beyond lie vast salons, notably the Salón de los Espejos (the Mirror Room), a replica of that in Versailles, and the Salón Dorado (the Gold Room), decorated with yellow marble. The building contains fine works of art.

Rooms are divided chronologically, from the colonial period to the modern day. It is necessary to follow the route room by room through the mazelike corridors. Detailed maps describe the battles and progress of the revolutionary war. Hundreds of guns and rifles are displayed alongside grisly photos of dead and tortured heroes. The Moncada Room displays the bloodstained uniforms of the rebels who attacked the Moncada barracks in Santiago in 1953. Another section is dedicated to the revolutionaries who died in an assault on the palace on 13 March 1957 (Batista escaped through a secret door to a secure apartment reachable only by a private elevator, frustrating an action that turned into a bloody debacle). A room labeled "El Triunfo de la Revolución" bears the red flag of MR-26-7 and other revolutionary groups along with a photo

of an ecstatic Castro. Che Guevara is there in the form of a lifelike statue, sweating, rifle in hand, working his way heroically through the jungle. Don't miss Ronald Reagan satirized alongside other notable adversaries of the Cuban state in the museum's "Corner of Cretins."

At the rear, in the former palace gardens, is the **Granma Memorial,** preserving the vessel that brought Castro, Guevara, and other revolutionaries from Mexico to Cuba in 1956. The *Granma,* a surprisingly muscular launch that embodies the powerful, unstoppable spirit of the revolutionary movement, is encased in an impressive glass structure—a simulated sea—with a roof held aloft by great concrete columns, rather like Lenin's tomb (for some strange reason, soldiers prevent you from photographing it, but you can steal a photo from the street). It is surrounded by vehicles used in the revolutionary war: strange armored vehicles, the bullet-riddled "Fast Delivery" truck used in the student commandos' assault on the Presidential Palace in 1957, and Castro's green Land Rover with *Comandancia General Sierra Maestra* stenciled in red on the door. There's also a turbine from the U-2 spy plane downed during the missile crisis in 1962, a naval Sea Fury, and a T-34 tank supposedly used by Castro himself against the counterrevolutionaries at the Bay of Pigs.

You can take photos of the exhibits from the street, but to get closer to the *Granma,* you must enter the museum through the main entrance.

Monumento al General Máximo Gómez

This massive monument of white marble supported by classical columns dominates the waterfront at the base of Agramonte. The monument, erected in 1935, honors the Dominican-born hero of the Cuban wars of independence who led the Liberation Army as commander-in-chief. Although a foreigner, Gómez dedicated himself to the cause of Cuban independence and displayed Napoleonic brilliance in his tactics. He survived the war and died in Havana on 17 June 1905. Generalissimo Gómez (1836-1905) is cast in bronze, with his bare head aloft and reining in his horse. Designed and made by sculptor Aldo Gamba, its base contains three reliefs depicting the Patria, the People, and Freedom.

Cabaña, the access road to the Havana harbor tunnel that leads to Parque Morro, as well as

Monumento Máximo Gómez

of Cuban music since early colonial days; it displays many antique instruments, including a beautiful collection of venerable pianos and the huge collection of drums once owned by Fernando Ortíz, a renowned Africanist. In a separate room, you can listen to old scores drawn from the record library. The museum also hosts concerts. Open Mon.-Sat. 9 a.m.-4:45 p.m. Entrance is US$2.

Immediately to the south, three all-important governmental buildings face west onto the Plaza 13 de Mayo: the **Comité Nacional de UJC** (the Union of Communist Youth), the **Asemblea Provincial de Poder Popular** (Havana's local assembly), and the **Organización de Pioneeros José Martí** (the communist youth pioneers, Cuba's equivalent of Boy Scouts with a political twist). Rousing socialist murals adorn the walls.

Here, too, immediately east of the Presidential Palace, is the **Iglesia del Santa Ángel Custodio,** sitting atop a rock known as Angel Hill. There's a virginal purity to this shimmering white church with its splendid exterior. Actually, the lavishly gothic facade is the rear of the church, which was founded in 1687 by builder-bishop Diego de Compostela. The tower dates from 1846, when a hurricane toppled the original, while the facade was reworked in neo-gothic style in the mid-19th century. It's immaculate yet simple within: gray marble floor, modest wooden gothic altar, statues of saints all around, pristine stained-glass windows. Cuba's national hero, José Martí, was baptized here on 12 February 1853. The church has appeared in several movies and was the setting for the tragic marriage scene that ends in the violent denouement on the steps of the church in the 19th-century novel *Cecilia Valdés,* by nationalist Cirilo Villaverde. A bust of the author stands in the *plazuela* outside the church entrance, which is on the corner of Calles Compostela and Cuarteles, one block east.

It's worth continuing along Cuarteles one block to a junction known as **Las Cinco Cuarteles de El Ángel** (Five Corners of the Angel). Here you can admire an agglomeration of ancient houses, some with beams of round trunks that attest to their age.

Monserrate continues south three blocks to **Plazuela de Supervielle,** commemorating Dr. Manuel Fernández Supervielle, mayor of Havana during the 1940s. His principal election promise—to resolve the city's ongoing water

to Playas del Este, Matanzas, and Varadero, curls and nosedives beneath the monument.

CALLE MONSERRATE

Calle Monserrate—Avenida de Bélgica—parallels Agramonte one block to the east (if driving, Monserrate is one-way downhill) and follows the space left by the ancient city walls after they were demolished last century. A semi-derelict watchtower—**Baluarte de Ángel**—erected in 1680 still stands in front of the Presidential Palace at Refugio and Monserrate as a lone reminder of the fortified wall that once surrounded Habana Vieja.

At the base of Monserrate, at its junction with Calle Tacón and facing onto the Gómez monument, is the **Museo de la Música,** tel. (61) 9846 and (63) 0052. It's housed in the sober Casa de Pérez de la Riva, which was built in Italian Renaissance style in 1905 and for a short time served as a jail. The museum traces the evolution

CUBA'S COCKTAIL

The daiquiri is named for a Cuban hamlet 16 miles east of Santiago de Cuba, near a copper mine where the mining firm's chief engineer, Jennings S. Cox, first created the now world-famous cocktail that Hemingway immortalized in his novels. Cox had arrived in 1898, shortly after the Spanish-American War, to find workers at the mines anxious about putatively malarial drinking water. Cox added a heartening tot of local Bacardi rum to boiled water, then decided to give his mixture added snap and smoothness by introducing lime juice and sugar.

The concoction was soon duplicated, and within no time had moved on to conquer every high-life watering hole in Havana. It is still most notably associated with El Floridita, and Hemingway's immortal words: *"Mi mojito en La Bodeguita, mi daiquiri en El Floridita."*

Shaved—frappéd—ice, which gave the drink its final touch of enchantment, was added by Constante Ribailagua, El Floridita's bartender, in the 1920s. The frozen daiquiris, "the great ones that

Constante made," wrote Hemingway, "had no taste of alcohol and felt, as you drank them, the way downhill glacier skiing feels running through powder snow and, after the sixth and eighth, felt like downhill glacier skiing feels when you are running unroped."

A daiquiri should include all of Cox's original ingredients (minus the water, of course). It may be shaken and strained, or frappéd to a loose sherbet in a blender and served in a cocktail glass or poured over the rocks in an old-fashioned glass. The "Papa Special," which Constante made for Hemingway, contained a double dose of rum, no sugar, and a half ounce of grapefruit juice.

The *Perfect* Daiquiri

In an electric blender, pour half a tablespoon of sugar, the juice of half a lemon, 1.5 ounces of white rum. Serve semifrozen blended with ice (or on the rocks) in a tall martini glass with a maraschino cherry.

---

supply problem—went unfulfilled (the allocated money ended up in private pockets), causing him to commit suicide.

The plazuela is shadowed on its north side by a uniquely inspired building at the corner of Neptuno. The structure—the **Edificio Bacardi**—was formerly the headquarters of the Bacardi rum empire. Finished in December 1929, this magnificent art deco edifice is clad in Swedish granite and local limestone. Terra-cotta of varying hues accents the design, with motifs showing Grecian nymphs and floral patterns. It is crowned by a Lego-like bell tower topped in turn by a wrought-iron, brass-winged gargoyle that is the famous Bacardi motif. The building is difficult to appreciate at street level; to better admire it, nip inside the Hotel Plaza, where it is best seen from the *azotea* (the rooftop plaza). The Edificio Bacardi, surely one of the world's finest art deco inspirations, was receiving a much-needed restoration at press time.

Plazuela de Albear, a tiny plaza on Monserrate, one block east of Parque Central at the west end of Calle Obispo, is hallowed ground. Not because of the bust to Francisco de Albear,

who last century engineered the Malecón and Havana's first water drainage system (still in use). Rather, here—on the southwest corner—is El Floridita.

El Floridita

This famous restaurant and bar has been serving food at this location since 1819, when it was called Pina de Plata. Its name was later changed to La Florida, and then, more affectionately, El Floridita. It is said to be haunted by Ernest Hemingway's ghost. The novelist's seat at the dark mahogany bar is preserved as a shrine. His bronze bust watches over things from its pedestal beside the bar, where Constante Ribailagua once served frozen daiquiris to Hemingway (he immortalized both the drink and the venue in his novel *Islands in the Stream*) and such illustrious guests as Gary Cooper, Tennessee Williams, Marlene Dietrich, and Jean-Paul Sartre. (Rum authority Francisco Campoamor's book, *The Happy Child of Sugar Cane,* tells the tale of El Floridita.)

El Floridita was recently spruced up for tourist consumption with a 1930s art-deco polish. Waiters hover in tux jackets and bow ties. You expect a spotlight to come on and Desi Arnaz to appear conducting a dance band, and Papa to stroll in as he would every morning when he lived in Havana and drank with Honest Lil, the Worst Politician, and other real-life characters from his novels. "When we went to the Floridita bar in those days it wasn't like Orson Welles entering the lobby of the Grand Hotel, as Hotchner described Papa's public excursions in later years," recalls Hemingway's son, Gregory. "It was just a nice bar where my father knew the staff and could drink with us and his friends." They've overpriced the place, even for the package tourist crowd. But, what the hell—sipping a daiquiri at El Floridita is a must.

CALLE TACÓN AND THE HARBOR CHANNEL

Throughout most of the colonial era, sea waves washed upon the beach that lined the southern shore of the harbor channel, known as the Playa de las Tortugas for the marine turtles that came ashore to lay eggs. The beach bordered what is today **Calle Tacón,** which runs along the site of the old city walls forming the original waterfront. In the early 19th century, the area was extended with landfill, and a broad boulevard—**Avenida Manuel de Céspedes** (Avenida del Puerto)— was laid out along the new harborfront, with a wide, shady park separating it from Calle Tacón. The park is divided in two: to the west is **Parque Anfiteatro**, with an open-air theater in Greek fashion and a *parque diversione* (children's fairground); to the east is **Parque Luz Caballero**, pinned by a statue of José de la Luz Caballero, "teacher of Cuban youth, 1800-62."

Calle Tacón is flanked with buildings of historic interest. At the western end, at the foot of Calle Cuarteles, is the **Palacio de Artesanía,** housed in a magnificent mansion—originally the Palacio Pedroso—built in Moorish style for nobleman Don Mateo Pedroso around 1780. Pedroso's home—a profusion of patterned tiles and foliate door arches—was a center for Havana's social life well into the 19th century. Today, duly restored, it houses craft shops and a bar, where you can soak up live music and soothing rum while enjoying a pronounced whiff of the *Arabian*

Nights. Folkloric and other entertainment is offered at night and on weekends.

Amazingly, no maps make any mention of the splendid little medieval-style fortress—**El Castillo de Atane**—a stone's throw east, at the foot of Chacón. This is because the *fortaleza* today houses a police headquarters, as it has since it was built in 1941 for the former Havana Police Department. Yes, it's only a pseudo-colonial confection.

Fronting the "castle," in the middle of Tacón, is a watchtower—a rare remnant of the original city wall. Waves once beat against this sentry box, now landlocked since construction of the Avenida del Puerto. During the British attack on Havana in 1762, this section of wall bore the brunt of the assault on the city, fired on from the heights of El Morro and La Cabaña after those fortresses had been conquered.

RECOMMENDED WALKING TOUR 2

At Parque Central, begin at the **Hotel Plaza,** then head east on Neptuno one block to the **Plazuela de Supervielle** and follow Monserrate north, downhill, to the **Iglesia Santo Ángel Custodio.**

Head east on Cuarteles two blocks to **Cinco Caminos,** then north along Habana to the **Museo de Música.** Follow Calle Tacón east past remains of the *muralles* (old city walls) to the **Palacio Pedroso.** Continue east past the **Seminario de San Carlos** to the end of Tacón and turn right into **Plaza de la Catedral.**

Browse the Plaza, including the **Catedral** and the **Casa del Conde de Bayone,** being sure to stop in for a *mojito* and meal at **El Bodeguita del Medio,** on Empedrado.

Exit the place along San Ignacio and turn left onto O'Reilly. Two blocks brings you to **Plaza de Armas.** A clockwise tour takes in the **Palacio del Segundo Cabo,** the **Castillo de la Real Fuerza, El Templete,** the **Hotel Santa Isabel,** the **Casa de Ron,** the **Museo de Ciencias Naturales,** and the **Museo de la Ciudad** in the **Palacio de Capitanes Generales.**

Return to Parque Central along **Calle Obispo,** calling in at the **Hotel Ambos Mundos** and **Museo de la Educación.**

The jewel in the crown of Tacón is the **Seminario de San Carlos y San Ambrosio,** a massive seminary due east of El Castillo de Atane, between Chacón and Empedrado. It was established by the Jesuits in 1721 and ever since has been a center for young men studying for an ecclesiastical career. The seminary was built in an irregular polygon shape during the second half of the 18th century, featuring a three-story gallery in varying styles and a massive banister of caoba wood with elaborate carvings. Its dramatic baroque facade—which amazingly dates from the 1950s, when it was remodeled in neo-baroque style like the Havana cathedral—is missed by most tourists, as is the serenity of the inner courtyard, because the seminary is closed to public viewing.

A large artisans' market takes up the length of Tacón directly in front of the seminary, where an excavated site shows the foundations of the original seafront section of the city walls—here called the **Cortina de Valdés**—against which the sea once lapped, no more than 10 yards from the seminary.

Tacón ends at a tiny *plazuela* at the foot of Empedrado, where a bevy of colorful old fishing boats that could have fallen from a painting by Hockney sit on the cobbled curbside in front of the **Casa de la Miniatura.** This former mansion now sells exquisite miniature soldiers and pirates, although the range (once vast) is now motley. Horse-drawn open-air cabs called *calezas* gather here, offering guided tours to tourists.

Around the corner to the south, on a narrow extension of Tacón that leads to Plaza de Armas, another restored mansion now houses **Bar y Restaurante D'Giovanni.** Its fabulous inner courtyard is graced by three tiers of balustraded balconies (note the stunning mural in the entranceway). Also worth a visit is the building next door, **Gabinete de la Arqueología** (the Archaeological Department of the Office of the City Historian), at Calle Tacón 12, tel. (61) 4469. Remarkably, the beautiful mansion (first mentioned in documents in 1644) was inherited in 1700 by a mulatta whose owner, Doña Lorenza de Carvajal, had granted her freedom (Doña Lorenza's own daughter had brought disgrace upon herself by becoming pregnant and was shuttled off to a convent). The mansion's most re-markable feature is a series of eccentric murals depicting life in bold technicolor as it was lived in Havana centuries ago (the murals, painted between 1763 and 1767, were revealed during a recent restoration from beneath 26 layers of paint and whitewash). It's open Tues.-Sat. 10 a.m.-5 p.m., Sunday 9 a.m.-1 p.m.

PLAZA DE LA CATEDRAL

You'll find yourself returning again and again to this exquisite cobbled square dominated by the intimate but imposing and decadently baroque 18th-century "Columbus Cathedral"—and, on the other three sides, aristocratic *palacios:* the Casa de Lombillo, Casa del Marqués de Arcos, Casa del Conde de Bayona, and Casa de Marqués de Aguas Claras.

This was the last (and finest) square to be laid out in Habana Vieja, for it occupied a lowly quarter where rainwater drained (it was originally known as the Plazuela de la Cienaga—Little Square of the Swamp). Its present texture dates from the 18th century, before which it served as a fish market and cattle watering station. A cistern was built here in 1587, and only in the following century was the area drained for construction.

The square is Habana Vieja at its most quintessential, the atmosphere enhanced by mulattas in traditional costume who will happily preen and pose for your camera for a small fee. Be sure to visit by night also, when the setting is enhanced by the soft glow of wan lanterns and the plaza is moody and dreamy. One night per month, the plaza is the venue for **Noches en la Plaza de la Catedral,** when tables are laid out in the square, dinner is served, and you get to witness a folkloric *espectáculo* with a stunning backdrop.

Catedral de la Habana

This splendid edifice is the maximum exemplar of Cuban baroque. Known colloquially as Catedral Colón and Catedral de San Cristóbal, this little stunner has an official name—Catedral de la Virgen María de la Concepción Inmaculada (her statue is installed in the High Altar), tel. (61) 7771. The cathedral was initiated by the Jesuits in 1748. The order was kicked out of Cuba by

Plaza de la Catedral

However, for a small tip, Marcelino the *campanero* (bell ringer) might lead you up the time-worn stairs of the bell tower where, like Quasimodo, you may run your fingers over the eight patinated bells of different sizes and peer down over the square. Take care up here, as nobody thinks to clean up the debris underfoot, and there are no guardrails. Marcelino even led me into the organ loft (also littered with debris), where I lay on a bed of dust and snapped photos down over the nave. Look, too, at the wooden image of Saint Christopher, patron saint of Havana, dating to 1633 and originally composed of 170 pieces (the original was too heavy to carry in processions, so a sculptor was commissioned to reduce its size; unfortunately, his hand was uneven and there is a noticeable disproportion between head and body).

Columns divide the rectangular church into three naves, with a marble floor, two side aisles supported by great pillars, and eight chapels off to the side (the oldest, the Chapel of Nuestra Señora de Loreta, consecrated in 1755, predates the conversion of the original church into a cathedral). The interior remains in excellent condition, although the murals (the work of renowned Italian painter Guiseppe Perovani) above the main altar are mildewed. Artist Jean-Baptiste Vermay, who was born in France around 1790, moved to Havana, and died—along with 8,000 other citizens—in the cholera epidemic of 1833, is also represented. The main altar is very simple and made of wood. More impressive is the chapel immediately to the left, with several altars, including one of Carrara marble inlaid with gold, silver, onyx, and carved hardwoods.

The Spanish believed that a casket that had been brought to Havana with due pomp and circumstance from Santo Domingo in 1796 and resided in the cathedral for more than a century held the ashes of Christopher Columbus. Casket and ashes—a "pile of dust and a bit of bone"—were returned to Spain in 1899. All but the partisan Habaneros now believe that the ashes were those of Columbus's son Diego. The *Gran Almirante*, the stone statue of Columbus that stood outside the cathedral, is gone also (Graham Greene, in *Our Man From Havana*, thought it looked "as though it had been formed through the centuries under water, like a coral reef, by the action of insects"), transferred to Spain with the casket.

Carlos III in 1767, but the building was eventually completed in 1777 and altered again in the early 19th century by Bishop José Díaz de Espada, who found many of the elements not to his liking. Thus, the original baroque interior is gone, replaced in 1814 by a new classical interior.

Describing the cathedral's baroque facade, adorned with clinging columns and rippled like a great swelling sea, Cuban novelist Alejo Carpentier wrote that it was "music turned to stone." The facade, which derives from Francisco Borromini's 1667 San Carlo alla Quattro Fontane in Rome, is so simple yet magnificent that a royal decree of December 1793 elevated the church to a cathedral because "the beautifully carved stones of the church . . . are clamouring from their walls for the distinction of cathedral."

On either side of the facade are mismatched towers (one fatter and taller than the other) containing bells supposedly cast with a dash of gold and silver, which is said to account for their musical tone. The eastern bell tower has in the past been open to tourists—not so in spring 1999.

At press time, the cathedral was open Mon.-Sat. 10 a.m.-3:30 p.m., Sunday 9 a.m.-10:30 p.m.

Casa de los Marqueses de Aguas Claras

If the heat and bustle of the square get to you, you should settle on the patio beneath the soaring *portal* of this splendid old mansion on the west side of the plaza. Here you can sip a cool beer or heady *mojito* (rum mint julep) and watch the comings and goings while being serenaded by musicians. The mansion was owned during the 16th century by Governor General Gonzalo Pérez de Angulo and has since been added to by subsequent owners. The inner courtyard, with its fountain and grand piano amid lush palms and clinging vines, today houses the Restaurante La Fuente del Patio.

The restaurant extends upstairs, where members of the middle classes once dwelled in apartments (since converted for diners' pleasure, enhanced by *mediopuntos* that by day saturate the floors with shifting fans of red and blue light). Novelist Enrique Fernandez, writing in 1994, recalled being able to look down from his grandmother's balcony and watch "the goings on in the plaza: the fruit vendors and bootblacks, the elegant men and women in white linen going into the restaurant (which was far too pricey for the second-floor tenants), and at the garishly dressed Americans buying stuffed baby alligators in the tourist shops that festooned the other two *palacios*." You can still steal out onto the rickety balconies to look down on the colorful action; when the crowds disappear, note the patterned cobbles.

Casa del Conde de Bayona

For the best view and photos down over the square, ascend the steps to the upper level of Casa del Conde de Bayona, the simple two-story structure that faces the cathedral on the south side of the square. Dating from 1720, it's a perfect example of the traditional Havana merchant's house of the period, with side stairs and an *entresuelo* (mezzanine of half-story proportions) tucked between the two stories and used to house servants and slaves. It was built in the 1720s for Governor General Don Luís Chacón and today houses the **Museo de Arte Colonial**, tel. (62) 6440. The museum is an Aladdin's cave of colonial furniture, glass, porcelain, Baccarat crystal, ironwork, musical instruments, and other sumptuous artifacts from the colonial period. One room is devoted to the stunningly colorful stained-glass *vitrales* and *mediopuntos* unique to Cuba. There's even an array of chamberpots—handy if you get taken short! Open daily except Tuesday 9:30 a.m.-7 p.m.; entrance costs US$2 (cameras cost US$2, guides cost US$1).

Other Sites

On the southwest corner of the square, at the junction with Calle San Ignacio, is the **Callejon de Chorro**, a tiny cul-de-sac with a plaque denoting where a bathhouse was once located at the terminus of the Zanja Real (the "royal ditch," a covered aqueduct that brought water from the Río Almendares, some 10 km away). A small sink and spigot are all that remain. At the end of Callejon de Chorro is the **Taller Experimental de la Gráfica**, where you can watch art students making impressive prints. At the corner of the square and Callejon sits the **Casa de Baños**, looking quite ancient but built this century in colonial style on the site of a 19th-century bathhouse erected over an *aljibe* (water reservoir) fed by the Zanja Real. Today the Casa contains the **Galería Victor Manuel**, tel. (61) 2955, which sells exquisite quality arts.

On the plaza's east side is the **Casa de Lombillo.** Built in 1741, this former home of a slave trader still houses a small post office (Cuba's first), as it has since 1821. Note the mailbox set into the outside wall; it is a grotesque face—that of a tragic Greek mask—carved in stone, with as its slit a scowling mouth that looks like it might take your fingers or at least spit back your letter. In spring 1999, the house was being restored and will eventually house the Oficina del Historidades de la Ciudad (office of Eusebio Leal Spengler, the city historian), returning to a role it played 1947-64.

Casa de Lombillo adjoins the **Casa del Marqués de Arcos,** built in the 1740s for the royal treasurer. The mansion today houses the **Nelson Domínguez Experimental Graphics Art Gallery**, its walls virtually obliterated by large canvases by Domínguez, a noted Cuban artist whose exquisite mind seems to be inhabited, suggests Eusebio Leal, by "strange officiating priests of myth and religious fantasy."

The two houses are fronted by a wide *portal* supported by thick columns and today used as a venue for artists to display their works.

CALLE EMPEDRADO

Cobbled Calle Empedrado leads west from the north side of the Plaza de la Catedral.

Anyone with an interest in art should call in at the **Centro Wilfredo Lam,** on San Ignacio, tel. (61) 2096 and (61) 3419, fax (33) 8477, e-mail: wlam@artsoft.cult.cu, immediately west of the cathedral at the corner of Empedrado and San Ignacio, in the restored former mansion of the Counts of Peñalver. The center, named for the noted Cuban artist, displays works by Lam, other Cuban artists, and artists from throughout the Third World. The cultural institution studies, researches, and promotes contemporary art from around the world. It sponsors workshops and the biennial Havana Exhibition, in which up-and-coming artists have a chance to exhibit. It also features a library on contemporary art, a large music store, and a collection of 1,250 art pieces. Open Mon.-Fri. 8:30 am.-3:30 p.m.; for guided visits, Mon.-Sat. 10 a.m.-5 p.m.

La Bodeguita del Medio

No visit to Havana is complete without at least one visit to Ernest Hemingway's favorite watering hole, at 207 Calle Empedrado, tel. (62) 6121, half a block west of the cathedral. This neighborhood hangout—Hemingway's "little shop in the middle of the street"—was originally the coachhouse of the mansion next door (that of the Contesa de la Reunión). Later it was a bodega, a mom-and-pop grocery store where Spanish immigrant Angel Martínez served drinks and food over the counter. According to Tom Miller in *Trading with the Enemy,* Martínez hit upon a brilliant idea: he gave writers credit. The writers, of course, wrote about their newfound hangout, thereby attracting literati and cognoscenti from around the world. (After the Revolution, Martínez stayed on as manager.)

You enter La Bodeguita through a saloon-style swinging door. The bar is immediately on your right, with the restaurant behind (note the beautiful tilework along the passageway wall). The bar is usually crowded with tourists, who ebb and flow. Troubadors move among the thirsty *turistas.* Between tides, you can still savor the proletarian fusion of dialectics and rum. The house drink is the US$3 *mojito,* the rum mint julep that Hemingway brought out of obscurity and turned into the national drink; the concoction is insipid, about as bad as you'll find in Havana.

The rustic wooden bar is carved with names. Miscellaneous bric-a-brac adorns the walls: posters, paintings, and faded black-and-white photos of Papa Hemingway, Carmen Miranda, and other famous visitors. The walls look as if a swarm of adolescents has been given amphetamines and let loose with crayons. The most famous graffiti is credited to Papa: "Mi Mojito En La Bodeguita, Mi Daiquiri En El Floridita," he supposedly scrawled on the sky-blue walls. Errol

CUBA'S PICASSO: WILFREDO LAM

Wilfredo Lam, a Cubist and student of Pablo Picasso, was one of the greatest painters to emerge from Cuba during this century. His heritage is a mixture of Cuban, African, and Chinese blood. He was born in 1902, in Sagua La Grande, and studied at Havana's San Alejandro School of Painting. In 1936, he traveled to Paris and developed close ties with the surrealists. Picasso took Lam under his wing and offered the young Cuban his studio to work in. Lam lived briefly in Marseilles before returning to Havana. In 1956, he returned to Europe, although he continued to visit Cuba periodically. He died in Paris on 11 September 1982.

Lam's work distills the essence of Afro-Antillean culture. He broke with the traditional rules and created his own style using the myths, rituals, customs, and magic of his background to explore a world of Caribbean negritude. His most important works are considered to be *La Silla,* painted in 1941, and *La Jungla,* painted in 1943. Many of his etchings, sketches, and canvases are exhibited in Havana's Bellas Artes museum. His *La Manigua,* painted in Haiti in 1956, hangs in the Museum of Modern Art in New York. And one of his paintings, *La Mañana Verde,* sold at Sotheby's in 1995 for US$965,000. You can even walk on his work, which is inset on the sidewalks of Calle 23 (La Rampa) in Vedado.

Flynn thought it "A Great Place to Get Drunk." They are there, these ribald fellows, smiling at the camera through a haze of cigar smoke and rum. Stepping from La Bodeguita with rum in your veins, you may feel an exhilarating sensation, as if Hemingway himself were walking beside you through the cobbled streets of this most literary of Havana's terrain.

Other Sites
The **Casa del Conde de la Reunión,** at Empedrado #215, 50 meters west of La Bodeguita, was built in the 1820s, at the peak of the baroque era. The doorway opens onto a courtyard surrounded by rooms in which Alejo Carpentier, Cuba's most famous novelist (and a dedicated revolutionary), once worked. A portion of the home, which houses the **Centro de Promoción Cultural,** is dedicated to his memory as the **Museo Carpentier,** tel. (61) 5500. One entire wall bears a display under sloping glass of Carpentier's early works. His raincoat is thrown stylishly over his old desk chair, suggesting that the novelist might return home at any moment. The novelist's widow dedicated his posthumous royalties to establish and maintain the museum. It's open weekdays 8:30 a.m.-4:30 p.m. Entry is free.

Two blocks west, you'll pass **Plazuela de San Juan de Díos,** a small, unkempt plaza between Calles Habana and Aguiar centered on a white marble monument erected in 1906. The life-size facsimile of Miguel de Cervantes, the great Spanish author of *Don Quixote,* sits in a chair, book and pen in hand, looking contemplatively down upon rose bushes, lending the plaza its colloquial name: Parque Cervantes.

CALLE O'REILLY AND VICINITY

Calle O'Reilly runs from the northwest corner of Plaza Armas and, although today quite sedate, was before the Revolution a major commercial thoroughfare. "The bells were ringing in Santo Christo, and the doves rose from the roof in the golden evening and circled away over the lottery shops of O'Reilly Street and the banks of Obispo," wrote Graham Greene in *Our Man in Havana.* It is named not, as you may suspect, for an Irishman but rather for a Spaniard, Alejandro O'Reilly, who arrived to represent the Spanish crown after the British returned the city to Spain in 1763.

Catercorner to Plaza de Armas, at the corner of O'Reilly and Tacón, is a plaque inset in the wall that reads, "Two Island Peoples in the Same Seas of Struggle and Hope. Cuba and Ireland." The building is the **Empresa Cubana del Tabaco,** O'Reilly #104, tel. (61) 5759, fax (33) 5463, the headquarters of Habanos S.A., which oversees Cuba's production and sale of cigars. Visitors are welcomed into the lobby to admire its exhibit, including display cases of Cuba's finest cigars.

Walking west, you'll pass **Calle San Ignacio,** a narrow, cobbled thoroughfare that's loaded with atmosphere, leading 50 meters north to Plaza de la Catedral. Half a block west of Calle San Ignacio is **Café O'Reilly,** O'Reilly #205, a charming streetside café with an ornate cast-iron spiral staircase that leads up to a tiny bar. Here you can sit on a balcony and sip a coffee or beer while watching the tide of people flooding O'Reilly.

CUBA'S LATE, GREAT WRITER, ALEJO CARPENTIER

Alejo Carpentier (1904-80) is acclaimed as Cuba's greatest latter-day writer. Carpentier (his name is pronounced in the French manner) is known for his erudite and verbally explosive works. A favorite is "Journey Back to the Source," a brilliant short story chronicling the life of Don Marcial, Marqués de Capellanías, but told chronologically backward from death to birth. Carpentier was born in Havana to a French father and Russian mother. In 1946, during the violent excesses of the Batista era, he fled Cuba for Venezuela, where he wrote his best novels (one year before, he published a seminal work called *Music in Cuba*). When the Castro revolution triumphed, the gifted novelist and revolutionary patriot returned as an honored spiritual leader. Alas, say some critics, Carpentier became a bureaucrat and sycophant; under his influence, the National Printing Press even reworked *Moby Dick* to make it palatable to the socialist masses (Captain Ahab, Ishmael, and Queequeg were still there, but "you couldn't find God in the labyrinth of the sea," wrote Guillermo Cabrera Infante).

Worth a look, too, is the neoclassical **National City Bank of New York,** at O'Reilly and Compostela, where, "passing through great stone portals, which were decorated with four-leaf clovers," Greene's Wormold was reminded of his meager status.

O'Reilly continues westward without buildings of further note.

PLAZA DE ARMAS

The most important plaza in Habana Vieja, and the oldest—originally laid out in 1519—is this handsome square at the seaward end of Calles Obispo and O'Reilly, opening onto Avenida del Puerto to the east. Plaza de Armas was the early focus of the settlement and later became its administrative center, named Plaza de Iglesia for the church that once stood here (demolished in 1741 after it was destroyed when an English warship, the ill-named HMS *Invincible,* was struck by lightning and exploded, sending its main mast sailing down on the church). The square derived its contemporary name following a dispute in 1581 between the Cuban governor, Gabriel Luján, and Diego Quiñones, governor of the Castillo de la Real Fuerza, who competed for command of the castle garrison. Luján won the day by taking over the square for military exercises: hence, Plaza de Armas.

It is still rimmed by four important buildings constructed in the late 18th century, when the ca-pacious square was reconstructed with "buildings appropriate to the grandeur of this city." The plaza seems still to ring with the cacophany of the past, when military parades, extravagant fiestas, and musical concerts were held under the watchful eye of the governor, and the gentry would take their formal evening promenade. The lovely tradition has been revived on Sunday, when by day the plaza hosts a secondhand book fair and, by night, musical concerts. It is lent a romantic cast by its verdant park shaded by palms and tall trees festooned with lianas and epiphytes, lit at night by beautifully filigreed lamps. At its center stands a statue of Manuel de Céspedes, hero of the Ten Years' War, with a tall palm at each corner.

The following are described in clockwise order around the plaza, beginning at the Palacio de los Capitanes Generales.

Palacio de los Capitanes Generales

Commanding the square is this somber, stately palace fronted by a cool loggia, shadowed by a facade of Ionic columns supporting nine great arches. The tall loggia boasts a life-size marble statue of Fernando VII, holding in one hand a scroll of parchment that from the side appears jauntily cocked (pardon the pun) and is the butt of ribald jokes among locals. In his other hand, he holds a plumed hat.

Spain's stern rule was enforced from here: the Palacio de los Capitanes Generales was home to 65 governors of Cuba between 1791

On Sunday, the Plaza de Armas hosts a secondhand book fair.

and 1898 and, after that, the early seat of the Cuban government (and the US governor's residence during Uncle Sam's occupation. Between 1920 and 1967, it served as Havana's city hall. Originally the parish church—La Parroquial Mayor, built in 1555—stood here. The holy structure was demolished when the mast and spars of the *Invincible* came through the roof—an unfortunate "act of God."

The palace is a magnificent three-story structure surrounding a courtyard (entered from the plaza), which contains a statue of Christopher Columbus competing for the light with tall palms and a veritable botanical garden of foliage. Don't be alarmed by any ghoulish shrieks—a peacock lives in the courtyard. Arched colonnades rise on all sides, festooned with vines and bougainvillea. Several afternoons each week, an orchestra plays decorous 19th-century dance music, while pretty girls in crinolines flit up and down the majestic staircase, delighting in the ritual of the *Quince*, the traditional celebration of a girl's 15th birthday. On the southeast corner, you can spot a hole containing the coffin of an unknown nobleman, one of several graves from the old Cementerio de Espada (a church that once stood here was razed to make way for the palace; note the plaque—the oldest in Havana—commemorating the death of Doña María de Cepero y Nieto, who was felled when a blunderbuss was accidentally fired while she was praying—another unfortunate "act of God").

Today, the palace houses the **Museo de la Ciudad de La Habana** (the City of Havana Museum), 1 Calle Tacón, tel. (61) 2876. The entrance is to the side, on Calle Obispo. The great flight of marble stairs leads to high-ceilinged rooms as gracious and richly furnished as those in Versailles or Buckingham Palace. The throne room, made for the King of Spain but never used, is of particularly breathtaking splendor and brims with treasures. The countless curiosities include two enormous marble bathtubs in the shape of nautilus shells, Máximo Gómez's death mask, and a cannon made of leather. The museum also features a Hall of Flags, plus exquisite collections illustrating the story of the city's (and Cuba's) development and the 19th-century struggles for independence. Even here you can't escape the ubiquitous anti-Yankee expositions: one top-floor room contains the shattered wings

of the eagle that once crested the Monumento del Maine in Vedado, along with other curios suggestive of US voracity and fragility.

The museum also has a model of an early 20th-century sugar plantation at 1:22.5 scale, complete with steam engine, milling machines, and plantation grounds with workers' dwellings, a church, and a hotel—all transporting you back in time on the world's smallest sugar plantation. A railroad runs through the plantation, with two steam locomotives pulling sugarcane carriers, water tanks, and passenger carriages.

The museum is open daily 9:30 a.m.-6:30 p.m. Entrance costs US$3 tourists (US$2 extra for cameras, US$10 for videos, US$1 for a guide). You can purchase a US$9 ticket here, good for *all* museums in Havana. The museum also offers guided tours of the plaza and Old Havana (US$5, or US$6 for both the tour and museum entry).

Palacio del Segundo Cabo

This quasi-Moorish, pseudo-baroque, part neoclassical Palace of the Second Lieutenant, on the north side of the square on Calle O'Reilly, dates from 1770, when it was designed at the city Post Office. Its use metamorphosed several times until it became the home of the vice-governor general (Second Lieutenant) and, immediately after independence, the seat of the Senate. Today, it houses the Instituto Cubano del Libro (the Cuban Book Institute) and, appropriately, the Bella Habana bookstore. The Institute hosts occasional public presentations but is otherwise generally not open to public perusal. At press time, it was being renovated.

Castillo de la Real Fuerza

This pocket-size castle, begun in 1558 and completed in 1582, is the second oldest fort in the Americas and the oldest of the four forts that guarded the New World's most precious harbor. Built in medieval fashion, it was almost useless from a strategic point of view, being landlocked far from the mouth of the harbor channel and hemmed in by surrounding buildings that would have formed a great impediment to its cannons in any attack. With walls six meters wide and 10 meters tall, the castle forms a square with enormous triangular bulwarks at the corners. I never cease to marvel at its solidity, simple sophistication, sharp angles (that slice the dark waters of the moat like the prows of galleons), and beauty, especially at night, when it is haloed in ghostly light. The governors of Cuba lived here until 1762.

Visitors enter the fortress on the northeast corner of Plaza de Armas via a courtyard full of patinated cannons and mortars. Note the royal coat of arms representing Seville, Spain, carved in stone above the massive gateway as you cross the moat by a drawbridge. The entrance to the vaulted interior features two suits of armor in glass cases.

Stairs lead up to the storehouse and battlements, now housing an impressive **Museo y Taller de Cerámica,** tel. (61) 6130, featuring pottery both ancient and new. You can climb to the top of a cylindrical tower rising from the northwest corner; the tower contains an antique brass bell gone mossy green with age and weather. Originally, the bell was rung to signal the approach of ships, with differing notes for friends and foes. The tower is topped by a bronze weathervane called La Giraldilla de la Habana—a reference to the Giralda weathervane in Seville. While rather a pathetic looking thing, much is made of it—it's the symbol of Havana and also graces the label of Havana Club rum bottles. The vane is a copy—the archetype, which toppled in a hurricane, resides in the city museum. The original was cast in 1631 in honor of Inéz de Bobadilla, the wife of Governor Hernando de Soto, the tireless explorer who fruitlessly searched for the Fountain of Youth in Florida. De Soto named his wife governor in his absence, and she became the only female governor ever to serve as such in Cuba. Every afternoon for four years she climbed the tower and scanned the horizon in vain for his return; and it is said that she died of sorrow. In memory of his widow, the residents of Havana commissioned the weathervane and placed it atop the tower. The Giraldilla is a voluptuous albeit small figure with hair braided in thick ropes, bronze robes fluttering in the wind. In her right hand she holds a palm tree and in her left a cross.

The castle is open daily 8 a.m.-7 p.m.; entry costs US$1.

The Northeast Corner
Immediately east of the castle, at the junction of Avenida del Puerto and O'Reilly, is an obelisk to the 77 Cuban seamen killed during World War II by German submarines (five Cuban vessels were sunk by German U-boats). Cuba formally declared war on Nazi Germany in late 1941. The Nazis placed a spy in Cuba—Heinz August Kenning, alias Enrique Augusto Lunin—to report on the arrival and departure of shipping, which could then be hunted by submarines. Kenning was discovered and executed on 10 November 1942. There is no memorial to him. (Hemingway added to his adventures by converting his sportfishing vessel, the *Pilar,* to hunt submarines on behalf of the US Navy.)

HEMINGWAY HUNTS THE U-BOATS

In May 1942, Ernest Hemingway showed up at the US embassy in Havana with a proposal to fit the *Pilar* out as a Q-boat, a vessel disguised as a fishing boat to decoy Nazi submarines within range but armed with .50-caliber machine guns, other armaments, and a trained crew (with himself at the helm, of course). The boat would navigate the cays off the north coast of Cuba, ostensibly collecting specimens on behalf of the American Museum of Natural History but in fact on the lookout for German U-boats, which Hemingway intended to engage and disable. The writer was "quite prepared to sacrifice his beloved vessel in exchange for the capture or sinking of an enemy submarine."

Hemingway's friend, Col. John W. Thomason Jr., was Chief of Naval Intelligence for Central America and pulled strings to get the plan approved. The vessel was "camouflaged" and duly set out for the cays. Gregorio Fuentes—who from 1938 until the writer's death was in charge of the *Pilar*—went along (and served as the model for Antonio in *Islands in the Stream,* Hemingway's novel based on his real-life adventures).

They patrolled for two years. Several times they located and reported the presence of Nazi submarines that the US Navy or Air Force were later able to sink. Only once, off Cayo Mégano, did Hemingway come close to his dream: a U-boat suddenly surfaced while the *Pilar* was at anchor. Unfortunately, it dipped back below the surface and disappeared before Hemingway could get close.

A charming copy of a Doric temple—**El Tem-plete**—sits on the square's northeast corner. It was built in the early 19th century on the site where the first mass and town council meeting were held in 1519, beside a massive ceiba tree. The original ceiba was felled by a hurricane in 1828 and replaced by a column fronted by a small bust of Christopher Columbus. The tree has since been replanted and today still shades the tiny temple, which wears a great cloak of bougainvillea. Its interior, with a black-and-white checkerboard marble floor, is dominated by trip-tych wall-to-ceiling paintings depicting the first Mass, the first town council meeting, and the in-auguration of the Templete. In the center of the room sits a bust of the artist, Jean-Baptiste Ver-may, whose ashes (along with those of his wife, who also died in the cholera epidemic of 1833) are contained in a marble urn next to the bust. Entry costs US$1 with an interpretive guide.

The Southeast Corner

The grand building immediately south of El Tem-plete is the former Palacio del Conde de San-tovenia, built in the style of the Tuileries Palace in France and today housing the **Hotel Santa Isabel** on Calle Barratillo. The *conde* (count) in question was famous for hosting elaborate par-ties, most notoriously a three-day bash in 1833 to celebrate the accession to the throne of Isabel II that climaxed with an ascent of a gaily decorated gas-filled balloon (he was less popular with his immediate neighbors, who detested the reek of oil and fish that wafted over the square from his first-floor warehouses). In the late 19th centu-ry, the palace was bought and sanitized by a colonel from New Orleans. He reopened it as a resplendent hotel, a guise it resumed in 1998.

Half a block east of the hotel, on narrow Calle Baratillo, is the **Casa del Café,** tel. (33) 8061, serving all kinds of Cuban coffees, and, next door, the **Taberna del Galeón,** tel. (33) 8476, better known as the House of Rum. Inside, where it is as cool as a well, you can taste various rums at no cost, although it is hoped you will make a pur-chase from the wide selection (a free *mojito* awaits your arrival). The place is popular with tour groups, which periodically pack the place like sardines. It's open Mon.-Sat. 9 a.m.-5 p.m., Sun-day 9 a.m.-3 p.m. The door is usually closed, but only to keep the air-conditioned air chill.

The South Side

On Calle Obispo, on the east side of the square, is the **Biblioteca Provincial de la Habana,** Ha-vana's spanking new provincial library, which houses a surprisingly paltry (and dated) array of books. Next to it is an art gallery—**Galeria Villena.** And adjoining it to the west is **Museo de Ciencias,** formerly in the Capitolio. This museum shows off the collection of the Academía de Ciencias and encompasses the Museo de Cien-cias Naturales (Museum of Natural Sciences) and the Museo de Ciencias y Técnicas (Museum of Science and Technology). The museum also houses superb collections of Cuban flora and fauna, many in clever reproductions of their nat-ural environments, plus stuffed tigers, apes, and other beasts from afar.

The Southwest Corner

Facing the plaza, at the junction with Calle Oficios, is **Restaurante Cubano,** housed in a green and ocher 17th-century mansion that was originally the college of San Francisco de Sales for orphan girls. Its central patio, surrounded by galleries of stocky columns and wide arches enclosing slatted doors and *mediopuntos,* is now roamed by pea-cocks that beg tidbits from diners. The outside patio facing the plaza is occupied by the lively **Café Mina,** where you may sit beneath shady canopies on the sidewalk while dining as Cuban musicians entertain. Next door, the **Casa del Agua la Tinaja** sells mineral water (US 25 cents a glass—the source was discovered in 1544, and early explorers made use of the water; in 1831, an aqueduct was built to carry it to the burgeoning town, thereby solving the water shortage).

Facing the south side of the Palacio de Capi-tanes Generales, along a 50-meter-long cob-bled section of Calle Obispo, is a series of gems, beginning at Obispo #113. Here, massive metal-studded doorways open into what was once a stable, which now contains a bakery—**Dulcería Doña Teresa**—selling custards, ice creams, and other delights. Next door is the **Museo de Plata,** crammed with silver and gold ornaments from the colonial era, including old clocks, coins, medals, and plates. Upstairs you'll find cande-labras, a dining set that includes a massive silver *ponchera* (punch bowl), a beautiful replica in sil-ver of Columbus's *Santa María,* walking sticks, and a splendid collection of swords and firearms.

Downstairs, a silversmith is occasionally on hand to demonstrate his skills. Entry costs US$1 (plus US$1 for a guide, optional).

Next door is the **Oficina del Historidades de la Ciudad** (Office of the City Historian), Obispo #117-119, with a copper galleon hanging above its door and an old cannon standing upright outside. Appropriately, this is the oldest house in Havana, dating from around 1570. Inside you'll find books on Cuban history and culture for sale and, behind a grilled gate, venerable artifacts including a *quitrín*, a two-wheeled conveyance with a moveable bonnet to protect passengers from the elements, made to be pulled by a single horse (usually ridden by a *calesero*, a black slave, who dressed in high boots, top hat, and a costume trimmed with colorful ribbons). With luck, the city historian, Eusebio Leal, may appear to regale visitors with fascinating tales of his restoration plans for the city. However, his office was due to move to the Casa de Lombillo, in Plaza de la Catedral.

Opposite, look closely at the two cannons outside the south side of the Palacio de Capitanes Generales, and you'll note the monogram of King George III. The cannons are relics of the brief English occupation of Cuba in 1762.

At the end of the cobbled pedestrians-only block is a fabric store in a beautiful blue and cream mansion, the former Casa del Marques de Casa Torre, Obispo #121; and, around the corner, on Mercaderes, the **Casa de las Infusiones**, still selling refreshing cups of tea today as it has since 1841.

CALLE OBISPO

Calle Obispo has been one of the city's busiest thoroughfares since its inception in the early colonial era. The name means "Bishop's Street," supposedly so named because it was the path favored by ecclesiastics of the 18th century. It became Havana's premier shopping street early on and was given a boost when the city walls went up in the mid-1700s, linking the major colonial plaza with the Monserrate Gate, the main entranceway to the city built into the city wall. Cafés and taverns arose to serve the merchants and mendicants. Calle Obispo is still Habana Vieja's bustling thoroughfare, linking Plaza de Armas

---

RECOMMENDED WALKING TOUR 3

Begin in Plaza de Armas and walk south down **Calle Oficios**, calling at the **Casa del Arabe** and **Hostal Valencia**, one block south of which you emerge on **Plaza de San Francisco.**

After visiting the **Iglesia y Convento de San Francisco de Asís,** walk down Oficios to Muralles, and turn left for Avenida del Puerto. At the corner, visit the **Museo de Ron,** then head south one block to the **Bar Dos Hermanos** to commune with Ernest Hemingway's ghost.

Retrace your steps west up Muralles to **Plaza Vieja,** being sure to visit the **Casa del Condes de Jaruco.** Exit the square to the northeast along **Calle Mercaderes,** which leads past **La Cruz Verde** to the **Plaza Simón Bolívar** and the **Casa de África, Casa de la Obra Pía,** and **Casa de Benito Juárez.**

Mercaderes returns you to Plaza Armas, passing the **Museo de Tabaco** and **Museo de Asia.**

---

with today's Parque Central. Every visitor to Havana ought to walk its length. Its most important structures date from the 1920s, when Obispo became a center for banking—a kind of Cuban Wall Street.

Fortunately, the street provides shade (despite a lack of balconies), for it was designed in the colonial fashion typical in tropical climes: extremely narrow, with tall buildings to provide shadow for most of the day.

On the corner of Calles Mercaderes and Obispo is the rose-pink **Hotel Ambos Mundos,** tel. (66) 9592, built in the 1920s and recently reopened after a long restoration. Off and on throughout the 1930s, Hemingway laid his head in Room 511, where the plot of *For Whom the Bell Tolls* formed in his mind. After the Revolution, the hotel was turned into a hostelry for employees of the Ministry of Education across the way. However, Hemingway's room—"a gloomy room, 16 square meters, with a double bed made of ordinary wood, two night tables and a writing table with a chair," recalled Colombian author and Nobel laureate Gabriel García Márquez—has been preserved, down to an old Spanish edition of *Don Quixote* on the night table. His room is open to view Mon.-Sat. 10 a.m.-5 p.m. (entrance US$1).

A plaque on the exterior wall reads, "The novelist Ernest Hemingway lived in this Hotel Ambos Mundos during the decade of the 1930s," when it formed a perfect base for forays to El Floridita and La Bodeguita, and the novelist could be seen day or night strolling my favorite street. Another plaque tells you that "In this site, on 3 January 1841, George Washington Halsey inaugurated the first photographic studio" in Cuba.

Across the street, on the northwest corner of Obispo and Mercaderes, is the **Museo de la Educación,** tel. (61) 5468, dedicated in part to telling the tale of the remarkable and inspirational literacy campaign of 1961, when university students and teachers went to the far corners of Cuba to create a "territory free of illiteracy." Almost one million people were taught to read and write during the epochal program. The ugly modern building here today sits atop what was formerly the Convent of Santo Domingo. Rooms are arranged in chronological order. Open Mon.-Fri. 8:15 a.m.-4:45 p.m. Entry is free.

Note the **antique bell** held aloft by modern concrete pillars immediately east of the museum. Its plaque in Spanish commemorates the fact that this was the original site of the University of Havana, founded in January 1728, and housed in the convent. It was demolished in the mid-19th century; all that remains is the bell, which once tolled to call the students to class.

The **Maqueta de Habana Vieja,** slated to open in 1999 immediately west of Ambos Mundos, will feature a 1:500 scale model of Habana Vieja measuring eight by four meters, with buildings color-coded by use. Don't confuse it with the Maqueta de La Habana in Miramar.

Havana is replete with dusty old apothecaries, but the **Museo y Farmácia Taquechel,** Obispo #155, tel. (62) 9286, immediately south of the Maqueta, is surely the most interesting, with its colorful ceramic jars decorated with floral motifs full of herbs and potions. Dating from 1898, it's named for Dr. Francisco Taquechel y Mirabal. The place is exquisite and sparkles behind modern glass doors after a recent restoration. It also sells Cuba's range of Elguea creams and lotions, such as anti-cellulitis cream.

Another site of interest along Calle Obispo is the **Banco Nacional de Cuba,** in a splendid neoclassical building—that of the Comite Estatal de Finaza—fronted by fluted corinthian columns and portals decorated with four-leaf clovers. It's three blocks west of Plaza de Armas, at Calle Cuba. After the Revolution, Che Guevara was named president of the bank and Minister of Finance. He loved to tell the joke of how he'd gotten the job. Supposedly at a cabinet meeting to decide on a replacement of bank president Felipe Pazos, Castro asks who among them is a "good *economista.*" Guevara raises his hand and is sworn is as Minister of Finance and head of the National Bank. Castro says: "Che, I didn't know you were an economist." Guevara replies, "I'm not!" Castro asks, "Then why did you raise your hand when I said I needed an economist?" to which Guevara replies, "Economist! I thought you asked for a communist!" He stayed true to his beliefs, determined to do away with money altogether. When new banknotes were issued, it was Guevara's job to sign them, which he did dismissively by simply scrawling "Che."

Today the old bank houses in its basement vaults the **Museo de Finanzas,** dedicated to telling a corrupted tale of the history of banking in Cuba from the colonial era to the tenure of Guevara's reign as the bank's president in the early 1960s. The museum features the enormous safe within which—when Cuba had such—the nation's gold reserves were held for more than half a century.

The most resplendent building along Obispo is the former Palacio de Joaquín Gómez, catercorner to the bank, between Calle Cuba and Aguiar. It's now the **Hotel Florida,** with a stunning lobby dating from 1838. Also worth a peek is **La Casa del Consomé La Luz,** five blocks west of Plaza de Armas, at Calles Obispo and Havana. This is another moody apothecary with a white marble floor and old glass cabinets faded with age, filled with chemist's tubes, mixing vases, and mortars and pestles, and lined with bottles of oils, herbs, and powders.

CALLE OFICIOS

Calle Oficios leads south from Plaza de Armas three blocks to Plaza de San Francisco. Its newly restored colonial buildings are confections in stone; walking this street, you may fall under a spell from which you may never escape.

The first noteworthy building is **Casa del Árabe** (Arab House), Oficios #12, tel. (61) 5868. This mansion, an appropriately fine example of Moorish-inspired architecture, is the only place in Havana where Muslims can practice the Islamic faith. It now houses a museum dedicated to all things Arabic. You enter into a beautiful place bursting with foliage—a softly dappled courtyard radiating ineffable calm. The prayer hall is decorated with hardwoods inlaid with mother-of-pearl, tempting you to run your fingers across the floral and geometric motifs to sense the tactile pleasure. Please resist! The museum displays exquisitely crafted camel saddles and Oriental carpets, an exact replica of a *souk* (market), models of Arab *dhows* (traditional sailing vessels), and a superb collection of Arab weaponry. Open daily 9 a.m.- 7 p.m. Entrance costs US$1. Cultural activities are hosted in the evenings.

Coin lovers should call in next door at the **Museo Numismático** (the Coin Museum), in the former 17th-century bishop's residence at Oficios #8, tel. (61) 5811. This fascinating collection of coins dates back to the earliest colonial days and includes "company store" currency printed by the sugar mills. Open Tues.-Fri. 10 a.m.-5 p.m., Saturday 10 a.m.-4 p.m., Sunday 9 a.m.-1 p.m.

Across the street, at Calle Oficios 13, Havana's **Museo de Autos Antiguo** includes an eclectic range of antique automobiles, from a 1905 Cadillac to a 1960s-era Daimler limousine. Several vehicles once belonged to famous figures, such as Che Guevara's jeep and Cuban novelist Alejo Carpentier's Volkswagen Beetle. A number of classic Harley-Davidson motorcycles are also exhibited. By the way, the first car arrived in Havana in 1898. Open daily 9:30 a.m.-7 p.m. Entrance costs US$1 (US$2 extra for cameras, US$10 for videos).

Around the corner, in the Casa Garibaldi at Calle Justíz #21, is **El Caserón del Tango**, which opened in July 1993 to promote the melancholic Argentinian dance. There's a theater opposite—**Casa de la Comedia** (also known as Salón Ensayo)—in the headquarters for the Teatro Anaquillé, in a former slave quarters. It hosts children's theater and comedy events from 7 p.m. on weekends.

Make sure to call in at **Hostal Valencia,** a picturesque Spanish-style *posada* that looks as if it's been magically transported from some Manchegan village. It originated in the 17th century as the home of Governor Count Sotolongo, an aristocrat of pure Spanish pedigree. The hotel, on the corner of Oficios and Obrapia, could have been used as a model by Cervantes for the inn where Don Quixote was dubbed a knight by the bewildered innkeeper. The *hostal* sets out to attract tourists with a liberal coating of green and white paint, various bits and pieces of armor, a handsome bar and courtyard, and a splendid restaurant looking onto Oficios through full-length *rejas* (turned wooden rails). One look and you may want to check in.

PLAZA DE SAN FRANCISCO

The cobbled Plaza de San Francisco, at Oficios and the foot of Amargua, faces onto Avenida del Puerto and the inner shore of Havana harbor, of which it was once an inlet. During the 16th century, long before the Franciscan convent and church were built here, the area was the great waterfront of the early colonial city. Here, Iberian emigrants disembarked with their dreams, slaves were unloaded, and Spanish galleons, their holds groaning with treasure, were replenished with water and victuals for the passage to Europe. A market developed on the plaza, which became the focus of the annual Fiesta de San Francisco. In the 17th century, the customs house and prison were built here, while nobles built their homes on surrounding streets. The plaza has been fully restored, including the cobbles, relaid in 1999.

At its heart is a beautiful fountain, **Fuente de los Leones** (Fountain of the Lions), erected in 1836, moved to different locations at various times, but finally ensconced where it began life. The muscular five-story neoclassical building on the north side is the **Lonja del Comercio** (the "Goods Exchange"), dating from 1907, when it was built as a center for trading in food commodities. It now sparkles after a complete restoration: the shell is original, but the interior is state-of-the-art futuristic and houses offices of international corporations, news bureaus, and tour companies. Note the beautiful dome crowned by a bronze figure of the god Mercury.

Across the way, where Spanish galleons once tethered, the **Terminal Sierra Maestra** cruise terminal faces onto the plaza. (It's a fantastic location—imagine arriving by sea. No other cruise terminal in the world opens so immediately onto the heart of such an incredible colonial city.)

Iglesia y Convento de San Francisco de Asís

Dominating the plaza on the south is the great church whose construction was launched in 1719. It began humbly but was reconstructed in 1730 in baroque style with a 40-meter bell tower—one of the tallest in all the Americas, crowned by St. Helen holding a sacred Cross

of Jerusalem. The church was eventually proclaimed a Minorite Basilia, and it was from its chapel that the processions of the *Vía Crucis* departed every Lenten Friday, ending at the Iglesia del Santo Cristo del Buen Viaje. The devout passed down Calle Amargura (Street of Bitterness), where stations of the cross were set up at street corners and decorated with crucifixes and altars (the so-called Passion emerged from the Third Order of Saint Francis and was adopted by many cities in Spain and the Americas). You can still see the first of the stations—**Casa de la Cruz Verde**—at the corner of Calles Amargura and Mercaderes; it's shaded beneath the eaves, above the Mudejar-style balcony.

CUBAN ARCHITECTURAL TERMS: A BRIEF GLOSSARY

Cuba's colonial mansions—with their tall, generously proportioned rooms and shallow-stepped staircases—were usually built on two main floors (the lower floor for shops and warehouses, the upper floors for the family) with a mezzanine between them for the house servants. Colonial homes typically featured two small courtyards, with a dining area between the two, parallel to the street. The arrangement—termed *obra cruzada* (transverse construction)—gave a more formal character to the first patio, with laundry and other service functions relegated to the inner, second patio, or *traspatio*. Life centered on the inner courtyard, hidden behind massive wooden doors often flanked by pillars. The homes were heavily influenced by traditional Spanish and *mudejar* (Moorish) styles, and evolved quintessential Cuban features that included:

Alfarjes: Pitched wooden roofs combining parallel and angled beams to create additional definition for interiors, providing a conceptual shift in emphasis to enhance the sense of space. Normally found in churches and smaller homes, they adopted a star pattern.

Antepechos: Ornamented window guards flush with the building facade.

Cenefas: Italianate bands of colored plasterwork used as decorative ornamentation on interior walls.

Entresuelo: Shallow mezzanine levels between ground and upper stories, usually housing slaves' living quarters.

Lucetas: Long rectangular windows that run along the edges of doorways and windows. They usually contain stained or marbled glass.

Mamparas: Double-swing half doors that serve as room dividers or as partial outer doors to protect privacy while allowing ventilation. The *mampara* was described by 20th-century Cuban novelist Alejo Carpentier as "a door truncated to the height of a man, the real interior door of the Creole home for hundreds of years, creating a peculiar concept of family relations and communal living."

Patio: An open space in the center of Spanish buildings—a Spanish adaptation of the classic Moorish inner court—which permits air to circulate through the house. The patios of more grandiose buildings are surrounded by columned galleries.

Persianas: Slatted shutters in tall, glassless windows, designed to let in the breezes while keeping out the harsh light and rains.

Portales: Galleried exterior walkways fronting the mansions and protecting pedestrians from sun and rain. The grandest are supported by stone Tuscan columns and have vaulted ceilings and arches. Later, North American influences led to a more sober approach, with square wooden posts (à la the porch).

Postigos: Small doors set at face level into massive wooden doors of Spanish homes.

Rejas: Wooden window screens of rippled, lathe-turned rods called *barrotes* that served to keep out burglars (later *rejas* were made of metal).

Vitrales: Arched windows of stained glass laid out in geometric designs that fan out like peacock's tails and diffuse the sunlight, saturating a room with shifting color. A full 180-degree arch is called a *mediopunto*.

After the Protestant English used the church briefly for worship during their tenure in Havana in 1762, the Catholics refused ever to use the Iglesia de San Francisco de Asís again as a church.

The church and adjoining convent were reopened in October 1994 after a complete restoration. The main nave, with its towering roof, looks as if it will stand for another 500 years. During the restoration, I watched muralists painting the marvelous trompe l'oeil that extends the perspective of the nave. Note the Tiffany grandfather clock (in working order), dating from the 1820s, on the far right. On the left side, inset into the walls, are the morbid remains of Teodoro—a Franciscan brother of high regard—pickled in glass jars next to a statue of St. Francis. Members of the most aristocratic families of the times were buried in the crypt, which includes the body of Capitan Don Luís de Velasco, heroic defender of the Castillo de los Tres Reyes de Morro, who fell in battle during the British attack on Havana in 1762. You may peer into the crypts through a glass window in the terra-cotta tile floor.

Unfortunately, the sumptuously adorned altars are gone, replaced by a huge crucifix suspended above a grand piano. Yes, the nave has metamorphosed into a concert hall; the music program is posted in the entrance. Performances (usually classical) are given each Saturday at 6 p.m. and Sunday at 11 a.m.

The nave opens to the right onto the cloisters of a convent, to which the church belonged (it had 111 cells for members of the religious community). Today it contains the **Museo de Arte Religioso,** featuring fabulous silverwork, porcelain, and other treasures of the Spanish epoch, including a room full of ornately gilded hymnals of silver and even mother-of-pearl displayed in glass cases. In the late 1840s, the liberal government expropriated and secularized the property, which became a customs office, a post office, and, in this century, a warehouse serving the nearby wharfs. A music school occupies part of the building. The church and museum are open daily 9 a.m.-7 p.m. Entrance costs US$2 plus US$1 extra for the campanile, which offers marvelous views of the city (cameras cost US$2 extra; videos cost US$10).

South of the Plaza

Dating from the 16th century, the beautiful colonial buildings on Calle Oficios south of the plaza possess a marked Mudejar style, exemplified by their wooden balconies. The entire block has been magnificently restored and many of the buildings converted into art galleries. What a remake! One of the gems is the pink and green **Casa de Carmen Montilla,** 50 meters south of the square. Only the front of the house remains, but the architects have made creative use of the empty shell. Through the breezy doorway, you can catch sight of a fabulous 3-D mural by famous Cuban artist Alfredo Sosabravo at the back of an open-air sculpture garden. Fabulous art is portrayed within, in the two-level art gallery, and next door is the **Estudio Galerai Los Oficios,** offering revolving art exhibitions; open Mon.-Sat. 9:30 a.m.-5 p.m. Entry is free.

Further south, the 19th-century building housing the **Asemblea Provincial Poder Popular** (the local government office) was being restored at press time. The interior lobby is striking for its ornate baroque and neoclassical stucco work.

In spring 1999, a railway carriage—the *Mambi*—was parked on rails on the narrow lane between the convent and the Asemblea. Apparently, it will become a museum, but of what I don't know.

CALLES MERCADERES

Intimate Calle Mercaderes links Plaza de Armas with Plaza Vieja, four blocks south. Now restored to grandeur, it brims with handsome buildings and museums of interest.

The block immediately south of Calle Obispo and the Hotel Ambos Mundos includes the **Tienda de las Navegantes,** Mercaderes #117, a beautiful wood- and glass-fronted building featuring a ship's wheel inlaid with a copper galleon above the door. This incongruously positioned store sells maps and nautical charts, including the best selection of road and city maps available in Cuba. A hearse-size glass case contains a three-meter-long scale model of the *Juan Sebastian Elcano,* made in 1928 for La Compañia Transatlantica de Barcelona.

Across the street are the **Casa de Puerto Rico** and **Casa del Tabaco,** both at Mercaderes

#120. Besides a fine stock of cigars, the latter also houses the **Museum of Tobacco,** tel. (61) 5795, upstairs. The first room, part of which is decorated as a typical middle-class sitting room, with rocking chairs and a cigar displayed on a silver ashtray, contains a collection of lithos from cigar-box covers. Other exhibits include pipes and lighters from around the world. Look out for the stunning silver cigar box engraved with script that reads: "To my godfather Dr. Fidel Castro Ruz from Fidel Charles Getto, August 9, 1959." Open Tues.-Sat. 10 a.m.-5:30 p.m., Sunday 9 a.m.-1 p.m.; no entrance charge.

At the end of the block, at the corner of Obrapía, the pink building with a wraparound wrought-iron balustrade and Mexican flag fluttering above the doorway is the **Casa de Benito Juárez,** housing the Sociedad Cubano Mexicana de Relaciones Culturales, tel. (61) 8166, marvelously displaying artwork and costumes from different Mexican states. Open Tues.-Sat. 10:30 a.m.-5:30 p.m., Sunday 9 a.m.-1 p.m. Entrance costs US$1. The house faces a tiny landscaped *plazuela,* containing a larger-than-life bronze statue of Simón Bolívar atop a marble pedestal and a fabulous mural behind.

On the next block is the **Museo de Asia,** tel. (63) 9740, which downstairs seems unimpressive, holding a few inlaid bowls, rugs, musical instruments, and a marble model of the Taj Mahal. The best rooms are upstairs, containing an astonishing array of carved ivory, silverware, mother-of-pearl furniture, scimitars, kukris, and other Oriental armaments, plus exquisite kimonos. Most of the collection comprises gifts to Fidel from Asian nations. The foyer features an engraved rock—a gift from the citizens of Hiroshima. The museum also includes a small bonsai garden, and one of the rooms downstairs doubles as a school class, a crafty ploy to remind visitors of the success of Cuba's education program. Open Tues.-Sat. 10 a.m.-5:30 p.m., Sunday 9 a.m.-1 p.m. Entry costs US$1 (plus US$2 for a camera, US$10 for video).

Half a block south is a sign for the **Armería 19 de Abril,** Mercaderes #157, tel. (61) 8080, no longer a museum (the collection is now incorporated into the Museo de la Revolución) but important in contemporary history, for here four members of MR-26-7 were killed in an assault on the armory on 9 April 1959. A sign outside reads,

"Armaments Company of Cuba, hunting supplies and explosives." The company was a subsidiary of DuPont, the US munitions giant.

Across the street is **Casa del Libertador Simón Bolívar,** Mercaderes #156, tel. 61- 3988, housing the Venezuelan embassy and containing the **Museo de Simón Bolívar,** which displays cultural works and art from Venezuela (open Tues.-Sat. 10 a.m.-5 p.m., US$1).

If heading down to Plaza Vieja, check out the stunning lobby in the building on the southwest corner of Mercaderes and Amargura. Now part of the **Banco de Crédito y Comercio,** the lobby is a mix of art nouveau and neoclassical, with a dramatic skylight.

CALLE OBRAPIA

The two blocks of Calle Obrapia between Oficios and San Ignacio contain several beautifully restored buildings of historic appeal. The street is named for the *obra pía* (pious act) of Don Martín Calvo de la Puerta, who devoted a portion of his wealth to sponsoring five orphan girls every year.

The most important building is the **Casa de la Obra Pía,** Obrapia 158, tel. (61) 3097. This splendid mansion with lemon-meringue-yellow walls on the northwest corner of Obrapia and Mercaderes was owned by the Calvo de Puertas family, one of the most important families in Cuba in early colonial days. It dates from the early 17th century, with additions in baroque style, such as voluptuous moldings and dimpled cherubs, as late as 1793. Visitors can see the arms of the Castellón family (which bought the house after Martín Calvo de la Puerto's death), surrounded by exuberant baroque stonework, emblazoned above the carved entrance of regal proportions. As much as any house in Habana Vieja, Casa de la Obra Pía exemplifies the Spanish adaptation of a Moorish inner courtyard, with a serene, scented coolness illuminated by daylight filtering through *mediopuntos* fanning out like a peacock's tail. It features a permanent exhibition of works by Alejo Carpentier in the foyer; other rooms contain miscellaneous art. Open Tues.-Sun. 9:30 a.m.-2:30 p.m.; entrance US$1.

Across the way is the **Casa de África,** Obrapia #157 e/ Mercaderes y San Ignacio, tel.

(61) 5798. When flung open wide, its large wooden doors reveal breezy courtyards full of African artwork and artifacts, masks, and cloth. On the third floor, you'll find a fabulous collection of paraphernalia used in *santería,* including statues of the leading deities in the Yoruban pantheon, dancing costumes of the Abakuá, and *otanes* (stones) in which the *orishas* (the gods of *santería*) are said to reside. Much of the collection was contributed by the 17 African embassies in Havana. The museum guides are well versed, but for a more in-depth recitation, ask for the museum's director, Claudia Mola Fernández, or the curator, Raísa Fornaguera. Open Mon.-Sat. 10:30 a.m.-5 p.m., Sunday 9:30 a.m.-1 p.m. Entrance costs US$2.

One block farther west, at the corner of Calle Cuba, the **Casa de Gaspar Riveros de Vasoncelos** is esteemed for its corner balcony with delicately curved balustrades. Though restored in 1985, it is not open to the public. Between Mercaderes and Oficios is the **Casa Guayasamú,** Obrapia 111, housing a museum of plastic arts and photographs from Ecuador, with changing exhibitions of art from other Latin American countries. A huge dugout canoe sits in the entrance lobby. Open Tues.-Sat. 10:30 a.m.-5:30 p.m., Sunday 9 a.m.-1 p.m. Entrance costs US$1.

PLAZA VIEJA AND VICINITY

The last of the four resplendent main squares in Habana Vieja is Plaza Vieja, the old commercial square (bounded by Calles Mercaderes, San Ignacio, Brasil, and Muralla), surrounded by mansions and apartment blocks from where residents could look down on processions, executions, bullfights, and wild fiestas. The plaza originally hosted a market where peasants and free Negroes sold all manner of produce. At its center sat a stone fountain, with a wide bowl and four dolphins that gushed "intermittent streams of thick, muddy liquid which Negro water vendors eagerly collected in barrels to be sold throughout the city," recorded a French visitor in the 19th century.

Lamentably, President Machado built an underground car park here in the 1930s, and the cobbles and fountain fell afoul of the wrecking ball. Time and neglect brought near ruin this century, and many of the square's beautiful buildings sank into a sorry state of disrepair. Fortunately, Eusebio Leal and his maestros have waved a magic wand over the plaza, which was in the midst of being restored to former grandeur in early 1999. Even the fountain has reappeared, now gurgling clear water. *Magnificent!* Renowned for its acoustics, the square is often used for concerts.

A café, a bar, and a fashion boutique have opened, and soon enough, two hotels, a cinema (**Cine Habana**), and a classy bar (**Taberna Benny Moré**) featuring the personal effects of renowned composer and singer Benny Moré will be added. On the east side of the square is the headquarters of **Fototeca,** tel. (62) 2530, the state-run agency that promotes the work of Cuban photographers, which offers international photo exhibitions in the Salón Nacional de Fotografia. It's open Tues.-Sat. 10 a.m.-5 p.m.

The most important building, on the south side of the square, is the **Casa de los Condes de Jaruco,** an impressively restored 18th-century structure highlighted by mammoth doors opening into a cavernous entrance hall. It was built between 1733 and 1737 by the father of the future Count of Jaruco, who gave the building its name. Today it houses several magnificent *galerias* and boutiques under the umbrella of the **Fondo Cubano de Bienes Culturales** (BFC), tel. (62) 3577, the organization responsible for the sale of Cuban art. The BFC headquarters is upstairs, in rooms off the balcony. Whimsical murals are painted on the walls, touched in splashy color by the undulating play of light through *mediopuntos* and by the shifting of shadows through *rejas.* Upstairs, various galleries sell an eclectic range of creative arts and crafts. The downstairs is occupied by three galleries, including the **Galeria Pequeño Formato,** with some fascinating miniature modernist paintings and sculptures. A *joyeria* next to the entrance sells high-class jewelry by Raúl Valladares. In the inner courtyard, surrounded by lofty archways festooned with hanging vines, visitors can snack at wrought-iron tables.

On the northwest corner is the **Casa de las Hermanas Cárdenas,** recently restored with faux brickwork and marble. The building—named for two sisters, María Loreto and María

Ignacia Cárdenas, who lived here in the late 18th century—houses the **Centro de Desarollo de Artes Visuales,** tel. (62) 3533 or (62) 2611. Through the towering doors, immediately on the left, is a craft workshop where young women can be seen making cloth dolls and naive animals gaudily painted in the pointillist fashion now common throughout the Caribbean. The inner courtyard is dominated by an intriguing sculpture—a kind of futuristic skyscraper in miniature—crafted by Alfredo Sosabravo. Art education classes are given on the second floor, reached via a wide wooden staircase that leads to the top story, where you'll find an art gallery in a wonderfully airy loft. If the tiny yellow door is locked, ask for the key downstairs. Open Tues.-Sat. 10 a.m.-5:30 p.m.

Next door is the **Casa del Conde de San Estéban de Cañongo,** at San Ignacio #356. This former mansion of a nobleman today houses an intriguing artisans' factory—**Artesanías Para Turismo Taller**—where workers use stems of the *malanbueta* plant to weave baskets, wall hangings, and dozens of other items. The supervisor, Ana Ester García Calbert, will be happy to give you a guided tour (in Spanish). You can watch the acid being squeezed from the thick reeds, which are pressed into flat yet flexible fibers woven into durable mats on simple looms worked by a foot pedal. Other workers sit to the side conjuring the stems into baskets, purses, *zapatas* (shoes), and intriguing wall hangings depicting scenes of old Havana. The items are not for sale here, but you'll be directed to various *tiendas artesanias* (including El Travesí, next door to El Floridita restaurant).

The old **Palacio Vienna Hotel** (also called the Palacio Cueto), on the southeast corner of Plaza Viejo, is a phenomenal piece of Gaudiesque art nouveau architecture, fabulously ornate and dating from 1906. The frontage is awash in surf-like waves and ballooning balconies. It is scheduled for renovation.

Physicians and scientists inclined to a busman's holiday might walk one block west and one north of the plaza and check out the impressive **Museo Histórico de las Ciencias Carlos Finlay,** Cuba #460, tel. (63) 4824, between Amargura and Brasil. The building, which dates from 1868 and housed the Royal Academy of Sciences, today contains a pharmaceutical collection and tells the tales of various Cuban scientists' discoveries and innovations. The Cuban scientist Dr. Finlay is honored, of course, for it was he who discovered that yellow fever is transmitted by the Aedes aegipti mosquito. The museum also contains a medical library of 95,000 volumes. Albert Einstein spoke here in 1930. Open Mon.-Fri. 8:30 a.m.-5 p.m., Saturday 8:30 a.m.-3 p.m. Entrance is US$2.

The church immediately north of the museum, across Lamparilla, is the **Iglesia de San Agustín,** built in 1633 but much altered since. It was consecrated anew in 1842 when it was given to the Franciscans after they lost their tenure at the Church of Saint Francis of Assisi in the eponymous square. Unlike other churches in Havana, this one bears the influence of the Augustine monks who came to Cuba from Mexico, imbuing their own style with rich Mexican murals. The curves and countercurves of the undulating pinion facade likewise is of Mexican influence. The church also boasts a fine organ and six altars.

PLAZA DEL CRISTO

The disheveled Plaza del Cristo lies at the west end of Amargua, between Lamparilla and Brasil, two blocks east of Avenida de Bélgica (Monserrate). During the 19th century, the square was named for "the washerwomen," a lively and colorful clique of black women who washed others' clothes for a living and congregated here to seek custom from the wealthy merchants leaving the church after Mass. It was here that Wormold, the vacuum-cleaner salesman turned secret agent, was "swallowed up among the pimps and lottery sellers of the Havana noon" in Graham Greene's *Our Man in Havana.* Wormold and his wayward daughter Millie lived at 37 Lamparilla. Alas, the house was fictional.

The square is slated to receive a complete restoration.It is dominated by the tiny, utterly charming **Iglesia de Santo Cristo Buen Viaje.** This church is one of Havana's oldest, dating from 1732, but with a Franciscan hermitage—called Humilladero chapel—dating from 1640. Buen Viaje was the final point of the *Vía Crucis* (the Procession of the Cross) held each Lenten Friday and beginning at the Iglesia de San Francisco de Asís. The church, which is in a splendid state of repair and has an impressive cross-beamed wooden ceiling and stained-glass windows, was named for its popularity among sailors and travelers, who used to pray in it for safe voyages. It contains several exquisite little altars, including one to the Virgen de la Caridad showing the three boatsmen being saved from the tempest. Open daily 9 a.m.-noon.

If hungry, call in at the **Restaurante Hanoi,** on Calle Brasil (Teniente Rey) and Bernanza, at the southwest corner of the square, tel. (57) 1029. The restaurant is in one of the oldest houses in Havana and is colloquially known as La Casa de la Parre (Grapevine House) for the luxuriant grapevine growing in the patio.

THE ECCLESIASTICAL CORE

Southern Habana Vieja is worth visiting for its 18th-century ecclesiastical buildings, concentrated within a few blocks in the heart of the region.

Closest to the colonial core to the north, midway along Calle Brasil at Compostela, two blocks east of Plaza del Cristo, you'll find the handsome **Iglesia y Convento de Santa Teresa de Jesús,** the third of Havana's monasteries. Built by the Carmalites in 1705, the separate church and convent both have outstanding baroque doorways. The church has ever since performed its original function (call in on Saturday afternoon, when Afro-Cuban music and dance is hosted in the courtyard), although the convent ceased to operate as such in 1929, when the nuns were moved out and the building was converted into a series of homes.

Across the road, on the east side of Compostela, is the **Farmácia Roturno Permanente** (formerly the Drogerría Sarrá), whose magnificently carved wooden shelves seem more fitting as the altarwork for the church across the way. The paneled shelves bear painted glass murals and are stocked with herbs and pharmaceuticals in colorful old bottles and ceramic jars.

Three blocks south on Compostela is the **Iglesia y Convento de Nuestra Señora de Belén,** a huge complex occupying the block between Calles Luz and Acosta, and Compostela and Aguacate. Until recently, it was a derelict shell. The convent was built to house the first nuns who arrived in Havana in 1704. Construction took from 1712 to 1718. The first baroque religious structure erected in Havana, it served as a refuge for poor convalescents under the tenure of Bishop Compostela. In 1842, Spanish authorities ejected the religious order—the Order of Bethlehem—and turned the church briefly into a government office before making it over to the Jesuits. They in turn established a college for the sons of the aristocracy here. Famously, it is linked to contiguous buildings across the street by an arched walkway—the **Arch of Bethlehem,** unfortunately in decrepit condition—spanning Acosta. As you enter, note the ornate facade decorated with a nativity scene set in a large niche framed with a shell. The United Nations and the Swiss government are helping pay for its restoration. The church will supposedly become a religious community again, while a portion of the building will house a home for the aged. Part of the cloisters is slated to become a hotel.

Two blocks east of Belén, on Calle Cuba between Luz and Sol, you'll discover the **Convento de Santa Clara de Asís,** tel. (61) 3335, fax (33) 5696, a massive nunnery—the first in Havana—begun in 1638 and completed in 1644. It also once was a slaughterhouse and later housed hundreds of nuns and slaves. It was a refuge for girls unfortunate enough to possess an insufficient dowry to attract suitors. Only thus could the hapless females preserve their self-respect. It is a remarkable building, with a lobby full

Iglesia y Convento de Nuestra Señora de Belén

RECOMMENDED WALKING TOUR 4

From Parque Central, head east one block to **Plazuela de Albear** and turn south, passing El Floridita (which we'll save for later). Follow **Monserrate** for six blocks or so (it becomes Egido en route) to the **Agropecuario Egido,** the farmers' market. Continue south to the **Estación Central de Ferrocarril** (the main railway station) and, facing it, the **Casa Natal de José Martí** (Martí's birthplace).

Continue down Egido past the **Cortina de los Muralles,** the remains of the old city walls, and turn left onto Desamparados.

Turn up Cuba and visit the **Iglesia y Convento de Nuestra Señora de la Merced.** Return to Desamparados for the **Iglesia de San Francisco de Paula** (be careful crossing the street here), then continue north along **Avenida del Puerto** and the **Alameda de Paula.**

At the end of the Alameda, follow Calle Acosta west to **Iglesia Parroquial del Espíritu Santo.** Then follow Calle Cuba north three blocks to the **Convento y Iglesia de Santa Clara.**

Calle Luz then takes you west to the **Iglesia y Convento de Belén,** from where you'll turn north along Compostela three blocks to the **Iglesia y Conventode Santa Teresa.**

From here, follow Brasil (Teniente Rey) west three blocks to the **Plaza del Cristo.** Return to Monserrate (one block west on Brasil) and turn right.

End your walk at **El Floridita** with a well-earned daiquiri.

of beautiful period pieces. Its inner and outer cloistered courtyard, awash in divine light, is surrounded by columns, one of which is entwined by the roots of a *capulí* tree, whose fruits resemble large golden pearls and taste ambrosial. Steady yourself before gazing up at the breathtaking cloister roof carved with geometric designs: a classic *alfarje*. Indeed, stunning wooden carvings abound. The second cloister contains the so-called Sailor's House, built by a wealthy pirate—he later became a respectable shipowner—for his daughter, whom he failed to dissuade from a life of asceticism. It's open Mon.-Fri. 9 a.m.-4 p.m.; entrance US$1.

The convent has been restored to pristine condition and now, fittingly, houses the **Centro Nacional de Conservación y Museología,** plus nine charming rooms for rent. The center offers courses for architects, planners, conservationists, and the like. A café serves basic refreshments. Peek inside the **Salon Plenario,** a marble-floored hall with a lofty beamed wooden ceiling of imposing stature and used to teach classes in international culture.

Havana's oldest church, the **Iglesia Parroquial del Espíritu Santo,** lies two blocks south of Santa Clara de Asís, at the corner of Calles Cuba and Acosta. The church, which dates from 1638 (the circa 1674 central nave and facade, and circa 1720 Gothic vault are later additions), was originally a hermitage "for the devotions of free Negroes." Later, continuing in liberal tradition, King Charles III issued a royal decree giving the right of asylum here to anyone hunted by the authorities (a privilege no longer bestowed today). The church reveals many surprises, including a gilded, carved wooden pelican in a niche in the baptistery. The sacristy, where parish archives dating back through the 17th century are preserved, boasts an enormous cupboard full of baroque silver staffs and incense holders. Catacombs to each side of the nave are held up by subterranean tree trunks. While exploring the eerie vault that runs under the chapel, peek between the niches (still containing the odd bone) and you will see, almost erased by time and damp, a series of paintings of skeletons crowned with tiaras and holding mitres. They represent the dance of death. One look is enough to send you scurrying to escape what Juliet Barclay called a "grim place full of bones, dust and spiders." The body of Bishop Gerónimo Valdés had been laid to rest in the church. He remained in a kind of limbo, his whereabouts unknown, until he turned up, buried under the floor, during a restoration in 1936. Today, he rests in a tomb beside the nave, which boasts a carved wooden altar. The sturdy tower holds four bells. Steps lead up to the gallery, where you may turn the handle of a carillon.

Finally, two blocks south on Calle Cuba, is another small handsome church—**Iglesia y Convento de Nuestra Señora de la Merced**—tucked into the corner of Cuba and Calle Merced.

Trompe l'oeil frescoes add color to the ornate interior, which contains romantic dome paintings (added during a remodeling in 1904) and an alcove lined with fake stalactites in honor of Nuestra Señora de Lourdes. It is one of the most resplendent of the city's church interiors. The church, begun in 1755, has strong Afro-Cuban connections, and it is not unusual to see devotees of *santería* kneeling in prayer. In its heyday, it was the favored church for weddings of the aristocracy. Try to time your visit for 24 September, when scores of gaily colored worshippers cram in for the Virgen de la Merced's feast day. More modest celebrations are held on the 24th of each other month.

AVENIDA SAN PEDRO (DESAMPARADOS)

South of the Plaza de San Francisco, Havana's waterfront boulevard swings along the harborfront, changing names as it curves (Avenida San Pedro, Leonor Pérez) and overshadowed by portside warehouses and sailors' bars.

The Fundación Destilera Havana Club, or **Museo de Ron,** was under construction at press time in a harborfront colonial mansion on San Pedro, between Churruca and Sol. It will host an audiovisual presentation on the history and production of Cuban rums, with a free rum sampling to boot. A mini-production unit is to be installed that will demonstrate the process, from the growing of sugarcane and fermentation to the distillation and aging process that results in some of the world's finest rums. A bar—**Bar Havana Club**—will let you tipple the wares. Open 9:30 a.m.-6 p.m. (the bar will be open 11 a.m.-2 a.m.).

Be sure to call at **Dos Hermanos,** the simple bar at the foot of Sol once favored by Hemingway and, in earlier days, by Spanish poet Frederick García Lorca. A strong *mojito* will provide a pick-me-up and steel you for a close look at the harbor, named by the United Nations as one of the world's 10 most polluted. When the tides ebb sufficient to draw out the harbor waters, petroleum scums the ocean fronting the Malecón, and the stench hangs over the port city like Banquo's ghost. This is nothing new—the plight dates back to prerevolutionary days, when, Hemingway wrote, "the smoke blew straight across

the sky from the tall chimneys of the Havana Electric Company and . . . the water was as black and greasy as the pumpings from the bottom of the tanks of an oil tanker . . . and the scum of the harbor lay along the sides blacker than the creosote of the pilings and foul as an unclean sewer." Nothing has changed, though a cleanup is supposedly in the works.

Further south, at the junction with Calle Oficios, San Pedro takes a name change: Leonor Pérez, which runs alongside the **Alameda de Paula.** The Alameda, a 100-meter-long raised promenade, is the first such boulevard within the ancient city walls. Lined with marble and iron street lamps, on weekdays it's the setting for alfresco tuition and physical education for schoolkids. Bring your camera. Midway along the Alameda stands a carved column with a fountain at its base, erected in 1847 to pay homage to the Spanish navy, although it bears an unlikely Irish name: **Columna O'Donnell,** named for the Capitan-General of Cuba, Leopoldo O'Donnell, who dedicated the monument. It is covered in relief work on a military theme and crowned by a lion with the arms of Spain in its claws.

Leonor Pérez leads south to **Plazuela de Paula,** a small circular plaza with the **Iglesia de San Francisco de Paula** in the middle of the road. This twee little place was abandoned ages ago as a church and today houses a little museum full of oil paintings and oversized photographs of early-20th-century bands. It is also used for the study of popular Cuban music. Note the national hymn, "La Bayamesa," inscribed in metal on the interior wall to the left. It was in the midst of restoration in early 1999.

West of the plazuela, at the foot of Calle San Isidro, were the old P&O docks where the ships from Miami and Key West used to dock and where Pan American World Airways had its terminal when it was still flying the old clipper flyingboats. Before World War II, when the US Navy took over the docks, San Isidro had been the great whorehouse street of the waterfront. According to Hemingway, many of the women were Europeans. After the war, the Navy closed the brothels and "shipped all the whores back to Europe. Many people were sad after the ships had gone and San Isidro had never recovered. . . . There were gay streets in Havana and there were some very tough streets and tough quarters, such as Jesús y María, which was just a short distance away. But this part of town was just sad as it had been ever since the whores had gone."

South of the plazuela, the harborfront boulevard becomes Desamparados, which runs south to the **Cortina de la Habana,** a remnant section of the old fortress wall enclosing Habana Vieja in colonial days. Desamparados continues south from here past the docks to the Vía Blanca, the road for San Francisco de Paula, Regla, and Playas del Este. One hundred meters south of the Cortina, you'll see a monument made of twisted metal parts—fragments of *La Coubre,* the French cargo ship that exploded in Havana harbor on 4 March 1960 (the vessel was carrying armaments for the Castro government, and it is generally assumed that the CIA or other counterrevolutionaries blew it up). The **Monumento Mártires del Vapor La Coubre** honors the seamen who died in the explosion.

AVENIDA DE BÉLGICA (EGIDO)

Avenida de Bélgica, colloquially called Egido, follows the hollow once occupied by Habana Vieja's ancient walls. It is a continuation of Monserrate and flows downhill from two blocks east of Parque de la Fraternidad to the harbor. It has the appearance of being rundown, but a closer look reveals that it is lined with beautiful buildings constructed during the urbanization that followed demolition of the walls. Though built during the mid-19th century, the buildings have the appearance of being much older, as with the **Palacio de la Contesa de Villalba,** a Renaissance-style edifice facing onto the **Plazuela de los Ursulinos.** Similarly, the **Palacio de los Marqueses de Balboa,** one block south, speaks of erstwhile beauty through a layer of grime and decay.

The street's masterpiece is the **Estación Central de Ferrocarril,** Havana's impressive Venetian-style railway station, at the corner of Calle Arsenal. Sitting on rails in its lobby is an 1843-model steam locomotive called *La Junta,* said to have been Cuba's first. The station was designed in 1910 by a North American architect, blending Spanish Revival and Italian Renaissance styles. It is built atop what was once the Arsenal, or Spanish naval shipyard.

On the station's north side is a small shady plaza—**Parque de los Agrimensores** (Park of

HAVANA'S CITY WALLS

Construction of Havana's fortified city walls began on 3 February 1674. They ran along the western edge of the bay and, on the landward side, stood between today's Calle Egido, Monserrate, and Zulueta according to a plan by Spanish engineer Cristóbal de Rodas. To pay for construction, the Court of Spain voted an annual budget from the Royal Chests of Mexico and even decreed a tax on wine sold in Havana's taverns.

Under the direction of engineer Juan de Siscaras, African slaves labored for 23 years to build the 1.4-meter-thick, 10-meter-tall city wall that was intended to ring the entire city using rocks hauled in from the coast. The 4,892-meter-long wall was completed in 1697, with a small opening for the mooring of ships, and a perimeter of five km. The damage inflicted by the British artillery in 1762 was repaired in 1797, when the thick wall attained its final shape. It formed an irregular polygon with nine defensive bastions with sections of wall in-between, and moats and steep drops to delay assault by enemy troops.

It was protected by 180 cannons and garrisoned with 3,400 troops. In its first stage, it had just two entrances (nine more were added later), opened each morning upon the sound of a single cannon and closed at night the same way.

As time went on, the *intramuros* (the city within the walls) burst its confines. In 1841, Havana authorities petitioned the Spanish Crown for permission to demolish the walls. Just 123 years after the walls went up, they came down again. The demolition began in 1863, when African slave-convicts were put to work to destroy what their forefathers had built under hard labor. The demolition wasn't completed until well into the 20th century.

Regrettably, only fragments remain, most notably at the junction of Calle Egido and Avenida del Puerto, near the railway station at Avenida del Puerto and Egido, and at Monserrate and Teniente Rey streets. Sentry boxes still stand in front of the Presidential Palace, between Calles Monserrate and Zulueta, and at the west end of Calle Tacón.

the Surveyors)—pinned by a large remnant of the old city wall.

A shining star in southern Habana Vieja's constellation is the **Casa Natal de José Martí,** Leonor Pérez #314 (also called Calle Paula), tel. (62) 3778, at the junction with Egido and facing the railway station. This simple house—painted ocher, with green windows and door frames and terracotta tile floors—is a shrine for Cuban schoolchildren. They flock to pay homage to Cuba's National Hero, who was born on 28 January 1853 and spent the first four years of his life here. As you may imagine, the house and museum are splendidly kept. The entrance lobby displays letters from Martí in glass cases and a beautiful bronze bust on a simple wooden pedestal. Many of his personal effects are here, too, including a beautiful lacquered *escritorio* (writing desk) and a broad-brimmed Panama hat given to him by Ecuadorian President Eloy Alfaro (Panama hats don't come from the country of Panama—they're made in Ecuador). Many of his original texts, poems, and sketches are on display. There's even a lock of the hero's hair from when he was only four years old. There are more guides (one per room) than you can shake a stick at. They follow you around creepily, although at a discreet distance. Open Tues.-Sat. 9 a.m.-5 p.m., Sunday 9 a.m.-1 p.m. Entrance US$1 (US$1 extra for guides, US$2 for cameras, US$10 for videos). The building across the street houses a *Salón de Expocisiones,* where piano recitals and other cultural activities are hosted.

Egido slopes south to the Cortina de la Habana at the junction with Desamparados, and is lined with remnants of the **Murallas de Habana,** the original city walls. Just north of Desamparados is the **Puerta de la Tenaza,** the only ancient city gate still standing. Here a plaque inset within a still extant remnant of the old wall shows a map of the old city and the extent of the original walls and fortifications.

PARQUE HISTÓRICO MORRO Y CABAÑA

Looming over Habana Vieja, on the north side of the harbor channel, is the rugged cliff face of the Cabaña, dominated by two great fortresses that constitute **Morro-Cabaña Historical Park,**

tel. (62) 7653. Together, the castles comprise the largest and most powerful defensive complex built by the Spanish in the Americas. It is very windy up here, but the views over Habana Vieja and toward Vedado are spectacular, especially at dawn and dusk. Maintained in a superb state, the two castles are must-sees on any visitor's itinerary (you should visit by both day and night).

The first military structure dated back to 1563, when Governor Diego de Mazariegos ordered a tower built on the *morro* (headland) to extend the vision from the heights and to serve as a reference for galleons. To aid in navigation, the tower was whitewashed. Cannons and a sentry post were later added. However, Havana's treasures were never safe from marauding pirates, against which the feeble tower (and the Castillo de la Real Fuerza, below on the harbor channel) proved inconsequential. Thus, in 1589 King Philip II approved construction of a fortress: the Castillo de los Tres Reyes del Morro.

Entrance to the park ostensibly costs US$1 (entrance to the castles is extra), but no charge was being levied in spring 1999.

The Cabaña looms over the village of **Casablanca,** which clings to the shore on the northeast side of Havana harbor, in the easterly lee of the Castillo de San Carlos de la Cabaña. Casablanca's narrow main street is overhung with balconies, and from here tiers of houses rise up the hillside. Today, a few rusting freighters sit in dry dock, and fishing boats bob along the waterfront. Casablanca is also fascinating as the departure point for the "Hershey Train," a three-car passenger train once belonging to the Hershey-Cuban Railroad.

Getting There: Visitors arriving by car reach Loma Cabaña via the tunnel (no pedestrians) that descends beneath the Máximo Gómez Monument off Avenida de Céspedes. The well-signed exit for the Morro and Castillo San Carlos is immediately on your right after exiting the tunnel on the north side of the harbor. Buses from Parque de la Fraternidad pass through the tunnel and will drop you by the fortress access road (the *ciclobus* permits bicycles).

You can also get there by day by taking the little ferry that bobs its way across Havana harbor to Casablanca every 20 minutes or so from the Muelle la Luz (10 centavos) on the south side of the Terminal Sierra Maestra, at the foot of Calle

Santa Clara. From here you can walk uphill (it's a steep 10-minute climb) to an easterly entrance gate to the Foso de los Laureles in the Cabaña. However, the easterly access gate closes at dusk, so don't take this route if you plan on seeing the *cañonazo.*

Casablanca is also reached by car from the Vía Monumental; the exit is marked about one km east of the tunnel. The road follows the eastern ridge of the *cabaña* and switchbacks down to Casablanca.

Castillo de los Tres Reyes del Morro

This handsome, ghost-white castle, tel. (63) 7941, is built into the rocky palisades of Punta Barlovento, crowning a rise that drops straight to the sea at the entrance to Havana's narrow harbor channel. Canted in its articulation, the fort—whose construction began in 1589—follows a tradition of military architecture established by the Milanese at the end of the Middle Ages. It forms an irregular polygon that follow the contours of the rocky headland on which it was built, with a sharp-angled bastion at the apex, stone walls 10 feet thick, and a series of batteries stepping down to the shore. Hundreds of slaves toiled under the lash of whip and heat of the sun to cut the stone *in situ,* extracted from the void that forms the moats. El Morro took 40 years to complete and served its job well, repelling countless pirate attacks and withstanding for 44 days a siege by British cannon in 1762.

The castle has been marvelously restored to former glory and has lost none of its commanding composure, with plentiful cannons on trolleys in their embrasures. A still-functioning lighthouse was constructed beside the fortress in 1844.

Originally the castle connected with the outside world principally by sea, to which it was linked via the **Plataforma de la Estrella,** the wharf at the southern foot of the cliff. Today you enter via a drawbridge across the deep moat that leads through a long tunnel—the **Tunel de Aspillerado**—to the vast wooden gates. The gates open to the **Camino de Rondas,** a small parade ground (Plaza de Armas) with, to the right, a narrow entrance to the **Baluarte de Austria** (Austrian Bastion), a covered area with cannon embrasures for firing down on the moat (it is named for the period when the Austrian House of

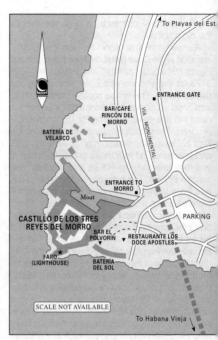

Hapsburgs ruled Spain). A cobbled ramp—also to the right—leads up from the plaza to the **Baluarte de Tejeda,** a wide, windswept platform with further embrasures and a splendid view east past the **Batería de Velasco** (with cannons added in the 19th century) and along the coast. On the seaward side of the Tejeda Bastion (named for the governor and military leader who began work on the castle), you can look down into the crevasse caused by the explosion that breached the Caballero del Mar wall in the 1762 siege by the British. Various plaques inset in the bastion commemorate heroic figures of the siege—even the Royal Navy is honored on a plaque placed by the British Embassy. From here you can walk the curtain wall where rusting cannons of the **Morrillo** (High Battery) are in place, with the Low Battery on the level below. Do not be tempted to walk the wind-battered battlements, which are canted seaward and have no guardrails. One false step, and you could easily tumble onto the wave-swept rocks below.

To the left of the Plaza de Armas is the **Surtida de los Tinajones,** where giant earthenware vases

PARQUE HISTÓRICO MORRO-LA CABAÑA

are inset in stone. They once contained rape-seed oil as fuel for the 15-meter-tall lighthouse, reached by a small ramp over the *surtida*. The original wood-fired lantern was eventually replaced by one fueled by rapeseed; then, in 1928, by an acetylene lantern; and, finally in 1945 an electric lantern that still flashes its light every 15 seconds, sending a beam 18 miles long.

The Camino de Rondas surrounds a central building built in 1763 atop the cisterns that supplied the garrison of 1,000 men with water. The galleries of this two-story structure are now exhibition rooms, including the **Museo Navigación** with expositions on the colonial sea voyages of Portugal and Spain. Another room exhibits relics recovered from the bottom of Havana harbor, including mementos from the USS *Maine,* which mysteriously exploded in the harbor on 5 February 1898, providing a pretext for US entry into the Spanish-Cuban war.

All maritime traffic in and out of Havana harbor is controlled (as it has been since 1888) from the **Sala de la Estación Semafórica,** the semaphore station atop the castle, accessed via the Baluarte de Tejeda. With luck, Fernando, the station master, may invite you in to scan the city using his 20 x 120-power Nikon binoculars. Note the flagpole outside: it was used to signal information to the city fortresses and harbormasters about approaching traffic. It was here, too, that the English raised the Union Jack to proclaim their capture of Cuba—and where the Spanish flag was raised again one year later. The flagpole came to take on political significance, so it was here that the Stars and Stripes replaced the flag of Spain when the latter came down for the last time in 1898. Today, the tradition of adorning the flagpole with multicolored signal flags is continued on public holidays.

Below the castle, facing the city on the landward side and reached by a cobbled ramp, is the **Battery of the Twelve Apostles.** It boasts massive cannons and a splendid little bar—El Polvorín (The Powderhouse)—and restaurant.

The Morro is open daily 9 a.m.-8 p.m. (entrance US$2, plus US$1 for a guide, US$2 for cameras, US$5 for videos). Entry to the lighthouse ostensibly costs US$2 extra.

CHE GUEVARA

Ernesto "Che" Guevara was born into a leftist middle-class family in Rosario, Argentina, in 1928. He received a medical degree from the University of Buenos Aires in 1953, then set out on an eight-month motorcycle odyssey through South America that had a profound influence on his radical thinking.

In 1954, he spent a brief period working as a volunteer doctor in Guatemala and was on hand when the Arbénz government was overthrown by a CIA-engineered coup. Guevara helped organize the leftist resistance (his experience left him intensely hostile to the US). He fled Guatemala and went to Mexico where, in November 1955, he met Fidel Castro and, seeing in him the characteristics of a "great leader," joined the revolutionary cause.

The two had much in common. Guevara was a restless soul who, like Castro, was also daring and courted danger. They were both brilliant intellectuals (Guevara wrote poetry and philosophy and was probably the only true intellectual in Cuba's revolutionary leadership). Each had a relentless work ethic, selfless devotion, and an incorruptible character. Although the handsome, pipe-smoking rebel was a severe asthmatic, with an acute aller-

gic reaction to mosquitoes, Guevara also turned out to be Castro's best field commander, eventually writing two books on guerrilla warfare that would become standard texts for Third World revolutionaries. He commanded the Third Front in the Sierra Escambray and led the attack that on 28 December 1958 captured Santa Clara and finally toppled the Batista regime. It was Guevara who took command of Havana's main military posts on New Year's Day 1959.

Shaping the Revolution

The revolutionary regime declared Guevara a native Cuban citizen as an act of gratitude, rendering him legally entitled to hold office in Cuba. He became head of the National Bank of Cuba and Minister of Finance and, in 1961, Minister of Industry. He also led the execution squads that dispensed with scores of Batista supporters—Guevara never flinched from pulling the trigger himself—and was instrumental in the general repression that was meant to crush "counter-revolutionaries."

Guevara supervised the radical economic reforms that swept through Cuba and, embracing the Soviet model with innocent fervor, negotiated the trade deals with the Soviet Union and COMECON countries and the carefully crafted maneuvering that led to the seizing of US assets (Soviet representative Alexandr Alexiev said, "Che was practically the architect of our relations with Cuba").

Creating the "New Man"

Guevara was a "complete Marxist" (he had an obsessive hatred of bourgeois democracy) who despised the profit motive and US interests. He believed that the selfish motivations that determine behavior in a capitalist system would become obsolete when collective social welfare became the stated goal. Guevara set out his thoughts in an essay, "Man and Socialism in Cuba," in which he explained the difference in motivation and outlook between people in capitalist and socialist societies. He believed that the notion of material value lay at the root of capitalist evil. Man himself became a commodity. Meanwhile, liberty eroded moral values: individualism was selfish and divisive, and essentially detrimental to social development.

To build socialism, a new ethos and consciousness must be built. By removing market forces and profit or personal gain, replacing these with production for the social good and planning instead of market "anarchy," a new individual would emerge, committed to a selfless motivation to help shape a new society. Castro agreed with Guevara, and a revolution to create the New Man was launched. It called for collective spartanism shaped by Castro's personal belief in sacrifice.

The government moved to censure work for personal benefit. Bonuses and other financial incentives were replaced with "moral incentives"; consumerism was replaced by the notion of "collective and individual satisfaction" from work. Private enterprise and trade were banned. Ideological debate was quelled. Apathy was frowned on. And psychological and other pressures bore down on anyone who refused to go along with the new values imposed from above.

For many Cubans, the idea of the New Man struck a resonant chord, because the Revolution came from the people themselves, not against their will or in spite of them. This nourished the concept of collective responsibility and duty, subordinating liberty (to do as one wishes) for the common good. There was nothing the Cubans wouldn't do. The state didn't even need to ask. "No one worked from eight to five," a 59-year-old woman told reporter Lynn Darling. "You worked around the clock. The horizons were open. We had a world to conquer, a world to give to our grandchildren."

An intrinsic sense of egalitarianism and dignity was nourished and seeped into the Cuban persona, as many individuals strove to embody the New Man ideal. Cubans spread their spirit throughout the Third World, helping the poor and the miserable.

Fall from Grace
However, Guevara was greatly at odds with Castro on fundamental issues. Castro's scheme to institutionalize the Revolution hand-in-hand with the Soviets, for example, ran counter to Guevara's beliefs (Guevara considered the Soviet Union as rapacious as the capitalists).

Although they were intellectual equals, in many ways Guevara and Castro were unmatched. Where Castro was pragmatic, Guevara was ideological. Guevara was fair-minded toward Cubans critical of the Castro regime, unlike Castro. Guevara gradually lost his usefulness to Castro's revolution. His frankness eventually disqualified him, forcing him into suicidal exile.

Guevara left Cuba in early 1965. He renounced all his positions in the Cuban government as well as his honorary Cuban citizenship. Guevara apparently severed his ties with Cuba voluntarily, although the reasons have never been adequately explained.

Death and Eternal Glory
Che (the word is an affectionate Argentinean appellation, literally "you" but colloquially meaning "pal" or "buddy") fought for a short time in the Congo with the Kinshasa rebels before returning briefly in secret to Cuba. He reemerged in 1966 in Bolivia, where he unsuccessfully attempted to rouse the Bolivian peasantry to revolutionary passions—reflecting his ambition, in his own words, "to create another Vietnam in the Americas" as a prelude to another—and, he hoped, definitive—world war in which socialism would be triumphant. He was betrayed to the Bolivian Army Rangers by the peasants he had hoped to set free. He died on 9 October 1967, ambushed and executed along with several loyal members of the Cuban Communist Party.

Castro has since built an entire cult of worship around Guevara. He has become an icon, exploited as a "symbol of the purest revolutionary virtue" and lionized for his glorious martyrdom and lofty ideals. Guevara became the official role model of the *hombre nuevo,* the New Man. The motto *seremos como Che* ("we will be like Che") is the official slogan of the Young Pioneers, the nation's youth organization. In 1997, Guevara's remains were delivered to Cuba and interred in Santa Clara.

His image is everywhere, most notably the five-story metal motif adorning the facade of the Ministry of the Interior in Havana's Plaza de la Revolución. The photographer Korda shot the famous image that will live to eternity—"The Heroic Guerrilla"—showing Guevara wearing a windbreaker zippered to the neck, in his trademark black beret with five-point revolutionary star, his head tilted slightly, "his eyes burning just beyond the foreseeable future," wrote Tom Miller.

Guevara has been turned into a modern myth the world over. He became a hero to the New Left radicals of the 1960s for his persuasive and purist Marxist beliefs. He was convinced that revolution was the only remedy for Latin America's social inequities ("revolution cleanses men") and advocated peasant-based revolutionary movements. He believed in the perfectibility of man, although his own mean streak and manically irresponsible actions are glossed over by leftists. The ultimate tribute perhaps came from French philosopher Jean-Paul Sartre, who honored Guevara as "the most complete man of our age."

Castillo de San Carlos de la Cabaña

This massive fortress lining Cabaña hill half a kilometer east of the Morro enjoys a fantastic strategic position, with a sloping vantage to the north out to sea, and a clifftop balcony over the city and harbor to the south. It is the largest fort in the Americas, covering 10 hectares and stretching 700 meters in length. It was built 1764-74 following the English invasion, and cost the staggering sum of 14 million pesos (when told the cost, the king after whom it is named reached for a telescope; surely, he said, it must be large enough to see from Madrid). From the very beginning, the castle was powerfully armed and could count in the mid-19th century some 120 bronze cannons and mortars, plus a permanent garrison of 1,300 men (the castle was designed to hold 6,000 troops in times of need). While never actually used in battle, it has been claimed that its dissuasive presence won all potential battles—a tribute to the French designer and engineer entrusted with its conception and construction. The castle has been splendidly restored.

The fortress is reached from the north. You pass through two defensive structures before reaching the monumental baroque portal (flanked by great columns and a pediment etched with the escutcheon of Kings Charles III and plaques dedicated to various colonial governors) and massive drawbridge over a 12-meter-deep moat, one of several moats carved from solid rock and separating individual fortress components.

Beyond the entrance gate, a paved alley leads to the **Plaza de Armas,** centered on a grassy, tree-shaded park fronted by a 400-meter-long curtain wall. The area to the right is off-limits. But immediately ahead upon entering the plaza is the **Comandancia de Che,** where Che Guevara had his headquarters in the months following the Triunfo del Revolution (his guerrilla army occupied the fortress on 3 January 1959). The small structure now houses the **Museo Che Guevara,** dedicated to saluting the Argentinian doctor-turned-revolutionary who played such a key part in the Cuban Revolution (though some negative aspects of his tenure in Cuba are overlooked).

To the west, the cobbled street leads past a small **chapel** with a charming vaulted interior containing a beautifully carved wooden altar, plus a spired belltower and an even more impressive baroque facade surrounding blood-red walls. Venerated here were three saints: Santa Carlos, patron saint of the fortress; Santa Barbara, patron saint of artillerymen; and Nuestra Señora del Pilar, patron saint of sailors.

Immediately west, on the north face of the plaza, is a building that contains a **history museum** tracing the castle's development. The museum features a room containing various torture instruments and dedicated to the period when political executions took place, and another containing uniforms and weaponry from the colonial epoch (including a representation of the *cañonazo* ceremony). A portal here leads into a garden—**Patio de Los Jagüeyes**—that while today a place of repose, once served as a *cortadura,* a defensive element once packed with explosives that could be ignited to foil the enemy's attempts to gain entry.

A long building runs west from here, following the slope of the plaza. Today, its various rooms make up the impressive **Museo de Fortificaciones y Armas,** containing an impressive collection of suits of armor and weaponry that spans the ancient Arab and Asian worlds and stretches back through medieval times to the Roman era. Never seen a battering ram or ballistic catapult? Check 'em out here. The museum does a magnificent job of tracing the development of weaponry through the ages. A model of the Cabaña helps in understanding the concepts that made this fortress so formidable.

To the rear of the armaments museum is the **Calle Marina,** a handsome cobbled street lined with former barracks, armaments stores, and cells of condemned prisoners. The former vaults have been converted and now contain two worthy restaurants: **Restaurant Doña Yulla,** serving pizzas and Cuban dishes for 12-38 pesos (open 2-10 p.m.), and the more upscale **Bodegón de los Vinos,** serving Spanish cuisine with traditional entertainment. Another of Havana's finest restaurants—**La Divina Pastora**—lies below and 200 meters west of the Morro, by the wharf where supply ships once berthed.

Midway down Calle Marina, a gate leads down to the **El Foso de los Laureles.** The massive Moat of the Laurels contains the execution wall where hundreds of nationalist sympathizers were shot during the wars of independence, when the fortress dungeons were used as a prison for Cuban patriots—a role that Generals Machado and Batista continued. Following the Revolution, scores of Batista supporters and "counterrevolutionaries" met the same fate, with Guevara commanding the execution squads (it was here that *Comandante* Che set up his revolutionary tribunals for "crimes against the security of the state"). A plaque is inset in the wall in memory of Cuban nationalists and leftists executed prior to the Revolution, and a cenotaph commemorates one in particular: Juan Clemente Zenea, executed in 1871. Today goats nibble the grass where scores of "traitors" were shot.

On the north side of the moat is a separate fortress unit, the recently reopened **San Juliá Revellin**. It contains examples of the missiles installed during the Cuban Missile Crisis (called the October 1962 Crisis by Cubans), among them a Soviet nuclear-tipped R-12 rocket.

At the north end of the Plaza de Armas, a covered path leads to the **Semi-baluarte de San Lorenzo,** an expansive and maze-like fortification offering vast views over the harbor from the cannon embrasures. Note the sentry box of San Lorenzo at the far end—it makes a great foreground for a picture-perfect photo over Habana Vieja

The curtain wall—**La Cortina**—runs the length of the castle on its south side and formed the main gun position overlooking Havana. It is still lined with ceremonial cannons engraved with lyrical names such as *La Hermosa* (The Handsome). Here, every night at 9 p.m., a small unit assembles in military fashion, dressed in scarlet 18th-century garb and led by fife and drum. Soon enough, you'll hear the reverberating crack of the *cañonazo*—the nightly firing of a cannon, which used to signal the closing of the city gates

and the raising of the chain to seal the harbor mouth. Today, it causes unsuspecting visitors to drop their drinks.

The castle is open daily 10 a.m.-10 p.m. Entry costs US$3, children US$1.50 (plus extra US$1 for guide, US$2 for cameras, US$10 for videos) and includes the *cañonazo* (you can visit the castle by day and return at night on the same ticket). The rest of the fortress grounds is still used as a military base, making most of the surrounding area off-limits.

Excursions are available to witness the *cañonazo,* usually followed by dinner at La Divina Pastora. You can make reservations through any of the tour agencies listed in the Getting Around section of the Transportation chapter.

El Cristo de Casablanca

A great statue of Jesus Christ looms over Casablanca, dominating the cliff face immediately east of the Castillo, with the domed National Observatory behind. The 15-meter-tall statue, erected in 1958, stands atop a three-meter-tall pedestal and was hewn from Italian Carrara marble by noted female Cuban sculptor Jilma Madera. The figure stands with one hand on his chest and the other raised in a blessing. From the *mirador* (viewing platform) surrounding the statue, you have a bird's-eye view of the deep, flask-shaped harbor. The views are especially good at dawn and dusk, and it is possible, with the sun gilding the waters, to imagine great galleons slipping in and out of the harbor, a conduit for the wealth of a hemisphere.

The statue is accessible by a 10-minute uphill walk from Casablanca. Either climb the staircase beginning in the plazuela 100 meters north of the ferry terminal or take the winding roadway that leads west from the plazuela.

CENTRO HABANA

Centro Habana (Central Havana—pop. 175,000) lies west of the Prado and Habana Vieja. Laid out in a near-perfect grid, Centro is mostly residential, with few sights of note. Many houses along and inland of the Malecón, having been battered by waves and salt air over decades, are in a tumbledown state. Parts of Centro are so dilapidated that they conjure up images of what Dresden must have looked like after it was bombed in World War II.

In prerevolutionary days, Centro was the heart of Havana's red-light district, and scores of prostitutes roamed such streets as the ill-named Calle Virtudes (Virtues). Today, southern Centro is the great commercial heart of the city—if a bit faded from the days when there were more goods to sell. Still, in spring 1999, the main shopping streets of San Rafael, Neptuno, and Galiano had sprung back to life, and modern US-style shopping centers had opened, stocked with mostly imported goods sold for dollars only.

Believe it or not, there's also a small Chinatown—Barrio Chino—delineated by Calles Zanja, Dragones, Salud, Rayo, San Nicolás, and Manrique.

The two major west-east thoroughfares are the Malecón to the north, and the Zanja and Avenida Salvador Allende through the center; plus two important shopping streets - Calles Neptuno and San Rafael between the Malecón and Zanja. Cutting south from the Malecón run three major thoroughfares: Calzada de Infanta, forming the western boundary; Padre Varela, down the center; and Avenida de Italia (Galiano), farther east.

MALECÓN AND VICINITY

How many times have I walked the Malecón? Twenty? Thirty? Once is never enough, for Havana's six-lane seafront boulevard curving east to west enigmatically seems to represent all of Havana. When questioned by an immigration official as to why he had come to Cuba and stayed for 10 years, Costa Rican composer Ray Tico replied: "I fell in love with Havana's seafront drive." The Malecón (more properly the Muro de Malecón, literally "embankment," or "seawall") was designed as a jetty wall in 1857 by Cuban engineer General Francisco de Albear but not laid out until 1902, by US governor General Woods. It fronts sinuously and dramatically along the Atlantic shoreline between the Castillo de San Salvador de la Punta and Río Almendares. It took 50 years to reach the Río Almendares, almost five miles to the west.

"Silver lamé" was what composer Orlando de la Rosa called the boulevard. The metaphor has stuck, although it is today only a ghostly reminder of its former brilliance—what Martha Gellhorn called a "19th century jewel and a joke." The Malecón is lined with once-glorious houses, each exuberantly distinct from the next. Unprotected by seaworthy paint, they have proven incapable of withstanding the salt spray that crashes over the seawall in great airy clouds and then floats off in rainbows. Their facades—green trimmed with purple, pink with blue, yellow with orange (many of the seaside homes belonged to millionaires and were painted red, blue, or yellow according to the owner's political allegiance)—are now decrepit, supported by wooden scaffolding, while the broad limestone walkway is now pitted and broken.

By late 1998, the restoration of the Malecón was well underway; in spring 1999, one-third of the buildings was fronted by scaffolding. The renovation includes the interiors, too. Families have been moved out temporarily while the plumbing and electrical cables are relaid.

All along the shore are the worn remains of square baths—known as the "Elysian Fields"—hewn from the rocks below the seawall, originally with separate areas for men, women, and Negroes. Since the Revolution, they are more democratic. These Baños de Mar precede construction of the Malecón and were cut into the steps of rock alongside the Calzada de San Lazaro. Each is about 12 feet square and six to eight feet deep, with rock steps for access and a couple of portholes through which the waves of this tideless shore wash in and out.

The Malecón is the city's undisputed social gathering spot. It offers a microcosm of Havana life: the elderly walking their dogs; the shiftless looking for tourists; the young passing rum among friends; fishermen tending their lines; and always, scores of couples, for the Malecón is a mecca for love affairs. All through the night, lovers' murmurings mingle with the crash and hiss of the waves.

Literature buffs may be intrigued by the **Museo Lezama Lima,** three blocks inland from the Malecón at Trocadero 162 e/ Crespo y Industria, two blocks west of the Prado. The museum, which opened in 1995, is in the former home of prodigious writer José Lezana Lima, author of *Paradiso,* which was made into a renowned movie. The building evokes the rich and varied universe of the writer, variously described by Guillermo Cabrera Infante as a "fat man with a perennial cigar" and a "deeply mystical influence."

Dominating the Malecón to the west is the massive bronze **Monumento Antonio Maceo,** atop a marble base in a plaza in front of the **Hospital Hermanos Ameijeiras.** The hospital was built atop what was intended to be the Banco Nacional de Cuba, but Guevara, as the revolutionary Minister of Finance, nixed the plans, despite which local rumor has it that the vaults still contain Cuba's meager gold reserves. The motley tower that stands at the west end of the plaza is the **Torreon de San Lazaro,** with loopholes for snipers aiming along the Malecón (fortunately, today it's unmanned).

Barrio Cayo Hueso

Immediately west of the Plaza Antonio Maceo is a triangular area bordered by the Malecón, Calle San Lazaro, and Calzada de Infanta, forming the northwest corner of Centro Habana. Known as Barrio Cayo Hueso, the region dates from the early 20th century, when tenement homes were erected atop what had been the Espada cemetery (hence the name, Cay of Bones). Some 12,000 homes are squashed into the compact and deteriorated region, accessed by a warren of irregular alleyways comprised of sagging walls and peeling paint—an area in lamentable decline.

In 1995, because of its deteriorated state, Cayo Hueso became the first area of Havana earmarked for an experimental program to halt its decline based on a humanistic and manageable approach to public housing. A new microbrigade effort was launched to renovate existing buildings, providing experts to guide inhabitants in the rehabilitation of their own units and utilizing supplies that are placed in their hands. Almost 20 government agencies are involved in the restoration (each agency has adopted a street), and an effort has been made to educate the local community as to its own history and culture.

The area, indeed, is a cultural treasure. On Calle Hornos, the first cultural center dedicated to tango was formed; today, it still hosts tango dancing. Other cultural events are hosted on Friday nights on Calle Hamel, one block south of San Lazaro, where the renowned artist Salvador González has adorned walls with evocative murals inspired by *santería.* Nearby, at Calle Hamel 108, lived the singer-songwriter Angel Díaz, credited as the "inventor" of the musical genre called *filin* (feeling).

The **Iglesia de San Nicolas,** one block west of Máximo Gómez, on Calle San Nicolas, is a splendidly restored yet tiny church with ocher walls and a circular bell tower.

The plazuela at the junction of Infanta, between Calles Jovellar and San Lazaro, honors students of the University of Havana who were murdered or otherwise lost their lives during the fights against the Machado and Batista regimes. San Lazaro rises to the *escaleras,* the wide staircase at the entrance to the university that was the center for student demonstrations. The junction of Infanta and San Lazaro was an important scene of battles between students and police. A memorial plaque in the plazuela recalls that it was from Calle Jovellar 107 that Castro set out for Santiago de Cuba on 25 July 1953 in a blue Buick sedan, initiating the attack on the Moncada barracks that would launch his revolution.

CALLES SAN RAFAEL AND NEPTUNO

The major commercial thoroughfare of Centro is **Calle San Rafael,** which for five blocks leads west from Parque Central as a pedestrian precinct lined with department stores, many of which still bear prerevolutionary neon signs promoting US brand names from yesteryear, such as Hotpoint and Singer. The pedestrian precinct stretches to Galiano, where it reverts to traffic and the stores give way to residences. Those stores selling Cuban-made goods are reminders of how pitiful is the domestic output, with chintzy plastic and metal knick-knacks and clothing of the most rough manufacture. Many other department stores—such as La Epoca on Neptuno and Galiano—are now almost as well-stocked with Western goods as their Northern American and European counterparts, with the goods for sale in dollars, of course.

Paralleling San Rafael to the south, Calle Neptuno is a secondary shopping node for several blocks west of Galiano. Fans of tango might check out the **Casa del Tango,** 303 Neptuno, honoring the tradition of the Argentinian dance and run by an elderly couple that keeps no regular hours. Within, it is festooned with magazine covers, record covers, and other mementos to tango.

If strolling down Neptuno, be sure to pop into the **Cine América,** tel. (62) 5416, at the junction of Galiano. Dating from 1941, the interior is a model of art deco grace. Its tiers of ballooning balconies and curvilinear box seats melt into the walls of the vaulted auditorium, which boasts a moon-and-stars ceiling. The foyer features a terrazzo floor with zodiac motifs and an inlaid map of the world, with Cuba, which lies at the very center, picked out in polished brass. Nancy Stout says wonderfully: "Other heavenly symbols populate the space as spheres become a theme echoed in railings, ceilings, and the proscenium arch. America is the theme endorsed, and so ships emerge from the walls, highlighted by light. At the auditorium's soffit, diminutive sources of illumination skillfully emulate the firmament, bathing the hall's more sculptural components with a faint glow, as if determined to underline the many instances in which space is purposefully engirdled." Albeit severely deteriorated and crying out for restoration, it remains one of the world's great modern-style theaters.

Another tiny gem is the **Iglesia de Nuestra Señora de Monserrate,** dating from 1843, on Galiano one block north of Neptuno.

BARRIO CHINO AND VICINITY

After the end of slavery in 1886, landowners imported 150,000 Chinese as indentured laborers to work the fields. They were contracted to labor

STRAITS OF FLORIDA

To Regla, Guanabacoa, and San Francisco de Paula

PALADAR TORRESÓN

EON DE LAZARO

CONVENTO DE LA IMACULADO CONCEPCIÓN

MONUMENTO MÁXIMO GÓMEZ ★

RUMBOS CAFÉ

AVENIDA MACEO (MALECÓN)

HOTEL DEAUVILLE ●

HOTEL CARIBBEAN ●

HABANA VIEJA

HOSPITAL CLÍNICO QUIRÚRGICO HERMANOS AMEIJEIRAS ■

CASA DE LA CULTURA ★

SAN LAZARO

TROCADERO

BLANCO

AGUILA

CRESPO

COLÓN

REFUGIO

MORRO

PASEO DE MARTÍ (PRADO)

ZULUETA

LAGUNAS

ANIMAS

PALADAR LA GUARIDA ▼

PRESERVANCIA

CAMPANARIO

MANRIQUE

SAN NICOLAS

VIRTUDES

HOTEL LINCOLN ●

MUSEO LEZAMA LIMA ■

AGRAMONTE

AVENIDA DE LAS MISIONES

GONZÁLEZ

LUCENA

PADRE VARELA (BELASCOAIN)

ESCOBAR

LEALTAD

CONCORDIA

NEPTUNO

EL RÁPIDO ●

IGLESIA MONSERRATE ■

HOTEL LIDO ●

INDUSTRIA

CONSULADO

GERVASIO

OPTICAS MIRAMAR ★

CINE AMÉRICA ★

BURGUÍ ★

AGUACATE

RUMBOS CAFÉ ●

SAN MIGUEL

SAN RAFAEL

CASA DE LA CULTURA ★

BAR NAUTILUS ▼▼▼

Parque Central

HOTEL INGLATERRA

VILLEGAS

CENTRO

SAN MARTIN (SAN JOSE)

RESTAURANTE TIEN-TAN ▼

ETECSA BOOTH ■

AMISTAD

LA CALESCA CAFETERIA

BERNAZA

HABANA

RESTAURANTE PACÍFICO ▼

AVENIDA DE ITALIA (GALIANO)

CASAS PARTICULARES ★★

BARCELONA

CAPITOLIO ★

BRASIL

AVENIDA DE BELGICA (MONSERRATE)

(TENIENTE REY)

FREEMASON'S LODGE ■

CASA ABUELO LUNG-KONG ★

RESTAURANT SONG SAI LI ▼

HOTEL NUEVA YORK ●

FÁBRICA DE TABACO H. UPPMANN ■

ISIA SAGRADO ZÓN DE JESUS ★

AVENIDA SIMÓN BOLIVAR (REINA)

DRAGON GATE ▼

FÁBRICA DE TABACO PARTAGAS

DRAGONES

Parque de la Fraternidad

ESCOBAR

LEALTAD

CAMPANARIO

MANRIQUE

SAN NICOLAS

RAYO

PALACIO DE ALDAMA ■

HOTEL ISLA DE CUBA ●

SITIO

PENALVER

IGLESIA DE SAN NICOLAS ■

A DE TABACO O Y JULIETA ■

CONDESA

CONCEPCIÓN DE LA VALLA

MÁXIMO GÓMEZ (MONTE)

APÓDACA

APONTE

SOMERUELOS

CIENFUEGOS

CÁRDENAS

ECONOMÍA

ZUINONA

CONSERVATORIO MUNICIPAL DE HABANA ■

FIGURAS

SAN NICOLAS

MISIÓN

ESTACIÓN CENTRAL DE FERROCARRIL ■

CORRALES

GLORIA

ESPERANZA

EGIDO

NUEVA DEL PILAR

LINDERO

AVENIDA DE ESPAÑA (VIVES)

FLORIDA

ALAMBIQUE

FACTORÍA

REVILLAGIGEDO

SUÁREZ

AGUILA

TERMINAL LA COUBRE ■

ROYO (AVENIDA MANGLAR)

To Estación Cristina

PUERTO GERRADA

DESAMPARADOS

CUATRO CAMINOS ★

ESTACIÓN CRISTINA ■

© AVALON TRAVEL PUBLISHING

GRAHAM GREENE~OUR MAN IN HAVANA

No contemporary novel quite captures the tawdry intrigue and disreputable aura of Batista's Havana than does Graham Greene's *Our Man in Havana*, published in 1958, on the eve of the revolutionary triumph, and set amid the torrid events of Havana in 1957.

The comic tale tells of Wormold, an English vacuum-cleaner salesman based in Havana and short of money. His daughter has reached an expensive age, so when approached by Hawthorne, he accepts the offer of £300 a month and becomes Agent 59200/5, MI6's man in Havana. To keep his job, he files bogus reports based on Lamb's *Tales from Shakespeare* and dreams up military apparatus from vacuum-cleaner parts. Unfortunately, his stories begin to come disturbingly true, and Wormold becomes trapped by his own deceit and the workings of a hopelessly corrupt city and society.

Graham Greene (1904-91) was already a respected author when he was recruited to work for the Foreign Office, serving the years 1941-43 in Sierra Leone, in Africa. In the last years of the war, he worked for the British Secret Service dealing with counterespionage on the Iberian peninsula, where he learned how the Nazi Abwehr (the German Secret Service) sent home false reports—perfect material for his novel, in which he also poked fun at the British intelligence services. He traveled widely and based many of his works, including *Our Man in Havana*, on his experiences. He visited Havana several times in the 1950s and was disturbed by the mutilations and torture practiced by Batista's police officers and by social ills such as racial discrimination: "Every smart bar and restaurant was called a club so that a negro could be legally excluded." But he confessed to enjoying the "louche atmosphere" of Havana and seems to have savored the fleshpots completely. "I came there . . . for the brothel life, the roulette in every hotel. . . . I liked the idea that one could obtain anything at will, whether drugs, women or goats," he later wrote.

Castro condoned *Our Man in Havana* but complained that it didn't do justice to the ruthlessness of the Batista regime. Greene agreed: "Alas, the book did me little good with the new rulers in Havana. In poking fun at the British Secret Service, I had minimized the terror of Batista's rule. I had not wanted too black a background for a light-hearted comedy, but those who had suffered during the years of dictatorship could hardly be expected to appreciate that my real subject was the absurdity of the British agent and not the justice of a revolution." Nonetheless, Castro permitted the screen version, starring Alec Guinness as Wormold, to be filmed in Havana in 1959.

Greene returned to Cuba in the years 1963-66. Although initially impressed by Castro's war on illiteracy (he called it "a great crusade"), he later soured after witnessing the persecution of homosexuals, intellectuals, and Catholics. Perhaps for this reason, the author isn't commemorated in Cuba in any way.

---

for eight years for miserable wages insufficient to buy their return. Most stayed, and many intermarried with blacks. The Sino-Cuban descendants of those who worked off their indenture gravitated to Centro Habana, where they settled in the zones bordering the Zanza Real, the aqueduct that channeled water to the city. Here they worked as domestics or opened vegetable shops, laundries, and restaurants. They were later joined by other Chinese fleeing persecution in California, including a wealthy group of California Chinese who arrived with investment opportunities in mind. In time, Havana's Chinese quarter, Barrio Chino, became the largest in Latin America—a mini-Beijing in the tropics. The Chinatown flourished and became wealthy—many Chinese profited immensely during the "Dance of the Millions" sugar boom of the 1920s—and rich merchants sponsored masquerades and other exotic Chinese festivities.

During the "sordid era," Barrio Chino became a center of opium dens and prostitution houses. At the infamous Shanghai theater, for US$1.25 one could see a "nude cabaret of extreme obscenity with the bluest of blue films in the intervals," wrote Graham Greene, who "watched without much interest Superman's performance with a mulatto girl (as uninspiring as a dutiful husband's)," then "smoked marijuana, and [saw] a lesbian performance at the Blue Moon," before snorting a little cocaine. Superman—also known as El Toro (The Bull)—had a 14-inch penis and earned US$25 nightly. He became so famous that he was immortalized in *The Godfather II,* in the scene in which the mobsters are in Cuba watching a live sex show. Greene made the Shanghai a setting in *Our Man in Havana,* when Wormold wisely opts to take Beatrice to the Tropicana instead.

Today, Barrio Chino is a mere shadow of its former self, with about 400 native-born Chinese and perhaps 2,000 descendants still resident in the area. The vast majority of Chinese left Cuba in the years immediately following the Revolution. Barrio Chino has since lost much of its personality along with its colorful characters, who were encouraged to become "less Chinese and more Cuban." Nonetheless, there's enough to remind you of how things once were. Chinese lanterns still hang outside the doorways, alongside signs written in Chinese. You'll recognize Chinese features, too, in the lively free market held daily (except Wednesday) on tiny Calle Cuchillo. In 1995, the government of China agreed to help rebuild Havana's Chinatown and funded a dragon gate across Calle Dragones, announcing visitors' entry from the east.

The most overtly Chinese street is diminutive, pedestrian-only **Calle Cuchillo,** which runs less than 100 meters and is lined with a dozen genuine Chinese restaurants. Be sure to visit Calle Cuchillo at night, when the Chinese lanterns are aglow. The most interesting of restaurants is **Restaurante Pacifico,** on Calle San Nicolas and Cuchillo. Hemingway used to eat here, on the top floor of the five-story building to which Castro is still an occasional visitor. "To get there," recalls Hemingway's son, Gregory, "you had to go up in an old elevator with a sliding iron grille for a door. It stopped at every floor, whether you wanted it to or not. On the second floor there was a five-piece Chinese orchestra blaring crazy atonal music. . . . Then you reached the third floor, where there was a whorehouse. . . . The fourth floor was an opium den with pitifully wasted little figures curled up around their pipes."

Perhaps the most interesting contemporary site in Barrio Chino is the **Casa Abuelo Lung Kong,** at Manrique y Dragones. The social club exists to support elders in the Chinese community and offers a genuine Chinese ambience. Oldsters sit in their rockers in the front *sala,* gossiping and reading newspapers, while others dine on free breakfasts and lunches in a basic restaurant at the rear on Chinese fare using *parrillas* (chopsticks). You could be in Hong Kong. It has a more elegant restaurant upstairs. Visitors are usually made welcome, but it's a common courtesy to ask permission before burying your nose inside. Similarly, check out the **Sociedad Chung Shan,** another Chinese cultural society on Dragones between San Nicolas and Rayo.

If you can, time your visit to coincide with Chinese New Year at the end of January into early February, when the streets are charged with the staccato pop of firecrackers meant to scare away evil spirits and the lion comes out to leap and dance through the streets of Barrio Chino.

Fábrica de Tabaco H. Upmann

This cigar factory, on Calle Amistad, e/ Barcelona y Dragones, tel. (62) 0081, one block west of the Capitolio, is officially known as the José Martí factory. It was begun by the erstwhile London-based banking house of H. Upmann in 1844, when it registered its name as a cigar brand (beginning in the 1830s, it had imported Cuban cigars in the first embossed cedar boxes; the firm also introduced the cedar-lined aluminum tube in the 1930s). In its heyday at the turn of the century, the factory was by far the largest producer of cigars in the country. The Upmann name remains synonymous with the highest quality Havana cigars—mild to medium-flavored, very smooth and subtle, and available in more than 30 sizes (not to be confused with H. Upmanns made in the Dominican Republic). Cigar connoisseurs consider that the best Montecristos come from this factory, including the mammoth Montecristo A and Cohiba Robusto and Esplendido.

The factory's almost 50 rollers are all rated "grade seven," the highest ranking a cigar roller can possess in Cuba, although only three rollers possess the skills and strength to roll the whopping Montecristo A, of which only about 15,000 are made annually. Many Habano cognoscenti, says *Cigar Aficionado,* "scour cigar shops around the world for boxes with the coveted 'JM' initials printed on the bottom." Nearly two million rare grade seven cigars annually are created at the Upmann factory.

It's open Mon.-Fri. 8 a.m.-4 p.m. for call-by visitors. Tours are offered at 10:30 a.m. and 1:30 p.m. (US$10).

AVENIDA SALVADOR ALLENDE AND VICINITY

This wide boulevard was laid out in the early 19th century by Governor Tacón, when it was known officially as Carlos III and colloquially as the Paseo. It runs east-west as a westerly extension of Avenida Reina (today's Avenida Simón Bolívar), which connects it to Parque de la Fraternidad. The governor built his summer house on Carlos III, setting a trend for many of Havana's nobility.

The boulevard has a few sites of note, but of interest only in passing. One such is the **Gran Templo Nacional Masonico,** the Grand Masonic Temple established on 25 March 1951. Though no longer a Freemason's lodge, it still retains a fading mural in the lobby depicting the history of masonry in Cuba. It competes for attention with a larger-than-life statue of José Martí.

Farther west, at Salvador Allende y Arbol Seco is the **Casa del Cultura Centro Havana,** hosting cultural activities for the local community and containing the **Galeria Kahlo** in a colonial mansion of note. An intriguing curiosity one block west, at Hospital #707, one block north of Salvador Allende, is the **Evangelical Temple** that draws a crowd of curious onlookers who peer in the windows to witness Cuban believers clutching their bibles within.

Avenida Salvador Allende continues its march westward of Calzada de Infanta through the Vedado district. Luring you north along Calzada de Infanta is the distant warbling of birds, and at the junction of San Rafael, you'll discover a tiny enclosed plaza where members of the Asociación Nacional Ornithológica de Cuba, colloquially termed the **Canary Cultivators of Havana,** gather to make bird talk and buy cages and seed. Their headquarters is half a block away, at Infanta 402, tel. (33) 5749. Here, ANOC members display as well as buy and sell their rainbow-hued birds, and the place is full of the chirping of finches and parakeets. The members breed birds, which the association exports. It's open Mon.-Fri. 8:30 a.m.-5:30 p.m.

Eastward, Avenida Simón Bolívar slopes to Parque de la Fraternidad, with a sweeping view down the scalloped avenue. Simón Bolívar is lined with once-impressive colonial-era structures gone to ruin. One of the few structures not seemingly on its last legs is the **Iglesia del Sagrado Corazón de Jesús,** a gothic inspiration in stone that could have been transported from medieval England. Its beamed ceiling is held aloft by great marbled columns, and its stained-glass windows rival the best in Europe. The church, one of the most active in Cuba, also boasts a fabulous soaring altar of carved wood. Services are offered Mon.-Sat. 7 a.m. and 4:30 p.m.; Sunday 7 a.m., 9:30 a.m., and 4:30 p.m.

CALLE PADRE VARELA

Calle Padre Varela is sadly diminished since being laid out last century with tall buildings on each side. Many edifices are ready for the wrecking ball, but there are at least two structures of contemporary note.

The first, four blocks down from Salvador Allende, is the **Fábrica de Tabaco Romeo y Julieta,** the famous cigar factory founded in 1875 by Inocencia Álvarez and officially today the Antonio Briones Montoto factory. It's in an exquisite three-story building with ironwork balconies on Padre Varela e/ Desague y Peñal Verno, tel. (78) 1058 or (79) 3927. Green glazed tiles cover the interior walls of the lobby, and an iron staircase twirls gracefully toward the ceiling, decorated with classical moldings with pink and green laurel wreaths. The factory specializes in medium-flavored brands such as El Rey del Mundo (King of the World) and, since 1875, the fine Romeo y Julieta. It also makes the heavyweight, high-quality, and limited-quantity Saint Luís Rey cigars favored by actor James Coburn and the late Frank Sinatra. Like most Havana cigar factories, duties vary by floor, with leaf handling on the ground floor, and stemming, sorting, rolling, box decorating, and ringing on the upper two floors. Its trademark label is world-renowned and one that, says Nancy Stout, "is particularly successful at conveying the discriminating gentleman's relationship with his cigar"—that of a love affair, however ill-fated. The factory is open for visits by permit only, Mon.-Fri. 7 a.m.-4 p.m. Permission must be requested from the Cubatabaco (the Empresa Cubana del Tabaco), O'Reilly #104 e/ Tacón y Mercaderes, Habana Vieja, tel. (62) 5463.

Another cigar factory—**Fábrica El Rey del Mundo**—hides behind the Romeo y Julieta factory at Calle San Carlos 816, tel. (70) 9336. Currently known as the Carlos Balino factory, and formerly as the Díaz Brothers, Cuesta Rey & Co., this small factory produces cigars under the El Rey del Mundo label.

One block south of Fábrica de Tabaco Romeo y Julieta, on Padre Varela and Carmen, is the **Conservatorio Municipal de Habana,** a music conservatory boasting a well-preserved classical facade, gleaming white and quite a shocker amid the decay and dishevelment.

Padre Varela continues south four blocks to Cuatro Caminos, an all-important junction where six major thoroughfares meet.

CERRO

South of Centro, the land rises gently to Cerro (pop. 130,000), a separate administrative district (the word means "hill"). During the last century, Cerro developed as the place to retire during the torrid midsummer months; many wealthy families maintained two homes in Havana—one in town, another on the cooler hill. The region is terribly deteriorated, and the majority of buildings transcend sordid, reminding you perhaps of the worst tenements of New York or Glasgow. Cerro spreads out expansively and is renowned for some of the more disreputable areas of the city, including centers of drug trading. Avoid the Barrio Canal and Sucel districts.

The district is anchored by Avenida Máximo Gómez (popularly called Monte or Calzada de Cerro), which snakes southwest from Parque de la Fraternidad and is surely one of the saddest streets in all Havana. During the 19th century, scores of summer homes in classical style were erected here, each more extravagantly Italianate than the next. Many of the luxurious houses went up along Avenida Máximo Gómez. The avenue—lined with colonnaded mansions like an endless Greek temple—ascends gradually, marching backward into the past like a classical ruin. Alas, today it looks as Herculaneum must have looked during its decline. Monte's once-stunning arcades are now in desperate condition, and houses are decaying behind lovely facades. To my mind, it is the saddest sight in Havana.

Novelist James Michener, exploring Cerro while looking for a house in which to set the Cuban portion of a novel on the Caribbean, was told "in elegiac tones" by his guide: "The steps went down by decades. 1920s the mansions are in full flower. 1930s the rich families begin to move out. 1940s people grab them who can't afford to maintain them, ruin begins. 1950s ten big families move into each mansion, pay no rent, and begin to tear it apart. 1960s during the first years of the Revolution, no housing elsewhere, so even more crowd in, ruin accelerates. 1970s some of the weakest begin to fall down. 1980s many gone beyond salvation." Heartrending.

A drive along Máximo Gómez will provide a lasting memory. But don't judge Havana by this, for the famous avenue is in the early stage of renovation—most notably at its lower end, near Parque de la Fraternidad. Supposedly, facades are to be renovated and building materials distributed to residents according to the housing conditions, with the aim of restoring Monte as one of the city's major shopping streets. Almost two dozen restaurants and shops reopened here in 1995, but in spring 1999, there was little sign that local residents had received any assistance.

One of the few buildings of interest is the **Cuatro Caminos** farmers' market, at the junction of Máximo Gómez with Manglar and Cristina (also called Avenida de la México). This much-dilapidated 19th-century market hall still functions as such and is worth a visit for its bustling color and ambience.

At the other end of Máximo Gómez, one block south of the avenue on Calle Peñon, is the tiny **Plaza de Galicia.** Shaded by venerable ceiba trees and bougainvillea bowers, the square features the diminutive **Iglesia de Peñon** at its heart. The church bears a Corinthian frontage and is topped by a round spire. It is open most afternoons and for mass on Sunday. The plaza was dedicated in 1991 to the Pueblo Gallego (the Galician people).

Fábrica de Ron Bocoy
The most intriguing site in Cerro is this venerable former home-turned-rum factory with a two-tone

pink facade and the legend "BOCOY" above the wide, handsome door, on Máximo Gómez between Patrio and Auditor, tel. (70) 5642, immediately east of Hospital Salvador Allende. Its facade is decorated with four dozen cast-iron swans painted blue-and-white and marching wing to wing, "each standing tall and slim, its long neck bent straight down in mortal combat with an evil serpent climbing up its legs to sink its fangs," wrote James Michener. For his book *Caribbean*, the author chose this building to be the model for the house in which lived "once-intimate liberal relatives" of a conservative Cuban exile family living in Miami.

Beyond the swan-filled portico, the mansion is one of Havana's most important distilleries, containing great oak casks up to seven meters tall stacked in dark recesses—"something out of Piranesi, a ghostly affair with a single unshaded lightbulb"—and making Cuba's famous Legendario rums and liquors (a comparative taste test

betrays the fact that Legendario is one of Cuba's least prestigious rums). The distillery manufactures five types of rum, three brandies, sweet wine (*vinos dulces*), and liqueurs made of plantain, anis, cacao, mint, and coffee. The atmosphere is heady.

Bocoy also manufactures one of the choicest rums in Cuba, intended solely for Fidel Castro to give as gifts to notable personalities. The special libation is packaged in a bulbous earthenware bottle inside a miniature pirate's treasure chest labeled La Isla del Tesoro (Treasure Island). The bottles are guarded assiduously—I was not permitted even a peek at the sole example in the distillery.

The guide, Yemsis Cardoso, leads free tours of the distillery. It has a showroom upstairs and a separate bar for tippling the goods as a prelude—it is hoped—to buying. There's also a Casa del Tabaco. Open Mon.-Sat. 9 a.m.-5 p.m., Sunday 9 a.m.-2 p.m.

VEDADO AND PLAZA DE LA REVOLUCIÓN

The conclusion of the brief Spanish-American-Cuban War, in 1898, brought US money rushing in to Havana. A new age of elegance evolved in Cuba's capital, concentrated in hilly Vedado, between Centro Habana and the Río Almendares. Fine parks and monuments to generals were added, along with the Malecón, the wide promenade anchoring the waterfront. Civic structures, large hotels, casinos, department stores, and lavish restaurants sprouted like mushrooms alongside nightclubs displaying fleshly attractions.

Vedado—today's commercial heart of Havana—has been described as "Havana at its middle-class best." The University of Havana is here. So are the fabulous Cementerio de Colón, many of the city's prime hotels and restaurants, virtually all its main commercial buildings, and block after block of handsome mansions and apartment houses in various states of decay or repair. (While exploring, watch for stone lions flanking the gates of large mansions. These revered symbols denote the home of a nobleman. Some time late last century, a commoner who had amassed a fortune bought himself a title and erected lions. The proper grandees of Spain were so outraged that they tore theirs

down in a protest known as La Muerte de los Leones—The Death of the Lions.) The streets are lined with jagüey trees dropping their aerial roots to the ground like muscular tendrils.

Vedado is administered as part of Plaza de la Revolución (pop. 165,000), which includes Nuevo Vedado, a distinct district south of Vedado. The area, much of which has been rebuilt since the Revolution, is centered on the Plaza de la Revolución, surrounded by ministry buildings, the Palacio de la Revolución (the seat of government), and the towering José Martí monument, now containing an eponymous museum.

For a grand view of Vedado, head to the top of the Habana Libre. Alternately, take time for a cocktail or meal at La Torre, atop the 35-story **Focsa,** a prerevolutionary apartment building that later was used to house East European and Soviet personnel and has since reverted to its former role.

ORIENTATION

The sprawling region is hemmed to the north by the Malecón, to the east by Calzada de Infanta, to the west by the Río Almanderes, running in a deep canyon, and to the southeast by the Calzada de Ayestaran and Avenida de la Independencia.

Vedado follows a grid pattern aligned NNW by SSE and laid out in quadrants. Odd-numbered streets (calles) run east-west, parallel to the shore. Even-numbered calles run perpendicular. (To confuse things, some "calles" are "avenidas," although there seems to be no logic as to which these are; and west of Paseo, calles are even-numbered; east of Paseo, calles run from A to P). The basic grid is overlain by a larger grid of broad boulevards averaging six blocks apart. Dividing the quadrants east-west—running through the heart of Vedado—is the all-important Calle 23, which rises (colloquially) as La Rampa from the Malecón at its junction, with Calzada de Infanta to the northeast. Paralleling it to the north is a second major east-west thoroughfare, Calle 9 (Linea), five blocks inland of the Malecón, which it also intersects to the northeast. Four major roadways divide the quadrants north-south: Calle L to the east, and Avenida de los Presidentes, Paseo, and Avenida 12 further west. Vedado slopes gently upward from the shore to Calle 23 and thence gently downward toward Cerro.

Nuevo Vedado has an irregular pattern. Avenida de los Presidentes, Paseo, and, to the west, Avenida 26, connect Vedado to Nuevo Vedado. Most roadways converge on the Plaza de la Revolución, which divides Avenida Carlos M. de Céspedes on its north side and Avenida de Rancho Boyeros on its south side. The two meet westward to form Avenida de la Independencia, which runs to the international airport.

THE MALECÓN

The Malecón runs along the bulging, wave-battered shorefront of northern Vedado, curling east-west from La Rampa in the east to the Río Almandares in the west, a distance of three miles, where the seafront boulevard meets Calzada (7ma) and dips under the tunnel that links it with Miramar. This portion of the Malecón is less dramatic than that along the shoreline of Centro Havana. However, there are several important sights, not least the **Hotel Nacional,** dramati-

cally perched atop a small cliff at the junction of La Rampa and the Malecón (entrance is on Calle O). Now a national monument, this grande dame hotel with its Moorish-influenced architecture is worth a peek. It was designed by the same architect who designed The Breakers in Palm Beach, which it closely resembles. General Machado signed off on the showplace hotel—a monument to his surging self-importance—meant to be majestic enough to entertain government guests in grand style. It opened on December 30, 1930, in the midst of the Great Depression.

The elaborately detailed, Spanish-style hotel suffered from bad management and was badly in need of refurbishment when mobster Meyer Lansky persuaded General Batista to let him build a grand casino and convert some of the rooms to luxurious suites for wealthy gamblers. In 1955, the casino and nightclub opened, drawing society figures from far and wide. Luminaries from Winston Churchill and the Prince of Wales to Marlon Brando have laid their heads here, as attested by the photos in the lobby bar. The sweeping palm-shaded lawns to the rear slope toward the Malecón, above which sits a battery of cannons from the Wars of Independence, and a network of defensive tunnels built in modern times.

Fronting the hotel by the shore is the **Monumento ál Maine,** dedicated by the republican Cuban government to the memory of the 260 sailors who died when the US warship exploded in Havana harbor in 1898, creating a prelude for US intervention in the Wars of Independence. Two rusting cannons are laid out beneath 40-foot-tall corinthian columns dedicated in 1925 and originally topped by an eagle with wings spread wide. Back then, relations between the two nations were warm, and when a hurricane toppled the eagle, it was replaced by a more aerodynamic sibling (the original now resides in the Cubanacán district, in the former residency of the US Ambassador, still occupied by the head of the US Interests Section). Following the Revolution, the monument was a point for anti-Yankee rallies. Immediately after the failed Bay of Pigs invasion in 1960, it was desecrated by an angry mob that toppled the eagle from its roost and broke its wings (its body is now in the Museum of the City of Havana, while the head hangs on the wall of the cafeteria in the US Interests Section). The Castro government later dedicated a

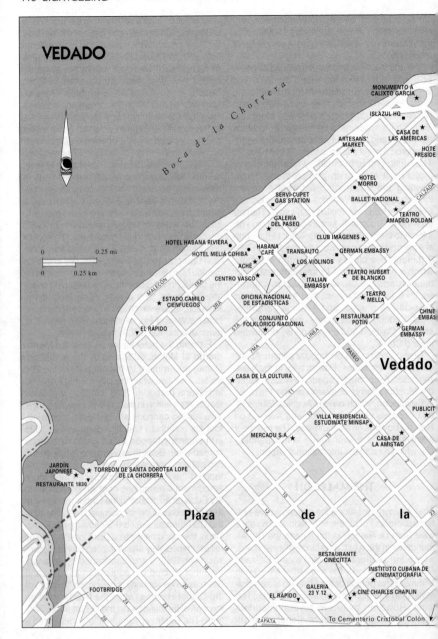

MALECÓN
POLICE
DAR EL BISTROT
U.S. INTERESTS SECTION
"SEÑOR IMPERIALISTAS..." BILLBOARD
REX RENT-A-LIMOUSINE
STRAITS OF FLORIDA
ESTADIO JOSÉ MARTÍ
SERVI-CUPET GAS STATION
MONUMENTO DEL MAINE
PANAUTOS RENT-A-CAR
CLÍNICA CAMILO CIENFUEGOS/FARMÁCIA INTERNACIONAL
BANCO FINANCIERO INTERNACIONAL
RUMBOS CAFÉ
CABARET PARISIENNE
PALADAR MARPOLY
RUMBOS (HQ)
JAPANESE EMBASSY
CAFÉ CONCERT GATO TUERTO
HOTEL NACIONAL
MINREX
PALADAR GRILL
FOCSA BUILDING
AIRLINE OFFICES
ETECSA BOOTH
HOTEL UNIVERSARIO
HOTEL CAPRI
SALA ROJA
TEATRO BRECHT
PALADAR NEREZ
HOTEL VICTORIA
CLUB 21
BISART
RUMBOS CAFÉ
PATRONATO
HORIZONTES (HQ)
PIZZERIA MILANO
MUSEO DE LA DANZA
CASA DE TABACO
PABELLÓN CUBA
JAZZ CLUB LA ZORRA
PALADAR HURÓN AZUL
CRAFTS MARKET
FOTOVIDEO
HOTEL ST. JOHN
CASA PARTICULAR DOÑA TATA
TECH STORE
CASA PARTICULAR MARTA VITONTE
INDIAN EMBASSY
Parque Coppelia
COPPELIA
LA RAMPA
HOTEL VEDADO
CABARET LAS VEGAS
UNEAC
COPPELIA (DOLLARS)
TOUR AND TRAVEL OFFICE
MERCADO AGROPECUARIO
RESTAURANTE SIETE MARES
LAS BULERIAS
HOTEL HABANA LIBRE TRYP
DE ARTES ATIVAS
CASA PARTICULAR DE JORGE COLLA POTTS
ETECSA BOOTH
HOTEL COLINA
PIZZERIA
SAN LÁZARO
LAS ESCALERAS
CONCORDIA
CASA DE LA PRENSA
TEATRO EL SÓTANO
UNIVERSIDAD DE LA HABANA
TABERNA DON PEPE
EL COCHINITO
NEPTUNO
MUSEO DE CIENCIAS NATURALES FELIPE POEY Y MUSEO ANTROPOLÓGICO MONTANTE
PALADAR LOS HELÉCHOS
CINE RIVIERA
SARACEN ARMORED CAR
MUSEO NAPOLEÓNICO
SAN MIGUEL
LA RAMPA
HOSPITAL CALIXTO GARCÍA
CALZADA DE INFANTA
PALADAR EL AMOR
POST OFFICE
MONUMENTO A MÁXIMO GÓMEZ
ESTADIO JUAN ABRAHANTES
ZANJA
HOSPITAL ORTOPEDICO
JARDÍN BOTÁNICO
CASTILLO DEL PRINCIPE
QUINTA DE LOS MOLINOS
Revolución
AV. SALVADOR ALLENDE
ROSENBERG MONUMENT
ZAPATA
BRUZÓN
HOTEL BRUZÓN
SALA POLIVALENTE RAMON FONST/MUSEO DEPORTIVOS
TERMINAL DE ÓMNIBUSES INTERPROVINCIALES
To José Martí Int'l Airport

plaque that reads, "To the victims of the *Maine,* who were sacrificed by imperialist voracity in its eagerness to seize the island of Cuba." Recent evidence, however, suggests that the explosion was an accident.

Three blocks west, at the bottom of Calle L, is the unmarked **US Interests Section** (formerly the US Embassy), where low-profile US diplomats and CIA agents serve Uncle Sam's whims behind a veil of mirrored-glass windows. Facing it, to the east, is what must be Havana's most photographed site: a huge, brightly painted billboard showing a fanatical Uncle Sam growling menacingly at a Cuban soldier, who is shouting, *"Señores Imperialistas: ¡No les tenemos absolutamente ningún miedo!"* ("Imperialists: You don't scare us at all!"). It faces the Interests Section as a purposeful taunt. The building is well guarded by Cuban military figures—is it a coincidence that there's a police headquarters adjoining?—who will shoo you away if you attempt to sit on the seawall within 100 meters or so of the US Interests Section. Nor are you permitted to walk past the US Interests Section on the inland side of the road.

Westward, the Malecón curls in much denuded state past an open-air sports stadium, the **CVD José Martí,** of a strange Bauhaus design in concrete. Immediately to the west, at the foot of Avenida de los Presidentes, is the **Monumento Calixto García,** with a tall bronze figure of the 19th-century rebel general on horseback atop a black marble pedestal. The statue is surrounded by a wall with verdigris-coated bronze plaques showing battle scenes from the Wars of Independence. Cannons lie rusting amid an intriguing grotto-like landscape.

Immediately to the west is a massive apartment tower dating from 1967, interesting as one of the most sophisticated built since the Revolution, although it makes evident the city's atrocious construction standards. Continuing on, you'll reach the spic-and-span **Hotel Cohiba,** a late-1990s edifice whose contemporary face launched Havana toward the Millennium; and the **Hotel Riviera,** the Mafia's last and most ambitious attempt to eclipse Las Vegas. Mobster Meyer Lansky owned the hotel but was registered as the kitchen manager to evade taxes. When opened in 1958, it was considered a marvel of modern design. It boasted an egg-shaped, gold-leafed casino and a nightclub whose opening was headlined by Ginger Rogers. Recently restored, it still functions as one of Havana's leading hotels.

The last bend of the Malecón brings you to the mouth of the Río Almandares, guarded by a small fortress, the **Torreon de Santa Dorotea.** It was built to guard the western approaches to Havana following the English invasion in 1762. Today, it houses a restaurant.

LA RAMPA AND VICINITY

Millionaires, mafiosi, presidents, paupers, and pimps all once walked the five blocks of Calle 23 which rises steeply—and heavily American in style—from the Malecón to the Hotel Habana Libre. La Rampa was the setting of *Three Trapped Tigers,* Guillermo Cabrera Infante's famous novel about swinging 1950s Havana, for it was here that the ritziest hotels, casinos, and nightclubs were concentrated in the days before the Revolution. You may still find yourself enthralled by the verve of La Rampa.

Not until the 1950s did La Rampa begin to acquire its present look (prior to that, it was a shantytown). In 1963, multicolored granite tiles created by Cuba's leading artists—Wilfredo Lam, René Portocarrero, and others—were laid at intervals in the sidewalks. It is art to be walked on (or respectfully skirted).

La Rampa's flavor is that of a tree-lined boulevard in Buenos Aires or even Spain, with its candy-stripe awnings shading faded restaurants and nightclubs from the heyday of sin. Modern, vital, and busy, it climbs steadily past the offices of Cubana, Havanatur, the television station, and art-deco apartment buildings mingling with high-rise office buildings. It crests at Calle L, pinned by Parque Coppelia, Cine Yara, and the **Hotel Habana Libre,** the national landmark hotel that was once *the* place to be after opening in 1958 on the eve of the Revolution. Castro even had his headquarters here briefly in 1959, and for years the hotel teemed with shady foreigners—many of them, reported *National Geographic,* "not strictly tourists" and all "watched by secret police agents from the 'ministry,' meaning MININT, the Ministry of the Interior." The lobby contains many fine contemporary art pieces, in

COPPELIA~CUBA'S DELICIOUS CONFECTION

Coppelia is the name of a park in Havana, the flying saucer–like structure at its heart, and the brand of excellent ice cream served there.

In the bad old good old days, the trendy area at the top of La Rampa was full of ice cream parlors. But, as Tom Miller claims in *Trading with the Enemy*, the lower classes and blacks weren't welcome, so in 1966 the government built a big, lush park with a parlor in the middle as the ultimate democratic ice cream emporium—surely the biggest ice creamery in the world, serving an estimated 30,000 customers a day. Cuba's rich diversity is to be found standing in line at Coppelia on a sultry Havana afternoon.

Before the Revolution, Cuba relied on its northern neighbor for much of its ice cream supply, and Baskin-Robbins' 28 flavors were the ice cream of choice. Castro, however, promised to outdo the Yanks with 29 flavors (a boast Cuba failed to achieve). Before the Special Period, you used to be able to choose anything from a one-scoop cone to complex sundaes as well as more than two-dozen flavors, including exotic tropical fruits that Ben and Jerry have never heard of. In 1996, after five years of the Special Period, Coppelia could manage only one flavor a day. It was doing a bit better in 1999, but everyone swears the quality is not what it once was.

The strange concrete structure that looms over the park, suspended on spidery legs, shelters a marble-topped diner-bar where Cubans sit atop tall bar stools and slurp ice cream from stainless steel bowls. A series of circular rooms is arranged overhead like a four-leaf clover, offering views out over three open-air sections where *helados* can be enjoyed beneath the dappled shade of fulsome yagüey trees. Each section has its own *cola* (line) proportional in length to the strength of the sun. Even on temperate days, the *colas* snake out of the park and onto nearby streets like lethargic serpents. The *colas* move forward at a pace barely distinguishable from rigor mortis. Just when you are about to give up all hope, the line will surge briskly forward. Trying to make sense of the lines is a puzzle, and determining the last person in line—*el último*—is never easy. Cuban lines are never static. Habaneros wander off willy-nilly to sit in the shade while others disappear from view completely, lending the impression of having given up. But always they reappear at the critical moment, and your *cola* will coalesce in perfect order, thanks to some unfathomable and puissant osmosis. Young waitresses in red tartan miniskirts seat you at communal tables made of local marble. Coppelia is a family diner.

Coppelia featured in Tomás Gutierrez's Alea's trenchant classic movie, *Fresa y Chocolate*, which was based on Senel Paz's short story, *The Woods, the Wolf, and the New Man*, and is named for the scene at Coppelia where Diego, the homosexual, had ordered strawberry ice cream, much to the consternation of David, the loyal Fidelista: "Although there was chocolate that day, he had ordered strawberry. Perverse." After the success of the movie, Cuban males, concerned with their macho image, had taken a cue from the movie and avoided ordering *fresa*.

cluding a mosaic mural by René Portocarro. The hotel is fronted by a spectacular contemporary mural—*Carro de la Revolución* (the Revolutionary Car)—by ceramist Amelia Peláez made of 525 pieces in the style of Picasso. The mural was originally created in 1958, but falling tiles killed a hotel guest and injured several others, so it was removed. It was refabricated and remounted more securely (we hope) by Mexican experts and reinaugurated in January 1997 during the Pope's visit.

Anyone interested in Cuba's revolutionary history should step south one block to Calle 25 164 e/ Infanta y O, the address of the **Casa Abel Santamaría**, tel. (70) 0417, where the martyr—brutally tortured and murdered following the attack on the Moncada barracks in 1953—once lived. Prior to the attack, the simple two-room apartment (no. 603) was used as the headquarters of Fidel Castro's nascent revolutionary movement, the MR-26-7. The original furnishings are still in place: a roped-off sofa bed, a small bookcase, Fidel's work desk with a statue of José Martí, and a kerosene fridge. You'd have to be a serious leftist or student of history to thrill to this place, but it's interesting in passing. The adjoining room (no. 604) has a small exhibition—mostly photos—of Abel's sister Haydee Santamaría, Fidel, and other revolutionaries (curiously, the only photo of Abel is as a two-year-old). Open Mon.-Fri. 9 a.m.-12:30 p.m. and 1-5 p.m., Saturday 9 a.m.-1 p.m. Entry costs US$1, or US$2 with the guide, who gives an enthusiastic spiel.

Catercorner to the Hotel Habana Libre, at the top of the hill at Calle L, is **Parque Coppelia,** an entire block devoted to the consumption of ice cream, of which Cubans are consummate lovers. The ice cream is excellent and worth the long wait in line.

Universidad de la Habana

Follow Calle L south from La Rampa three blocks, and you arrive at an immense stone staircase at Calle 27—the famous *escalinata*—that leads up to the university. The 50-meter-wide steps are topped by a porticoed, columned facade beyond which lies a peaceful square surrounded by more columned arcades. The tree-shaded campus was loosely modeled after New York's Columbia University and is centered on a quadrant surrounded by classical buildings. A patinated statue looks down upon the *escalinata,* which in Batista days was famous as a setting for political rallies and riots.

The university was founded by ecclesiastics in 1728 and was originally situated on Calle Obispo in Habana Vieja. Admission back then was based on "purity" of bloodline: Jews, Moors, other non-Christians, and, of course, blacks and mulattoes were barred. The university was secularized in 1842, although admission remained the privilege of the privileged classes.

During the 20th century, the university was composed of 13 schools, each with its own president. The presidents elected the president of the University Students' Federation, the pillar of student political activity and an extremely influ-

THE JEWS OF HAVANA

Havana's Jewish community once thrived. Today it is thought to number only about 1,300, about five percent of its prerevolutionary size, when Havana's Jewish community supported five synagogues, several schools, and a college.

The first Jews are thought to have traveled to Cuba with Columbus and were followed in the 16th century by Sephardic Jews escaping persecution at the hands of the Spanish Inquisition (many Jews fled to the Caribbean under assumed Christian identities). Later, Jews coming from Mediterranean countries felt at home in Cuba and were joined by Jews from the United States, who arrived at the end of the last century. They concentrated in southern Habana Vieja, where many started out selling cloth and gaining a monopoly based around Calles Bernaza and Muralla, and across the bay in Guanabacoa. They were joined at the turn of this century by Jews from Florida, who founded the United Hebrew Congregation. Other Ashkenazic Jews emigrating from Eastern Europe passed through Havana en route to the United States in significant numbers until the US slammed its doors in 1924, after which they settled in Cuba. Arriving during a time of destitution, they were relatively poor compared to the earlier Jewish immigrants and were disparagingly called *polacos.* Many were sustained by the largesse of the United Hebrew Congregation.

Sephardic Jews came as families and were profoundly religious. They formed social clubs, opened their own schools, and married their own. By contrast, Ashkenazim most often were single men who went on to marry Cuban (Catholic) women and eventually were assimilated into Cuban society, says Robert M. Levine in his book *Tropical Diaspora: the Jewish Experience in Cuba* (University Press of Florida, 1993). The Ashkenazim were fired with socialist ideals and were prominent in the founding of both the labor and Cuban communist movements.

Cuba seems to have been relatively free of anti-Semitism (Batista was a friend to Jews fleeing Nazi Europe). Levine, however, records how during the late 1930s, the US government bowed to isolationist, labor, and anti-Semitic pressures at home and convinced the Cuban government to turn back European Jews. It is a sordid chapter in US history, best told through the tragic story of the SS *St. Louis* and its 937 passengers trying to escape Nazi Germany in 1939. The ship languished in Havana harbor for a week while US and Cuban officials deliberated on letting passengers disembark; tragically, entry was refused, and the ship and passengers were sent back to Europe and their fate.

By the 1950s, Cuban Jews had prospered in the

ential group amid the jungle of Cuban politics. The university was an autonomous "sacred hill" that neither the police nor the army could enter (although gangsters and renegade politicians roamed the campus). Its most notable of many notable students was Castro, who enrolled in the law school in October 1945 and was involved in the gangsterism. A Saracen armored car sits in the quadrant—it was captured in 1958 by students in the fight against Batista.

The dour modernist monument of concrete across the street facing the steps contains the ashes of Julio Antonio Mella, a student leader (and founder of the Cuban Communist Party) assassinated by the Machado regime in 1929. Ironically, the contemporary edifice dates from the Machado era, when the dictator-president signed bills to fund construction of the Acropolis-like buildings and staircase.

Fortunately, today the campus is a peaceful place. Visitors are allowed to stroll the grounds, although peeking into the classes requires advance permission. The campus is off-limits on weekends, and access is restricted by conscientious *custodios* to Mon.-Fri. 8 a.m.-6 p.m. The campus and museums are closed in July.

The university contains two museums, foremost the **Museo Anthropológico Montane** (Montane Anthropology Museum), tel. (79) 3488, on the second floor of the Felipe Poey Science Building, to the left (south side) of the quadrant beyond the portico at the top of the *escalitas*. The museum contains a valuable collection of pre-Columbian artifacts, including carved idols and turtle shells. Open Mon.-Fri. 9 a.m.-4 p.m. Entry costs US$1.

The **Museo História Naturales Felipe Poey** (Felipe Poey Museum of Natural History), down-

---

clothing trade and enjoyed a cosmopolitan life. The Revolution "had elements of tragedy for the Jewish community," writes Rosshandler, author of the autobiographical novel *Passing Through Havana* (St. Martin's Press, 1984). Castro shut down all business but gave them "the option of staying and keeping their homes. But they had devoted their energy to business and they could not bear to live in a society that looked down on what they prized." Havana's Jews became part of the Cuban diaspora, and only perhaps as many as 2,000 remained (a few joined the Castro government; two became early cabinet members).

It has been claimed that "Castro's Jews" have been better treated in Cuba than anywhere else in the world. Jewish religious schools were the only parochial schools allowed to remain open after the Revolution (the government provided school buses). The Cuban government has always made matzoh available and even authorized a kosher butcher shop in Habana Vieja to supply meat for observant Jews. The Jewish community also has its own cemetery, atop a hill in Guanabacoa, east of Havana, dating from 1910.

A renaissance in the Jewish faith is occurring in Cuba. Synagogues are being refurbished and new ones opened. In 1994, the first bar mitzvah took place in more than 12 years and the first formal bris in more than five years. And the recently reopened Hebrew Sunday School—for children and adults—in the Patronato teaches Hebrew and Hebrew traditions.

To learn more, look for screenings of the documentary film *Havana Nagila: the Jews of Cuba* (57 minutes, 1995), directed by Laura Paull, which traces the history of Jews in Cuba from their immigration in the early 1900s to the current resurgence of Jewish life. Also look for screenings of *Next Year in Havana,* a documentary by Lori Beraha about Havana's Jewish community.

The **Cuban-Jewish Aid Society,** 44 Mercury Ave., Colonia, NJ 07607, tel. (908) 499-9132, sends medicines, humanitarian aid, and religious articles to Cuba, as does the **American-Joint Jewish Distribution Committee,** tel. (212) 687-6200, which sends rabbis and teachers who lead services and make conversions.

Jewish Heritage Tours
The following organizations offer Jewish study tours to Havana: **Center for Cuban Studies,** 124 W. 23rd St., New York, NY 10011, tel. (212) 242-0559, fax (212) 242-1937, e-mail: cubanctr@igc.apc.org, website: cubaupdate.org; **Cuba Travel,** Ave. Quintana Roo, Suite TIJ-1173, Zona Centro, Tijuana, Mexico 22000, tel. (66) 865-298 (Mexico), (310) 842-4148 (US answerphone), e-mail: info@cuba-travel.com.mx, website: www.cubatravel.com.mx; and **Cuban-Jewish Aid Society,** 44 Mercury Ave., Colonia, NJ 07607, tel. (908) 499-9132.

stairs in the same building, tel. (32) 9000, fax (32) 1321, displays an excellent array of pre-Columbian artifacts and the inert remains of dozens of endemic species, stuffed or pickled for posterity within glass cases. There's even a pilot whale suspended from the ceiling, while snakes, alligators, and sharks hang in suspended animation on the walls. The museum—the oldest in Cuba—dates from 1842 and is named for its French-Cuban founder. Poey (1799-1891) was versed in every field of the sciences and founded the Academy of Medical Sciences, the Anthropological Society of Cuba, and a half-dozen other societies. Open Mon.-Fri. 9 a.m.-4 p.m. Entry costs US$1.

Museo Napoleónico

Who would imagine that so much of Napoleon Bonaparte's personal memorabilia would end up in Cuba? But it is, housed in the splendid Ferrara mansion on the south side of the university, at Calle San Miguel 1159, tel. (79) 1412. The collection was the private work of a politician, Orestes Ferrara, who brought back from Europe such precious items as the French emperor's death mask, toothbrush, and the pistols Napoleon used at the Battle of Borodino (other items were seized from Julio Lobo, the former National Bank president, when he left Cuba for exile). The three-story museum is replete with portraits of the military genius. A library is organized chronologically to trace the life of the "Great Corsican." (The large antenna next door is supposedly used to block the signals of TV Martí, beamed from the US.) Open Mon.-Fri. and alternate Sundays 9 a.m.-noon and 1-4 p.m. Entrance costs $5.

Other Sites

The Gothic **Iglesia San Juan de Letran,** Calle 19 e/7 I y J, is hidden away in the residential district southwest of Coppelia. It dates from the 1880s and is one of Havana's most impressive ecclesiastical edifices, equally as impressive within as the Catedral de la Habana, with some of the finest stained-glass windows in Cuba. It is actively used, but rarely open to view.

One block west of the church is a small and charming park (between 21 and 19, and I and H) centered on a pergola. On its northeast corner is a memorial to Leanor Pérez Cabrera, mother of

José Martí, with a letter from Martí to his dearly beloved mamá inscribed in metal. One block north, at the corner of 17 and I, is **UNEAC,** the Unión Nacional de Escritores y Artistes de Cuba (National Union of Writers and Artists), tel. (32) 4551, fax (33) 3158.

Cuba's Jewish heritage is maintained with a passion, as demonstrated by the dedication of Adela Dworin—the doyenne—and her staff at **El Patronato,** otherwise known as the **Casa de la Comunidad Hebrea de Cuba,** which works to preserve Hebrew traditions and pride. The edifice at Calle I between 13 y 15, tel. (32) 8953, abuts the **Bet Shalon Sinagogo** (where you can witness services with permission). It contains an active community center and a large library on Judaica, Israel, and related themes. Tom Miller provides a splendid review of the *Patronato* and Jewish heritage in Havana in his *Trading with the Enemy.*

The black marble column at the corner of Linea and L was erected in 1931 to commemorate Havana's *chinos* who fought for Cuban independence.

AVENIDA DE LOS PRESIDENTES AND VICINITY

Avenida de los Presidentes is a wide boulevard that might be considered Vedado's backbone. It runs perpendicular to Avenida 23 and flows downhill to the Malecón—a distance greater than the length of Habana Vieja. A wide, grassy, tree-lined median runs down its spine, dividing separate roadways running uphill and downhill. To each side are grand colonial homes in various states of repair and disrepair. Many now function as schools or government departments. The leafy residential streets of northern Vedado are a joy to walk along.

One of the more extravagant mansions is at Calle 17 e/ D y E, two blocks west of Avenida de los Presidentes. The villa, which formerly belonged to a Cuban countess, now houses the stunning **Museo de Artes Decorativas** (Museum of Decorative Arts), tel. (32) 0924, which brims with a lavish collection of furniture, paintings, textiles, and chinoiserie from the 18th and 19th centuries. Most of the furniture, however, is European, not Cuban. No matter, it's staggering in its sumptuous

BALLERINA CUBANA ALICIA ALONSO

Cubans love ballet, which is associated in Cuba with one name above all—Alicia Alonso. Ballet appeared in Cuba as early as 1842, and throughout the 19th century, foreign ballet companies performed, notably at the Teatro Tacón. Finally, in 1931, Havana got its own ballet company: the Sociedad Pro-Arte Música, with a conservatory that produced many outstanding ballet dancers, including Alonso, born to an aristocratic family in Havana on 21 December 1921 and christened Alicia Ernestina de la Caridad del Cobre Martínez Hoyo.

Alonso studied in her youth with the American Ballet following its inception in the 1940s and became a prima ballerina with the company. In 1948, she returned to Cuba and, sponsored by Batista (who hated ballet but considered her star status a propaganda bonus), that year founded the Ballet Alicia Alonso, which in 1955 became the Ballet de Cuba. Alonso was outspoken in her criticism of the "Sordid Era," and she went into exile in 1956 when Batista withdrew his patronage. The Revolution later adopted her, and her ballet company was re-formed and renamed the Ballet Nacional de Cuba, which became a showpiece for the Cuban Revolution, making regular forays abroad (including to the US in 1978).

Alonso is revered as a national icon and an exemplar of the cultural achievements of the postrevolutionary years. There is no doubting her technical excellence and her inspirational character, and her company is renowned worldwide for its original choreography and talent, although Alonso has been accused of maintaining a lily-white dance corp.

The **Museo de la Danza,** in a restored mansion at the corner of Linea and Avenida de los Presidentes, opened on the 50th anniversary of the Ballet of Cuba. Its diverse salons are dedicated to Russian ballet, modern dance, the National Ballet of Cuba, and other themes. Exhibits include wardrobes, recordings, manuscripts, and photographs relating to the history of dance. Alicia Alonso, founder and *prima ballerina absoluta* of the Ballet of Cuba, contributed her valuable personal collection, including her first ballet shoes and the costume she wore in *Carmen.* The museum contains a library and video archives. It was not yet open to the public at press time.

Near the base of Avenida de los Presidentes, pause at #220 to admire the beautiful blue tilework and stucco, and the columns like twirled candy sticks. Nearby is the **Casa de las Américas,** at Avenida 3ra and the corner of Calle G, tel. (55) 2706, fax (33) 4554, e-mail: casa@artsoft.cult.cu, a cultural center formed in 1959 by revolutionary heroine Haydee Santamaría to study and promote the cultures of Latin America and the Caribbean. It has a large library and exhibits in two nearby galleries—the **Galeria Haydee Santamaría** (Avenida 5ra and G) and the **Galería Mariano** (15 #607 between B and C)—containing the Art Collection of New America. This collection comprises more than 6,000 pieces of sculpture, engravings, paintings, photographs, and popular art representing artists throughout the Americas and the Caribbean. The center contains a silkscreening shop and hosts concerts, film screenings, and theater and dance programs. It also has a small bookstore with a focus on the arts. Open Mon.-Fri. 10 a.m.-5 p.m.

Midway between Avenidas de los Presidentes and Paseo is the recently restored **Parque Villalon,** between 5ra y Calzada (7ma) and C y D. While there's nothing noteworthy about the park, it's surrounded by some important edifices, including, on its southeast side, the grandiose Romanesque **Teatro Amadeo Rohoan,** recently restored to haughty grandeur as a concert hall. Next door, at Calzada #1510, is the headquarters of the **Ballet Nacional de Cuba,** tel. (55) 2946, founded and run by Alicia Alonso, a national icon. Understandably, the ballet school is closed to visitors (who might disturb the dancers' concentration), but sometimes you can spot the

quality. Upstairs, where the landing is festooned with ivory figures, you'll find a boudoir decorated Oriental style, its furniture inlaid with mother-of-pearl. Highly recommended. Open Tues.-Sat. 11 a.m.-6:30 p.m. Entrance costs US$2 (US$5 extra for cameras, US$10 for videos).

Following the Avenida de los Presidentes north, note the handsome bronze statue of Alexandro Rodriguez y Velasco on a granite pedestal, guarded by a bronze figure of Perseus at Linea and Avenida de los Presidentes.

dancers practicing their pirouettes if you peek through the gate.

South of Calle 23, Avenida de los Presidentes climbs to the **Monumento al General Máximo Gómez** (not to be confused with a similar monument in Habana Vieja), topped by nubile figures in classical style. The road then drops down to meet the westward extension of Avenida Salvador Allende through a canyon lined with ancient and giant jagüey trees, which form a fantastical glade over the road. Hidden from sight on the bluff above (to the west) is the **Castillo del Principe,** built in the 1770s following the English invasion. The castle is off-limits and rarely mentioned in Cuban tourist literature because it houses a prison.

On the north side of Salvador Allende, about 100 meters east of Avenida de los Presidentes, is the unkempt **Botanical Gardens.** This was a popular recreation spot in colonial days, when it was the site of the pleasure gardens of the governor's summer palace. Slaves newly arrived from Africa were kept here in barracoons, where they could be displayed to passersby. The gardens surround the once-graceful **Quinta de los Molinos,** reached via a decrepit cobbled, gladed drive. The old mansion is named for the royal snuff mills that were built here in 1791 to take advantage of the waters of Zanza Real; you can still see part of the original aqueduct—inaugurated in 1592—to the rear of the time-worn *quinta*. It now houses the **Museo de Máximo Gómez,** tel. (79) 8850, honoring the Dominican-born hero of the Cuban Wars of Independence. His sword and a few other personal effects are on display, and maps show his progress during the wars. The collection is motley and poorly presented. Open Tues.-Sat. 9 a.m.-5 p.m., Sunday 9 a.m.-1 p.m. (US$1). Lectures, art classes, and other activities are hosted here for community members.

PASEO AND WESTERN VEDADO

Paseo parallels Avenida de los Presidentes seven blocks to the west; like the Avenida de los Presidentes, the Paseo is a linear park flanked by two avenues considered as one, being one way in either direction. Although itself a pleasant stroll, Paseo offers little of touristic interest. An exception is the **Casa de la Amistad**, on Paseo between 17 and 19. This old mansion of generous proportions is run by the Cuban state as a "friendship house" with rooms for entertaining, plus a Casa del Tabaco and a meager snack bar out back overlooking the unkempt gardens. It seems to be a popular trysting spot for more mature Cubans and makes a good place to break your perambulations with a cool drink.

On the southern end of Paseo, at the junction of Paseo and Zapata, and at the top of the rise that continues southeast to Plaza de la Revolución, is the **The Rosenberg Monument,** a curiosity in passing. Here a small park is pinned by a tree shading an inconspicuous red-brick wall bearing cement doves and an inset sculpture of Julius and Ethel Rosenberg, the US couple executed in 1951 for passing nuclear secrets to the Soviet Union. An inscription reads, "Murdered June 19, 1953." Julius's final words are engraved, too: "For Peace, Bread, and Roses, We Face the Executioners."

Paralleling Paseo six blocks to the west is Calle 12. **Galeria 23 y 12,** at the corner of Calles 23 and 12, marks the spot where on 16 April 1961, Castro announced—on the eve of the Bay of Pigs invasion—that Cuba was henceforth socialist. The anniversary of the declaration of socialism is marked each 16th April, when Castro speaks on the corner. The facade bears a patinated bronze plaque showing the heroes who were killed in the US-sponsored strike on the airfield at Marianao that was a prelude to the invasion. The plaque, of course, also features Castro, shown most prominently in his usual defiant pose. Today the building houses an art *salón*.

While walking down Calle 12, you'll pass a couple of Castro's "safe houses," such as the one between Linea and 13, where the road is cordoned off as a "Zona Militar."

One block south, at the junction of Calle 12 and Zapata (a sinuous westward extension of the Zanja, following the course of the ancient aqueduct) is Vedado's pride and joy, the Cementerio de Colón.

Cementerio de Colón

Described as "an exercise in pious excesses," Havana's Necrópolis Cristóbal Colón is renowned worldwide for its flamboyant mausoleums, vaults, and tombs embellished with angels, griffins, cherubs, and other ornamentation, with poppies, hibiscus, bougainvillea, and other cut flowers adding notes of bright color. The cemetery, covering 56 hectares on land once owned by the Catholic Church, contains more than 500 major mausoleums, chapels, family vaults, and galleries (in addition to countless gravestones). It was laid out between 1871 and 1886 in 16 rectangular blocks, or *insulae*, like a Roman military camp, with an ocher-colored, octagonal Greek Orthodox-style church—the **Capillo Central**—at its center. The designer, a Spaniard named Calixto de Loira, divided the cemetery by social status, with separate areas for non-Catholics and for victims of epidemics (appropriately, Loira was among the first to be buried here). It was originally open only to nobles, who competed to build the most elaborate tombs, with social standing dictating the size and location of plots. The cemetery represents Havana's major architectonic expression of the era and has been declared a national monument.

Here the wealthy vied for immortality on a grand scale. The cemetery is a petrified version of society of the times, combining, says the *Guía Turística* (available at the entrance gate), a "grandeur and meanness, good taste and triviality, popular and cosmopolitan, drama and even an unusual black humor, as in the gravestone carved as a double-three, devoted to an emotional elderly lady who died with that domino in her hand, thus losing both game and life at a time." The *doble tres* was that of Juana Martin, a domino fanatic who indeed died as described.

Famous *criollo* patricians, colonial aristocrats, and war heroes such as Máximo Gómez are

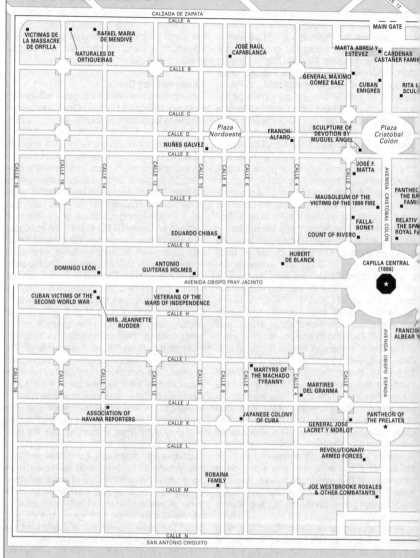

CEMETERIO CRISTÓBAL COLÓN

CALLE 14
CALLE 12

CALZADA DE ZAPATA
CALLE A

MAIN GATE

VICTIMAS DE LA MASSACRE DE ORFILLA

RAFAEL MARIA DE MENDIVE

NATURALES DE ORTIGUEIRAS

JOSÉ RAÚL CAPABLANCA

MARTA ABREU Y ESTÉVEZ

CÁRDENAS CASTAÑER FAMI

CALLE B

GENERAL MÁXIMO GÓMEZ BÁEZ

CUBAN EMIGRÉS

RITA L SCUL

CALLE C

Plaza Nordoeste

FRANCHI-ALFARO

SCULPTURE OF DEVOTION BY MUGUEL ANGEL

Plaza Cristóbal Colón

CALLE D

NUÑES GÁLVEZ

CALLE E

JOSÉ F. MATTA

MAUSOLEUM OF THE VICTIMS OF THE 1890 FIRE

PANTHEO THE BA FAMI

CALLE F

FALLA-BONET

RELATIV THE SPA ROYAL F

EDUARDO CHIBAS

COUNT OF RIVERO

CALLE G

HUBERT DE BLANCK

CAPILLA CENTRAL (1886)

DOMINGO LEÓN

ANTONIO GUITERAS HOLMES

AVENIDA OBISPO FRAY JACINTO

CUBAN VICTIMS OF THE SECOND WORLD WAR

VETERANS OF THE WARS OF INDEPENDENCE

MRS. JEANNETTE RUDDER

CALLE H

FRANCIS ALBEAR Y

CALLE I

MARTYRS OF THE MACHADO TYRANNY

MÁRTIRES DEL GRANMA

CALLE J

ASSOCIATION OF HAVANA REPORTERS

JAPANESE COLONY OF CUBA

GENERAL JOSE LACRET Y MORLOT

PANTHEON OF THE PRELATES

CALLE K

CALLE L

REVOLUTIONARY ARMED FORCES

ROBAINA FAMILY

CALLE M

JOE WESTBROOKE ROSALES & OTHER COMBATANTS

CALLE N

SAN ANTONIO CHIQUITO

CALLE 18
CALLE 16
CALLE 14
CALLE 12
CALLE 10
CALLE 8
CALLE 6
CALLE 4
CALLE 2

AVENIDA CRISTÓBAL COLÓN
AVENIDA OBISPO ESPADA

THE CUBAN GOVERNMENT

Cuba is an independent republic. The Cuban Constitution, adopted in 1975, defines it as a "socialist state of workers and peasants and all other manual and intellectual workers" (it is really a *Fidelista* state, one in which Marxist-Leninism has been loosely grafted onto Cuban nationalism, then tended and shaped by one man). Dr. Fidel Castro Ruz is head of both state and government. The constitution names Castro as first secretary of the Communist Party, president of the Republic, chairman of the State Council, chairman of the Council of Ministers, and commander in chief of the armed forces (he is normally referred to as *Comandante-en-Jefe,* or Commander in Chief). His younger brother, Raúl, is first vice president of both the Council of State and the Council of Ministers, the second secretary of the Communist Party, defense minister, and General of the Army.

All power and initiative are in the hands of the Communist Party (*Partido Comunista de Cuba,* or PCC), which controls the labyrinthine state apparatus. There are no legally recognized political organizations independent of the party. Steering the party is the Comité Central (Central Committee), whose members are selected by Castro (at the base of the PCC chain is the party cell of 10 members organized at work and educational centers). Policy emanates from Castro, who has used his own charismatic qualities and inordinate tactical skills to consolidate almost hegemonic authority. The PCC has no program—Castro defines the flavor of the day.

The highest-ranking executive body is the Council of Ministers, whose Executive Committee administers Cuba on a day-to-day basis. The council is accountable to the National Assembly of People's Power, which "elects" the members at the initiative of the head of state. However, it is mostly a rubber-stamp legislature and meets only twice annually.

The Council of State is modeled on the Presidium of the former Soviet Union and functions as the Executive Committee of the National Assembly when the latter is not in session.

Local Government

The country is divided into 14 provinces and 169 municipalities *(municipios),* dominated by the city of Havana (a separate province). Havana is governed by an Assembly of Delegates of People's Power, representing state bodies at the local level. The Assembly is headed by Esteban Lazo, the tall, girt black First Secretary of the Communist Party of Habana, a position equivalent to City Mayor. Since 1992, members have been elected by popular ballot and serve two-and-a-half-year terms.

Committees for the Defense of the Revolution

The linchpins in maintaining the loyalty of the masses and spreading the Revolution at the grassroots level are the *Comités para la Defensa de la Revolución* (CDRs), created in 1960 as neighborhood committees designed to protect the Revolution from internal enemies. There are 15,000 CDRs in Havana, and 100,000 throughout the island (66% of the population are members). Every block has one.

On one hand, the CDRs perform wonderful work: they collect blood for hospitals, take retired people on vacations, discourage kids from playing hooky, organize graduation parties, and patrol at night to guard against delinquency. But they are also the vanguard in keeping an eye on the local population, watching and snitching on neighbors (the CDRs are under the direction of MININT, the Ministry of the Interior, which handles most aspects of state security). Anyone nay-saying the Revolution, mocking Castro, or dealing on the black market (economic crimes are political crimes, seen as a security threat to the state) is likely to be reported by the block warden, a loyal revolutionary who records what he or she hears from colleagues and neighbors.

People face harsh retribution if they cross the line into political activism. In 1991, Rapid Response Detachments were formed, ostensibly made up of volunteers from local CDRs but under the purview of MININT, to deal with public expressions of dissent. This they do through distasteful pogroms called *actos de repudios,* beating up dissidents, much as did Hitler's *Blockwarts.* Like Nazi street gangs, the brigades are said to be a spontaneous reaction of outraged Cubans.

Other Mass Organizations

Citizen participation in building socialism is manifested through a number of mass organizations controlled by the PCC. Prominent among them are the **Federation of Cuban Women,** the **Confeder-**

ation of Cuban Workers, Organization of Small Farmers, and the Union of Communist Youth. Although ostensibly representing their members' interests, the bodies subordinate these to national goals.

The Judiciary

The highest court in the land is the People's Supreme Court in Havana. Its president and vice president are appointed by Castro; other judges are elected by the National Assembly. There are seven courts of appeal, 14 provincial courts, and 169 municipal courts for minor offenses. The provinces are divided into judicial districts with courts for civil and criminal cases.

Courts are a fourth branch of government and are not independent. The judiciary is not charged with protecting individual rights but rather, according to Article 121 of the Constitution, with "maintaining and strengthening socialist legality." Thus, they are subject to interference by the political leadership. And interpretation of the Constitution is the prerogative solely of the National Assembly, not the courts.

A State of Acquiescence

Castro has engineered a state where an individual's personal survival requires a display of loyalty and adherence to the Revolution. A margin of public criticism is allowed, to vent political pressure. The headiest steam is periodically allowed to leave for Florida on rafts and inflated inner tubes. Otherwise, jail or "spontaneous" acts of repudiation by gangs of "citizens" quickly silence the dissident and serve to put others on notice.

The government maintains a file on *every* worker, a labor dossier that follows him or her from job to job. Cubans have to voice—or fake—their loyalty. To become *integrado* (integrated) is essential to get by. Transgressions are reported in one's dossier. If "antisocial" comments are noted, the worker may be kicked out of his or her job, or blackballed. Cuban citizens can hardly make a move without accounting for it to the authorities.

Most Cubans have accommodated themselves to the parameters of permissible behavior set out years ago. The hardcore opponents left for Miami long ago. Most of the rest go along. Nonetheless, dissidence and vocal opposition to both the state of affairs and the Castro government have grown markedly in recent years. The overwhelming majority of Habaneros are tired of sacrifice, foolhardy experiments, and the paternalism that tells them how to live their lives. The constant opening and closing of society has taken its toll, raising and then dashing Cubans' hopes. In recent years, occasional riots have broken out on the streets of Havana, and harassment and jailing of dissidents has risen sharply, with periodic crackdowns on Cubans—deemed "counter-revolutionaries"—having too-close contact with foreigners.

Wrote James Michener, "Perhaps only the kindness of the climate prevents the smoldering of revolt that might accompany the same conditions in a cold and relentless climate."

buried here alongside noted intellectuals, merchants, and corrupt politicians (as well, of course, as the rare honest one, such as Eduardo Chibás). The list goes on and on: José Raúl Capablanca, the world chess champion 1921-27; Alejo Carpentier, Cuba's most revered contemporary novelist; Hubert de Blanck, the noted composer; and Celia Sánchez, Haydee Santamaría, and a plethora of revolutionaries killed for the cause. Its many collective vaults reflect Cuba's heterogeneous roots. You'll even find Greco-Roman temples in miniature, an Egyptian pyramid, and medieval castles, plus Baroque, Romantic, Renaissance, Art Deco, and Art Nouveau art, allegories, and metaphors of human life by a pantheon of Cuba's leading sculptors and artists. You could take all day to discover all the gems. Fortunately,

benches are provided beneath shade trees. Still, wear your sunglasses against the glare of the incandescent sun bouncing off a surfeit of Carrara marble. Says Nancy Stout: "Eclecticism is the key to cosmetics here."

The most visited grave is the flower-bedecked tomb of Amelia Goyri de Hoz, revered as *La Milagrosa* (The Miraculous One), to whom miraculous healings are attributed as a protector of sick children. According to legend, she died during childbirth in 1901 and was buried with her stillborn child at her feet. When her sarcophagus was later opened, the baby was supposedly cradled in her arms. Ever since, superstitious Cubans have paid homage by knocking three times on the tombstone with one of its brass rings, before touching the tomb and requesting a favor (one must not turn one's back on the tomb when departing). Many are the childless women who pray here in hopes of a pregnancy.

The **Tobias Gallery** is one of several underground galleries; this one is 100 meters long and contains 256 niches containing human remains.

The impressive Romanesque-Byzantine entrance gate of locally quarried coral stone is at the top of Calle 12 and Calle Zapata, which runs along its north face. The triple-arched gate was inspired by the Triumphal Arch in Rome that alludes to the Holy Trinity, with reliefs in Carrara marble that depict the crucifixion and Lazarus rising from the grave. It is embellished with a marble sculpture of the coronation stone representing *The Theological Virtues:* Faith, Hope, and Charity. The major tombs line the main avenue that leads south from the gate.

To the right of the entrance is an information office; you must pay an entrance fee here (US$1). Guided tours are available free of charge, but tips would be welcome. It is worthwhile buying a guidebook containing a map (US$5). Open 7:30 a.m.-5 p.m.

Chinese Cemetery

Immediately southwest of Cementerio Colón, on the west side of Avenida 26, the Chinese built their own cemetery, with graves that appeal to an Asian culture. The circular gateway derives from the *pai lou,* the monumental Chinese arches erected by custom at the entrance to processional ways, palaces, and tombs. Traditional lions stand guard over hundreds of graves beneath highly pitched burial chapels with upward-curving roofs of red and green tile in the traditional *xuan-shan* (hanging mountain) gabled style. It is a place, says Nancy Stout, of "cultural contradistinctions," with plenty of Christian crosses and a "malleable classical vocabulary." There's no charge to enter, but the gates are usually locked.

PLAZA DE LA REVOLUCIÓN

Havana's largest plaza is a must-see for two defining edifices, although the plaza itself is a rather ugly tarred square accurately described by P.J. O'Rourke as "a vast open space resembling the Mall in D.C., but dropped into the middle of a massive empty parking lot in a tropical Newark." You can't blame the Revolution. The trapezoidal complex measuring one km in length was laid out during the Batista era, when it was known as the Plaza Cívica, and all the major edifices (including the José Martí monument and statue) date back to the 1950s.

It's a 30-minute walk from the Habana Libre Hotel, but you can take bus no. 84 from the bottom of La Rampa, at Calle 0 and Humboldt.

On the plaza's northwest corner, across Avenida Céspedes, is the modern but rundown and poorly constructed **Teatro Nacional,** with a glass-plated facade. The theater is underutilized—"waiting," wrote novelist Donald Westlake, "for a theatrical season that had never quite arrived."

The plaza is the center of government, highlighted by the **Palacio de la Revolución,** tel. (79) 6551, immediately behind the José Martí monument to the south. This is where Castro and the Council of Ministers and their underlings work out their policies of state. The labyrinthine, ocher-colored palace adjoins the buildings of the Central Committee of the Communist Party and is fronted by a broad staircase built by Batista for the Cuban Supreme Court and national police headquarters. It boasts fine marble floors, and an enormous ceramic-tile mosaic of birds, animals, and flowers dominates the reception hall. The artist apparently cast the intricately etched tiles while the architect was still designing the interior, and, through a misunderstanding, the ceiling was built too low. The top two rows wouldn't fit, robbing the mosaic of its crown. Castro's study is a "simple room with several couches, chairs, and potted plants spread throughout." An entire wall is fronted by a bookcase with bound books gifted by the president of Mexico. One door leads from here to the cabinet meeting room; another leads to Castro's office, containing a desk lined with telephones, a bookcase, sofa, two lounge chairs, and a small conference table. No visitors are allowed.

To the north and east are government ministries in soulless post-Stalinist style, including, on the northwest side, the tall **Ministerio del Interior** (the ministry in charge of national security), with a windowless wall bearing a soaring black-metal "mural" of Che Guevara and the words "Hasta la Victoria Siempre" (Until the Victory Forever). To the east of the Ministry of the

Interior is the **Ministerio de Comunicaciones,** containing the **Museo Postal Cubano** (on the ground floor), tel. (70) 5581. Serious philatelists will find it fascinating. The well-cataloged collection is kept in vertical pull-out glass file drawers. A complete range of Cuban postage stamps (including the first, dating from 1855) is on display, plus a large collection of stamps from almost 100 other countries, including numerous "penny black" and other valuable stamps from England. Check out the little solid-propellant rocket that was launched in 1936 by a group of enthusiastic philatelists eager to promote rocket propulsion to speed up mail delivery. The museum has a well-stocked *filatelica* (stamp shop) selling stamps. Open Mon.-Fri. 9 a.m.-4 p.m.; entrance US$1.

Across Avenida Rancho Boyeros, on the southeast side, is the **Ministerio de Defensa** and, behind, the headquarters of *Granma,* the national daily newspaper of the Cuban Communist Party. On the northeast corner of the square is Cuba's largest library, the **Biblioteca Nacional.**

One block north, in the Sala Polivatente Ramón Fonst sports stadium on Rancho Boyeros between 10 de Mayo and Bruzón, you'll find the **Museo de História del Deportivo,** tel. (81) 4696, which tells the history of Cuban sports. Open Tues.-Sun. 10 a.m.-5 p.m.; entrance US$1.

Parking is strictly controlled at Plaza de la Revolución, with a designated parking zone on the east side of the plaza. If you park on the plaza or along the road, soldiers will quickly move you along.

Monumento y Museo José Martí

This spectacular monument, made entirely of gray granite and marble, sits atop a 30-meter-tall base that spans the entire square. It acts as a massive reviewing stand and podium, from which Castro tutors, harangues, and encourages the masses. To each side, great arching stairways lead to a huge granite statue of the National Hero sitting in a contemplative pose, like Rodin's *The Thinker.*

Behind looms a slender, 109-meter-tall Babylonian edifice stepped like a soaring ziggurat from a sci-fi movie. The tower—the highest point in Havana—is made entirely of gray marble quarried from the Isle of Youths. The top bristles with antennas. Vultures soar overhead and roost on the narrow ledges, lending an added eerie quality to the scene. Its construction is said to have cost every citizen in Cuba one centavo.

Until early 1996, soldiers barred the way up to the monument, from where sentries surveyed passersby—and often icily shooed them away. The guards have since departed, and the edifice has been opened as a museum dedicated to José Martí, within the base of the tower. The museum, tel. (82) 0906, is splendid, depicting everything you could wish to know about Martí. Among the exhibits are many first-edition works, engravings, drawings, and maps, as well as reproductions of significant artifacts in Martí's life. Of course, the largest photograph of all depicts Castro, shown in saintly homage on the beach at Cojababo, the site in Guantánamo province where Martí put ashore in 1896 after a 16-year exile.

The museum also displays the original plans for the design of the monument and plaza, including a Parthenon-like scheme that seems a copycat version of Washington's Lincoln Memorial. Planning, construction, and urbanization of the area around the plaza is traced with large black-and-white photos that display key moments that have occurred here since the Revolution. New Age music plays in the background, drawing you to a multiscreen broadcast on the wars of independence and the Revolution. One of the four exhibition rooms is dedicated to traveling exhibits, which change every three months. To one side is a small art gallery featuring portraits of Martí by numerous leading artists.

The museum is open Mon.-Sat. 10 a.m.-6 p.m., Sunday 10 a.m.-2 p.m. Entrance costs US$5 (US$5 extra for cameras, US$10 for videos). For an additional US$5, you can take the elevator to a viewing gallery at the top (open Mon.-Sat. 9 a.m.-4 p.m., Sunday 2-4 p.m.). From above, you can see that the entire structure is designed as a five-pointed star. Each star in the *mirador* contains windows on each side, providing a 360-degree view over Havana. On a clear day, you can see 50 miles. Inset in the floor of each point is a compass showing the direction and distance of national and international cities (New York, for example, is 2,100 km away, and the North Pole is 7,441 km away).

JOSÉ MARTÍ

He is the most revered figure in Cuban history. His name has been appropriated by the Castro government *and* the fiercely anticommunist exiles in Florida. He is José Martí, avatar of Cuba's independence spirit and the ideological architect of the Cuban Revolution. There is hardly a quadrant in Havana that does not have a street, square or major building named in his honor.

Martí was born in 1853 in a small house on Calle Paula in Habana Vieja. Martí came from peninsular stock. His father was from Valencia, Spain; his mother from the Canary Islands. He spent much of his youth in Spain before his parents returned to Cuba. When the War of Independence erupted in 1868, Martí was 15 years old. Already he sympathized with "the cause."

At the age of 16, he published his first newspaper, *La Patria Libre*. He also wrote a letter denouncing a school friend for attending a pro-Spanish rally. The letter was judged to be treasonous, and Martí was sentenced to six-years' imprisonment, including six months' hard labor at the San Lázaro stone quarry in Havana. In 1871, he was exiled to Spain, where he earned a law degree and gravitated to the revolutionary circles then active in Madrid.

In 1878, as part of a general amnesty, he was allowed to return but was then deported again. He traveled through France and, in 1881, to the US, where he settled for the next 14 years with his wife and son, working as a reporter in New York.

The Pen and the Sword
Dressed in his trademark black suit and bow tie, with his thick moustache waxed into pointy tips, Martí devoted more and more of his time to winning independence for Cuba. He wrote poetry heralding the liberation of his homeland during a "time of fervent repose," the years fol-

NUEVO VEDADO

Nuevo Vedado is a spawling complex of mid-20th-century housing, including ugly high-rise, postrevolutionary apartment blocks, arrayed in irregular grids interlinked (unusual for Havana) by serpentine thoroughfares.

The main site of interest is the **Jardín Zoológico de la Habana,** Havana's provincial zoo (not to be confused with the national Parque Zoológico on the city's outskirts), on Avenida 26 and Zoológico, tel. (81) 8915. The zoo is a sad affair that suffers from poor management and lack of attention. The hippopotamus, crocodiles, caimans, flamingoes, and other water-loving species wade and wallow in polluted lagoons. It has many monkeys and chimpanzees, but tragically they are kept apart, and though their cages abut each other, they are separated by walls so that no monkey or ape has a view of its neighbors. Other species on view include Andean condors, water buffalo, jaguars, leopards, lions (thankfully in a large pit), and a gorilla, which suffered a stoning from a child when I was last there. The animals and visitors alike are further tormented by modern music piped over loudspeakers at deafening levels. A children's playground offers pony rides, and there's a basic snack bar. Open Tues.-Sun. 9:30 a.m.-5:30 p.m. (US$2).

From the city zoo, you can follow Avenida Zoológica west to the bridge over the Río Almendares, and by turning right at the end, enter the **Bosque de la Habana.** This woodsy parkland stretches along the canyon and plain of the river, and can still be enjoyed in a virtually untouched state, for which it is popular with lovers seeking a private spot—a veritable Garden of Eden. To the south, the woods extend to **Los Jardines de la Tropical,** a landscaped park built 1904-10 on the grounds of a former brewery and designed by the Tropical beer com-

lowing the Ten Years' War. His writing wedded the rhetoric of nationalism to calls for social justice, fashioning a vision of a free Cuba that broke through class and racial barriers.

Prophetically, Martí's writings are full of invocations to death. It was he who coined the phrase *La Victoria o el Sepulcro* (Victory or the Tomb), which Fidel Castro has turned with great success into a call for *"Patria o Muerte"* (Patriotism or Death), and more recently, *"Socialismo o Muerte."*

Martí is revered as much for his poetry, which helped define the school of modern Latin American poetry. His voluminous writings are littered with astute critiques of US culture and politics. He despised the expansionist nature of the US, arguing that US ambitions toward Cuba were as dangerous as the rule of Spain. "It is my duty . . . to prevent, through the independence of Cuba, the USA from spreading over the West Indies and falling with added weight upon other lands of Our America. All I have done up to now and shall do hereafter is to that end."

Theory into Action

In 1892, Martí met with leading Cuban exiles and presented his "Fundamentals and Secret Guidelines of the Cuban Revolutionary Party," outlining the goals of the nationalists: independence for Cuba, equality of all Cubans, and establishment of democratic processes. That year, Martí began publishing *Patria.* Through dint of passion and idealism, he had established himself as the acknowledged political leader. He melded the various exile factions together, formulated a common program, and managed to integrate the cause of Cuban exile workers into the crusade (they contributed 10% of their earnings to his cause). He founded a revolutionary center, Cuba Libre (Free Cuba), and La Liga de Instrucción, which trained revolutionary fighters.

In 1895, Martí presented the *Manifesto de Montecristi,* outlining the policy for the war of independence that was to be initiated later that year. Martí was named major general of the Armies of Liberation, while General Máximo Gómez was named supreme commander of the revolutionary forces.

On 11 April 1895, Martí, Gómez, and four followers landed at Playitas, in a remote part of eastern Cuba. Moving secretly through the mountains, they gathered supporters and finally linked up with Antonio Maceo and his army of 6,000. The first skirmish with the Spanish occurred at Dos Ríos on 19 May 1895. Martí was the first casualty. He had determined on martyrdom and committed sacrificial suicide by riding headlong into the enemy line. Thus, Martí brought the republic to birth, says Guillermo Cabrera Infante, "carrying a cadaver around its neck."

pany for promotional purposes (a free round of drinks was offered to picnickers). The park was paid for by Catalonians resident in Cuba and, appropriately, found its inspiration in Antoni Gaudí's Parque Güell in Barcelona, with winding paths shaded by almond trees and ficus snaking like castaway ropes through the 12.5-acre site. It features gazebos, watchtowers, pergolas, a castle, a pigeon house, and other attractions along the way, including Gaudíesque concrete columns shaped as tree trunks and railings resembling logs.

PLAYA (MIRAMAR AND BEYOND)

West of Vedado and the Río Almendares stretches a vast and vital region where, prior to the Revolution, the wealthy and middle classes lived in low-rise apartments, and columned and balustraded mansions. The *municipio*—called Playa—extends west to the far reaches of Havana, beginning in the east, with the seaside district of Miramar extending west about four miles as far as the Río Quibu. Miramar is still exclusive—leafy and secluded. The rich who fled or were forced to depart left their grandiose homes and classy apartments as valuable "gifts" to the Revolutionary government (in reality, of course, the properties were seized), which turned many into clinics, kindergartens, and clubs. Those for which no public use could be found were divided up into private apartments and communal dwellings for multiple families flooding in from the countryside. Unfortunately, most Habaneros have lacked the resources to maintain them, and many of the mansions have degenerated into slums.

Miramar is at the forefront of Cuba's quasi-capitalist remake. Even upscale condominiums had gone up in 1999, with ritzy apartments for sale to foreigners (Cubans, ironically, are not permitted to buy or sell property). Cuba's future can be seen here, with dozens of cranes and construction crews at work erecting new hotels and offices. In spring 1999, they built the **Miramar Trade Center,** a 27,000-square-meter complex with adjoining offices—many of them complete and ready to rent—opposite the gleaming new Meliá Habana hotel on Avenida 3ra. This area, an undeveloped flatland between Calles 70 and 84, was also being developed, with Havana's largest hotel complex—the Hotel Miramar (on Avenida 5ra) and Hotel Panorama (on Avenida 3ra), both well underway at press time.

Inland of Avenida 5ra—the main east-west boulevard—Miramar slopes south, uphill to the suburban Marianao district, accessed fromVedado via Avenida 31, which begins at the junction of

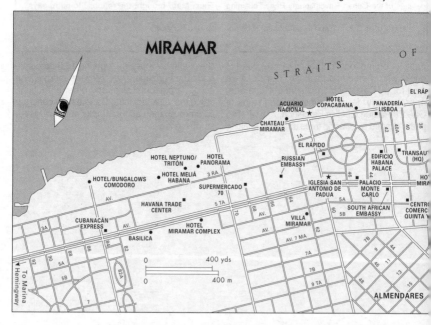

Avenida 7ma and Calle 10 and runs southwest to the famous Tropicana nightclub at Calle 70. From downtown, access to Miramar is via tunnels under the Río Almendares at the west end of both the Malecón (at its junction with Calle 7, or Calzada) and Calle 9; and via a steel footbridge—**Puente de Hierro**—at the west end of Calle 9.

West of Miramar, Playa boasts the city's *balnearios* (bathing areas), which line the shore of the Nautico and Flores districts, cut through by Avenida 5ta. Playa also boasts Havana's most luxurious residences, concentrated along the leafy boulevards of the hilly Cubanacán district, on the slopes inland of the shore. Adjacent Siboney is now a center for biogenetic research.

There's an **Infotur** tourist information office located (oddly) on the north side of the traffic circle (roundabout) on Avenida 5ra at 112. It has a minimal stock of literature.

AVENIDA 1RA (PRIMERA)

Avenida 1ra (Primera) runs along the Miramar seafront. It's a lively spot, popular with Havana's youth. It's Havana's answer to Santa Monica—without the sand and the pier, but with the occasional girl in skin-tight hot pants being pulled along on roller blades by a dog. However, the shoreline is grotesquely ugly and lacks beaches.

Avenida 1ra is witnessing a boom, with many embassies, restaurants, and commercial entities opting for a locale by the sea. Even surfing has come to Cuba; the surfing crowd finds its waves in the coastal section fronting the Hotels Neptuno/Tritón on Avenida 1ra between 70 and 84.

Decrepit *balnearios* are found all along Miramar's waterfront, cut into the coral shore. Most are concentrated west of the Hotel Comodoro, beginning at Calle 84. They are exceedingly time-worn, battered by one-too-many Caribbean storms, and of no appeal. More appealing beaches—the Playas del Oeste—begin half a kilometer farther west in the Nautico district and extend west to Flores (Jaiminito).

A stroll along the avenue is pleasant (don't underestimate its length, about two miles), but there are only two sites of interest. First comes the Maqueta de La Habana.

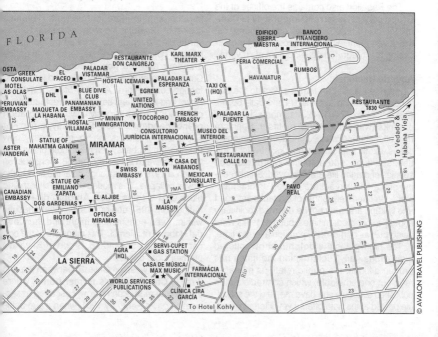

Maqueta de La Habana Vieja

The must-see *maqueta* (model) is a 1:1,000 scale replica of the city. It is housed in a lofty, hangar-sized, air-conditioned building—the Pabellón—at Calle 28 #113, e/ Avenida 1 y 3, tel. (33) 2661. The Pabellón contains a balcony for viewing the model from on high. The 144-square-meter model represents 144 square km of Havana and its environs. It is impressive—but, more important, a visit here puts the entire city in accessible 3-D perspective, allowing you to understand the layout.

The *maqueta*—one of the largest city models in the world—took nine experts more than 10 years to complete and shows Havana in the most intimate detail. Every contour is included, every building, every bump on every hill, even the balconies on buildings are there. It is color-coded by age: historic buildings are painted crimson; postrevolutionary buildings are ivory. The model is made of sections that can be moved on rails to allow access for changes.

It's open to the public Tues.-Sat. 10 a.m.-5:30 p.m.; entrance costs US$3 (US$1 for students, seniors, and children).

The Pabellón also contains the offices of the **Grupo para el Desarrollo Integral de la Capital,** tel./fax (33) 2661, e-mail: gdic@tinored.cu, the government institution responsible for overseeing the integrated development of Havana.

Acuario Nacional

On weekends, Cuban families flock to the National Aquarium on Avenida 1ra and Calle 60, tel. (23) 6401, fax (24) 1442. Its impressive array of tanks (with educational motifs in Spanish) hold all manner of sea life, including anemones, corals, exotic tropical fish, sharks, hawksbill turtles, sea lions, and dolphins. More than 300 species of marine life are displayed. Shark feeding and a sea lion act are offered as entertainment. Unfortunately, some of the tanks are aged and ill-kept, and may not be deemed "politically correct" in our modern times, but new tanks were being built as part of an expansion at press time.

The highlight is the **dolphin show,** offered eight times daily (determining the times has proven difficult: the public relations manager read out one timetable, which contradicted the published schedule she gave me, and the schedule posted at the gate offered yet different times).

However, it's about the only thing in Cuba that runs on time to the minute. Call ahead for times. The show lasts 20 minutes and features four trained dolphins that belong to the species *Tursiop trucaus,* commonly known as "mule" dolphins. The dolphins belie that misnomer by performing synchronized leaps through hoops, dances to music, and other enthralling tricks while a commentator offers an educational program in Spanish. It's impressive. Take the kids, who have an opportunity to participate.

A small library upstairs caters to marine topics; open Monday 10 a.m.-1 p.m., Tues.-Fri. 10 a.m.-5 p.m., Saturday 10 a.m.-9 p.m. Facilities include public toilets and a basic snack bar.

The aquarium is open Monday 6-11 p.m., Tues.-Thurs. 10 a.m.-6 p.m., Friday 10 a.m.-10 p.m., Sat.-Sun. 10 a.m.-6 p.m.

Rumbos S.A., tel. (66) 9713 or (24) 9626, offers an evening at the aquarium, with sea lion and dolphin shows and shark feeding Monday and Friday 6-10 p.m.

AVENIDA 5TA (QUINTA)

Miramar's main thoroughfare (and Havana's busiest boulevard) is the wide fig-tree-lined boulevard called Avenida 5ta, flanked by mansions, many of which have been restored to an earlier grandeur and are now occupied by various Cuban commercial agencies or leased (or sold) to foreign corporations. Avenida 5ta is "Embassy Row," and also offers several fine restaurants. A curiosity is the monstrously ugly **Confederation of Independent States' Embassy,** a peculiar Cubist tower—formerly the Soviet Embassy, now the Russian Embassy—in the middle of Avenida Quinta between Calles 62 and 66. Construction began in 1978 and was ongoing at the time of the Soviet collapse. The modernist-style church one block east is **Iglesia San Antonio de Padua,** dating from 1951 and quite simple yet peaceful within. Even nonsmokers might find the **Casa del Habana** of interest. This mansion, at the corner of Avenida 5ta and 16, is one of Havana's premier cigar outlets.

One block west, on Calle 18 between 5ta and 7ma, is **Che Guevara's former home,** where the revolutionary icon narrowly escaped assassination on 24 February 1961, when a gun battle erupted outside his home a few moments after he had set out for work.

The **Plaza Emiliano Zapata,** spanning Avenida 5ta between Calles 24 and 26, is shaded by massive jagüey trees, seemingly supported by their aerial roots dangling like cascades of water. On the south side of the road is a life-size stone statue of Zapata, Mexico's revolutionary hero, appropriately surrounded by cacti; on the north side is a parthenon and behind it a bronze bust to Mahatma Gandhi.

Two blocks south, on Avenida 9ta between 24 and 28, is a fortified cash depository in the most unlikely of places. A sturdy steel wall has been built around the entire block, with electric gates and plenty of security. Havana's dollar assets are stored here. It's best to refrain from taking photos.

The **Museo Marcha del Pueblo Combatiente,** housed in the former Peruvian embassy at 5ta and 72, tel. (29) 1497, tells the official version of the events that took place here in April 1980, culminating in the Mariel Boatlift, when some 120,000 Cubans—the Castro regime calls them *gusanos,* or worms—fled the island for Florida, causing President Carter no end of grief. It all began when 12 Cubans walked through the embassy gates and requested asylum. The Peruvians agreed and refused to hand them over to the Cuban police. Carter announced that the United States would welcome Cuban political refugees with "open arms." In a fit of pique, Castro removed the embassy guards, and 11,000 Cubans rushed into the embassy. Castro let them all leave and added to the swelling numbers by emptying his prisons of criminals and other "antisocial elements." Open Mon.-Sat. 9:30 a.m.-5:30 p.m.

The intriguing Byzantine-style church immediately to the west is the **Iglesia Jesús de Miramar.**

Museo de Ministerio del Interior

The Museum of the Ministry of the Interior, tel. (23) 4432, is dedicated to the CIA's decades of inept villainy and efforts to dethrone Fidel. The seal of the CIA looms over a room full of photos and gadgets—oddities straight from a spy movie. It displays lots of small arms, bazookas, and the like. It also features exhibits honoring MININT's good work in solving homicides (there's even a stuffed German shepherd that was used by police in their sleuthing). As always, Fidel is there in black and white.

The CIA's attempts (now defunct) to oust Castro were set in motion by President Eisenhower as early as March 1959. The bitter taste left by the CIA's botched Bay of Pigs invasion led to an all-out secret war against Castro, an effort code-named Operation Mongoose, headed by Bobby Kennedy. Mongoose eventually involved 500 case workers handling 3,000 anti-Castro Cubans at an expense of more than $100 million a year. The CIA's plans read like a James Bond novel—or a comedy of errors. In true James Bond fashion, the agency even recruited Cuban embassy staff by "dangling stunning beauties . . . exceptionally active in amorous adventures." James Bond's creator, Ian Fleming, even volunteered a few ideas. Some plots were straightforward, such as the attempt to kill Castro with a bazooka. The CIA's Technical Services Division (TSD) was more imaginative. It impregnated a box of cigars with botulism (they were tested on monkeys and "did the job expected of them") and hoped—in vain—to dupe Castro into smoking one. No one knows whether they reached Castro or whether some innocent victim smoked them. The spooks also tried to damage Castro's image by sprinkling his shoes with thallium salts (a strong depilatory), hoping that his beard would fall out, apparently in the belief that his beard was the source of his strength. Another box of Castro's favorite cigars was contaminated with a chemical that produced "temporary disorientation."

Eventually, the CIA turned to the Mob. It hired assassins handpicked by Johnny Rosselli, who had run the syndicate's Sans Souci casino in Havana. The killers were on both the FBI's 10-most-wanted-criminals list and Bobby Kennedy's target list of organized crime figures. The marksmen disguised as Marxmen didn't fool Castro, who correctly assumed the CIA would hire assassins. He considered them inefficient, claiming that an assassin "does not want to die. He's waiting for money, so he takes care of himself." Several assassins were caught and executed.

Meanwhile, Havana's El Encanto department store blew up (along with a Cubana Aviation plane, killing all 82 passengers), and terrorist organizations such as Operation 40 were funded and armed. All this, of course, backfired miserably. The secret war to oust Castro caused the Russians to increase their military commitment to Cuba. In the end, it provoked the missile crisis, bringing the world to the brink of nuclear disaster.

A police helicopter and speedboat stand in a lot across the road from the museum. Open Tues.-Fri. 9 a.m.-5 p.m., Saturday 9 a.m.-4 p.m. Entry costs US$2 (plus US$1 for a guide).

Playas del Oeste and Marina Hemingway
Avenida 5ta continues west beyond the Río Quibu and passes into the old Flores district, a shorefront region lined with *balnearios.* These beaches are small, and most are nothing to write home about, but they're extremely popular with Cubans on weekends, when they get crowded. Most of the aging *balnearios* date from prerevolutionary days (many went up in the 1920s and '30s, during the early years of Havana's tourist heyday, when there was even an eponymous mini-version of New Jersey's famous Coney Island theme park).

The shining star is **Club Habana,** Avenida 5ta between 188 and 192, in Reparto Flores, Playa, tel. (24) 5700, fax (24) 5705. This palatial private "nautical and social club" is operated by Palco (the Conference Center agency) and managed by Sol Meliá. It used to be the famous Havana Biltmore Yacht and Country Club, dating from 1928. It covers 10 hectares and boasts a fine beach of white sand, plus a handsome pool with sundeck. The main clubhouse is regally appointed and features a business center with Internet service, elegant restaurant, plush bar with marble floors, separate piano bar, and a Casa del Tabaco and cigar lounge. A fitness center offers sauna and massage, and a nursery takes care of the kids. Sports facilities include yacht, surfboard, Aqua bike, and sea kayak rental; scuba diving; a golf range; and beach volleyball. It offers shows and cabarets on Saturday nights.

The club serves its members, made up mostly of foreign diplomats and businesspeople, but nonmembers are welcome (entrance costs US$10 Mon.-Fri., US$15 Sat.-Sunday).

You can also swim at **Marina Hemingway,** Avenida 5ta and Calle 248, tel. (24) 1150, fax (24) 1149, e-mail: comercial@comermh.cha.cyt.cu. It's one km west of Club Habana in the Santa Fe district and 15 km west of downtown, with several swimming pools sprinkled about the vast yachting marina. The best pool is that of the Hotel El Jardín del Edén. Take you pick of numerous restaurants and bars, including the Bar Parillada Piscina and Cabaret Marina, which get lively with Cubans on weekends, drawing flirty *cubanas* eager to find positions as captains' mates (weekdays, entry costs US$3; a US$10 *consumo minimo*—minimum purchase charge—applies on weekends). Deafening music is played constantly, and the cabaret hosts shows at night.

Additional beaches lie west of the marina along the Santa Fe waterfront.

CUBANACÁN AND VICINITY

Cubanacán is—or was—Havana's Beverly Hills, a rolling area on the west bank of the Río Quibu. It was developed in the 1920s in a "garden-city" style, with winding tree-lined streets and enormous lots on which grandiose mansions and houses arose. An 18-hole golf course at the Havana Country Club served Havana's middle and wealthy classes, lending the name Country Club Park to what is now called Cubanacán, then as now the most exclusive address in town.

Bus no. 32 operates between La Rampa in Vedado and Cubanacán (five pesos), as does the **Vaivén Bus Turístico.**

Following the Revolution, most of the area's homeowners decamped and fled Cuba. Many mansions have since fallen into ruin, reminding novelist James Michener of "an Arthur Rackham painting of a country in which a cruel king has laid waste the mansions of his enemies." After the Revolution, other mansions were dispensed to party officials, many of whom still live in glorious isolation. Others have been splendidly maintained amid neatly trimmed lawns and serve either as "protocol" houses—villas where foreign dignitaries and VIPs are housed during visits to Cuba—or as foreign embassies and ambassadors' homes. Among them is the US Residency, heavily guarded for obvious reasons, on immaculate and spacious grounds where, at the end of a long promenade, the eagle that once stood atop the Monumento del Maine on the Malecón spreads its magnificent wings. And on "Embassy Row," house #6 (known locally as La Casa de Gabo), with the black Mercedes Benz 280, belongs to Gabriel García Márquez (Castro's Colombian novelist friend). It stands next to the mansions given to Robert Redford and Harry Belafonte on their recent visits to Cuba. Castro himself maintains several homes here, too, and security is strict.

The erstwhile exclusive Havana Country Club was converted following the Revolution to house Cuba's leading art academy. The club building became the Faculty of Music. Additional buildings (most rather grim) were added to house other faculties that together make up the **Instituto Superior de Arte,** featuring the Escuela de Música (School of Music), Escuela de Ballet (Ballet School), Escuela de Baile Moderno (School of Modern Dance), and Escuela de Bellas Artes (School of Fine Arts). The brick and concrete buildings "deliquesce," says Nancy Stout, "into the surrounding topography without need of camouflage; their vaulted roofs are a most fitting metaphor for nature's own mounds and hills. No other buildings in Havana are so forcefully driven to the tellurian." I find no aesthetic appeal whatsoever, and apply here Stout's words: "Disrespectful building has, unfortunately, not forsaken Havana," though she speaks of somewhere else in the city. Access is from Avenida 5ta via Calle 120.

The **Palacio de las Convenciones**—Havana's impressive convention center—is also here, on Calle 146, e/ 11 y 13, tel. (22) 6011, fax (21) 9496, e-mail: palco@palco.get.cma.net, website: www.cubaweb.cu/palco. It was built in 1979 for the Non-Aligned Conference, and the main hall (one of 15 halls), seating 2,200 delegates, hosts meetings of the Cuban National Assembly. Nearby, at Avenida 17 and 180, is **Pabexpo,** with four exhibition halls for hosting trade shows.

Cuba's admirable biotechnology industry also is centered here, south and west of Cubanacán in the flatter districts of La Coronela and Siboney respectively, where dozens of ugly high-rise apartment blocks have risen during the past four decades. The **Centro de Ingenieria Genética y Biotecnología,** is at Avenida 31 and 190, tel. (21) 6022, fax (21) 8070. The **Centro Nacional de Investigaciones Científicas** is nearby at Avenida 25 and 158, tel. (21) 8066; it was here that PPG, or Ateromixol, Cuba's homespun anticholesterol wonder drug, was developed. You can arrange visits that will duly impress you with Cuba's phenomenal commitment to—and success with—cutting-edge research in the field.

HAVANA'S BIOTECHNOLOGY CENTERS

Cuba is a biotech minipower. In 1965, there were said to be only 12 research scientists in Cuba; today there are more than 25,000. Under Fidel Castro's personal patronage, Cuba has evolved one of the world's most advanced genetic engineering and biotechnology industries, with large-scale investment coming from public sources such as the Pan American Health Organization and the World Food Program.

The program is led by the **Centro de Ingenieria Genética y Biotecnología** (Center for Genetic Engineering and Biotechnology), Avenida 31 y 158, in the Havana suburb of Cubanacán, tel. (21) 6022. The center, perhaps the most sophisticated research facility in the Third World, opened in 1986 as one of more than two-dozen Cuban institutes dedicated to the biological sciences. Together they supply state-of-the-art health products to the world (sold through the marketing entity Heber Biotec), bringing in more than US$100 million annually.

Cuba has developed nearly 200 products, both innovative and derivative. It invented and manufactures vaccines for cerebral meningitis, cholera, hepatitis B, interferon for the treatment of AIDS and cancer, and a skin growth factor to speed the healing of burns. For years, Cuba has touted a cure for the skin disease vitiligo. Recently it developed PPG, a "wonder drug" that reputedly washes cholesterol out of blood and, incidentally, is said to increase sexual potency (the source of a brisk black market for peddlers selling the drug to tourists). In 1996, CIGB scientists even began testing a vaccine to prevent HIV infection.

Other advances have been made in agriculture and industrial bioengineering. Unfortunately, US law denies these lifesaving wonders from being sold in the United States and prohibits the export to Cuba of any product (including foreign-made products bearing a US patent) that might aid the development of medicines and biotechnology on the island.

La Coronela offers the **Museo del Aire** (Air Museum) on Avenida 212. The gamut of civilian and military aircraft displayed includes helicopters, missiles, bombers, and fighter planes. It features Soviet MiGs and a turn-of-the-century biplane hanging from the ceiling, plus three main rooms replete with aviation mementos. A section dedicated to the Bay of Pigs battle evokes poignant memories; remnants of planes destroyed in the fighting and black-and-white photos speak with mute eloquence of the Cuban pilots who died defending the island. There's also a collection of model aircraft, and a space section honoring Yury Gagarin and Col. Arnaldo Tamayo Méndez, the first Cuban cosmonaut. The museum also has a restoration program. An artisans' shop and restaurant are planned. Open Tues.-Sun. 9 a.m.-5 p.m. Entrance US$2. The museum is hard to find: from Avenida 5ta, take 17-A south to the roundabout; take the first exit to the right, heading west on Avenida 23; then the first left, onto 198; then the first right onto 212, disregarding the sign that reads 27; the museum is 100 yards to your left.

About 100 yards down Avenida 212 is the **Fundación del Nuevo Cine Latinamericano,** the Havana branch of the film institute presided over by Gabriel García Márquez.

For a swim and refreshments, call in at **Complejo Turístico La Giradilla,** at Calle 272 e/ 37 y 51 in the La Coronela district, tel. (33) 6062. Popular with the Cuban elite, this restaurant and entertainment complex occupies a huge 1920s mansion on expansive grounds. In spring 1999, the gardens were receiving a Versailles-type remake that includes construction of a huge swimming pool and sundeck plus a covered stage for floor shows and concerts.

Fábrica El Laguito

This cigar factory, at Avenida 146 #2302, Cubanacán, tel. (21) 2213, one block south of the Palacio de las Convenciones, opened in 1966 as a training school. Built in 1910 near the old country club as the home of the Marquez de Pinar del Río, it was adorned with 1930s art deco glass and chrome, a spiral staircase, and abstract floral designs in the stucco detailing, and took its name from this part of the city. Because of its origins as a fabulous turn-of-the-century mansion, the factory components are dispersed eccentrically, with some store and selection rooms located at the end of long palm-lined paths. El Laguito makes Montecristos and the majority of Cohibas, *the* premium Havana cigar. It has been said that Che Guevara initiated production while in charge of the Cuban tobacco industry; his objective was to make a cigar that surpassed every other prerevolutionary cigar. However, Nancy Stout (in her splendid book, *Habanos*) says that it was started by revolutionary heroine Celia Sánchez as a place of employment for women (men have been employed as rollers here only since 1994), while Guevara had his own little offshoot factory in the Cabaña fortress.

Since Cohibas are made from only the finest leaves, El Laguito is given first choice from the harvest ("the best selection of the best selection," says factory head Emilia Tamayo). The Cohiba was initially made solely for distribution to foreign diplomats and dignitaries. Since 1982, it has been available for general consumption (bodybuilder-turned-actor Arnold Schwarzenegger prefers Cohibas, as did Castro before he stopped smoking). Today, 3.4 million Cohibas are produced annually—about one percent of Cuban production. Cohibas, rich, rather spicy cigars that come in 11 sizes, are considerably more expensive than other Havana cigars.

El Laguito also makes the best cigar in the world—the Trinidad, a cigar you'll not find in any store. The seven-and-a-half-inch-long cigar is made exclusively for Castro, who presents them to diplomats and dignitaries. The 2,000 Trinidads produced monthly are, says Tamayo, "the selection of the selection of the selection."

Call ahead for an appointment if you wish to visit.

MARIANAO

This untouristed *municipio*, on the heights south of Miramar, began life as an old village. By the mid-19th century, wealthy Spaniards began to build fine summer homes along newly laid streets on its breeze-swept slopes. Sections still bear the stamp of the colonial past. Following the US occupation of Cuba in 1898, the US military governor, General Fitzhugh Lee, established his headquarters here and called it Camp Columbia. During the 1920s, Cuban developers promoted the area and established the Marianao Country Club, the Oriental Park racetrack, and the Grand Nacional Casino. Marianao became a center of tourism, being given a boost on New Year's Eve 1939, when the Tropicana nightclub opened as the ritziest establishment Havana had ever seen. Marianao remained a pleasure center until the Revolution, when **Las Fritas,** Marianao's erstwhile three-block-long strip of restaurants, beer parlors, shooting galleries, peep shows, and cabarets, was shut down.

Camp Columbia later became headquarters for Batista's army; it was from here that the sergeant effected his *golpes* (coup d'etats) in 1933 and 1952. Camp Columbia—renamed Ciudad Libertad following the Revolution—continued to operate as a military airstrip, although Castro, true to his promise, had since turned Batista's barracks into a school. In an attempt to destroy Castro's air force, the airstrip was bombed on 15 April 1960 by B-26 light bombers (falsely painted in Cuban colors) during the prelude to the CIA-run Bay of Pigs invasion. The attack failed, although five of Castro's planes were destroyed. The bombers had struck houses in the densely packed neighborhood of Ciudad Libertad, killing seven people and wounding 52, giving Castro a grand political victory in his calls for solidarity against US aggression (one of the dying men wrote Castro's name in blood on a wall). The following day he announced for the first time that Cuba was undergoing a "socialist revolution."

Today, the former Campamento Columbia army camp houses the **Museo de la Alfabeti-** **zación,** at the junction of Calle 31 and Avenida 100, tel. (20) 8054. It is dedicated to the literacy campaign of 1961. Open weekdays 8 a.m.-5 p.m.; US$1. A tower outside the entrance is shaped like a syringe in honor of Carlos Finlay, the Cuban who in 1881 discovered the cause of yellow fever.

A visit to the **Tropicana,** off Calle 72 between 41 and 45, tel. (27) 0110, fax (27) 0109, is a *must*. The whirlwind show began in 1939 in an open-air theater in the gardens of a mansion that once housed the US ambassador. The Tropicana quickly eclipsed Havana's other nightclubs in grandeur and extravagance, enhanced by the most beautiful female dancers in Cuba (teams of producers traditionally hunted the island for the best-looking talent; today, posters islandwide announce recruitment drives). Most of the structures date from 1951, in modernist style with thin-shell concrete vaults held up by five arches spanning up to 30 meters. They frame two circular dance floors, with curving bands of glass to fill the intervening space, and sliding doors across the base. Visitors are not welcome by day, when the dancers practice. They must visit at night, when the lavishly costumed, statuesque showgirls perform beneath the stars. The lush entrance grounds offer a fittingly sensuous statue of the Greek maenads by Cuban sculptor Rita Longa (the maidens first floated on a pond of the Gran Casino Nacional), with the bacchants performing a wild ritual dance to honor Dionysius at night amid the woods, as in the original myth.

The only other site of tourist interest in Marianao is the **Fábrica Heroes del Moncada** cigar factory, Avenida 57 #13402, Marianao, tel. (20) 9006. This modest-scale factory was established in 1952, when it was moved by its owner from Las Villas Province (today's Villa Clara). All the major brands of export cigars are manufactured here. Leaf processing takes place on the ground floor, and the rolling upstairs. The factory receives very few visitors, and you must call ahead.

SUBURBAN HAVANA

In addition, a number of metropolitan Havana's prime attractions lie on the city's outskirts and are well worth the drive. The following are presented in counterclockwise order, beginning with southern Havana.

BOYEROS

Boyeros, south of the Playa district and southwest of Havana, is a vast, mostly undeveloped area with few sites of touristic appeal. It is accessed from downtown Havana via Avenida de la Independencia, which runs south through the industrial area of **Rancho Boyeros** to the José Martí International Airport. South of the airport, Avenida de la Independencia becomes Avenida de los Mártires, and you suddenly find yourself in Santiago de las Vegas, a colonial-era rural town in the midst of the country.

The **Havana Golf Club** is hidden east of Avenida de la Independencia in the industrial-residential area called Capdevilla, midway between Havana and Santiago de las Vegas. The golf club was opened as the Rover's Athletic Club in 1948 by the British community and maintained by the British Embassy until given to the Cuban government in 1980. The place is popular on weekends with Cuban families, who flock to the swimming pool, not the golf course. Its nine holes were being extended to 18, and at press time, the entire course brought up to international par.

Santiago de las Vegas

This small town, 20 km south of Havana, is the nearest provincial town to Havana and a worthy destination for an excursion. It straddles Avenida de los Mártires (Avenida Rancho Boyeros), about three km south of the airport. It is steeped in sleepy bucolic charm. Its allure lies in strolling the narrow streets lined with red-tile-roofed colonial houses painted in faded pastels. Take time to sit on the tiny main square, where children play hoop and senior citizens gather to debate and gossip beneath shade trees. At its core is a marble statue of a local Mambí hero, Juan Delgado Gonzales, and the other local citizenry who formed a regiment of Mambí (insurgent nationalist troops) during the Wars of Independence. A quaint whitewashed church faces onto the plaza from the west.

Santiago's streets are horrendously potholed with huge troughs big enough to swallow Cuba's hefty homegrown cattle.

The main road rises abruptly south of Santiago de las Vegas, and soon you find yourself amid pine forests in an area containing several camps utilized by the Cuban military. At **El Cacahual,** about two km south of Santiago de las Vegas, General Antonio Maceo Grajables (1845-96)—the black general and hero of the Wars of Independence—slumbers in an open-air mausoleum in a circular park the size of a football field and shaded by trees full of birdsong. The memorial holds two tombs: Maceo's and that of Capitán Ayudante (Captain-Adjutant) Francisco Gómez Toro (1876-1896), General Máximo Gómez's son, who gave his life alongside Maceo at the Battle of San Pedro on 7 December 1896, near here. The granite tombs are engraved in the style of Mexican artist Diego Rivera. An adjacent pavilion features a small exhibit with photos and maps showing the black general's route during the war.

The park forms a giant traffic circle, on the east side of which stands a monument in bronze to Coronel (Colonel) Juan Delgado, chief of the Santiago de las Vegas regiment, who recovered Maceo's body. The tiny hamlet of **Cacahual** lies hidden from sight no more than 200 yards east, behind the pine trees.

Getting There and Away: A train (40 centavos) runs to Santiago de las Vegas from the Estación Cristina at Avenida México and Arroyo in southwest Habana Vieja, tel. (78) 4971, at 6:05 and 10:40 a.m., and 2:50 and 7 p.m. Return trains depart Santiago de las Vegas for Cristina at 7:57 a.m. and 12:30, 4:54, and 8:40 p.m.

Turistaxi has an office on General Peraza, tel (683) 3007.

Sanctuario de San Lazaro

One of Cuba's most important pilgrimage sites is the Sanctuary of San Lazaro, half a kilometer west of the village of Rincón and three km southwest of Santiago de las Vegas. The well-maintained complex comprises an impressive church and, behind, a leprosy and AIDS sanatorium. The church has a gray marble floor and various altars (the main one is a popular roosting site for local birdlife).

On any given day, the church is busy with mendicants, especially on Sunday, when Cubans come in droves to have their children baptized, while others fill bottles with holy water from a fountain behind the church. San Lazaro is the patron saint of the sick, and as such the **Procession of the Miracles** takes place 17 December, when hundreds of pilgrims—up to 50,000 in some years—make their way to the sanctuary to give thanks to the saint for miracles they imagine were granted. The villagers of Rincón do a thriving business selling votive candles and flowers to churchgoers. Limbless beggars, lepers, and other mendicants crowd at the gates and plead for a

charitable donation, while penitents crawl on their backs and knees, and others walk ahead of them and sweep the road ahead with palm fronds. "A man inched along painfully on his back, with cinder blocks tied to his feet," wrote Andrei Codrescu in *Ay Cuba!* "I asked the man coiling and uncoiling on his back with the cinder blocks tied to his feet what he was going to ask San Lazaro. 'To help me walk,' the man replied."

Here, too, is **Los Cocos,** Cuba's first sanatorium built to house patients infected with HIV.

To get there, follow the signed road that leads east from El Cacahual, or take Carretera Santiago de las Vegas, which begins at the bus station on the southwest edge of town.

Getting There and Away: Bus M2 runs from Parque de la Fraternidad in Havana and stops on the southeast corner of the square. The *terminal de autobus* is on the southwest side of town, at Calle 12 and Avenida 17, on the road to Rincón and Santiago de los Baños.

CUBA'S WAR ON AIDS

Cuba has one of the world's most aggressive and successful campaigns against AIDS. The World Health Organization (WHO) and the Pan-American Health Organization have praised the program as exemplary.

Cuba's unique response to the worldwide epidemic that began in the early 1980s was to initiate mass testing of the population and a "mandatory quarantine" of everyone testing positive. By 1994, when the policy of mandatory testing was ended, about 98% of the adult population had been tested. Voluntary testing continues. The program stemmed an epidemic that rages only 50 miles away in Haiti and kept the spread of the disease to a level that no other country can equal. By the turn of 1996, Cuba had recorded 1,196 cases of HIV, and 287 people had died of AIDS (Puerto Rico has only one-third Cuba's population but 8,117 reported cases of AIDS).

At first, the purpose was to keep the disease from spreading. The objective was to develop AIDS sanatoriums throughout the island, where people who tested HIV-positive could be evaluated medically and psychologically, and educated in the ethics and biology of AIDS prevention—then go out and lead a normal life, using the sanatorium as an out-

patient facility. Twelve sanatoriums exist on the island. Residents live in small houses or apartments, alone or as couples (straight or gay).

Cuba has defended its sanatorium policy as a way of guaranteeing first-class health care for patients while protecting the rest of the population. "When you think about the amount of money they spend on each of us, and that we don't pay one cent!" an AIDS-positive hemophiliac told journalist Karen Wald, "and apart from that, we receive our complete salary. What other country in the world has done that? You're asking if the Revolution violates my rights by sending me to a sanatorium? I'm alive because of the Revolution!"

Mandatory confinement was ended in early 1994. Instead, an outpatient program has been implemented. The new emphasis is on personal responsibility. The Ministry of Health has established the National Center for Sex Education to offer safe-sex workshops.

The **Cuba AIDS Project,** 465 SW 62nd Court, Miami, FL 33144, tel. (305) 531-3973, e-mail: cubaidspr@aol.com, delivers medications to Cubans who suffer from HIV/AIDS on the islands. Donations and couriers are needed.

Parque Zoológico

Cuba's national zoo is about 10 miles south of central Havana, at the west end of Avenida Soto, one km west of Calzada de Bejucal, in Boyeros, tel. (44) 7613 or (57) 8054, fax (24) 0852. Opened in 1984, it covers 340 hectares, and contains more than 800 animals and more than 100 species.

Tour buses (0.40 centavos) depart the parking lot about every 30 minutes and run through the African wildlife park—**Pradera Africano**—and lion's den, but you can also drive your own car further into the park. The guided bus trip is the highlight, taking you through an expansive area not unlike the savanna of east Africa. Elephants come to the bus and stick their trunks in through the window to glean tidbits handed out by tourists. There are rhinos, two species of zebra, wildebeests, ostriches, and two hippos that spend most of their daylight hours wallowing in a deep pool. Gawkers gather at the low wall, where they can simply reach over and stroke the elephants. Amazingly, there's no security fence nor moat, and you sense that the animals could simply leap or step over the four-foot-high wall any time they wanted. Scary! No park staff are on hand, so visitors feed the animals all manner of junk food.

The lion pit—**Foso de Leones**—is a deep quarry on the north side of the park. The bus makes a quick loop through the pit, but you can also sit atop the cliff on a viewing platform and look down upon the lions fornicating (which is all they seem to do when they're not snoozing; 30 times a day for the males is an average performance, explains the guide).

A walk-through section houses a leopard, tiger, chimps, monkeys, and birds, but the cages are small and bare (there are no natural habitats), many of the animals look woefully neglected, and the conditions are deplorable.

The zoo also reproduces more than 30 endangered species and includes a taxidermist's laboratory.

A map of the zoo is posted at the entrance gate, where there's a snack bar. A children's area provides pony rides. It's open Wed.-Sun. 9:30 a.m.-4:30 p.m. Entrance costs US$3 per person (US$2 per child, US$5 for a vehicle).

Getting There: By car, the quickest way to the park is via Avenida de la Independencia (Avenida Rancho Boyeros) to Avenida San Francisco—the Parque is signed at the junction—which leads to the village of Arroyo Naranjo. The main entrance gate is off Calzada de Bejucal, which runs south through Arroyo Naranjo. A taxi will cost about US$12 each way.

Buses no. 31, 73, and 88 operate between La Vibora and Arroyo Naranjo.

ARROYO NARANJO

This *municipio* lies due south of Havana and offers three sites of unique appeal.

Parque Lenin

Parque Lenin, tel. (44) 2721, at Calle 100 y Carretera de la Presa, southeast of the village of Arroyo Naranjo, was created from a former hacienda and landscaped mostly by volunteer labor from the city (and maintained by inmates from a nearby psychiatric hospital). The vast complex, open Wed.-Sun. 9 a.m.-5:30 p.m., features wide rolling pastures and small lakes surrounded by forests and pockets of bamboo, ficus, and flamboyants, or *guira*, from which maraccas are made. What Lenin Park lacks in grandeur and stateliness, it makes up for in scale and scope. You'll need a long study to get an idea of the full scope of the park, which is laid out around the large lake, **Presa Paso Sequito,** with a huge reservoir—Ejército Rebelde—to the east. Cuban families flock to the park on weekends for the children's park, with carousels and fairground pleasures, horseback riding, rodeos, and all the fun of the fair.

The park is bounded by the Circunvalación to the north and Calzada de Bejucal to the west. The official entrance to the park is off Calzada de Bejucal. A second road—Calle Cortina de la Presa—enters from the Circunvalación and runs ruler-straight down the center of the park; most sites of interest lie at the south end of this road, south of the lake. Calle Cortina is linked to Calzada de Bejucal by a loop road that passes most of the recreational sites north of the lake.

Sites, Galleries, and Museums: Begin with a visit to **Galería del Arte Amelia Peláez,** at the south end of Calle Cortina. It displays Paláez's works (she was responsible for the ceramic mural on the facia of the Hotel Habana

Libre, in Vedado) along with changing exhibitions of other artists. Behind the gallery is a series of bronze busts inset in rock.

Nearby is the **Monumento Lenin,** a huge granite visage of the communist leader and thinker in Soviet-realist style. Moving west, you'll pass an **aquarium** displaying freshwater fish and turtles, including the antediluvian garfish (*marijuarí*) and a couple of Cuban crocodiles, Pepe and Rosita, in lagoons and tanks. Open Wed.-Sun. 9 a.m.-5 p.m. Entry costs US$1.

About 400 meters farther west is the **Monumento á Celia Sánchez,** with a trail that follows a wide apse of large natural slabs to a broad ampitheater lined with ferns. At its center is a bronze figure of Sánchez ("the most beautiful and endemic flower of the Revolution"), inset in a huge rock. Sánchez set up the secret system that supplies arms, etc., to Castro's Rebel Army in the Sierra Maestra. She was Castro's secretary, lover, and most intimate advisor, and played a steadying influence on the fickle Cuban leader until her death from cancer in 1980. A small museum exhibits portraits of the heroine alongside her personal items.

Also worth a visit are the **Taller Cerámica** (ceramic workshop); **Casa de la Amistad Cubano Soviético** (Cuban-Soviet Friendship House), farther west; and the **Che Guevara Pioneer Palace,** full of stainless-steel sculptures of the revolutionary hero.

Activities, Recreation, and Entertainment:
Horseback riding: There's an equestrian center—**Centro Ecuestre** (often called Club Hípico)—immediately east of the entrance off Calzada de Bejucal. It offers riding lessons (a course of 10 one-hour riding lessons costs US$102), one-hour horseback trips (US$15), and even trips in a *coche* (colonial horsedrawn coach). You can also rent horses. The riding club covers 20 hectares and has stables for 30 horses, a training racetrack and paddock, several dressage paddocks, a smithy, veterinary clinic, changing rooms, showers, and even sauna and massage facilities. Open 9 a.m.-4:30 p.m.

Train Rides: A narrow-gauge railway circles the park, dropping passengers at various sites. The old steam train dates from 1870 and departs the **Terminal Inglesa** daily at 8 and 10 a.m., noon, and 2 and 4 p.m. (three pesos), and takes 30 minutes to circle the park. Another old steam train dating from 1915 is preserved under a red-tiled canopy in front of the station.

Bicycle and Rowboat Rental: The park is a splendid place to bicycle. A bike rental shop, east of Calle Cortina, was not functioning in spring 1999 but has in the past. You can also rent rowboats on the lake at El Rodeo.

For Children: A **parque diversiones** (amusement park) located in the northwest quarter includes carousels, a miniature "big dipper," and pony rides.

Rodeo: You can watch cowboys lasso cows at **El Rodeo,** which offers *rodeo cubano* in a horse ring (entry costs three pesos).

Theater and Music: Classical and other concerts are held at the **Anfiteatro,** a magnificent setting formed of a raised half-moon ampitheater facing down over the lake from its south side. Patrons sit in steeply banked seats hollowed from natural rock while the bands play on a floating stage.

Other Facilities: There's also a doll museum (Colina de los Muñecos), a drive-in movie theater (Ciné Césped; not operating at press time), and even a motocross circuit (not operating at press time).

Casa de la Popularidad is an information center with a small bar and restaurant. It's just off Calle Cortina at the junction with the loop road that leads along the north shore of the lake from Calzada de Bejucal. A tourist map of the park (US$1) will prove handy; you may be able to buy one at Tienda las Navigantes in Habana Vieja.

Getting There: See Parque Zoológico, above, for instruction on getting there by car (the official signed entrance is opposite the turnoff for the zoo on Calzada de Bejucal, south of the village of Arroyo Naranjo). However, the easiest route is to take the Avenida San Francisco 100 highway and turn south directly into the park. In addition to the Arroyo Naranjo entrance to the west, the Circunvalación runs past the north side of Parque Lenin, with a spur road running south through the park. A taxi will cost about US$15 each way.

Buses no. 31, 73, and 88 operate between La Vibora and the park entrance.

A train runs hourly from the Cristina Station in Havana to Galápago de Oro station (on the northwest side of the park), which is served by bus no. 31.

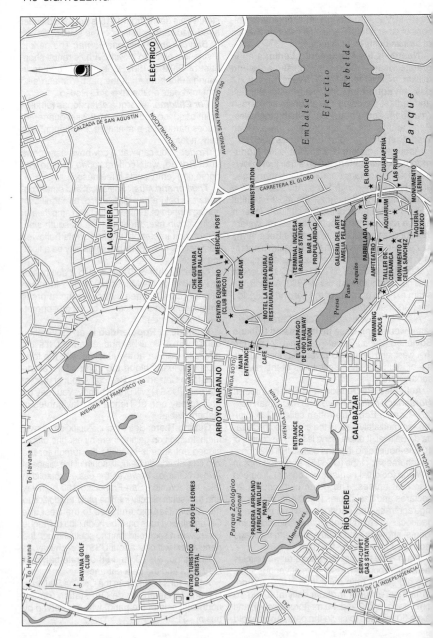

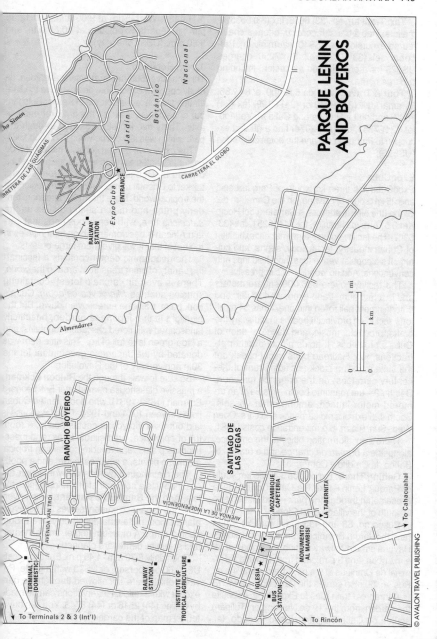

PARQUE LENIN
AND BOYEROS

© AVALON TRAVEL PUBLISHING

Taxi Transtur, tel. (33) 6666, fax (33) 5535, e-mail: taxihab@transtur.com.cu, offers a chauffeured excursion for US$40 (car/minivan). **Palcocar,** tel. (33) 7235, fax (33) 7250, charges US$25 for a chauffeured excursion, including two free hours.

Tour & Travel, Avenida 5 #8409, e/ 84 y 86, Miramar, tel. (24) 9200 or (24) 9199, fax (24) 1547, and on La Rampa and Calle M, Vedado, tel. (24) 7541, fax (24) 2074, has a guided excursion to Parque Lenin and the botanical garden (US$25).

ExpoCuba

ExpoCuba lies three km south of Parque Lenin and 25 km south of Havana, on the Carretera del Globo (the official address is Carretera del Rocío Km 3.5, Arroyo Naranjo), tel. (44) 6251, fax (33) 5307. The facility houses a permanent exhibition of Cuban industry, technology, sports, and culture. It's a popular venue for school field trips and conventions. And no wonder—it's impressive.

The facility covers 588,000 square meters and is a museum, trade expo, world's fair, and entertainment hall rolled into one. It has 34 pavilions, including provincial booths that display the crafts, products, music, and dance of each of Cuba's provinces. It holds plenty of other attractions, too. Railroad buffs might check out the vintage rolling stock (including turn-of-the-century carriages) on the entrance forecourt. Booth #9—the maritime booth—displays an armored motor launch, among other vessels. Booth #25 exhibits old carriages and cars. Open Wed.-Sun. 9 a.m.-6 p.m.; entrance costs US$1.

There's an information office at the entrance, alongside a *bureau de change* and a branch of Banco de Credito y Comercio.

Getting There: ExpoCuba is three km south of Parque Lenin—take the Calle Cortina de la Presa south through the park—and immediately south of the village of El Globo.

Buses no. 88 and 113 leave for ExpoCuba (and the Jardín Botánico) from the north side of Havana's main railway station weekends at 10 a.m., noon, and 3 p.m., and from Havana's Terminal de Ómnibus at 9 a.m., 11 a.m., and 4 p.m. Bus no. 80 also serves the park, from Lawton.

A three-car train runs to ExpoCuba, opposite the garden, from the 19 de Noviember (Tulipán) station on Calle Tulipán, Nuevo Vedado, tel. (81) 4431, Wed.-Sun. at 9:05 a.m. and 12:35 p.m.; it departs ExpoCuba at 10:50 a.m. and 3:50 p.m. (US$1 one way).

Jardín Botánico

This massive (600-hectare) botanical garden, directly opposite ExpoCuba, doesn't have the fine-trimmed herbaceous borders of Kew or Butchart, but nonetheless is worth the drive for enthusiasts. Thirty-five km of roads lead through the park, which was laid out between 1969 and 1984.

The expansive garden consists mostly of wide pastures planted with copses of trees and shrubs divided by Cuban ecosystems (from coastal thicket to Oriental humid forest) and by regions of the tropical world. More than 100 gardeners tenderly prune and mulch such oddities as the satchicha tree, with pendulous pods that certain African tribeswomen rub on their nipples in the belief that it will give them large breasts.

The geographic center contains a fascinating variety of palm trees from around the world. There is even an "archaic forest" containing species such as *Microcyca calocom,* Cuba's cork palm, from the antediluvian dawn. But the highlight is the **Japanese garden,** beautifully landscaped with tiered cascades, fountains, and a jade-green lake full of koi. This little gem was donated by the Japanese government for the 30th anniversary of the Revolution.

Be sure to walk through the **Rincón Eckman,** a massive glasshouse named after Erik Leonard Eckman (1883-1931), who documented Cuban flora between 1914 and 1924. The glasshouse is laid out as a triptych: a cactus house; a room full of epiphytes, bromeliads, ferns, and insectivorous plants; and a room containing tropical mountain plants, a small cascade, and a pool.

The glasshouse (which has wheelchair access) boasts a souvenir stall and café, plus toilets. And the **Bambú Restaurant,** which overlooks the Japanese garden, serves the best vegetarian food in Havana (lunch only; Wed.-Sun noon-3 p.m.). A museum, motel, amphitheater and scientific center are planned.

Open daily 8:30 a.m.-4:45 p.m. Entrance costs US$0.60 per person, or US$3 with a guide. Private vehicles are *not* allowed through the park except with a guide. Reservations can be made by calling (44) 2516 or (44) 8743. You can buy a tourist map of the garden for US$1.

Getting There: See "Getting There" under ExpoCuba," above. **Tour & Travel,** Avenida 5ta #8409 e/ 84 y 86, Miramar, tel. (24) 9200, fax (24) 1547, and on La Rampa and Calle M, Vedado, tel. (24) 7541, fax (24) 2074, has a daily excursion to the garden (US$15, or US$25 with lunch).

SAN MIGUEL DE PADRON

The *municipio* of San Miguel de Padron, which extends south of the Bahía de La Habana, is mostly residential, with ugly modern factory areas in the lowlands by the harbor and time-worn colonial housing on the hills south of town. None is a draw in itself, with the exception of **San Francisco de Paula,** on the city's outskirts, 12.5 km south of Havana (about 20 minutes from Habana Vieja). En route, you pass through the suburb of Luyano, four km southeast of Habana Vieja. Chugging up Calzada de Luyano when heading north, there is a view, off to the left, of El Cerro that reminded Hemingway's character Thomas Hudson in *Islands in the Stream* of Toledo: "Not El Greco's Toledo. But a part of Toledo itself seen from a side hill. They were coming up on it now, as the car climbed the last of the hill and he saw it again clearly and it was Toledo all right, just for a moment." In Hemingway's day, Luyano was a shantytown so squalid that Hudson carried drink against the shock when passing through. (Up until the Triumph of the Revolution, the deplorable shantytowns—there were others ringing the hills—were the most unfortunate spots in Havana. They were torn down after the Revolution, and new housing was built. But Luyano still looks far from pretty.)

San Francisco de Paula moves at a bucolic pace befitting its small wooden houses of colonial vintage. Rising above the village, but hidden from view, is Hemingway's must-see former home, Finca Vigía.

Finca Vigía

In 1939, Hemingway's third wife, Martha Gellhorn, was struck by Finca Vigía (Lookout Farm), a one-story Spanish-colonial house built in 1887 and boasting a wonderful view of Havana. They rented it for $100 a month. When Hemingway's first royalty check from *For Whom the Bell Tolls*

arrived in 1940, he bought the house for US$18,500 because, like his character Ole Anderson in "The Killers," he had tired of roaming from one place to another. In August 1961, his widow, Mary Welsh, donated the house and most of its contents to the Cuban state, in accordance with Hemingway's will.

On 21 July 1994, on the 95th anniversary of Papa's birthday, Finca Vigía reopened its doors as a museum, tel. (91) 0809 or (55) 8015, following nearly two years of repairs and remodeling. The house is preserved in suspended animation, just the way the great writer left it. His presence seems to haunt the large, simple home.

Bougainvillea frame the gateway to the 20-acre hilltop estate. Mango trees and sumptuous jacarandas line the driveway leading up to the gleaming white house. No one is allowed inside—reasonably so, since every room can be viewed through the wide-open windows, and the temptation to pilfer priceless trinkets is thus reduced. (Two years after Hemingway died, someone offered $80,000 for his famous Royal typewriter which sits on a shelf beside his workroom desk; today, you can buy it for $7—inscribed in gray on a T-shirt that reads "Museo Ernesto Hemingway, Finca Vigía, Cuba").

Through the large windows, you can see trophies, firearms, bottles of spirits, old issues of *The Field, Spectator,* and *Sports Afield* strewn about, and more than 8,000 books, arranged higgledy-piggledy the way he supposedly liked them, with no concern for authors or subjects. The dining-room table is set with cut crystal, as if guests were expected.

It is eerie being followed by countless eyes—those of the guides (one to each room) and those of the beasts that had found themselves in the crosshairs of Hemingway's hunting scope. "Don't know how a writer could write surrounded by so many dead animals," Graham Greene commented when he visited. There are bulls, too, everywhere bulls, including paintings by Joan Miró and Paul Klee; photographs and posters of bullfighting scenes; and a chalk plate of a bull's head, a gift from Picasso.

Here is where Hemingway wrote *Islands in the Stream, Across the River and Into the Trees, A Moveable Feast,* and *The Old Man and the Sea.* The four-story tower next to the house was built at his fourth wife's prompting so that he

ERNEST HEMINGWAY AND HAVANA

Ernest Hemingway first set out from Key West to wrestle marlin in the wide streaming currents off the Cuban coast in April 1932. Years later, he was to sail to and fro, on the Key West-Havana route, dozens of times. The blue waters of the Gulf Stream, chock-full of billfish, brought him closer and closer until, eventually, "succumbing to the other charms of Cuba, different from and more difficult to explain than the big fish in September," he settled on this irresistibly charismatic island.

Hemingway loved Cuba and lived there for the better part of 20 years. It was more alluring, more fulfilling, than Venice, Sun Valley, or the green hills of Africa. Once, when Hemingway was away from Cuba, he was asked what he worried about in his sleep. "My house in Cuba," he replied, referring to Finca Vigía, in the suburb of San Francisco de Paula, 15 km southeast of Havana.

The Cult of Hemingway

Havana's city fathers have leased Papa's spirit to lend ambience to and put a polish on his favorite haunts. Havana's marina is named for the prize-winning novelist. A special rum, "El Ron Vigía," was even introduced to coincide with the author's 95th birthday, on 21 July 1994. Hemingway's room in the Hotel Ambos Mundos and Finca Vigía are preserved as museums. His name is attached to fishing tournaments and sugar-free daiquiris, and his likeness adorns T-shirts and billboards.

Yet the cult of Hemingway is very real. Cubans worship him with an intensity not far short of that accorded Che Guevara and nationalist hero José Martí. The novelist's works are required reading in Cuban schools. His books are best-sellers. "We admire Hemingway because he understood the Cuban people; he supported us," a friend told me. "He was very simple. His friends were fishermen. He never related to high society," adds Evelio González, one of the guides at Finca Vigía. The Cuban understanding of Hemingway's "Cuban novels" is that they support a core tenet of Communist ideology—that humans are only fulfilled acting in a "socialist" context for a moral purpose, not individualistically. (Many of Hemingway's novels appear to condemn economic and political injustices.)

"All the works of Hemingway are a defense of human rights," claims Castro, who knows Papa's novels "in depth" and once claimed that *For Whom the Bell Tolls*, Hemingway's fictional account of the Spanish Civil War, inspired his guerrilla tactics. Castro has said the reason he admires Hemingway so much is that he envies him the adventures he had. In July 1961, after Hemingway's death, his widow, Mary Welsh, returned to Finca Vigía to collect some items she wanted. Castro came to visit. Recalls Welsh: Fidel "headed for Ernest's chair and was seating himself when I murmured that it was my husband's favorite. The Prime Minister raised himself up, slightly abashed." The two headstrong fellows met only once, during the Tenth Annual Ernest Hemingway Billfish Tournament in May 1960. As sponsor and judge of the competition, Hemingway invited Cuba's youthful new leader as his guest of honor. Castro was to present the winner's trophy; instead, he hooked the biggest marlin and won the prize for himself. Hemingway surrendered the trophy to a beaming Castro. They would never meet again. One year later, the great writer committed suicide in Idaho.

Papa and the Revolution

There has been a great deal of speculation about Hemingway's attitude toward the Cuban Revolution. Cuba, of course, attempts to portray him as sympathetic (Gabriel García Márquez refers to "Our Hemingway" in the prologue to exiled Cuban novelist Noberto Fuente's *Hemingway in Cuba*).

Hemingway's Cuban novels are full of images of prerevolutionary terror and destitution. "There is an absolutely murderous tyranny that extends over every little village in the country," he wrote in *Islands in the Stream*.

In 1960, Hemingway wrote to a friend, "I believe completely in the historical necessity of the Cuban revolution." Papa was away from Cuba all of 1959, but he returned in 1960, recorded *New York Times* correspondent Herbert Matthews, "to show his sympathy and support for the Castro Revolution." Papa even used his legendary 38-foot sportfishing boat, the *Pilar,* to run arms for the rebel army, claims Gregorio Fuentes, the weatherbeaten sailor-guardian of the *Pilar* for 23 years. In his will, the great author dedicated his home and possessions—including his Nobel prize—to the Cuban state; but the *Pilar* he left to Fuentes.

Nonetheless, with the Cold War and the United States' break with Cuba, Hemingway had to choose. Not being able to return to Cuba contributed to Hemingway's depression, says his son Patrick: "He really loved Cuba, and I think it was a great shock to him at his age to have to choose between his country, which was the United States, and his home, which was Cuba."

Hemingway's widow, Mary, told the journalist Luís Báez that "Hemingway was always in favor of the Revolution," and another writer, Lisandro Otero, records Hemingway as saying, "Had I been a few years younger, I would have climbed the Sierra Maestra with Fidel Castro." These comments, alas, can't be validated. But Hemingway's enigmatic farewell as he departed the island in 1960 is illuminating. "*Vamos a ganar. Nosotros los cubanos vamos a ganar.* [We are going to win. We Cubans are going to win.] I'm not a Yankee, you know." But what would he have made of the outcome?

---

could write undisturbed. Hemingway disliked the lower and continued writing amid the comings and goings of the house, surrounded by papers, shirtless, in Bermuda shorts, with any of 60 cats at his feet as he stood barefoot on the hide of a small kudu.

Beside his toilet is a penciled diary with entries recording his morning weight, one of the few fights he continually lost.

Finca Vigía's sprawling grounds are equally evocative. Hemingway's legendary cabin cruiser, the *Pilar,* is poised loftily beneath a wooden pavilion on the former tennis court, shaded by bamboo and royal palms. Nearby are the swimming pool where Ava Gardner swam naked and the graves of four of the novelist's favorite dogs.

The museum, headed by a trained curator, offers free tours. Open Mon.-Sat. 9 a.m.-4 p.m., Sunday 9 a.m.-noon. Closed Tuesday and rainy days. Entrance costs US$3 for foreigners. A gift shop sells portraits, T-shirts, and other souvenirs.

Getting There: By car, from Havana, begin at the foot of Calzada de Infante, at its junction with Vía Blanca. From this junction, take Calzada Diez de Octubre south half a kilometer to Calzada de Luyano, which leads east to the Calzada de Güines, the Carretera Central that leads south to San Francisco de Paula. The museum is signed; turn left at Barbería Peluquería.

Alternately, you can take the Circunvalación (Vía Monumental), which circles Havana and runs through San Francisco de Paula, linking it directly with Cojímar, too.

Bus no. 7 departs from Parque de la Fraternidad in Habana Vieja. Bus no. 404 departs from Avenida de Bélgica (Monserrate) and Dragones. Both travel via San Francisco de Paula en route to Cotorro and Havana.

Trains ostensibly run from the Cristina station at Avenida de México and Arroyo, at Cuatro Caminos, Cerro Habana, tel. (78) 4971. Take the train for Cotorro (four times daily) via San Francisco de Paula.

If you're interested in an organized tour, contact **Paradiso: Promotora de Viajes Culturales,** Calle 19 #560 esq. C, Vedado, tel. (32) 6928, fax (33) 3921, e-mail: paradis@turcult.get.cma, website: www.cult.cu/paradiso/index.html, which offers a five-hour guided excursion to Finca Vigía (US$35, including lunch). And **Cubanacán,** Calle 146 esq. 9na, Playa, tel. (33) 9884, fax (33) 0107, also has a "Re-encounter with Hemingway" trip.

REGLA

Regla developed into a smugglers' port in colonial days, a reputation it maintained until recent days, when pirates (who made their living stealing off American yachts anchored in the harbor) were known as *terribles reglanos.* It was also the setting for Havana's bullfights. Today, the

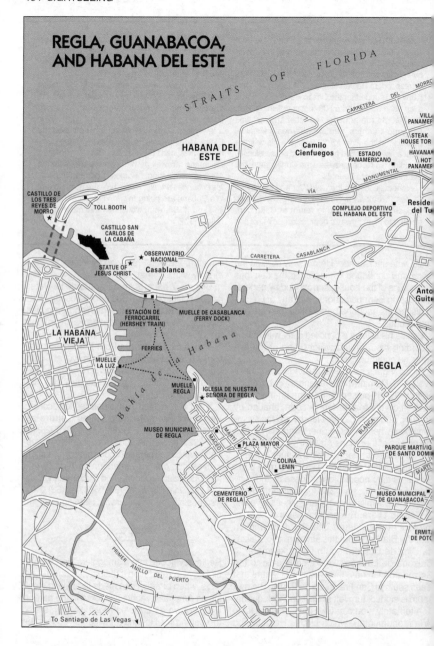

REGLA, GUANABACOA, AND HABANA DEL ESTE

STRAITS OF FLORIDA

MORRO

CARRETERA DEL MORRO

VILLA PANAMER

STEAK HOUSE TOR

HABANA DEL ESTE

Camilo Cienfuegos

ESTADIO PANAMERICANO

HAVANA

HOT PANAMER

VÍA MONUMENTAL

CASTILLO DE LOS TRES REYES DE MORRO ★

TOLL BOOTH

COMPLEJO DEPORTIVO DEL HABANA DEL ESTE

Reside del Tu

CASTILLO SAN CARLOS DE LA CABAÑA

OBSERVATORIO NACIONAL ★ Casablanca

CARRETERA CASABLANCA

STATUE OF JESUS CHRIST

Anto Guite

ESTACIÓN DE FERROCARRIL (HERSHEY TRAIN)

MUELLE DE CASABLANCA (FERRY DOCK)

LA HABANA VIEJA

FERRIES

Bahía de la Habana

MUELLE LA LUZ

MUELLE REGLA ★

IGLESIA DE NUESTRA SEÑORA DE REGLA

REGLA

MUSEO MUNICIPAL DE REGLA

MARTÍ

MACEO

PLAZA MAYOR

VÍA BLANCA

PARQUE MARTÍ/IG DE SANTO DOMI

COLINA LENIN

MARTÍ

CEMENTERIO DE REGLA ★

MUSEO MUNICIPAL DE GUANABACOA

★

ERMIT DE POTO

PRIMER ANILLO DEL PUERTO

To Santiago de Las Vegas ↓

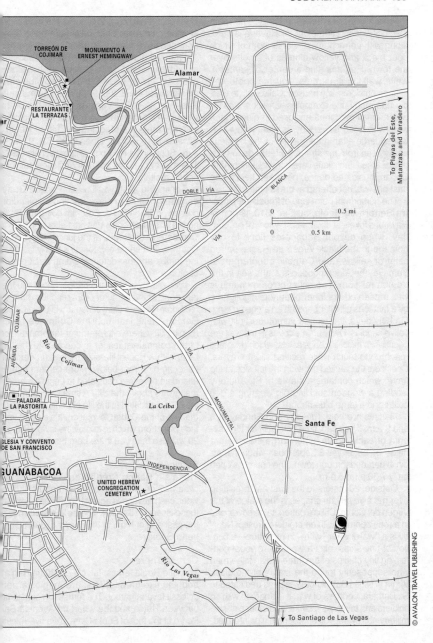

TORREÓN DE COJÍMAR
MONUMENTO Á ERNEST HEMINGWAY

Alamar

RESTAURANTE LA TERRAZAS

To Playas del Este, Matanzas, and Varadero

DOBLE VÍA

BLANCA

VÍA

0   0.5 mi

0   0.5 km

AVENIDA COJÍMAR

Río Cojímar

VÍA

MONUMENTAL

La Ceiba

Santa Fe

PALADAR LA PASTORITA

IGLESIA Y CONVENTO DE SAN FRANCISCO

GUANABACOA

INDEPENDENCIA

UNITED HEBREW CONGREGATION CEMETERY

MOON

Río Las Vegas

To Santiago de Las Vegas

© AVALON TRAVEL PUBLISHING

town is a major center of industry. The main electricity-generating plant for Havana is here, along with petrochemical works, both of which pour black and yellow plumes of smoke over the town. Regla is also a center of *santería;* while walking its streets, you may note tiny shrines outside many houses. Calle Calixto García has many fine examples. Check out #116, with a small madonna enclosed in glass in the wall, with fresh flowers by its side; and #114, whose large altar in the middle of the house is easily seen from the street. A **Fiesta de los Orishas,** a quasi-religious ceremony featuring Afro-Cuban music and dance, has been held in the past but was not offered at press time.

The harborfront hermitage of **Iglesia de Nuestra Señora de Regla,** built in 1810, is one of Havana's loveliest churches. Try to visit on Sunday, when devout Habaneros flock to pay homage to the black Virgén de Regla, patron saint of sailors (and Catholic counterpart to Yemayá, the African goddess of the sea in the Yoruba religion). The ocher-colored church is well preserved. Its inner beauty is highlighted by a fabulous gilt altar beneath an arched ceiling. On holy days, the altar is sumptuously lit with votive candles. Dwelling in alcoves in the wall are figurines of miscellaneous saints, which devotees reach up to touch while reciting silent prayers. Check out the vaulted niche on the left side of the nave, which contains a statue of St. Anthony leading a wooden suckling pig wearing a dog collar and a large blue ribbon.

Masses are held Tuesday and Sunday at 8 and 9 a.m. If you can, time your visit for the seventh of each month, when large masses are held—or, better yet, 8 September, when the Virgin is paraded through town. The church is open daily 7:30 a.m.-6 p.m.

Outside, 20 meters to the east and presiding over her own private chapel, is the statue of the Virgen del Cobre, Cuba's patron saint, enveloped in a robe adorned with embroidered roses. Nearby is a **"water altar"** with—in miniature—a convoy of tiny ships, plus a wooden rowboat containing tiny effigies of the three Indian fishermen who supposedly found the statue of the black Virgin in Nipes Bay. Another altar is dedicated to St. Barbara, goddess of war. It is adorned with tin soldiers and toy tanks, planes, and other pint-size military hardware—all appropriately painted red,

Chango's ritual color. With luck, you may arrive to witness an Afro-Cuban *batá*-drum recital being pounded out beneath the altar.

From the harborfront plaza, the tidy, well-preserved main street (Calle Martí) leads two blocks east past a small plaza to the **Museo Municipal de Regla,** at #158, tel. (97) 6989. The museum tells the tale of the Virgin of Regla and of the city's participation in revolutionary struggles. It also presents an intriguing exhibit on Regla's *santería* associations. Open Mon.-Sat. 9 a.m.-6 p.m., Sunday 9 a.m.-1 pm. Entrance costs US$2. The museum hosts cultural activities such as poetry recitals.

Continuing east, you'll reach **Parque Guaycanamar,** the main plaza fronting a splendidly preserved Georgian edifice with columns. From here, Calle Martí continues east about one km to **Cementerio de Regla,** at the junction with 10 de Octubre. The cemetery contains many fascinating tombs and headstones dating back over a century.

Immediately beyond the bridge, about 400 meters north of the cemetery (but reached more directly from Parque Guaycanamar via Calle Calixto García), steps lead uphill to **Colina de Lenin** (Lenin Hill), where a three-meter-tall bronze face of the communist leader is carved into the cliff face, with a dozen life-size figures (in cement) cheering him from below. More cement figures attend an olive tree dedicated to Lenin's memory that grows above the cliff. A small museum atop the hill is dedicated to the life of Lenin and various martyrs of the Cuban revolution. It's a good vantage point from which to survey the town. (Bus no 29 will also take you there from the ferry).

Services

There's a **Banco Crédito** on Calle Martí between 27 de Noviembre and Arangura. It provides cash advances against credit cards (except those issued in the US). The **police station** is a the east end of Martí at the corner of Juan Gualberto Gómez.

Getting There

The little Regla ferries, tel. (97) 9130 (in Regla) bobbing like green corks, are magic carpets across Havana harbor. The ferries run constantly between Regla and the wharf on Avenida San Pedro at the foot of Santa Clara; it's a five-minute crossing (10 centavos). Other ferries depart Regla's wharf for Casablanca.

You can catch buses from Habana Vieja. Bus no. 6 departs from Agramonte (Zulueta) and Genios; bus no. 106 departs from Agramonte and Refugio.

GUANABACOA

Guanabacoa, about three km east of Regla, developed in colonial days as a major landing area for slaves for more than a century. Thus, a strong Afro-Cuban culture evolved here. Guanabacoa remains Cuba's most important center of *santería*, and there are plentiful signs of this on the streets. As such, it is a popular pilgrimage site for Habaneros, but its various touristic attractions await restoration. It is currently of interest only to those with a serious interest in *santería* or a bent for ecclesiastical history.

Cuba's recently established **La Zona Franca** (Free Trade Zone), Carretera de Berroa, Km 1, Municipio del Este, Ciudad de La Habana, AP 6965, tel. (33) 8137, fax (33) 8140, website: www.zfranca.cubaweb.cu, is being constructed three km east of Guanabacoa. It is hoped that the zone will become a major center for foreign-owned industry.

The sprawling town is centered on a small square: the tree-shaded **Parque de Guanabacoa.** The square is dominated by the columned **Palacio Municipal** and the recently restored **Iglesia Parroquial Mayor.** The church features a beautiful baroque gilt altar dripping with gold, with pink walls and a lofty wooden roof painted sky blue.

Between San Antonio y Maceo on the west side of the church sits the **Museo Histórico de Guanabacoa** (Historical Museum of Guanabacoa), Calle Martí #108, tel. (90) 9117, which tells the tale of Guanabacoa's development. The 33-room museum outlines the evolution of Afro-Cuban culture, with emphasis on the slave days and *santería*. Open Mon.-Sat. 8 a.m.-6 p.m., Sunday 2-6 p.m. If the museum is closed—as it was in spring 1999—try the **Bazar de Reproduciones Artísticas** down the road at Calle Martí 175, with a shrine to Yemaya and rooms brimming with *santería* regalia. It's open Mon.-Sat. 9:30 a.m.-5:30 p.m.

CASTRO AND *SANTERÍA*

Even Fidel Castro, a highly superstitious person, is said to be a believer in *santería*. He had triumphed on 1 January, a holy day for the *orishas*. The red and black flag of the revolutionaries was that of Elleguá, god of destiny. Then, on 8 January 1959, as Castro addressed the nation from Camp Columbia, suddenly two doves flew over the audience and circled the brightly lit podium; miraculously, one of the doves alighted on Castro's shoulder, touching off an explosion from the ecstatic onlookers: *"Fee-del! Fee-del! Fee-del!"* In *santería*, doves are symbols of Obatalá, the Son of God. To Cubans—and perhaps Castro himself—the event was a supreme symbol that the gods had chosen him to guide Cuba.

Over the ensuing years, Castro's dogma of scientific communism and his need to emasculate rival sources of power translated into an attempt to convert *santería* into a folkloric movement. Religious rites were restricted. As Marxism lost its appeal in the late 1980s, *santería* bounced back, offering relief from the "propogandistic realism" of the socialist world.

The desperate conditions of the Special Period have caused millions to visit their *babalaos* (priests). In 1990, the Castro government began to co-opt support for the faith—it is said that Castro also encourages *santería* as a counterpoint to the rising power of the Catholic Church—by economically and politically supporting the *babalaos*. Reportedly, many *babalaos* have been recruited by MININT, for they above all know people's secrets.

The list of religious sites is long: **Convento de Santo Domingo,** at Calles Santo Domingo and Lebredo; **Convento de San Francisco** (still used to train priests, apparently, two centuries after its founding; it lost a side tower in 1884, knocked off by a hurricane); **Iglesia Los Escolapios;** and **Iglesia de Santo Domingo,** at Bertemati and Jesús María and Lebredo, designed in 1728 and constructed by artisans from the Canary Islands, with one of the most complicated *alfarjes* (intricately pieced, Moorish-inspired ceilings layered with geometric and star patterns) in Cuba, comprising thousands of fitted wooden pieces without nails. Also check out the **Palacio de Gobierno,** at Pepe Antonio and Jesús María.

Some touted sites are not worth the walk, such as the **Baños de Santa Rita.** Where once stood the colonial *balneario,* today only a few crumbling vestiges remain overlooking a disgustingly littered stream. And the tiny, red-tiled **Hermitage Potosí** and its overgrown cemetery, atop a hill at Calzada Vieja Guanabacoa and Potosí, is in a sad state of neglect, despite its tremendous potential. The hermitage dates back to 1644—one of the oldest in Cuba.

At the corner of San Juan Bosco and San Joaquín is a small shrine to Santo Lazarus beneath a fulsome bougainvillea bower. Pilgrims flock here each 17 December, bearing flowers and *promesas* (pledges). Mirella Acosta, who lives at San Juan Bosco #118, catercorner to the shrine, will happily recite details in Spanish.

Last but not least, Guanabacoa boasts a Jewish necropolis—the **United Hebrew Congregation Cemetery**—on the eastern outskirts of town, on Avenida Martí, entered by an ocher-colored Spanish-colonial frontispiece with a Star of David and Hebrew spelling on the pediment giving the game away. The tombs are packed in tight. A **Holocaust memorial** stands in somber memory of the millions who lost their lives to the Nazis, with emotionally stirring text: "Buried in this place are several cakes of soap made from Hebrew human fat, a fraction of the six million victims of Nazi savagery in the 20th century. May their remains rest in peace."

If you linger through the afternoon and evening, call in at the **Casa de la Trova,** Martí e San Antonio y Versalles, to see if any Afro-Cuban music and dance is happening. Before leaving, also call in at the **Centro Gráfico de Reproducciones Para el Turismo,** at San Juan Bosco and Barreto. The center displays ceramics and other artwork.

The **Dirección Municipal de Cultura,** at the juncture of San Andres and Martí, can offer information on the town's culture.

Services

East of town, the **Banco Financiero Internacional** has a branch on Carretera de Berroa, Km 1, tel. (33) 8680, fax (33) 8681. It offers foreign exchange services.

Getting There

Bus no. 3 departs for Guanabacoa from Parque de la Fraternidad in Habana Vieja, and bus no. 95 from the corner of Corrales and Agramonte (Zulueta). From Vedado, you can take bus no. 195; from the Plaza de la Revolución, take bus no. 5.

HAVANA DEL ESTE

Beyond the tunnel under Havana harbor, you pass through a toll booth (no toll was being charged in 1999), beyond which the six-lane Vía Monumental dual-carriageway leads east to Ciudad Panaméricano and Cojímar. One km east of the second (easternmost) turnoff for Cojímar, Vía Monumental splits awkwardly. Take the narrow Vía Blanca exit to the left to reach Playas del Este, Matanzas, and Varadero; the main Vía Monumental swings south so that you'll end up circling Havana on the *Circunvalación*.

The coastal vistas along the Vía Blanca soon open up with some splendid views to the south as you drive along the coast road between Havana and Matanzas and look down upon wide valleys with rolling hills, tufts of royal palms, and *mogotes* far to the south.

Warning: The tunnel is monitored by cameras and dozens of police eyes; fines are dispensed to tourists for the slightest transgression. *Keep your speed down to the posted limits!* Motorcycles are *not* allowed through the harbor tunnel; if you're on two wheels, you'll have to take the Vía Blanca from its origin in Havana, which skirts around the bay.

CIUDAD PANAMERICANO

Three km east of Havana, you'll pass the Ciudad Panamericano complex, built at great cost in 1991 for the Pan-American Games, which Cuba won convincingly. A high-rise village was built to accommodate the athletes, spectators, and press. Today, it is a residential community for Cubans, built in the hurried, jerry-rigged style of postrevolutionary years and, although but a decade old, already betraying the third-rate construction techniques. Crumbling concrete, rusting metal door frames, etc., hint that it's on its way to becoming a slum.

Ciudad Panamericano is also pushed prominently in tourist literature, despite its ugly countenance. It offers nothing but regret for tourists. There's no reason to visit unless you have an abiding interest in sports or want a base close to the funky fishing village of Cojímar nearby.

Avenida Central is the main boulevard, sloping down toward the shore. Everything you'll need can be found along here.

If you're staying here and need entertainment, the night spot of choice seems to be the disco of the Panamericano (open 10 p.m. until 6 a.m.).

Services

A Banco de Credito y Comercio is on the right, 100 meters downhill from the hotel (open Mon.-Fri. 8:30 a.m.-3 p.m., Saturday 8:30-11 a.m.). There's a post office (open 7 a.m.-10 p.m.) at the bottom of the main street. **Cadeca**, on the east side of the street, one block downhill from the hotel, can change dollars into pesos, but it's hard to imagine what you'd buy with pesos around here.

You can make domestic and international calls from the modern *telecorreo* on the east side of the main street, two blocks downhill from the hotel. The post office is next door (open Mon.-Fri. 8 a.m.-noon and 2-6 p.m., Saturday 8 a.m.-noon).

There's a pharmacy and optician (**Óptica Miramar**) on the main street, one block downhill of the hotel. The medical center is one block east of the main street, 50 meters downhill of the hotel.

You'll find several supermarkets on the main street selling Western goods.

Getting There and Around

From the Vía Monumental heading east, take the first exit to the right—marked Cójimar—which will take you back over the freeway into the Pan-American complex and the Hotel Panamericano. (Another exit, two km farther, leads directly to the old village of Cójimar). Ciudad Panamericano is well served by buses from Havana. Bus no. 204 arrives and departs from the main street in Ciudad Panamericano, bus M1 from the Vía Monumental.

A free shuttle departs the Hotel Panamericano for Havana at 9:30 a.m., 11:30 a.m., 2:30 p.m., and 5:30 p.m., dropping passengers off downtown at the Hotel Caribbean on the Prado (20 minutes) and Hotel Capri in Vedado (40 minutes). The bus for Ciudad Panamericano departs the Hotel Capri at 10:20 a.m., 12:20 p.m., 3:20 p.m., and 6:20 p.m., and from the Hotel Caribbean 20 minutes later.

Havanautos has a car rental office, tel. (33) 8113, near the post office. **Transauto** also has an office in Villa Panamericana, tel. (33) 8802. You can rent scooters at **Rent-a-Scooter,** opposite the coffee shop, one block west of the Hotel Panamericano. The scooters are new Italian Aprilla Gullivers (US$10 per hour, US$24 per day) and Yamaha Razzes (US$8 per hour, US$24 per day). A US$50 deposit is required.

The Hotel Panamericano offers a Hemingway Tour (US$3, including sandwich), on Monday, Wednesday, and Saturday.

COJÍMAR

For Hemingway fans, a trip to the fishing village of Cojímar is a pilgrimage. For everyone else, it's a treat. Here, the author berthed his legendary sportfishing boat, the *Pilar.*

The forlorn village spreads out along the shore and rises up the hill behind it; an old church on the hilltop has seen better days. The waterfront is lined with weather-beaten, red-tile-roofed cottages with shady verandas. Whitecaps are often whipped up in the bay, making the Cuban flag flutter above **El Torreon,** the pocket-size fortress guarding the cove's entrance. It was here in 1762 that the English put ashore their invasion army and marched on Havana to capture Cuba

for King George III. The fortress, built in the 1760s to forestall another fiasco, is still in military hands, and you will be shooed away from its steps if you get too close. Unfortunately, Hurricane George did a number on the fort when it ripped through in 1997, tearing away much of its foundations.

When Hemingway died, every fisherman in the village apparently donated a brass fitting from his boat. The collection was melted down to create the bust of the author—**Monumento Ernest Hemingway**—that has stared out to sea since 1962 from atop a large limestone block within a columned rotunda at the base of El Torreon. A plaque reads: *"Parque Ernest Hemingway. In grateful memory from the population of Cojímar to the immortal author of* Old Man and the Sea, *inaugurated 21 July 1962, on the 63rd anniversary of his birth."* The brass bust occasionally receives a spit and polish, and the classical rotunda was recently renovated. It is a stirring site, and the royal blue sky and hard windy silence make for a profound experience as you commune alone with Papa.

After exploring, appease your hunger with fisherman's soup and paella at Hemingway's favorite restaurant, **La Terraza,** tel. (65) 3471, on the main street 200 meters south of El Torreon. After Hemingway's death, the restaurant went into decline. Apparently, Castro, passing through in 1970, was dismayed to learn of its condition and ordered it restored. The gleaming mahogany bar at the front, accepting dol-

The bust of Hemingway at his monument (just across from pocket-size El Torreon fortress) is made of brass from melted-down boat fittings donated by Cuban fishermen upon the author's death.

lars only, gets few locals—a pity; what a hangout it could be. You sense that Papa could stroll in at any moment. His favorite corner table is still there. He is there, too, patinated in bronze atop a pedestal, and adorning the walls in black and white, sharing a laugh with Castro.

Cojímar's most famous resident is Gregorio Fuentes, Hemingway's old pal and skipper after whom the novelist modeled the proud fisherman in *The Old Man and the Sea*. Travelers come from far and wide to hear Fuentes recall his adventures. When I last saw him, in May 1999, the centegenarian was frail but still going strong. He will be delighted to smile for your camera and answer questions; however, please refrain from knocking on his front door at Calle Pesuela #209. The old man can often be found regaling travelers in La Terraza, and this is where you should arrange any meeting with him. Regardless, you should toast his good health with a turquoise cocktail—"Coctel Fuentes"—appropriately named after Cojímar's venerable homegrown hero. His grandson, Rafael Valdés, charges visitors $50 for 15-minute "consultations," although haggling can cut the price by more than half.

Cojímar is fascinating by night, too, with every house door and window wide open; families sitting on sofas watching TV; dogs roaming for morsels; figures gently rocking, suffused by the soft glow of 40-watt lights; the moonlight reflecting on the bay. Zig-zagging through these streets one evening, I chanced upon a garden full of villagers sitting beneath the stars watching a movie projected onto a house wall.

The post office is two blocks west on Calle 98; open Mon.-Sat. 8-11 a.m. and 2-6 p.m.

Getting There
By car, the exit from the Vía Monumental is well marked (coming from Havana, take the *second* exit marked Cojímar).

You can catch buses no. 58, 116, 195, 215, and 217 from the bottom of the Prado, at the junction with Avenida de los Estudiantes (10 centavos). Bus 58 departs from the west side of Parque de la Fraternidad, two blocks west of the Capitolio.

Virtually every major hotel in Havana offers excursions to Cojímar through its tour desk. **Paradiso: Promotora de Viajes Culturales,** Calle 19 #560 esq. C, Vedado, tel. (32) 6928, fax (33)

3921, e-mail: paradis@turcult.get.cma, website: www.cult.cu\paradiso\index.html, includes Cojímar on a five-hour guided excursion called Hemingway: The Mystery of a Footprint, offered daily from Havana.

ALAMAR AND CELIMAR

Immediately east of Cojímar, you'll pass a modern, self-contained dormitory city long prized by the Cuban government as an example of the achievements of socialism. Alamar (pop. 100,000) is a sea of ugly concrete high-rise complexes—what Martha Gellhorn considered "white rectangular factories"—jerry-built with shoddy materials by microbrigades of untrained "volunteer" workers borrowed from their normal jobs and taught on-site. Alamar sprawls east to its sister city, Celimar.

In April 1959, Alamar emerged on the drawing board as the first revolutionary housing scheme in postrevolutionary Cuba. The initial plan for 10,000 people in four- to 11-story prefabricated concrete apartment blocks was to be fully self-contained in self-sufficient "superblocks." These were partly inspired by the British postwar models for fixed-rent, low-cost housing run by the state, already discredited in Europe. The apartment units, built in four-story blocks, are virtually identical: two small bedrooms, a small living room, bathroom, kitchen, and balcony. Alamar was vastly expanded beginning in 1976 and today covers four square miles.

Castro was a regular visitor during the early years of construction: Alamar was a matter of pride and joy for him. He touted the project as a model for future revolutionary housing schemes. Later, Cuban planners came to acknowledge its isolating nature and overwhelming deficiencies (the plumbing came from the Soviet Union, the wiring from China, the stoves from North Korea; there were no spare parts budgeted for upkeep). Today, the city wears a patina of mildew and grime, and, by any standards, is a virtual slum. Refuse litters the potholed roads, and the roadside parks are untended. There are no jobs here, either, and few stores, so that locals tend their own vegetable plots enclosed by rough walls and steel rods. There's also no proper transportation. It is difficult to find any redeeming fea-

THE OLD MAN: GREGORIO FUENTES

Gregorio Fuentes, born in 1897, no longer has his sea legs and now walks with the aid of a crutch. But his memory remains keen, particularly when it comes to his old fishing companion, Ernest Hemingway. "His absence is still painful for me," says Fuentes, the now-ancient captain who from 1938 until Hemingway's death was in charge of the writer's boat, the *Pilar.*

Fuentes was the model for "Antonio" in *Islands in the Stream,* and is considered by many—albeit more contentiously—to be the model for Santiago, the fisherman cursed by *salao* (the worst form of bad luck) in *The Old Man and the Sea,* a simple and profound novel that won Hemingway the Nobel Prize for Literature. Fuentes—who says that the "Santiago" in the novella was partly modeled after another Cuban fisherman, Anselmo Hernández—looks the part: "The old man was thin and gaunt with deep wrinkles in the back of his neck. The brown blotches of the benevolent skin cancer the sun brings from its reflections on the tropic sea were on his cheeks. . . . Everything about him was old except his eyes and they were the same color as the sea and were cheerful and undefeated."

Fuentes started his sea life at Lanzarote, in the Canary Islands, when he was four years old. He came to Cuba at age 10 and met Hemingway in 1931 on Tortuga, in the Bahamas, when the two men were sheltering from a storm (Fuentes was captain of a smack). The two men were virtually inseparable from 1935 to 1960. During World War II, they patrolled the coast for German U-boats. Years later, says Fuentes, he and Hemingway patrolled the same coast to assist Castro's rebel army. Their birthdays were 11 days apart and, reports Tom Miller, the two would celebrate each together with a bottle of whiskey. Fuentes kept the tradition alive after Hemingway's death by pouring a whiskey over the latter's bust down by the harbor.

The old skipper is regarded with awe by Cubans. He dines daily at Las Terrazas, where his meals have been free since 1993, courtesy of Castro, who named him a national treasure and gifted him a color TV and a doubling of his pension. In 1999, he celebrated his 102nd birthday and was still going strong.

Hemingway's friend, fishing buddy, and inspiration

tures in Alamar, although the bleakness is broken in springtime by bright-yellow blossoms lining the roads.

The singular saving grace is **Playa Bacuranao,** a small horseshoe cove with a white-sand beach backed by seagrape and palms at the east end of Alamar. It's popular on weekends with Habaneros escaping city life for a day by the sea in the sun. The Spanish built a watchtower here (still extant), where they could watch for pirate ships and signal to Havana with smoke fires. Later, it was used as a lookout station to signal contraband boats at sea, letting them know whenever the *rurales* (soldiers on horseback) were around by hanging out clothes on the clothesline. Hemingway also used to berth his *Pilar* here, and it was here that his fishermen in *To Have and Have Not* had squeezed "the Chink's" throat until it cracked. A tourist resort here is now closed.

The area is good for **scuba diving.** The wreck of an 18th-century galleon lies just off the tiny beach, and there's another wreck farther out (a popular playpen for turtles). Coral grows abundantly on both sides of the bay, so if you have **snorkeling** gear, bring it.

Getting There

Plenty of *camellos* (camels, or *tren buses*, towed passenger cars that serve as public transportation) leave from Parque de la Fraternidad: look for the M1. Buses no. 62 and 162 pass by Bacuranao, departing from Parque Central in Havana.

Most residents hitch. The junctions of the two major access roads off the Vía Blanca are major hitching points.

TARARÁ

Two km farther east, you'll cross the Río Tarará and pass by the village of Tarará, at Vía Blanca Km 19. Tarará is famous as a summer camp and health resort, with a splendid beach. Before the Special Period, it was used by Cuban schoolchildren, who combined study with beachside pleasures and stayed at Tarará's **José Martí Pioneer City,** replete with soccer pitch, cinema, and other services. Here, too, several thousand young victims of the Chernobyl nuclear disaster in the Ukraine in 1988 were treated free of charge, as they still are; blonde, blue-eyed children still abound.

It was here, too, that Castro operated his secret government in the early stage of the Revolution. Che Guevara was convalescing here after his debilitating years of guerrilla warfare in the Sierra Maestra, and the location away from Havana proved perfect for secret meetings to shape Cuba's future while Castro played puppeteer to the weak and demoralized "official" democratic government of President Urrutia. It was here that INRA (the Agrarian Reform Institute) was created and operated as the main instrument for enforcing a communist revolution.

Today, Servimed operates Tarará as a health tourism facility with limited success. The place fell on hard times in recent years, but in spring 1999, a far-reaching renovation was half complete, promising to bring life back to the villas in the hopes that Tarará can be promoted as a tourist resort. The land slopes gently down to the shore. The upper half of the complex remains a bit decrepit, but the lower half nearer the shore offers a pleasing ambience, albeit a bit lonesome.

Tarará has two beaches. To the west is a delightful pocket-size beach that forms a spit at the rivermouth. Popular with locals, it features a volleyball court and shady *palapas*. The channel is renowned for its coral—great for snorkeling and scuba diving, as large groupers and snappers swim in and out of the river mouth. A second, larger white-sand beach—the westernmost extent of Playas del Este—spreads along the shoreline farther east. It, too, is popular with locals and a few tourists, and also has a sand volleyball court, shade umbrellas, and lounge chairs.

Entry is free, but gaining access exemplifies the worst form of petty Cuban bureaucracy. Cubans and tourists alike must show ID. Tourists also must bring their passports (a photocopy will *not* suffice); the two mule-minded female *custodios* refused my two photo IDs and turned me away.

Marina Puertosol Tarará

Marina Puertosol Tarará, tel. (97) 1510, fax (97) 1499, channel VHF 77, is behind the spit, on the east side of the river. The marina, whose formerly impressive facilities were beginning to look threadbare in early 1999, is headquarters for Puertosol marinas nationwide. The marina has 50 berths, with water and electricity hookups, plus diesel and gas. It also has a dry dock. (The Marina Puertosol head office is in Edificio Focsa, Calle 17 y M, Vedado, tel. 33-4705, fax 33-4703.)

Each July, the marina hosts the **Old Man and the Sea Fishing Tournament.** Registration costs US$200 for up to three *pescadores* (fishermen). Boats are made available for US$180 - 300 per day, depending on size. The marina also hosts the **La Hispanidad Fishing Tournament** in October (registration costs US$250, but boat charter fees are the same).

Boat Rental: Yachts can be rented for US$250 for nine hours. You can also rent one of three live-aboard motorboats. Weekly rentals range from US$2,100 (May-Oct.) to US$2,800 (mid-Dec. to mid-January). You can rent **Hobie-Cats** on the beach, and **pedal boats** at the marina for forays along the river estuary (US$4 per 30 minutes).

Scuba Diving: The *buceo* (scuba diving) office, tel. (97) 1501, ext. 239, faces the marina. Trips cost US$30 (one dive) or US$50 (two dives). A four-day certification program costs US$400. Initiation dives (three hours) are also offered, and equipment rental costs US$10.

Sportfishing: You can charter a boat for four hours' sportfishing for US$200-250, depending on the vessel (one to four people). Other fishing trips cost US$20.

Snorkeling: Three-hour **snorkeling** excursions cost US$30 based on a minimum of four people per boat.

Yacht Cruises: Yacht excursions include six-hour "seafaris" that depart at 9:30 a.m. and cost US$50, featuring fishing, snorkeling, and lunch on board, based on a minimum of four passengers. A three-hour nocturnal cruise costs US$15 with dinner on board, plus music and dancing.

Other: Banana boats, jet skis, and catamaran trips are also available.

Services and Entertainment

The **Discoteca La Sirena,** near the marina, offers a laser show and disco from 9 p.m. onward. There's a **go-cart** track beside the Vía Monumental at the turnoff for Tarará. A six-minute spin on a zesty 260 cc Honda costs US$5, and 13 minutes costs US$10. A *parque diversion* (amusement park) on the west side of the Río Tarará offers carousels and other rides; access

is by a separate exit from the Vía Monumental west of the river.

Getting There

Tarará is at Km 17 Vía Blanca, 27 km east of Havana. It is signed off the Vía Blanca. A taxi will cost about US$17.

PLAYAS DEL ESTE

"A sense of the island's racial history and diversity wasn't to be culled from the telephone directory," wrote Carlo Gébler in *Driving Through Cuba,* "but was to be seen at first hand on the sand by the edge of the sea." Cubans are great beachgoers, and nowhere on the island proves the case more than the Playas del Este. On hot summer weekends, all of Havana seems to come down to the beach (well, at least they did before the Special Period, when gas and money were more widely available). The beaches of Playas del Este are temples of ritual narcissism: young Cubans congregate here to meet friends, tan their bodies, play soccer or volleyball, and flirt.

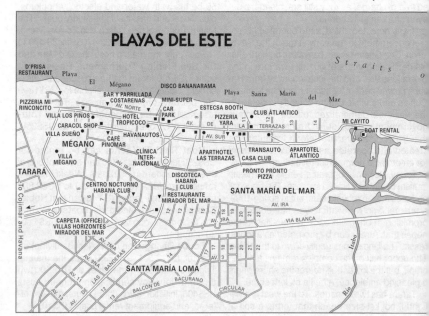

The beach action concentrates in front of the main hotel, the Tropicoco.

A nearly constant tropical breeze is usually strong enough to conjure surf from the warm turquoise seas—a perfect scenario for lazing, with occasional breaks for grilled fish or fried chicken from thatch-roofed *ranchitas,* where the drinks are strong and you can eat practically with your feet in the water. After a sun-stunned day, everyone seems to curl up for a recuperative snooze in preparation for the reappearance of the bohemian spirit, which stirs around eight.

Playas del Este is pushed as a hot destination for foreign tourists and, in the mid-1990s, enjoyed some success, bringing tourists (predominantly Italian and male) and Cubans (predominantly young and female) together for rendezvous under *palapas* and palms. The beach was considered by *jineteras* to be a great place to find single Italian males, for whom the resort has become a virtual colony. When a ban was placed on Cuban women in hotel rooms, private room rentals rocketed. (Many *casas particulares*—private houses—rent rooms by the hour to couples seeking a place of coital conve-

nience.) The police crackdown in early 1999 knocked the wind clear out of Playas del Este's sails. Young Cubanas were arrested and, as of May 1999, remained wary of the heavy police presence and harassment. As a result, Italians canceled their vacation plans in droves.

By international standards, it's a nonstarter other than for a day visit. This isn't Cancún or even Negril. Although upscale villas are available, the hotels are dour. The nightlife and services are desultory. And though Playa Santa María is a beautiful beach and offers bars and watersports, forget any other hopes of aesthetic appeal. Playas del Este will probably go through a year or two of deterioration—in spring 1999, with tourists few and far between, it looked rundown, and several buildings were derelict. For now, it conjures up the worst images of a communist beach resort. Until Playas del Este is revitalized, skip it as a vacation destination and use it merely as a daytime (or weekend) sojourn from Havana.

The beaches of Playas del Este stretch unbroken for six km east-west. The area is divided into the purely touristy Mégano and Santa María

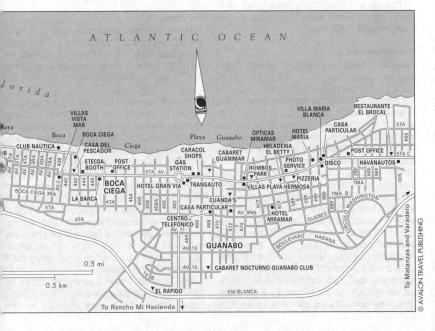

del Mar district to the west of the Río Itabo, with Boca Ciega (comprising mostly rental units for Cubans) and the village of Guanabo to the east. Separating these two distinct regions is a large mangrove swamp reaching inland from the mouth of the river, where egrets, herons, and other waterfowl can be admired. (**Warning:** Puddles collect in mangroves and pastures on the lowlands inland, forming perfect breeding habitats for mosquitoes; when the rains come, the bloodsuckers are voracious. By day, you're usually okay, but lather up with insect repellent at night.) The main beach—Playa Santa María—is several kilometers long, with light-golden sand shelving into stunning aquamarine and turquoise waters. Playa Boca Ciega, backed by dunes, is also beautiful.

Guanabo is a Cuban village with many plantation-style wooden homes. Playa Guanabo is the least-attractive beach. Local Cubans use it for recreation, including old men looking like salty characters from a Hemingway novel standing bare-chested, reeling in silvery fish from the surf. It has few restaurants and no hotels to Western standards, but is slowly accruing tourist facilities.

The village of Santa María Loma is one km inland, atop the hill that parallels the shore. It offers many modest rental units.

Dude Ranches

Dude ranches at the beach? Not exactly. About four km inland, near Minas, are two *fincas de recreo* (dude ranches) in the heart of the Cuban countryside: **Finca de Recreo Guanabito**, Calzada de Jústiz, Km 3.5, Guanabo, tel. (96) 4610, and just up the road, **Rancho Mi Hacienda**, Calzada de Jústiz, Km 4, Guanabo, tel. (96) 4711. Rancho Mi Hacienda is a 13-hectare *finca* that raises animals and vegetables used in the ranch's restaurant. It offers horseback riding, as well as boats rides on a lake. Take your camera to record the flurry of feathers during ferocious yet bloodless cockfights (fortunately, in deference to tourists' politically correct modern tastes, the bird's spurs are covered to prevent them from seriously hurting each other). Rancho Mi Hacienda hosts an Afro-Cuban cultural show once a week. Accommodation is provided in six handsome albeit rustic cabins connected by suspension bridges on the banks of the Río Itabo, plus three rooms in what was once a posh mansion. Each a/c unit has a telephone, satellite TV, and minibar. There's a dining hall and swimming pool amid lush gardens.

Recreation

Several outlets on the beach rent **jet skis** (US$15 for 15 minutes) and **Hobie-Cats** (US$20 per hour). You can also rent shade umbrellas (US$3 per day) and beach chairs and lounge chairs (US$2 per day). **Go-cart racing** is offered on a circuitous track beside the Vía Blanca at the turnoff for Tárara. Each six minutes costs US$5. **Horses** can be rented on the beach in front of Tropicoco. If the kids tire of the beach, take them to the basic children's playground— **Parque Diversiones**—on Avenida Quinta and Calle 470 in Boca Ciega. The kids (and adults) can take potshots at cutouts of soldiers (*yanquis,* perhaps?) at a fairground rifle range one block east, at Calle 472.

Scuba diving is available from the watersport stand on the beach in front of the Hotel Tropicoco. A coral reef runs offshore at a depth of no more than 20 feet, with lots of brain, elkhorn, and staghorn formations.

Services

You can purchase postage stamps and make international calls at the Hotel Tropicoco. There's also a post office in Boca Ciega, on Avenida 5ta and Calle 448; and one in Santa María in Edificio Los Corales, on Avenida de las Terrazas at Calle 11, open 8 a.m.-1 p.m.

There are plenty of ETECSA phone booths, including on Avenida de las Terrazas in Santa María in front of Hotel Tropicoco and also immediately west of Club Átlantico; on the beachfront road and Calle 442 in Boca Ciega; and in Guanabo at Calle 468 and Avenida 9na.

Servimed operates the **Clínica Internacional**, on Avenida de las Terrazas, 100 yards east of Hotel Tropicoco, tel. (97) 1032. It's open 24 hours. A visit to the clinic costs US$25 (US$30 at night). The doctor also makes hotel visits if needed (US$50). It boasts a well-stocked pharmacy and even a clinical laboratory and an ambulance. Asistur can arrange credit payment if you're in financial straits.

The **Tropical Travel Agency** can advise on and make travel arrangements. It's in Edificio Los Corales, next to the post office, on Avenida de las Terrazas in Santa María. There's also a tourism desk in the lobby of Hotel Tropicoco.

Photo Service has two small stores where you can buy instamatic cameras, batteries, and film: in the lobby of the Hotel Tropicoco, and on Avenida 5ta in Guanabo, at Calle 480.

Entertainment

There's not much nightlife. The hottest thing is the **Disco Bananarama,** a palenque bar-cum-disco right on the beach in Santa María. **Hotel Tropicoco** also has a late-night disco (entrance free to hotel guests, US$2 to others). **Aparthotel Atlántico** offers entertainment at 1 p.m., which at press time included an Afro-Cuban show on Thursday, a campesina show on Tuesday, and a Caribbean theme on Saturday. The **Casa Club Atlántico** has a pool hall and dance club upstairs with a bar, TV, and karaoke. Open 2 p.m.-2 a.m. It offers a *cabaret espectáculo* on weekends, with free entry.

Several down-to-earth places cater to the local Cuban populace. Try **Centro Nocturno Habana Club,** on Calle 10 e/ 1 y 3ra; **Cabaret Nocturno Guanabo Club,** on Calle 468; **Cabaret Guanimar,** at Avenida 3ra and Calle 468; or **Cabaret Pino del Mar,** on Avenida del Sur e/ Calles 5 y 7ma.

Western camp classic films dubbed in Spanish are shown at **Cine Guanabo** on Calle 480 (one peso).

Getting There and Away

Playas del Este is well served by bus from Havana. Buses no. 62, 162, and 262 operate from Parque Central; bus no. 219 departs from the main bus terminal, and bus no. 400 departs from near the railway station, at the junction of Agramonte and Glória (one peso). You can also hire a *maquina* (a *colectivo* taxi) from outside the railway station and at Dragones in Havana. They'll charge anywhere upward of US$5 to Playas del Este, depending on the number of passengers.

Licensed taxis cost about US$20 one way. Taxi and car rental companies offer chauffeured excursions. For example, **Palcocar,** tel. (33) 7235, fax (33) 7250, charges US$69 for an excursion with hotel pickup and five free hours at the beach.

In summer, a train runs four times daily to Guanabo (July-Aug. only) from Estación Cristina, at Avenida de México and Arroyo, in Habana Vieja, tel. (78) 4971.

Cubatur and Havanatur, in Hotel Tropicoco, offers excursions that include a Havana city tour (US$15), the Bay of Pigs (US$44), Viñales (US$46), and "Hemingway's Route" (US$14, Thursday only), plus a nocturnal excursion to the Tropicana nightclub.

Getting Around

You can walk virtually anywhere in Mégano/Santa María or Boca Ciega/Guanabo, although you will want wheels to get between them.

In Santa María, **Havanauto** has a car-rental office in the parking lot of Hotel Tropicoco. It also rents scooters for US$10 per hour, US$24 per day (with a US$50 deposit). **Transauto** has a scooter-rental office in the Aparthotel Atlántico, renting Suzuki scooters for US$15 per day (gas costs US$5.50 extra).

In Guanabo, **Havanauto** has two offices on Avenida 5ta, next to the gas station at Calle 464, and also at Calle 500, tel. (96) 2694. **Transauto** rents scooters from its office next to the Hotel Gran Vía and opposite Havanauto on Avenida 5ta at Calle 464, tel. (33) 2917.

There's a **Cupet gas station** on Avenida 5ta, two blocks east of the traffic circle at the foot of Calle 462.

ENTERTAINMENT, RECREATION, AND SHOPPING

Don't believe anything you've read about communism having killed the capital city's zest. Habaneros love to paint the town red (so to speak). You can still find as much partying as party line in Havana—a city of spontaneity and the undisputed cultural epicenter of the Caribbean—especially in the realm of music.

Author Norman Mailer scolded President Kennedy for the Bay of Pigs defeat by asking, "Wasn't there anyone around to give you the lecture on Cuba? Don't you sense the enormity of your mistake—you invade a country without understanding its music." Cuba's musical influence reverberates around the world, from Kinshasa to Tokyo, with Havana as its hub.

Music—the pulsing undercurrent of Cuban life—is everywhere. Dance, from the earliest *guaguanco* (an erotic rumba in which the man tries to make contact with the woman's groin

with whatever part of his body he can, and the woman dances defensively, like a female *matador* with a bull) to the *mambo* craze, has always been a potent expression of an enshrined national tradition—Cuban sensualism. Girls are whisked onto the dance floor and whirled through a flurry of complicated steps and sensuous undulations, the intensity of which makes their North American counterparts look like butlers practicing the waltz. Young or elderly, every Cuban undulates with coquetry, swaying to the rhythm just a little closer than cheek to cheek. It's a wonder Havana's birth rate isn't higher.

At night, the pace quickens and Havana pulsates with the Afro-Latin spirit, be it energy-charged musical sessions or the sacred chantings of *santería*. Nowhere else in the Caribbean has as many discotheques, cinemas, and cabarets to choose from. Sure, the city has lost the Bar-

bary Coast spirit of prerevolutionary days, when, according to Graham Greene, "three pornographic films were shown nightly between nude dances" in the Shanghai Theater. Many of the famous clubs from the "sordid era," which ended in the 1950s, remain in name, their neon signs reminders of what was. Many—those still used by Cubans—are seedier (albeit without the strippers) than they were three decades ago—and often somewhat surreal, too, because in many the decor hasn't changed. Cubans even enjoy the anguished, melancholy verses of the tango, which sprang from Buenos Aires's brothels almost a century ago but perfectly fits Cuba's mood today.

More cultured entertainment is present aplenty. Since the Revolution, the government's sponsorship of the arts has yielded a rich harvest in every field. The **Centro Nacional de Escuelas de Arte** (National Center of Schools of Art), created in 1960, has 41 schools in Havana under its umbrella, including the national Escuela de la Música, a national folkloric school, two ballet schools, two fine arts schools, and a school of modern dance. Unfortunately, since the Special Period, many schools have been affected immensely, suffering great shortages of instruments, sheet music, leotards, dance shoes, paints, brushes, and other materials. *Donations are welcome.*

During the mid-1980s, Cuba was a rest-and-relaxation capital for the Latin Left. (Havana is still popular with South Americans, who flock to the Latin American Film Festival, Havana Jazz Festival, and other annual world-class cultural extravaganzas.) Ballet is much appreciated by Habaneros. Each region has a *Casa de la Trova,* where you can hear traditional ballad-style *trova* (love songs rendered with the aid of guitar and drum), often blended with revolutionary themes; and a *Casa de la Cultura,* which hosts movies, art exhibitions, and other cultural events. Havana also has ongoing music concerts, choral recitals, and art and sculpture exhibits. The only fault to be found is the quality of Cuban theater, although there's plenty of comedy theater.

On the bar scene, a fistful of atmospheric spots recall the heyday of the 1950s, such as Dos Hermanos, La Bodeguita del Medio, and El Floridita, all haunted by Hemingway's ghost. Hip cigar lounges, trendy bistro-bars, and take-offs on the internationally renowned Hard Rock Café are beginning to blossom (Gato Tuerto and the Habana Café come to mind). Otherwise, the bar scene is relatively dull.

The city is relatively devoid of the kind of lively sidewalk bars that make Rio de Janeiro buzz and South Beach hum. Most major hotels have bars; some, such as the lobby bar of the Hotel Ambos Mundos, are splendid. And most such bars have live music, everything from salsa bands to folkoric trios. Romantic crooners are a staple, wooing local crowds with dead-on deliveries of Benny Moré classics while sensual all-female bands entice tourists with the ubiquitous *"beseme, beseme mucho . . . "* and "the Che song" (*"Querido Comandante Guevara/La transparencia de su presencia . . . "*). Take your pick between dollars-only haunts, where drinks will set you back at least US$3 a pop, to grim local bars where one peso will buy a beer. Havana also offers earthy discos (called cabarets) and *centros nocturnos* (open-air discotheques), often with laser light shows, serving the locals, who in 1999 had (with the exception of Cuba's nouveau riche) been driven from tourist spots by high dollar prices.

The scene is fluid. Many venues herein described may have closed or be operating on a threadbare budget due to the Special Period; others, to which entrance was once free, now have a cover charge.

More and more clubs and discos have begun to apply a *consumo minimo* (minimum charge policy), which sometimes applies to the entire evening and sometimes to the first purchase. Watch out for abuses: for example, if a US$5 *consumo minimo* applies to your first purchase and you order several beverages during the evening, be sure that the first drink you order is a more expensive drink—you'll be charged US$5 even for a mineral water—and that any inexpensive item you might order later in the evening doesn't appear as the first drink on your bill.

The restrictions imposed by police in late 1998 and early 1999 put a severe damper on Havana's nightlife for locals, who were forced to be more creative—which means that the birth rate will spike. Some discos remain closed.

Resources

The best resource is *Guia Cultural de la Habana,* published monthly by Centro de Desarrollo y Comunicación Cultural (CREART), Calle

4 #205 e/ Linea y 11, Vedado, tel. (32) 9691, fax (66) 2562. It provides up-to-date information on what's on in town. You can pick up free copies at tour desks in leading hotels.

The weekly newspaper *Cartelera* publishes similar information on exhibitions, galleries, and performances. It's available in many hotel lobbies. *Granma,* the daily Communist Party newspaper, also lists the forthcoming week's events.

And the Ministry of Culture sponsors a bimonthly magazine, *Revolución y Cultura,* containing interviews, fiction, poetry, essays, photography, and profiles on the arts, plus news on cultural events. It is hard to come by today (past issues—US$3 each—can be obtained from the Center for Cuban Studies, 124 W. 23rd St., New York, NY 10011).

Paradiso: Promotora de Viajes Culturales, Calle 19 #560 esq. C, Vedado, tel. (32) 6928, fax (33) 3921, e-mail: paradis@turcult.get.cma, website: www.cult.cu\paradiso\index.html, promotes artistic and cultural events, festivals, courses, seminars, workshops, and conferences in the arts, sciences, and technology. It also arranges participatory courses for foreigners in cultural courses.

Idea Bank Z (BIZ) is a nonprofit group of artists, writers, and intellectuals that champions Cuban culture. For example, it publishes limited editions of unpublished writers (incorporating visual art), among them *Libros-Arte* and *Libros-Eventos Especiales.* BIZ is preparing a databank of contemporary Cuban art (donations can be sent to Banco de Ideas Z, Calle 19, No. 1362, Apto. 15, e/ 24 y 26, Vedado, Havana 4, C.P. 10400, tel. 3-7327).

Dance classes for the casual tourist are offered at the Hotel Lincoln Tuesday 4-6 p.m. Alternately, contact Gilberto Capote, Calle O'Reilly #362, Apto. 6, 3ra piso (third floor), e/ Habana y Compostela, tel. (61) 7080. He's been recommended as a one-on-one dance instructor.

FESTIVALS AND EVENTS

The Special Period took its toll on popular festivals, cultural celebrations, and *cumbanchas,* the Cuban equivalent of street parties or sprees that might go on all night. Fortunately, festival life is now rebounding.

Religious parades are very few. The noted exception is the **Procession of the Miracles** each 17 December, when hundreds of pilgrims—many of them dragging stones or crawling on their knees—make their way to the Santuário de San Lazaro, the "leper of the miracles," to give thanks to the saint (known as Babalu Aye in *santería*) for miracles they imagine she has granted. The sanctuary, a national monument, is at Rincón, southwest of Havana, on the outskirts of Santiago de las Vegas.

For a list of forthcoming festivals, conferences, and events, contact **Paradiso** (see address above) or the **Palacio de Convenciones,** Calle 146 e/ 11 y 13, Playa, tel. (22) 6011, fax (21) 9496, e-mail: palco@palco.get.cma.net.

Daily Events

Be sure to attend the **Ceremonia del Cañonazo** (Cannon Ceremony), held nightly at 9 p.m. at the Castillo de San Carlos de la Cabaña, where troops dressed in 18th-century military garb light the fuse of a cannon to announce the closing of the city gates, maintaining a tradition going back centuries. You are greeted at the castle gates by soldiers in traditional uniform, and the place is lit by flaming lanterns. Very atmospheric. About 8:50 p.m., a cry rings out, announcing the procession of soldiers marching across the plaza bearing muskets, while a torchbearer lights flaming barrels. The soldiers ascend to the cannon, which they prepare with ramrod, etc. (Latter-day soldiers have pre-prepared the explosives and are on hand to guard the show.) When the soldier puts the torch to the cannon, you have about three seconds before the thunderous boom. Your heart skips a beat. But it's all over in a millisecond, and the troops march away.

You can visit on your own; your US$3 entrance to the castles includes the ceremony and museums. Be sure to get there no later than 8:30 p.m. if you wish to secure a seat close to the cannon. The ceremony is popular with Cuban families, and the place gets jam-packed. Latecomers (there are usually several hundred) are relegated to the lawns or the roof a good distance away.

You can book excursion tours from any hotel tour desk. Several tour agencies combine an excursion to witness the *cañonazo.* For example, **Tour & Travel,** tel. (24) 9200 or (24) 9199 in

Miramar, tel. (24) 7541 in Vedado, charges US$15 (US$25 with dinner). Some agencies combine the ceremony with a cabaret.

Monthly Events

Habaguanex puts on the **Noche en la Plaza de la Catedral** on the third or fourth Saturday of every month. It's a glorious evening in the plaza, when a *criollo* dinner is served and a folkloric *espectáculo* takes place on the steps of the cathedral. The wide-ranging entertainment includes the Conjunto Folklórico JJ, ballet, and *boleros* (ballads). Tickets cost US$30 and can be booked in advance at tour agencies throughout the city; at the Restaurante El Patio in the plaza, tel. (57) 1034; or at Habaguanex's office at Calle Oficios #110 between Lamparilla and Amargura, tel./fax (66) 9761 or (33) 9585, website: www. habaguanex.cubaweb.cu/habaguan.

Annual Events

January: Recently reintroduced to kick off the year is the **Cabildos** festival on 6 January, when Habana Vieja resounds with festivities recalling the days when Afro-Cuban *cabildos* danced through the streets in vivid costumes and painted faces. Contact the City Historian's office at Calle Tacon #1, tel. (33) 8183; or Habaguanex (see above).

February: The star-studded annual **International Havana Jazz Festival** is held in mid-February, highlighted by the greats of Cuban jazz, such as Chucho Valdés and Irakere, Los Van Van, Juan Formell, Silvio Rodríguez, and Grupo Perspectiva. Concerts are held in the Hotel Riviera's Salón Internacional (formerly the Palacio de Salsa), at the Casa de Cultura de Plaza (an open-air courtyard with bleacher seating at Calzada #909 esq. 8, Vedado, tel. 31-2003), and at José Echeverría Stadium, which hosts the All Stars Concert. You can buy tickets in pesos at the Casa de Cultura. Prearranged group tours to the festival are offered through **Caribbean Music and Dance Programs,** 12545 Olive St. #241, St. Louis, MO 63141, tel. (314) 542-3637 or toll free (877) 665-4321, fax (314) 469-2916, e-mail: caribmusic@igc.apc.org, website: www.caribmusic.com. **Wings of the World,** 1200 William St. #706, Buffalo, NY 14240-0706; or 1636 3rd Ave. #232, New York, NY 10128, tel. (800) 465-8687, fax (416) 486-4001, also offers

an annual weeklong tour to the festival. Both programs include jazz workshops and reserved seating at jazz concerts.

Carnival in Havana! was revived in 1996 after a five-year hiatus. It's held in mid-February, when thousands of Habaneros take to the streets. For an entire week, the Malecón becomes a stage for the island's hottest folkloric, salsa, and jazz groups. Tourists throw inhibitions to the wind and join local residents in colorful pre-Lenten revelry as traditional *comparsas* (music and dance troupes originally tied to slaves' tribe of origin) parade through the streets. The party mood is highlighted by outdoor concerts, street fairs, conga lines, and colorful parades. While many folks go lavishly gowned, others ecstatically flaunt their freedom, having cast off customary controls along with most of their clothing. Caribbean Music and Dance Programs (see above) offers seven-day group study programs to Carnival.

Literati and bookworms should time their visit to coincide with the **Havana Book Fair,** also held in February, organized by the Cuban Book Institute and the Cuban Book Chamber. For information, contact either the Center for Cuban Studies, 124 W. 23rd St., New York, NY 10011, tel. (212) 242-0559, fax (212) 242-1937, or Cámara Cubana del Libro, Feria Internacional del Libro Habana, Calle 15 #604, Vedado, Havana, Cuba, tel. (32) 9526, fax (33) 8212.

April: 4 April is the **Day of Children,** when various venues throughout the city host special entertainment for kids.

May: When 1 May rolls around, thousands of Habaneros head to the Plaza de la Revolución for the **May Day Parade.** The day is meant to honor workers and is intended to appear as a spontaneous demonstration of revolutionary loyalty, although in reality it is a carefully choreographed affair and scores of buses bring loyal workers and children from surrounding regions. Cuban stooges use the tannoys to work up the crowd with chants of "Viva Fidel!" The disaffected scoff and stay home. The military parade of yesteryear has been replaced of late; in recent years, the overriding theme has reflected the political flavor of the day (thus the 1999 parade was heavily imbued with denunciations of NATO's bombing campaign in Yugoslavia). You'll be surrounded by as many as 200,000 people waving colorful banners and placards and wearing T-shirts painted with revolutionary slogans. Everyone is eager for a glimpse of Castro, who applauds lightly in saintly fashion.

Each May, the city hosts the prestigious **Havana Biennale,** hosted by the Centro Wilfredo Lam, on San Ignacio, tel. (61) 2096 and (61) 3419, fax (33) 8477, e-mail: wlam@artsoft.cult.cu. The show features artists from more than 50 countries around the world and is hosted in almost two dozen venues throughout Habana Vieja. They hold practical workshops in printmaking and other disciplines, as well as soirées and other activities.

The **Havana Cup** is an annual boat race from Florida to Havana that goes back to 1930 (with a respite 1960-94). In 1999, some 250 yachts competed from Tampa to Havana's Marina Hemingway.

June: The **International Boleros Festival** (Festival Internacional Boleros de Oro), sponsored each June by UNEAC (the National Union of Writers and Artists of Cuba), features traditional Cuban folk music.

July: The **International Hemingway Colloquium** takes place in early July every two years.

August: Every second August (odd years) sees the **Festival Internacional de Música Popular Benny Moré,** named for the popular Cuban composer-singer referred to as *lo mas barbaro del ritmo* (the guy with the most terrific rhythm) and featuring a panorama of popular Cuban music. The festival takes place in Havana concurrently with events in Cienfuegos.

September: The biennial **International Theater Festival of Havana,** sponsored by the National Council of Scenic Arts, features international theater companies covering drama, street theater, musicals, and contemporary and traditional dance.

October: The annual **Havana Festival of Contemporary Music** traditionally spans a week in early October. Venues include the Teatro Nacional, Gran Teatro, La Casa de las Américas, and the Basilica de San Francisco de Asís, with a focus on choral and orchestral works by Cuban and international performers.

The **International Festival de Ballet** is an established part of Havana's annual events calendar. In 1998, the festival featured dancers and choreographers from more than 26 coun-

tries—including the Bolshoi, New York City Ballet, and Opera de Paris—who helped the Ballet Nacional de Cuba celebrate its 50th anniversary. Performances are held at the Gran Teatro, Teatro Nacional, and Teatro Mella. Contact the Ballet Nacional de Cuba, Calzada #510 e/ D y E, Vedado, Ciudad Habana, C.P. 10400, tel. (55) 2953, fax (33) 3117.

November: The annual **Festivities of San Cristóbal de la Habana** celebrates the anniversary of the founding of the city with a wide range of musical, theatrical, and other performances. Also in November, the **Festival of African Races,** which honors African folkloric traditions, takes place at venues throughout Guanabacoa.

December: At the **International Festival of New Latin-American Cinema** (also known as the Latin American Film Festival), a star-spangled guest list is no longer wined and dined at the Cuban state's expense, as in days of yore, and the all-night parties for which the festival had earned fame were replaced in 1994 by more sober soirées. But the festival, held in mid-December, is still one of Cuba's most glittering events. Castro is usually on hand, schmoozing with Hollywood actors and directors in the lobbies of the Hotel Nacional and Habana Libre. The menu of movies—shown at more than 20 cinemas and theaters across the city—includes films from throughout the Americas and Europe. For further information, contact the Instituto de Cinematográfía in Havana, tel. (55) 2841, fax (33) 4273, e-mail: festival@icaic.inf.cu, or the Center for Cuban Studies, 124 W. 23rd St., New York, NY 10011, tel. (212) 242-0559, fax (212) 242-1937, website: www.cubaupdate.com.

FOLK MUSIC AND DANCE

The capital city fairly vibrates to the pounding of the bongo drum and the strumming of guitars. Many hotels host touristy shows on specific days of the week, while virtually any bar worth its salt will feature at least one musician singing *"Guan-tan-a-mera!"* Each district also has its own **Casa de la Cultura,** where traditional music and dance can be heard.

Watch for performances by **Los Muñequitos de Matanzas**—literally, the dolls of Matanzas but signifying the "kings of rumba"—who tour nationwide from their base in Matanzas.

Habana Vieja

If you're visit coincides with the once-per-month (usually the third or fourth Saturday) **Noches en la Plaza de la Catedral,** be sure to attend.

One of the more active **casa de la culturas** is that in Habana Vieja at Aguilar #509 esq. Teniente Rey (also called Brasil), tel. (63) 4860, with entertainment nightly. It offers *peñas* on Tuesday, dancing on Wednesday, plus *boleros y poesia,* comedy, and even karaoke. Performances of Afro-Cuban rumba by Grupo Saranbanda are offered on Tuesday (free), and folk music is featured on Friday. The performances, which begin at 8 p.m., are given in the courtyard of the Iglesia San Agustín, where every Saturday at 3 p.m. the Compañia "JJ" Túrarte also performs rumba and popular music and dance. This is traditional Cuban entertainment at its best! You'll probably be the only tourists there to watch the mulatta dancers dressed in daffodil yellows, flamboyant reds, and morning-sky blues, whirling and shaking to the rhythms of a band dressed in magenta shirts and white shade hats. Entrance costs US$1.

Each Monday and Friday night, Dulce María, an intoxicatingly warmhearted singer and songwriter, hosts a soirée called **Encounter with Cuban Music,** at 78 Calle San Ignacio, tel. (61) 0412. Climbing a rickety staircase to the top of the dilapidated three-story building, you emerge on her apartment *azuela* (rooftop) overlooking the Plaza de la Catedral. Hands are extended. You are hugged warmly by Cubans you do not know. Dulce's band, Son de Cuba, gears up with a rumba. The rhythms of the marimbas, bongos, and a guitar called a *tres* pulse across the rooftops of Habana Vieja. Rum and beer are passed around, and soon you are clapping and laughing while Dulce belts out traditional Cuban compositions, her hips swaying to the narcotic beat. The ice is broken. The infectious beat lures you to dance. It is like the plague—you can only flee or succumb. Each song is introduced, with the history and meaning behind the song explained. You're invited to bring your own instrument. Says Dulce: "If we don't know it, we'll invent it." Entry costs US$5, including a drink.

The **Palacio de las Artesanias,** at the west end of Tacón, also offers a *noche Afrocubana* Fri.-Mon. 9:30 p.m. (US$3), plus what it calls *salsa espectáculos* (US$4).

Dozens of musicians and bands play on an impromptu basis around town. Look for **Las Mulatas del Caribe,** an all-female group of drummers and singers that play rumba and guaguanco at their base at Calle Obispo #213A.

The **Casa de 10 Octubre,** at Calzada de Luyanó and Calle Reforma in the Luyanó district, south of Habana Vieja, is active on weekends.

Centro

The **Casa de la Trova,** San Lazaro #661, Centro Habana, tel. (79) 3373, is especially active on weekends, as is the **Casa de la Cultura** on San Miguel, one block east of Avenida de Italia. It has a lively bamboo bar to the rear that draws a more mature Cuban crowd for live music.

The **Galeria Kahlo** of the Casa de Cultura at 720 Salvador Allende, tel. (78) 4727, hosts *peñas* and posts a list of forthcoming events on the outside wall. It's open Mon.-Sat. 11 a.m.-6 p.m. (except Friday).

Vedado

My favorite nightspot is **Café Concerto Gato Tuerto** (one-eyed cat), on O between 17 y 19, tel. (55) 2696 or (66) 2224, where they play *música filin* (feeling music). This former colonial home has been grandly restored with a thoroughly contemporary decor, bringing a new level of sophistication to Havana's nightclub scene. It has *trova* and *bolero* nightly, featuring Havana's leading performers, including Alden Naigt, a dramatic storyteller and poet. Occasionally, Carlos, one of the barmen, breaks out his trumpet and plays a superb rendition behind the bar while the barmaids demonstrate with choreographed and exquisite care the correct formula for making a drink called an "orgasm." Gato Tuerto is popular with a sophisticated, monied Cuban crowd; foreign males and their Cuban consorts fill the empty seats. There's no cover charge, but it has a *consumo minimo* policy: you're charged US$5 for your first drink, regardless. If you order a *mojito,* be sure to ask for a *mojito internacionál* made from two types of rum, including *añejo.* The music plays nightly until 4 a.m. The restaurant upstairs serves until 2 a.m., and the grilled fish and *criollo* meals are good.

CUBAN MUSIC

The development of Cuban music styles since 1800—from *contradanza, danzón, habanera,* mambo, and *son* to *nueva trova*—is the story, writes Erroll McDonald, "of a swinging dialectic between West African choral and percussive genius and European melodic and harmonic sophistication." Here's a historical rundown to help you appreciate the sounds and moves of Havana.

Folkloric Music and Dance

The earliest influence was Spanish. The colonists brought the melodies (such as the *bolero*), guitars, and violins from which evolved early *criollo* folk music. Most of Cuba's folk music, or *guajira* (such as the all-important *danzón,* the *punto,* and the *zapateo,* all popular in past centuries among white country people and accompanied by small accordions, kettledrums, gourds, and calabashes), is European music that has been influenced through contact with black culture.

The fusion gave rise to *punto campesinas* (peasant dances), still performed in country towns, including the slow and sensual *yambú* and the *columbia,* a solo men's dance performed blindfolded with machetes. The melancholic love song *Guantanamera* is undoubtedly the most famous of Cuban *guajiras,* recorded by everyone from Pete Seeger (who in May 1999 was awarded the Felix Varela Medal, Cuba's highest cultural honor) to Julio Iglesias (who is barred from Cuba, as are his recordings, for offending Castro's sensibilities with comments he made years ago).

From Europe, too, came the *trovas,* poetic songs concerned with great historical events and, above all, with love. *Trovas,* which were descended from the medieval ballad, were sung in Cuba throughout the colonial period. *Trovadores* performed for free, as they still do at Casas de la Trova. The Matamoros Trio is perhaps the best known in the genre. This century has seen the evolution of *trovas nuevas,* songs about contemporary life. The movement has ties to the American folk-protest song movement of the 1960s and often includes outspoken criticism of current situations. The contemporary works of Pablo Milané and Silvio Rodríguez, for example, echo the revolutionary dreams and restlessness of the current generation.

The African Influence

Almost from the beginning, the Spanish guitar (from the tiny *requinto* to the nine-stringed *tres*) joined the hourglass-shaped African *bata* and *bongo* drum, *claves* (two short hardwood sticks clapped together), and *chequerí* (seed-filled gourds) to give Cuban music its distinctive form. Slaves played at speakeasies in huts in the slaves' quarters. Their jam sessions gave birth to the *guaguancó,* a mix of flamenco guitar and African rhythm that is the mother of Cuban dance music. Later, slaves would take the *guaguancó* a few steps farther to create the sensuous rumba, a sinuous dance from the hips (the rumba has African roots, but the melody is very Spanish) and from which tumbled most other forms of Cuban music; and the *tumba francesa,* a dance of French-African fusion.

Rumba, which evolved around the turn of the century, remains deliriously popular. From it came *son,* originally a sugar-workers' dance adopted by urban musicians for their large percussion and horn sections. Such contemporary groups as Los Van Van have incorporated the *son,* which has its own variants, such as the fast, infectious, overtly sexual *son changüí* from Guantánamo province, typified by the music of Orquestra Revé.

The **mambo,** like the cha-cha, which evolved from it, is a derivative of the *danzón,* jazzed up with rhythmic innovations. Mambo is a passé but still revered dance, like the jitterbug in the US, danced usually only by older people. Created in Cuba by Orestes López in 1938, mambo stormed the United States in the 1950s, when Cuban performers were the hottest ticket in town. Though the craze died, mambo left its mark on everything from American jazz to the old Walt Disney cartoons where the salt and pepper shakers get up and dance. People were titillated by the aggressive sexual overtures required of women in the elegant but provocative dance. Captivated by the earthy break from the more modest swing, Americans created a simpler but equally risqué spin-off—"dirty dancing."

The mix of Cuban and North American sounds created blends such as *filin* ("feeling") music, as sung by Rita Montaner and Nat "King" Cole, who performed regularly in Havana; and *Cu-bop,* which fused bebop with Afro-Cuban rhythms, epitomized by Benny Moré—*el bárbaro de ritmo* (the Barbarian of Rhythms)—a theatrical showman who was considered the top artist of Cuban popular music. His more famous tunes include *Rebel Heart* and *Treat Me as I Am.*

Modern Sounds

The Revolution put a crimp in the music scene. Foreign performers stayed away, while many top performers left Cuba, such as Celía Cruz, "queen of salsa." **Salsa** (a derivative of *son*) has flourished since the 1980s, when the government began to lighten up. It is the heartbeat of most Cuban nightlife and a musical form so hot it can cook the pork. Los Van Van—one of Cuba's hottest big, brassy salsa-style bands—and Irakere have come up with innovative and explosive mixtures of jazz, classical, rock, and traditional Cuban music that have caused a commotion in the music and entertainment circles. They regularly tour Europe and Latin America, earning the country scarce hard currency.

For a long time, the playing of **jazz** in Cuba was completely discouraged (it was seen as "representative of Yankee imperialism, the music of the enemy"). Cuban musicians missed out on the Latin Jazz effervescence of the 1960s. Paquito D'Rivera, for example, was discouraged from playing jazz when he became director of the Orquestra Cubana de Música Moderna in 1970. Today, Cuba boasts wonderful jazz players of every stripe, and there is a growing stable of places where jazz can be heard.

Cuban jazz zigzags from bebop to fusion and European classical to Afro-Caribbean rhythms. It is "a bravura, macho form of jazz; trumpeters playing the highest notes and pianists going as fast as they can go." Cuban jazz musicians are admired the world over for their unique creativity and spirit. "When this is over and the musicians start coming out of Cuba, we'll all have to go back to school to catch up," says North American jazz maestro Tito Puente. Many leading international stars are Cuban. Celebrated trumpeter Arturo Sandoval left Irakere and Cuba in 1990, and D'Rivera left Cuba for New York in 1980. Like many artists, however, his departure had nothing to do with politics. "I fell in love with being a jazz musician in New York since first listening to a Benny Goodman record," he says. (Nonetheless, both groups' music was pulled from the shelves in Cuba. Those who leave Cuba take their *cubanidad* with them; they become nonpersons at home.)

Rock and roll was once officially banned. In recent years, the Young Communists have lassoed the popularity of modern music to corral disaffected youth (you'll see many long-haired youths—*roqueros*—wearing Led Zeppelin and Metallica T-shirts; heavy metal fans are known as *metálicos,* while "hippies" are called "freakies"). Hence, the state sponsors rock concerts, and state television and radio stations generously broadcast pirated videos of everyone from Nirvana to Sinéad O'Connor. However, the government keeps its own rock musicians (such as heavy-metal group Zeus) on short leashes. Playing unofficial venues can get *roqueros* arrested. To a large degree, the state decides what music can be played. Electricity rationing also sometimes pulls the plug on rehearsals and concerts, which are advertised through the grapevine.

Many Cubans are also avid fans of American rap artists, and they can gracefully execute the latest hip-hop steps. You'll find many reggae fans sporting dreadlocks (such as Carlos Alfonso Valdés, the leader of a popular Cuban funk band, Sintesis, with dreadlocks nearly down to his waist) and Bob Marley T-shirts (Cuban youth have scarce resources but possess a dead-on fashion sense gleaned from MTV).

Classical Music

"In the realm of classical music Cuba has been an inspirational locale rather than a breeding ground for great composers and instrumentalists," says noted pianist Daniel Fenmore. Nonetheless, it is astounding how many contemporary Cubans are accomplished classical musicians. Everywhere you go, you will come across violinists, pianists, and cellists serenading you for tips while you eat.

Cuba boasts several classical orchestras, notably the National Symphony Orchestra, under the baton of Manuel Duchesne Cuzán. It first performed in November 1960 and has a repertoire ranging from 17th-century works to the most contemporary creations, with a special emphasis on popularizing works by Latin American and Cuban composers, such as Amadeo Roldán and Alejandro García Caturla. It may not be on a par with the London Philharmonic or the San Francisco Symphony Orchestra, but a performance is stirring nonetheless. Watch, too, for performances by Frank Fernández, Cuba's finest classical pianist.

In a similar vein, try **Club Imágenes,** a stylish piano bar at the corner of Calzada y C, tel. (33) 3606. Open 3 p.m.-4 a.m.

Cabaret Pico Blanco, in the Hotel St. John, features traditional Cuban *trova* nightly, 10 p.m.-4 a.m. And the **Bar Hurón Azul,** of the Unión Nacional de Escritores y Artistes de Cuba (UNEAC, or National Union of Cuban Writers and Artists), at the corner of Calle 17 and I, tel. (32) 4551, fax (33) 3158, hosts *boleros* and *trovas* on Saturday night (US$3). A listing of upcoming events is posted on the gate. It's a great place to meet Cuban intellectuals.

Traditional Afro-Cuban dance is also the focus of **Sábado de Rumba,** held each Saturday afternoon, beginning about 2 p.m., in the inner courtyard of the **Conjunto Folclórico Nacional,** Calle 4, e/ Calzada y Linea, tel. (31) 3467. Entrance costs US$1. The National Folklore Dance Group performs nationwide and was founded in 1962 to revive Cuban folk traditions because it was thought that the populace had lost touch with its folkloric past. Every major city has a performance group supported by the national umbrella body.

Also check out the **Riviera Azúl,** in the Hotel Deauville on the Malecón and Galiano. The Afro-Cuban folkloric group Oni Ire performs Friday at 10 p.m., preceding the disco. Entrance costs US$5.

A friend has recommended **Joya's,** the eponymous home of the host at the corner of San Lazaro and Infanta. Joya puts on *peñas* with dancing on Friday, Saturday, and Sunday nights. Apparently she's a Josephine Baker type and has been described as "a bit of a character" and a "mix between Marilyn Monroe and Muhammad Ali."

Playa (Miramar and Beyond)

For a bit of melancholy, head to **Boleros,** in the Dos Gardenias complex on Avenida 7ma and Calle 26. Here, Isolina Carrillo hosts some of the best singers of the *bolero* nightly 10:30 p.m.-3 a.m. Carrillo was a cinema pianist at the age of 10, entered the conservatory at 13, and composed the famous song "Dos Gardenias" after which the complex is named.

CABARETS *(ESPECTÁCULOS)*

One of the first acts of the revolutionary government was to kick out the Mafia and close down the casinos and brothels. "It was as if the Amish had taken over Las Vegas," wrote Kenneth Tynan in a 1961 edition of *Holiday.* Not quite! The Cubans are Caribbean—and Latin. They seem to love showy spectacles and overt displays of flesh—the bread-and-butter of cabarets, which are a staple of Cuban entertainment.

Although the term "cabaret" sometimes refers to a disco, more frequently, it refers to *cabarets espectáculos,* Las Vegas-style song-and-dance routines highlighted by long-legged women (usually mulattas) with glistening copper-colored bodies, wearing high heels and skimpy costumes with lots of sequins, feathers, and frills, who gyrate into an erotic frenzy. Usually, they are accompanied by smaller dance troupes of bare-chested male performers. Singers, magicians, acrobats, and comedians are often featured. Cuban couples delight in these shows. Cubans shake their heads at the concept that these shows are sexist.

By far the most spectacular cabaret is that at the Tropicana. Most of the larger hotels have their own *espectáculos,* as do any number of major restaurants. The largest and showiest are reserved for tourists. Several tour agencies offer visits to a cabaret in association with the **cañonazo** ceremony (see above). You can also book excursions to the cabarets through hotel tour desks. You may need to reserve seats on weekends.

One of the best ways to enjoy the cabarets is to go with a group and to reserve a table. Have your hotel concierge call ahead. Otherwise a tip to the maître d' should do the trick. A bottle of Havana Club rum, cans of Coke, and ice bucket and glasses will be delivered to your table when you arrive.

Cabarets are usually followed by discos.

Habana Vieja

Most nights, the rooftop bar of the **Hotel Inglaterra** features live music, often with a small cabaret *espectáculo* (US$5). Weekend evenings are your best bet.

Habaneros without dollars to throw around get their cabaret kicks at **El Colmao,** on Calle Aramburu between San José and San Rafael in Centro Habana. The traditional floor show is highlighted by Spanish flamenco. Open 8 p.m.-2 a.m. Cubans pay in pesos, but you may be required to pay in dollars.

Vedado

The most lavish show in Vedado is the **Cabaret Parisién,** in the Hotel Nacional, tel. (33) 3564, second only to the Tropicana, which still overshadows it by a mile. Shows are offered Fri.-Wed. at 10 p.m., with a smaller show at 12:30 a.m. Entrance costs US$30. Although the show ostensibly starts at 9 p.m., you first have to sit through a tedious musical trio; the real show doesn't start until about 10:30 p.m. The wait is worthwhile—the two-hour show is excellent.

Club Turquino, in the Hotel Habana Libre, tel. (33) 4011, offers a medley of entertainment varying nightly, with a **cabaret espectáculo** Wednesday and Thursday (US$15), followed by a disco. Open 10:30 p.m.-4:30 a.m.

Slightly cheaper, but still exotic, is the **Cabaret Capri,** in the **Salon Rojo,** in Vedado's Hotel Capri at N y 21, tel. (33) 3747, fax (33) 3750, nightly except Monday at 10 p.m. (US$10).

There's no entry fee to the **Habana Café,** tel. (33) 3636, next to the Hotel Meliá Cohiba, at the foot of Paseo, which offers cabaret nightly and is one of the best all-around nightspots in town.

Many discos also have cabaret, such as **Club 1830,** which hosts its flurry of flesh and feathers outdoors at midnight. It's a small affair but draws many Cubans, and is particularly popular with models from La Maison and a coterie of *jiniteras,* who hang out at the gates hoping to score with male tourists. Entrance costs US$10.

A smaller, cheesier alternative is the **Cabaret Las Vegas,** Infanta, e/ Calles 25 y 27, tel. (70) 7939, with a show at 10 p.m. followed by a disco (US$5 per couple). The *espectáculo* is a feeble, short-lived affair with two dancers, and not worth the billing. And the set-up can take an excrutiatingly long time. *Mojitos* cost a whopping US$5! The gloomy bar has a pool table.

Cubans also have access to the **Disco Tango** at the Hotel Bruzón, where a small *espectáculo* is presented Thursday at 11 p.m. (foreigners pay US$5); and to **Club Sofia,** on La Rampa at Calle O, a modest place with a disco and an *espectáculo* Saturday and Sunday at midnight (US$2).

The Hotel Riviera has hosted cabarets in the past, but did not do so at press time.

Playa (Miramar and Beyond)

The shining star in Havana's cabaret constellation is the **Tropicana,** at Linea del Ferrocarril y 72, Marianao, tel. (27) 0110, fax (27) 0109. Cuba's premier Las Vegas-style nightclub, boasting more than 200 performers, has been described as "like looking at a Salvador Dali painting come to life" and is a *de rigueur* night out for every tourist wanting a jaw-dropping treat.

The **Hotel Comodoro,** on Avenida 1ra y Calle 84, tel. (33) 2703, features an *espectáculo* as part of its entertainment for guests. It's very good. **Discoteca Habana Club,** behind the Hotel Comodoro, tel. (24) 2902, also has a cabaret. You might try the **Club Ipanema,** adjacent to the Hotel Copacabana, tel. (24) 1037, with a "Noches Azules" *espectáculo.* And the **La Cecilia** restaurant complex, Avenida 5ta, e/ 1110 y 112, tel. (24) 1562, has a small *espectáculo* Thurs.-Sun. 9:30 p.m., with disco afterward.

Likewise, the *"Espectáculo Dos Gardenias"* in the **Salon Bolero** of the Dos Gardenias complex, Avenida 7ma at 26, has shows at 9 p.m. and 11 p.m. (US$10; US$5 extra for cameras, US$10 for videos). The program changes nightly. Call ahead. The **Salon La Tarde,** adjacent the Bolero in the same complex, offers nightly entertainment from 7:30 p.m. (US$5).

Cabaret Chévere, at Club Almendares on Avenida 49C in Reparto Kohly, tel. (24) 4990, has an open-air cabaret with a band and fashion parade (but no *espectáculo*) Fri.-Sun. 10 p.m.-6 a.m. (US$5). The bar is open 24 hours, and there's a pool hall (US$1 per game).

Young adult Cubans—particularly females seeking foreign sailors—flock to **Cabaret Marina,** at Marina Hemingway, tel. (24) 1150, ext. 120, which hosts shows Tues.-Sun. 10 p.m.-4 a.m. (a US$10 cover applies, plus there's a US$15 *consumo minimo* policy). It features a laser disco.

DISCOTHEQUES AND DANCING

There's no shortage of discos in dance-crazy Havana. The "best" are money-milking machines serving well-heeled foreigners but also popular with Cubans. Male foreigners can expect to be solicited outside the entrance to these dollars-only discos: Cuban women take a stranger's arm and beg to be escorted in *("por favor!"),* because entry (perhaps US$10) is beyond their means. Some places only admit couples; many discos

THE TROPICANA NIGHTCLUB

A visit to the Tropicana nightclub, Calle 72 e/ 41 y 45, Marianao, tel. (27) 0110, fax (27) 0109, is a *must*. The prerevolutionary extravaganza now in its sixth decade of Vegas paganism—girls! girls! girls!—has been in continuous operation since New Year's Eve 1939, when it opened (in the gardens of a mansion that once housed the US ambassador) as the most flamboyant nightclub in the world. The casino has gone, but otherwise neither the Revolution nor the recent economic crisis have ruffled the feathers of Cuba's most spectacular show.

The Tropicana quickly eclipsed all other clubs in the grandeur and imagination of its productions, which featured colored smoke and lighting, and special effects such as waterfalls, enhanced by various moods conjured up by the resident orchestra and dancers. The floor shows were meticulously researched (for one Asian-flavored floor show, two Japanese professors coached the dancers to create the perfect rhythmic sound with their feet, made by moving sugarcane stalks on the stage floor). In its heyday, during the 1950s, the Tropicana spent more than US$12,000 nightly on its flamboyant shows, which ranged widely from the "Asian Paradise," portraying the exotic Orient, to choreographed Haitian voodoo rituals. The casino also offered a daily US$10,000 bingo jackpot and a free raffle giveaway of a new automobile every Sunday. International celebrities such as Nat "King" Cole, Josephine Baker, and Carmen Miranda headlined the shows. Then as now, however, the key attraction was the sensual mulatta parade; talent scouts scoured Cuba for the most beautiful models and dancers. The more than 200 performers are still hand-picked from the crème-de-la-crème of Cuba's dancers and singers. And famous international entertainers still occasionally perform.

The "paradise under the stars," which takes place in the open air, begins with the "Dance of the Chandeliers," when a troupe of near-naked showgirls parades down the aisles wearing glowing chandeliers atop their heads. The rest of the show consists of creative song and dance routines, and a never-ending parade of stupendous mulattas sashaying and shaking in sequined bikinis, ruffled frills, sensational headdresses, and feathers more ostentatious than peacocks'.

The show, enhanced by a fabulous orchestra, takes place in the Salón Bajo Las Estrellas Tues.-Sun. at 9 p.m. Patrons supposedly get their money back if it rains (if the rains are intermittent, the show merely takes a break, then resumes).

The Tropicana is a favorite venue for Cuban families and couples, who pay 70 pesos entrance or from 232 pesos for a full package, including a meal and a bottle of rum. Only a limited number of seats are reserved for Cubans—to the rear—and then usually only for workers who have outperformed their co-workers.

There are two zones: US$50 for the outer fringe (including a Cuba libre), US$60 for closer to the stage (including one drink). You're charged US$5 for cameras, US$15 for videos. Cocktails cost US$3. The ticket booth, tel. (27) 0110, is open 10 a.m.-6 p.m. You can order tickets here by telephone, or purchase tickets directly at the entrance from 8:30 p.m. (call ahead to check availability), but

heat and light at the Tropicana

it's always best to book in advance through your hotel tour desk or Havanatur because the show is often sold out.

The Tropicana features two eateries: the elegant sky-lit **Los Jardines** (named for its surfeit of tropical plants, harboring mosquitoes), serving tasty continental fare and beef tenderloin with lobster as the house specialty (US$14.50; open 6 p.m.-1 a.m.); and the 1950s-diner-style **Rodney Café,** serving salads, soups, burgers, and tortillas to a mostly Cuban crowd (open noon-2 a.m.). The Tropicana also has a discotheque—Arcos de Cristal—open midnight-5 a.m. It was closed for renovation at press time.

---

have a strange policy of not letting single women in (the opposite of some Western discos).

Most of the hotel discos are open 10 p.m.-5 a.m. There's little point in arriving before midnight; few discos get in the groove before the clock strikes 12, and many go on until dawn. Most discos usually play a mix of Latin, techno, and world-beat music.

Drink prices in the touristy discos can give you sticker shock. The best bet is usually to buy a bottle of rum—but expect to fork out at least US$20 for a bottle—and Coca-Cola.

Don't worry about getting back to your hotel in the wee hours. There are always taxis hovering outside the entrances of the best discos, and freelancers are on hand to run you home for a negotiable fare.

Habana Vieja

Marlin S.A., Calle 184 #123, Flores, Havana, tel. (33) 6675, operates a floating disco with karaoke aboard the *XIV Festival,* which departs the wharf on San Pedro at the foot of Luz, Tues.-Sun. 8:30 p.m., 10:30 p.m., and 12:30 a.m. (US$5).

Centro

You can kick up the dust with impecunious Cubans at the gloomy and basic **Club Nocturno El Volcán,** which jams on weekends. Entry costs seven pesos.

The **Casa Abuelo Lung Kong,** at Manrique y Dragones in Barrio Chino, has a disco upstairs on the outside patio on weekends.

Cuban youth without dollars head to **Cabaret Las Olas** on the Malecón, 100 meters east of La Rampa, tel. (70) 3735, with an outdoor disco Fri.-Sun. 9 p.m.-1 a.m. (10 pesos). It's operated by UjoteCa (the Union of Communist Youth).

La Pampa, opposite the Torreon de San Lázaro at the Malecón and Vapor, features dancing nightly except Monday; US$1, including cabaret. It's on the edge of the rough Cayo Hueso district and has a decidely earthy appeal. Leave your jewelry at home. Another earthy local favorite is **Palermo,** at San Miguel y Amistad (nightly except Wednesday).

Vedado

The **Salón Internacional** (formerly the Palacio de Salsa), in the Hotel Havana Riviera, tel. (33) 4051, specializes in the Latin beat and often features the top names in live Cuban music. I haven't checked it out, but as the Palacio de Salsa, it was *the* place for serious salsa fans. Open daily 10 p.m.-3 a.m. Also try the **Pico Blanco,** on the top floor of the Hotel St. John's on Calle 0 (US$5). It has salsa on Monday and rumba on weekend afternoons.

Tiny **Las Bulerias,** on Calle L opposite the Hotel Habana Libre, is a smoky, moody place that plays a lot of reggae. It's popular mostly with black Cubanas (there are few Cuban males). It doesn't get going until about 11 p.m. Entrance costs US$3; beers are US$1.

UjoteCa runs the **Pabellon,** on La Rampa at Calle N. The Pabellon features a gamut of activities Wed.-Sun.: typically salsa on Wednesday, disco and rap Thurs.-Sat. (US$5), and disco with rock music on Sunday (US$7).

Cubans also kick up the dust at the **Café Cantante Mi Habana,** in the Teatro Nacional at Paseo, one block west of the Plaza de la Revolución, tel. (33) 5713 or (79) 6011. Entry costs US$3. **Club Scherazada,** a small, dingy, and smoky basement bar on the southwest side of the FOCSA building at the junction of 19 y M, offers a medley of musical offerings each night from 6 p.m., with *trovas* and *boleros,* plus more lively sounds. It has a US$2.50 per-person cover (the sign outside says "US$5 por pareja," but the doorman sometimes tries to con solo guests who don't know that this means "per pair"). It

SEX AND TOURISM

" 'What effect is dollarization having on families and society?' asked one of [the journalists]. Said Maruetti [a Cuban economist], looking bureaucratically oblivious, 'Number One: foreign investment. Two: intensive development of tourism. Three: opening to foreign trade.' Sis had been out hitchhiking and someone made a foreign investment in her. It's all part of Cuba's intensive development of tourism. And, boy, is she open to foreign trade."

—P.J. O'ROURKE

Before the Revolution, Batista's Babylon offered a tropical buffet of sin. During the 1950s, it is said there were more than 10,000 prostitutes in Havana, a city of 1.2 million people. In 1959, the revolutionary government closed down the sex shows and porn palaces, and sent the prostitutes to rehabilitative trade schools, thereby ostensibly eliminating the world's oldest trade. (Prostitution reappeared, however, within a few years of the Triunfo. Fred Ward recorded in 1977 how "a few girls have been appearing once again in the evenings, looking for dates, and willing to trade their favors for goods rather than money." He thought it "more a comment on rationing than on morals.")

Today, tourism-generated prostitution is proliferating again beneath a general complacency. At night, on dimly lit streets, perfumed Cubanas in high heels and tight Spandex call out to unaccompanied males.

But the situation is not a simple one and needs some explaining.

A Chance to Get Ahead—and Get Away

Today, prostitution in Cuba is mostly an amateur affair. The *jiniteras* (the word comes from *jineta,* which means horsewoman or jockey) who form intimate relationships with tourists are a far cry from the uneducated prostitutes of Batista days. Studies by the Federation of Cuban Women (FMC) have shown that "Most [*jiniteras*] have the benefit of extensive economic and educational opportunity compared to the lot of their sisters before the Revolution. Most are not ashamed [and] few have low self-esteem. . . . . *Jiniteras,* with very few exceptions, don't need to practice commercial sexual relations to survive. Instead, what motivates these women . . . is the desire to go out, to enjoy themselves, go places where Cubans are not allowed to go."

Young mulattas, including educated, morally upright girls who would laugh to be called *jiniteras,* hang out by the hotel doorways or parade the tourist beaches, seeking affairs—*lucha un yuma*—and invitations to be a part of the high life. A pretty Cubana attached to a generous suitor can be wined and dined and get her entrance paid into the discos, drinks included. Many women hook up with a man for the duration of his visit in the hope that a future relationship may develop. Many succeed in snagging foreign husbands. Their dream is to live abroad—to find a foreign boyfriend who will marry them and take them away.

In 1995, the Congress of the Federation of Cuban Women concluded, too, that the rise in *jiniterismo* has an equal amount to do with Cuban youth's permissive attitudes toward sex. It recognized *jiniterismo* as an expression of a moral crisis and stressed the need to emphasize the role of the family, to help dissuade young women who have discovered the power of their sexuality from living it out to the full.

In a society where promiscuity is rampant and sex on a first date is a given, any financial transaction—assuredly, more in one night in *fula* (dollars) than she can otherwise earn in a month's salary in worthless pesos—is reduced to a charitable afterthought to a romantic evening out.

The Government's Response

The Cuban government has been slow to admit that prostitution is prevalent (some critics even claim that the government sponsored Cuba's image as a cheap-sex paradise to kick-start tourism). "The state tries to prevent it as much as possible. It is not legal in our country to practice prostitution, nor are we going to legalize it. Nor are we thinking in terms of turning it into a freelance occupation to solve unemployment problems. [Laughter.] We are not going to repress it either," Castro told *Time* magazine. Nonetheless, in 1996 Cuban women were barred from guest rooms in tourist hotels under all circumstances. In January 1999, the government initiated a crackdown. That month alone, about 7,000 women were picked up on the streets of Havana.

But the situation has always been fluid. The Cuban government, claims Guillermo Cabrera Infante, has always made stupendous state *mulattas* available to foreign dignitaries. No one blinks an eye, says Humberto Werneck, at "the French temptations that are whispered at the exit of the legendary [Tropicana] cabaret," whose showgirl-hookers (a minority of the dancers, to be sure) charge a "guild" rate of US$100 and brazenly have the doorman hail the cab for her and her partner.

Fortunately, Cuba has not yet come full circle. True, professional prostitution (and pimping) is on the rise, and the first worrisome signs of child prostitution have appeared, with girls as young as 13 hanging around outside the Hotel Habana Libre Tryp. But the Cuban situation is not like Asia, where a whole generation is being exploited for commerce by governments hungry for tourist dollars. There are no brothels, and none of the porn palace fiefdoms of Batista days, nor the rural misery of the old republic that drove families to sell their young daughters into vice to service poor men in backwater towns for 40 cents a day. Nor is it New York, where, in the words of Lynn Darling, "underclass addicts ply their trade under the watchful eye of the men who manage them."

Sex and Underage

Sex is legal at the age of 16 in Cuba, but under Cuban and international law, foreigners can be prosecuted for sex with anyone under 18.

The **Center for Responsible Tourism,** 1765-D Le Roy Ave., Berkeley, CA 94709, e-mail: crtourism@aol.com, publishes a leaflet, *What You Should Know About Sex Tourism Before You Go Abroad,* dealing with sex with minors.

If you know of anyone who is traveling to Cuba with the intention of sexually abusing minors, contact the US Customs Service, International Child Pornography Investigation and Coordination Center, 45365 Vintage Park Rd., Suite 250, Sterling, VA 20166, tel. (703) 709-9700, e-mail: icpicc@customs. sprint.co.

---

has a *peña yoruba* with rumba and other Afro sounds Saturday 3-8:30 p.m. A disco cranks up at 10:30 p.m. Farther west, the **Turf Club** on Calzada (Avenida 7) and F is a popular nightclub among the locals.

Cuban rock fans head to **Patio de María,** on Calle 37 and Paseo, near the Teatro Nacional, where the disco combines Latin sounds with rock Friday and Saturday nights. Rock concerts are hosted Sunday evenings.

For dancing outdoors, make sure to check out **Club 1830,** on an oceanside terrace behind the Restaurante 1830 (walkways lead through a grotto that includes a Chinese-style pagoda and a mosque-like structure with a Japanese garden). The nightly disco is very popular on weekends and includes a fashion show and undistinguished cabaret *espectáculo.* Entrance costs US$10. It's open 10 p.m.-4 a.m., but doesn't start jumping until well past midnight. It's a popular pickup spot for *jiniteras.* Adjacent, the **Torreon La Chorrera** also has a disco popular with Cuban youth.

Other spots to consider include **Salón Caribe,** in the Hotel Habana Libre, tel. (33) 4011, open Wed.-Mon. 9 p.m.-4 a.m.; and **Centro Vasco,** at the corner of Avenida 3ra and 4, tel. (3) 9354, near the Hotels Meliá Cohiba and Riviera, with an upstairs disco and video bar popular with Cubans.

Playa (Miramar and Beyond)

If you have money to blow, the classiest disco by far is **Discoteca Habana Club,** behind the Hotel Comodoro on Avenida 1ra and Calle 84 at the west end of Miramar, tel. (33) 2703. Ostensibly, it's open 10 p.m.-5 a.m., but it stays open later. Entrance costs US$10. Drinks are outrageously priced (Cokes and beers cost US$5; fruit juices cost US$7; a *cuba libre* will set you back US$10). It attracts a chic in-crowd—mostly a blend of Cubans, Mexicans, and other Latins—who bop to yester-decade's Abba tunes and pop hits (with a hint of salsa) played at top volume between cabaret floor shows.

The **Club Ipanema,** at the Hotel Copacabana, tel. (29) 0601, plays mostly techno music (or it did in spring 1999). The clientele is mostly Cuban, and the atmosphere subdued. There's no entry charge, but a *consumo minimo* of US$6 applies. It's open 10 p.m.-4 a.m.

Farther out, **Salón Rosado Benny Moré,** on

Luís Duvalon e/ Avenida 41 y 42, tel. (29) 0985, is an open-air concert arena popular for dancing on weekends, when top-billed Cuban singers perform. **La Cecilia,** on Avenida 5ta y 110, Miramar, tel. (33) 1562, also hosts salsa and other music and dance after the restaurant closes (Thurs.-Sun. 9:30 p.m.-2 a.m.). **Papa's** and the **Cabaret Marina,** way out west at Marina Hemingway, on Avenida 5ta at Calle 248, tel. (33) 1150, are discos popular with young Habaneras seeking foreign seafarers.

Its open-air stage was still being built at press time, but the **Complejo Turística La Giradilla,** Calle 272 e/ 37 y 51 in the La Coronela district of La Lisa, tel. (33) 6062, should become one of the most popular disco venues in town for Cubans with *fula* (dollars).

Cubans without dollars find their fun at such spots as **Juventud 2000 Discoclub,** in the Karl Marx Theater Complex at Avenida 1ra y 10, tel. (30) 0720 (open Fri.-Sun. 9 p.m.-2 a.m.), or the open-air amphitheater on the Malecón, 200 meters west of the Hotel Meliá Cohiba. This popular spot gets thronged with a mostly black crowd. There is usually a heavy police presence due to the frequent fights.

TANGO AND FLAMENCO

Into tango? The **Caserón de Tango** at Calle Justíz #21, one block south of Plaza de Armas in Habana Vieja, highlights the Argentinian music and dance form.

THE GAY SCENE

Cuban gays must find irony that the heart of the homosexual world is Castro Street in San Francisco. It is assuredly not named in El Jefe's honor, as gays—called "queens," *maricónes,* or *locas* in the Cuban vernacular—were persecuted following the Revolution. Castro (who denies the comment) supposedly told journalist Lee Lockwood that a homosexual could never "embody the conditions and requirements of . . . a true revolutionary."

However, by the mid-1980s, Cuba began to respond to the gay-rights movement that had already gained momentum worldwide. Officially, the new position was that homosexuality and bisexuality are no less natural or healthy than heterosexuality. The reckoning with the past was underscored in 1994 by the release of Tomas Gutierrez Alea's Oscar-nominated film, *Fresa y Chocolate.* The movie is understood as a universal plea for tolerance. It could not have been produced without official approval, and therefore exemplifies an acknowledgment of how the prejudice against homosexuals harmed Cuba's cultural life. Nonetheless, prejudice still exists throughout society, and there is still a restriction on gays joining the party. The Cuban gay community does not have representative organizations, although the first gay men's group on the island, Cubans in the Struggle Against AIDS, was recently formed.

Gay Cuba, by Sonja de Vries, is a documentary film that looks candidly at the treatment of gays and lesbians in Cuba since the Revolution. You can order copies from Frameline, 346 Ninth St., San Francisco, CA 94103, tel. (415) 703-8654, fax (415) 861-1404, e-mail: frameline@aol.com, website: www.frameline.org. Also check out *Machos, Maricónes, and Gays: Cuba and Homosexuality,* by Ian Lumsden (Philadelphia, PA: Temple University, 1996) for a study of the relationship between male homosexuality and Cuban society.

Gay Gathering Spots

Gay life in Havana has expanded noticeably in recent years, and male homosexuals act with more demonstrable confidence (lesbianism has not become quite so accepted). There are cruising sections, such as on the Malecón opposite the Fiat Café two blocks east of La Rampa, where the party spreads along the seafront boulevard in the wee hours. The corner of La Rampa and L, outside the Cine Yara, is a lesser cruising spot. The Café Monseigneur, on Calle O between La Rampa and 21, is a gay hangout. Parque de la Fraternidad has a late-night cruising scene. There are also private gay parties, known as *fiestas de diez pesos,* which charge a 10 peso cover.

A good place to find out that night's happening spot is to ask the gay crowd that congregates at night outside the Cine Yara.

For gay beaches, head to the Boca Ciega section of Playas del Este, east of town. In town, try Playita de 16, the rocky *balneario* at Calle 16 in Miramar; and Playa Tritón, in front of the Hotel Neptuno/Tritón.

Also in Habana Vieja, **La Zaragoza,** on Monserrate at Obrapía, offers tango, bolero, and flamenco Thursday and Saturday night at 9:30 .m.

Fans of tango might also check out the **Casa el Tango,** a tiny shop at Neptuno #303, where cratchy old recordings and tapes are played. Dance is not hosted here.

JAZZ VENUES

Despite the fame and popularity of Cuba's jazz musicians, Havana is a far cry from Chicago. Following the Revolution, jazz was discouraged as a bourgeois form of music. But things are changing, and the city is picking up more and more dedicated jazz joints.

Watch for a terrific jazz fusion group called Cuarto Espacio, a jazz singer named Xiamara, and pianists Chucho Valdés and Gonzalo Rubalava.

Habana Vieja

A jazz trio performs in the **Café del Oriente,** at the corner of Oficios and Amargura on the west side of Plaza de San Francisco, tel. (66) 6686, where you can enjoy cocktails at the ritzy marketop bar.

Centro

Cine América, on Galiano at Neptuno, tel. (62) 4416, is a rather rundown place that hosts jazz and ballet.

Vedado

The **Jazz Café** on the third floor of the Galeria del Paseo, facing the Hotel Meliá Cohiba at the base of Paseo, is a classy joint with plate-glass windows, contemporary decor, and some of the best jazz in town, including from resident maestro Chucho Valdés. The US$5 cover includes a cocktail.

The basement **La Zora y el Cuevo,** at the bottom of La Rampa, between N y O, offers jazz of modest standard in English-pub style surrounds (the entrance is a giant English phone booth). Occasional foreign bands perform here. Open 10 p.m.-4 a.m. (US$5).

Jazz and salsa are staples at the **Jazz Cafería,** in the Casa de Cultura, Calle 7 y Avenida 4/6, Vedado. The Casa de Cultura is one of the venues for the annual **International Havana Jazz Festival.**

Cuba's particularly vivacious version of jazz can also be heard at the **Salón Internacional** (formerly the Palacio de Salsa) in the Hotel Riviera, and **Café Turquino Salsa Cabaret,** in the Habana Libre Hotel. The lobby bar of the Hotel Copacabana also has a jazz trio that performs nightly.

Playa (Miramar and Beyond)

A jazz group performs at the **Tocororo** restaurant at Calle 18 y Avenida 3ra, tel. (33) 4530.

BARS

Havana has scores of bars, but you can count the classic bars on your fingers. Though every hotel has a bar, few are outstanding.

Habana Vieja

The lobby bar in the **Hotel Ambos Mundos** is one of the liveliest and most pleasant in town. A pianist entertains, and you can watch the flood of pedestrians down Calle Obispo through the lofty French windows.

No visit to Havana is complete without sipping a *mojito* at **La Bodeguita del Medio,** Calle Empredado #207, tel. (62) 4498, as Ernest Hemingway did almost daily. You won't want to make La Bodeguita a regular haunt, however, as the *mojitos* are abysmally weak, the mint usually wilted, and the glass far too small for the US$4 tab. Hemingway would throw a fit if he tasted the consistently insipid concoctions served to tourists today by consistently surly bar staff. No cigars are sold here—bring your own.

Another Hemingway favorite—and one offering far better (and cheaper; US$2) *mojitos*—is the **Dos Hermanos,** a wharf-front saloon where Hemingway bent elbows with sailors and prostitutes at the long wooden bar, open to the street through wooden *rejas.* The down-to-earth bar, at San Pedro and Sol, is perfect for unpretentious tippling with locals, although it draws the occasional tour group! It offers the advantage of being open 24 hours. The *mojitos* (US$2.50) are good, served by friendly staff, and there's often live music, plus bar snacks.

MOJITO: THE BODEGUITA'S CLASSIC DRINK

Here's the official version of how to make a killer *mojito:*

With a stirrer, mix half a tablespoon of sugar and the juice of half a lime in a highball glass. Add a sprig of *yerba buena* (mint), crushing the stalk to release the juice; two ice cubes; and 1.5 oz. of Havana Club Light Dry Cuban rum. Fill with soda water. ¡Salud!

Hemingway enjoyed his daily daiquiri at **El Floridita,** at Calle Obispo esq. Monserrate, tel. (63) 1060, a fabulous place to sit at the bar smoking a premium *habano,* listening to the jazz quartet, and pretending you're Papa himself. The frosty daiquiri for which the bar is famous is a perfect pick-me-up after a hot stroll through town, but be sure to ask for the "Daiquiri Nature, "a hand-shaken version (the regular daiquiris are today made in an electric blender). It may not quite live up to its 1950s aura, when *Esquire* magazine named it one of the great bars of the world, but to visit Havana without sipping a daiquiri here would be like visiting France without tasting the wine.

The moodily atmospheric wood-paneled **Bar Monserrate,** just south of El Floridita at Avenida de Bélgica (Monserrate) and Obrapía, has long been popular with Cubans and is noted for its *Coctel Monserrate* (one teaspoon of sugar, two ounces of grapefruit juice, five drops of grenadine, two ounces of white rum, ice, and a sprig of mint).

The **Galeria La Acera del Louvre,** the patio bar of the Hotel Inglaterra, was once the informal meeting point for budget and independent travelers, but has lost its edge since the hotel's room rates have skyrocketed. It remains a good spot to sip a beer or *cuba libre* and watch the comings and goings around Parque Central. A Mexican *mariachi* band performs Sunday at 8:30 p.m.

La Lluvia de Oro and the always buzzing **Café Paris,** both on Obispo (at Calle Habana and San Ignacio, respectively), are lively, down-to-earth bars popular with a mix of Cubans and wayward foreigners, who frequent these bars to sample the live music and pick up wayward Cubans. If you follow Obispo west to Villegas,

you can even purchase takeout daiquiris for one and-a-half pesos, served in cardboard cups from a small shop, **El Huevino,** on the corner.

Another favorite of locals is the **Bar Lafayette** on Aguiar between O'Reilly and Empedrado. Its house cocktail is rum and tomato juice.

By the time you read this, **Taberna Benny Moré** should be open on the northeast side of Plaza Vieja. It promises to be an upscale bohemian affair, its walls festooned with the personal effects of Cuban's renowned singer-composer, for whom the bar is named.

Across the harbor channel, the atmospheric **Bar La Tasca,** on the harborfront facing Havana between the Morro and La Cabaña fortresses, is well worth a visit. It's an intimate oak-beamed place, full of Spanish weaponry, with a friendly barman and a terrace where you can sip your *mojito* while enjoying the views. Nearby, and in a similar vein, are the **Mesón de los Doce Apóstoles** and **El Polvorín,** at the foot of the Morro castle. El Polvorín is wonderful, offering patio dining with a view past the cannons and across the harbor mouth toward Havana. Inside is as cool as a well, with an early colonial ambience to boot.

For a truly down-to-earth experience, check out **Bar Actualidades** on Monserrate, behind the Hotel Plaza. This compact and dingy little bar is favored by Cubans and offers an insight into the nocturnal pleasures of impecunious Cubans. Its red light and raffish Afro-Cuban quality might have appealed to Sammy Davis Jr. and the Rat Pack.

The **Club Los Marinos,** overhanging the harbor on Avenida Carlos M. Céspedes one block east of Plaza de Armas, tel. (57) 1402, is popular with a younger Cuban crowd that flocks for karaoke. It offers music on the jukebox and has a large-screen TV. Open nightly 7 p.m.-2 a.m. Entry costs US$1 (US$2 for karaoke). Karaoke also the forté of the **Disco Karaoke** in the Hotel Plaza, packing the Cubans in thick as sardines nightly 10:30 p.m.-5 a.m. (US$4).

Centro

This area has few bars of note. To commune with locals, try **Bar Nautilus,** a moody and gloomy place, yet quite lively, with fish tanks in the wall. It's on Calle San Rafael, one block west of Parque Central.

edado

spring 1999, the in-vogue spot was the **Ha-
ana Café,** next to the Hotel Meliá Cohiba, at the
ot of Paseo, tel. (33) 3636. Havana's home-
oun version of the Hard Rock Café is a must-
sit at least once, rekindling the zesty (but tamer)
pirit of the 1950s, and luring everyone from
ur groups to cigar-chomping bigwigs with slen-
er Cubanas on their arms. Cuban couples with
ollars attend, as well as ambitious Cubans
cavenging for tourists of the opposite gender.
eating is theater style around the stage. The
950s decor includes walls festooned with mu-
ical instruments and photos of famous per-
ormers from the era. A classic Harley-David-
on, an old Pontiac, and a 1957 open-top ca-
ary-yellow Chevy add a dramatic effect, as do
eriod gas pumps and a small aeroplane with
Cubana motif suspended from the ceiling.

This is a classic nightclub, with nonstop en-
ertainment 8 p.m.-3 a.m., including a small Trop-
cana-style cabaret, drummers, a splendid jug-
ling act, and a Benny Goodman-style band. A
roup plays traditional music noon-4 p.m., and a
ianist playing *bolero* music keeps patrons
mused 4-8 p.m. Dress up if you wish. The code
s casual, but a suit is not out of place. *Mojitos*
ost US$5.50. Try an "afrodisíaco" made of egg
olk, honey, milk, and vanilla (US$4.50). A con-
umo mínimo applies: US$5 at the bar, US$10 at
table—but be careful to ensure that you don't
et ripped off as I did. This "minimum consump-
on" charge (plus 10% service charge) applies to
he first drink, for which you'll be charged
JS$5.50 even if it's a glass of soda water, so it
ays to order a more expensive drink or food
em first—but make sure that the bar staff bills
ccordingly and doesn't scam you by charging
he cheapest drink first (followed up in my case
y heavy-handed Mafia-style treatment from the
ouncers and manager).

The ground-floor **El Relicario Bar** of the Hotel
Meliá Cohiba is popular with a monied, cigar-
oving crowd and offers an elegant Edwardian
mbience and relative serenity. In an entirely
lifferent vein is the cramped and raffish **La Roca,**
n Calle 21 esq. M, tel. (33) 4501, the kind of
lark yet appealing dive where the Rat Pack
night have hung out in the 1950s.

The **Bar Vista del Golfo** in the Hotel Nacional
as music on an old jukebox, and walls festooned with famous figures such as Errol Flynn,
Johnny Weismuller, and assorted mobsters.

The sparkling new **Bar Elegante** in the Hotel
Riviera, adjacent to the Meliá Cohiba, now features the Disco Karaoke, nightly 8 p.m.-4 a.m.

More radical youth elements congregate at
the **Casa de los Infusiones,** at Calles 23 y G,
Vedado, where *aguardente* (neat rum) shots
cost US50 cents each.

Several bars offer superb views of the city:
try the rooftop bar at the Hotel Nacional, as well
as those at the Hotel Inglaterra and Hotel Riviera,
and La Torre, atop the FOCSA Building at Calles
17 y M (entrance US$1). The best, perhaps, is
the **Turquino,** on the 25th floor of the Hotel Habana Libre, with its fabulous views. The US$2
admission includes one drink.

Playa (Miramar and Beyond)

The hotels here all have bars, although none
stand out. The **Dos Gardenias** complex, on
Avenida 7ma at 26, features a piano bar.

Try the tasteful bar of the elegant sky-lit **Los
Jardines** in the Tropicana nightclub, Calle 72
e/ 41 y 45, Marianao, tel. (27) 0110, fax (27)
0109. It gets few patrons, despite the popularity
of the cabaret. The fish tanks behind the black
marble-topped bar can keep you amused.

CINEMA

Cubans are passionate moviegoers, and Havana is blessed with cinemas—by one account
more than 170—showing current Hollywood
movies (normally within one year of release)
plus Cuban films. Hollywood culture saturated
the Havana of the 1930s, and the bloom of movie
houses coincided with the heyday of art deco
and moderne styles. Overnight, Havana was
blessed with a crop of streamlined, futuristic facades suggestive of fantasy. Most striking, perhaps, is the 1941 Cine América, on Calle de
Italia, tel. (62) 5416, in streamlined moderne design, with curvilinear box seats melting into the
walls of the vaulted auditorium.

Entrance usually costs two pesos (foreigners
are rarely charged in dollars), and the menu is
surprisingly varied, albeit a bit campy. Leading
Hollywood productions (classic and contemporary) and cartoons are shown, as are Westerns,

CUBA'S MOVIE GREAT

Undoubtedly the most respected of Cuba's film-makers is Tomás Gutiérrez Alea, one of the great masters of Cuban cinema, whose work is part of a general questioning of things—part of the New Latin American Cinema. The Film Institute has granted a relative laxity to directors such as Gutiérrez, whose populist works are of an irreverent picaresque genre. For example, his Memorías del Subdesarrollo (Memories of Underdevelopment), made in 1968, traced the life of the bourgeoisie disrupted by the Revolution. He followed it with Death of a Bureaucrat, a satire on the stifling bureaucracy imposed after the Revolution; and La Última Cena (The Last Supper), which dealt with a member of the upper class confronting the emerging social phenomenon that was about to topple them.

Gutiérrez, born in 1928, started filming in 1947 and made his first serious work in 1955, filming a documentary on the plight of charcoal workers, earning him black marks with the Batista regime. He contributed to the Revolution at an early stage at the fore of the cinematic section of the Revolutionary army and, following Castro's triumph, the first postvictory documentary, Esta Tierra Nuestra (This Land of Ours).

His later films are criticisms of the Revolution, in the sense that they are "part of the public dialog as to how the Revolution should proceed." Gutiérrez's work was frequently misinterpreted outside Cuba, and the critical, parodying nature of his films led to the producer being regarded incorrectly as an arch anti-Castroite, much to his own dismay. The extra-ordinary subtleties of films such as the masterly Memories of Underdevelopment, a study of a bourgeois intellectual adrift in the new Cuba, proved too sophisticated for Cold War mentalities to the north and had been seized upon by US propagandists in ways that were never intended.

Gutiérrez's finest film, a true classic of modern cinema, is Fresa y Chocolate (Strawberries and Chocolate), which when released in 1994 caused near-riots at cinemas in Havana because the crush for entry was so great. The poignant and provocative movie, set in Havana during the repressive heyday of 1979, explores the nettlesome friendship between a flagrant homosexual and a macho Party member, reflecting the producer's abiding questioning of the Revolution to which he was nonetheless always loyal. It portrays the marginalization of intellectuals, the implementation of prejudices, the idealization of "norms" of behavior, the struggles to be different in a rigid revolutionary context. It is less an indictment than a social analysis of the purge against homosexuals that climaxed in the 1970s, profoundly affecting Cuba's cultural movement.

Fresa y Chocolate and the subsequent movie, Guantanamera, the producer's last, starred his wife, Mirta Ibarra, in a leading role.

Gutiérrez died of lung cancer on 16 April 1996. His passing still weighs heavily upon Habaneros, to whom he was an intellectual hero. Gutiérrez's faith in the Revolution never faltered. Like Castro, he clung to the thread of his dream as the health of his country deteriorated alongside that of his own.

kung fu flicks, and other foreign productions, particularly those of socially redeeming quality. Movies are often subtitled in Spanish (others are dubbed, to enjoy which you'll need to be fluent in Spanish). Age restriction is 16 years. Children and youths can attend screenings at the **Cinemateca Infantil y Juvenil,** at Cinema 23 y 12, every Saturday at 2:30 p.m. Adult films are banned, as are certain politically "offensive" movies (one movie you will not see in Havana, for instance, is The Wonderful Country, starring Robert Mitchum; it was banned because the villains were called the Castro brothers).

In 1959, Cuba established a high-quality cinema institute to produce feature films, documen-taries, and newsreels with heavy revolutionary content. All movies in Cuba—their making, importation/exportation, and distribution—are under the control of the **Instituto de Cinematográfi** (Film Institute), Calle 23 #1109, Vedado, Havana, tel. (33) 4634, fax (33) 3281, next to the Charli Chaplin movie house on Calle 23 e/ Calles 10 12. It often has preview screenings of new Cuba releases in its studios. The Chaplin has bee called the largest theater in the world.

You'll find several movie houses clustere along La Rampa in central Vedado. The most im portant cinemas in town are:

Cine Acapulco: Avenida 26 e/ 35 y 37, Veda do, tel. (3) 9573. Daily from 4:30 p.m.

Cine Charles Chaplin: Calle 23 e/ 10 y 12, edado, tel. (31) 1101. Daily except Tuesday t 5 and 8 p.m. (box office opens 30 minutes rior). Also here is **Video Charlot** (same times), lso showing first-run movies.

Cine Payret: Prado and Calle San José, Habana Vieja, tel. (63) 3163. Daily from 12:30 p.m.

Cine La Rampa: Calle 23 e/ O y P, Vedado, l. (78) 6146. Daily except Wednesday from :40 p.m.

Cine Riviera: Calles 23 y H, Vedado, tel. (30) 564. Daily from 4:40 p.m.

Cine Yara: Calle 23 y Calle L, Vedado, tel. 32) 9430. Open from 12:30 p.m.

The latest issue of *Granma* will list what's currently showing.

French films are shown Saturday at 2 p.m. at e **Alliance Française,** at Calle G No. 407 e/ 17 19 in Vedado, tel. (33) 3370. Entrance is free.

THEATER AND CLASSICAL PERFORMANCES

lavana has seven major theaters, although the ity is *not* a thespian's dream. Theater is the east developed of Cuba's cultural media and as been usurped by the Revolution as a medim for mass consciousness raising. As such, it ecame heavily politicized. In recent years, an vant-garde theater offering veiled political critcism has begun to evolve. Many theaters host litte drama and are used mostly for operatic, symhonic, and other concerts.

Although legitimate or live theater has yet to ake off, Cubans are enthusiastic lovers of ballet nd classical music. Audiences are known to se to their feet and yell with delight at the end of oncerts.

The most important theater is the baroque Gran Teatro de la Habana, on the west side f Parque Central, tel. (62) 9473. It is the main tage for the acclaimed Ballet Nacional de Cuba Calzada #510 e/ D y E, Vedado, tel. 55-2953, ax 33-3117) as well as the national opera comany. The building has two theaters—the **Sala García Lorca,** where ballet and concerts are eld, and the smaller **Sala Antonin Artaud,** for ess-commercial performances. Jazz and other erformances are often given, and most weeks hroughout the year, you can even see Span-

ish dance here Thurs.-Sat. at 8:30 p.m. and Sunday at 5 p.m. (US$10). A dress code (no shorts) applies for performances.

Look, too, for performances of the National Symphony—the orchestra is excellent, if you excuse the occasional pings of dropped bows and triangles—and other classical and contemporary performances at the modern **Teatro Nacional,** on Avenida Carlos M. de Céspedes, one block west of the Plaza de la Revolución, tel. (79) 6011. It has two performance halls—the **Sala Avellaneda,** for concerts and opera, and the **Sala Covarrubias.** It also hosts important Communist Party functions and revolutionary celebrations.

The **Basílica de San Francisco de Asís** in Habana Vieja also hosts classical concerts, normally Thursday at 6 p.m.

The **Teatro Mella,** on Linea (Calle 7ra) y A, tel. (3) 5651, is noted for its contemporary dance and theater, including performances by the **Danza Contemporánea de Cuba.** Many of Cuba's more contemporary and avant-garde plays are performed here.

Gran Teatro de la Habana

The **Casa de la Música** at Calle 17 y E in Vedado offers concerts by soloists and chamber ensembles—and so does the **Casa de la Música** on Calle 20 e/ Avenida 33 y 35 in Miramar, tel. (24) 0447, which has different performances nightly at 10 p.m. except Monday in the *sala de espectáculos* (US$10 cover). The **Museo de la Música** at the north end of Monserrate, at its junction with Cuba, in Habana Vieja, offers classical concerts Saturday and Sunday at 4 p.m. (US$2).

The **Teatro Amadeo Rohoan** on Parque Vi lalon, between 5ra y Calzada (7ma) and C y D was recently restored to haughty grandeur—th restoration was ongoing in spring 1999—an will feature classical concerts year-round. Nea by is the **Teatro Hubert de Blanck,** on Calzad e/ Calles A and B, tel. (30) 1011, known for bot modern and classical plays.

Watch, too, for performances by Xiomar Palacio, a puppet-show artist recognized a Cuba's leading figure in children's theater. On

TUNING WITH THE ENEMY

When Benjamin Treuhaft first visited Cuba, he marveled at the ability of young musicians to raise beautiful sounds from decrepit pianos—Wurlitzer short uprights from the turn of the century, unpromising 1970s Russian Tchaikas, and pre-1959 US instruments eaten by salt air and termites.

Treuhaft, a piano tuner who has tuned on behalf of Steinway, vowed to collect pianos and ship them to Cuba. He sent letters to dealers across the nation soliciting parts and soon had pledges for dozens of pianos. His mission of musical mercy, however, struck a dissonant note with the US Commerce Department, which declared that pianos are not humanitarian aid and were therefore barred. When Treuhaft replied in jest that the Cubans might use the pianos for military purposes, the case was shifted to the department's Office of Missile and Nuclear Technology! Due considerations were presumably given to piano throw weights and trajectories before official permission was given to ship his pianos, providing that they were not "used for the purpose of torture or human rights abuse"—proof that US policy toward Cuba is overdue for its own major tuning.

The first 22 pianos (plus an organ and half a ton of spare parts) reached Havana in December 1995, to be dispersed to deserving students and teachers by the Instituto Cubano de la Música (Cuban Institute of Music). More than 60 pianos have thus far been shipped, along with 20 piano tuners. Treuhaft has even installed a German wire-spinning machine in Havana.

Treuhaft needs piano wire, tuning pins, and tools, but most of all that old piano (in rebuildable condition) languishing in your basement. Monetary donations are also requested (make checks payable to Havapiano). Contact Benjamin Treuhaft, 39 E. St.

#3, New York, NY 10003, tel. (212) 505-3173, e-mail blt@igc.org.

Watch for *Tuning with the Enemy,* an hour-long documentary filmed in Havana and Berkeley, about Treuhaft's project. It was made for British TV and has appeared on cable TV throughout the United States.

Ben Treuhaft, tuner with a mission

of Cuba's premier choral groups, Schola Cantorum Coral, known also as Coralina, trains children and youth in chorale.

Comedy

Comic theater is popular with Cubans. It is considered part of the national culture and was an important element in 19th-century life. However, you'll need to be fluent in Spanish to get many giggles out of the shows, which are heavy on burlesque. Most cabaret shows also feature stand-up comedy. Look for announcements for forthcoming shows posted outside the Cine Yara in Vedado.

In Habana Vieja, head to **Casa de la Comédia** (also called Salón Ensayo), at the corner of Calles Justíz and Baratillo, tel. (63) 1160, one block southeast of Plaza de Armas. It hosts comic theater on weekends at 7 p.m., performed by the Teatro Anaquillé (US$2).

In Vedado, the **Teatro Bretch** specializes in comedy, which it offers every Tuesday at 8:30 p.m. The **Teatro Guiñol** on the west side of the FOCSA building, on M e/ 17 y 19, also offers comedy; as does the **Teatro El Sótano**, at Calle K #514 between 25 and 27, every Thursday evening.

The **Salón Internacional** in the Hotel Habana Riviera, Avenida Paseo y Malecón, tel. (33) 4051, presents a weekly "Gran Fiesta" of comedy and music (US$5 cover). **Cabaret Las Olas,** a simple outdoor facility on the Malecón, one block east of La Rampa, hosts comedy Wednesday at 8 p.m.

Comedy is also sometimes performed at the **Café Cantante Mi Habana,** in the Teatro Nacional at Paseo, one block west of the Plaza de la Revolución, tel. (33) 5713 or (79) 6011, and in the bar beside Casona del 17 at Calles 17 and M, in Vedado.

MUSEUMS AND GALLERIES

Few cities in Latin America can match Havana's showcase museums and galleries. Havana has almost 40 museums and at least 14 major art galleries and countless minor ones. Typically, you'll find at least 30 major exhibitions in Havana at any one time.

The bimonthly *Galerías de Arte Programación,* available from the **Centro de Desarrollo de las Artes Visuales,** at San Ignacio #352, in Plaza Vieja, lists openings. Likewise, the *Guia Cultural de la Habana, Cartelera,* and *Granma* publish current information on exhibitions and galleries, as does the bimonthly magazine *Revolución y Cultura.*

Museums

You'll find many natural history museums and "decorative arts" museums, but by far, the majority of Havana's museums are dedicated to one form or another to the glories of the Revolution. Entrance for foreigners usually costs US50 cents to US$3. Almost always, you are accompanied by a guide, who either trails a short distance behind or offers a sometimes stirring, other times turgid précis of socialism. Many museums support a variety of cultural activities, such as theater and ballet.

Art Galleries

You'll find an incredible array of revolving art, sculpture, and photo exhibitions. The shows often draw top international artists as well as Cubans of stature: an exhibition of sculptures by famous English genius Henry Moore highlighted Havana's calendar in 1997. Although official proscriptions keep a tight rein on avantgarde exhibitions, things had loosened enough in 1998 for an exhibition of nude photography by Roberto and Oswaldo Salas, Havana's first

---

AN INSIGHT INTO CUBAN ART

Everyday Art is a 50-minute video portrayal of Cuba's folkloric traditions and contemporary art scene, focusing on the everyday life of Cuban musicians, dancers, and artists. It reflects the strong presence of folk art in social institutions such as religion and education.

The Center for Cuban Studies, 124 W. 23rd St., New York, NY 10011, tel. (212) 242-0559, fax (212) 242-1937, e-mail: cubanctr@igc.apc. org, website: www.cubaupdate.org, maintains the **Cuban Art Space,** the largest collection of contemporary Cuban art in the United States, with more than 800 paintings, drawings, and graphics, plus about 5,000 posters, and a library on art.

HAVANA ART GALLERIES

Centro Wilfredo Lam: San Ignacio 22 esq. Empedrado, Habana Vieja, tel. (61) 2096; Mon.-Sat. 10 a.m.-5 p.m. Temporary exhibits with contemporary art from the Third World.

Galeria del Arte galiano: Calle Galiano #258 esq. Concordia, Centro Habana, tel. (62) 5365; Tue.-Sat. 10 a.m.-4:30 p.m.

Galeria del Arte Latinoamericano: Calle G, e/ 3ra y 5ta, Vedado, tel. (32) 4653; Mon.-Fri. 10 a.m.-5 p.m.

Galeria Forma: Calle Obispo #255 e/ Cuba y Aguiar, Habana Vieja, tel. (62) 2103; Mon.-Sat. 10 a.m.-4 p.m. Small-format sculptures by prominent Cuban artists. Also paintings by leading artists.

Galeria Habana: Calle Linea e/ E y F, Vedado, tel. (32) 7101; Mon.-Sat. 10 a.m.-4:30 p.m., Sunday 9 a.m.-1 p.m. Paintings, silkscreen prints, and drawings by young Cuban artists.

Galeria Haydee Santamaría: Calle G e 3ra y 5ta, Vedado, tel. (32) 4653; Mon.-Fri. 10 a.m.-5 p.m. Graphics, prints, drawings, and photography from throughout the Americas.

Galeria Horacio Ruíz: Calle Tacón No.4 esq. Empedrado, Habana Vieja; Mon.-Sat. 10 a.m.-5:30 p.m. Leather, metal, glass, papier-mâché, and other materials.

Galeria Francisco Javier Baez: Plaza de la Catedral, Habana Vieja; Mon.-Fri. 10 a.m.-5 p.m.

Galeria La Acacia: Calle San José 114 esq. Consulado y Industria, Centro Habana, tel. (63) 9364; Mon.-Sat. 10 a.m.-4 p.m. Fine collection of antiques and works by the great masters of Cuban plastic arts.

Galeria Marinao: Calle 15 #607, e/ B y C, Vedado; Mon.-Fri. 10 a.m.-5 p.m., Saturday 10 a.m.-3 p.m.

Galeria Nelson Dominguez: Calle Obispo #166, e/ Amargura y Churruca, Habana Vieja, tel. (63) 9407; Mon.-Sat. 10 a.m.-5:30 p.m.

Galeria Plaza Vieja: Calle Muralla No.107 esq. San Ignacio, Habana Vieja, tel. (62) 6295; Mon.-Fri. 9 a.m.-3:30 p.m. Specializes in Afro-Cuban influences in the works of celebrities like Manuel Mendive, Zaida del Río, and Armando Laminaga.

Galeria Roberto Diago: Muralla 107 esq. San Ignacio, Habana Vieja, tel. (33) 8005; Mon.-Sat. 10 a.m.-5:30 p.m. Permanent exhibits of primitive artists.

Galeria UNEAC: Calle 17 esq. H, Vedado, tel. (32) 4551; Mon.-Fri. 9 a.m.-5 p.m. Exhibits by contemporary Cuban artists.

Galeria Victor Manuel: Plaza de la Catedral, Habana Vieja, tel. (61) 2955; Mon.-Sat. 10 a.m.-4 p.m. Cuban landscapes, pottery, and applied arts.

Taller de Seregráfia Rene Portocarrero: Calle Cuba #513, e/ Teniente Rey y Muralla, Habana Vieja, tel. (62) 3276; Mon.-Fri. 9 a.m.-4 p.m. Silkscreen printing workshop; serigraphy applied to art reproduction.

Taller Experimental de la Gráfica: Callejón del Chorro, Plaza de la Catedral, Habana Vieja, tel. (62) 0979; Mon.-Sat. 10 a.m.-4 p.m. Traces the history of engraving. Exclusive pieces for sale.

---

such exposition in many decades (surprisingly, a government that endorses a mature liberalism with regard to sexuality and sensualism has long prohibited photographic explorations of the nude).

Cuba makes great efforts to display art from other countries, notably the Caribbean and Latin America, as for example the **Art of Our Americas** collection, housed in Havana's Casa de las Américas, Calle 3ra and G, tel. (55) 2706, fax (33) 4554, e-mail: casa@artsoft.cult.cu, a nongovernmental institution that has studied and promoted every aspect of Latin American and Caribbean culture since 1959. The collection comprises more than 6,000 pieces encompassing sculpture, engravings, paintings, photographs, and popular art.

Likewise, the **Centro Wilfredo Lam,** at the

corner of Empedrado and San Ignacio in Habana Vieja, tel. (61) 2096 and (61) 3419, fax (33) 8477, e-mail: wlam@artsoft.cult.cu, has a collection of 1,250 contemporary art pieces from Cuba and around the world. Open Mon.-Fri. 8:30 am.-3:30 p.m., but Mon.-Sat. 10 a.m.-5 p.m. for guided visits. If you can, time your visit for May to coincide with the prestigious **Havana Biennale,** an annual art show hosted by the Centro Wilfredo Lam.

Needless to say, the **National Arts Museum** in Havana's Palacio de Bellas Artes houses a tremendous collection of both classical and modern art, featuring works by Renoir, Picasso, Rodin, and other masters. But there are dozens of other smaller galleries.

CITY OF BOOKWORMS

Habaneros as a whole are incredibly literate. They're avid readers, and not just of home-country writers. The works of many renowned international authors are widely read throughout Cuba: Ernest Hemingway, Tennessee Williams, Gabriel García Márquez, Günter Grass, Isabel Allende, Jorge Amado, Mark Twain, Raymond Chandler, and Dashiell Hammett.

During the first years of the Revolution, Castro relished being the "bohemian intellectual." Artists and writers enjoyed relative freedom. As the romantic phase of the Revolution passed into an era of more dogmatic ideology, hard-line Marxists took over the Culture Council. In 1961, the government invited intellectuals to a debate on the meaning of cultural liberty at which Castro offered his "Words to the Intellectuals," which he summed up with a credo: "Within the Revolution, everything. Against the Revolution, nothing!" The government acquired full control of the mass media. Many talented intellectuals, writers, and artists were intimidated into ideological straitjackets. Thousands chose to leave Cuba.

Cuba's goals and struggles have been a breeding ground for passions and dialectics that have spawned dozens of literary geniuses whose works are clenched fists that cry out against social injustice. Says writer Errol McDonald, "The confluence of the struggle against Spanish and American imperialism, the impact of the cultivation of sugar and tobacco, a high appreciation of the 'low-down' sublimities of Afro-Cuban and Hispanic peasant life, a deep awareness of European 'high' and American popular culture, and the shock of the revolution has resulted in a literature that is staggering for its profundity and breadth—its richness."

Cuban literature was born in exile. The most talented Cuban writers, such as Cirilo Villaverde (whose spellbinding novel *Cecilia Valdés* was writ-

ten in exile in the 1880s), Virgilio Piñera, Guillermo Cabrera Infante, and Alejo Carpentier, all produced their best works abroad, including many, such as Piñera and Infante, cast into purgatory as "contagious political bacteria" during the Revolution. The worst years ended when the Ministry of Culture was founded in 1976, ushering in a period of greater leniency. Still, although postrevolutionary Cuba has had its literary figures of note, it has not produced a definable literature of its own.

Many talented individuals stayed, of course, and produced rich and lively works (despite ideological restraints, there is a genuine commitment on the part of the Cuban government to culture and the arts). The past few years have seen a considerable thaw. The current Cuban cultural policy is to salvage those artists and writers who, having produced significant works, were never allowed to publish. Many writers previously reduced to "nonpersons" are now being treated with kindness and, often, postmortem canonization.

Ironically, this new openness coincides with the hardships of the Special Period, which have caused a severe paper shortage affecting Cuba's publishing industry. By 1993, books were as scarce as the food. Many state-employed writers found themselves among the ranks of the unemployed. Prompted by the economic and political openings of the early 1990s, they banded together to form the **Unión de Escritores y Artistas de Cuba** (UNEAC), or Union of Freelance Writers and Artists. Alas, Cuba's political climate runs hot and cold. In spring 1996, the government began to cool authors down a bit, and freelancers reported a new tug on the leash. The government continues to harass freelance writers who, since the promulgation of a new law in 1999 aimed as a sword at their hearts, must now be cautious against writing anything that can be implied to be "supporting the enemy" (i.e., Uncle Sam).

OTHER ENTERTAINMENT

Aqua Espectáculos

Swimming pool *espectáculos* (also called *aquaticas danzas*) are choreographed water ballets with son et lumière and are offered at the Hotel Meliá Cohiba Wednesday nights, and the Hotel Nacional, which offers *Swan Lake* nightly at 9:30 p.m.

The **Qualton El Viejo y el Mar,** in the Marina Hemingway complex in the Barlovento district of western Havana, also offers an *aquatica danza* Tuesday at 9 p.m.

Fashion Shows

La Maison, Calle 16 #701 esq. Avenida 7ma, Miramar, tel. (24) 1543, fax (24) 1585, is touted by Cuban tourist agencies. *Presentación de modas* (fashion shows) are held beneath the stars in the terrace garden of an elegant old mansion, on a stage lit by a son et lumière. Live music is provided. It's enjoyable, albeit a bit strained. Reservations are recommended. Entrance costs US$10 (US$15 including transportation and a bottle of rum). A 4 p.m. matinee show is offered on weekends. Meals are served alfresco during the show beneath the flame-of-the-forest trees. There's a piano bar in a separate a/c building (US$2), open after the show.

The disco at **Club 1830** also hosts a fashion show, including formal evening wear and see-through wedding gowns (the brides are "dressed" for the honeymoon under their gowns) that would give a vicar a heart attack. The show is included in the US$5 entrance price.

Poetry Readings and Literary Events

The Special Period has had a devastating impact on the publication of Cuban literature. Prior to the period, prominent writers and poets gathered at **La Moderna Poesía** bookstore, at the west end of Calle Obispo, each Saturday at noon to sign copies of their latest releases. But literary events have begin to appear again.

Literary readings are offered at the **Unión Na-** cional de Escritores y Artistes de Cuba at the corner of Calle 17 and I UNEAC, tel. (32) 4551, fax (33) 3158. The mansion's porch is now the union's café, where you may mingle with Cuba's literati. UNEAC publishes a bimonthly magazine, *La Gaceta;* subscriptions (US$40) are available through Pathfinder, 410 West St., New York, NY 10014, tel. (212) 741-0690, fax (212) 727-0150.

Poetry readings are also given at the **Casa de las Américas,** Calle 3 and G, Vedado, tel. (55) 2706, fax (33) 4554, e-mail: casa@artsoft.cult.cu,; the **Fundación Alejo Carpentier,** Empedrado No. 215, Habana Vieja, tel. (61) 3667; and **La Madriguera,** a popular hangout for university students, on Avenida Salvador Allende and Calles Luaces. The **Museum of Fine Arts,** on Tracadero and Agramonte (Zulueta), also hosts literary events, as well as film screenings and musical presentations.

Dolphin Show

A dolphin show is offered eight times daily at the National Aquarium, Avenida 1ra and Calle 60, Miramar, tel. (23) 6401. The 20-minute show features four trained dolphins that cavort and leap and do tricks while a commentator offers an educational program in Spanish. The schedule seems to change constantly, so call ahead for times. Shark feeding and a sea lion show are also offered on a scheduled basis. The aquarium is open Monday 6-11 p.m., Tues.-Thurs. 10 a.m.-6 p.m., Friday 10 a.m.-10 p.m., Sat.-Sun. 10 a.m.-6 p.m. (US$2, children US50 cents; in addition to US$5 entrance to the aquarium).

Transvestite Shows

Cubans have a tremendous sense of satire, and transvestite humor is a staple of any comedy show. Dedicated transvestite shows are hosted upstairs in the **Centro Cultural de Árabe** on the Prado e/ Calles Refugio y Trocadero, Fri.-Sun. 9 a.m.-midnight (US$15). Cabarets are hosted nightly (US$5). Another *tranvestis* show is hosted at the **Rosalia Castro,** around the corner from the Restaurant Hanoi, on Plaza del Cristo.

SPORTS AND RECREATION

Havana has many *centros deportivos* (sports centers), although most are very rundown or otherwise dour. The largest is the **Panamericano** complex, in Habanas del Este, tel. (97) 4140. It includes an Olympic athletic stadium, tennis courts, swimming pool, and even a velodrome for cycling.

Cubadeportes, Calle 20 #705, e/ 7 y 9, Miramar, tel. (24) 0945 or (24) 7230, fax (24) 1914, manages Cuban sports and access to them for foreigners. It publishes a list of international events hosted in Cuba (the 1999 program listed more than 70).

Organized Tours

Agencia de Viajes Cubadeportes, Calle 20 #705, e/ 7 y 9, Miramar, tel. (24) 0945, fax (24) 1914, specializes in sports tourism and arranges visits to international sporting events, training facilities, etc., including lodging, transfers, and other necessities.

Last Frontier Expeditions, 4823 White Rock Circle, Suite H, Boulder, CO 80301, tel. (303) 530-9275, fax (303) 530-9275, e-mail: CopaBob@aol.com, specializes in trips to Cuba for sporting enthusiasts. For example, it offers a trip to the **Ernest Hemingway International Sports Classic** *(Clásico Internacional Hemingway)*, a 10K race through Habana Vieja that the company helped initiate in 1995. The race occurs each May and is part of "national sports week," which includes baseball, basketball, and volleyball events; sports symposia; and visits to sports medicine clinics. Last Frontier also offers the Ernest Hemingway Sportfishing Tournament, the Havana Open Golf Tournament, hunting and fishing trips, baseball fantasy camps, and motorcycle tours using BMWs and escorted by your author.

In Canada, **Eleggua Project,** 7171 Torbram Rd., Suite 51, Mississauga, ON L4T 3W4, tel. (800) 8181-8840, fax (905) 678-1421, e-mail: cancuba@pathcom.com, website: www.pathcom.com/~cancuba, specializes in athletic and sports study programs to Cuba and provides travel services.

PARTICIPATORY ACTIVITIES

Bicycling

Bicycling offers a chance to explore the city alongside the Cubans themselves. Since the demise of the Soviet Union severed the gasoline pipeline, Cubans have taken to bicycling with zeal. The roads are a bit dodgy, with bullying trucks and buses pumping out fumes, plus potholes and other obstacles to contend with (a helmet is a wise investment). But repairs are never a problem: scores of Cubans now make a living repairing *poncheras* (punctures) and mechanical problems. Nonetheless, you should still bring spares.

The University of Havana's **Club Nacional de Cicliturismo Gran Caribe** (alias the Havana Bicycle Club), Lonja del Comercio, Calle Oficia, Habana, tel. (96) 9193, fax (66) 9908, trans@mail.infocom.etecsa.cu, welcomes foreigners to join students on weekend cycle trips into the countryside surrounding Havana. Contact club president Ignacio Valladares Rivero.

Airlines generally allow bicycles to be checked free of charge (properly packaged) with one piece of luggage. Otherwise, a small charge may apply. Leave your racing bike at home and bring a touring bike or, better yet, a mountain bike.

Most Cubans get around on clunky old Chinese contraptions, but an increasing number have lightweight road-racing bicycles. Cuba fields a competitive race team, which trains at the **Velodromo Reynaldo Passiero,** at Ciudad Panamericano, tel. (97) 3776.

If you're interested in joining groups of Cuban students, mostly English speaking, contact the **Club Ciclocaribe Olímpico,** Comité Olímpico Cubano, Calle 13 #601 esq. C, Vedado, Havana, Cuba CP 10400, or **Club Nacional de Cicliturismo Gran Caribe,** Lonja del Comercio, Calle Oficia, Habana, fax (66) 9908, e-mail: trans@ mail.infocom.etecsa.cu (alias the Havana Bicycle Club) of the University of Havana, which welcomes foreigners to join students on weekend cycle trips into the countryside surrounding Havana. Contact club president Ignacio Valladares Rivero, home tel. (98) 9193 or, at Estadio Juan Abrantes, tel. (78) 3941, for more information.

A good resource for cycling information is Cuba's **Federación de Ciclismo,** in Havana, tel. (68) 3776 or (68) 3661.

The only place that currently seems to be renting bicycles in Havana is the **Hotel Jardín del Eden,** Marina Hemingway, tel. (24) 1150, ext. 371. It charges US$1 per hour, or US$12 per day for mountain bikes.

Organized Tours: Global Exchange, 2017 Mission St. #303, San Francisco, CA 94110, tel. (415) 255-7296 or (800) 497-1994, fax (415) 255-7498, e-mail globalexch@igc.org, website: www.globalexchange.com, offers a "bicycle adventure in Cuba" in association with the Cuban Bicycle Club (US$850, including airfare from Cancún).

Lucie Levine, 15543 Maplewood Dr., Sonoma, CA 95476, tel./fax (707) 996-1731, also offers annual bike trips in association with the Havana Bicycle Club and the Instituto Cubano de Amistad con los Pueblos.

Active Journeys, 4891 Dundas St. W, Suite 4, Toronto, ON M9A 1B2, Canada, tel. (416) 236-5011 or (800) 597-5594, fax (416) 236-4790, e-mail: journeys@pathcom.com, also offers bicycle tours; as does **McQueen's Bicycle Shop & Travel,** 430 Queen St., Charlottestown, Prince Edward Island C1A 4E8, Canada, tel. (902) 368-2453 or (800) 969-2622, fax (902) 894-4547, e-mail: biketour@peinet.pe.ca.

In the UK, **Hazel Pennington Bike Tours,** P.O. Box 75, Bath, Avon BA1 1BX, England, tel. 01225-480130, fax 01225-480132, offers bike tours of Cuba.

Bowling

You can practice your 10-pin bowling at an alley in the **Hotel Kohly,** at Avenida 49 esq. 36A, Reparto Kohly, Vedado, tel. (24) 0240, fax (24) 1733, e-mail: reserva@kohly.gav.cma.net; or at the **Havana Golf Club,** tel. (55) 8746, way south of town at Carretera de Vento, Km 8, off Avenida Rancho Boyeros. The club has a fully mechanized two-lane bowling alley and full-size pool tables. They're very popular with local youth.

Golf

Yes, Havana offers golf—near Boyeros, about 20 km south of Havana, at the **Havana Golf Club,** hidden east of the Avenida de la Independencia, at Carretera de Vento, Km 8, Capdevila Havana, tel. (55) 8746 or (33) 8919, fax (33) 8820. Of four courses in Havana in 1959, this is the only one remaining. Also called the "Diplo Golf Course," the nine-hole course—with 18 tees and 22.5 hectares of fairway—is no Palm Springs. It's a bit rundown, despite a recent facelift, but it retains the unmistakable air of a private club reflecting the days when it opened in 1948, built by British residents who felt homesick for Turnberry (they called their Cuban course the Rover's Athletic Club). The two sets of tees, positioned for play to both sides of the fairway, make the holes play quite differently. A second set of nine holes is planned to open by the year 2001, when it will be a 6,257-yard course (the layout of the current nine holes will be changed). The course, a "woodland parkland-style layout" that is compared to Pinehurst in North Carolina, starts off badly, but the fifth and sixth holes are described as "well-designed holes that could hold their own on almost any course of the world."

"Golfito"—as the locals know it—has a minimally stocked pro shop, plus five tennis courts, a swimming pool, and two restaurants set amid landscaped grounds. The pleasant Bar Hoy 19 (19th Hole), with a small TV lounge, overlooks the greens.

The club hosts golf competitions. Membership costs US$70 plus US$45 monthly (US$15 for additional family members). A round costs nonmembers US$20 for nine holes (US$30 for 18). You can rent clubs for US$10. Caddies cost US$3 per nine holes. A US$3.50 fee is charged to use the pool, US$2 for the tennis facilities. Jorge Duque is the affable resident golf pro; he charges US$5 per 30 minutes of instruction.

The **Club Habana** at Avenida 5ta between 188 and 192, Reparto Flores, Playa, tel. (24) 5700, fax (24) 5705, has a practice range. The club serves its members, made up mostly of foreign diplomats and businessmen, but nonmembers are welcome (entrance costs US$10 Mon.-Fri., and US$15 Sat.-Sunday).

Four additional courses are planned in Cuba over the next few years, including an 18-hole course in Havana.

Wings of the World and **Last Frontier Expeditions** both offer occasional golf tours from North America.

Gymnasiums

Only a few tourist hotels have gyms. The best are at the Hotels Meliá Cohiba and Parque Central. Havana, however, is replete with gymnasiums and other sports centers. Contact Cubadeportes, Calle 20 #705, e/ 7 y 9, Miramar, tel. (24) 0945 or (24) 7230, fax (24) 1914, for information.

Horseback Riding

Club Hípico, tel. (33) 8203 or (44) 1058, fax (33) 8166, in Parque Lenin, in the *municipio* of Arroyo Naranjo on Havana's southern outskirts, is a *centro ecuestre* (equestrian center) that offers horseback rides plus instruction in riding, jumping, and dressage. A course of 10 one-hour riding lessons costs US$102. You can take one-hour horseback trips (US$15), and rent horses if you're already proficient. Open 9 a.m.-4:30 p.m.

Horseback riding is also offered near Playas del Este at **Finca de Recreo Guanabito,** Calzada de Jústiz, Km 3.5, Guanabo, tel. (96) 4610, and nearby at **Rancho Mi Hacienda,** Calzada de Jústiz, Km 4, Guanabo, tel. (96) 4711, near Minas. These working "dude ranches" offer you a chance to get covered with dust and manure.

Running

The Malecón is a good place to jog, although you need to beware the uneven surface and occasional pothole. Try using the bicycle lane. For wide-open spaces, head to Parque Lenin, where the road circuit provides a perfect running track. Serious runners might head to the track at the Panamericano complex, tel. (97) 4140; the **Estadio Juan Abrahantes,** on Zapata, south of the university; **Centro Deportivo Claudio Argüellos,** at the junction of Avenida de la Independencia, Avenida 26, and Vía Blanca; or **CVD José Martí** stadium (which has a running track) at the base of Avenida de los Presidentes, in Vedado.

Sailing

Yachts and motor vessels can be rented at **Marina Hemingway,** Avenida 5ta and Calle 248, Santa Fe, Havana, tel. (24) 1150, fax (24) 1149, e-mail: comercial@comermh.cha.cyt.cu, which has 27- and 33-foot *Piraña* yachts and larger motorboats for bareboat or crewed rental.

Club Habana, Avenida 5ta between 188 and 192, in Reparto Flores, Playa, tel. (24) 5700, fax (24) 5705, also offers yacht rental.

Marina Puertosol Tarará, tel. (97) 1510, fax (97) 1499 (in Havana: Marinas Puertosol, Avenida 1ra #3001 esq. 30, Miramar, tel. 24-5923, fax 24-5928), rents yachts for US$250 for nine hours. It also offers live-aboard motorboats. Weekly rentals range from US$2,100 (May-Oct.) to US$2,800 (mid-Dec. to mid-January).

Scuba Diving

Cuba is a diver's paradise, with extensive coral reefs and countless cays and islets. But there's also good diving offshore of Havana. The Gulf Stream and Atlantic Ocean currents meet west of the city, where many ships have been sunk through the centuries, among them the wreck of the *Santísimo Trinidad,* off Santa Fé, west of Marina Hemingway; a merchant ship called the *Coral Island;* and the *Sanchez Barcastegui,* an armored Spanish man-o'-war that foundered in 1895. Their wooden and iron hulls make for fascinating exploration. This western shore, known as **Barlovento,** is unusual in that the island shelf drops by steps into the abyss, each forming a prairie with corals, gorgonians, sponges, and caves in addition to shipwrecks.

Also, the so-called **"Blue Circuit"** is a series of dive sites (with profuse coral and shipwrecks) extending east from Bacuranao, about 10 km east of Havana, to the Playas del Este. Visibility ranges from 15 to 35 meters. Water temperatures average 80° F to 85° F. The traditional critters of the Caribbean abound: barracuda, rays, sharks, tarpon, and turtles. The star-studded cast also includes angels, bigeyes, butterflies, damsels, drums, gobies, groupers, grunts, jacks, parrotfish, snappers, triggerfish, and wrasses, all of which seem perfectly content to ignore the human presence. Dozens of morays peer out from beneath rocky ledges.

Cuban divemasters are all trained by internationally recognized organizations and are highly skilled. The standard of equipment is good. Nonetheless, it's a good idea to bring your own equipment (leave tanks and weight belts at home, as all scuba diving centers have steel 12- or 15-liter tanks). If you need to replace O-rings, batteries, straps, etc., most supplies are available. Both European and North American tank fittings and equipment can be found in Cuba.

There's a decompression chamber in Havana at Hospital Luís Díaz Soto, Habanas del Este, tel. (60) 2804.

Publicitur publishes a 60-page booklet, *The Cuban Caribbean: Scuba-Diving Guide,* by Feliberto Garrié Fajardo. However, serious divers should consult *Diving and Snorkeling Guide to Cuba,* by Diana Williams (Lonely Planet, 1996), which provides detailed accounts of major dive sites. Cubanacán and Marlin Marinas jointly publish a *Scuba Cuba* brochure with a section on Havana.

Spearfishing is strictly controlled. Spearguns and gigs are *not* allowed through customs.

Dive Centers: Marina Hemingway offers scuba diving from **La Aguja Scuba Center,** tel. (21) 5277 or (33) 1150, fax (33) 6848 or (33) 1536, which has professional guides and also rents equipment. La Aguja charges US$28 for one dive, US$50 for two dives, US$60 for a "resort course," and US$360 for an open-water certification. It offers dive excursions to Playa Girón (Bay of Pigs) and Varadero for US$70, and rents equipment for US$5. Open daily 8:30 a.m.-4:30 p.m.

The **Blue Dive Club** is at Avenida 1ra and 24 in Miramar. The **Blue Reef Diving Center** at the Hotel Cocomar in Caimito, 23 km west of Havana, tel./fax (80) 5089, also has a scuba facility, as does **Club Habana,** Avenida 5ta between 188 and 192, Reparto Flores, Playa, tel. (24) 5700, fax (24) 5705, where entrance costs US$10 for non-members Mon.-Fri., US$15 Sat.-Sunday.

The Hotel Copacabana, Avenida 1ra e/ Calles 44 y 46 in Miramar, tel. (33) 1037, fax (33) 3846, offers beginning and advanced scuba diving lessons as well as trips. The water sports concession here rents underwater video and photography equipment.

The scuba center at **Marina Puertosol Tarará,** at Tarará, near Playas del Este, tel. (97) 1501, ext. 239, offers one-dive (US$30) and two-dive (US$50) trips, a four-day certification program (US$400), plus three-hour initiation dives.

Equipment rental costs US$10. World immersion record-holder Debora Andollo trains here (she claims four world records).

Havanatur offers a "Scuba in Cuba" program, tel. (23) 9783, fax (24) 1760, e-mail: adolfov@cimex.com.cu.

In North America, **Scuba in Cuba,** Ave. Quintana Roo, Suite TIJ-1173, Zona Centro, Tijuana, Mexico 22000, tel. in Mexico (66) 865298, in US (310) 842-4148, e-mail: scuba@cubatravel.com.mx, website: www.cubatravel.com/mx/scuba, offers scuba packages in conjunction with the Caribbean Diving Center and Puertosol.

Sportfishing

So many gamefish run offshore, streaming through the Gulf Stream that Hemingway called his "great blue river," that deep-sea fishing here has been compared to "hunting elk in the suburbs." You'll discover far more fish than fishhooks off the coast of Cuba, where snagging the *really* big one comes easy. Hardly a season goes by without some IGFA record being broken. Unfortunately, in this Cuba of food shortages, the Cubans aren't yet into tag-and-release, preferring to let you sauté the trophy (for a cut of the steak). Be sure to do the cooking yourself because your skipper, like most Cubans, is sure to prefer his fish cooked until it resembles a sole—of a shoe.

The big marlin run begins in May, when they swim against the Gulf Stream current close to the Cuban shore. In places, the stream begins only a quarter-mile offshore, with the depth sounder reading 1,000 feet; another quarter-mile and the bottom plummets another 5,000 feet.

Marlin S.A., on Canal B at Marina Hemingway, tel. (24) 1150, ext. 735, offers sportfishing using a variety of boats (US$130-290 for four hours, US$185-470 six hours, depending on the craft).

Puertosol, Casa Matriz, Avenida 1ra #3001 esq. 30, Miramar, tel. (24) 5923, fax (24) 5928

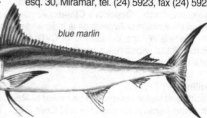

blue marlin

in Playas del Este at Calle Cobre #34404, e/ 2da y 4ta, Villa Marina, Tarará, Havana, tel. 97-1510, fax 97-1499), offers sportsfishing excursions. Typical four-hour *pesa a fondo* (light-tackle excursions) cost US$15-30 per person; four-hour deep-sea excursions cost US$150-250 for up to four passengers.

Also see Tarará in the "Habanas del Este" section, and Marina Hemingway in the "Playa Miramar and Beyond)" section of the "Sightseeing" chapter.

Fishing Tournaments: Cuba hosts several sportfishing tournaments. The big three competitions are based in Havana's Marina Hemingway: **The Currican Tournament** is held the first or second week of April, when the surface species take to Hemingway's "great blue river." **The Ernest Hemingway International Marlin Tournament** is the granddaddy of tournaments. It's held each May or June and offers trophies for the biggest marlin and the highest score. The Ernest Hemingway Cup may well be the world's most sought-after fishing trophy. **The Blue Marlin Tournament** also entices fisherfolk from around the world each August or September.

Wings of the World, 1200 William St. #706, Buffalo, NY 14240-0706; or 1636 3rd Ave. #232, New York, NY 10128, tel. (800) 465-8687, fax (416) 486-4001, offers eight-day fishing trips timed to coincide with each of the three tournaments. The US$2,495 price includes air, hotel, entrance fee, and all other aspects of competing—and their trips are fully legal for all US citizens. **Last Frontier Expeditions,** 4823 White Rock Circle, Suite H, Boulder, CO 80301, tel. (303) 530-9275, fax (303) 530-9275, e-mail: CoBaBob@aol.com, also offers trips to the Ernest Hemingway tournament.

Swimming

Most large tourist hotels have pools that are open for the use of nonguests. One favorite in Habana Vieja is the small rooftop pool in the **Hotel Parque Central.** Nearby is **Club Sevilla,** which offers access to the ground-floor, open-air figure-eight pool to the rear of the Hotel Sevilla. Entry costs US$5 (free to guests of the Hotel Sevilla, US$2.50 for children and guests of the Hotel Plaza), plus a gym (US$2), sauna (US$3.50), and massage (US$15-25). The entrance is on the corner of the Prado and Animas.

One of the best pools in Vedado is at the **Hotel Nacional** (US$5 per nonguest). Nonswimmers need to beware the sudden steep drop to the deep end, which plunges to three meters (a common fault in the design of Cuban swimming pools). Also try the small rooftop pool of the **Hotel Capri** and the attractive, outdoor mezzanine pool in the **Hotel Habana Libre Tryp.**

In Miramar, the **Club Almendares,** on Avenida 49C in Reparto Kohly, tel. (24) 4990, has a large, well-kept pool (US$3 adults, US$1 children) with sundeck that proves popular with Cuban families. Two other favorites are the pools at the **Hotel Copacabana** and the large, freeform pools in the **Hotel Comodoro** bungalow complex.

The best facility in Havana, however, is **Club Habana,** at Avenida 5ta between 188 and 192 in Reparto Flores, Playa, tel. (24) 5700, fax (24) 5705, a private members-only club that opens its doors to nonmembers for US$10 weekdays and US$15 weekends. It has a splendid beach that shelves gently into calm waters, as well as a large pool built to Western standards. Likewise, the **Marina Hemingway** is very popular with Cubans as well as foreign sailors who arrive by private yacht. It has two pool complexes, the best being that of the Hotel Jardín del Eden. And the **Complejo Turístico La Giradilla,** at Calle 272 e/ 37 y 51 in the La Coronela district, just west of Cubanacán, tel. (33) 6062, now offers a splendid swimming pool.

Farther afield, there are public swimming pools in Parque Lenin, and also an Olympic pool, **Piscina Olímpica,** Avenida 99 #3804, Lotería, southeast of Havana in the *municipio* of Cotorro. In Habana del Este, try the **Hotel Panamericano** pool.

Forsake joining the locals who bathe and snorkel in the waters off the Malecón. The rocks are sharp, and the waters often rough and badly polluted (when the ebbing tide drains Havana harbor, the sea off the Malecón can seem like pure gasoline). Far better is to head out to Bacuranao, Tarará, or Playas del Este, where you can swim in the warm sea; or to the *balnearios* of the Playa del Oeste extending from western Miramar to Barlovento. Care should always be taken when swimming in the waters off Tarará and Playas del Este, where the waves are often powerful and rip currents are common.

BEISBOL: CUBA'S NATIONAL PASTIME

*B*eisbol (or *pelota*) is as much an obsession in Cuba as it is in the US—more so, in fact; in 1909, Ralph Estep, a salesman for Packard, journeyed through Cuba and found the country "baseball crazy." The first officially recorded baseball game was played in Cuba, in 1874, at what is now the world's oldest baseball stadium still in use.

Just watch Cuban kids, playing, writes author Randy Wayne White, "without spikes, hitting without helmets, sharing their cheap Batos gloves, but playing like I have never seen kids play before. It wasn't so much the skill—though they certainly had skill—as it was the passion with which they played, a kind of controlled frenzy." No wonder Cuba traditionally beats the pants off the US team in the Olympic Games.

Needless to say, the US professional leagues are well aware of this enormous talent pool. Many black Cubans found positions in the US Negro leagues. (The flow went both ways. Tommy Lasorda, for example, played five seasons in Cuba and, in 1959, pitched the national team into the Caribbean world series.) Players who make the Cuban national team and barnstorm the Olympics earn about 400 pesos a month—about the same as the average laborer—and it's not surprising that many are still tempted by the prospect of riches in the US. More than 30 Cuban baseball stars have fled Cuba since 1991. Rene Arocha, now a star pitcher for the St. Louis Cardinals, split from the Cuban team during a stopover in Miami in July 1991. In Sep-

tember 1995, Cuban pitcher and national team member Osvaldo Ferná left Cuba and signed a $3.3 million deal with the San Francisco Giants. Cuban pitcher Rolando Arrojo defected during the 1996 Olympics. That same year, Livan Hernández left and was snatched up for $4.5 million by the Florida Marlins.

The defection of Hernández so rankled Castro that in a fit of pique, Livan's half-brother, Orlando "El Duque" Hernández, one of the world's greatest pitchers, was barred from playing for life (Castro—who, as a youth, used to storm off the field if his team was losing—even forbade the Cubans to watch the 1997 World Series that year); Hernández was relegated to work in the Havana Psychiatric Hospital for US$8 a month. Understandably, in January 1998 he fled Cuba on a homemade raft and was signed by the Yankees for US$6.6 million. Imagine the fury of Castro, who, says Andrei Codrescu, "has railed against Yankee imperialism for years."

Still, not every player is eager to leave. In 1995, Omar Linares, slugging third baseman for the Pinar del Río team and considered to be one of the best amateur baseball players in the world, rejected a $1.5 million offer to play for the New York Yankees. "My family and country come first," said Linares. "I'm aware of what a million-and-a-half dollars means, but I'm faithful to Fidel."

Ah, yes, Fidel. Cuba is led by a sports fanatic. In the early years of power, Castro would often drop in at Havana's Gran Stadium (in 1971 it was renamed

Juan Abrahantes baseball stadium, Havana

Estadio Latinoamericano and holds 55,000 people; it was state-of-the-art when opened in 1946 with 35,000 seats) in Cerro in the evening to pitch a few balls at the Sugar Kings' batters. And everyone knows the story of how Castro once tried out as a pitcher for the old Washington Senators. How different history might have been had his curveball curved a little better!

Plans for a Cuba-US match were hatched many times during the past several decades, but politics always got in the way. Finally, in March 1999, the Baltimore Orioles fielded a team in Havana and beat the Cuban national team, 3-2. The latter got revenge in May when they trounced the Orioles 12-6 at Oriole Park in a game that had all Havana glued to the TV.

Cuba's stars play more than 100 games a season on regional teams under the supervision of the best coaches, sports doctors, and competition psychologists outside the US big leagues. Each province has a team on the national league (Liga Nacional),

and two provinces and the city of Havana have two teams each, making 18 teams in all. The last game of every three-game series is played in a pueblo away from the provincial capital so that fans in the country can see their favorite team play live. The season runs Dec.-June. The teams play a 39-game season, with the top seven teams going on to compete in the 54-game National Series.

Stadiums are oases of relaxation and amusement. There are no exploding scoreboards or dancing mascots, and beer and souvenir hawkers are replaced by old men wandering among the seats with thermoses, selling thimble-size cups of sweet Cuban espresso. Spam sandwiches replace hot dogs in the stands, where the spectators, being good socialists, also cheer for the opposition base-stealers and home-run hitters. Balls (knocked out of the field by aluminum Batos bats made in Cuba) are even returned from the stands, because everyone understands they're too valuable to keep as souvenirs.

SPECTATOR SPORTS

Cuba is a world superstar in sports and athletics—out of all proportion to its diminutive size. In 1971, the Cuban government formed the National Institute for Sports, Physical Education, and Recreation. The state invested huge sums in bringing sports to the Cuban people. Sports training is incorporated into every school curriculum and many adult education programs. Baseball, chess, dominoes, and martial arts are the real national pastimes, but virtually every other conceivable sport and recreation is available, too.

Rough, often weed-covered basketball courts are everywhere, and Havana is replete with baseball stadiums, gymnasiums, and athletic facilities. Most facilities are basic by North American standards, but, hey, it's the results that count—and in that, Cuba is David to the US's Goliath.

Baseball
Cubans are baseball fanatics. The baseball season runs Dec.-June at the 60,000-seat **Estadio Latinoamericano,** the main baseball stadium, hidden in Cerro on Avenida 20 de Mayo and Calle Pedrosa, tel. (70) 6526. Games are played Tues.-Thurs. at 8 p.m., Saturday at 1:30 and 8 p.m., Sunday at 1:30 p.m. (three pesos). The

entrance is at Calle Zequeira.

You can also watch games being played at the **Estadio Juan Abrahantes** (also called Estadio Universitario), below the university at the end of Zanja, at Avenida 27 de Noviembre.

Boxing and Martial Arts
Little Cuba has always punched above its weight, and never more so than in the world of boxing: Cuba is a heavyweight in this sport, and as of 1999 held 23 Olympic titles, 45 senior world titles, 42 junior world titles, and 25 world cups.

The main boxing training center is the **Centro de Entrenmiento de Boxeo** at Carretera Torrens in Wajay, in the municipio of Boyeros, tel. (22) 0538, southwest of the city.

You can watch boxing and martial arts at the **Gimnasio de Boxeo Rafael Trejo,** Calle Cuba #815, Habana Vieja, tel. (62) 0266, and at **Sala Polivalente Kid Chocolate,** on the Prado opposite the Capitolio, tel. (62) 8634. It's intriguing to pop inside to watch kids and adults sparring. They may even welcome you onto the court or into the ring. Likewise, martial arts are hosted at the **Sala Polivalente Ramón Font** on Avenida de la Independencia y Bruzón, in Plaza de la Revolución, tel. (82) 0000; and at the **Estadio Universitario Juan Abrantes,** at San Rafael y Ronda, Vedado, tel. (78) 6959.

The week-long **International Conference on Olympic Style Boxing,** held in November 1999 at Havana's Instituto Superior de Cultura Física Manuel Fajardo, is intended to be an annual event. Contact Agencia de Viajes Cubadeportes, Calle 20 #705, e/ 7 y 9, Miramar, tel. (24) 0945, fax (24) 1914.

Other Sports

Volleyball and basketball are hosted at the **Sala Polivalente Kid Chocolate** and **Sala Polivalente Ramón Font** (see above).

For **fencing,** head to **ExpoCuba,** in the *municipio* of Arroyo Naranjo, tel. (44) 6251.

For **hockey,** head to the **Terreno Sintético de Hockey,** in Santiago de las Vegas.

The **Complejo de Pelota Vasca y Patinodromo,** at the junction of Avenida de la Independencia, Avenida 26, and Vía Blanca, tel. (81) 9700, has a **roller-skating** track.

Soccer games are played at the **Estadio Pedro Marrero,** Avenida 41 #4409 e/ 44 y 50, Cerro, tel. (23) 4698.

FOR THE KIDS

The Cuban government likes to look after its children and has outfitted Havana with plenty of children's play parks.

Pony rides are offered in Parque Luz Caballero, between Avenida Carlos M. Céspedes and Tacón in Habana Vieja. The ponies make a circuit around a statue of José de la Luz Caballero, "el maestro de la juventud cubana, 1800-62." Immediately west is a *parque diversione* (children's fairground) in front of the Castillo de Atane on Calle Tacón. It offers electric train rides plus all the fun of the fair.

There are plenty of other *parques diversiones* in town. In Vedado, try **Jalisco Parque** on Calle 23 at 18. **Club Almendares,** on Avenida 49C in Reparto Kohly, tel. (24) 4990, offers miniature golf and a kiddy's pool. **Parque Lenin** has plenty of attractions to keep the kids amused, from an old steam train ride and pony rides to a *parque diversion* with a miniature big dipper and other rides.

Take them to see the dolphin show at the **Acuario Nacional** (National Aquarium), Avenida 1ra and Calle 60, Miramar, tel. (23) 6401, fax (24) 1442, which is extremely popular with Cuban families on weekends.

Casa de la Comedia, on Calle Justíz in Habana Vieja, hosts children's theater and comedy events on weekend afternoons.

Both the **Jardín Zoológico de la Habana** (Havana's zoo) in Vedado and the **Parque Zoológico** (the national zoo) offer pony rides, *parque diversiones,* and, of course, the animals.

SHOPPING

Havana is a trove of bargain buys. True, you don't come here for factory outlets of designer boutiques. But for high-quality art and crafts, Havana is unrivaled in the Caribbean. The two big-ticket items are, of course, cigars and rum, readily available throughout the city, with the world's best cigars selling for one-third or less of their sale price in North America. Stunning silver and gold jewelry belies Cuba's images as a stodgy vacuum of creativity. Other great bargains include dolls, musical instruments (although few are made in Cuba), and music cassettes and CDs.

You're not going to find anything of interest in peso stores, which are half full (or half empty) of shoddy Cuban-made plastic and tin wares—or at Cuban pawn shops, called *casas comisionistas,* where Cubans place items for sale on consignment and pocket a commission (the state takes the rest). If your curiosity runs to it, check out a Cuban take on the modern department store, or one of the illicit shops run by Habaneros, often concentrated along streets colloquially named *Calle Ocho* for the famous Eighth Street in Miami, where Cuban exiles established their businesses during the first years of exile. For obvious reasons, their existence is advertised by word of mouth.

Outside Cuba, telephone and fax numbers need to be preceded by 53-7, the codes for Cuba and Havana respectively.

ANTIQUES

Havana's museums and private homes overflow with colonial-era antiques—to the degree that armed robbers have been known to raid houses and make off with the family jewels. Regrettably, there are few antique stores, partly because the government is keen to prevent a wholesale exodus of the country's treasures (it has been buying up antiques and gold from its own populace—for a fraction of their market value). Nonetheless, you *can* find antiques for sale. Perhaps the best place is **Galería la Acacia,** 114 San José, Centro Habana, tel. (63)

9364 (open Mon.-Sat. 9 a.m.-4:30 p.m.), whose trove includes everything from 18th-century ceramics to grand pianos. Some of it is merely kitschy, and much is in a sorry state. But for the knowledgeable, there are some gems certified by the National Heritage Office, Calle 4 #251, Vedado, tel. (55) 2272, from which you'll need an export license.

ARTS AND CRAFTS

Cuba's strong suit is arts and crafts, sold freely for dollars by artisans at street stalls, and also in art and craft stores by state agencies such as the Fondo de Bien Culturales and ARTEX. The best stuff is sold in the gift stores of the upscale hotels, which mark up accordingly; often you can find identical items on the street at half the price (as with *papier-mâché* baseball figures).

Great imagination is evident in the wares for sale. Cubans are supremely artistic, and the shortest walk through Habana Vieja can be a magical mystery tour of homegrown art. In recent years, art has been patronized by the tourist dollar, so the city is overflowing with whimsical Woolworth's art: cheap canvas scenes, busty cigar-chomping ceramic *mulattas,* kitschy erotic carvings, *papier-mâché* masks and vintage Yankee cars, and animal figurines painted in pointillist dots. But there is plenty of true-quality art, ranging from paintings and tapestries to handworked leather goods and precious wood carvings in Afro-Cuban realism but representing a solid investment. You'll also see *muñecitas* (dolls) everywhere, mostly representing the goddess of the *santería* religion (Cuban women are great doll collectors and often keep their childhood dolls into late adulthood).

Avoid the appalling *cineceros* (ashtrays) made of stuffed frogs doing various acrobatic maneuvers. *Don't buy these*—doing so contributes to the devastation of Cuba's endemic wildlife.

Pottery is outstanding also. You'll find everything from small rough-clay ashtrays with a clay cigar attached, and Castro in figurine form, to creative vases and ceramicware. Also look for

ARTISTS IN CUBA

Cuban artists express an intense Afro-Latin Americanism in their passionate, visceral, colorful, socially engaged art. Painters and other artists imaginatively stretch their limited resources to produce widely interpretive modern and postmodern works. The work is eclectic, but there is energy in it all.

In the late 1960s, the government tried to compel Cuban artists to shun then-prevalent decadent abstract art and adopt the realistic style of the party's Mexican sympathizers such as Diego Rivera and David Alfaro Siqueiros, who turned from easel painting to wall murals because, in the words of Siqueiros: "While it is technically possible to play a revolutionary hymn on a church organ, it is not the instrument one would prefer." The artists who grew up *after* the 1959 revolution—the "generation of the '80s"—have been given artistic encouragement, reflecting Cuba's liberal notion that artists are no less socially useful than masons, storekeepers, and bus drivers.

Cuba has 21 art schools, organized regionally with at least one per province. The **Instituto Superior de Arte** (Higher Institute of Art), Calle 120 #1110, Cubanacán, Havana, tel. (21) 0288 or (24) 6633, Cuba's premier art school, remains key as an educational center and gateway to the world of Cuban art.

The art educational system is both traditional and modern, with fundamental classical drawing and painting techniques at its core. The Cuban state has always fostered academic training in still life, landscape, and figure form. On attaining mastery of these skills, artists are encouraged to depart on experiments in expression to the extent of their imaginations (and without overstepping Castro's 1961 dictum to think more of the message than the aesthetic). As a result, says critic Tina Spiro, "most Cuban artwork, regardless of its style, is informed by a precision of line and a beautiful technical finish."

Upon matriculation from art school, artists receive the support of the **Fondo Cubano de Bienes Culturales**, Muralla #107 esq. San Ignacio, Habana Vieja, tel. (62) 3577, fax (33) 8121, in marketing and presenting their work to the public. The Cuban Cultural Fund offers gallery exhibitions, cataloging services, shipping, and transportation, and is currently trying to transform itself into a more marketing-oriented entity.

Until recent years, artists were employed by various Cuban state institutions and received a small portion of receipts from the sale of their work. In 1991, the government finally recognized that copyright belongs with the artist. It has created independent profit-making, self-financing agencies, such as ARTEX, to represent individual artists on a contractual basis whereby the agency retains 15% of sales receipts. Regulations provide that artists (including performers) can, ostensibly, retain up to 85% of earnings from the sale or licensing of copyrights abroad. A portion of the retained earnings goes to the Ministry of Culture's Fund for Educational and Cultural Development, which provides resources for arts training and public arts programs.

The artists themselves are increasingly shaking off their clichés and conservatism. In 1980, when the Cuban government began to loosen up, it even sponsored a show of avant-garde work influenced by international formats. Artists began holding unofficial exhibitions in their homes. By the late 1980s, the artists were overstepping their bounds (*The Orgasm on the Bay,* by Tomás Esson, for example, depicted an ejaculating cigar in Castro's mouth). Armando Hart, Minister of Culture, decided that the Cuban artists' enthusiasm should be promoted from afar. Mexico City was selected, and a community of deported artists has evolved—quixotically, with official Cuban sponsorship. In recent years, Cuban artists have taken the Western art world by storm. Says *Newsweek,* "Like the German and Italian neoexpressionists who took over the scene in the '70s and '80s, the Cuban artists may be on the brink of changing the face of contemporary art."

A new religious element is also taking root in art (where Afro-Cuban faith was basic to art in the 1980s, religious art today is inclining toward Roman Catholicism). Much of current art subtly criticizes the folly of its sociopolitical environment, but usually in a politically safe, universal statement about the irony in human existence—for example, Juan-Carlos Amador Machado has broken through the restrictions and paints the world of rotting Habana Vieja outside his door, expressing the hardships of daily life in a dark, surreal way. Within limits, this artistic dissent is not censored.

artfully delicate, copper-toned wind chimes and high-quality graphics by Cuba's top artists printed on recycled paper, including reproductions of classic Cuban painters, such as Wilfredo Lam, Victor Manuel, Mariano Rodríguez, and Amelia Peláez. Keep your eyes peeled for originals by up-and-coming talent such as Tomás Sanchez, Manuel Mendive, and Zaida del Río, with their very Cuban vision of landscapes, myths, and reality.

Among Cuba's most revered contemporary artists is Alfredo Sosabravo—a painter, draftsman, engraver, and ceramist born in 1930—and the most versatile and complete artist among those making up the plastic-arts movement in Cuba today. He's also perhaps the most prolific: you'll come across his works (and influence) everywhere, including a permanent exhibition at Havana's Museo Nacional and the Palacio de Bellas Artes. He is dramatically present in hotel lobbies and other touristed spots. Look, too, for the erotic art of Chago Armada and the sensual landscapes of Lester Campa, painted in almost hallucinogenic detail.

The security staff at Havana's international airport checks all artwork for its value. Anything deemed of antique value or high value will either be confiscated or taxed. An export permit is required for all works of art not purchased from state galleries and shops where official receipts are given. If you buy from independent artists, you'll need to acquire a permit (good for up to five works of art) for US$10 from the National Registry of Cultural Goods, Calle 17 #1009, e/ 10 y 12, Vedado. Allow up to two days for processing. Without it, you run the risk of Cuban customs taking the art. However, customs seems more interested in guarding against precious works leaving the country, and for kitschy paintings sold on the street, you should be fine.

Souvenir Stores

You'll find **ARTEX** shops throughout the city. All of them stock postcards, books, music cassettes and CDs, T-shirts, arts and crafts, rum, cigars, and other souvenirs. In Vedado, check out the shop at the junction of Calle L and La Rampa. Nearby, at La Rampa and P, is a **Bisart** store with a similar range of goods.

Manzana de Gómez is a shopping complex on the northeast side of Parque Central, in Habana Vieja. It contains several souvenir stores selling carvings, leather goods, and intriguing wall hangings, belts, purses, and posters. The store called **Monsieur** is particularly good. Several souvenir stores cluster around Plazuela de Albear, immediately east of the Manzana de Gómez.

Open-Air Markets

Artists sell their works freely on the streets, often for remarkably low prices. A limited amount of bargaining is normal at street markets. However, most prices are very low to begin with, and Cubans are scratching to earn a few dollars. Be reasonable. Don't bargain simply to win a battle. If the quoted price seems fair—and it usually

*open-air market,
Plaza de la Catedral*

is—then pay up and feel blessed that you already have a bargain. Feel free to visit the artists' studios, of which there are several on Calle Obispo in Habana Vieja.

There are plenty of markets to choose from. The best is undoubtedly the arts and crafts market held on Calle Tacón in Habana Vieja, selling everything from little ceramic figurines of Castro, miniature bongo drums, and **papier-mâché** figures of Cuban baseball players, to banana-leaf hats and fabulous bronzes and paintings.

In Vedado, a small open-air flea market on La Rampa e/ Calle M y L sells woodcarvings, jewelry, shoes, and leather goods. It's open daily 8 a.m.-6 p.m. A better bet is the larger **Carnaval de la Calle** market, on the Malecón e/ Calles D y E, where about 300 artisans exhibit and sell handicrafts, including corals delicately spun into bracelets (note, however, that coral is endangered), beaten copper pieces, quality leather sandals, woodcarvings, paintings, quaint ceramics, carved ox horns, plates showing 3-D landscapes, and even live parakeets. Avoid buying the stuffed marine turtles and turtle heads—there's an international ban on the sale and transport of turtle products.

Galleries

You're spoilt for choice, notably in Habana Vieja, which has a score of good galleries. Havana is home to a dizzying galaxy of galleries, most with both permanent and revolving exhibitions as well as art for sale. Pick up a copy of the weekly tourist guide, *Cartelera,* for complete listings. You can also pick up a bimonthly program, *Galerías de Arte Programación,* from the **Centro de Desarrollo de las Artes Visuales,** San Ignacio #352, Plaza Vieja. Its calendar of openings usually lists at least 30 major exhibitions taking place in Havana at any given time. For more complete information on workshops and galleries, contact the **Fondo Cubano de Bienes Culturales,** also in Plaza Vieja at Muralla #107, tel. (33) 8005, fax (33) 8121, with excellent artwork for sale in its galleries (see below). Most galleries are open Mon.-Sat. 10 a.m.-4 p.m.

One of the best places is **Galería la Acacia,** 114 San José, e/ Industria y Consulado, Centro Habana, tel. (63) 9364, an art gallery with first-class contemporary works. Expect to pay US$1,000 or more for the best works. Other top-

Roberto Fernández Martinez in his studio

quality art is sold a short distance away at **Galería del Centro Gallego,** next to the Gran Teatro on Parque Central. This Aladdin's cave includes superb bronzes by Joel del Río, imaginative ceramics, some truly stunning silver and gold jewelry, Cuban Tiffany-style lamps, and wooden and papier-mâché animals painted in bright Caribbean colors and pointillist dots, in Haitian fashion. This is high-quality work, priced accordingly. Bring your US$100 bills.

Of a similar standard is the **Galería Victor Manuel,** tel. (61) 2955, on the west side of Plaza de la Catedral, displaying fine landscapes and ceramic pieces. Around the corner, on Calejón del Chorro, is the **Taller Experimental de la Gráfica,** which traces the history of engraving and has exclusive prints for sale.

The galleries in the **Casa de los Condes de Jaruco,** on Plaza Vieja, tel. (62) 2633, sell work of unparalleled beauty and quality. Upstairs, and most impressive of all, is **Galería de la Casona,** with, among its many treasures, fantastic *papier-mâché* works of a heavily spiritualist nature. Be sure to walk through into the back room, where the works on display include Tiffany lamps, sculpted wooden statues, ceramic pieces, jewelry of truly mesmerizing creativity, and superb leatherwork in a uniquely Cuban style. Also upstairs is **Galeria de la Plaza Vieja,** where you will find some of the strongest statements in Cuban art. Similarly, you'll find experimental art for sale at the **Centro de Desarrollo de las Artes Visuales,** in the Casa de las Hermanas Cárdenas on the west side of Plaza Vieja, tel. (62) 3533 or (62) 2611.

Calle Obispo is famed for its art galleries. The highest quality works are displayed at **Galería Forma,** Calle Obispo #255, tel. (62) 0123, fax (33) 8121, selling artwork of international standard, including intriguing sculptures, ceramics, and copper pieces. The **Taller de Pintura,** Obispo #312, has a small gloomy room full of paintings of a more explorative, radical nature, including Daliesque paintings and copies of the great Spaniard's works. A gallery at Obispo #366 offers more native works; that at Obispo #408 has some fantastical ceramics. At Obispo #515, you'll find the studio of experimental ceramist Roberto Fernández Martinez, a lively old man with a spreading white beard who explores the influences of African and Indo-Cuban mythology. His eclectic paintings range through a variety of styles from Klee to Monet. The **Asociación Cubana de Artesana Artistas** has a store on Obispo where individual artists have small booths selling jewelry and arts and crafts. Check out the fantastical, museum-scale wall hangings and fabulous statuettes in the gallery at the rear. Open Tues.-Fri. 1- p.m., Saturday 10 a.m.-4 p.m.

The **Palacio de Artesanía Cubana,** on Calle Tacón, tel. (62) 4407, is replete with quality arts and crafts. You can also buy cigars and rum here. Open daily 9 a.m.-6 p.m.

The **Galeria Horacio Ruíz,** in the Palacio del Segundo Cabo on the north side of Plaza de las Armas, has a large selection of *muñecas* (dolls) and papier-mâché masks.

The **Centro Wilfredo Lam,** on San Ignacio, tel. (61) 2096 and (61) 3419, fax (33) 8477, e-mail: wlam@artsoft.cult.cu, exhibits works by the great Cuban master as well as other artists from around the Americas. It hosts the famous Havana Arts Biennial each May, when leading works are for sale. Likewise, the **Casa de las Américas,** on Calle 15 e/ B y C, Vedado, tel. (55) 2706, hosts exhibitions with works for sale. Its permanent Art of Our Americas collection is housed in newly refurbished galleries at the corner of Calle 3 and Avenida de los Presidentes in Vedado (photographic and graphic collections are grouped in the mansion at the corner of Calle 5). Also in Vedado, check out **Galeria Mariano,** part of the Casa de las Américas, named in honor of Mariano Rodríguez, a founder of the Cuban school of contemporary art.

The small gallery in the lobby of the Hotel Nacional also exhibits and sells paintings by the Cuban masters. The Hotel Meliá Cohiba's **Galeria Cohiba,** tel. (33) 3636, is another good source.

Jewelry

Most of the open-air markets offer silver-plated jewelry at bargain prices. Check out the weekend market at Calle 25 e/ Calles I y H in Vedado; some of the simple pieces for sale here (especially the necklaces) display stupendous creativity and craftsmanship, at ludicrously low prices.

Most upscale hotels have *joyerías* (jewelry stores) selling international-quality silver jewelry, much of it inlaid with black coral and in a distinctly contemporary style.

In Habana Vieja, head to the *joyería* in the **Casa de los Condes de Jaruco** on Plaza Vieja, tel. (62) 2633, where the stunning works by Raúl Valladeres are for sale. Other good places to find upscale jewelry include the store in the **Museo de Plata,** on Calle Obispo in Habana Vieja; and the **Palacio de las Artesanias,** at the west end of Calle Tacón in Habana Vieja. Also try the **Galeria del Centro Gallego** and **Galeria Victor Manuel** (see above).

In Vedado, try the **Joyería La Habanera,** Calle 12 #505, e/ Avenida 5ta y 7ma, Vedado, tel. (33) 2546, fax (33) 2529, which has an exquisite array of gold and silver jewelry.

One of the best upscale jewelry stores in town is the **Joyería Balla Cantando** in the Club Habana, west of Miramar in the Playas district. Likewise, the jewelry store upstairs in the **Casa de Habana** on Avenida 5ra and Calle 16 in Miramar offers top-notch creations.

Much jewelry, sadly, is of tortoiseshell, in spite of the international ban on the sale and transport of turtle products. *Don't buy it!*

Ceramics

You'll find many artists producing fantastic sculptural ceramics, such as those of Teresita Gómez or Roberto Fernández Martinez, whose works—often totemic—are heavily influenced by African myths. Look, too, for the works of women artists such as Antonia Eiriz and Amelia Peláez, and US-born Jacqueline Maggi, now professor of engraving at the Advanced Institute of Art in Havana, who "tackles the problem of women" in her woodcarvings and sculptures. **Galeria Villena,** on the south side of the plaza, sells ceramic works by leading artists such as Alfredo Sosabravo, Amelia Peláez, and Carballo Moreno.

More down-to-earth, whimsical pieces are a staple of the arts and crafts markets (see above).

Miscellany

Miniaturists and military buffs will find a few tiny soldiers, pirates, and other figurines in the **Casa de la Miniatura** on Tacón, one block east of Plaza de la Catedral, but the collection is not what it once was. (Those that were antiques certified by the National Heritage Office are no longer for sale.)

Lovers of Tiffany lamps should look for Gilberto Kindelán's transparent art nouveau lamps with bucolic landscapes featuring butterflies, which Kindelán describes as very visual and lending themselves well to poetry and movement in glass. The artist gets his glass, pewter, copper, and bronze from old mansions, recycling pieces rescued from beneath the wrecking ball.

BOOKS

For a city of two million literate and cultured people, Havana is appallingly short of books, which are severely restricted by the Cuban government. The few bookstores that exist stock only Spanish-language texts, including the classics of international literature (at least those on the right side of politics), but most works are socialist texts glorifying the Revolution. Castro's own writings are the most ubiquitous works, alongside those of José Martí. Most gift stores sell coffee-table books on Cuba, as well as a range of leftist, English-language texts and, occasionally, pulp fiction novels.

Two stores stand out, but don't get your hopes up—Havana is desperately in need of a Barnes & Noble. The first is **Librería La Internacional,** at the top of Calle Obispo #528, Habana Vieja tel. (61) 3238. It stocks a reasonable selection of historical, sociological, and political texts in English, plus a small selection of English-language novels. Open Mon.-Sat. 9 a.m.-4:30 p.m. The city's largest bookstore is **Fernando Ortíz,** near the university on Calle L esq. 27, Vedado, tel (32) 9653. Its collection spans a wide range o subjects, although almost entirely in Spanish (including translations of inspirational books by Anthony Robbins and Wayne Dwyer, plus a range of popular novels), as well as a limited range of pulp fiction, English dictionaries, and sightseeing books on Cuba. It also sells magazines, including a smattering of international periodicals. Open Mon.-Fri. 10 a.m.-5 p.m., Saturday 9 a.m.-3 p.m.

You'll also find a small selection of English-language novels at **La Bella Habana,** in the former Palacio del Segundo Cabo on the north side of Plaza de Armas, Habana Vieja, tel. (62) 8092. Open Mon.-Sat. 9 a.m.-4:30 p.m.

Other small outlets include **Librería Casa de las Américas,** at Calle G esq. 3ra, Vedado, tel (32) 3587, open Mon.-Fri. 9 a.m.-5 p.m.; **Librería de la UNEAC,** in the Cuban Writers' and Artists Union at Calle 17 esq. H, Vedado, tel. (32) 4551 open Mon.-Fri. 8:30 a.m.-4:30 p.m.; and **Librería Internacional José Martí,** Calzada #I259 e/ J y I, Vedado, tel. (32) 9838, open Mon.-Fri. 9 a.m. 4 p.m.

The **La Moderna Poesia** bookstore, opposite Librería La Internacional on Calle Obispo promotes works by lesser-known Cuban authors. Readings and book signings are held here on Saturday, although less frequently since the advent of the Special Period. Also here is the **Librería Cervantes,** a venerable but depressing secondhand bookstore.

For books on art and film, check out **Tienda Chaplín,** on Calle 23 e/ 10 y 12, tel. (31) 1101; it specializes in works related to the cinema but also has books on art and music, as well as posters and videos. Open Mon.-Sat. 2-9 p.m.

Centro de Desarollo de Artes Visuales, in the Casa de las Hermanas Cárdenas on Plaza Vieja, tel. (62) 3533, (62) 2611, sells artwork posters, and art and photography books.

If all else fails, you can pick from the dreary collection of faded texts at the secondhand book fair in Plaza de Armas. You'll find all kinds of tattered tomes, including atlases of Cuba, books o and by Ernest Hemingway, and a panoply of works by and about Che Guevara and Fidel Castro.

The only stationery store I know of is **La Papeleria,** 102 O'Reilly, catercorner to the Plaza de las Armas. It sells pens, paper stock, and other basic office supplies.

CLOTHING

Cuba isn't renowned for its fashions and offers little in the way of boutiques.

Most likely, if you're male, you'll want to purhase a *guayabera,* Cuba's unique short-sleeved, embroidered shirt worn outside the pants, draped to hide any figure flaw. It is designed of light cotton to weather tropical heat, with eight to 10 rows of embroidered tucking, and is outfitted with four pockets to stock enough robustos for a small store. This cultural icon was designed in Cuba more than two centuries ago and represents a symbol of masculine elegance, although it is disdained by Cuban youth for its associations with government figures (it has become a virtual uniform for state employees). You can buy *guayaberas* at any ARTEX store, or for pesos in the Cuban department stores along Calle San Rafael or Galiano.

The woman's fashion boutique **La Belleza Cubana,** on the west side of Plaza de San Francisco, specializes in wedding wear. Next door, on Oficios at the foot of Amargura, is a **United Colors of Benetton** outlet.

Casa 18, also called Exclusividades Verano,at Calle 18 #4106 e/ Calles 41 y 43, Miramar, tel. (23) 7040, sells Cuban-designed clothes, including beautiful one-of-a-kind Verano dresses and straw hats. Nearby, at Calle 6 y Avenida 11, is **La Flora,** which sells fine Cuban crafts and clothing, including *guayaberas* with the Pepe Antonio label and Verano dresses (other quality items include leatherware, stained-glass lamps, carved statues, and ceramic tableware).

The most famous fashion stores are found in **La Maison,** Calle 16 esq. 7ma Avenida, Miramar, tel. (24) 1543, a former colonial mansion known for its nightly fashion shows. The rooms have been converted into shops selling upscale imported clothing and deluxe duty-free items such as perfumes and jewelry. There's a shoe and clothing store upstairs. I bought a beautiful pair of leather sandals here for US$25 (made in Mexico).

For embroideries and lace, head to **El Quitrín,** at the corner of Obrapía and San Ignacio in Habana Vieja.

You can even buy military uniforms—a Soviet sailor's jacket, perhaps?—at **El Arte,** on Avenida Simón Bolívar on the east side of Parque de la Fraternidad.

Lost those Ray-Bans? Then head to **Ximeres** on the forecourt of the Hotel Habana Libre in Vedado; it stocks a range of Western designer shades.

DEPARTMENT STORES AND *DIPLOTIENDAS*

All foreign goods are imported by Cimex, headquartered in the former Hotel Sierra Maestra on Avenida 1ra in Miramar. You may be amazed by the number of department stores and shopping malls that Cimex is opening up all over town, selling all manner of Western goods, from Nikes and Reeboks to Japanese electronics. The malls are a far cry from their North American or European counterparts, but they point the way of the future.Security is tight, and a guard at the door will usually search your bags and correlate the contents against your itemized receipt after purchase.

Once known as *diplotiendas,* the original dollars-only outlets were exclusively for diplomats and other foreign residents. Today, Cubans are also welcome—as long as they have dollars to spend. One of the original complexes is **Quinta y 42,** at Avenida 5ta and Calle 42, which includes a sporting goods store, toy store, bakery, and general supermarket. Larger, more modern malls include the **Galerias de Paseo,** facing the Malecón at the foot of Paseo in Vedado. It even has a car showroom with new Fiats and Japanese cars (but it's for show, as Cubans can't legally buy new vehicles).

A new **Centro Comercial Sierra Maestra,** at Avenida 1ra and Calle 0, was under construction at press time. Need a TV, microwave oven, or diesel-powered lawnmower? This is the place to come.

Havana's most important commercial thoroughfares have traditionally been Calles San Rafael and Neptuno, immediately west of Parque Central. This is where the major department stores were located in Cuba's heyday before

1959. They remained open throughout the Revolution, each year growing more dour and minimalist in what they sold until, by the mid-1990s, their shelves were bare. Their vitality is coming back, however, and both streets are thronged again with shoppers hoping to find something worthwhile to buy with their pesos and dollars. Foreigners will find little of interest among the peso stores, as the Cuban-made items for sale here are for the most part shoddy in the extreme. But several department stores have reopened, stocked with imported goods for dollars.

If you need toiletries and general supplies, head for any of the smaller **Tiendas Panamericanos** that serve Cubans with dollars. You'll find them all over Havana, including at the foot of the FOCSA building on Calle 17 e/ M y N in Vedado.

MUSIC AND MUSICAL INSTRUMENTS

You'll find cassettes and CDs for sale at every turn, at rates comparable to the US and Western Europe. Few outlets offer bargains. Musicians in restaurants will offer to sell you cassette tapes of their music for US$5-15.

You can buy a quality guitar for US$200 or a full-size conga drum for US$100. But check that they're Cuban-made. You'll be amazed how many stores sell drums made in the US.

In Habana Vieja, **Longina,** Calle Obispo #360, tel. (62) 8371, offers a splendid collection of drums (a *bata*—set of three—costs about US$400), plus guitars, and even trombones (from China). It also features a large CD collection. The **Museo de la Música** at the junction of Calle Cuba and Monserrate in Habana Vieja, also has a wide selection of CDs.

In Miramar, check out the **Estudios de Grabaciones** (the recording studio of EGREN, the state recording agency), at Calle 18 between 1ra and 3ra. It has a large music store, tel. (24) 1473. However, for the widest selection, head to **Max Music,** Calle 33 #2003 e/ 20 y 22, Miramar, tel. (24) 3002, fax (24) 3006; or **Casa de la Música,** Calle 20 #3309 esq. 35. Both have huge collections of cassettes and CDs running the Cuban gamut, plus musical instruments. Instruments are sold upstairs in the Casa de la Música, but don't expect those drums (they're all

made in the US) or guitars (Japanese) to be Cuban. When I called by in May 1999, only the claves and maraccas were island-made.

Farther out, **Imágenes S.A.,** 5ta Av. #18008 esq. 182, Reparto Flores, Playa, tel. (33) 6136 fax (33) 6168, also has a large stock of CDs and cassettes, plus videos of live performances.

POSTERS

Posters make great souvenirs. Cuba is the world leader in political art, and you can find stunning examples for sale at ARTEX and similar stores throughout the city. Check out the shop at **Cinemateca,** Calle 23 e/ 10 y 12, Vedado—it sells superb film posters.

For reproduction prints, head to **Galería Exposición,** in Manzana de Gómez on Calle San Rafael, tel. (63) 8364. It has famous pictures of Guevara plus a huge range of posters and prints representing works by Cuba's best painters (US$3 to US$10).

RUM AND LIQUORS

Virtually every hotel store sells rum and other Cuban spirits. About one dozen distilleries operate in Cuba today, producing some 60 brands of rum. They vary widely (the worst can taste like paint thinner). Each brand generally has three types of rum: clear "white rum," labeled *Carta Blanca,* which is aged three years and costs less than US$5 a bottle; the more asserting "golden rum," labeled *Dorado* or *Carta Oro,* aged five years, and costing about US$6; and *"añejo,"* aged seven years and costing US$10 or more.

The best in all three categories are undoubtedly Havana Club's rums, topped only by Matusalem Añejo Superior, described by a panel of tasting experts as showing "a distinctive Scotch whisky-like character, with peaty and smoky aromas and flavors accented by orange-peel notes dry on the palate and long in the finish." A few limited production rums, such as Ron Santiago 45 Aniversario (US$20) and the 15-year-old Havana Club Gran Reserva (US$80) approach th harmony and finesse of fine Cognacs.

Two stores in Habana Vieja specialize in rum and offer tastings before you buy. The first i

Casa de Ron, above El Floridita restaurant at the top end of Calle Obispo, tel. (63) 1242. Open daily 10 a.m.-8 p.m. The second is the **Taberna del Galeón,** tel. (33) 8061, off the southeast corner of Plaza de Armas. The tavern—a favorite of tour groups—offers samplers in the hope that you'll purchase a bottle or two. But you can tipple upstairs in solitude, sampling from any of a zillion types of rum (and even Cuban whisky). Try the house special, *puñetazo,* a blend of rum, coffee, and mint.

Another preferred spot for a tipple, albeit a bit out of the way, is the **Fábrica de Ron Bocoy,** at Calzada de Cerro (Máximo Gómez), e/ Patrio y Auditor, Cerro, tel. (70) 5642. It makes the famous Bocoy and disappointing Legendario rums, and has a showroom upstairs and a separate bar for tasting the goods as a prelude to buying. You can tour the tiny factory, heady with the aromas of rum aging in centenarian casks. There's also a Casa del Tabaco. Open Mon.-Sat. 9 a.m.-5 p.m., Sunday 9 a.m.-2 p.m.

At press time, the **Museo de Ron** was under construction on Avenida del Puerto (San Pedro), e/ Churruca y Sol. It will feature the Bar Havana Club, where you can taste the wares after visiting the museum and mini-distillery. It will have a well-stocked store. Open 9:30 a.m.-6 p.m. (the bar will be open 11 a.m.-2 a.m.).

FOR CHILDREN

The past few years has seen a blossoming of stores selling children's wear and toys. Most **Tiendas Panamericanos** sell a limited range of kiddie's toys and supplies. In Habana Vieja, try the **Tienda Pedagógica** on Calle O'Reilly at Mercaderes. In Vedado, try the children's store in the gallery of the Hotel Habana Libre Tryp. Unfortunately, most of the toys are made in China and are of poor quality.

El Mundo de los Niños (Children's World) is a small, sparsely stocked children's store on Calle San Rafael and Oquendo, six blocks east of Calzada de Infanta, in Centro Habana.

CUBAN POSTER ART

Cuba's strongest claim to artistic fame is surely its unique poster art, created in the service of political revolution. Cuban poster art has blossomed, thanks to state support—a situation comparable to the United States in the 1930s, when the government paid artists to produce individual work.

The three leading poster-producing agencies—the Organization of Solidarity with the Peoples of Africa, Asia and Latin America; the Cuban Film Institute (ICAIC); and the Editora Política, the propaganda arm of the Cuban Communist Party—have produced more than 10,000 posters since 1959. Different state bodies create works for different audiences: artists of the Cuban Film Institute, for example, design posters for movies from Charlie Chaplin comedies to John Wayne westerns; Editora Política produces posters covering everything from AIDS awareness, baseball games, and energy conservation to telling children to do their homework.

Cuba's most talented painters and photographers rejected Soviet realism and developed their own unique graphic style influenced by Latin culture and the country's geography. The vibrant colors and lush imagery are consistent with the physical and psychological makeup of the country, such as the poster urging participation in the harvest, dripping with psychedelic images of fruit and reminiscent of a 1960s Grateful Dead poster.

Cuban posters are typically graceful, combining strong, simple concepts and sparse text with ingenious imagery and surprising sophistication. One poster, for example, warns of the dangers of smoking: a wisp of smoke curls upward to form a ghost-like skull.

The vast collection—acclaimed as "the single most focused, potent body of political graphics ever produced in this hemisphere"—provides a lasting visual commentary of the Revolution. Since the onset of the Special Period, however, output has plummeted due to a shortage of materials and money.

In the US, you can order posters—or a CD collection of posters—from the **Cuba Poster Project,** c/o Inkworks, 2827 7th St., Berkeley, CA 94710, tel. (510) 845-7111, fax (510) 845-6753, e-mail: lcushing@igc.apc.org.

CUBAN CIGARS

"There is no substitute for our tobacco any-where in the world. It's easier to make good cognac than to achieve the quality of Cuban tobacco."

—FIDEL CASTRO

It seems ironic that Cuba—scourge of the capitalist world—should have been compelled by history and geography to produce one of the most blatant symbols of capitalist wealth and power, the cigar. Yet it does so with pride. The unrivaled reputation of Cuban cigars as the best in the world transcends politics, transubstantiating a weed into an object capable of evoking rapture. And Cubans guard the unique reputation scrupulously.

"Havana" cigars are not only a source of hard currency—they're part and parcel of the national culture. Although Castro gave up smoking in 1985 (after what he called a "heroic struggle"),

Cubans still smoke 250 million cigars domestically every year. Another 160 million are exported annually through Habanos, S.A. Although some 20% of Cuban cigars are machine-made, the best are still hand-rolled.

A BIT OF HISTORY

This cigar tradition was first documented among the indigenous tribes by Christopher Columbus. The Taino Indians made monster cigars (at the very least, they probably kept the mosquitoes away) called *cohiba* (the word "cigar" originated from *sikar,* the Mayan word for smoking, which in Spanish became *cigarro*).

The popular habit of smoking cigars—as opposed to tobacco in pipes, first introduced to Europe by Columbus—began in Spain, where cigars made from Cuban tobacco were first made in Seville in 1717. Demand for higher quality cigars grew, and *Sevillas* (as Spanish cigars were called) were superseded by Cuban made cigars. King Ferdinand VI of Spain encouraged production—a state monopoly—in the Spanish colony. Soon, tobacco was Cuba's main export and received a boost after the Peninsula Campaign (1806-12) of the Napoleonic wars when British and French veterans returned home with the cigar habit. Cigar smoking soon became fashionable in their home countries.

By the mid-19th century, there were almost 1,300 cigar factories throughout Cuba.

A US Addiction

Israel Putnam, an officer in the British Army (later an American general in the Revolutionary War) introduced the cigar to North America in 1762 when he returned from Cuba to his home in Connecticut with a selection of Havana cigars. Soon Cuban cigars were being imported. Domestic cigar production also began, using Cuban tobacco (even the American cigars were known as Havanas, which by then had become a generic term). By the late 19th century, several US presidents practiced the habit and helped make cigar smoking a status symbol.

an early cigar

The demand fostered a full-fledged cigar-making industry in the United States (by 1905, there were 80,000 cigar-manufacturing businesses in the US, most of them mom-and-pop operations run by Cuban émigrés). But it was to Cuba that the cognoscenti looked for the finest cigars of all. "No lover of cigars can imagine the voluptuous pleasure of sitting in a café sipping slowly a strong magnificent coffee and smoking rhythmically those divine leaves of Cuba," wrote American pianist Arthur Rubinstein.

Bundled, Boxed, and Boycotted

Cuban cigars were sold originally in bundles covered with pigs' bladders, later in huge cedar chests. The banking firm of H. Upmann initiated export in cedar boxes in 1830, when it imported cigars for its directors in London. Later, the bank decided to enter the cigar business, and the embossed cedar box complete with colorful lithographic label became the standard form of packaging. Each specific brand evolved its own elaborate lithograph, while different sizes (and certain brands) even evolved their own box styles.

The Montecristo was the fashionable cigar of choice. In the 1930s, any tycoon or film director worth the name was seen with a whopping Montecristo A in his mouth (half of all the Havanas sold in the world in the 1930s were Montecristos, by which time much of Cuba's tobacco industry had passed into US ownership). Among the devotees of Cuban cigars was President Kennedy, who smoked Petit Upmans. In 1962, at the height of the Cuban missile crisis, Kennedy asked his press secretary, Pierre Salinger, to obtain as many Upmans as he could. Next day, reported Salinger, Kennedy asked him how many he had found. Twelve hundred, replied his aide. Kennedy then pulled out and signed the decree establishing a trade embargo with Cuba. Ex-British premier Winston Churchill also stopped smoking Havanas and started smoking Jamaican cigars, but after a time he forgot about politics and went back to Havanas. His brand was Romeo y Julieta.

The embargo dealt a crushing blow to Cuba's cigar industry. Castro nationalized the cigar industry and founded a state monopoly, Cubatabaco. Many dispossessed cigar factory owners immigrated to the Dominican Republic, Mexico, Venezuela, and Honduras, where they started up again, often using the same brand names they had owned in Cuba (today, the Dominican Republic produces 47% of the handmade cigars imported into the US). Experts agree, however, that these foreign "Cuban" brands are inferior to their Havana counterparts.

At the time of the Revolution, about 1,000 brands and sizes of Havanas existed. There are now about 35 brands and 500 cigar varieties. Only eight factories make handmade export-quality cigars in Cuba today, compared with 120 at the beginning of the century. All cigar factories produce various brands. Some factories specialize in particular flavors, others in particular sizes—of which there are no fewer than 60 standard variations, with minor variations from brand to brand.

THE PRODUCTION PROCESS

You'll forever remember the pungent aroma of a cigar factory, a visit to which is de rigueur. The factories, housed in fine old colonial buildings, remain much as they were in the mid-19th century. Though now officially known by ideologically sound names, they're still commonly referred to by their prerevolutionary names, which are displayed on old signs outside. Each specializes in a number of cigar brands of a particular flavor (the government assigns to certain factories the job of producing particular brands). And revolutionary slogans exhort workers to maintain strict quality—"Quality is respect for people."

From Leaf to Cigar

The tobacco leaves, which arrive from the fields in dry sheets, are first moistened and stripped.

The leaves are then graded by color and strength (each type of cigar has a recipe). A blender mixes the various grades of leaves, which then go to the production room, where each *tabaquero* and *tabaquera* receives enough tobacco to roll approximately 100 cigars for the day.

The rollers work in large rooms, where they sit at rows of *galeras* (workbenches) resembling old-fashioned school desks. Two workers sit at each desk, with piles of loose tobacco leaves at their sides. The rollers take great pride in their work, and it's a treat to marvel at their manual artistry and dexterity. The rollers' indispensable tool is a *chaveta*, a rounded, all-purpose knife for smoothing and cutting leaves, tamping loose tobacco, "circumcising the tips," and sometimes banging a welcome to factory visitors on their desks in rhythmic chorus like a percussion orchestra. Most workers are born to their tasks, following in the footsteps of other family members, carrying on their traditional skills from one generation to the next.

While they work, a *lector* (reader) reads aloud from a strategically positioned platform or high chair. Morning excerpts—beginning promptly at 8 a.m.—are read from the *Granma* newspaper; in the afternoon, the *lector* reads from historical or political books, or short stories and novels (Alexandre Dumas, Agatha Christie, and Ernest Hemingway are favorites; Dumas' novel *The Count of Monte Cristo* was such a hit in the 19th century that it lent its name to the famous Montecristo cigar). The practice dates back to 1864, when the unique institution was set up to alleviate boredom and help the cause of worker education. *Lectores* are auditioned and hired on their reading ability, and the tradition has for more than a century carried great political weight, while serving to produce astutely versed workers. Says city architect Mario Coyula: "In Cuba before the Revolution, men who were completely illiterate knew the classics, the plays of Shakespeare, and most modern novels. And even though they could not read or write, they were well versed in current political issues."

Rolling the Cigar

The *torcedore* (cigar roller) fingers his or her leaves and, according to texture and color, chooses two to four filler leaves, which are laid end to end and gently yet firmly rolled into a tube, then enveloped by the binder leaves to make a "bunch."

The rough-looking "bunch" is then placed with nine others in a small wooden mold that is screwed down to press each cigar into a solid cylinder. Next, the *tabaquero* selects a wrapper leaf, which he or she trims to size. The "bunch" is then laid at an angle across the wrapper, which is stretched and rolled around the "bunch," overlapping with each turn. A tiny quantity of flavorless tragapanth gum (made from Swiss pine trees) is used to glue the *copa* down. Now the *tabaquero* rolls the cigar, applying pressure with the flat of the *chaveta*. Finally, a piece of wrapper leaf the size and shape of a quarter is cut to form the cap; it is glued and twirled into place and the excess is trimmed.

The whole process takes about five minutes. Hence, a good cigar maker can roll about 100 medium-sized cigars a day (the average for the largest cigars is far less).

Cigar rollers serve a nine-month apprenticeship (each factory has its own school). Many fail. Those who succeed graduate slowly from making petit corona cigars to the larger and specialized sizes. Rollers are paid piece rates based on the number of cigars they produce. They receive on average 350-400 pesos for a six-day workweek. In addition, they can puff as much as they wish on the fruits of their labor while working.

Today, the majority of rollers are women. Prior to the Revolution, only men rolled cigars; the leaves were selected by women, who often sorted them on their thighs, giving rise to the famous myth about cigars being "rolled on the dusky thighs of Cuban maidens."

And So to Market

The roller ties cigars of the same size and brand into bundles—*media ruedas* (half-wheels)—of 50 using a colored ribbon. These are then fumigated in a vacuum chamber. Quality is determined by a *revisador* (inspector), according to eight criteria, such as length, weight, firmness, smoothness of wrappers, and whether the ends are cleanly cut. *Catadores* (professional smokers) then blind test the cigars for aroma, draw, and burn, the relative importance of each varying according to whether the cigar is a slim panatel (draw is paramount) or a fat robusto (flavor being more important). The *catadores* taste only in the morning and rejuvenate their taste buds with sugarless tea.

Once fumigated, cigars are placed in cool cabinets for three weeks to settle fermentation and remove any excess moisture. The cigars are then graded according to color and then shade within a particular color category.

A trademark paper band is then put on by an *anillado*. (A Dutchman, Gustave Bock, introduced the band last century to distinguish his cigars from other Havanas. Later, bands served to prevent gentlemen smokers from staining their white evening gloves.)

Finally, the cigars are laid in pinewood boxes, with the lightest cigar on the right and the darkest on the left (cigars range from the very mild, greenish-brown *double claro* to the very strong, almost black *oscuro*). The boxes are then inspected for alignment and uniformity. A thin leaf of cedar wood is laid on top to maintain freshness, and the box is sealed with a green-and-white label guaranteeing the cigars are genuine Havanas, or *puros Habanos* (today *puro* is a synonym for cigar).

VISITING HAVANA'S CIGAR FACTORIES

The five major cigar factories in Havana (altogether, there are 42 throughout Cuba) all now welcome visitors. Unfortunately, the tours are not well organized and often crowded with tour groups, few of whom have any genuine appreciation for cigars. Explanations of tobacco processes and manufacturing procedures are also sparse. Tours usually bypass the tobacco preparations and instead begin in the *galeras* (rolling rooms), then pass to the quality-control methods. Visitors therefore miss out on seeing the stripping, selecting, and dozens of other processes that contribute to producing a handmade cigar.

Although the government has considered banning tours (it did so briefly in 1997 at the Partagas and La Corona factories), the income comes in handy. A portion is given to the factories and used to improve workers' conditions.

You can book tours through tour desks in major hotels or call the factories direct. Be sure to book ahead, for every entrance is guarded by

a cigar factory in Havana, circa 1900

an ever-present, stern-faced female concierge determined to stop you from entering. Writes Nancy Stout: "These women are tougher than the civil guard nearby, in his green khakis with a tie-on red armband and pistol around his waist."

Habanos S.A. has its headquarters at **Empresa Cubana del Tabaco,** O'Reilly #104 e/ Tacón y Mercaderes, Habana Vieja, tel. (62) 5463; open 7:45 a.m.-3:45 p.m.

Fábrica La Corona, Calle Agramonte #106, e/ Refugio y Colón, Habana Vieja, tel./fax (62) 6173, is open to the public Mon.-Sat. 7 a.m.-5 p.m.

Fábrica Partagas, Calle Industria #520, e/ Dragones y Barcelona, Habana Vieja, tel. (62) 4604, offers guided tours daily at 10 a.m. and 2 p.m. (US$10).

Fábrica H. Upmann, one block west of Partagas, at Calle Amistad #407, e/ Dragones y Barcelona, Centro Habana, tel. (62) 0081, is open Mon.-Fri. 8 a.m.-4 p.m. for call-by visitors. Tours are offered at 10:30 a.m. and 1:30 p.m. (US$10)

Fábrica Romeo y Julieta, on Padre Varela e/ Desague y Peñal Verno, Centro Habana, tel. (78) 1058, is open for visits by permit only, Mon.-Fri. 7 a.m.-4 p.m. Permission must be requested from the Empresa Cubana del Tabaco, O'Reilly #104 e/ Tacón y Mercaderes, Habana Vieja, tel. (62) 5463.

Fábrica El Laguito, Calle 146 #2302, Cubanacán, tel. (21) 2213, allows visits by permit only. Permission must be requested from the Empresa Cubana del Tabaco, O'Reilly #104 e/ Tacón y Mercaderes, Habana Vieja, tel. (62) 5463.

Organized Tours

Cuban Adventures, 4823 White Rock Circle, Suite H, Boulder, CO 80301-3260, tel. (303) 530-9275, fax (303) 530-9275, e-mail: CopaBob@ aol.com, website: www.clubhavana.com, operates cigar tours to Cuba, including tours of the legendary cigar factories. Likewise, **Wings of the World Travel,** 1200 William St. #706, Buffalo, NY 14240-0706; or 1636 3rd Ave. #232, New York, NY 10128, tel. (800) 465-8687, fax (416) 486-4001, offers a Cuban Cigar Adventure.

In the UK, Havana cigar merchant **Peter Lloyd,** 25 Terrace Rd., Aberystwyth SY23 1NP, Wales, tel. (01970) 612-254, e-mail: a_e_lloyd@compuserve.com, website: www.cubawe1.com; and **Captivating Cuba** collaboratively offer cigar tours (the trips are fully hosted in Cuba, so US citizens can legally join; from US$980). **Intro-Cuba,** 500 High Rd., Woodford Green, Essex IG8 0PN, tel. (181) 505-9656, fax (181) 559-0215, offers a similar 14-day guided Cigar Connoisseur Tour.

SHOPPING AND BUYING

Cigars are among the most coveted Cuban products for tourists. Quality cigars can be bought at virtually every restaurant, hotel, and shop that welcomes tourists. There are now more than two dozen **Casas de Tabaco** throughout the city, plus scores of other cigar outlets. The best shops now offer the type of selection previously only available in top stores in London or Geneva—everything from cedar boxes of 100 Hoyos de Monterrey Double Coronas to five-packs of Corona Lanceros. A good bet is to combine your purchase with a visit to a cigar factory.

The quality of Cuban cigars declined significantly in the mid-1990s as the government set to

CIGAR BOX CRYPTOGRAPHY: READING THE CODE

On the underside of every box of cigars is a code, printed as a series of letters. If you know the code, it can tell you a fair amount about the cigars inside. Even if you're not attuned to every nuance of specific factories, you can still determine at least the provenance and date of cigars, which vary markedly.

The first two or three letters usually refer to the factory where the cigars were made (for example, FPG refers to the Partagas factory); the next four letters give the date of manufacture (OASC, for example, means 0697—June 1997—though the 0 in front of single-digit months is often omitted).

Newly created cigars will have a different code.

DATE CODE

1	N
2	I
3	V
4	E
5	L
6	A
7	C
8	U
9	S
0	O

FACTORY CODE

BM	Romeo y Julieta (Briones Montolo)
CB	El Rey del Mundo (Carlos Balino)
EL	El Laguito
FR	La Corona (Fernandez Rey)
FPG	Partagas (Francisco Perez German)
HM	Heroes de Moncada
JM	H. Upmann (José Martí)
PL	Por Larrañaga (Juan Cano Sainz)

boost production (160 million handmade premium cigars were produced in 1998, more than double the number produced in 1995). By 1999 the quality and consistency had recovered, although the government was aiming for 240 mil-

MADE IN HABANA, CUBA

In addition, there are styles, sizes, and brands of cigars that have not been made in Cuba since shortly after the Revolution. They're the most valuable (a Belinda corona from the late 1930s will sell for $100 or more). It's not unusual for a box of 100 Montecristo No. 1s from the late 1950s to sell for $4,500 or more. Connoisseurs opt for "cabinet cigars," which come in undecorated cedar boxes.

Fatter cigars—the choice of connoisseurs—are more fully flavored and smoke more smoothly and slowly than those with smaller ring gauges. As a rule, darker cigars are also more full-bodied and sweeter. The expertise and care expressed in the cigar factory determines how well a cigar burns and tastes, and a visit to a factory is a must for anyone wishing to gain a true appreciation of Havana cigars.

ion cigars in 2000. As such, prices have increased in recent years. Accordingly, reported the June 1999 issue of *Cigar Aficionado:* "Where-is not too long ago one could find a box of 25 Partagas Serie D No. 4s for US$68 or a box of Punch Double Coronas for US$86, cigar lovers can now expect to pay about US$100 to US$150, respectively, for such cigars. On the right side, cigars purchased in Havana are anywhere from one fourth to one half the price of similar cigars in London or Geneva and about 15 percent less than prices in Spain."

If you're buying for speculation, buy the best. The only serious collectors' market in cigars is in prerevolutionary cigars, according to Anwer Bati in *The Cigar Companion.* Older cigars produced before the 1959 Revolution are commonly described as "pre-Castro." Those made before President Kennedy declared the US trade embargo against Cuba in February 1962 are "pre-embargo." Pre-Castro or pre-embargo cigars are printed with MADE IN HAVANA-CUBA on the bottom of the box instead of the standard HECHO EN CUBA used today. Since 1985, handmade Cuban cigars have carried the Cubatabaco stamp plus a factory mark and, since 1989, the legend "Hecho en Cuba. Totalmente a Mano" (Made in Cuba. Completely by Hand). If it reads "Hecho a Mano," the cigars are most likely hand-*finished* i.e., the wrapper was put on by hand) rather than and*made*. If its states only "Hecho en Cuba," they are assuredly machine-made.

Cigars, when properly stored, continue to ferment and mature in their boxes—an aging process similar to that of good wines. Rules on the topic don't really exist, but many experts claim that prime cigars are those aged for six to eight years. Everyone agrees that a cigar should be smoked either within three months of manufacture or not for at least a year (the interim is known as a "period of sickness").

Several of Cuba's 42 factories might be producing any one brand *simultaneously,* so quality can vary markedly even though the label is the same. Experts consider cigars produced in Havana's La Corona, El Laguito, and Romeo y Julieta factories the best. The source is marked in code on the underside of the box. The year of production is also indicated there—remember, as with wines, the quality of cigars varies from year to year.

In 1998, the Cuban government upped the export allowance to US$2,000 worth of cigars with documentation (you'll need receipts). If you don't have your receipts, Cuban customs permits only two boxes. In 1999, the US government also upped *its* allowance: persons with licenses to travel to Cuba may purchase US$185 of Cuban cigars or other goods, but the cigars may only be purchased in Cuba.

Street Deals

Street deals are no deal. Everywhere you walk in Havana, *jiniteros* will offer you cigars at discount prices. You'll be tempted by what seems the deal of the century. Forget it! You might get lucky and get the real thing, but a huge percentage are low-quality, machine-made cigars sold falsely as top-line cigars to unsuspecting tourists. Don't be taken in by the sealed counterfeit box, either. Fortunately, the crackdown by police initiated in early 1999 has significantly reduced the problem. (*Cigar Aficionado,* which estimates that up to 90% of "Cuban" cigars sold in the US are fakes, also reports, however, that international crime syndicates are muscling in on the counterfeit act.)

You can buy inferior domestic cigars—called "torpedoes"—for about one peso (US$1) in bars and restaurants and on the street.

Where to Buy

There are hundreds of outlets for cigars in Havana, but most shops have poorly informed and uninterested clerks who know little about *tabacos* (the Cuban term for *habanos*). Your best bet if you're a serious smoker is to buy at a serious outlet. Most of the upscale hotels now feature *casas del tabaco,* notably the Hotel Parque Central and the Hostal de Habana in Habana Vieja; the Hotel Meliá Cohiba, Hotel Habana Libre, Hotel Riviera, and Hotel Nacional in Vedado; as well as a score of others.

Most shops sell by the box only. Due to high demand, cigars are often on back order. For example, Cohibas were rare abroad in 1996 (one major London cigar merchant told me that the Cubans are holding back supply to raise prices). Prices can vary up to 20% from store to store, so shop around. If one store doesn't have what you desire, another surely will. You should inspect your cigars before committing to a purchase. Most shops don't allow this, but the best shops do.

My list of outstanding cigar shops would include eight endorsed by *Cigar Aficionado:*

Habana Vieja: La Casa del Habanos in the Partagas factory at Industria #520, e/ Barcelona y Dragones in Habana Viejo, tel. (33) 8060, has a massive walk-in humidor and accounted for the largest percentage of the 14 million cigars sold by Cuban tobacconists to tourists in 1998. The store has a front room catering to the bus-loads of tourists; hidden away to the rear is a lounge with a narrow humified walk-in cigar showcase for serious smokers. Manager Abel Díaz oversees the service-oriented staff.

Palacio del Tabaco, in the Fábrica La Corona at Agramonte #106, e/ Colón y Refugio, tel. (33) 8389, offers rare cigars such as figurados and double coronas. It has a small bar.

La Casa del Habano, below the Museo de Tabaco at Mercaderes #120, esq. Obrapia, tel. (61) 5795, has a selection fairly limited in range but high in quality. There's no smoking on-site.

La Casa del Tabaco y Ron, at Calle Obispo esq. Monserrate, tel. (33) 8911, is to the rear of this rum store. The sales staff is knowledgeable and friendly, and prices are the best in town. You can smoke upstairs in the bar.

La Casa del Habano, in the newly opened Hostal Habana at Calle Mercaderas esq. Lamparilla, tel. (62) 9682, aims (as does the hotel) to lure serious cigar smokers. It offers a large range of quality cigars and a sumptuous smoker's lounge with TV and plump leather seating. It was gearing up to open at press time.

La Casa del Tabaco Parque Central, at Neptuno e/ Prado y Zulueta, tel. (66) 6627, a small outlet in the recently opened Hotel Parque Central, has "the potential to be one of the best." Manager Emilio Amin Nasser oversees the friendly staff, and the hotel offers one of the finest smoking lounges in Cuba upstairs.

Vedado: At press time, Habaguanex was restoring an old mansion opposite the Hotel Victoria, on Calle 19 in Vedado, and converting it into a Casa del Habano. It is sure to be the best in Vedado. (Until then, try the **Casa del Tabaco** in the forecourt of the Hotel Habana Libre Tryp and those in the Hotel Nacional and Hotel Meliá Cohiba.

Playa (Miramar and Beyond): La Casa del Habana, at the corner of Avenida 5ra and 16, tel. (24) 1185, is perhaps the flashiest place in town. This impressive colonial mansion recently received a facelift that includes stained-glass windows of cigar label motifs. It boasts a vast humidor, executive rooms, bar and lounge, and good service. Manager Pedro Gonzalez will be happy to offer his recommendations.

La Casa del Habano, in Marina Hemingway on Avenida 5ta y 248 in the Santa Fe district, tel. (24) 1151, has "a good selection of cabinet cigars" plus "helpful and friendly" young staff. No smoking on-site.

Suburbs: A new **La Casa del Habano** was due to open in mid-1999 at Avenida 5ta, e/ 188 y 192, tel. (24) 5700, to be run by Enrique Mons, whom *Cigar Aficionado* magazine has termed the maestro of cigar merchants in Havana," and who for most of the 1970s and '80s was in charge of quality control for the Cuban cigar industry.

FURTHER READING

For a comprehensive synopsis of individual cigar brands and types, refer to the *Cigar Companion:* *A Connoisseur's Guide,* by Anwer Bati (Running Press, Philadelphia, PA), or *Cigar Aficionado* (M. Shanker Communications Inc., 387 Park Ave. S., New York, NY 10016). Two books—*Holy Smoke,* by Guillermo Cabrera Infante, and *Cuban Counterpoint,* by Fernando Ortíz—tell the tale of Cuban cigars.

To learn more on the production process, refer to Nancy Stout's *Habanos* (Rozzoli, New York, 1997), a splendid coffee-table book on the subject.

A complete range of books about Cuban cigars is available at a discount online at www.cuba-books.com—which also retails humidors and Cuban cigars.

ACCOMMODATIONS

Outside Cuba, all telephone and fax numbers given here need to be preceded by 53-7, the codes for Cuba and Havana respectively.

Havana is blessed with accommodations of every stripe. The motley and dowdy hostelries of a few years ago have been upstaged by a blossoming of deluxe and boutique hotels, and skyrocketing demand has fostered the arrival of foreign name-brand hotels (50/50 joint ventures with Cuban state-owned tourism agencies), with more coming online every year. Havana also has some appallingly dreary options, and although the cash-strapped government is working hard to upgrade its hotels, even the best are second-rate by global standards. Upkeep and lousy management are the main problems, so that hotels rapidly deteriorate and a newly constructed or renovated hotel today might appear rundown a year or two later. Says *Cigar Aficionado:* "A number of hotels in Havana still look like low-income housing or urban crack houses." You can go horribly wrong in your choice of hotel.

Cuban hotels are graded by the conventional star system, but the ratings are far too gener-

ous. Although Havana on the eve of the Revolution boasted a fine stock of international-standard hotels, most of them spanking new, they were allowed to deteriorate. Following the Revolution, virtually all hotel construction was for the use of Cubans. Most such hotels rate as one- or two-star on the international scale and are usually dreary cement post-Stalinist properties described as having "all the plaintiveness of an Olympic facility two decades after the games have ended." Many of these Bulgarian-designed Bauhaus structures have been given facelifts, with potted plants, fresh paint, and new furnishings. Others, however, retain lumpy beds and dour utility furniture. Tiled floors are the norm.

In lower-grade properties, rooms are generally small by North American standards. Lighting tends to be subdued (usually because the wattage is low). Virtually every hotel room has a/c. Most hotels have both a "regular" restaurant (generally with buffet service) and a specialty restaurant. A swimming pool is usual, most often with a bar. Hotels also supply towels and soap, but only the most deluxe ones provide shampoo, conditioner, and body lotion. Bring your own sink plug, especially for less expensive accommodations.

Hotels built in recent years reflect standards necessary to attract a foreign clientele (most would be rated three- or four-star). Since 1994, when six hospitality enterprises were created, niche hotels have begun to appear, including many five-star deluxe properties. International hotel companies have made inroads in joint ventures with the Cuban hotel groups. However, none of Havana's so-called luxury hotels—designated as such below by virtue of pricing—would be considered deluxe hotels by international standards. Even the more upscale hotels are not entirely free of Cuban quirks. All of which makes the unduly high prices doubly annoying.

Fawlty Towers?

Cuba's hotel foibles conjure up déjà vu for viewers of Fawlty Towers, the BBC's hilarious sitcom. Most hotels have a few petty annoyances. For example, after a hot, sticky day, you return to your room to find no hot water—a plight for which you're supposed to get 10% off your bill. No running water at all? Twenty percent off. Ah! The water is running—but, alas, there's no plug. In theory, you're entitled to a well-defined refund for each such contingency. A sorry mattress is worth a 10% discount, according to the State Prices Commission.

The number of faults is usually in inverse proportion to price: at the cheapest places, you'll find gurgling pipes, no toilet seat (quite likely), no bathplugs (virtually guaranteed), and sunken mattresses (guaranteed). You'll fare much better at the newer, more expensive hotels. In bare-bone hotels, even hot water may only be tepid—and available at certain times of day. Shower units are often powered by electric heater elements, which you switch on for the duration of your shower. Beware! It's easy to give yourself a shock from any metal objects nearby.

Though many of the staff are mustard-keen, far too many hotels have abysmal service. (Castro agreed: "Cubans are the most hospitable, friendly, and attentive people in the world. But as soon as you put a waiter's uniform on them, they become terrible.") Sometimes the opposite is true. Chambermaids, for example, often rearrange your belongings until you can no longer find them—which may be the whole point (I've "lost" several items of clothing this way).

To be fair, things are improving. Cuba is aggressively addressing the deficiencies and has set up hotel management training schools run by Austrians—world leaders in the hospitality industry. However, hotel management still leaves much to be desired, very few Cubans seem to care about their clients or jobs, and there rarely seems to be a manager on-site. It's enough to make you wonder if Basil Fawlty is running the show.

Which District

Location is important in choosing your hotel.

In **Habana Vieja,** you're in the heart of the old city, within walking distance of nearly all the sights there are to see. Here you'll find two Spanish-style posadas, two exquisite colonial palaces-turned-hotel, and (around Parque Central) a fistful of turn-of-the-century hotels that have all been, or are being, upgraded.

Vedado's mid-20th-century offerings tend to be larger and still well-situated for sightseeing. There are several first-class hotels from which to choose. In eastern Vedado, you'll be in the midst of Havana's reenergized night life, with Old Havana a 30-minute walk along the Malecón. Farther out, in western Vedado, are the Riviera and the tony Cohiba, beloved by cigar-chomping businessmen. Vedado also has plenty of casas particulares (private rooms for rent in family-run homes). Habana Vieja is a 10- to 15-minute taxi ride away.

Playa (Miramar), which is a considerable distance from sites and attractions, has a number of hotels popular with tour groups, such as the Comodoro, Copacabana, and Kohly, plus an increasing number of moderate to upscale business hotels. But all are far away from the main tourist sights, leading to whopping taxi bills. You're well over a one-hour walk to Old Havana and will need wheels to get around. Habana Vieja is a 15- to 20-minute taxi ride away.

The Suburbs are represented by the hotels of Ciudad Panamericano and Playas del Este. Avoid these at all costs unless you're determined to have a second-rate beach holiday (in Ciudad Panamericano, you'll find yourself out on a limb, without even a beach to amuse you).

Prices

Hotels in this book are classified as: **Budget** (less than US$35), **Inexpensive** (US$35-60), **Moderate** (US$60-85), **Expensive** (US$85-110), **Very Expensive** (US$110-150), and **Luxury** (US$150 and above). Each price category is divided by district: **Habana Vieja, Centro Habana, Vedado, Miramar,** and **Suburban Havana.** All prices refer to double rooms, high season.

Your accommodation will be your biggest-ticket item in Cuba. Prices have shot up in recent years, and Havana no longer represents a bargain. Most hotels are vastly overpriced, so it pays to do your research.

Prices at many hotels vary for low and high season. Usually low season is May-June and Sept.-Nov., high season is Dec.-April and July-August. However, this varies. Some hotels have four rates, adding peak high season and low low season. Usually, single rooms cost about 20% less than double rooms. Cuba imposes no room tax or service charge to guests' bills (this may change, however). It pays to book through a travel agent such as Cuba Travel, tel. (66) 865-298 (Mexico) or (310) 842-4148 (US answerphone), e-mail: info@cubatravel.com.mx, website: www.cubatravel.com.mx, or any of Cubatour's or Havanatur's international representatives, since Cuban hotels offer discounts as much as 50 percent to wholesalers. Canadians and Europeans can keep costs down by buying a charter package tour with airfare and hotel included (tour operators usually buy hotel rooms in bulk and pass the savings on to you). They represent tremendous bargains, although standards vary widely. If you book your hotels from abroad, you'll be issued hotel vouchers that you exchange upon arrival in Cuba for a coupon (usually through the Cubatur represenative at the airport) or present at your hotel.

There are few options for accommodations below US$35. The few that exist serve a primarily Cuban clientele and tend to get full. They usually have two prices: a peso price for Cubans and a dollar price for foreigners. See the caveats under "Fawlty Towers?" above. (The following budget hotels, shown on some maps and listed in some guidebooks, were closed at press time: Hotel Bristol, Hotel Real, and Hotel Nueva Isla.)

The best way to keep costs down is to rent a *casa particular,* a private room in a family home.

What Type of Acccommodation?

Camping: The Cuban term *campismo* refers to basic huts at established sites. There are no campsites in or around Havana.

Peso Hotels: Peso hotels cater to Cubans and are extremely cheap—usually the equivalent of less than US$1 for Cubans, who pay in pesos. Most are run by Islazul, which has finagled things so that tourists now pay in dollar equivalent. Although a few are quite attractive, most are dour by Western standards. The worst are little more than mildewed nests of foul bedclothes.

You cannot book peso hotels through any state tourism organization; you will have to do this face-to-face in Cuba. Most peso hotels refuse to accept foreigners; others charge a minimal dollar rate; some will take your pesos. Don't believe it if you're told that a pesos-only hotel is full. That's a standard answer given to foreigners. Be persistent. Be creative. Be nice about it. If the receptionist warms to you, a room can magically be found. But don't count on it, as things have tightened up in recent years.

Aparthotels: Aparthotels are also a bargain, offering rooms with kitchens or kitchenettes (pots and pans and cutlery are provided), and sometimes small suites furnished with sofas, tables and chairs. One- or two-bedroom units are the norm. Aparthotels are particularly economical for families. Most are characterless: it's all a matter of taste. Many are linked to regular hotels, giving you access to broader facilities.

Villas, Apartments, and *Protocolos:* Self-catering apartments are available for rent, as are fully staffed villas, including *protocolos—*special houses reserved for foreign dignitaries. Most of the *protocolos* are splendid mansions in the Cubanacán region.

Private Rooms: My favorite way to go is to seek out a *casa particular* (literally, private house), a room in a family home. Since the triumph of the Revolution, the Urban Reform Law explicitly prohibited the rent of housing, despite which *casas particulares* began to blossom in the mid-1990s following the restrictions on having Cuban guests in hotel rooms (foreign guests turned to renting private rooms for their liaisons). In 1996 the law was reformed: Cubans are now permitted to rent out up to two rooms. A new tax code was also introduced, regulating *casas particulares* to ensure that those renting out their houses "fulfill their social duty" by paying taxes, which vary according to district (US$100 monthly in a nontourist zone, and US$200 in a tourist zone, plus a yearly percentage of their earnings extra). Your host now must record your passport number and, ostensibly, the particulars of any of your guests.

Since legalization, *casas particulares* have sprouted like mushrooms on a damp log; you'll have no difficulty finding a place. You'll not be five minutes in the city before being approached by touts working on commission. Many Habaneros are quick to recommend a particular place. Since conditions vary remarkably, it's important not to agree to rent until you've checked a place out and compared it with others.

The going rate is US$20-40, often with breakfast and dinner included. Some families are willing to vacate their entire homes on a moment's notice! Heavy taxation (as intended) has forced many *casas particulares* to close, and the situation is fluid.

Reservations

Officially, it's *de rigueur* to book at least two nights' accommodation prior to arrival, which you can do abroad through accredited tour agencies. Since 1997, Cuba immigration officials have been more assiduous in ensuring that arriving visitors have prebooked rooms. You can give a private address if you have reservations at a *casa particular*. (Tourist visas state that tourists must receive express permission from immigration authorities if wishing to stay at other than a hotel or "authorized accommodation," which includes *casas particulares*. Some immigration officials don't seem clear about this and attempt to force tourists to book a hotel room regardless. If this happens to you, point out that registered *casa particulares* pay taxes and are legal; stick to your guns!) Otherwise, expect to be directed to the tourist information booth to secure a hotel reservation.

Havana is in the midst of a tourism boom, and many hotels are often fully booked (including the less expensive hotels that also cater to Cubans). Finding a hotel room without a reservation can pose a problem, especially during peak winter season. The Christmas and New Year's season is particularly busy. It's wise to secure accommodation in advance.

HOW ABOUT A LITTLE CUBAN PIED-À-TERRE?

Think Cuba is such a fine place to visit that it might also be a great place to live (though perhaps just for part of the year)? Although Cubans are still barred from buying and selling houses, foreigners *can* now purchase a piece of the action. Forget that old mansion you've been coveting. At press time, only foreign residents in Cuba can buy such homes, and then only in the names of their Cuban girlfriends or spouses. But remarkably, the Cuban government is now building condominiums for sale to foreigners.

At press time, at least five separate developments were underway in the Miramar and Siboney districts, plus a separate development at Playas del Este. Starting prices were US$67,000. At the upper end of the market are the condominiums at **Monte Carlo Palacio,** a ritzy, spanking new block of apartments on Avenida 5ra between 44 and 46, selling for more than US$200,000 apiece. Also check out Edificio Habana Palace, on Calle 42 at Avenida 3ra.

For information, contact **Re/Max,** Avenida 7ma esq. 14, Miramar, tel. (24) 5005, fax (24) 5006, e-mail: information@realestate.cuba, website: www.realestatecuba.com; or **Real Inmobiliaria,** Calle 3 #3407 esq. 36, Miramar, tel. (24) 9871, fax (24) 9875, e-mail: realin@colombus.cu.

A handy resource is *Living and Investing in the New Cuba,* by Christopher Howard, Costa Rica Books, Suite #1 SJO 981, P.O. Box 025216, Miami, FL 33102-5216, e-mail: crbooks@racsa.co.cr, website: www.costaricabooks.com.

Don't rely on mail to make reservations—it could take several months to confirm. Call direct, send a fax or e-mail, or have a Cuban state tour agency or a tour operator abroad make your reservation. Normally, a deposit will not be required.

Cuban Hotel Groups

Six Cuban hotel entities compete for business (operating in cooperative management agreements with foreign hotel groups). The corporations all publish directories available through Cuban tourist offices abroad. You may need to double-check telephone numbers—they change frequently.

Cubanacán, Avenida 7ma #6624 e/ 66 y 70, Miramar, tel. (24) 6316, fax (24) 6313, e-mail: dirmark@reserva.cha.cyt.cu, website: www.cubanacan.cu, has about 12 hotels in Havana, from modest to luxury.

Gaviota, Edificio La Marina, Avenida del Puerto y Justiz, Habana Vieja, tel. (66) 6765, fax (33) 2780, e-mail: gaviota@nwgaviot.gav.cma.net, website: www.gaviota.cubaweb.cu. Gaviota (a branch of the Cuban military!), owns three three-star hotels in Havana.

Gran Caribe, Avenida 7ma #4210 e/ 42 y 44, Miramar, tel. (24) 0575, fax (24) 0565, e-mail: armando@grancaribe.gca.cma.net, has mostly top-end establishments, including the landmark Hotel Nacional.

Horizontes, Calle 23 #156 e/ N y O, Vedado, tel. (33) 4042, fax (33) 3161, e-mail: crh@horizontes.ht.cma.net, website: www.horizontes.cu, has nine hotels in Havana, in the two- and three-star categories.

Hoteles Habaguanex, Calle Oficios #110 e/ Lamparilla y Amargura, Habana Vieja, tel. (33) 8693, fax (33) 8697, operates four historic hotels in Habana Vieja, with more being added.

Islazul, Malecón y G, Vedado, tel. (57) 1286, fax (33) 3458, operates basic hotels primarily for national tourism, but they also accept tourists.

Hotel Booking Agents

For US citizens, Cuba Travel, tel. (66) 865-298 (Mexico), (310) 842-4148 (US answerphone), e-mail: info@cubatravel.com.mx, website: www.cubatravel.com.mx, can handle bookings. Licensed travelers should book through Tico Travel or Marazul Tours.

In the UK, **Regent Holidays,** 15 John St., Bristol BS1 2HR, tel. (0272) 211-711, fax (0272) 254-866, acts as a booking agent for hotels throughout Cuba.

Havanatur's international offices also act as booking agents.

Security

Most hotel lobbies now have MININT security agents in dark suits with microphones tucked in their ears. They were posted following the spate of bombs planted in Havana's hotels in 1997 and serve to prevent a repeat performance, but also do double duty to keep Cubans from slipping upstairs with foreign guests. Unfortunately, they lend a prison-like atmosphere and are not above bothering hotel guests and their legitimate friends.

Theft is an issue, especially in budget hotels. Most tourist hotels have safe-deposit boxes at the front desk or in individual guest rooms. Be sure to use it for any valuables, especially your passport, camera, and money. Clothing is often stolen. Consider locking *all* your items in your suitcase each time you leave your room. Before accepting a room, ensure that the door is secure and that your room can't be entered by someone climbing in through the window. *Always* lock your door.

Guest Cards

Upon registering, you'll be issued a *tarjeta de huesped* (guest card) at each hotel, identifying you as a hotel guest. Depending on your hotel, the card may have to be presented when ordering and signing for meals and drinks, when changing money, and often when entering the elevator to your room.

Cuban Guests

The presence of young Cuban women on the arms of foreign men (and Cuban men with foreign women) became a fixture of most hotel lobbies in the early 1990s. In 1995, the government began to clear them out, and there are now strictures against young Cuban women (and men) entering hotel lobbies alone. At press time, no Cubans were permitted in guest rooms in tourist hotels. Period. A kind of tourist apartheid is in force. Even Cubans with pockets full of *fula* (dollars) can't register in the better hotels, under the pretext that this protects tourists (another reason may be that in-room TVs carry international news that runs counter to official jargon). Unless you can prove that a Cuban companion is your spouse, rest assured that hotel staff will turn your partner away.

Cubans and foreigners are allowed to share hotels run by Islazul, where the clientele is *primarily* Cuban; foreigners and Cubans generally come and go and interact without restriction. However, the policy is in flux as the government finesses its handling of *jiniteras* (prostitutes) and *jiniteros* (illicit marketeers) in hotels, and at press time even Islazul hotels did not permit Cubans to enter the rooms of foreign hotel guests (the hotel staff go to ridiculous lengths to prevent such occurrences).

Fortunately, it is still legal to have a Cuban as your guest if you're staying in a *casa particular*. Your Cuban partner must be at least 18 years of age. And your host is supposed to record his or her name and other pertinent details for inspection by authorities. Ostensibly, he or she should be your steady *novio* or *novia* (boyfriend or girlfriend), not a *jinitera*. Your host may insist on this, but most hosts (being Cuban and thereby sexually liberal) will not care, as Cuban couples often rent rooms by the hour in someone else's home to consummate their love unions—accepted practice in overcrowded Havana, where several families often share the same apartment and couples need some privacy.

Of course, the government is sensitive to the needs of every man and woman, and has created state-run, 24-hour love hotels (*posadas*), which exist to provide relief for the large percentage of Cubans who live together with aunts, uncles, parents, and even grandparents along with the children, often in conditions in which rooms are subdivided by curtains. At these hotels, couples can enjoy an intimate moment together, although conditions are often dour. Most couples are married, sometimes to each other. (In most, conditions are modest, to say the least. More upscale, congenial facilities have gardens, a/c, and music in the rooms, such as El Monumental—12 km west of Havana—which is favored by government officials). Rooms are usually rented for three hours, typically for five pesos (25 cents), for which the state thoughtfully provides a bottle of rum by the bed.

HABANA VIEJA

Habana Vieja is in the midst of a hotel boom, with many colonial-era mansions and erstwhile grande dame hotels having come online after splendid makeovers. They have the advantage of superb locations to add to their considerable charms.

Habaguanex (see above), the state corporation that administers tourist commercial enterprises in Habana Vieja, is slated to open 16

hotels in Habana Vieja in the next few years: the **Hotel Telegrafo** was due to open in 2000 adjacent to the Inglaterra on the west side of Parque Central; the 150-room **Gran Hotel Saratoga** was scheduled to open opposite the Capitolio, on the corner of Dragones and the Prado; an aparthotel is to be built behind the Hotel Parque Central; and a residential complex with villas and a hotel is planned for the Parque Morro-Cabaña.

Casas Particulares

I have yet to find an agreeable *casa particular* in Habana Vieja, where so much of the housing is in decrepit condition. But hardier travelers might not be so fussy. Touts will approach you on the street. Here are a few to consider:

Aguacate #356, e/ Amargura y Lamparilla, tel. (63) 7448 (Leonardo Mayor)

Galiano #564, Apto. H25, e/ Salud y Reina

Calle San Juan de Ríos #102, Apto. 4C, e/ Aguacate y Compostela

Prado #20, Apto. 6A, e/ San Lazaro y Carcel, tel. (61) 7932 (Guidelia y Estanislao)

San Ignacio #78, tel. (61) 9277 (Salvador Guiterrez Trujillo)

Budget (Less Than US$35)

One of the best bargains in town is the simple **Residencia Académica Convento de Santa Clara,** in the former convent on Calle Cuba between Luz and Sol, tel. (61) 3335, fax (33) 5696. The restored building is beautiful and today houses the National Center for Conservation and Museology (Centro Nacional de Conservación y Museología), which offers residential courses to foreign and Cuban academics. It has nine charming, modestly furnished but well-kept rooms for US$25 s/d. A café serves basic refreshments.

A good barebones bet is the **Hotel Isla de Cuba,** an Islazul property on Máximo Gómez on the south side of Parque de la Fraternidad, tel. (57) 1128. It is used almost entirely by Cubans and is usually full. The hotel was not accepting foreigners at press time, when it was scheduled to receive a facelift. However, it has accepted foreigners in the past and may do so again. The atmospheric colonial building is aged and gloomy but has antique charm. Beyond the massive 10-meter-tall mahogany doors, its narrow, soaring atrium has balconies and is surrounded by 64 simple but adequate rooms (two with a/c, the rest with fans). Rooms have telephones and clean bathrooms (with cold water only). *Refresquerías* selling ice cream and sodas lie close at hand, on the corner of Máximo Gómez and Cienfuegos.

Alternately, consider the **Hotel New York,** on Dragones, one block west of Parque de la Fraternidad, tel. (62) 5260. This Islazul property serves a mostly Cuban clientele and has 75 rather dour rooms with ceiling fans, private bathrooms, and cold water (US$9.80 s, US$12.05 d, US$15.45 t, US$18 q high season); a small bar and restaurant in the lobby; and a popular patio bar and restaurant on the corner outside the hotel.

The **Hotel Ferrocarríl,** facing the railway station on Egido, is reserved solely for railway employees.

Inexpensive (US$35-60)

You may be excused for having a flashback to the romantic *posadas* of Spain the moment you walk into **Hostal Valencia,** Oficios #53, e/ Obrapía y Lamparilla, tel. (57) 1037, fax (33) 5628. Appropriately, this quaint 12-room hotel is owned by a Spanish firm in partnership with the government. The recently restored 18th-century mansion (Casa de Sotolongo) exudes splendid charm, with its lobby—entered through a tall doorway—of hefty oak beams, Spanish tiles, magnificent wrought-iron chandeliers, hardwood colonial seats, and statuettes. The inner courtyard, surrounded by a lofty balcony, is a setting for live music and has a bar that teems with atmosphere and locals enjoying the US$1 beers. The 12 spacious rooms have cool marble floors but are furnished, regrettably, in modern utility style (US$40 s, US$52 d, US$65 suite). All have private bathrooms and TVs, telephones, refrigerators, and walls decorated with pretty ceramic plaques. Some have French doors that open onto the street. To the left as you enter is the equally atmospheric La Paella restaurant (reservations suggested), and to the right the charming Bar Entresuelo. *Recommended.*

The **Hotel Caribbean,** Paseo de Martí #164, a Horizontes hotel on the corner of Colón and Prado, tel. (33) 8233 or (66) 9479, is a favorite of budget travelers, and rightly so after a splendid renovation. It has 38 rooms (five with a/c), small and meagerly yet adequately furnished in pleasing Caribbean colors, with silent a/c, tiny TVs,

telephones, in-room safe-boxes, and small yet nicely renovated bathrooms with all-new plumbing. The hotel has a small, simple bar. Rates are US$33 s, US$43 d low season, US$36 s US$48 d high season. There's no sign for the hotel: the entrance is immediately next to the Café del Prado (open 7 a.m.-3 a.m.), which serves the hotel and passersby with pizza, sandwiches, and spaghetti.

Nearby is the **Casa de Científicos** at Prado #212, e/ Calles Trocadero y Colón, tel. (62) 4511 fax (33) 0167. This lofty-ceilinged, four-story colonial mansion—the old Casa José Miguel Gómez— is like a mini-Versailles, sumptuously adorned with rococo ceilings and marble floors. A rickety elevator and a marble staircase with a magnificen stained-glass atrium ceiling lead upstairs to 12 a/c rooms modestly furnished with a medley o antiques and utility furniture, plus satellite TVs and large, well-lit bathrooms with white tilework The vast suite boasts a bathroom in black marble A rooftop bar sometimes hosts entertainment Downstairs, the elegant Restaurant Los Vitrales is replete with exquisite antiques. Rates are US$25 s, US$31 d, US$37 t with shared bathroom with cold water only, US$45 s, US$55 d, US$64 t with private bathroom.

Moderate (US$60-85)

Want to rest your head where Ernest Hemingway found inspiration? Then try the **Hotel Ambos Mundos,** splendidly situated one block west o Plaza de Armas on Calle Obispo, e/ San Ignacio y Mercaderes, tel. (66) 9530, fax (66) 9532. The hotel, which originally opened in 1920, reopened in 1997 after a terminally long restoration. The compact lobby is airy and breezy, with tall French doors running the length of its walls. A pianist plays, adding notes to the tinkling fountain, and the mahogany lobby bar is always lively. The hotel offers 49 a/c rooms and three junior suites arranged atrium style, each with cable TV and international telephone lines. Most rooms are small and dark, but feature modern albeit undistinguished furnishings. Some have windows looking out; others face the interior courtyard, which are quieter in early morning when the street cacophony can intrude. Facilities include a modest rooftop restaurant and solarium with views over Habana Vieja. Hemingway's room—511—is preserved in suspended animation. Avoid the fifth oor, which is a thoroughfare for sightseeing hawkers, who fill the single, rickety old elevator (the wait is interminable) and amble up and down the narrow marble stairs. The food in the rooftop restaurant is fairly good, but breakfast is said to be "weak" (there's a splendid bakery a one-minute walk away). Rates are US$65 s, US$90 d, US$110 t, US$120 suite.

Hostal de Habana is an intimate *bogeda*-style hotel in the former home of the Conde de Villanueva at Calle Mercaderas esq. Lamparilla, tel. (62) 9682. A splendid remake has restored the colonial mansion to former grandeur. Breezes waft through lofty doors, cooling the spacious lobby-lounge, with its bottle-green sofas and blood-red cushions, terra-cotta floor, and beamed ceiling with chandeliers. Beyond is an intimate courtyard, with caged birds, tropical foliage, and rockers beneath *porticos*. The eight large, airy, and simply appointed rooms and one suite (with jacuzzi) are arranged all-around on two levels, with *ventrales* on the upper balcony diffusing sunlight in rainbow hues. A small restaurant and bar to the rear has a fountain and TV. The hotel aims at cigar smokers with a Casa de Habanos outlet and a sumptuous smokers' lounge. Rates in early 1999 were US$53 s, US$68-77 d, US$135 suite, but they probably will be jacked up. For now, it remains one of the few real bargains in town. *Recommended*.

Expensive (US$85-110)
Parque Central is a privileged location offering several options. The first is the atmospheric **Hotel Plaza,** Calle Agramonte #267, tel. (33) 8583, fax (33) 8869, built in 1909 in the grand old style. The small entrance lobby is quite stunning with its lofty ceiling supported by Corinthian columns and festooned with plaster motifs. Squawking parrots fly free in the lobby. A venerable marble stairway leads upstairs to the 186 lofty-ceilinged a/c rooms (18 suites), furnished with dark hardwood antiques and reproductions, TVs (with US cable channels), radios, safe-deposit boxes (US$5), and heaps of closet space. The sky-high ceilings help dissipate the heat. Although the rooms are kept spotlessly clean, some are rather gloomy, and rooms facing onto the street can be noisy. The gracious lobby bar is lit by four stained-glass skylights during the day, and by gilt chandeliers at night, when a pianist hits the ivories. The Restaurant Real Plaza serves superior cuisine in a classically chic setting. To the left, tucked away, is another restaurant serving grim breakfasts and set buffet meals. The top (fifth) floor has a terrace restaurant offering views over the city. Service stops at 10 a.m. on the dot, when even the coffee and juice machines are promptly unplugged. The fifth-floor *azuela* features a gift store and a solarium with lounge chairs and a splendid eye-to-eye view of the top of the old Bacardi building. Unhappily, prices have skyrocketed of late without justification. Rates are US$75 s, US$100 d low season, US$80 s, US$120 d high season.

On the west side of Parque Central is the **Hotel Inglaterra,** Paseo del Prado #416, tel. (33) 8993 or (62) 7071, fax (33) 8254, with its ornate wedding cake facade. It was a particular favorite of visitors in the 19th century, although travelers' accounts—such as those of Winston Churchill, who laid his head here in 1895—"reverberate with wails about the hard mattresses and the offhand service." The hotel has been named a National Monument and, prior to its recent price hike, was very popular with younger, independent travelers, for whom it became the unofficial meeting point in Havana; they have since been driven away by the stiff rate increases, unjustified despite a recent renovation. The extravagantly decorated lobby is loaded with atmosphere. Musical interludes emanate from the lobby bar and restaurant, cool havens of stained glass and patterned tiles that whisk you off to Morocco with their arabesque archways and mosaics of green, blue, and gold. Of the 83 a/c rooms, three offer panoramic views from their balconies. Noise from the square can be a problem, especially in the early morning. All rooms have a telephone, satellite TV, safe-deposit box, hair dryer, and minibar, but they remain dark and musty. Take time to sip a *mojito* at the entrance patio bar or rooftop **La Terraza** bar, where cabaret is performed at night. Unfortunately, the hotel has no swimming pool. Rates are US$75 s, US$100 d low season, US$80 s, US$120 d high season. *Overpriced*.

Very Expensive (US$110-150)
An intimate and resplendent option is the **Hotel Florida,** in a stunning colonial building—the Casa de Joaquín Gómez, built in 1835 for a

wealthy merchant—at Calle Obispo #252 esq. Cuba. The 35-room hotel will be opened sometime in late 1999 by Habaguanex (see above). It will be aimed primarily at businesspeople, and you can bet it will be sumptuously furnished.

Luxury (US$150+)

One peek inside the lobby of the **Hotel Sevilla,** Trocadero #55, between the Prado and Zulueta, tel. (33) 8560, fax (33) 8582, and it could be love at first sight, despite its outrageous pricing. The landmark hotel—famous as the setting for Graham Greene's *Our Man in Havana* (Wormold stayed in room 501)—has filigreed balconies and a newly touched-up facade straight out of *1,001 Arabian Nights.* You enter via a lofty arched doorway of Gaudiesque proportions to what may strike you as a Moroccan medina, with spiral columns augering up from a marble floor. French louvered windows open fully so that the breeze blows freely, mingling with piped music and the sunlight pouring in through tinted *vitrales.* The hotel was built in 1924, and its uninspired rooms and filthy walls suggest that it hasn't had a spring cleaning all the while, despite a recent remake. The 178 rooms are disappointing: small, low on light, and furnished with tacky outdated furniture, although each has a safe, minibar, telephone, and satellite TV. The top-floor restaurant is a sumptuous gem—the food was until recently abysmal but has improved markedly with the arrival of a French chef. The French Accor group recently took over management,

so hopefully things will improve. On-site you'" find a tour and car-rental desk, as well as a swimming pool, four bars, a beauty parlor, and assorted shops. Taxi service can be slow, particularly at night. Room rates are US$84 s US$128 d low season, US$97 s, US$154 d high season. *Overpriced.*

The **Golden Tulip Parque Central,** tel. (66 6627, fax (66) 6630, e-mail: sales@gtpc.cha cuy.cu (in The Netherlands, Golden Tulip, Stationsstraat 2, P.O. Box 619, 1200 AP Hilversum tel. 35-284588, fax 35-284681; in Canada, tel 800-344-1212; in the UK, tel. 181-770-0333), a joint venture of Cubanacán and the Dutch Golden Tulip hotel chain, sits at the top of the Prado on Neptuno and Agramonte (Zulueta), on the north side of Parque Central. This ultra-modern hotel is one of the best in town, with a management and staff that seems to understand the concept of service. The exterior is hardly inspirational, but the gracious lobby offers a surfeit of marble and lively decor in ocher and bottle green blending a contempo style with colonial hints. It has 281 rooms done up in a fashionable contemporary style with a soothing color scheme of soft greens and creams. They come with all modern conveniences, including satellite TV (CNN, HBO, etc.), antique reproduction furnishings, and king-size beds (a deluxe rarity in Havana), plus marble bathrooms with separate tub and shower, vanity mirrors, ceilings inset with halogen bulbs, and heaps of fluffy towels. Avoid the second- and third-floor rooms on the south-

More than 60 years old (it's hosted luminaries from Winston Churchill to Marlon Brando), the majestic Hotel Nacional is still a commanding presence.

west corner, which have tiny windows at waist level (the integration of the colonial frontage into the design of guest rooms is ill-conceived). Many rooms have no views whatsoever, so be sure to ask for an exterior room. The suites are vast. A mezzanine has an upscale cigar lounge-bar with plump leather seats, plus executive meeting rooms, a business center, and a top-class restaurant that was due to open in mid-1999. An art gallery was also in the works. Topping it all off is a rooftop swimming pool and jacuzzi in a rotunda with glass walls offering views over the city. Here, too, is a fitness room and a splendid rooftop grill in Italianate style (terra-cotta floor, wrought-iron posts) serving snacks, including a traditional Dutch dish called *bitterballen*. Introductory rates in spring 1999 were US$115 s, US$165 d, US$250 suite. Expect these to rise.

The Plaza de Armas provides a fabulous setting for the **Hotel Santa Isabel,** Calle Baratillo #9 e/ Obispo y Narciso López, tel. (33) 8201 or (66) 9619, fax (33) 8391, a small and intimate hostelry recalling days of yore when it was *the* place to be. The splendid building, facing both westward onto the plaza and eastward onto the harbor, began life as a lodging at the end of the 17th century. It later became a palace of the Countess of Santovenia and, in the second half of the 19th century, the Hotel Santa Isabel, which today recaptures the colonial ambience and is regarded as the most elite hotel in Habana Vieja. Decor includes plush velvet sofas, antiques, and modern art in the marble-floored lobby. The hotel has 27 lofty-ceilinged, a/c rooms (10 of them suites) arrayed around an airy atrium with fountain, with sunlight streaming in rainbows through stained-glass *mediopuntos*. The standard rooms occupy the third floor; 10 suites occupy the second floor. Rooms are furnished in pinks and blues, with marble or stone and ceramic floors, poster bed, reproduction antique furniture, satellite TV, direct-dial telephone, and safety box, plus leather recliners on wide balconies. Choose from twin or king-size beds. Suites have a jacuzzi tub. There's an elegant restaurant, a small lobby bar with a fountain, and a rooftop *mirador*. The Bar El Globo offers a pleasant spot to relax beneath the shade of the *portico* facing the square. A rooftop swimming pool was planned. In spring 1999, however, management was abysmal (I witnessed several faults, including the most disturbing treat-

ment of a guest I've ever encountered in two decades of travel reporting), and two readers have written to complain about reservations not being honored. Rates are US$110 s, US$150 d, US$135 s and US$190 d for junior suites, including breakfast.

CENTRO HABANA

Casas Particulares

One of the best *casas particulares* in Havana is located at Barcelona #56, e/ Aguila y Amistad, tel. (63) 8452. Jesús Deiro Raña, the host, offers one antique-filled room upstairs in his well-kept home, with a lofty ceiling and private bathroom with hot and cold water. He charges US$20, representing a great bargain. Call ahead. (Jesús and his family may move to San Rafael #312, e/ Galiano y San Nicolas, same telephone number. He promises that this house is even better.)

A neighbor, Augusto Estanque, also offers three rooms for rent in his home at Barcelona #304, tel. (63) 0122 or (40) 7471. Rooms are relatively small and dark, and share a clean but simple bathroom with hot and cold water. They can be rented singly for US$25 or you can take the entire house, which has lofty ceilings and *vitrales*, plus a TV lounge. It had minimal furniture when I visited, but Augusto claims that more furniture is to be put in, along with a/c and a second bathroom. Guests can use the meager kitchen.

A reader has recommended a "comfortable" *casa* run by Orlandito and Tati at Industria #270, e/ Neptuno y Virtudos, tel. (63) 5690, on the sixth floor, and conveniently placed close to Parque Central. Another recommends a house at Calle Escobar #43, close to Barrio Chino, where the English-speaking owner, Patricia, charges US$25 ("a bit overpriced").

In western Centro, near Vedado, try the following *casas particulares:* Juana Duran's at San Rafael #967, Apto. 75 (seventh floor), e/ Espado y Hospital, tel. (79) 4241; Pila Cotero's, in the same building at San Rafael #967, Apto. 83 (eighth floor), e/ Espada y Hospital, tel. (70) 7920; Jacobo León's at Infanta #113, Apto. 1, e/ San Fransisco y Espada; Ninfa Milian Cruz's at Espada #5, Apto. 211, e/ Infanta y 25, tel. (78) 2478; Dr. Alejandro Oss's on the Malecón #163, Apto. #1, e/ Aguila y Crespo, tel. (63) 7359; Celia y Fidel's at Calle 25 #9, Apto. 7, tel. (78) 5355; Miriam Rodríguez's at San Lazaro #621, altos, e/ Gervasio y Escobar; and at Hospital #707, one block north of Salvador Allende. None of these have been reviewed.

Inexpensive (US$35-60)

The basic **Hotel Lido,** near the Prado at Animas and Consulado, tel. (57) 1102, fax (33) 8814, awaits a renovation and is overpriced at US$25 s, US$35 d low season. The modest a/c rooms feature utility furniture, telephones, radios, and tiny balconies. The bathrooms have cold water only. Safety boxes are available (use them—the Lido has a reputation for theft), and a bar serves snacks in the dreary lobby. The fifth-floor *azuela* (rooftop) bar is open until 4 a.m. and has a view over Havana. This Islazul hotel serves both Cubans and tourists.

A better bet is the **Hotel Lincoln,** Galiano esq. Virtudes, tel. (33) 8209, an Islazul hotel also open to both Cubans and foreigners (but the latter are prohibited from carousing in their rooms with the former) and famed as the spot where world champion racecar driver Fangio was kidnapped by Castro's revolutionaries in 1958. This modest, 139-room hotel dates from 1926 and features graceful public arenas, including a lobby boasting chandeliers and Louis XVI-style furnishings. It also offers 16 suites. The a/c rooms are clean and pleasant, with radio, telephone, satellite TV, and mini-fridge (in suites). Facilities include the elegant Restaurant Colonial in the lobby, a rooftop terrace bar, and nightly entertainment that runs from Afro-Cuban cabarets to dance classes. Foreign guests are reminded that no *chicas* are permitted in their rooms, to which effect an attendant is imprisoned in the tiny elevator to prevent any subterfuge. Rates are US$22 s, US$29 d low season, US$27 s, US$36 d high season.

Moderate (US$60-85)

Though utilized by package-tour groups, the **Hotel Deauville,** tel. (33) 8812, fax (33) 8148, is a gloomy cement tower that journalist Martha Gellhorn called "a postwar, prerevolutionary blight on the Malecón." True enough. Gellhorn "came to dote" on the hideous hotel, though I'm not sure why. It lies in limbo at the foot of Avenida Italia (Galiano), midway between Habana Vieja and Vedado, and is as ugly within as without. The 148 a/c rooms have TV, radio, and telephone, but dreary furnishings. Facilities include a rooftop swimming pool and a disco, with a cabaret on Saturday. Service is terrible. At least the views over the city are splendid from upper-level rooms. The exterior was undergoing a facelift at press time, and hopefully the interior will receive the same. Until then, it's best avoided. Rates are US$40 s, US$52 d, US$67 t low season, US$48 s, US$62 d, US$78 t high season.

VEDADO AND PLAZA DE LA REVOLUCIÓN

Casas Particulares

Vedado is blessed with possibility, and the majority of private rooms for rent in Havana are concentrated here.

I've rented four or five *casas particulares* and inspected a score of others, and eventually settled on a pleasing ground-floor unit in a modern apartment block with a large, well-lit, and well-furnished bedroom with ceiling fan, a/c, telephone, and refrigerator, and a beautifully tiled bathroom with piping hot water, a secure garage for my motorcycle, and the company (whenever I chose) of a wonderful family—for US$25-30 daily. Contact Jorge Coalla Potts, Calle I #456, Apto. 11, e/ 21 y 23, tel. (32) 9032. His apartment is superbly situated two blocks from Coppelia and the Habana Libre, and is by far the best I've seen. Jorge speaks broken English. There's a gas stove if you wish to cook for yourself. *Recommended.*

Another splendid option is a three-room, two-bath apartment run by Martha Vitonte at Avenida de los Presidentes #301, tel. (32) 6475, e-mail: rida@jcce.org.cu. Her apartment takes up the entire 14th floor with wraparound glass windows on a balcony that offers fabulous views over the city. Her lounge has plump leather sofas, lounge chairs, and antiques. The three rooms are clean and beautifully kept, featuring antique beds and private bathrooms. Martha— a retired civil servant (she formerly worked in Havana's International Press Center) and an engaging conversationalist who speaks fluent English and has an answerphone—charges US$35 per room. The only drawback is the rickety escalator.

In far east Vedado, try **El Rinconcito Azúl**, run by Doña Tata, at Calle P #110 e/ Humboldt y Infanta, tel. (70) 4239. She has two a/c rooms with a shared bath with hot water for US$20 apiece. The rooms are simple and dark, but boast plentiful furnishings, and there's a kitchen and tiny lounge with TV.

Around the corner is **Casa Particular #156**, on Calle 25 and Infanta, tel. (70) 7613. Here, Dolores Lopez offers four rooms with fans in a house with lofty ceilings, a kitchen, and a patio out back. Two rooms have private baths, two share a bath. The place is always busy with family members shooing in and out.

The *casa* at Calle 21 #203, between J and K, tel. (32) 1066, is in a timeworn house of palatial proportions and full of antiques, but with filthy walls screaming for a fresh pot of paint. The owners offer one room in the house with a firm mattress and a shared bathroom with hot water and a bidet. Two other rooms are in a more modern addition upstairs and reached by an outside stairway. They're not particularly attractive and have tiny bathrooms, but also have a/c and telephone, and a refrigerator in the small kitchenette. Each room costs US$25.

A reader, Joanna Swanger, recommends Mercedes Gonzalez, who has two rooms in a house at Calle 21 #360, Apto. 2A, e/ G y H, Vedado, tel. (32) 5846. Both rooms have a/c, ceiling fans, and hot water, and are described as "very clean" and "safe and secure." Another reader recommends Aleida García at Calle 28 #270, e/ 21 y 23, for US$20 with a/c. The place is said to be clean. A third recommends an unidentified *casa*, e-mail: la_superabuela@hotmail.com, with TV and VCR, a/c, and safety box, plus "electronic security."

In eastern Vedado, a North American friend who lives in Havana recommends Teresa Isidrón's place at Calle 28 between 21 and 23, tel. (3) 9732, near Cementerio Colón. It's described as a "family environment," and Teresa hosts musicians on the rooftop terrace. She's "very plugged into the music and dance scene." She prepares meals and charges US$20-25.

Casa Blanca, Calle 13 #917, entre 8 y 6, Vedado, tel. (3) 5697, e-mail: duany@casa.caspar.net, website: www.caspar.net/casa/, has an a/c room with hot water, terrace, telephone, and e-mail service for US$20 per night (US$3 for breakfast).

Many of the occupants of the seven-story edifice at the corner of O and 21, opposite the entrance to the Hotel Nacional, advertise *casas particulares* for rent. Their signs hang above the front door.

Others to consider include: Calle B #83, tel. (30) 2237 (Eladra Hernandez); Calle 21 #21, Apto. 1, e/ N y O, tel. (32) 3260 (Angel Milian Paredes); and Calle J #52, between 23 and 25.

Budget (Less Than US$35)

If you're on a serious budget and don't mind being a one-hour walk from things, consider the modest **Hotel Bruzón**, an Islazul property between Pozos Dulces and Boyeros, just north of the Plaza de la Revolución, tel. (57) 5684. There's nothing appealing about this 46-room hotel, with barebones utility furniture, a/c, small TVs and radios (local stations only), and basic bathrooms with cold water only. Still, it will do in a pinch for hardy budget travelers. It has a small bar and a disco (with cabaret on Thursday). Rooms cost US$14 s, US$18 d low season, US$18 s, US$23 d high season.

The Ministry of Public Health runs **Villa Residencial Estudiantil del MINSAP**, on Calle 2 between 15 and 17, tel. (30) 9830 or (30) 8411, in an old mansion with simple rooms for about US$20 s, US$25 d. It has a small restaurant and a broad, breeze-swept veranda with rockers.

Inexpensive (US$35-60)

The **Hotel Morro**, at Calles D and 3ra, tel./fax (33) 3907, is a no-frills property run by Horizontes. Each of its 20 a/c rooms has basic utility furniture plus a TV, telephone, and refrigerator, and a clean bathroom boasting two rarities: hair dryers and plenty of towels. Rooms offer no views through louvered windows with frosted glass. The small Bar Arrecife serves snacks, and the hotel offers laundry service. Rates are US$21 s, US$28 d, US$37 t low season, US$29 s, US$38 d, US$47 t high season.

The Ministry of Education runs the **Hotel Universitario**, at Calle L y 17, tel. (33) 3403 or (32) 5506, fax (33) 3022, formerly open to Cuban and foreign teachers (it had separate dining rooms for Cubans and foreigners) but today solely for foreign tourists. It's a basic, wood-paneled affair with a gloomy student-union-style bar and a pleasant restaurant downstairs behind the glum lobby. Its 21 rooms offer the essentials but lack noteworthy ambience. Rates are US$30 s, US$40 d, US$50 t year-round.

A popular, moderately priced bargain in the thick of Vedado is Horizontes' **Hotel St. John's,** on Calle O one block south of La Rampa, tel. (33) 3740, fax (33) 3361. Beyond the coldest air-conditioned lounge in the world, this 14-story property has 96 recently renovated a/c rooms, each with radio, telephone, and TV (US$25/32 s, US$33/43 d, US$45/54 t low/high season). A cabaret is offered in the Pico Blanco Room (Tues.-Sun.), plus there's a rooftop swimming pool and a tourism bureau. It was receiving ongoing restoration at press time.

Moderate (US$60-85)
The recently renovated 194-room **Hotel Vedado,** tel. (33) 4062, at Calle O e/ 23 y 25, is of reasonable standard, albeit overpriced. It has a tiny, uninspired a/c lounge and minimal facilities, including a small tour desk. Rooms are small but done up in pastel colors, with satellite TV, telephone, tile floors, and small bathroom. The El Cortijo Restaurant specializes in Spanish cuisine, and there's a disco and cabaret. Rates are US$44 s, US$58 d low season, US$53 s, US$70 d high season, including breakfast.

In a similar vein, try the modest 79-room **Hotel Colinas,** on Calle L, tel. (33) 4071, fax (33) 4104, two blocks south of the Habana Libre, one block from the University of Havana. The a/c rooms are depressingly hokey but feature TV and telephone. The modest facilities include a small tour desk, modest mezzanine restaurant, and patio snack bar good for watching the world go by. A renovation is slated for 1999-2000. Rates are US$38 s, US$50 d, US$65 t low season, US$46 s, US$60 d, US$78 t high season, including breakfast.

Expensive (US$85-110)
In central Vedado is the charmless **Hotel Capri,** Calle 21 y N, tel. (33) 3747, fax (33) 3750. The airy lobby is flooded with light from plate-glass windows, as are the 215 a/c rooms, which are dowdily furnished but feature TV, telephone, and safety box; they were slated for refurbishment in late 1999. The 18th-floor *azuela* swimming pool and La Terraza Florenta restaurant both offer spectacular views. The Capri was built

by mobster Santo Traficante Jr. Its gambling casino was, until 1959, run by George Raft, the mobster-movie actor. (A favorite hangout of the Mafia, the Capri was the setting for a scene in Mario Puzo's *The Godfather*.) When revolutionaries arrived on 1 January 1959 to destroy the gaming tables, Raft stood at the door and snarled, "You're not comin' in my casino!" The casino is long gone (it is now a drab dining room), but the hotel features the Salon Rojo cabaret *espectáculo*. It has a tour booth. Rates are US$65 s, US$80 d low season, US$78 s, US$94 d high season. *Overpriced.*

Farther out, at the foot of Avenida de los Presidentes, is the **Hotel Presidente,** tel. (33) 4074, a tall, 144-room, art deco-style 1930s property with a maroon exterior and—in 1998— a carnal-red and pink interior lent jaded elegance by its sumptuous Louis XIV-style furnishings and Grecian urns and busts that rise from a beige marble floor. The hotel was closed for renovation in spring 1999.

Luxury (US$150+)
The grandest of Havana's Old World-style hotels, and Gran Caribe's flagship, is the **Hotel Nacional,** on Calle O off La Rampa, tel. (33) 3564, fax (33) 5054. Luminaries from Winston Churchill and the Prince of Wales to Marlon Brando have laid their heads here, and this city icon—which dates from the 1930s—still dominates important events, when celebrities flock. The property recently emerged from a thorough restoration that revived much of the majesty of the 60-plus-year-old neoclassical gem, perched haughtily on a cliff overlooking the Malecón with a postcard view of Havana harbor. It is entered via a long, palm-lined driveway, while to the rear the hotel's magnificent greenswathe, studded with slender Royal palms and pale ceibas, is perfect for a romantic stroll. The vast vaulted lobby with mosaic floors boasts Arab-influenced tilework and lofty wood-beamed ceilings, Moorish arches, and extravagant nooks and crannies where whispered confidences were once offered.

Most of the Nacional's 457 a/c rooms (15 are suites) boast ocean views. They are large and appointed with cable TV, telephone, safe, and self-service bar; however they don't live up to the billing (nor high prices) and could do with more regal furnishings. The hotel was being renovated floor by floor at press time, when the only floor that was complete was the sixth floor, termed an Executive Floor, housing 63 specially appointed rooms and suites (for which a US$30 premium applies). The Comedor de Aguiar restaurant serves good Cuban and continental dishes. In 1955, a casino and nightclub was opened and managed by mobster Meyer Lansky. Today the club—Cabaret Parisien—hosts one of the hottest cabarets in town. The top-floor cocktail lounge (closed for repair in spring 1999) in the turrets offers a magical view; and the lobby-level bar offers a yellowing collage of luminaries, including Mob titans Lansky, Santo Trafficante, and others. There are five bars, two swimming pools, and a full range of facilities, including upscale boutiques, beauty salon, spa, tennis courts, and tour desk. Service is reasonably attentive by Cuban standards. Rates are US$100 s, US$140 d low season, US$120 s, US$170 d high season. Suites cost US$180-260 low season, US$215-315 high season. Special suites are US$400-1,000 year-round.

The landmark high-rise **Hotel Habana Libre Tryp,** at Calles L, e/ 23 y 25, tel. (33) 4011, fax (33) 3141, e-mail: comer@rllibre.com.cu, is synonymous with the heyday of Havana. It was built in the 1950s by the Hilton chain and soon became a favorite of mobsters and high rollers. After the Revolution, Castro set up his headquarters here in January 1959. You used to hear that the whole place was bugged. The good ol' bad ol' days are long gone, and it is now managed by the Spanish Tryp group. The Habana Libre is still popular with foreigners and Cuban VIPs (and, despite the security, with *jiniteras* prowling for foreign dates). It recently emerged from a renovation that included replacing the formerly capricious plumbing. The atrium lobby now shines beneath its glass dome and features a fountain and popular bar with a hip '50s retro feel. The 533 rooms come equipped with satellite TV, direct-dial telephone, minibar, safety box, and hair dryers in the bathrooms. It also offers 36 junior suites and three suites, plus 24-hour room service. The hilltop location is splendid, and the hotel is loaded with facilities—all-important tour desks, a bank, airline offices, boutiques, post office, and international telephone exchange, as well as a snack-bar-style café, two full-service restaurants, a patio bar under a

futuristic 1950s-era skylight, a bar with cabaret on the 25th floor, and an all-important underground parking lot. The swimming pool is at mezzanine level, overlooked by a handsome bar. Rates are US$90 s, US$130 d low season, US$106 s, US$163 d high season.

A good bet and one favored by business travelers is the small and charming **Hotel Victoria,** splendidly located at Avenida 19 y Calle M, tel. (33) 3510, fax (33) 3109. This Victorian-style, neoclassical building began life in the 1920s as a small guesthouse and retains its personal feel. It has only 31 elegant, albeit somewhat small a/c rooms refurbished with 1970s decor, with hardwoods and antique reproduction furnishings. Relaxation is offered in a small swimming pool and an intimate lobby bar. The elegant restaurant is one of Havana's finest. It's a reasonable bargain at US$80 s, US$100 d low season, US$90 s, US$120 d high season.

The **Melía Cohiba,** on Paseo e/ Calles 1 y 3, tel. (24) 3636, fax (33) 3939, e-mail: sec_com_mlc@cohiba1.solmelia.cma.net, is a hotel of international deluxe standard, bringing Havana squarely into the 21st century with its handsome postmodern European design and executive services, and adding a shine to the drab grays at the base of Paseo. The 22-story, 462-room hotel is *the* hotel of choice for foreign businesspeople, who gather to smoke their stogies in the **El Relicario** bar. It is run by the Spanish Grupo Sol Meliá. There's no Cuban ambience whatsoever, except in the traditional cuisine of the **Abanico de Cristal** restaurant—one of four eateries in the hotel. The spacious lobby hints at the luxe within, with its marble, splendid artwork, and magnesium-bright lighting. Its spacious and elegant rooms feature brass lamps; marble floors; Romanesque chairs with contemporary fabrics; a mellow color scheme of beige, gold, and rust; and mirrored walls behind the bed. They were beginning to look tired in spring 1999, however, despite the hotel's youth. The bathrooms are dazzling, with bright halogen lights and huge mirrors. Bidets and hair dryers are standard, as are fluffy towels and piping hot water in torrents. There are three standards of suites. Facilities include two swimming pools, gym, solarium, shopping center, business center, four restaurants, five bars, and the Habana Café—Havana's take on the Hard Rock Café. Service is far better than in any other Havana hotel. Rates are US$155 single, US$190 double, US$235-350 suites on standard floors; US$200 s, US$235 d, US$300-550 suites on the executive floor.

The **Hotel Habana Riviera,** on the Malecón at the base of Paseo, tel. (33) 4051, fax (33) 3739, now operated by Gran Caribe, is one of the more famous legacies from the heyday of sin. Meyer Lansky's old hotel recently underwent restoration to recapture its 1950s luxe, *sans* casino (his 20th-floor suite, stripped of memorabilia, is available for US$200 a night). The idiosyncratic '50s lobby was replaced with contemporary-style furnishings and a pleasant cocktail lounge, and features acres of marble and plate glass. The spacious rooms received a total remake in 1998 and now come up to international standards, although one still must ask if the hotel is worthy of the price. Room decor is in soothing pastels, with conservative contemporary furniture, satellite TV, safety box, and minibar. The 20-story hotel boasts a large seawater pool, tour desk, boutique, modest restaurant, coffee shop, a Casa de Habanos, and the newly renovated Salón Internacional (formerly the Palacio de Salsa) nightclub for entertainment. Rates are US$84 s, US$127 d low season, US$93 s, US$154 d high season. *Overpriced.*

PLAYA (MIRAMAR AND BEYOND)

Miramar's hotels are utilized by tour groups and businesspeople. You're a long way from the sightseeing action, so expect to fork out plenty of *dinero* for taxi fares into town. Although many of the hotels sit on the shore, this section of Havana's coastline has few beaches and is ugly and barren (although the beaches of Playas del Oeste lie close at hand).

Miramar is slated to receive many new upscale hotels over the next few years. The 427-room **Novotel Miramar,** on Avenida 5ta between 70 and 84, tel. (62) 8308, fax (62) 8587, is a joint project with Gaviota and the French Accor group and was halfway complete in mid-1999. The complex will include the huge hotel plus the **Apartotel Monteverde** and the **Sofitel Quinta Avenida,** all squarely aiming at a business clientele. **Hotel Casa Habana** is a 175-room business hotel going up at press time on the south

side of Avenida 5ra at Calle 96. And the German LTU company's **LTI-Panorama Hotel Havana,** on the shorefront next to the Hotel Neptuno/Triton, will have 306 rooms when completed in 2000.

Casas Particulares

Jorge Pérez and his family offer an a/c room with private entrance, TV, telephone, mini-refrigerator, private bathroom with hot water, plus garage in western Miramar at Calle 96 #535 e/ 5ta y 7ma, tel. (80) 2313, fax (22) 4136, e-mail: borbone@mail.infocom.etecsa.cu. Three generations of the Pérez family live here, and Jorge is fluent in English and Italian.

Casa Miramar, Calle 30, No. 3502, e/ 35 y 37, Miramar, tel. (29) 5679, in Canada (604) 874-4143, e-mail: mail@casamiramar.com, website: www.casamiramar.com, is an exquisite colonial-style 1926 home with original marble floors and vaulted ceilings that owners Marco and Daulema are restoring to its original character and form (aided by Daulema's Vancouver- based sister and her Canadian architect-husband). It has three a/c rooms upstairs with one shared bathroom. Each room has its own character and is appointed with early 1900s art nouveau furnishings, a queen-size boxspring and mattress, goose down pillows, and a private balcony. The master suite has its own mission-style library. Bedding and towels are changed daily. Breakfast is served on the terrace, and dinner is available by request (Marco cooks up an awesome baked Pargo). There's even a safety deposit box that you can program with your own PIN. A one-car garage is available for parking. Rates are US$35 per room, or US$38 including breakfast.

Budget (Less Than US$35)

Motel Las Olas, overlooking the ugly shore on Avenida 1ra at Calle 32, tel. (29) 4531, serves Cubans and impecunious foreigners. The meagerly appointed rooms cost US$20 s, US$30 d, US$42 t, US$52 q. Despite its "motel" status, it's not a love hotel: it's a workers' hotel and has a small pool, video games, and bar. It offers a meal plan for US$31 daily, but you'll do better dining elsewhere. The constant din of piped music in the pool forecourt may prove too much to bear. *Overpriced.*

Inexpensive (US$35-60)

Students will fit right in at the modest **Hostal Cemar,** Calle 16 e/ 1 y 3, tel. (29) 5471, fax (22) 5244, operated by MINET, the Ministry of Education, and mostly utilized by foreign students. However, anyone can check into this 1950s Miami-style hotel that was renovated in 1998. It has 54 large a/c rooms with TV and hot water. Check out several rooms, and take one facing the sea; they have more light. It offers a meal plan. Rates are US$27 s, US$44 d, US$66 t high season. You can also select any of six apartments across the road (same rates as rooms). They're huge (some sleep up to eight people), but some are rather gloomy and minimally furnished.

Two similar options are **Hotel Universitaria Ispaje,** at Avenida 1 and Calle 22, tel. (23) 5370, offering eight rooms with private baths for US$25 s, US$35 d, including breakfast, and **Villa Universitaria Miramar,** at Calle 62 #508 esq. Avenida 5ta, tel. (32) 1034, offering 25 rooms with private baths for US$15 s, US$18 d. There's a bar with pool table, popular with Cuban students and expats.

The **Villa Costa** on Avenida 1ra e/ Calles 34 y 36, just east of the Hotel Copacabana, tel. (29) 2250, fax (24) 4041, is a very handsome seafront villa with lots of louvered windows topped by *ventrales* filtering the sunlight into rainbow colors. Caged songbirds chirp and chatter, adding their musical tones. The rooms are simply furnished, though roomy and adequate (US$27, including breakfast). You can also choose a nicely furnished a/c suite with a spacious bathroom (US$37). There's a comfortable lounge with a TV and VCR. It even has a swimming pool and sundeck of sorts overlooking the ocean. The elegant little restaurant serves set meals for US$5. *Recommended.*

Also worth considering is the **Hostal Villa-mar,** on Avenida 3ra at the corner of 24, tel. (23) 3778, in a colonial mansion built castle style within and without. The four upstairs a/c rooms are spacious and nicely furnished with modern accoutrements, plus TV (local stations only), radio, and mammoth tiled bathrooms. It has a rustic bar and restaurant with wood-beamed ceilings and a fireplace, serving *criollo* food and open 24 hours. Rates are US$29 s, US$48 d.

Moderate (US$60-85)

The dreary **Hotel Kohly,** Avenida 49 esq. 36A, Reparto Kohly, Playa, tel. (24) 0240, fax (24) 1733, e-mail: reserva@kohly.gav.cma.net, run by Gaviota, is a modest 1970s-style property popular with tour groups. Its out-of-the-way location offers no advantages. The 136 a/c rooms are pleasant enough, nicely though modestly furnished, with satellite TV, radio, telephone, minibar, safety box, and spacious shower. Most have a balcony. The patio restaurant serves excellent rice and beans, pork or chicken, and brothy shallots for US$4. The main restaurant is less appealing. Facilities include a tour desk, car rental, and a bar popular with the local youth, who come for the live music and to play pool on the full-size pool tables and 10-pin bowling in the automated bowling alley. Rates are US$50 s, US$62 d low season, US$54 s, US$68 d high season. It was scheduled to be refurbished in late 1999-2000.

You can also choose any of five Mediterranean-style houses next to the hotel, with three to six bedrooms.

Gaviota also runs the recently refurbished and attractive **Hotel el Bosque,** sitting above the Río Almendares in the Reparto Kohly district of Miramar, on 28A one block east of Avenida 47, tel. (24) 9232, fax (24) 5637, e-mail: reservas@bosque.gav.cma.net. The breezy lobby has a bar with pool tables and opens to the rear onto a hillside patio where snacks are served. Its 61 rooms are pleasingly albeit modestly furnished with bamboo, and include a/c, satellite TV, telephone, safety box, and large, louvered French windows opening to balconies (some rooms only), plus small bathrooms with modern glass-enclosed showers. The outside patio has a Mediterranean feel. The Villa Diana restaurant plus the restaurants of the Club Almendares lie close at hand. There are taxis and rent-a-car, a laundry, and tour desk. Rates are US$49 s, US$61 d low/high season.

Also try **Hotel Mirazul,** on Avenida 5ta at Calle 36, tel. (33) 0088, fax (33) 0045. This Wedgwood blue mansion is owned by the Ministry of Higher Education, which offers 10 rooms of varying sizes for tourists as well as educators and students. Rooms vary, but most are spacious and have modest bamboo furnishings, satellite TV, a/c, telephone, and bathroom with hot water. Facilities include a restaurant, pool table, and rooftop sauna and sundeck. It's popular with expats in the know. Rates are US$40-60 s, US$50-70 d, depending on the room. A suite costs US$50 s, US$60 d, US$70 t, and US$80 q. Lower rates are offered to students and teachers.

The **Hotel Bellocaribe,** in Cubanacán at Calle 158 e/ 29 y 31, tel. (33) 9906, fax (33) 6838, predominantly serves the nearby Convention Center and biotech facilities, and is too far out from tourist attractions to offer any appeal for the general traveler. It's a faceless modern property in drab communist style, with 120 pleasantly yet modestly furnished a/c rooms (including 15 suites) featuring satellite TV, radio, telephone, safe-deposit box, and minibar. A full range of facilities includes car rental, tour desk, tennis court, shops, Casa del Tabaco, and beauty salon. There's also an attractive pool and sundeck with separate kiddy's pool, plus the appealing La Estancia restaurant. Rates are US$45 s, US$64 d, US$77 suite low season, US$57 s, US$81 d, US$93 suite high season.

Cubanacán also runs the **Mariposa,** a faceless, uninspired hotel on the Autopista del Medidodía midway between the airport and downtown Havana, in Arroyo Arenas west of the Cubanacán district, tel. (33) 6131 or (20) 0345. It's handy for the Havana Convention Center but too far out to consider otherwise. The 50-room hotel has four junior suites that run US$28 s, US$40 d year-round.

Expensive (US$85-110)

A favorite of tour groups is the **Hotel Comodoro,** Avenida 1ra and Calle 84, tel. (24) 5551, fax (24) 2028, website: www.cubanacan.cu, a Spanish-Cuban joint venture at the west end of Miramar. Originally built for the Cuban armed forces, it was revamped and is now a training school for apprentice Cuban hotel staff. It has 134 a/c rooms, including 15 suites. The ugly 1960s-style exterior belies the appeal of the large a/c rooms, with pleasant modern furnishings plus satellite TV and telephone. Some rooms have a balcony. Safety boxes cost US$2 per day. It has a bathing area in a natural ocean pool protected by a pier, with its own little beach and spacious, elevated sun terrace shaded by almond trees. Facilities include a selection of bars and restaurants, and the famous Havana Club disco. There's a travel

agency, clothes boutique, Red Cross clinic, and beauty salon. In spring 1999, however, the hotel had deteriorated markedly, looked very rundown and was in the early stages of yet another renovation. Scuba diving gear and jet-skis are available. Rates are US$65 s, US$90 d, US$135 suite low season, US$80s, US$110 d, US$155 suite high season.

Far better are the Comodoro's bungalows which are recommended (see below).

A recent restoration of the **Hotel Neptuno/Tritón,** Avenida 3ra y Calle 72, tel. (33) 1483 o (33) 1606, fax (33) 0042, has done little to assuage the dreary nature of this ugly twin-tower high-rise complex run by Gran Caribe. It has 524 a/c rooms and suites, each with modest furnishings, satellite TV, telephone, radio, safe-deposit box, and refrigerator. The tennis courts, large pool, and sun terrace with funky plastic furniture lack appeal, as does the horribly ugly rocky shoreline. At least the hotel has shops, a pleasant bar, and three restaurants. Rates are US$55 s US$70 d, US$90 t low season, US$70 s, US$90 d, US$110 t high season. *A hotel to avoid.*

Farther west in Barlovento, on the fringe o the city, Marina Hemingway offers the **Qualton El Viejo y el Mar,** tel. (24) 6336, fax (24) 6823, e mail: reservas@oldman.cha.cyt.cu, a modern hotel with 186 rooms boasting modern furnishings, as well as satellite TV, telephone, radio minibar, security box, and balcony. Its attractive lobby features a piano bar, shop, tour desk, and restaurant serving ho-hum food. The marina offers plenty of facilities, including watersports Rates are US$68 s, US$95 d low season US$84 s, US$105 d high season; junior suites cost US$95/116 s/d low season, US$100/121 s/d high season; suites cost US$118/138 s/d low season, US$129/149 s/d high season; bungalows cost US$93/124 s/d low season US$103/144 high season.

Cubanacán's newly built **Hotel El Jardín de Edén,** tel. (24) 7628, fax (24) 4379, e-mail: comercial@comermh.cha.cyt.cu, on Intercanal B a Marina Hemingway, has 314 a/c rooms including eight suites and 12 junior suites, all with satellite TV, telephone, radio, minibar, safety box, and balcony. Facilities include a buffet restaurant café, two bars, splendid swimming pool, shop games room, bicycle rental, and tour bureau Rates are US$60 s, US$80 d, US$95 junio suite, US$110 suite low season, US$70 s, US$90 d, US$110 junior suite, US$130 suite high season.

Cubanacán's **Spa La Pradera,** at Calle 230 y 15, Reparto Siboney, tel. (24) 7473, fax (24) 7198, e-mail: aloja@pradera.cha.cyt.cu, offers an advantageous position for conventioneers and scientists visiting the local biotech facilities but is otherwise out-of-the-way. The modern, 164-room low-rise hotel is attractive, however, and looks out over a large pool and gardens. All rooms feature a/c, satellite TV, telephone, minibar, and security box. The resort hosts entertainment and features squash, basketball, and volleyball courts plus a tiny gym with sauna. The hotel specializes in medical and spa treatments focusing on "life enhancement" and holistic treatments.

Very Expensive (US$110-150)

European tour groups favor the modern **Hotel Copacabana,** Avenida 1ra e/ Calles 34 y 36, tel. (24) 1037, fax (24) 2846, whose oceanfront location offers a unique advantage over other hotels. The hotel was opened in 1955 by a fervent admirer of Brazil. The atmosphere still has a Brazilian flavor and uses names from that country—the Itapoa steak house, the Do Port pizza and snack bar, the Caipirinha bar and grill. Not surprisingly, the place does a healthy trade with package groups from Brazil and Argentina but remains too far away from touristic sites. The 170 rooms boast hardwood furnishings, floral bedspreads, small TV, telephone, and safety box. The Restaurant Tucano (prix-fixe meals cost US$15) looks out over the huge swimming pool—popular with Cuban day-visitors—and the ocean. A separate bar serves the pool, and there's a pizzeria. A discotheque, tourism bureau, car-rental office, and boutique round out the facilities, and scuba diving is offered. Rates are US$75 s, US$110 d low season, US$80 s, US$120 d high season. *Overpriced.*

The most appealing apartment-villas in town are the **Comodoro Bungalow Apartments,** in an aesthetically striking Spanish-style village to either side of the Hotel Comodoro on Avenida 1ra and Calle 84, tel. (24) 5551 or (24) 2028, website: www.cubanacan.cu. Set amid lush foliage are 320 beautiful posada-style, two-story, one-, two-, and three-bedroom villas facing onto two massive amoeba-shaped swimming pools.

Very atmospheric. Rooms have a balcony or patio, plus kitchen, living room, and minibar. Facilities include a 24-hour coffee shop, business center, Photo Service outlet, upscale boutiques, travel agency, pharmacy, and restaurant. A cabaret *espectáculo* and other entertainment are offered. Rates are US$89 s, US$118 d low season, US$98 s, US$137 d high season for one bedroom; US$153-184 low season, US$180-216 high season for two bedrooms; and US$188-204 low season, US$220-248 high season for three bedrooms.

Chateau Miramar is a Cubanacán property on the ugly coral shorefront next to the aquarium on Avenida 1ra at Calle 62, tel. (33) 1915 or (33) 0224, fax (24) 0224. The handsome five-story, 50-room hotel was recently refurbished but cannot justify its room rates. Rooms, although a bit sterile, are neatly furnished and feature satellite TV, minibar, radio, and safety box. Nine of the rooms are one-bedroom suites with jacuzzi tub. Facilities include a seaside pool, elegant restaurant, two bars, executive office, small shop, Casa del Tabaco, massage, plus entertainment. The sea spray reaches up to the top-floor windows. It's popular with businessfolk. Rates are US$106 s, US$130 d, US$190 suites.

Aiming at businessmen and conventioneers is the **Hotel Palco,** at Avenida 146 e/ 11 y 13, tel. (33) 7235, fax (33) 7250 or (33) 7236, e-mail: info@hpalco.gov.cu, website: www.cubaweb.cu/palco, adjoining the Palacio de Convenciones (Convention Center). This purpose-built, five-story hotel has an expansive lobby and stylish modern decor (albeit hints of second-rate construction). The 180 rooms include 36 junior suites and are arrayed around an atrium with a skylit roof with stained glass and, at the base, a botanical garden and still-water pool with carp (mosquitoes breed and feed—on guests—copiously). Rooms are spacious and up to par, with modern decor in calming ochers, a/c, satellite TV, telephone, minibar, safety box, tile floors, and large, attractive bathroom with hair dryer. Facilities include a business center, elegant restaurant, outdoor snack bar, split-level pool, small sauna, and smaller gym. Rates are US$74 s, US$94 d low season, US$91 s, US$111 d high season, US$130-150 junior suites year-round.

You can rent attractive two-story waterfront apartments, bungalows, and villas in the **Cuba-**

nacán **Paraíso** complex in Marina Hemingway, tel. (24) 1150, ext. 85. It has about 100 houses and bungalows with one, two or three bedrooms. All have terraces, TV and video, safe-deposit box, and kitchen. In a touch of strange Cuban logic, the *carpeta* (reception office) is the *last* building at the far end of Pier 1. A one-room bungalow costs US$130 s/d; *casas* cost US$140 s/d for one room, US$200 for two rooms for up to four people, and US$250 for three rooms for up to six people.

Luxury (US$150+)
The **Hotel Meliá Habana,** haughtily perched atop a manmade mound on Avenida 3ra, 200 meters east of Calles 84, tel. (24) 8500, fax (24) 8505, e-mail: depres@habana.solmelia.cma.net, is Havana's most recent addition to the luxury hotel market and aims squarely at a business clientele. Although its disharmonious concrete and plate-glass exterior jars, the expansive lobby is beautiful, with a surfeit of gray and green marbles and ponds, and a sumptuous lobby bar plus the elegant Bosque Habana restaurant. The 405 a/c rooms and four suites are arrayed in a sinfully ugly complex fronting the shore. All come up to international standards, featuring balconies, satellite TV, telephone with fax and modem lines, and safety boxes. The executive floor offers more personalized service. Facilities include four restaurants, five bars, swimming pool, tennis courts, hairdresser, gym, and business center, plus up-to-date meeting facilities. Rates are US$140 s, US$175 d standard floors, US$185 s, US$220 d executive floor (US$15 extra with ocean view; suites US$15 extra). *Overpriced.*

SUBURBAN HAVANA

Budget (Less Than US$35)
Parque Lenin: The **Motel La Herradura,** tel. (44) 1058, on the south side of the Centro Ecuestre, offers seven a/c rooms with TV (local stations only) and utilitarian decor for US$17 s/d.

HABANA DEL ESTE

The Playas del Este have traditionally been the spot of choice for Habaneros on weekends, and despite the rigors of the Special Period, many Cubans still find the resources to vacation here. Many places are ugly concrete carbuncles that don't serve current tourism needs well. Some are terribly rundown. This has led to a growing trade in private room rentals. The entire complex is divided into *zonas,* each with a *carpeta* for rental units. Horizontes runs the show in Santa María; Islazul has a monopoly in Boca Ciega and Guanabo.

Casas Particulares
Playas del Este—Boca Ciega and Guanabo: There are many *casas particulares* from which to choose. Look for the signs or ask for a recommendation on the street. One of the best is an attractive colonial home at the corner of Avenida 7ma and Calle 472. Also try Angela Rico Terrera, tel. (96) 2885; and Marisela Dieguez at Calle 490 #5C.

Budget (Less Than US$35)
Alamar: Villa Bacuranao, on the eastern shore of the cove at Playa Bacuranao, was closed at press time. No restoration was slated, but stay tuned.

About one km east of Celimar is a dour tourist complex for Cubans called **Campismo Popular Celimarina,** with small and basic self-catering huts sprinkled amid pasture nibbled by goats. The shore isn't particularly appealing.

Playas del Este—Boca Ciega and Guanabo: Islazul's **Boca Ciega,** at the east end of 1ra, tel. (96) 2771, has 10 simple houses for rent at US$16 s, US$21 d. They were due for a restoration in late 1999. It has no facilities but rents volleyballs and footballs.

Hotel Gran Vía, another Islazul property, on the corner of Avenida 5ta and 462, tel. (96) 2271, offers five rooms for Cubans and five for foreigners at US$21 s/d low season, US$26 d high season. It has an a/c restaurant adjacent.

Also check out the simple **Islazul Hotel Miramar,** on Avenida 9 and Calle 478 in Guanabo, tel. (96) 2507, offering 23 rooms with cold water only, plus balcony, for US$20 s/d low season, US$26 d high season; and the **Islazul Villas Playa Hermosa,** on Avenida 5ta between 472 and 474. It features a cabaret Fri.-Sun. night.

Guanabo also has several extra-budget hotels (US$5 or so) that say they no longer accept foreigners. Among them are **Hotel María** and **Hotel**

Vía Blanca, opposite each other on Avenida 5ta at Calle 486. You may have better luck at the very basic Villa María Blanca.

Inexpensive (US$35-60)

Ciudad Panamericano: The **Hotel Panamericano Resort,** Calle A y Avenida Central, tel. (95) 1242, fax (95) 1021, features a hotel and two apartment complexes. The hotel's unappetizing lobby, full of dowdy utility furniture, is your first hint that a reservation here is a grave error. The rooms, likewise, cry out for a refurbishment, and in spring 1999 were still outfitted with modern but poorly made furnishings and maroon fabrics. Telephone and satellite TV are standard. The hotel has a large swimming pool that is a popular social scene on weekends. There's also a large gym plus sauna, car and moped rental, and tourism bureau. It offers a beach excursion to Playas del Este for US$20. Rates: US$55 s, US$60 d.

The only other option is to rent a meagerly furnished apartment in the **Apartotel Panamericano Resort,** opposite the hotel. It offers 421 two- and three-bedroom apartments popular with budget European charter groups. Facilities are meager, even dour, reminding me of a student union in a low-end Polytechnic. The lobby has a small bar and there's a basic restaurant. But you can't argue with the prices: US$46 low season, US$54 high season for a two-bedroom apartment; US$58 low season, US$68 high season for a three-bedroom apartment.

Jiniteros may approach you on the street and offer *casa particulares.* Expect to pay US$20-25 daily.

Playas del Este–Santa María: Horizontes runs the **Aparthotel Atlántico,** on Avenida de las Terrazas, tel. (97) 1494, fax (97) 1203, offering pleasantly furnished a/c apartments with TV and telephone. Facilities include a restaurant, swimming pool with bar, scooter rental, tour desk, tennis courts, and entertainment. One-room units rent for US$24 s/d low season, US$36 high season; two-room units cost US$32 and US$48 respectively.

If you don't mind being on a steep hill, a 10-minute walk from the beach, try **Villas Horizontes Mirador del Mar,** tel. (97) 1354, fax (97) 262. Its one- to five-bedroom a/c units in a self-contained complex feature a hilltop swimming pool, restaurant, and medical service that extends to massage in its *centro recreativo* (recreation center). Each has cable TV. It also rents rooms for US$36 d low season, US$40 d high season with breakfast. Villa rates run from US$45 for a one-bedroom unit to US$198 for a five-bedroom unit low season; US$52 to US$224 high season.

Villa Mégano, midway down Avenida de las Terrazas, tel. (97) 1610, at the far west end of Playas del Este, is a Horizontes property a 10-minute walk from the beach. The individual cabins received facelifts in 1997. The ambience and decor of the a/c cabins is simple yet appealing, with tile floors, bamboo furnishings, tiny satellite TV, small tiled bath with showers, and plate-glass doors opening to verandas. Larger cabins cost US$34 s, US$44 d low season, US$46 s, US$58 d high season; smaller cabins *(chicas)* cost US$28 s, US$36 d low season, US$38 s, US$48 d high season.

Another Horizontes option is **Aparthotel Las Terrazas,** Avenida Las Terrazas and Calle 9, tel. (687) 4910, fronting the shore. It has 144 a/c apartments with kitchen, TV, radio, and telephone for US$28 s, US$35 d. There's also a swimming pool.

Playas del Este–Boca Ciega and Guanabo: If you want a private villa in Boca Ciega, you can book one through **Villas Vista Mar,** on Avenida 1ra and Calle 438 in Boca Ciega. It has 69 *casas,* from US$44 for a two bedroom, US$63 for a three bedroom.

Cabañas Cuanda's, one block south of Avenida 5ta at Calle 472, tel. (97) 2774, has 37 a/c rooms, most with double beds and shower with tepid water. Rooms are overpriced at US$25 d.

Moderate (US$60-85)

Cojimar: A grand colonial mansion at the top of the hill at the entrance to the village was being restored and was slated to become a hotel, perhaps to open in 2000.

Playas del Este–Santa María: The most popular place in town is the rather gloomy **Hotel Tropicoco,** between Avenidas Sur and Las Terrazas and facing Playa Santa María, tel. (97) 1371, fax (97) 1389. The uninspired, communist-style, five-story building was recently renovated (you'd never know it), but no amount of tinkering can improve the appallingly designed and unwelcoming lobby. In spring 1999, it seemed overdue for a complete overhaul, yet remained popular with Canadian tour companies (but, one suspects, not their clientele). It has 188 a/c rooms with uninspired decor, telephone, and radio. Services include a restaurant, bar, tour desk, shop, Casa del Tabaco, post office, and car rental. Rooms cost US$40 s, US$53 d low season, US$52 s, US$65 d high season.

Much nicer is the **Sea Club Hotel Arenal,** on Laguna Itabo in the midst of the lagoon between Playas Santa María del Mar and Boca Ciega, tel. (97) 1272, fax (97) 1287 (in Europe, Pantravel, C.so Pestalozzi, 4a, 6900 Lugano, Switzerland, tel. 91-923-2043, fax 91-922-6286, e-mail: srosso@pantravel.ch. It relies mostly on Italian, German, and Austrian charters. Red-tile-roofed units surround a massive pool and lush lawns with thatched restaurant and bar. Rooms are spacious and offer eye-pleasing decor and furnishings. However, this all-inclusive property doesn't quite live up to the images presented in the slick brochure. It has a few shops, and the staff try hard to keep guests amused with canned *animación* (entertainment). Rates are US$65 per person (double occupancy) standard, US$75 superior Jan.-July and Sep.-Dec., and US$75 and US$95 July-August. A single supplement costs US$20 and US$30 respectively.

Very Expensive (US$110-150)

Tarará: Cubanacán Tarará, Via Blanca, Tarará, tel. (97) 1057, offers a range of villas—*casas confort*—for rent, with from one to four bedrooms. Most belong to Cubanacán. Others belong to Puerto Sol or to Islazul, which rents out to Cubans and tourists alike. The facility was in the midst of much-needed renovation at press time, when about half of the villas had received a thorough restoration that has brought them up to modern standards, although the grounds remain in need of a spruce-up. Each has a radio, satellite TV, telephone, and private parking. Nonregistered guests are strictly proscribed (none may

stay overnight without authority of the management, which even requires a list of guests attending "a social gathering"). A grocery, laundry service, and restaurants are on-site. Two-bedroom units cost US$160 low season, US$200 high season without a pool; US$200 low season, US$250 high season with pool. Three-bedroom units cost US$240/300 low/high season without pool; US$280/350 with pool. Four-bedroom units cost US$320/400 and US$360/450 respectively. The *carpeta,* tel. (97) 1462, fax (97) 1499 or (97) 1313, is 100 meters east of the marina.

Playas del Este–Santa María: A dreary option, but offering the advantage of being atop the beach, is the **Gran Caribe Club Atlántico,** tel. (97) 1085, fax (80) 3911. Until recently, it was leased entirely for use by an Italian tour company (Going One), but one suspects that the crackdown on *jiniteras* pulled the plug on the Italian market, forcing it to open its doors to all comers. This all-inclusive is a bit lowly by international all-inclusive standards and is dour in its public amenities. It has 92 a/c rooms with satellite TV, radio, and minibar. Facilities include a restaurant and snack bar, swimming pool, tiny gym, tennis court, and shop. Entertainment staff try to put a bit of pep into the scene. It may still be overpriced—even with meals included—for US$78 s, US$125 d low season, US$87 s, US$142 d high season.

The most elegant options are the **Villas los Pinos,** Avenida Las Terrazas y Calle 4, tel. (97) 1361, fax (97) 1524, e-mail: informatica@pinos gca.cma.net, run by Gran Caribe, which offers 46 two-and three-room villas. Some appear a bit fuddy-duddy, others are impressive and up to international standards, with their own private pools. Villa #35 even has its own squash court! They all have TV, VCR, radio, telephone, and kitchen. Rates are US$175-375 low season, US$200-425 high season for up to four people, including house maid service. Other staff are on hand, and baby sitters can be arranged.

FOOD

Cuba may take you on a culinary adventure, but it's not one that will usually leave you asking for more. You may have heard horror stories about its cuisine. Or jokes, such as, "What are the three biggest failures of the Revolution? Breakfast, lunch, and dinner." Or, "My wife thinks she's going blind. Whenever she opens the refrigerator, she doesn't see anything!"

For Cubans, rationing has become a permanent fixture of the past four decades. The collapse of the Soviet Union only made a bad situation much worse, since in 1989, an estimated 40% of rationed items were supplied by the former Soviet bloc. The Cuban government likes to blame the US embargo, but a sustained tour of the countryside inevitably leads to the conclusion that the inefficient communist system is mostly to blame. Whatever, the paucity is a constant source of exasperation for foreigners traveling independently beyond Havana. Even tourist hotels are subject to the shortages imposed by a mismanaged economy. After a while, you'll get bored of fried chicken, ham sandwiches *(bocaditos)*, and vegetables either overcooked or from a can. Bite the bullet. As a tourist, you're privileged to get the best that's available.

Before the Revolution, Havana also boasted many world-class restaurants. After 1959, many of the middle- and upper-class clientele fled Cuba along with the restaurateurs and chefs, taking their custom, knowledge, and entrepreneurship with them. Over the ensuing 40 years, Cuba's culinary landscape suffered for lack of international connections; let's face it: what could the Soviets offer?

Today, all but a handful of Cuba's restaurants are state owned, and the blasé socialist attitude toward dining, tough economic times, and general inefficiencies of the system are reflected in boring menus, low standards, and sketchy availability (the state system of food distribution is so inefficient that you'll rarely find fresh vegetables on your plate—expect fruits and veggies to be canned). Don't be fooled by extensive menus, as many items will probably not be available.

Now the Good News

Havana *does* still have some fine restaurants. Many of the best are in the top-class hotels—which usually have two or more to choose from, with specialty restaurants offering *à la carte* menus (meals in the hotel eateries are rarely

WHAT TO EAT AND DRINK

Cuban Dishes

Cuban *criollo* food is mostly peasant fare, usually lacking in sauces and spices (you'll be hard-pressed to find spicy food in Cuba). Pork *(cerdo)* and chicken *(pollo)* are the two main protein staples, usually served with rice and black beans *(frijoles negros)* and fried banana or plantain *(platanos)*. *Cerdo asado* (succulent roast pork), *moros y cristianos* (Moors and Christians—rice and black beans), and *arroz congrí* (rice with red beans) are the most popular and widely dispensed dishes. Another national dish is *ajíaco*, (hotchpotch), a stew of meats and vegetables.

By far the most common dish is fried chicken *(pollo frito)* and grilled chicken *(pollo asado)*. Grilled pork chops are also common. Beef is rare outside the tourist restaurants, where filet mignons and prime rib tend to be far below Western standards—often overcooked and fatty.

Occasionally, you'll find rabbit *(conejo)*, but where they get rabbits from I don't know, as I've never seen one in Cuba. Meat finds its way into snacks sold at roadside snack stalls, such as *empanadas de carne*, pies or flat pancakes enclosing meat morsels; *ayacas*, a kind of tamale made of a corn tortilla filled with meat and spices; and *piccadillo*, a snack of spiced beef, onion, and tomato. Crumbled pork rinds find their way into *fufu*, mixed with cooked plantain. Ham and cheese, the two most ubiquitous foods, find their way into fish and stuffed inside steaks as *bistec uruguayano*.

Fish had never been a major part of the Cuban diet and has made its way onto the national menu only in recent years. Sea bass *(corvina)*, swordfish *(filet de emperador)*, and red snapper *(pargo)* are the most commonly eaten species. You can find some splendid fish dishes, but all too often, Cuban chefs zealously overcook your fish steak until it resembles a boot sole.

Lobster and jumbo shrimps are readily available. If you avoid the expensive touristy haunts, you can enjoy a whole-lobster meal with trimmings and beer for US$10.

Vegetables

Cubans consider vegetables "rabbit food." Fresh vegetables rarely find their way onto menus, other than in salads. Mixed salads *(ensaladas mixta)* usually consist of a plate of lettuce or cucumbers *(pepinos)* and tomatoes (often served green, yet sweet) with oil and vinagrette dressing. *Palmito*, the succulent heart of palm, is also common as a salad. Often, you'll receive canned vegetables or a plateful of shredded cabbage *(col)*, usually alone. Beetroot is also common. So is yucca, which closely resembles a stringy potato in look, taste, and texture. It is prepared and served like a potato in any number of ways. A popular side dish is *boniato* (sweet potato), and other root vegetables such as *malanga*, a bland root crop rich in starch grown by the native Indian population and a rural staple.

Vegetables are most often used in soups and stews, such as *ajíaco*, a popular and tasty soup made with yucca, malanga, turnips, and herbs. Another common soup is garbanzo.

Beans are the most common vegetable and are used in many dishes. *Congrí oriental* is rice and red beans cooked together (the term refers to the Congo). *Frijoles negros dormidos* are black beans cooked and allowed to stand till the next day.

Fruits

Cuba's rich soils and amicable climate should nourish a panoply of fruits. But, alas, fruits are rare jewels outside hotel restaurant buffets. Even oranges and grapefruits, grown widely in Cuba, are about as common as gold nuggets. Virtually the entire fruit harvest goes to produce fruit juice. To buy fruits, head to the *mercado agropecuario* (farmers' market).

The most common fruit is the *platano*, a relative of the banana but used as a vegetable in a variety of ways, including as *tostones*, fried green plantains eaten as a snack, much like thick chips or English crisps.

In addition to well-known fruits such as papayas, look for such lesser-known types as the furry *mamey*

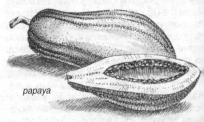

papaya

(continued on next page)

colorado, an oval, chocolate-brown fruit with a custardy texture and taste; the cylindrical, orange-colored *marañon,* the cashew-apple, whose seed grows *outside* the fruit; the oval, coarse-skinned *zapote,* a sweet granular fruit; and the large, irregular-shaped *guanábana,* whose thick skin is covered with briars (the pulp, however, is sweet and "soupy," with a hint of vanilla). *Canitel* (familiar to travelers to Jamaica as ackee) is also grown, through rarely found. Surprisingly, coconuts are rare.

Count yourself lucky to get your hands on mangoes, whose larger versions are referred to in the feminine gender, *mangas,* because of their size. And be careful with the word *papaya.* Habaneros refer to the papaya fruit as *fruta bomba* because in Cuba, "papaya" is a slang term for vagina.

Bread and Desserts
Havana has several bakeries making Cuba's infamously horrible bread (most often served as buns or twisted rolls), which Maurice Halperin found, whether toasted or not, "formed a sticky mass difficult to dislodge from between cheek and gum." I disagree— usually it's dry as a bone. (Cuba's reputation for lousy bread predates the Revolution. "Why can't the Cubans make decent bread?" Che Guevara is reported to have asked. Of course, Cubans eat rice, not bread, as they have since the early 19th century, when it became the staple food of black slaves; only well-to-do Cubans ate bread.) To be fair, some hotels and restaurants serve excellent bread, and the situation has improved markedly since the signing of a contract with a French company that now supplies breads to tourist hotels and sweet and tasty confections through outlets under the **Pain de Paris** banner.

Cubans make great desserts, often available for a few centavos at bakeries *(panaderias).* Hotel confections tend toward biscuits and sponge cakes (usually rather dry) topped with jam and canned cream. *Flan,* a caramel custard, is also popular (a variant is a delicious pudding called *natilla),* as is marmalade and cheese.

Also try *tatianoff,* chocolate cake smothered with cream; *chu,* bite-size puff pastries stuffed with an almost bitter cheesy meringue; and *churrizo,* deep-fried doughnut rings sold at every bakery and many streetside stalls, where you can also buy *galletas,* ubiquitous sweet biscuits sold loose.

The many coconut-based desserts include *coco quemado* (coconut pudding) and *coco rallady y queso* (grated coconut with cheese in syrup).

Of course, the best dessert of all is Cuban **ice cream,** most notably that made by Coppelia. Cubans use specific terms for different kinds of scoops. *Helado,* which means "ice cream," also means a single large scoop; two large scoops are called *jimagua;* several small scoops is an *ensalada;* and *sundae* is ice cream served with fruit. Want more? Ask for *adicionál.*

Nonalcoholic Drinks
Coca-Cola and Pepsi (or their Cuban-made equivalent, Tropicola), Fanta (or Cuban-made Najita), and other soft drinks are readily available at hotels, restaurants, and dollar stores. *Malta* is a popular nonalcoholic drink that resembles a dark English stout but tastes like root beer and is popular among young Habanaras.

Roadside snack stalls sell *refrescos,* chilled fruit juices (usually 20-50 centavos a glass), and *batidos,* delicious and refreshing fruit drinks blended with milk and ice. Just as thirst quenching and energy giving is *guarapo,* fresh-squeezed sugarcane juice, sold cold at roadside *guaraperias* (they're hard to find in Havana; ask around).

Coffee: Cubans take frequent coffee breaks, and no home visit is complete without being offered a *cafecito,* thick and strong, like espresso, served black in tiny cups and heavily sweetened. Unfortunately, much Cuban domestic coffee has been adulterated—*café mesclado*—since the Special Period with other roasted products, usually chicory. The best export brand is Cubita, sold vacuum-packed. *Café con leche* (coffee with milk) is served in tourist restaurants, usually at a ratio of 50:50, with hot milk. Don't confuse this with *Café americano,* which is usually diluted Cuban coffee.

Alcoholic Drinks
Beers: Cuba makes several excellent German-style beers, usually served just a little above freezing (US75 cents-US$3, depending on where you drink). Hatuey and Bucanero are full-flavored lagers. Cristal and Lagarto are lighter. The inexpensive and duller *Clara* is brewed for domestic consumption (typically one peso). You'll also find Heineken, Labatts, Ice, some US brands, and Tecate at most bars and in dollar stores (US$1.50-4).

Rums: Cuba's specialty is rum and rum-based cocktails. Cuban rums resemble Bacardi rums—not surprising, since several key rum factories in Cuba were originally owned by the Bacardi family—and come in three classes: light and dry *(ligero y seco)*

(continued on next page)

WHAT TO EAT AND DRINK
(continued)

Carta Blanca, aged for three years and also known as *tres años*; golden and dry *(dorado y seco) Carta de Oro*, aged for five years *(cinco años)*; and dark seven-year-old *Añejo (siete años)*. There are several brands, most notably the Habana Club label.

Golden and aged rums are best drunk straight (although many Cubans drink *tragos*—shots—of overproof *aguardiente*, cheap white rum). White rum is ideal for cocktails, such as a *piña colada, daiquiri*, and *mojito*, the latter two favorites of Ernest Hemingway, who helped launch both drinks to world fame. Recalling the Andrews Sisters' song, "Drinking Rum and Coca-Cola," you'll surely want to try a *Cuba libre* on its home turf. Dark rums are also used in cocktails such as the appropriately named *Mulatta*, with lime and cocoa liqueur.

Wines: Most upscale restaurants serve Chilean, French, Spanish, and even California wines, although generally twice the price or more of the US or Europe (expect to pay US$4 and upward for a tiny glass, from US$15 for a bottle). Most are poorly kept and prove disappointing. Avoid *vino quinado*, a sweet and unsophisticated Cuban wine. The most memorable thing about it is the hangover.

Forget hard liquors, which are readily available in touristy bars but usually very expensive. You can buy bottles of your favorite imported tipple at *diplo-tiendas*.

included in package prices). Many hotels also feature *Noches Cubana* (Cuban nights), showcasing typical Cuban specialties.

World-class restaurants, such as La Torre, are beginning to appear with the aid of foreign—primarily French—chefs who have arrived in recent years. Tasty traditional Cuban dishes are easy to find. Some restaurants are great values (El Aljibe comes to mind), while many others would give even the Japanese a nasty case of sticker shock.

Most restaurants serve seafood dishes, and several specialize in the food of King Neptune. But you have to search hard for cuisine of international standard (some are deplorably bad: Restaurante 1830, for example), and most "Chinese" and "Italian" dishes are really Cuban dishes with a twist. Cuba's Chinese restaurants make do as best they can with limited items. Italian restaurants are mostly limited to spaghetti bolognese and pizza. You'll find pizzerias serving local custom (you can buy a slice for five pesos). Even in dollar restaurants, most Cuban pizzas are dismal by North American standards—usually with a bland base covered with a thin layer of tomato paste and a smattering of cheese and ham (British people will recognize it).

As a rule of thumb, avoid the more sophisticated dishes, particularly with "international" menus, because few chefs have the ingredients or know-how to make them (the state provides the menus—many date from the 1960s—with explicit instructions on how particular dishes should be prepared, and chefs are barred from experimentation). "The fact that the favorite restaurants of many government officials are El Tocororo and El Ranchón underlines a misunderstanding in Cuba of what high-class restaurants are all about," notes *Cigar Aficionado*. Don't trust your hotel concierge—he's been instructed to point you to the high-priced government restaurants.

Fortunately, the country has begun to invest in culinary (and management) training in order to resolve the deplorable inadequacy of restaurant food.

State-run restaurants come in grades one to seven, one being the best. Fortunately, wherever you eat you're likely to be serenaded by troubadors to add cheer to even the dreariest meal.

A Few Practicalities
Be relaxed about dining; expect service to take much longer than you may be used to. Sometimes, the service is swift and friendly, sometimes protracted and surly. For a lunchtime pizza, you can wait 10 minutes for a waiter, another half-hour for the pizza to arrive, 15 minutes for the bill, and another 10 for the change. Plan up to two hours for dinner in a state-run restaurant. Many restaurants serve until midnight, some 24 hours.

Take a sweater—many restaurants have the air-conditioning cranked up to freezing. In general, avoid wines. Cuba's hot climate is hell on fresh wines, and few restaurants know how to store them. Stick to steadfast staples such as Torres and Concha y Toro. And bring your own cigars—few restaurants sell them.

Virtually all restaurants now charge tourists in dollars, even though Cubans may pay in pesos in the same restaurant (but not in tourist and other upscale restaurants). The price in pesos is usually converted one-to-one into dollars, which translates into vast overcharging of tourists without any commensurate preference in quality of food or service.

In the better restaurants, waiters expect to be tipped 10%, even where a service charge (now the norm in expensive restaurants) has been added to your bill. Check your bill carefully, however—bread is usually delivered to your table but is often charged to your bill extra even if you didn't order it. That, in fact, is one of several dastardly capitalistic tricks that the government has introduced to separate you from your dollars. Another is the *consumo mínimo* policy—a minimum-purchase charge applied in an increasing number of establishments (usually bars and nightclubs, but applying to meals, such as at the Habana Café) and ripe for abuse.

Havana's restaurant scene is in a constant state of flux. Many of the establishments listed below may have changed by the time you read this (so, too, their prices).

Remember that you can always dine for a pittance at streetside snack bars, which still accept pesos from tourists.

Self-Catering

For the average Cuban, shopping for food is a dismal activity. There are scant groceries, no roadside 7-Elevens. The state-run groceries, called *puestos,* where fresh produce—often of questionable quality—is sold, can make Westerners cringe. Cuba's best fruits and vegetables are exported for hard currency or turned into juices. Meat is equally scarce. As a result, most Cubans are forced to rely on the black market.

Since 1994, when free trading was legalized for farmers, Cuba has sprouted produce or farmers' markets *(mercados agropecuarios),* which

farmers' market

sell fruits, vegetables, and meats. Every district has at least one, selling in both dollars and pesos.

You can purchase Western goods at dollars-only stores, open to foreigners and Cubans alike and stocked with packaged and canned goods from all over the world. Havana even has a few supermarkets stocked with everything you'd expect to find in a Safeway or Sainsbury's. Cupet gas stations usually have dollars-only stores attached, where Western snack goods are sold.

Fresh fish is harder to come by. The government-run **Pescaderias Especiales** sell fish and other seafoods. Each municipality has one. The one in Vedado is next to the Hotel Vedado on Calle 25 between N and O; in spring 1999, it was selling shrimp for 22 pesos per pound, snapper *(pargo)* at 35 pesos per pound, and squid for 25 pesos per pound.

Health

Eating in Cuba doesn't present the health problems associated with many other destinations in Latin America. I've only once gotten sick eating in Cuba. However, in February 1999, at least 14 people died in Matanzas after eating from an unlicenced street stall, so *caveat emptor!*

And the water? Well, Christopher Columbus noted the quality of Cuba's water in 1494 on his second voyage to the New World: "The water is so cold and of such goodness and so sweet that no better could be found in the world."

That was then. Today, the state of Havana's plumbing is questionable, and tap water is best avoided. Bottled mineral water is widely available, and it's normal when you ask for water to receive bottled water, usually Ciego Montero Agua Mineral, produced by Cubagua. (It comes from Manatial de Ciego Montero, in Palmira in Cienfuegos province, and according to the label, "stimulates the digestion and facilitates the urinary elimination of uric acid.")

Breakfasts

Few places serve breakfast other than hotel restaurants, most of which serve variations on the same dreary buffets (*mesa sueca,* or Swiss table): ham, cheese, boiled eggs, and an array of fruits and unappetizing cakes and biscuits. The variety is usually limited by Western standards, and presentation often leaves much to be desired. Fruits—mangoes, papayas, pineapples—are most often frozen overnight and thawed (barely) for breakfast, thereby destroying the pulp and flavor. Top-class hotels often do a bit better. Nonguests are usually welcome, too; prices range US$4-12.

Don't leave your hotel breakfast (normally served 7-10 a.m.) until the last thing, or you'll arrive to find only crumbs.

Hotel room rates rarely include breakfast, although members of tour groups usually have breakfasts (and most dinners) included in the cost of their tour. Refunds are not made for meals not taken. Many hotels offer an *oferta especial* (special offer) that grants guests a discount up to 25% on buffet meals.

One of the best buffet breakfasts is served in the **Hotel Melía Cohiba.** Another good option (although the food is ho-hum) is the **Café La Rampa,** occupying the terrace outside the Hotel Habana Libre Tryp and offering a breakfast special of coffee and toast for US$2, with eggs, bacon, coffee, and juice for US$7.

Peso Eateries

Most restaurants admit both Cubans and foreigners, and charge the former in pesos and the latter in dollars. However, you can still find basic *criollo* dishes at pesos-only restaurants that aim at Cubans. Food availability tends to be hit and miss (usually only one or two items are available) and the cuisine undistinguished at best. In some, you may be refused service or asked to pay in dollars.

State-run *merenderos* (lunch counters) and private roadside snack stalls display their meager offerings in glass cases. A signboard indicates what's available, with items noted on strips that can be removed as particular items sell out. These accept pesos from foreigners and are an incredibly cheap way of appeasing your stomach with snacks.

You can still find plenty of *guarapos* throughout Havana producing fresh, sweet, empowering juice from crushed sugarcane.

Paladares

As everywhere in Cuba, the way to go is to eat at *paladares*—private restaurants whose owners often meld entrepreneurship with a sense for experimentation and culinary flair (the word *pal adar* means "palate," and comes from the name of the restaurant of the character Raquel, a poor woman who makes her fortune cooking, in a popular Brazilian TV soap opera, *Vale Todo*). Here you can fill up for US$5-15, usually with bloat-inducing meals. Often, the price includes a salad and dessert, as well as beer.

The owners put great energy into their enterprises, many of which are open 24 hours. Most serve both Cubans (often for pesos) and foreigners (always for dollars), and display an inventiveness in preparing good food and service that Castro himself has often complained about with regard to state restaurants. However, Castro says that the *paladares* are "enriching" their owners and has refused to dine at them. (*Paladares* were legalized in September 1994 to help resolve the food crisis but have always been fettered by onerous taxation and restrictive self-employment laws.) *Paladares* are not allowed to sell shrimp or lobster (a state monopoly). Nonetheless, most do, so ask: it's easy enough to find a huge lobster meal for US$10, including beer or soft drink. Restaurant owners re also allowed only to serve up to 12 people at one seating. Though relatives can assist, the owners cannot hire salaried workers.

At press time, the crippling monthly licensing fee had put many *paladares* out of business, as intended. Because they come and go, it's often difficult to monitor their sanitary standards. Feel free to check out the kitchen (often a stomach-churning experience) before choosing to dine.

Vedado has the greatest concentration of *paladares,* but you'll also find others scattered around town. Many are open 24 hours; some are closed or operate at restricted hours during the summer off-season. Your Cuban friends will be able to recommend their favorite places. Look for Christmas lights (the *paladares'* unofficial advertisement) hanging outside.

The shining star in the constellation is **La Guarida,** in Centro Habana (see below).

Fast Food

Thank goodness there are as yet no McDonald's or KFCs in Havana. However, in 1995, the government announced plans for a chain of 30 KFC-style, dollars-only fried-chicken joints called **El Rápido,** including a drive-in just off the Malecón with waitresses on roller skates (they proved too unstable and were short-lived).

Cuba's answer to McDonald's is **Burgui,** serving up uninspired burgers. It, too, has outlets throughout the city, open 24 hours. Hamburgers are popular, cheap, and usually not much worse than North American fast-food burgers (though some, to be sure, *are* worse—much worse—

TOP TEN PLACES TO EAT

Nowhere in Havana can rival the better restaurants outside the country, and you'll be hard-pressed to rank highly any additional restaurants beyond the following, which represents my recommended top 10 places to eat in Havana:

La Bodeguita del Medio, 207 Empedrado, Habana Vieja, tel. (62) 4498. This well-aged gem serves some of the best traditional Cuban food in Havana, but better still is the ambience steeped in a proletarian fusion of dialectics and rum. Commune with the ghost of Papa (Ernest Hemingway), who drank his *mojitos* here.

El Floridita, Monserrate y Obispo, Habana Vieja, tel. (63) 1063. The *other* Hemingway haunt, and the yin to the Bodeguita's yang, this restaurant specializes in seafood—notably lobster—served in opulent rococo surrounds. The food ranges from ho-hum to good, but what earns top marks is the only-in-Havana ambience.

La Paella, Hostal Valencia, Calle Oficios, e/ Obrapí y Lamparilla, Habana Vieja, tel. (57) 1037. A flashback to the *posadas* of Spain, this little charmer boasts provincial Spanish decor and tasty paellas, best washed down with a hearty Hatuey beer.

Roof Garden Restaurant, Hotel Sevilla, Trocadero #55, e/ Paseo de Martí y Zulueta, tel. (33) 8560. A splendid neoclassical fin-de-siecle atmosphere and—finally—recherché French cuisine to match under the watchful eye of a French executive chef.

La Guarida, Calle Concordia #418, e/ Garvasio y Escobar, Centro Habana, tel. (62) 4940. A tastefully conceived *paladar* with creative French-inspired cuisine, light on the palate and enhanced by the bistro-style setting, despite the condition of the rundown surroundings.

La Torre, FOCSA, Calle 17 e/ M y N, Vedado, tel. (55) 3089. Superbly executed French cuisine (considering the problem of obtaining fresh ingredients) prepared by a French chef, with spectacular vistas to boot.

Le Chansonnier, Calle 15 #306, e/ H y I, Vedado, tel. (32) 3788. A bistro-style *paladar* similar to La Guarida, albeit with simpler yet creative fare.

Coppelia, Calle 23 esq. L, Vedado. What, you ask, is an ice cream "parlor" doing in a list of best restaurants? Well, this is no ordinary ice cream store. Tremendous setting, tremendous atmosphere, tasty ice cream, a chance to commune with Habaneros, and the best damn bargain in town! For this, skip the dollar zone, and eat in the peso section.

El Aljibe, Avenida 7ma e/ 24 y 26, Miramar, tel. (24) 1583. The best *criollo* fare in town. Go for the house *chicken asado* prepared in a sweet sauce that is a well-guarded secret. Havana's chic in-crowd dines here (as well as any visiting Hollywood mavens) and the service is prompt.

Ranchón, Avenida 5ta esq. 16, Miramar, tel. (24) 1185. Steadfastly tasty Cuban fare, backed by well-prepared continental dishes served in handsomely rustic surroundings.

such as those sold at roadside stands for one peso. Are you sure that's even *meat?*).

Cafés and Snack Bars

Havana has plenty of splendid sidewalk cafés, although most of the prerevolutionary *cafeterías* (coffee stands) that used to make coffee on every corner have vanished, as have most of the former tea shops (*Casas de Té* or *Casas de Infusiones*). Most cafés are really snack bars-cum-restaurants; there are few in the purist Parisian tradition, and as of yet, no American-style coffee shops.

Rumbos S.A. has been opening up roadside snack bars at strategic points all over Havana, of an attractive uniform design with green-shade awnings. They serve a standard menu of *bocaditos, papa fritas,* and *criollo* staples such as fried chicken.

Ice Cream and Desserts

Cubans are renowned lovers of ice cream, and there are plenty of *heladerías* to appease them. You can buy ice creams for dollars in most tourist hotels and restaurants, or you can do as Cubans do and buy from *heladerías* on the street for a few pesos. Coppelia, everyone's favorite ice cream, still accepts pesos from tourists and is the best show in town.

Havana is blessed with numerous bakeries selling a wide range of desserts. The best are **Pain de Paris: Croissants de France,** tel. (33) 7669, fax (33) 7671, run with French instruction, with an increasing number of outlets throughout the city. Notable are those in Habana Vieja next to the Hotel Inglaterra and on Calle Obispo, just off Plaza de Armas.

HABANA VIEJA

Peso Eateries

Your peso pickings are slim in Havana's touristy heartland. To commune with a poorer class of locals, try the dingy and austere **Casa de los Vinos,** tel. (62) 1319, at the corner of Esperanza and Factoria, five blocks south of Parque de la Fraternidad and five blocks west of the railway station. This basic restaurant began life as a workers' canteen in 1912. Today, it is both a restaurant and a bar. With luck, you'll find

sausage and bean soup—two of its specialties—although it has fallen on hard times of late and offered a meager menu in spring 1999. The decor is highlighted by walls inlaid with tiles inscribed with love poems and proverbs, such as "The wind and women change by the minute."

La Casa Arencibia, on Calle San Miguel at Amistad, near the Capitolio, offers *platas* of chicken liver for US$1.

Paladares

My favorite *paladar* is the pocket-size **La Moneda Cubana,** at San Ignacio #77, one block south of Plaza de la Catedral, tel. (61) 0401. Although tiny, it's very well run, service is speedy, and the portions are huge. The menu offers the usual Cuban staples such as grilled chicken or fried fish (US$9) and even pork chops (US$10) served with rice and beans, mixed salad, and bread. It offers omelettes for US$8. Open daily noon- 11 p.m. Take your business card to add to the wall.

Try **La Rejita Mayéa,** Calle Habana #405, e/ Obispo y Obrapía, tel. (62) 6704. It has set meals—basic fare—for US$8. Open daily noon- 11 p.m. A friend recommends **EL Rincón de Eleggua** on Calle Aguacate. Apparently, it's renowned for its pastries.

The following have not been reviewed: **La Perla de Habana,** on Obispo e/ Habana y Cuba; **Las Tres Carabelas,** at Amargura #56, e/ San Ignacio y Mercaderes; **Paladar La Mulata del Sabor** at Calle Sol #153 e/ Cuba y San Ignacio; and **Paladar Sobrino** at Obrapia #358.

Breakfasts

Hotel restaurants welcome nonguests: the Hotel Parque Central is a good one to try. Most serve meager buffets for US$8-15. Budget travelers should check out **Monserrate** at Avenida de Bélgica (Monserrate) and Obrapía. It offers bacon and eggs (US$1.50), toast (US$1), and American-style coffee (US$0.75).

Criollo (Cuban)

No visit to Cuba is complete without a meal at **La Bodeguita del Medio,** 207 Empedrado, one block west of Plaza de la Catedral, tel. (62) 4498, a Havana legend favored by Ernest Hemingway. La Bodeguita was honored in 1992 with the "Best of the Best Five Star Diamond Award" by the North American Academy of Gastronomy,

The restaurant specializes in traditional Cuban dishes—most famously its roast pork, steeped black beans, flat-fried bananas, garlicky yucca, and sweet guava pudding—which are, as Nicolás Guillén (Cuba's national poet) once put it, "overflowing with surges of aged rum." Alas, the *mojitos* long ago lost their edge (be sure to ask for *añejo* rum). You may have to wait for an hour or more to be seated. The service is relaxed to a fault, and the atmosphere bohemian and lively. *Soneros* (popular dance-music performers) and troubadors (poet-musicians) in guayabera shirts entertain. The food is generally fresher at lunch than at dinner, for which you'll pay US$10-20 (a US$10 minimum applies). Reservations are strongly advised.

Virtually every foreigner passing through the Plaza de la Catedral also plonks his or her derriere at the **Restaurante El Patio,** tel. (57) 1034 or (61) 8504, if only to enjoy a refreshment in the El Portal patio bar. In addition to its bar and patio café, it features four dining rooms (one a folkloric dining room purportedly specializing in Mexican cuisine, open noon-11 p.m. The patio bar is open 24 hours and serves snacks such as an El Patio sandwich (US$3.50), hamburger (US$3), and steak palomilla with fries (US$2.75). Drinks are expensive. The main restaurant has three set menus and serves hideously expensive US$16-28) dishes such as shrimp *al ajillo* (in garlic) and even T-bone steak. But it is worth the price for the fabulous surroundings and the views over the plaza from upstairs.

The atmospheric **Café/Restaurante La Mina,** facing onto Plaza de Armas on Calle Obispo, tel. (62) 0216, offers shaded patio dining out front, where snacks and salads (US$3-5) and Cuban dishes (US$4-10) are served. To the rear, you'll find the **Restaurante Cubano,** where you dine in a courtyard with an arbor and free-roaming peacocks, caged birds, and saddles and other country artifacts for decor. The setting is wonderful, made more so by live musicians.

Around Parque Central, a favorite of budget travelers is the **Colonial Restaurant,** on the ground floor of the Hotel Inglaterra. It has a wide-ranging menu of Cuban dishes, such as shrimp in salsa roja (US$11), *pollo asado* (US$4.50), and fried beef in creole sauce (US$5.25).

Prado 264, on the Prado at Calle Animas, serves pizzas and soups, plus the normal range of undistinguished Cuban fare for US$3-7. Cubans have their own menu in pesos. Nearby, in the Casa de Científicos at Prado #212, is **Restaurant Los Vitrales,** impressive for its exquisite rococo decor, colorful *vitrales,* and fine antiques, though the menu is less distinguished, with the usual Cuban fare running to chicken, fish, and steaks (US$6-26).

Nearby, on Avenida de Bélgica (Egido), between Jesús María and Acosta, is **Puerto de Sagua,** tel. (57) 1026 or (63) 6186, a humble yet pleasant restaurant designed on a nautical theme and also beloved of local Cubans.

Open 24 hours, **La Zaragoza,** Calle Monserrate e/ Obispo y Obrapía, tel. (57) 1033, is a dark and moody Spanish-style bodega that maintains its Spanish ties with regional flags and soccer memorabilia. It serves *criollo* fare and specializes in seafoods such as squid rings (US$6), garlic shrimp (US$12), and *ceviche peruano* (US$2.50), but also offers lamb stew (US$9), tortillas (US$3), and pizza (from US$2).

Nearby is the **Castillo de Farnés,** also on Monserrate at #361 esq. Obrapía, tel. (57) 1030. This Havana landmark has been famous since its founding as a Spanish restaurant in 1896 (Castro used to frequent it while a student; he ate here again with Che Guevara on 9 January 1959, following his triumphal entry into Havana). Its menu includes omelettes (US$4), garlic shrimp (US$9), and lobster and steak (US$15-20). Be sure to take a sweater. It has a patio snack bar out front. Next door, the simpler **La Monserrate,** popular with Cubans and budget tourists, also has a grill open to the street and serves burgers, pizzas, and the like for US$1-2. Try its *Coctel Monserrate.* Open 11 a.m.-3 a.m.

The *posada*-style **Los Doces Apóstoles,** tel. (63) 8295, squats at the base of Morro Castle. Here, an African purée soup costs US$2, and creole chicken costs US$5.50. Open noon-11 p.m. Adjacent, the **El Polverín Bar** offers a charming little bar plus grand vistas from a breeze-swept patio beside the Twelve Apostles (the giant cannons guarding the harbor entrance). It's a perfectly lonesome spot to relax, and one popular with Cubans.

Arabic

Aiming mostly at tourists is **Restaurante al Medina,** in the Casa de los Árabes on Calle Oficios, one block south of Plaza de Armas, tel. (57) 1041. The menu used to be limited to standard *criollo* items such as fish and rice (US$3), salsa chicken (US$2.50), and vegetarian specialties for US$3. But they've added cous-cous and lamb dishes (US$6), as well as kebabs (US$5), kibbe (minced meatballs, US$4), and hummus (US$2.20).

Also try the **Restaurante Internacional Oasis,** in the Centro Cultural de Árabe on the Prado e/ Calles Refugio y Trocadero. Open 9 a.m.-midnight. Cabarets—often with transvestite shows—are hosted nightly (US$5).

Continental

You should be sure to eat at the huge, high-ceilinged, marble-floored **Roof Garden Restaurant** atop the Hotel Sevilla, tel. (33) 8560, not least for the sublime decor. Tall French doors open to balconies overlooking the city. Kemal Kairus, a Lebanese Cuban, plays piano. And the food—once mediocre at best—has improved by leaps since French chef Jean-Paul Gulotta took the helm in the kitchen, fusing Cuban into French, with mouth-watering recherché dishes for US$5-30.

The **Restaurante Real Plaza,** on the ground floor of the Hotel Plaza, is elegant, with gilt fittings and marvelous high-backed modern chairs. Here you can enjoy grilled fish for US$7.50.

In the heart of the old city, try the **Café Mercurió,** tel. (66) 6188, facing onto Plaza de San Francisco at the base of the Longa del Comercio. This elegant restaurant and bar—open 24 hours—offers a wide-ranging menu of continental and Cuban fare, including lobster (US$25) and grilled fish (US$8). It offers air-conditioned seating inside or shaded dining alfresco on the cobbled plaza. The regal **Restaurant El Condado,** in the Hotel Santa Isabel on Plaza de Armas, offers adventurous fare such as shrimp in mango sauce (US$19) and pork loin fried with orange and garlic (US$12). However, I've not eaten here and can't vouch for the quality.

Italian

The eponymous **A Prado y Neptuno,** which speaks of its situation, is a modern, air-conditioned place popular with Cubans and serving a range of pizzas and pastas (US$3.50-7), plus steaks, fish, and chicken dishes (US$4-25). It has a *heladería* to the rear.

The **Cantiluomo,** at the west end of Obispo, shares the kitchen with the Floridita (see below) and offers a simple Italianate ambience and ur ambitious pasta dishes from US$4. It has a goo wine list. Further down Obispo, **Via Venetto,** between Villegas and Aguacate, is a basic an gloomy Italian restaurant serving an exclusive Cuban clientele. Foreigners can pay in pesos.

The **Dominica,** at the east end of Calle Tacó tel. (66) 2917, serves pastas and pizzas (US$6 12) in elegant surroundings and, on some night offers the unusual distinction of Mexican mariac music. It is popular with Cubans.

Oriental

Cuba's erstwhile Chinese population has left i culinary legacy on the streets of Havana. A fis ful of restaurants boast genuine Oriental deco although the cuisine is usually disappointing more like Cuban cuisine with bamboo sprout. Most offer *parritas* (chopsticks).

In Habana Vieja, head first and foremost **Torre de Marfil,** Mercaderes #121 e/ Oficios Obrapía, tel. (57) 1038, which has all the tra pings: the Chinese lanterns, screens, and even banquet table beneath a mock temple. It's staffe by Chinese waiters, but the service is disorg nized and excruciatingly slow. The menu include chop suey, chow mein, won ton (US$1.50), ar shrimp and lobster dishes. Entrées range US$ 15. It serves set dinners from US$6.

Also consider **Restaurante Hanoi,** Calle T niente Rey at the corner of Bernaza, tel. (5 1029, also known as La Casa de la Par (Grapevine House) for the luxuriant grapevi growing in the patio. The restaurant—a symbol friendship with the people of Vietnam—is in or of the oldest houses in Havana. It has rattan fu niture, Chinese lanterns, and laquered woode wall hangings inlaid with mother-of-pearl. U happily, the menu is more Cuban than Chines but no single dish costs more than US$3.5 and it offers "combination specials" for belo US$3. Open 9 a.m.-11 p.m.

Surf and Turf

You *must* visit **El Floridita,** Monserrate y Obisp Habana Vieja, tel. (63) 1063, the favorite wate ing hole of one of America's favorite drinkers Ernest Hemingway—who immortalized th restaurant in *Islands in the Stream*. The circu estaurant to the rear wears a Romanesque livrie of red and gold—plus an original mural of the ld port—and still has a fin de siècle ambience, although today it is overly air-conditioned and ather sterile, cleansed of the heady atmosphere f the days when Papa drank here (it has been alled a "glitzy huckster joint" in *Travel & Leisure*). a 1992, El Floridita received the "Best of the est Five Star Diamond Award" by the North merican Academy of Gastronomy. Most of the ishes, alas, are disappointing. The menu feaares mostly overpriced seafood. The house pecial is *langosta mariposa* (lobster grilled with almonds, pineapple, and butter) chased with the Papa special" (a daiquiri), but it is best to stick ith simple dishes such as prawns flambéed in am. A shrimp cocktail costs US$15; oyster cockails cost US$5. You can even have frog's leg oufflé (US$19). Lobster costs a whopping S$36-42. The cheapest dish is grilled chickn (US$11). The wine list is perhaps the best the city, and choice cigars are offered. A string io serenades in the bar. Your daiquiri will set ou back a stiff US$6 (be sure to ask for the onnoisseur's *daiquiri natural,* shaken, without e brain-numbing ice).

At the other extreme is **La Casa del Esobeche,** a simple bar with flagstone floor and ejas open to the street, at the corner of Calles bispo and Villegas, serving a mostly Cuban ientele and, as its name suggests, offering deicious *escovitch* (cube chunks of fish marinated ith lime and salsa) for pennies.

One of the nattiest eateries in town is the **Café el Oriente,** at the corner of Oficios and Amarura on the west side of Plaza de San Francisco, l. (66) 6686. The ritzy marbletop bar, tux-clad aiters, and jazz pianist add to the regal tone ownstairs in the Bar Café (heck, you could be in ew York or San Francisco). The upstairs estaurant is yet more elegant, with sparkling arble and antiques, French drapes, and a agnificent stained-glass ceiling. Open 24 hours, offers mostly steaks and seafood dishes JS$12-30).

For views toward Havana—and splendid enrtainment—head to **La Divina Pastora,** tel. 3) 8341, 200 meters east of and below the lorro castle, directly across the harbor from astillo de la Real Fuerza. It's housed in a handome hacienda-style structure fronted by a battery of cannons and offers traditional entertainment such as bolero and cha-cha-cha. The atmosphere is splendid, especially on the patio in late afternoon. The menu includes such appetizers as Peruvian ceviche (US$4.50) and lobster cocktail (US$7), and such entrées as lobster creole (US$20) and grilled shellfish (US$25). Parking costs US$1. It's open noon-11 p.m. Behind the restaurant, on the harborfront, is the wonderful little bodega-type *Bar la Tasca,* with a breezy balcony offering fabulous views over the harbor. It's a great place to sit on a hot dayand features lances and medieval armor on the walls. The simple menu includes lobster and seafood dishes from US$8. Not many foreigners find this gem. It was closed for renovation at press time.

Spanish

My favorite Spanish restaurant in Havana is **La Paella,** in the Hostal Valencia on Calle Oficios, one block south of Plaza de Armas in Habana Vieja. It serves various paellas (ostensibly for two people only, although I have been served paella when dining alone) for US$7-15. The *caldo* (soup) and bread is a meal in itself (US$3). You can also choose steak, grilled fish, and chicken dishes (US$4-10), washing them down with Spanish wines (US$6-13). Try the excellent vegetable house soup. You'll dine beneath colonial chandeliers, surrounded by antique darkwood furnishings, with large, open windows to provide a cooling breeze.

Also in Habana Vieja, try modestly priced **La Tasca,** on the ground floor arcade of the Hotel Sevilla. Its decor replicates a Spanish bodega. The chef will whip up as good an omelette as you've ever had. Likewise, the newly renovated **El Baturro** on Avenida de la Bélgica (Egido) at Merced, tel. (66) 9078, offers *tapas* (US25 cents) and *escabeche* shrimp (US$3.50) as well as other Spanish and Cuban dishes amid Spanish surroundings: barrels, a bull's head, bullfight posters, ceramic murals, and brass lamps. The long bar serves a full range of liquors.

The **Bodegón de los Vinos** in the Castillo de San Carlos de la Cabaña offers perhaps the most genuinely Spanish experience in Havana. It's built into the vaults of the castle and has traditional *mantegan* (from La Mancha) decor. It serves *tapas,* sausages, and other Spanish dishes (US$2-17), washed down by sangria (US$3).

Flamenco dancers entertain. It occasionally fills with tour groups.

Cafés and Snack Bars

Most restaurants serve *cafecitos*—the thick, sweet Cuban version of espresso. Few serve coffee American style. For a wider range, head to **Restaurant La Luz,** on Calle Obispo between San Ignacio and Mercaderes, selling cappuccinos, espressos, and various coffees. The **Casa del Café,** on the southeast corner of Plaza de Armas, tel. (33) 8061, also sells cappuccinos (US$2), plus various grades of Cuban coffees. It's open Mon.-Sat. 10 a.m.-6 p.m., Sunday 9 a.m.-3 p.m.

Doña Isabel Cafetería, on Calle Tacón #4 esq. Empedrado, one block north of Plaza de Armas, tel. (63) 3560, serves sandwiches, pizzas, and other snacks. Next door, in a similar vein, is **Don Giovanni,** tel. (57) 1036, a café-restaurant in a beautiful colonial mansion. You can dine on the lower courtyard or upstairs in more elegant surroundings and look down over Calle Tacón and the harbor. It mostly serves snacks but also has a choice of pizzas and seafoods (US$4-15).

Another popular option for tourists is **El Patio Colonial,** on the Plaza de la Catedral. Its appeal is neither its ambience, the drinks, nor musicians, but rather that sitting beneath the cool *portrale* held aloft by tall columns, you can gaze out upon the whirligig of life on the plaza.

Café O'Reilly, on O'Reilly and San Ignacio, one block south of Plaza de la Catedral, has gone downhill in recent years and no longer serves cappuccinos or espressos. But it remains a good place to relax over Cuban coffee and simple snacks (mostly tapas and tortillas) on the upstairs balcony, which looks down over Calle O'Reilly. It's popular with the gay crowd and has a strong local clientele.

While exploring Plaza de Armas, you should relax at **Café Mina,** facing onto the square, the place to sip a cool beer or *mojito* (US$1.50) beneath shady umbrellas. It features good lemonades, and bands and troubadors perform alfresco. Next to it (part of the same complex) is the **Al Cappuccino** coffee house serving homemade pastries and custard for US$1.

The **Café Paris,** on the corner of Calles Obispo and San Ignacio, is a very lively social scene for both Cubans and tourists. You'll sit at rustic wooden furniture and look out through open trellised windows on life flowing down Obispo. Lively Latin music is usually playing from a jukebox. Fare includes fried chicken (US$2.50), hamburger (US$2), Spanish sausage with potato (US$2.50), and various sandwiches. Beers cos US$1. It's open 24 hours.

Another bar-cum-restaurant popular with Cubans is **La Lluvia del Oro,** at Obispo #316 on the corner of Calle Habana. La Lluvia reflects the city's rising bohemian life and remains lively into the wee hours (it, and Café Paris, remain the two major pickup spots for foreign male tourists and flirty cubanas). It serves snack food and pizzas.

Cubans congregate at **Café Habana** on Calle Mercaderes and Amargura; this pleasant little corner coffee shop sells cappuccinos and *cafecitos*.

The patio bar—the **Galeria La Acera del Louvre**—of the Hotel Inglaterra is the best place for coffee or snacks around Parque Central. I serves sandwiches, tortillas, tapas, and burgers (US$3-8), plus desserts and coffees. Service is slow.

Desserts and Ice Cream

Helado Tropical has small outlets throughout Havana, including an air-conditioned outlet a Calle Obispo #467, on the corner of Habana. Their ice cream is nowhere near the quality of Coppelia, but quite acceptable.

You'll also find *heladerías* on Calle Oficios attached to Café La Mina; and, in Centro Habana, the **Arlequin Cremeria** on Calle San Rafael, e/ Amistad y Industria.

The **Pasteleria Francesca,** a bakery du north of the Hotel Inglaterra on the west side of Parque Central, sells a marvelous array of confections for US10 cents upwards. Likewise, you' also find a bakery—**Panaderia San José**— catercorner to Café Paris, at Calles Obispo an San Ignacio. It, too, sells a tempting array of confections from US10 cents. A few blocks eas is **Dulcería Doña Teresa,** selling custards, ic creams, and other delights.

Shopping for Yourself

The largest—and most colorful—*agropecuari* (farmers' market) is **Cuatro Caminos,** in an ol Mercado building at Manglar and Cristina (also called Avenida de la Mexico) in the far south west corner of Habana Vieja. You may not want to buy a pig's head, or live ducks and chickens trussed on a pole, but if these—or herbs, vegetables, and fresh fruit or fish catch your fancy, you're sure to find it here. Watch for pickpockets.

Another large open-air market can be found on Avenida de la Bélgica (Egido) between Apodada and Corrales. It has separate section for meats, fish, and produce.

Imported salamis and meats are sold at **La Monserrate,** an air-conditioned butcher shop on Monserrate, e/ Brasil y Muralles, near the Egido *agropecuario*.

CENTRO HABANA

Paladares

Private restaurants are few and far between in residential Centro, but ironically, the area boasts the best *paladar* in town: **La Guarida,** on the third floor of an 18th-century townhouse on Calle Concordia #418, e/ Garvasio y Escobar, tel. (62) 4940. It's one of the hippest joints in Havana, reminding diners perhaps of a cozy bistro in New York's Soho (you may recognize it as a setting for scenes in the Oscar-nominated 1995 movie, *Fresa y Chocolate*). The decor is downsome comfy, and owners Enrique and Odeysis Nuñez serve up creatively conceived dishes with a perfectly delicate touch. The menu changes nightly and features such mouthwatering treats as fillet of snapper with beurre blanc sauce. A rary among Cuban chefs, the couple know how to make their food dance. Don't be put off by the dilapidated entrance and funky staircase. Budget US$10-20 apiece. *Recommended.*

Nearby, **Paladar Torresón,** on the Malecón one block west of the Prado, has a balcony dining room offering views along the seafront boulevard.

Criollo

The **Restaurant Colonial** in the Hotel Lincoln is one of the better restaurants in Centro and serves a 99% Cuban clientele with soups, fish,

mangoes

shrimp, and chicken dishes for less than US$4. The service is surprisingly swift and conscientious, and a piano player tickles the ivories.

Fast Food

El Rápido, Cuba's fried chicken chain, has an outlet on Calzada de Infanta at San Rafael. There's a **Rumbos** snack bar on the Malecón and Padre Varela.

Italian

Try **El Italiano,** at Calzada de Infanta and Allende, an unsophisticated place serving a local Cuban clientele.

Oriental

Barrio Chino boasts a score of restaurants, many staffed by Chinese waitresses in traditional costumes. The most famous is **Restaurante Pacífico,** on Calle San Nicolas, tel. (63) 3243, boasting genuine Chinese furniture and Cantonese favorites such as lobster or shrimp chow mein (US$7) and lobster chop suey (US$7). There are restaurants on all five floors, though the main restaurant is on the third. More exclusive guests gather on the fifth (Castro is an occasional visitor), where Hemingway used to eat.

Calle Cuchillo's 50-meter-length is lined with Chinese restaurants. The best is **Restaurante Tien-Tan,** cellular tel. (80) 6198, which offers more than 100 dishes—plus Tsing Tao beer from China. The menu includes such tantalizing offerings as sweet-and-sour fried fish balls with vinegar and soy (US$7), and pot-stewed liver with seasoning (US$7). This is probably the most genuinely Chinese cuisine in Cuba, and the only place that I've ever had highly spiced food on the island, though it still falls short of Chinese cuisine in New York or San Francisco. Chef Tao hails from Shanghai and speaks English. If he befriends you, he might offer a rice wine, but it is rough stuff. Stick to beer.

Also on Calle Cuchillo, consider **Restaurante Flamboyan** (entreés for US$1-3), **Restaurant Hueng-Hu** (entreés for US$15-20, though there is nothing special to justify these inordinate prices), and **Restaurant El Gran Dragon.**

The **Casa Abuelo Lung Kong,** at Manrique y Dragones, has a restaurant upstairs open to Cubans (pesos) and tourists (dollars). *Maripositas china* cost 10 pesos; chop suey and other entreés range 10-60 pesos. This is the real McCoy: Chinese staff, Chinese ambience, Chinese patrons.

One block east at Dragones 313 is the **Restaurant Song Sai Li,** tel. (62) 2757, with an authentic Chinese atmosphere in its upstairs restaurant. Balconies offer views along Dragones. Its simple Chinese menu offers *mariposita china* for 10 pesos and chow mein for 43 pesos.

Cafés

La Calesa Cafetería, one block west of Parque Central, on Calle San Rafael, is very popular with Cubans. Here you can sit in the open air beneath a shady canopy and watch the tide of shoppers flooding down San Rafael.

VEDADO AND PLAZA DE LA REVOLUCIÓN

Breakfast

Café La Rampa, beside the Hotel Habana Libre Tryp, is a good bet if you don't care for quality. It serves meager American-style breakfasts (US$2-6), plus tortillas (US$2.50-4), and has a breakfast special. The hotel also offers a breakfast buffet (US$9) in its mezzanine restaurant, 7-10 a.m.

Paladares

For creative fare with French-inspired food, try **Le Chansonnier,** at Calle 15 #306, e/ H y I, tel. (32) 3788, where the owners try hard to recreate a French bistro, with simple yet tasty fare such as roasted rabbit in mustard sauce and French fries. It's the best *paladar* in Vedado.

Another favorite is **Paladar El Amor,** on the third floor of an old mansion on Calle 23 e/ B y C, tel. (3) 8150. The place is full of fading antiques—porcelain, bronze figurines, silver pieces, and even a grand piano. The former mansion of a *condesa* (countess) is now owned by Amor, a young pop singer, and run by the delightful members of her family. Try the superb *pescado agridulce* (battered fish pieces with a sweet-and-sour sauce) served with salad and boiled potatoes for US$4.50. You'll dine off real Wedgwood china.

La Casa, hidden away at Calle 30 #865, e/ 2(y 41 in Nuevo Vedado, tel. (81) 7000, is wortl the drive, according to *Cigar Aficionado,* whicl offers this description: "Located in a 1950s-style house with a modish decor, La Casa serves such delicious dishes as fresh prawns sautéec in butter with garlic, and juicy roasted pork witl beans and rice."

A steadfast bargain is the tiny **Paladai Restaurant Monguito,** on Calle L directly op posite the Hotel Habana Libre Tryp, and for tha reason almost always full. *"China"* serves simple but filling Cuban dishes such as *pollo asadc* grill fish, and pork dishes (US$3-6).

The once-superb **Paladar Marpoly,** tel. (32 2471, in a colonial home at Calle K 154 (one block north of Linea), has gone downhill. Thє home is full of religious icons and other intriguing knick-knacks. You can dine in the parlor, or tc the rear, where a makeshift *bohio* is roofed ii thatch. The creative menu includes a house spe cial of seafood with pineapple and melted cheesє served in a pineapple (US$11, with salad anc side dishes). Alas, the place has been turned intc a tragic menagerie: watching you eat are twc monkeys, a dozen or so exotic dogs, a score c parrots and other birds, and a giant Galapago: turtle tethered to the wall. If ever Cuba offered a surreal dining experience, this is it. Hygiene i: now questionable. It's open noon to midnight. It': tricky to get to because of the one-way street: (refer to the map). Look for a house with rust-rec pillars and a mural of Santa Barbara on the wal illumined at night.

A reasonable bet is **El Balcón del Edén,** nea Coppelia, on Calle K e/ 19 y 21, tel. (32) 9113. I has dining upstairs on an open balcony. Try thє superb *marisco enchilada* in spicy tomato saucє (US$10, including accompanying dishes). Serv ings are plentiful, and it's open 24 hours. At nighl look for the red light illuminating the balcony.

Paladar Nerei, at the corner of 19 y I, tel. (32 7860, serves unremarkable but filling soups tuna salad (US$3.50), spaghettis, grilled fisl (US$7.50), calamari (US$8), and *criollo* dishe on a shaded terrace in a colonial home. It has ε more wide-ranging menu than most *paladares* including creative dishes such as duck witl onions (US$7.50) and lamb in tomato saucє (US$7.50). Open Mon.-Fri. noon-midnight, an Sat.-Sun. 6 p.m.-midnight.

Also try **El Bistro,** facing the Malecón at the base of **Calle K,** tel. (32) 2708. It's decorated with tasteful artwork, and you can dine on a balcony. Ostensibly it serves French food; in reality, it's Cuban cuisine with a quasi-French twist, such as *filete Roquefort* (US$12).

In eastern Vedado, near the Malecón, are **Paladar Huron Azúl** (not reviewed), at Humdbolt and P; and **Parillada L y 15,** Calle L #202 esq. 15, tel. (32) 1721, with terrace dining and usual Cuban staples served in filling portions for US$10. **Paladar 3B** is tucked away on the north side of Coppelia on Calle 21, between K and J. **Paladar Los Amigos** on Calle N between 19 and 21 is open noon-midnight.

A friend recommended **El Helecho,** at Calle 6 e/ Linea y Calle 11, and the **Festivál,** at the corner of Calle D and 27, tel. (30) 9549. A reader recommends **Bon Appetit,** at Calle 21 esq. M, tel. (32) 2072, near the Hotel Capri; here Ruben Pérez and his family make decent food, with dinners for US$4. The **Paladar Los Helechos,** on Avenida 23 and Avenida de los Presidentes, tel. (32) 3430, serves simple Cuban fare for US$5-10, but service is terribly slow. Another option nearby is **Paladar Puerto Isabel** on Calle 17 between B and C. Another reader recommends **Paladar Yiyo's,** Calle L #256, e/ 17 y 19, on the second floor, tel. (32) 8977, run by a retired doctor and his wife.

Criollo

A safe bet is the **Restaurante El Barracón,** in the Hotel Habana Libre Tryp. It serves *criollo* dishes (especially pork dishes, such as roast pork for US$12) and more adventurous fare such as "jerked horsemeat stew" for US$10) in atmospheric surroundings, with entrées US$7-15; open noon-midnight. Setting higher standards is the hotel's top-floor **Sierra Maestra** restaurant, offering splendid views over Havana. Food quality is acceptable at a reasonable price. Diners get free entrance to the Cabaret Turquino.

The **Polinesio,** on Calle 23 and also part of the Hotel Habana Libre Tryp, tel. (33) 4011, ext. 131, has plenty of Tahitian-style ambience, and hints of the South Seas find their way subtly into the menu. A meal will run upward of US$20, but it offers a lunch special for US$15 with *mariposas chinas*, cheese balls with sweet-and-sour sauce, barbecued chicken (mediocre), plus cocktail, dessert, and coffee. Open noon-midnight.

El Conejito, Calle M #206, esq. Avenida 17, tel. (32) 4671, is another splendid option, not least for its Old English or Teutonic ambience. A pianist plays while you dine on *conejo* (rabbit), served any of a dozen ways. Entrées average US$7. It also has fish and lobster dishes. Around the corner is the **Casona del 17** (formerly the Don Armagemnon) in an old mansion on Calle 17, e/ Calle K y L, tel. (33) 4529. It presents a tasty paella (US$7), lobster enchilada (US$10), and such staples as grill fish and pork, to be enjoyed on a breezy outdoor patio or within the a/c neoclassical building showing off contemporary art on the walls.

Taberna Don Pepe, at San Lazaro and Infanta, is a rustic bodega-style bar and restaurant where simple fare such as *pollo frito* averages US$2 a plate. **La Carreta,** next to Coppelia on 21 e/ J y K, offers similarly rustic ambience and simple Cuban fare, mostly to Cubans (in pesos; you'll pay dollars). At the other extreme, the **Wakama,** on Calle O, between La Rampa and Humboldt, once a famous prerevolutionary nightclub, has been turned into an ascetic restaurant-bar.

Continental

One of my favorite restaurants in Vedado is **La Roca,** on 21 at M, tel. (33) 4501, with modern stained-glass windows all around (no views) and Spanish turned-wood chairs. The French-inspired menu offers such intriguing appetizers as smoked salmon with escovitched grouper (US$7) and apple in red wine (US$3), plus lobster with coconut (US$25), creative seafood dishes, and pastas for the main course. The house specialty is Bavarian-style lobster. The results are hit-and-miss, but I've enjoyed some of the more pleasing dishes in town here, and the service has consistently been good. It has a large wine selection, but the wines are poorly kept. Pedro entertains on piano. A separate bar has been described as "the sort of place that Dean Martin and Frank Sinatra would have loved." Officially, La Roca is open noon-1:45 a.m., but tends to close at midnight. The place is named for the rock outside that occasionally spouts a meager fountain.

A good bargain is the classy **Restaurante Monseigneur,** tel. (32) 9884, opposite the entrance to the Hotel Nacional at the corner of Calle 21. Its elegant decor—a bit gauche for some tastes—is aided by violin and piano music. The large menu is heavy with seafood. Entrées are reasonably priced, with shrimp and lobster at US$12, but soups, salads, and tortillas are a real bargain at US$2-3. Bring a sweater. If you have a few more bucks to spend, try the acclaimed **Comedor de Aguiar**, in the Hotel Nacional. It serves international cuisine, highlighted by shrimp with rum flambé.

Another elegant, albeit expensive, option is the **Restaurante Hotel Victoria,** at Calles 19 and M. The place is conducive to romance, with lots of hardwoods, brass lamps, and gilt place settings. The menu—with an extensive wine list—offers grilled lobster (US$22), roasted snapper (US$12), filet mignon (US$11), and spaghetti with seafood (US$4).

The soaring FOCSA Building, at Calle 17 e/ Calles M y N, boasts two acclaimed restaurants. **El Emperador,** on the ground floor, tel. (32) 4998, is favored by Cuban VIPs, but its blood-red curtains and Louis XIV-style decor are a bit OTT (over the top). It serves soups and tortillas (US$2-4), plus Cuban staples and continental dishes such as filet uruguayano (US$8-25), but has lackluster service. Open 7-11 p.m.

The FOCSA building also boasts the equally costly but far more notable **La Torre,** tel. (55) 3089, a rooftop restaurant with splendid all-around views over the city and perhaps the best cuisine in the city. This restaurant has come a long way since iconoclastic French chef Frank Picol took over the kitchen. He's hampered by the difficulty of obtaining fresh ingredients, but his creative menu offers such tempting treats as roasted leg of lamb with garlic and rosemary (US$16), and filete de beef in pastry with onion confilore and red wine (US$27), backed by a large selection of wines. Open noon-midnight (the bar is open 11:30 a.m.-12:30 p.m.). *Recommended.*

Don't be fooled by the pretensions to French cuisine advertised by the **Bar/Restaurante Potín,** at the junction of Paseo and Linea. It serves Cuban fare.

Another expensive disappointment that is touted as a dining highlight is **Restaurante 1830,** in a 1920s mansion just east of the Almendares tunnel on Avenida 7ma (Calzada), at the junction with the Malecón, tel. (33) 4521. You can choose any of four plush dining rooms with huge bay windows overlooking the ocean. Service is often slow and surly, and the food can be equally bad. Open noon-11 p.m. Skip it.

Italian

In Vedado, check out the **Terraza Florentino,** the famous rooftop restaurant of the Hotel Capri, at Calle 21 y N, tel. (33) 3571. The pastas and risottos are inexpensive and tasty. Try the tangy spaghetti with shrimp in a white wine garlic sauce.

Don't be fooled by the **Terraza Restaurante Italiano Cinecittá,** at Avenida 23 y 12. It does serve pizza, but the menu is otherwise *criollo.*

Spanish

First and foremost, head to **Centro Vasco,** at the corner of 3ra and 4, tel. (3) 9354, near the Meliá Cohiba and Riviera hotels, which was opened by a Basque in 1954 and retains its original modestly elegant decor, including a wall-to-wall mural showing Basque mountain scenes. It claims Basque cuisine, such as escovitched octopus (US$6), paella (US$8.50), and seafood (US$5-20), but the preparation varies little from the usual Cuban fare.

The **Mesón La Chorrera** in the old fortress at the mouth of the Río Almendares at the west end of the Malecón, tel. (33) 4504, also specializes in Spanish cuisine and features ancient weaponry on the walls. The **El Cortijo Restaurant** in the Hotel Vedado offers paella and sangria (US$8) and a few other Spanish dishes on its mostly *criollo* menu.

Surf and Turf

The **Steak House Mirador Habana** on the 20th floor of the Hotel Habana Riviera offers all kinds of meat dishes, from steaks to sausage, pork and hams. It has a "Special Steak Porky" for US$10. Open 6 p.m.-6 a.m.

Cafés and Snack Bars

To call the **Habana Café** either a café or snack bar is to call a Rolls-Royce merely a "car." This is Havana's version of the internationally renowned Hard Rock Café, but with a distinctly Cuban twist. It serves tasty and good-sized burgers (from US$5) delivered American style with ketchup and mustard, plus sandwiches (US$6.50), caesar salad (US$7.50), filet mignon

US$17), and such desserts as a "banana split" US$5). You can also sit at the bar, where a larger-than-life cutout cardboard figure of Ernest Hemingway pours a glass of rum behind the bar. Entertainers amuse on the stage at lunchtime as well as at night. Suddenly the car horns beep and the headlamps flash, you hear the roar of an aeroplane taking off, then the curtains open and—voilá—the show begins. Entry is free, but a consumo minimo policy applies (US$5 at the bar; US$10 at a table, per person). Check our bill carefully, as scams are a hazard.

The **Café La Rampa,** outside the Habana Libre, is popular with Cubans and tourists alike. It has a special offer: sandwich, pizza, or burger with soft drink for US$5. The shaded patio of **Las Bulerias** nightclub, facing the Hotel Habana Libre Tryp on Calle L, serves *bocaditos, papas fritas,* and other simple fare for US$2-5.

Café 21, on Calle 21 opposite the Hotel Capri, has a shaded patio and serves sandwiches, tortillas, etc., for a few dollars. The dark, a/c restaurant next door—**Club 21**—has a dress code (no-shorts) and serves soups, salads, and *criollo* dishes.

Desserts and Ice Cream

The granddaddy of *heladerías* is **Coppelia,** at La Rampa and Calle L in Vedado (catercorner to the Hotel Habana Libre Tryp), which serves ice cream of excellent quality in stainless steel bowls and that even last-century traveler Albert Norton thought especially fine" (however, Cubans complain that the quality has deteriorated in recent years, and I agree). In 1998, a dollars-only section was opened up, and tourists are usually steered here. However, foreigners are still permitted to pay in pesos in any of half a dozen communal peso sections: forsake the dollar section and instead join the *cola* (line) to savor your ice cream with the Cubans—a far more rewarding experience. Be prepared for a lengthy wait on hot days. Although the small dollar section offers the advantage of immediate service, an *ensala-*

da here costs US$2.60 while the peso sections offer larger *ensaladas* (five scoops) for less than 10% that amount. A *jimagua* (two scoops) costs two pesos, and a *marquesita* (two scoops plus a sponge cage) costs 2.50 pesos. (It's difficult to fathom the pricing, which seems to change day by day. One day in spring 1999, an *ensalada* cost three pesos, but the next day an *ensalada* wasn't available, although you could buy as many *jimaguas* as you wished; on the third day, an *ensalada* cost five pesos.) Open daily 11 a.m.-11 p.m. (closed Monday).

Self-Catering

There's an *agropecuario* selling fruits and vegetables at Calle 19 between F and Avenida de los Presidentes, and a much smaller one at the corner of Calle 21 and J.

There's also a grocery stocking Western goods, plus a bakery, on the north side of the FOCSA building on Calle 17, e/ M y N.

canitel

PLAYA (MIRAMAR AND BEYOND)

Paladares

My favorite here is the well-known **La Cocina de Lillam,** at Calle 48 #1311, e/ 13 y 15, offering consistently tasty Cuban fare with a creative twist—call it nouvelle Cuban. Lillam, who is super-attentive, conjures up splendid appetizers such as tartlets of tuna-and-onion and chick pea-and-onion with three types of ham, plus fresh fish dishes and oven-roasted meats. You can opt to dine in the plant-filled garden or in the a/c dining room. Budget US$5-15 apiece.

Likewise, try **Paladar La Fuente,** in an atmospheric old mansion with mezzanine terrace at Calle 10 #303, e/ Avenida 3ra y 5ta, tel. (29) 2836. It specializes in superb fish dishes with cheese and ham, including *filete uruguayano* (US$6). The portions are huge, the preparation is creative, and the food tasty and filling.

Nearby is **Restaurante Calle 10,** in a floodlit mansion on Calle 10, e/ 3ra y 5ta, tel. (29) 6702. The menu includes ho-hum pizza (US$2), filete uruguayan (US$7), and fish with ham and cheese (US$5.50).

The **Paladar Vistamar,** at 1ra #2206, between 22 and 24, is popular. It serves continental fare as well as Cuban staples in a modern house on the seafront. Likewise, **Paladar Ristorante El Palio** at 1ra #2402, one block west at the corner of 24, serves Italian-*criollo* cuisine and is one of the most popular *paladares* in town for elite Cubans. Pastas, fettucines, and seafood dishes average US$5. You dine on a shaded patio to the rear, with suitably Italian decor. No telephone. It's open noon-midnight.

Paladar La Esperanza, is opposite the Hotel ICEMAR on Calle 16, between 3ra and 5ra; open daily (except Thursday) 8 a.m.-4 p.m. and 7-11:30 p.m.

Criollo

I find myself returning time and again to **El Aljibe,** Avenida 7ma between 24 and 26, tel. (24) 1583, absolutely my favorite restaurant in Havana and serving the best Cuban fare in town. It has recently been discovered by tour groups, but is also popular with the Havana elite and foreign businessmen showing off their beautiful Cuban girlfriends. This atmospheric charmer is run by Sergio and Pepe García Macías, former owners of the famous prerevolutionary Rancho Humo restaurant. You dine beneath a soaring bamboo roof. The superb house dish, the *pollo asado el aljibe,* is standard but far from ordinary—glazed with a sauce whose ingredients are closely guarded, then baked and served with fried plantain chips, rice, french fries, and black beans served liberally until you can eat no more. Feel free to take away what may be left over. It's a bargain at US$12 (desserts and beverages cost extra). Other *criollo* dishes are served (US$10-20). For dessert, try the flan, coconut pie, or chocolate cake. Check your bill carefully, however—the bread and salad side dish delivered to your table will be charged to your bill even if you didn't order it, and a 10% service charge is automatically billed. The service is prompt and ultra-efficient (even when the tour groups are in), so feel free to tip extra. Open noon-midnight.

Next to El Aljibe, at Calle 26, is the Dos Gardenias complex, tel. (24) 2353, a restored colonial mansion containing the modest **Restau-**rante Crillo.** You can enjoy a whole meal fo US$4, including bread, salad, beer (or soft drink and main course of chicken, *aporreodo de tern era,* or *picadillos à la criolla.* Soups and salads—a plate of cucumber—cost US$1. Dos Garde nias is open noon-midnight and offers chilly a/c interior or outdoor patio dining.

A more expensive option is the **Ranchón,** a Avenida 5ta esq. 16, tel. (24) 1185, acclaimed as one of Havana's best restaurants, although i serves traditional Cuban cooking, notably grilled fish and meats (the grilled pork chops are particularly good). More creative dishes include a delicious appetizer of stuffed red peppers with tuna. Chef Juan Luís Rosalas prepares a daily special, from roast beef to lamb chops. It has good mixed salads. The food is well prepared and the portions are huge. Don't confuse it with El Ranchón Palco. Open noon-midnight.

El Ranchón Palco, in jungly surroundings at Avenida 19 y Calle 140, tel. (23) 5838, in the heart of the tony residential district of Cubanacán is a handsome, open-sided *bohio* with terracotta floor, Tiffany-style lamps at the tables, and decor featuring saddles, umbrellas hanging from the thatch roof, and wooden toucans and parrots on swings. An octagonal bar is its heart. You can opt to dine on a patio or beneath thatch, or in a separate, more elegant dining room. It serves meat dishes (US$10-30), seafood (US$12-26) and the usual *criollo* fare, but the food is undistinguished at best; it serves canned vegetables frozen fries, and your standard grilled fare. It offers floor shows at night. Managed by the Palacio de Convenciones, it is popular among the government elite, who don't seem to have a clue what constitutes good dining.

La Estancia Restaurant adjoins the Hote Biocaribe, tel. (33) 7835, and offers a variety o frigid a/c rooms in an elegant colonial mansion The tables arrayed around the intimate courtyard are preferable. It serves *criollo* fare, plus boneless chicken (US$8), filet mignon (US$12) and such rarities as blood sausage (US$2) and tuna salad (US$4). It offers a lunch and dinner special (US$14 and US$20, respectively).

Seafood

Don Cangrejo on Avenida 1ra e/ 16 y 18, tel (24) 4169, offers some of the finest seafood in town (it should; it's overseen by the Ministry of

Fisheries), served in a converted colonial mansion with glass windows offering views over the flagstone patio—good on calm days for alfresco dining—toward the Straits of Florida. The large menu features such appetizers as crab cocktail (US$6), crab-filled wontons (US$3), house specialties such as crab claws (US$15), and garlic shrimp (US$12.50), plus paella, lobster, and fish dishes. However, the canned vegetables are dismaying. The wine list runs to more than 150 labels, and René Garcia is one of the few professional wine waiters in town. It's popular with the dollar-bearing Cuban elite and has been described as a "take on Joe's Stone Crab in Miami."

Argentinian

Meat lovers might try **La Pampa,** in the Hotel Comodoro, on Avenida 3ra y Calle 84, Miramar, tel. (33) 2028, fax (33) 1168. It specializes in Argentinian dishes such as *morcillas* (blood sausage) and *chinchulines* (grilled tripe stuffed with garlic).

Continental

The elegant a/c **Villa Diana** on Calle 28A in Reparto Kohly, tel. (24) 9232, ext. 621, offers an all-you-can-eat buffet for US$12. The fare, which claims to be continental, is really *criollo* with a hint of Europe. It has live music and is popular with Cubans. Open noon-6 a.m.

Prepare yourself for sticker shock if you dine at **Tocororo,** housed in a neoclassical mansion on the corner of Calle 18 y Avenida 3ra, tel. (33) 4530. This exquisite restaurant—an elitist luxury where ordinary Cubans can't even think of setting foot—is known as Gabriel García Márquez's favorite eatery (the Colombian novelist is known for his fondness for fine food, but here seems to have missed the beat). The walls bear the signatures of the rich and famous, although its reputation for fine food is undeserved. More fulfilling is the decor. The lobby is a cross between a museum, an art gallery, and a middle-class Victorian parlor full of rich treasures. Tocororo extends out into a garden patio—a delightfully tropical and relaxed place to eat, replete with rattan furniture, Tiffany lamps, and heaps of potted plants, along with painted wooden toucans and parrots hanging from gilt perches, and real *cotorros* (parrots) in cages. A pianist and an excellent jazz ensemble entertain.

The food is typical Cuban fare with an international twist. Or is it international with a *criollo* twist? Try the grilled lamb chops and mixed seafood brochette or local favorites such as *frijoles.* But it certainly isn't worth the outrageous price (expect to pay from US$25 for a run-of-the-mill grilled steak; and watch for the 10% service charge), and the wines, reputedly, are "normally in bad condition." Open noon-midnight.

A less-expensive option is **La Cecilia,** Avenida 5ta #11010, e/ 110 y 112, tel. (33) 1562, (22) 6700, another elegant and romantic restored mansion in the middle of a large garden. Most of the tables are outdoors and lit by Tiffany lamps surrounded by bamboo. It serves typical Cuban dishes such as *tasajo* (jerked beef), *churrasco* (broiled steak), and *pollo con mojo* (chicken with onion and garlic), as well as grilled lobster. Entrées cost US$10 and up. The place has a lengthy wine list at reasonable prices. At night, it hosts a *cabaret espectáculo* with sexy showgirls. Open noon-midnight (Thurs.-Sun. 9:30 p.m.-3 a.m. for cabaret).

In a similar vein is **La Ferminia,** at Avenida 5ta #18207, e/ 182 y 184, tel. (21) 0360, in a house full of anthuriums, chandeliers, and antiques. It has six private rooms, each in a separate color scheme (the pink room is full of Meissen porcelain), and you can also dine on an outside patio beneath a timbered roof. The menu includes soups (US$3), grilled chicken (US$8), and fish dishes (US$12); the house specialty is a mixed grill (US$28) with shrimp, lobster, fish, chicken, and scallops. (The chefs, unfortunately, have learned their vegetable preparation from the British—boiled to death.) A soda water and Coca-Cola will set you back US$4. Open noon-midnight.

If you'd like to watch a fashion show while you dine, try the touristy **La Maison,** Avenida 7ma and Calle 16, tel. (33) 1543 or (33) 0126. It offers a series of packages that include dinner; the cheapest is US$25 without alcohol. Open Mon.-Sat. 7 p.m.-1 a.m.

Italian

The **Ristorante Gambinas** in the Dos Gardenias complex on Avenida 7ma at 26 offers undistinguished pizzas, spaghettis, and raviolis for less than US$5. Take your sweater. Nearby, the Quinta y 42 commercial complex houses the flashy looking **Ristorante Italiano Rossini.**

For pizza, check out the **El Tucano** snack bar in the Hotel Copacabana. It's nothing to write home about, but the pizzas (average US$5) are the best I've had in Havana. Try the vegetarian pizza. It also has a buffet lunch for US$15. Alternately, try the **Pizzeria La Pérgola** in the Club Almendares on Avenida 49C in Reparto Kohly, where you can dine alfresco under an arbor or inside, where the a/c is cranked up (open noon-midnight).

By some accounts, **La Cova Pizza Nova,** in Marina Hemingway, Avenida 5ta y 248, tel. (24) 1150, has the best pizza in town.

Spanish and Mexican

I've yet to discover a Mexican restaurant in Cuba serving anything resembling Mexican food. The closest I know of is **Complejo Turística La Giraldilla,** at Calle 272 e/ 37 y 51 in the La Coronela district of La Lisa, southwest of Havana, tel. (33) 6062. It serves everything from tacos to chicken mole, washed down with sangría. It's popular with the political elite, who also flock to the clubby bar. Its grounds contain Versailles-type gardens, a huge swimming pool and sundeck, and a covered stage that hosts floor shows and concerts.

Oriental

Your best bet is **Pavo Real,** a little corner of China on Avenida 7ma #205 e/ Calle 2 y 4, tel. (24) 2315. Look for the huge Chinese neon sign outside. It also boasts Chinese decor, including art deco stained-glass doors. It serves undistinguished Chinese classics such as chow mein dishes for US$7 and up, plus Japanese tempura (US$9 and up), and Thai chicken (US$6.50). Try the spring rolls. Open noon-midnight.

A better bargain is the **Fonda China,** in Los Gardenias at Avenida 7ma and Calle 26. A good dish is the chop suey de camarones (US$8). Chopsticks are available. Entrées are US$4-9, complete meals US$8-10.

Hankering for grilled eels, *kim ch'i, chu'sok,* and other Korean specialties? Then head to **El Morambón,** on Avenida 5ta and 32, tel. (23) 3336. The cuisine is lackluster and overpriced, but you can eat it until 2 a.m.

Cafés and Snack Bars

Miramar lacks cafés. The **Parrillada La Fuente,** abutting the Casa de la Música on Calle 20 between 33 and 35, has an outdoor snack bar with shade trees; sandwiches and burgers cost below US$2, and fried chicken, steaks, and fish dishes run to US$16.

Desserts

You can buy delicious pastries, loaves, and iced cakes at **Nonaneli Pandería Dulcería,** a bakery in the Quinta y 42 complex at Avenida 5ta and Calle 42.

Self-Catering

The huge *supermercado* on Avenida 3ra and Calle 72 (100 meters east of Hotel Triton) in Miramar is Cuba's largest supermarket. It's like walking into a Safeway, with all the same Western consumer goods (at a hefty markup). It also has Cuba's best stock of fresh vegetables and fruits, canned goods, and other food items.

SUBURBS

Restaurants below are listed by region, rather than by type of fare, as above.

Boyeros (El Chico)

La Rueda, on the Carretera de Guajay, at Calle 294 in the village of El Chico, tel. (06) 8425, is a rustic yet acclaimed restaurant on a Ministry of Agriculture goose farm. Not surprisingly, the menu offers goose this and goose that. Be sure to accompany your *foie gras* with the house cocktail of rum and fruit juice. Set meals cost US$20. Despite its distance from the city, the place gets quite full. Reservations are recommended. Cockfights are hosted. Open noon-8 p.m.

Boyeros (Santiago de las Vegas)

The nicest place is **La Tabernita,** a *complejo turístico* (tourist complex) on Doble Vía Cacahual, on the main road to Cacahual, at the south end of town, tel. (683) 2033. It has a thatched restaurant serving *criollo* fare and is popular with Cuban families on weekends. In a similar vein is **Rincón Criollo,** about one km south of town, amid pine trees.

In town, try the **Mozambique Cafetería,** on the northeast corner of the town plaza; **Cafetería Amanecer,** at Avenida 411 #219; or **Cafetería Cocody,** one block north of the church. **Vesuvia Pizzeria** serves pizza slices for five pesos each.

Arroyo Naranjo (Parque Lenin)

The park boasts the noted **Las Ruinas** restaurant, tel. (44) 3336. It's well worth the drive, if only to admire the fabulous decor and setting. The building, which looks like something Frank Lloyd Wright might have conceived, was designed in concrete, encasing the ruins of an old sugar mill, with remnant free-standing walls overgrown with epiphytes and mosses (however, in typical communist fashion, it is also designed without any thought for patrons' safety; beware the lip at the top of the stairs, which have no guard rails). Downstairs is a bar and modestly elegant restaurant where a pianist plays, and the tables are lit by Tiffany lamps. Upstairs features stained-glass panels by the Cuban artist Portocarrero and louvered wooden French windows all around. The decor is elegant, with linens, silverware, classical urns full of flowers, and dozens of crystal chandeliers. It describes itself as serving international haute cuisine (lobster bellevue—US$20—is a specialty). The food has been described by readers as both "reminiscent of school dinners" and "the best in Havana." I rank it in-between; they make a tasty shrimp *enchilada* (US$12). Other dishes include pizza (US$4.50), blue cheese soup (US$2), shrimp brochette (US$12), and grilled fish uruguayano (US$11).

The **Restaurante Herradura** at the Centro Ecuestre offers a pleasant a/c ambience and serves garlic shrimp, pizzas, lobster, and *criollo* dishes for US$4-20. Abutting it is an outdoor grill—**La Rueda Parrillada**—with a pleasant patio.

The Mexican-style former home of the estate owner now houses a small and pleasing restaurant, the **Parillada 1740,** next to the Galeria de Arte. There are several other snack bars serving *bocaditos,* fried chicken, and the like. For a resuscitating fresh-squeezed cane juice, head to the *guarapera* opposite the entrance to El Rodeo.

Arroyo Naranjo
(ExpoCuba and Jardín Botánico)

A fistful of restaurants and cafés provide refreshment at ExpoCuba. The best is the elegant **Don Cuba Restaurant,** built around an inner courtyard with neoclassical Roman-cum-Arabic architecture. Flautists and singers perform in the courtyard. It offers a tasty grilled fish with rice and spiced vegetables for US$8.

The **Bambú Restaurant** overlooks the Japanese garden in the botanical garden. It bills itself as an "eco-restorán" and sells ice cream and sodas. It has been recommended by an expat in the know as the best vegetarian restaurant in Havana. However, it serves lunch only. Open Wed.-Sun. noon-3 p.m.

Regla

There are plenty of basic eateries to choose from here, though nothing stands out. Most are concentrated along Martí. Two pleasant restaurants sit on the southwest corner of Parque Guayacanamar, where an ice cream shop can help you beat the heat, and **Pizzeria Puerto Bello** is on the southeast corner. At Calle Martí and Pereira is a small bar, **La Casa del Daiquirí,** selling daiquiris for a few pesos.

Guanabacoa

Pickings are slim here. Try **Pizzería Bambino,** on the northwest corner of the main plaza, where there're also **Coppelia** and **Helado Tropical** outlets for ice cream. The dollars-only café fronting the entrance to the church is good for ice cream, sodas, and sandwiches. You're best bet is **Paladar La Pastorita,** on Calle 18 #21 esq. 6ta, in Reparto Guiteras (also known as the Bahía district) of northern Guanabacoa, tel. (97) 3732, serving huge portions.

Ciudad Panamericano

On the main street, **Steak House Toro,** tel. (33) 8545, offers clean, modern, a/c surroundings. It serves rib steak, filet mignon, T-bone steak, etc., and has an all-you-can-eat roast beef special for US$10. The village's other eateries are all dreary affairs, if not in decor, then in their menus. That of the hotel's **Restaurante Trópical** features soups (US$2), lobster and shrimp (US$13-21), and chicken roasted in fruit juices (US$6); breakfast at the hotel's Mesa Buffet is a lackluster affair. **Restaurante Allegro** offers pizzas and spaghetti for US$3-5, and **Restaurant Beit-Jing** makes a pitiful stab at Chinese food.

For ice cream desserts and shakes, head for the **Cremería,** 20 meters uphill from Tapatio. The **coffee shop** one block west of the hotel has a cool patio and is the hippest place to hang. A bakery is on the main street, 20 meters downhill from the hotel.

Cojímar

At **La Terraza** the food is good, with a wide-ranging menu that includes paella (US$7), grilled shrimp and fish (US$22), fish cocktail (US$2.50), and shrimp cocktail (US$8). The paella is inconsistent—from sublime to fair. Open noon-11 p.m. The bar is open 10:30 a.m.-11 p.m.

If you're feeling impecunious, there's a good *paladar*—**Restaurante Claro de Luna**—a few blocks north of the Hemingway statue. And the basic **El Torreón** serves unremarkable *criollo* fare.

Tarará

At the west end of Tarará, **Restaurante Cojímar** is next to the marina office and serves basic *criollo* fare, as does a handsome, thatched restaurant immediately west of the swimming pool near the marina.

A juice bar serves the east end of the beach, where there's also a restaurant 100 meters inland.

Prefer Chinese? Try **Restaurante El Chino** on the Via Monumental at the turnoff for Tarará.

Playas del Este (Santa María del Mar)

Most of the hotels have uninspired restaurants. Several *thatched* bars and eateries can be found on the beach, including two rustic places serving basic *criollo* fare in front of the Hotel Tropicoco. **Bar/Restaurante Bonanza,** on Playa Santa María, has a patio bar and modestly elegant indoor dining, too. You'll pay upward of US$5 for seafood and fried chicken dishes. It also has burgers and pizza noon-5 p.m. Dinner is served 6-9:45 p.m.

Another beach option is the **D'Prisa Centro Turístico,** at the west end of Playa El Mégano, with a thatched bar and grill. **Mi Casita de Coral,** 100 meters east of the Hotel Tropicoco, serves *criollo* fare 24 hours daily. Likewise, **Casa Club Atlántico** has a snack bar offering seafood, *criollo* dishes, and spaghettis (US$3.50), plus a chicken *oferta especial* (lunch special) for US$2. There's also **Costarenas Parrillada,** overlooking the beach on Avenida Norte, serving inexpensive grilled fare.

Pizzeria Mi Rinconcito, toward the west end of Avenida de las Terrazas, offers slices of pizza from US$1. Also catering to Italian tastes is **Pizzeria Yara,** on Avenida las Terrazas and Calle 10, with its own swimming pool. **Café Pinomar,** on Avenida Sur and Calle 5, also serves pizzas and burgers, and is open 24 hours.

For a breeze-swept view over the beach scene, head uphill to the **Restaurante Mirador del Mar,** on Calle 11 between Avenidas 1ra y 3ra.

Playas del Este (Boca Ciega and Guanabo)

El Bodegón, on 1ra in Boca Ciega, is a simple seafront restaurant with *criollo* fare served on a breeze-swept patio. Two blocks east is the handsome, thatched **Los Caneyes,** open 24 hours and also serving *criollo* dishes.

The most atmospheric place in Boca Ciega is **Casa del Pescador,** a Spanish-style bodega on Avenida 5ta esq. 442. It has fishing nets hanging from the ceiling. The menu is huge. Fish dishes average US$7, and shrimp and lobster start at US$8. The house specialty is *escabeche* (US$3.50). Open 10 a.m.-10 p.m.

In Guanabo, the simple **D'Prisa Cafetería La Barca,** on Avenida 5ta and 448, is popular with Cuban locals, perhaps for its stained-glass windows because its *criollo* fare is undistinguished. Another **D'Prisa Cafetería** on Avenida 5ta and 476 is a modish, pocket-size place serving sandwiches and basic Italian dishes from US$1.

One of the nicer eateries is **El Brocal,** at the corner of Avenida 5C and 500, in eastern Guanabo. This red-tile-roofed restaurant offers rustic ambience and simple *criollo* fare. **Pizzeria Italiano Piccolo,** nearby on 504 y Avenida 1ra, likewise offers colonial ambience near the shore.

The sparse **Cuanda's** on 474 y Avenida 5ta serves salads for US80 cents, rice dishes from US$1, and pastas for US$4.

For ice cream, head to the **Heladería El Betty,** on Avenida 5ta at Calle 480. There's a **bakery** next door.

TRANSPORTATION AND TOURS
GETTING THERE

BY AIR

The vast majority of flights to Cuba arrive in Havana. Havana's airport is the **José Martí International Airport** (see below), which in 1999 was served by more than two dozen airlines. Many leading international carriers have regular scheduled service from Europe, Canada, and Central and South America (the US government bans flights between the US and Cuba, except Miami-Havana charters for licensed travelers).

Cuba's national airline is **Cubana de Aviación,** Calle 63 #64, Vedado, Havana, tel. (33) 4949, fax (33) 4056, e-mail: ecacom@iacc3.get.cma.net, website: www.cubana.cu, which celebrated its 70th anniversary in 1999 and handles 30 percent of all traffic into Cuba. Cubana has been upgrading its fleet of late and now has 309-pas-

senger DC-10s and new A-320s that serve Europe and Mexico, and offer Business Class and First Class *(Clase Tropical)* service. However, the workhorses in the stable remain uncomfortable and poorly maintained Soviet-made aircraft (I've even seen cockroaches on board). Cubana's fares are generally lower than other airlines', but the airline is poorly managed: its attitude toward scheduled departures is cavalier (flight times change frequently, so double-check any published schedules); it is notorious for disposing of seats of passengers who arrive after the scheduled check-in time; its safety record is not good (crashes occurred in Cuba in 1997 and Ecuador in 1998); and nonsmoking regulations are rarely enforced. Says Michael Douglas of CubaTravel (website: www.cubatravel.com.mx): "The horror stories we hear from clients will make your hair stand on end."

CUBANA AIRLINE OFFICES OUTSIDE CUBA

Europe

Barcelona: Calle Fontanella 12B, Plaza Cataluña, Barcelona 08010, tel. (343) 318-8833, fax (343) 318-6091

Berlin: Frankfurter Tor 8-A, 10234 Berlin, tel. 589-3409, fax 589-2947763; Airport, tel. 678-8185

Brussels: Avenie Louise #272, BTE1, Brussels, tel. 640-2050, fax 640-0810

Cologne: Flughafen Köln-Bonn Postfach 980151, 51129 Koln, tel. (02203) 402-198, fax (02203) 412-197

Frankfurt: An der Hauptwache 7, 60313 Frankfurt am Main, tel. (069) 913-0980, fax (069) 913-09840

Las Palmas: Calle Galicia #29, Las Palmas 35007, Gran Canaria, tel. (928) 272-408, fax (928) 272-419

London: 49 Conduit St., London W1R 9FB, tel. (171) 734-1165, fax (171) 437-0681

Madrid: Calle Princesa #25, Edificio Exágono, 28008 Madrid, tel. (542) 2923, fax (541) 6642; Airport, tel. (205) 8448

Milano: Via Paolo de Cannobio 2-21122, Milano, tel. (6) 801-437, fax (672) 001-670

Moscow: Karovit Val 7, Corpus 1, Seccion 5, Moscow, tel. (237) 1901, fax (237) 8391; Airport, tel. (578) 7650

Paris: Tour Maine Montparnasse, 33 Avenue de Maine, B.P. 171, 75755 Paris Cedex 15, tel. (453) 83-112, fax (453) 83-110; Airport, tel. (48) 84-4060

Rome: Via Barberini 86, 4 Piano, Rome 00187, tel. (474) 1104, fax (474) 6836

Santiago de Compostela: Doctor Tejeiro #20, Santiago de Compostela, tel. (981) 581-415

Canada

Montreal: 4 Place Ville Marie #405, Montreal, PQ H3B 2E7, tel. (514) 871-1222, fax (514) 871-1227

Toronto: Lester B. Pearson Airport, tel./fax (416) 676-4723

Central America and Caribbean

Cancún: Av. Yaxchilan #23, SM-24 M-22 retorno 3, e/ Nit-Cheaven y Tanchacte, Cancún, tel. (86) 0192, fax (87) 7373, Airport, tel. (86) 0192

Fort-de-France: 50 Rue Schoelcher 97200, Fort-de-France, Martinique, tel. (60) 5200, fax (60) 3820

Kingston: 22 Trafalgar Road #11, Kingston 10, Jamaica, tel. (978) 3410, (978) 3406

Mexico City: Temistocles #246 esq. Homero, Colonia Polanco, C.P. 11550, Deleg. Manuel Hidalgo, Mexico, DF, tel. (255) 3776, fax (255) 0835; Airport, tel. (571) 5368

Nassau: Hotel British Colonial Beach Resort, Room 239, Nassau, tel. (242) 322-3301

Panama: Calle 29 y Av. Justo Arosemena No.4-14, tel. (507) 227-2122 or (27) 2291, fax (507) 272-2241

San José: De Canal 7, Carretera á Pavas, San José, tel. (290) 5095, fax (290) 5101

Santo Domingo: Av. Tiradente esq. 27 de Febrero, Plaza Merengue, Local 209, Dominican Republic, tel. (227) 2040, fax (227) 2044; Airport, tel. (549) 0345

South America

Bogotá: Carrera 14 #7920, Bogotá, tel. (621) 0793, fax (621) 0785

Buenos Aires: Sarmiento #552 e/ Florida y San Martin, Buenos Aires, tel. (326) 5291, fax (326) 5294; Airport, tel. (620) 0011

Caracas: Av. Rómulo Gallegos con Primera, Edificio Pascal Torre B #133, Palos Grandes, Caracas, tel. (285) 3548, fax (285) 6313

Guayaquíl: Centro Comercial Las Vitrinas, Local No.61, Calle H La Kenedy, Guayaquíl, tel. (39) 0727, fax (28) 9911

Lima: Jiron Tarata #250, Miraflores, Lima 18, tel. (41) 0554, fax (47) 1363

Montevideo: Boulevar Artigas 1147 #504, Montevideo, Uruguay, tel. (48) 1402

Quito: Avenida de los Shyris y 6 de Diciembre, Edificio Torre Nova Oficina 1A, Quito, Ecuador, tel. 5939-227463

Rio de Janeiro: Rua Teofilo Otono 81, CJ 901, CEP 20080, Rio de Janeiro, Brazil, tel. (021) 233-0960

Santiago de Chile: Calle Fidel Oteiza 1971 #201, Providencia, Santiago de Chile, tel. (274) 1819, fax (274) 8207

São Paulo: Rua da Consolacao 232, Conjunto 1009, Centro São Paulo, Brazil, tel. (214) 4571, fax (255) 8660

US LAW AND TRAVEL TO CUBA

Contrary to popular belief, US law does *not* prohibit US citizens from visiting Cuba. However, to visit Cuba legally you must either spend no money there, or qualify for a license issued by the US Treasury Department in order to buy goods (a meal at a hotel, for example) or services (an airline ticket, tour package, or hotel room). In order to apply, you need a good reason. Except as specifically licensed by the Office of Foreign Assets Control (OFAC), payments in connection with any other travel to Cuba are prohibited, whether travelers go directly or via a third country such as Mexico, Canada, or another Caribbean island.

US citizens and any person in the US is subject to these restrictions, regardless of citizenship. Under these restrictions, spending money relating to Cuban travel is prohibited unless the traveler is licensed. The regulations change frequently and are open to interpretation by the understaffed office (interpretation often shifts with the political breeze). For example, in May 1999, the Clinton administration announced new regulations that will expand travel opportunities. US universities and nongovernmental organizations may now apply for two-year travel permits to Cuba that will permit any of its members to travel to Cuba without requiring individual certification.

To determine if you or your organization qualify for a **general license** (which does not require prior government authorization) or a **specific license** (which does require prior government authorization), contact the Licensing Division, Office of Foreign Asset Control (OFAC), US Department of the Treasury, 1500 Pennsylvania Ave. NW, Washington, DC 20200, tel. (202) 622-2520 or (202) 622-2480, fax (202) 622-1657, website: www.ustreas.gov/ofac/ofactxt. Request the *Cuban Assets Control Regulations*. Alternately, check with the US-Cuba Trade and Economic Council, 30 Rockefeller Plaza, New York, NY 10112-0002, tel. (212) 246-1444, fax (212) 246-2345, website www.cubatrade.org, which stays abreast of latest regulations. Relevant information is contained within the Code of Federal Regulations (CFR)—31 CFR Part 515.

The Office of Cuban Affairs (OCA), Department of State, Washington, DC 20520, tel. (202) 647-9273, fax (202) 736-4476, website: www.state.gov, establishes the policies by which the OFAC interprets the regulations by which laws are enforced.

The following regulations applied at press time:

Who is an "Individual Subject to United States Law"

An individual subject to US law includes: any individual, wherever located, who is a citizen or resident of the US; any person who is within the US (a non-US citizen in transit at an airport, for example); any corporation organized under the laws of the US or of any state, territory possession, or district of the US; any corporation, partnership, or association, wherever organized or doing business, that is owned or controlled by an individual or individuals subject to US law. (Non-US citizens who have H-1 visas are generally considered to be subject to US law.)

General Licenses

The following categories of travelers are permitted to spend money for Cuban travel without the need to obtain special permission from OFAC, nor are they required to inform OFAC in advance of their visit to Cuba:

Official Government Travelers: US and foreign government officials, including representatives of international organizations of which the United States is a member, who are traveling on official business.

Journalists: Individuals who are regularly (full-time) employed by a news gathering organization (television network, television station, television production company, radio station, newspaper, newsletter, magazine, video production company, etc.), and persons regularly employed as supporting broadcast or technical personnel. Travelers are advised to have company identification (with photograph), business card, and/or a letter from the company confirming full-time employment.

Persons who are visiting close relatives: People with close relatives in Cuba may visit them in circumstances of humanitarian need. This authorization is valid only once every 12 months.

"Fully Hosted" Travelers: Individuals subject to US law traveling on a "fully hosted" basis can travel without a specific license so long as they do not spend any funds of their own while in Cuba. This includes travel on a prepaid, all-inclusive tour package with companies such as Wings of the World. Funds used to make payments for hotels, meals, ground transportation, sundries, etc., must originate from a) an entity within Cuba, b) an entity within another country, or c) an individual within another country. The use of indirect transfers is not permitted. A "fully

(continued on next page)

US LAW AND TRAVEL TO CUBA

(continued)

hosted" traveler may pay for transportation only if aboard a non-Cuban carrier such as Mexicana, Air Jamaica, Lacsa, or Iberia. Travelers whose expenses are covered by a person not subject to US jurisdiction may not bring back any Cuban origin goods, except for informational materials (books, magazines, posters, etc.) and an unlimited amount of artwork. Gifts from Cuba nationals may be brought into the US, but the gift must remain with the US Customs Service at the point of entry; the traveler subject must then request a license from the OFAC to take possession of the gift.

("Fully hosted" travelers are subject to increased scrutiny. As of March 1998, there is no longer a presumption of innocence; there is now a presumption of guilt. The OFAC now states that a letter from an individual or entity not subject to US law—or a letter from a US-based law firm—confirming that the individual was "fully hosted" will not be accepted as "proof" that a visit was "fully hosted." "Fully hosted" travelers are now required to produce receipts for all daily expenses within Cuba which demonstrate that all of the expenses were paid by an individual or entity not subject to US law, and to submit a signed letter to that effect.)

Amateur or semiprofessional athletes traveling to participate in athletic competition held under the auspices of an international sports federation.

Full-time professionals whose travel transactions are directly related to noncommercial, academic research and whose research will comprise a full work schedule in Cuba; plus full-time professionals whose travel transactions are directly related to attendance at professional meetings or conferences that do not promote tourism or other commercial activity involving Cuba or the production of biotechnological products.

Special Licenses

A specific license requires written government approval. Applicants should write a letter to OFAC stating the date of the planned visit and the length of stay; the specific purpose(s) of the visit; plus the name(s), title(s), and background(s) of the traveler. OFAC has been understaffed and is notoriously slow: allow two or three months. Special licenses are issued by OFAC on a case-by-case basis authorizing travel transactions by persons in connection with the following travel categories:

Humanitarian Travel: Persons traveling to Cuba to visit close relatives in cases involving hardship more than once in a 12-month period; persons traveling to Cuba to accompany licensed humanitarian donations (other than gift parcels); or persons traveling in connection with activities of recognized human rights organizations investigating human rights violations.

Educational Research: Travel in connection with professional research or similar activities, for clearly defined educational or religious activities, including academics intending to lecture at educational institutions or attend a meeting or conference, and activities related to study for an undergraduate or graduate degree sponsored by a college or university located in the United States.

Commercial "Opportunists": Individuals wishing to identify commercial opportunities in the fields of artwork, communications, entertainment, informational materials, medical equipment, medical instruments, medical supplies, medicated products, medicines, pharmaceuticals, and telecommunications; register trademarks and patents; organize and participate in trade shows; authorize consumer credit cards to be valid for use; and provide travel services and provide air transportation services.

Freelance Journalists: Many travelers have successfully been approved as "freelancers," particularly if traveling on arranged programs such as offered by the Center for Cuban Studies. If you want to go it alone and try the "journalist" or "researcher" angle, write to OFAC, which requires a written statement of why your proposed trip falls within the rules for permissible travel.

Others: Persons attending public performances, clinics, workshops, and exhibitions.

What You May Spend

Licensed travelers are authorized to spend up to US$195 per day. Exemptions to the US$195 per day authorization can be requested from OFAC. "Fully hosted" travelers are not subject to spending limits while within the Republic of Cuba. Journalists also may spend more than $195 daily (the amount is unspecified) to cover expenses incurred in the reporting of a story.

Money may be spent only for purchases of items directly related to travel such as hotel accommodations, meals, and goods personally used by the traveler in Cuba, or for the purchase of $195 worth of Cuban merchandise to be brought into the United States as accompanied baggage. Purchases of services related to travel, such as nonemergency medical services, are prohibited. The purchase of publications and other informational material is not restricted in any way.

Licensed travelers may return from Cuba with up to US$100 worth of Cuban products (such as cigars, rum, T-shirts, and crafts) for their personal use. For cigars, the US Customs Service permits up to 100 cigars, but the total value must not exceed US$100. For example, if a traveler returns with 100 cigars that cost US$1 each, the traveler would not be permitted to bring any other Cuban products (such as rum). Travelers should retain a receipt showing the amount paid for all Republic of Cuba-origin products.

Qualified Travel Service Providers

US law states, "US travel service providers, such as travel agents and tour operators, who handle travel arrangements to, from, or within Cuba must hold special authorizations from the US Treasury Department to engage in such activities."

OFAC has licensed the following companies as authorized Travel Service Providers (TSPs) legally entitled to make commercial travel arrangements to Cuba: **Tico Travel,** 161 E. Commercial Blvd., Ft. Lauderdale, FL 33334, tel. (954) 493-5335 or (800) 493-8426, fax (954) 493-8466, e-mail: tico@gate. net, website: www.destinationcuba.com; and **Marazul Charters,** Tower Plaza Mall, 4100 Park Ave., Weehawken, NJ 07087, tel. (201) 319-9670 or (800) 223-5334, fax (201) 319-9009, e-mail: bguild@marazultours.com, website: www.marazultours.com.

TSPs can only make reservations for licensed travelers. You must obtain approval before proceeding with a reservation. Qualified travelers should begin preparations two months in advance of their travel date. After you have determined which license you need, you must acquire a visa from the Cuban government.

However, referring to other travel agencies and tour operators (i.e., non-TSPs), "It is possible to provide travel services to US persons legally able to travel to Cuba for family visits, professional research, or news gathering," says Michael Krinsky, a partner in the law firm of Rabinowitz, Boudin, Standard, Krinsky and Lieberman, which represents the Cuban government in the United States.

US travel agencies can also provide services to third countries, from where a traveler makes his or her own arrangements for travel to and within Cuba. They may also be able to provide services, such as travel arrangements to Jamaica, where a component includes an excursion to Cuba. Treasury Department regulations do not "show a clear penalty against travel agents who book travel this way." *Travel agents should double-check the regulations,* however, with the US Department of the Treasury, or with Krinsky, 740 Broadway, New York, NY 10003, tel. (212) 254-1111, fax (212) 674-4614, e-mail mkrinsky@igc.apc.org.

Visas for Licensed Travelers

All licensed travelers to Cuba must have a visa from the Cuban government prior to reserving their flight. Tico Travel and Marazul (see above) can assist you in acquiring your visa. (Tico Travel charges US$120 for the visa and preparing the documents.) There are two different forms: one for those born in Cuba and one for those born outside Cuba. Allow 30 days for processing.

Cubans and Cuban-Americans: Anyone who permanently left Cuba after 31 December 1970 must have a valid Cuban passport (people born in Cuba who left Cuba permanently before that date don't need a Cuban passport). If you don't have a Cuban passport and you left Cuba after 31 December 1970, you must contact the Cuban Interests Section in Washington, DC, tel. (202) 797-8609 or (202) 797-8610, to get the required paperwork. Cubans who left Cuba permanently prior to 1959 can acquire a slightly less expensive 359 Visa, acquired directly with the Cuban Interests Section.

Illegal Travel

About 120,000 US citizens visited Cuba in 1998. The majority did so legally, while the rest slipped in through third countries and spent freely without a license. The US government has recently sought to tighten control of unsanctioned travel. Since May 1998, persons subject to US jurisdiction who travel to Cuba without a license bear a "presumption of guilt" and may be required to show documentation that all expenses incurred were paid by a third party not subject to US law.

In the five years since 1994, OFAC has fined 379 people. Trading with Cuba illegally is good for up to a US$55,000 fine, but most fines have been US$1,500 to US$5,000.

Many airlines operate a summer and winter timetable. Information below is based on winter (high season) schedules.

From the US

At press time, no regular commercial flights were permitted between the US and Cuba (for the exception, see below). Nor can any US airline, tour operator, or travel agent make arrangements for flights to Cuba without a license from the US Treasury Department.

Still, thousands of US citizens take advantage of the many scheduled commercial airline services to Cuba from third countries. Getting to Cuba from the US is no more difficult than flying, say, from Buffalo, New York, to Portland, Oregon. The most popular routes are through Canada or the Bahamas for East Coast residents and through Mexico for everyone else. Most Americans choose to fly through Mexico, specifically Cancún in the Yucatan Peninsula. From here, Havana is only an hour away, and flights leave twice a day (times vary slightly throughout the year). If you fly from the Bahamas and are transferring to flights into the US, you'll be greeted by US Immigration officers, who have an office inside Nassau airport. If you are quizzed whether you've been to Cuba and you are not licensed by OFAC, you may have a problem explaining your trip.

It is *essential* to have completely separate tickets and reservations for your travel into and out of Cuba from any third country: under the terms of the embargo, US citizens showing an airline reservation that includes an onward flight to Cuba will be refused boarding on the flight out of the US.

Licensed Charters: Licensed charter flights operate to Havana from Miami—the only permitted gateway—twice weekly for travelers with permission to travel to and spend money in Cuba (typically US$299 roundtrip, US$195 one-way; children under 12, US$175 roundtrip, US$115 one-way). Charter operators are only authorized to carry properly documented passengers as permitted by the US Treasury Department. Individuals who are hosted by the Cuban government are barred from taking charter flights through Miami and must travel on a non-Cuban carrier from outside the US. Flights must be authorized every month, and once authorized, they fill up almost immediately.

Licensed travel service providers (TSPs) include: **Marazul Charters,** Tower Plaza Mall, 4100 Park Ave., Weehawken, NJ 07087, tel. (201) 319-9670 or (800) 223-5334, fax (201) 319-9009 (and—for Cuban-Americans only—in Miami, tel (305) 232-8157), e-mail: bguild@marazultours com, website: www.marazultours.com, which operates Boeing 727s between Miami and Havana and **Tico Travel,** 161 E. Commercial Blvd., Ft Lauderdale, FL 33334, tel. (954) 493-5335 or (800) 493-8426, fax (954) 493-8466, e-mail tico@gate.net, website: www.destinationcuba.com which makes reservations; **Airline Brokers Company,** tel. (305) 871-1260, fax (305) 447-0965 e-mail tfre97a@prodigy.com; and **C&T,** P.O. Box 996091, Miami, FL 30351, tel. (305) 876-7660 fax (305) 871-1260. (The Miami-based commute carrier Gulfstream International Airlines also operates one flight a week to Havana exclusively for staff of the US Interests Section.)

By Private Aircraft: Owners of private air craft, including air ambulance services, who in tend to land in Cuba must obtain a temporary export permit for the aircraft from the US Department of Commerce prior to departure.

You must contact the **Instituto de Aeronáutica Civil de Cuba,** Calle 23 #64, e/ Infanta y P Vedado, tel. (55) 1047, fax (33) 4571, at least 10 days prior to arrival in Cuba and at least 48 hours before an overflight.

From Canada

More than 200,000 Canadians visited Cuba in 1998, and there are plenty of flights between Canada and Cuba (although most fly to Cuba's beach resorts rather than Havana). Toronto based charter tour operators are the driving force of the trade. You might find cheap airfares— about C$400 roundtrip—through **Travel Deals** tel. (416) 236-0125, or **Wholesale Travel Group,** tel. (416) 366-1000. **Canadian Universities Travel Service,** Travel Cuts, 187 College St., Toronto, ON M5T 1P7, tel. (416) 979-2406 sells discount airfares to students and has 25 offices throughout Canada.

Scheduled Flights: Cubana has three scheduled departures weekly using an A-320 from Montreal and Toronto to Havana (from about C$500 in low season and C$700 in high season). You can usually get rates lower than Cubana's published fares by booking with

Canadian tour agencies that block large numbers of seats.

Air Canada, tel. (800) 869-9000, website: www.aircanada.ca, flies three times weekly from Toronto to Havana, with connecting service to San José, Costa Rica. **Lacsa,** tel. (800) 225-272, offers a similar service.

You can also fly with **Air Jamaica,** 4141 Yonge St., Willowdale, ON M2P 2A6, tel. (416) 729-6024 or (800) 526-5585, which offers connecting flights to Havana through Montego Bay, Jamaica

Charter Flights: Air Canada Vacations, tel. 514) 422-5788, a division of Air Canada, has twice-weekly flights to Havana. Seven-night packages range from C$499 to C$1,099. **Air Transat,** tel. (514) 987-1616, fax (514) 987-750, and **Canada 3000,** tel. (416) 674-2661, also offer charters. Charter fares to Havana are approximately C$449. Tickets on both charter airlines are issued only via travel agencies.

Numerous air-hotel packages are offered by companies that utilize the above charter services. Such companies advertise in the travel sections of leading newspapers, such as the *Toronto Globe & Mail* and *Montreal Gazette.* For example, **Regent Holidays,** 6205 Airport Rd., Bldg. A, Suite 200, Mississauga, ON L4V 1E1, tel. (905) 673-3343 or (800) 263-8776, e-mail: general@regentholidays.com, website: www.regentholidays.com, offers charter flights and air/hotel packages using Air Transat, flying to Havana every Sunday.

From Europe

Direct air service to Cuba is available from most Western European countries. The cheapest fares are usually on direct flights, but you can also find cheap fares via Caribbean destinations or Miami, from where you can take a flight to the Bahamas and then to Cuba (see below). American Airlines, British Airways, Continental Airlines, United Airlines, and Virgin Atlantic fly from London to Miami. Note, however, that if flying aboard a US carrier, you must have your ticket for the Cuban portion issued on a separate ticket stock—and you must make your reservation for the Bahamas-Cuba leg separately.

From France: Air France, tel. (0802) 802-02, www.airfrance.com.fr, flies from Paris's Charles de Gaulle airport to Havana on Wednesday and Saturday using a Boeing 747 (US$934 low season, US$1,034 high season roundtrip, 30 day APEX). **AOM,** tel. (803) 001-234, www.aom.com, flies to Havana from Paris daily (except Tuesday). I was quoted US$1,464 for a six-month advance purchase! **Cubana,** tel. (45) 383-112, flies from Lyon via Orly airport in Paris on Monday, with additional twice-weekly service from Orly.

From Germany: Cubana, tel. (069) 913-0980, operates a DC-10 to Havana from Berlin via Frankfurt on Sunday. It also has charter service from Cologne to Havana on Friday. **Condor,** Postfach 1164, 65446 Kelsterbach, Germany, tel. (061) 079-390 or (07) 755-440, fax (061) 077-550, planned to introduce charters from Germany.

A travel agency called **Die Resisgalerie,** Myliusstr. 68, 60323 Frankfurt, Germany, tel. (69) 972-06000, fax (69) 972-06002, specializes in flights to Cuba. Also try **Kubareisen,** v.-Ossietsky-Str. 25, 48151 Münster, Germany, tel. (251) 790-077, fax (251) 798-363, e-mail: kubareisen@aol.com.

Discount fares are available through **Council Travel** in Düsseldorf, tel. (2113) 29-088, and Munich, tel. (0898) 95-022; and from **STA Travel,** tel. (69) 43-0191, fax (69) 43-9858, in Frankfurt.

From Italy: Air Europe, tel. (147) 848-130 or (02) 6711-8228, website: www.aireurope.it, flies from Milan to Havana via Rome on Sunday, and direct from Milan on Tuesday (US$800 roundtrip). **Cubana,** tel. (474) 1104, flies from Rome on Monday, Wednesday, and Friday using a DC-10.

Lauda Air, Strada Provinciale 52, 21010 Vizzola Ticino, Italy, tel. (0331) 7593, fax (0331) 230-467, website: www.laudaair.com, flies charters from Milan on Wednesday.

From The Netherlands: Martinair, website: www.martinair.com, planned to introduce in November 1999 direct flights from Amsterdam to Havana, continuing to Cancún, on Monday.

KLM, www.klm.com, has flights to Havana from Amsterdam on Wednesday and Sunday

From Russia: Aeroflot, 4 Frunzenskaya Naberezhnay, Moscow, tel. (095) 156-8019, flies from Moscow to Havana via Varadero for US$600 one-way, US$810 roundtrip. **Cubana** operates an Ilyushin once a week from Moscow.

From Spain: Cubana flies direct to Havana from both Madrid, tel. (542) 2923, and Barcelona, tel. (343) 318-8833, once weekly using a DC-10, and from Santiago de Compostela on Friday and Las Palmas (Canary Islands) using an Ilyushin. **Iberia,** tel. (587) 8785, also flies to Havana from Madrid, daily except Friday.

Air Europa, tel. (902) 401-501, www.aireuropa-online.com, flies from Madrid to Havana on Tuesday, Thursday, Saturday, and Sunday using a Boeing 767. One-way fare is US$480 low season, US$610 high season; roundtrip costs US$800 and US$940 respectively.

From the UK: British Airways, tel. (0345) 222-111, initiated direct flights to Havana from Heathrow in spring 1999. Fares are from £472 return. **Cubana,** 49 Conduit St., London W1, tel. (171) 734-1165, fax (171) 437-0681, flies to Havana from Gatwick four times weekly using a DC-10, with a connecting flight from Manchester on Wednesday.

Captivating Cuba, tel. (181) 742-1312, is the UK's largest travel agency handling air traffic to Cuba. Also try **Journey Latin America,** 12 Heathfield Terr., London W4 4JE, tel. (0181) 747-3108, fax (0181) 742-1312, e-mail: flights@journeylatinamerica.co.uk, website: www.journeylatinamerica.co.uk, offers roundtrip flights between London and Havana from £407 low season, £468 high season on Iberia.

Regent Holidays, tel. (0117) 921-1711, fax (0117) 925-4866, website: www.cheapflights.co.uk, also offers inexpensive flights to Havana.

You may be able to save money by buying your ticket through a "bucket shop," which sells discounted tickets on scheduled carriers. They usually have access to a limited number of tickets, so book early. Bucket shops advertise in London's *What's On, Time Out,* and leading Sunday newspapers. **Trailfinders,** 42 Earl's Court Rd., London W8 6EJ, tel. (181) 747-3108, specializes in cheap fares throughout Latin America. **STA Travel,** 74 Old Brompton Rd., London SW7, tel. (171) 937-9971, fax (171) 938-5321, specializes in student fares. STA also has offices throughout the UK. Alternately, try **Council Travel,** 28A Poland St., London W1V 3DB, tel. (171) 437-7767.

Online, one of the best resources for airfares to Havana is www.cheapflights.co.uk/Havana.html, which in July 1999 listed London-Havana roundtrip airfares for £329-534.

From Elsewhere: Cubana flies to Havana from Copenhagen on Thursday and from Brussels on Saturday using a DC-10; and from Las Palmas on Friday and Lisbon once weekly using an Ilyushin.

From the Caribbean

From The Bahamas: Cubana, tel. (242) 322-3301, offers a daily charter flight to Havana from Nassau. The flights generally leave around 4:30 p.m. but change frequently. Cuba's **Aero Caribbean** also flies between Nassau and Havana daily Wed.-Sunday.

You can book Cubana flights for US$179 roundtrip (plus US$20 visa and US$10 ticket tax) through **Bahatours,** based in the Graycliff Hotel, P.O. Box N-7078, Nassau, Bahamas, tel. (242) 361-6510, fax (242) 361-1336. Ask for Michael Larrow, whose services I've used several times: he'll meet you at the airport ticket counter with your ticket. Bahatours (also known as Havanatur Nassau) also offers two- to seven-night packages including airfare, transfers, and accommodations. You can guarantee your reservation with a credit card.

Likewise, **Cuba Tours,** P.O. Box N-1629, Nassau, Bahamas, tel. (242) 325-0042, fax (242) 325-3339, makes flight reservations and offers Cuba packages (its office is at Southland Shopping Centre, East St.), as does **Majestic Travel,** tel. (242) 328-0908, which has been recommended by a reader (US$208 roundtrip, including tourist visa). You can pick up your ticket at the office once you arrive in Nassau (Majestic Travel has vans at the airport that offer free transfers to the office and back to the airport), but if you plan to depart for Cuba the day you arrive, be sure to allow two or three hours in Nassau for the transaction.

Innovative Travel & Tours, tel. (242) 325-0042, fax (242) 325-3339, doesn't accept credit card reservations and requires you to pay a deposit in advance through a wire transfer or certified check, which has to be mailed. Your ticket is delivered to you at the airport (one reader reports that her booking went smoothly). Roundtrip tickets cost US$192 for up to 30 days (plus US$25 tourist visa); US$30 extra for an open-ended ticket.

Returning from Cuba, you pass through Bahamian immigration (there is no in-transit lounge). Bahamian Customs go "on notice" when the Cubana flight arrives and may search you

ags (although they're really interested in Ba-
amian nationals with bags stuffed full of cig-
rs). The departure terminal for flights to the US
s to the left of the exit from the arrivals hall. You
nust pass through US Immigration and Cus-
oms here. They, too, go "on notice." If you're a
JS citizen, they won't know that you've been in
Cuba unless you tell them. However, US offi-
ials may ask you outright if you've been to
Cuba, or where you stayed in the Bahamas and
ow long. If you choose to tell the truth, expect to
ave your Cuban purchases confiscated (one
of my friends had all her Cuban cigars snapped
1 two before her eyes). If you choose not to tell
ne truth, any hesitation may give the game
way.

From the Cayman Islands: Cuba's **Aero
Caribbean** flies between Grand Cayman and
Havana on Wednesday, Friday, and Sunday.
Eddy Tours, P.O. Box 31097, Grand Cayman,
el. (345) 949-4606, fax (345) 949-4095, operates
charters.

From the Dominican Republic: Cubana,
el. (809) 227-2040, has charter service to Ha-
ana from Santo Domingo on Thursday (via
Santiago) and Sunday. Cuba's **AeroGaviota,**
Calle 47 #2814, e/ 28 y 34 Reparto Kohly, Ha-
ana, tel. (81) 3068, fax (33) 2621, also operates
etween Puerto Plata and Havana.

From Jamaica: Air Jamaica, tel. (305) 670-
222 or (800) 523-5585 in the US; in Jamaica,
el. (876) 922-4661 (Kingston) or (876) 952-4300
Montego Bay), flies from Montego Bay to Ha-
ana on Monday, Thursday, and Saturday for
JS$156 one-way, US$188 roundtrip. **Cubana,**
el. (876) 978-3410 (Kingston), has scheduled
ights to Havana from Kingston and Montego
Bay on Friday, with additional charter service
rom Montego Bay utilized by several Jamaican
our companies.

Caribic Vacations, 69 Gloucester Ave., Mon-
ego Bay, Jamaica, tel. (876) 953-2600 or (876)
79-9387, fax (876) 979-3421, e-mail: car-
ouse@caribiconline.com, website: www.caribi-
online.com, offers Cubana charter flights from
Montego Bay to Havana on Friday and Sunday
JS$190 roundtrip, including Cuban visa). It also
ffers air-hotels packages to Havana from
JS$310, double occupancy.

Tropical Tours, tel. (876) 952-0440, fax (876)
52-0340, e-mail: tropical@cwjaimaica.com,

website: www.marzouca.com, offers charters to
Havana from Montego Bay and Kingston on
Monday, Thursday, and Sunday using Air Jamaica Express. A two-night "Weekend in Havana" package costs US$299.

From Elsewhere: Cubana operates service
between Havana and Curaçao (Monday), Fort-
de-France in Martinique (Friday), Pointe-a-Pitre
in Guadeloupe (Friday), Santo Domingo in the
Dominican Republic (Wednesday and Sunday),
and Sint Maarten (Sunday). **Aero Gaviota** also
offers charter flights from the Caribbean, and
Central and South America.

From Central America

From Belize: Cuba's **Aero Caribbean** flies between Belize and Havana on Monday.

From Costa Rica: LACSA, tel. (506) 296-
0909 in the US, 1600 NW LeJeune Rd. #20,
Miami, FL 33126, tel. (305) 870-7500 or (800)
225-2272, part of Grupo Taca (website: www.
grupotaca.com), flies from San José to Havana
daily (US$265 one-way, US$399 roundtrip), continuing to Toronto. Grupo Taca has a LatinPass
(e-mail: mail@latinpass.com, website: www.lat-
inpass.com) permitting multiple stops at cities
throughout the Americas, incuding Havana. The
cost varies according to number of cities and
their zone.

Cubana, tel. (506) 290-5095, operates flights
from San José to Havana on Thursday and Sunday (US$499).

Your best booking agent is US-owned **Costa
Rica's TravelnNet,** tel. (506) 256-7373, fax 256-
8412, e-mail: travelnet@centralamerica.net, web-
site:www.centralamerica.com, which specializes
in Cuba. **Tikal Tours,** tel. (506) 223-2811, fax
223-1916, e-mail: advtikal@sol.racsa.co.cr, also
specializes in Cuba.

From El Salvador: Grupo Taca has flights
from El Salvador to Havana three times weekly
(US$280 one-way, US$399 roundtrip).

From Guatemala: Grupo Taca flies from
Guatemala to Havana three times weekly
(US$280 one-way, US$399 roundtrip). Cuba's
Aero Caribbean flies between Guatemala and
Havana on Wednesday and Friday.

From Mexico: Mexicana, tel. (525) 448-0990
or (800) 502-2000, website: www.mexicana.com.
mx, flies from Mexico City to Havana daily, with a
second flight each Thursday and Saturday stop-

ping in Mérida (fares range from US$361 to US$601 roundtrip).

Cubana, Temistocles #246 B esq. Av. Homero, Colonia Polanca, tel. (5) 255-3776, fax (5) 255-0835, also offers service from Mexico City on Wednesday and Saturday using a DC- 10.

Far more popular among US travelers are the flights from Cancún. **Cubana,** Av. Yazchilán #23 SM-24 M-22, Retorno 3 e/ Nir-Cheaven y Tan-Chacte, tel. (87) 7333, flies daily from Cancún to Havana. Fares are about US$199 roundtrip, plus US$25 tax. These flights on ancient, dilapidated Russian jets are not for the weak-hearted. A much better alternative is **Aero Caribbean,** Ave. Cobá #5, Plaza América Local B, Cancún, Quintana Roo, tel. (98) 842-000, fax (98) 841-364, a regional airline of Mexicana (not to be confused with Cuba's Aero Caribbean), which flies from Cancún to Havana twice daily using a DC-9 for US$166 one-way, US$257 roundtrip. In the US, call (800) 531-7901.

Several companies offer charter flights and packages from Mexico. A good one is US-run **Cuba Travel,** Ave. Quintana Roo, Suite TIJ-1173, Zona Centro, Tijuana, Mexico 22000, tel. (66) 865-298 (Mexico), (310) 842-4148 (US answerphone), e-mail: info@cubatravel.com. mx, website: www.cubatravel.com.mx, which makes flight arrangements for US citizens from all points in Mexico serving Cuba. Cuba Travel books a large number of travelers with Aerocaribe and is thereby able to offer discounted roundtrip fares of $268, including tax, from Cancún to Havana.

Taino Tours, Avenida Coyoacán #1035, Col. del Valle, CP 03100, Mexico D.F., tel. (5266) 559-3907, fax 559-3951, e-mail: taino@pceditores.com, website: www.pceditores.com/taino, offers Cuba charters from Tijuana, Cancún, and Mérida. It has offices throughout Mexico.

Three other reputable wholesalers in Yucatán are **Merihabana Travel,** Calle 11 #114, local 7 entre 26 y 28, Col. Itzimna, Mérida, tel./fax (22) 6612, e-mail: merimid@mpsnet.com.mx; **Caribbean Tropical Tours,** tel. (98) 80-8160, fax (98) 80-8160, e-mail: cubatravel@mail.caribe.net.mx, website: www.cuba-travel.com.mx; and **Divermex,** Plaza Americas, Cancún, tel. (98) 84-2325, fax (98) 84-2325.

A good options for folks in California is a weekly **Aeromexico,** tel. (51) 33-4000 or (800) 021-4010, charter that flies Tijuana to Havana using an MD-80 every Saturday at 5:30 p.m., returning Sunday morning (available through Cuba Travel for US$535, including tax).

Note that for the return leg, you must obtain your tourist card for Mexico *before* arriving at Havana airport, where tourist cards are *not* issued; you can obtain one from the Mexican embassy at Calle 12 #518, Miramar, Havana, tel (33) 0856.

From Nicaragua: Cuba's **Aero Caribbean** flies between Managua and Havana on Friday.

From Panama: COPA, Ave. Justo Arosemena y Calle 39, Apdo. 1572, Zona 1, Panama, tel. (507) 227-2672, flies to Havana from Panama City daily.

From South America

From Chile: Ladeco, tel. 639-5053, fax 639 7277, flies to Havana from Santiago de Chile, as does **Lan Chile,** tel. 632-3442, website: www lanchile.com, using a Boeing 767 every Monday. **Cubana,** tel. 274-1819, flies from Santiago de Chile to Havana twice weekly

From Ecuador: TAME, tel. (2) 509-382, fax (2) 509-594, e-mail: tamecom@impsat.net.ec, web site: www.tame.com.ec, the national airline of Ecuador, flies to Havana from Quito on Thursday (from US$352 roundtrip). **Cubana,** tel. (9) 227 463, flies to Havana from Guayaquil and Quito on Saturday using a chartered Boeing 727.

From Venezuela: Aeropostal, tel. (800) 284 661 or (2) 708-6211, fax (2) 794-0702, flies from Caracas on Monday and Saturday (US$353). **Cubana,** tel. 285-3548, flies to Havana from Caracas on Monday and Wednesday.

From Elsewhere: Cubana has service to Havana from Bogota (Tuesday), Buenos Aires (thrice weekly), Montevideo (Saturday), and Rio de Janeiro and São Paulo (Saturday).

From Asia

There are no direct flights; travelers fly via London or the US. Flying nonstop to Los Angeles, then to Mexico City, Tijuana, or Cancún is perhaps the easiest route. Alternately, fly United or Malaysia Airlines to Mexico City (20 hours) and catch a flight next day to Havana (three hours). A roundtrip economy ticket is about HK$16,000 depending on the agent. Hong Kong is a good source for discount plane tickets.

From Macau, you can fly with **Iberia,** e-mail: nfoib@iberia.com, website: www.iberia.com, nonstop to Madrid and then on to Havana.

Travel Network, 11th Floor, On Lan Centre, 11-15 On Lan St., Central, Hong Kong, tel. (852) 2845-4545, fax (852) 2868-5824, has experience booking travel to Cuba. Ask for Alene Freidenrich, who can arrange visas (or contact the Cuban Honorary Consul, Room 1112, Jardine House, 1 Connaught Place, Central, Hong Kong, tel. 852-2525-6320; allow seven working days; HK$250).

STA Travel is a good resource for tickets and has branches in Hong Kong, Tokyo, Singapore, Bangkok, and Kuala Lumpur. You'll find a listing of international offices at its website: www. sta-travel.com.

From Australia and New Zealand

You'll find no direct flights to Cuba, nor any bargain fares. The best bet is to fly to Los Angeles or San Francisco and then to Cuba via Mexico. Air New Zealand (in Sydney, tel. 02-9223-4666; in Auckland, tel. 09-366-2400), Delta Airlines (in Sydney, tel. 02-9262-1777; in Auckland, tel. 09-379-3370), Qantas (in Sydney, tel. 02-9957-0111; in Auckland, tel. 09-357-8900), and United Airlines (in Sydney, tel. 02-9237-8888; in Auckland, tel. 09-307-9500), offer direct service between Australia, New Zealand, and California. Fares from Australia to California begin at about A$1,600 for special fares, about A$2,300 for regular APEX fares. Fares from New Zealand begin at about NZ$2,495.

A route from Sydney via Buenos Aires or Santiago de Chile and then to Havana is also possible. And a round-the-world (RTW) ticket offers the option for additional stopovers at marginal extra cost.

Cubatours, 235 Swan St., Richmond, Victoria 3121, Australia, tel. (03) 9428-0385, specializes in air-land packages to Cuba, as do Melbourne-based **Cuba World,** tel.(03) 9867-1200, and **Caribbean Destinations,** Level 4, 115 Pitt St., Sydney, Australia, tel. (800) 816-717.

Specialists in discount fares include **STA Travel,** in Sydney, tel. (02) 9212-1255; in Auckland, tel. (09) 309-9723, which has regional offices throughout Australia and New Zealand. Online, visit STA's website at www.sta-travel.com for a complete listing of offices. One of STA's offices is—get this—207 Cuba St., Wellington, New Zealand, tel. (04) 385-0561.

Arriving at José Martí International Airport

The airport is 25 km southwest of downtown Havana, in the Rancho Boyeros district. It has four terminals spaced well apart from each other and accessed by different roads (nor are they linked by a connecting bus service).

Terminal One serves domestic flights. Charter flights originating in Miami arrive at Terminal Two, tel. (44) 3300, carrying passengers with OFAC licenses. Services include car rental outlets. All international flights (except Miami-Havana charters) now arrive at the ritzy new Terminal Three, tel. (33) 5777, or (33) 5666, at Wajay, on the north side of the airport and linked to downtown Havana by a four- and six-lane freeway (only halfway complete at press time). This glitzy new facility is built to international standards and receives about 30 international airlines. Long-term plans call for two further expansions, each of which will permit the airport to serve another three million passengers annually (in 1998, the airport handled 2.5 million passengers). For information on arrivals and departures, call (45) 3133 or (70) 7701.

Immigration and Customs: Immigration procedures are straightforward and no more daunting than when arriving at any other Caribbean destination. Anticipate a long delay, however, as immigration proceedings are slow and long lines often develop. Personal carry-on baggage is X-rayed upon arrival.

Travelers arriving without prebooked accommodations are sometimes hassled and made to book—and pay for—at least two nights' hotel stay before being granted entry. It's a hit-and-miss thing: on occasion, I've arrived without prebooked lodging, but never had such problems.

Information and Services: There's an **Infotur** tourist information office immediately on the left after exiting the Customs lounge, tel./fax (66) 6101. It's poorly stocked with information and maps, but is staffed 24 hours. You should check in here if you have prepaid vouchers for accommodations or transfers into town.

There's a **foreign exchange** counter in the baggage claim area, but this serves mostly to change other foreign currency into US dollars. You'll not need Cuban pesos.

Getting into Town: There is no public bus service from either of the international terminals. Independent travelers must take a taxi (US$15-20 depending on destination), which can be found immediately outside the arrivals lounges. With luck, you might find a minibus operated by a tourist agency such as Cubanacán. Normally, they serve arriving tour groups, but often they're also happy to act as a shuttle service. You'll be charged about US$15 to get to downtown hotels. Most people arriving on package tours will have been issued prepaid vouchers for the shuttle.

A **public bus** marked "Aeropuerto" departs from **Terminal 1** for Vedado and Parque Central about 15 minutes after the arrival of domestic flights (one peso). Alternately, you can catch a "camel bus" (no. M-2 originating in Santiago de las Vegas) from the east side of Avenida de la Independencia, about 200 yards east of the terminal. The bus goes to Parque de la Fraternidad on the edge of Habana Vieja The journey takes about one hour, but the wait can be just as long. You can also take a private (albeit illegal) taxi for a negotiable fee (usually about US$8); touts will approach you.

Car Rental: Havanautos, tel. (33) 5197, **Panautos,** tel. (33) 0306 and (33) 0307, **Transauto Rent-a-Car,** tel. (33) 5177, and **Vía Rent-a-Car,** tel. (33) 5155, have offices outside the arrivals halls of both Terminals 2 and 3. **Cubacar,** tel. (33) 5546, also has an office at Terminal 3. **Rex,** tel. (33) 9160, fax (33) 9159, which offers Volvos and limousine service, also has offices at Terminals 2 and 3.

Check your car thoroughly before driving away. Many of the cars rented here are poorly maintained (in spring 1999, Havanautos gave me a battered 1996 model Daewoo with a faulty gas gauge and a dangerous gasoline leak). If you find a problem later on and want to exchange cars, you'll have to return to the airport office where you rented.

BY SEA

By Cruise Ship

At press time, three cruise companies offered regular cruises to Havana, which is destined to become one of the biggest ports of call in the world once the US embargo is lifted. (The embargo has restricted the cruise industry's access to Cuba. No US company can operate cruises to Cuba, and because foreign-owned vessels cannot dock in the US within six months of visiting Cuba or carrying Cuban passengers or goods most foreign cruise companies have shunned Cuba. The Italian company Costa Crociere initiated cruises to Cuba in October 1995 using the *Costa Playa* on weekly cruises out of the Dominican Republic; when Carnival Cruise Lines later bought the company, the US government forced it to cease operating the Cuba cruises.) The **Cruise Line Industry Association,** 500 5th Ave. #1407, New York, NY 10110, tel. (212) 921-0066, may be able to provide up-to-date information on regulations regarding cruising to Cuba

Italian **Nina Cruise Lines,** tel. (06) 428-84370 fax (06) 428-03540, e-mail: italia.prima@flash-net.it, www.italiaprima.co.it, operates the 520-passenger *Italia Prima* on weeklong cruises departing on Sunday from Havana to Playa de Carmen in Mexico, Montego Bay in Jamaica and Grand Cayman. You can join the cruise in Mexico, and "exceptionally in Jamaica."

A French company, **Nouvelle Frontieres,** www.nouvelles-frontieres.fr, operates the 650-passenger *Tritón,* a Greek vessel with departures from Havana on Sunday and calls at Grand Cayman, Montego Bay, Isla de la Juventud, and Calica in Mexico. Cruises are offered Dec.-April only. (The company's website and brochure provide no contact information You might have better luck at its Italian site—www.nouvelles-frontiers.it—where pages about the cruise were under construction at press time; e-mail: info@nouvelles-frontieres.it.) US citizens can also book these all-inclusive cruises through **Last Frontier Expeditions,** 4823 White Rock Circle, Suite H, Boulder, CO 80301-3260, tel. (303) 530-9275, fax (303) 530-9275 e-mail: CopaBob@aol.com, website: www.club-havana.com, boarding in Mexico, which makes the trip legal if you don't spend any money ashore.

A British company, **Sun Cruise,** operates the *Sundream.* And the *Aida,* from Germany, also calls in at Havana.

Terminal Sierra Maestra: Havana's spanking new cruise terminal, **Terminal Sierra Maestra**

el. (33) 6607, fax (33) 6759, inaugurated in December 1995, is a natty conversion of the old Customs building on Avenida San Pedro. Passengers step through the doorways directly onto Plaza de San Francisco and find themselves in the heart of Havana. The facility—owned and operated jointly by Cubanco S.A. (part of the Cuban Ministry of Transport) and a Curaçao-based Italian company called Milestone—is world-class, combining colonial-style architecture with ultramodern aluminum and plate glass. Pier 1 has two floors, each 8,000 square meters. Downstairs is a parking lot and bus terminal. Passengers are processed upstairs, which has wooden boardwalks outside and hardwood parquet floor inside, and a 1948 Dodge De Luxe D24 and 1958 Lincoln Continental on display. Facilities include a craft and souvenir store. Eventually, Pier 1 will also have an Italian restaurant and disco upstairs.

Pier 3 currently serves as a ferry terminal. Future plans include converting the pier at Mariel, west of Havana, into an international ferry terminal serving Florida.

By Private Vessel

Cuba offers a warm reception to visitors arriving by sea. Many guidebooks report that you must request permission at least two weeks in advance from Cuban authorities to call in. This is wrong. *No advance permission is required.* However, it is wise to give at least 72 hours advance warning if possible by faxing complete details of your boat, crew, and passengers to the harbormaster's office at Marina Hemingway, fax (537) 24-3104. (Anyone planning on sailing to Cuba should obtain a copy of Simon Charles's excellent *Cruising Guide to Cuba*.)

The US State Department advises that "US citizens are discouraged from traveling to Cuba in private boats" and permits such travel "only after meeting all US and Cuban government documentation and clearance requirements." (An executive order signed by President Clinton in spring 1996 states that vessels leaving Florida with the intention of entering Cuban territory may be confiscated by US authorities. The act was aimed at dissuading anti-Castro radicals from rash acts and was followed in July 1998 with a requirement that private boats of less than 150 feet obtain permits before leaving Florida and entering Cuban waters.) Nonetheless, scores of sailors—including US citizens in US-registered vessels—sail to Cuba each year without incident and without breaking the law (which for US citizens means spending no money there). Ostensibly, you'll need to find a non-US citizen to pay your berth fees, and presumably you will cater yourself with food brought from the US. Get the picture? Most US skippers I've spoken with have had no problems when they return to the US—as long as they don't have their holds full of Cuban cigars.

All persons subject to US law aboard vessels, including the owner, must be an authorized traveler to engage in travel transactions in Cuba. If you are not an authorized traveler, you may not legally purchase meals, pay for transportation, lodging, dockage, or mooring fees, and you may not bring any Cuban-origin goods back to the US. Any payments to the Marina Hemingway International Yacht Club would be considered a prohibited payment to a Cuban national and therefore in violation of the regulations. Vessel owners are prohibited from carrying travelers to Cuba who pay them for passage if the owner does not have a specific license from OFAC authorizing him or her to be a Service Provider to Cuba.

At the present time, the US and Cuba don't have a Coast Guard agreement. Therefore, although Cuban authorities have usually proven to be exceedingly helpful to yachters in distress, craft developing engine trouble or other technical difficulties in Cuban territorial waters cannot expect assistance from the US Coast Guard. Cuba's territorial waters extend 12 miles out. Unfortunately, there are reports of increasing corruption among Cuban officials involving foreign yachters, abetted by the fact that Cuban authorities may impound your vessel as collateral against the cost of rescue or salvage.

Yacht Charters and Crewing: US citizens should refer to Treasury Department regulations regarding chartering vessels for travel to Cuba. Charter companies in the Bahamas may permit travel to Cuba. Try **Nassau Yacht Haven,** tel. (242) 393-8173. In the UK, contact Alan Toone of **Compass Yacht Services,** Holly Cottage, Heathley End, Chislehurst, Kent BR7 6AB, tel. (0181) 467-2450. Toone arranges yacht charters and may be able to assist in finding a crewing position.

Traveling with Private Skippers: It's possible to find private skippers sailing to Havana from Florida, New Orleans, and other ports along the southern seaboard, as well as from the Bahamas. Boats leave all the time from marinas along the Florida Keys. You can call various marinas for recommendations. Be flexible. Pinpointing exact vessel departure dates and times is nearly impossible, especially in winter. As Ernest Hemingway wrote, "Brother, don't let anybody tell you there isn't plenty of water between Key West and Havana!" A nasty weather front can delay your departure as much as a week or more.

If you don't arrange a return trip with the same skipper, you'll find plenty of yachts flying the Stars and Stripes at Marina Hemingway in Havana. There'll usually be a skipper willing to run you back to Florida, but it can take days, or weeks, to find a skipper.

Warning: There's nothing illegal if passengers don't spend money in Cuba and if skippers don't charge for passage to or from Cuba. You may be questioned about this by US Customs or Immigration, who'll take a dim view of things. If a skipper asks for money, legally you must decline. Consider negotiating a *free* passage; of course, diesel fuel is expensive, so you may feel

charitably inclined (vessels seem to use anywhere from US$200 to US$400 worth of fuel for a trip across the Straits of Florida).

Maps and Charts: You'll need accurate maps and charts, especially for the reef-infested passage from the Bahamas. British Admiralty charts, US Defense Mapping Agency charts, and Imray yachting charts are all accurate and can be ordered from **Bluewater Books & Charts,** 1481 SE 17th St., Ft. Lauderdale, FL 33316, tel. (954) 763-6533 or (800) 942-2583, fax (954) 522-2278, e-mail: nautical-charts@bluewaterweb.com, website: www.bluewaterweb.com.

You can also order detailed National Oceanic & Atmospheric Administration charts from NOAA, Riverdale, MD 20737-1199, tel. (301) 436-8301 or (800) 638-8972, e-mail: distribution@noaa.gov, website: chartmaker.ncd.noaa.gov; or the Better Boating Association, P.O. Box 407, Needham, MA 02192. Most marine stores also stock US government charts of the region.

In Havana, you can purchase nautical charts from **El Navigante,** Calle Mercaderes #115, Habana Vieja; Cuba CP 10100, Gaveta Postal 130, tel. (61) 3625, fax (33) 2869, but its stock is relatively limited. It sells a complete set of nautical charts, including a "Chart Kit" containing maps of the entire Cuban coast (charts I and VII cost US$40; charts II, III, and VI cost US$45; charts IV and V cost US$35). Open Mon.-Fri. 8 a.m.-5 p.m., Saturday 8 a.m.-1 p.m.

Marina Hemingway: Private yachts and motor cruises berth at Marina Hemingway, Avenida 5ta and Calle 248, Santa Fe, tel. (24) 1150, fax (24) 1149, e-mail: comercial@comer-mh.cha.cyt.cu, on the western edge of metropolitan Havana, in Barlovento, 15 km west of downtown. The marina is a self-contained village and duty-free port with its own accommodations and restaurants, and complete services. US dollars are preferred, but all convertible currencies are accepted, as are credit cards (except those issued in the US). If you'd like, you can register your credit card and charge everything to your account while berthed.

The harbor coordinates are 23° 5'N and 82° 29'W. The seven-beam searchlight located five feet east of the entrance canal is visible for 17 miles. You should announce your arrival on VHF Channel 16, HF Channel 68, and SSB 2790 (expect a long wait for the reply). Arriving and dearting skippers should watch for snorkelers and surfers both within and outside the narrow entrance channel.

Upon arrival, you must clear Immigration and Customs at the wharf on the left just inside the entrance channel. If you plan to dock for less than 72 hours, visas are not required (your passport will suffice). The harbormaster's office will facilitate your entry and exit (ext. 2884), and visa extensions can also be arranged for US$25. Be patient!

The marina has four parallel canals—each one km long, 15 meters wide, and six meters deep—separated by *Intercanales* with moorings for 100 yachts. Docking fees, which include water, electricity, and custodial services, cost US35 cents per foot per day. Gasoline and diesel are available 8 a.m.-7 p.m. (tel. 24-1150, ext. 450), a mechanic is on hand, and your boat can be hauled out of the water if needed.

The marina has a tourism information center (8 a.m.-8 p.m., ext. 733, or tel. 24-6336) and harbormaster's office in Complejo Turístico Papa, the main service area at the end of channel B. The 24-hour medical post is here (ext. 737), as are a 24-hour laundromat (ext. 451), bathrooms with showers, soda bar, and TV lounge, storage room, ship chandler (or *avituallamiento,* ext. 2344), plus a beach-volleyball court and four tennis courts. The post office is at the entrance of Intercanal C (open 24 hours; ext. 448), where you'll also find the Hemingway International Nautical Club (ext. 701), which offers fax and telephone facilities, bar, and a quiet reading room. The shopping mall is at the east end of Intercanal B (ext. 739). Security boxes can be rented.

Many skippers bring their own bicycles, mopeds, or motorbikes to move around the marina and travel into Havana. Rental cars are also available (ext. 87), as are microbuses and taxis (ext. 85). The marina even has a scuba diving center (ext. 735) at Complejo Turístico Papa's at the west end of Intercanal B, where jet-skis can be rented (8:30 a.m.-4:30 p.m.).

Accommodation is provided at the Hotel Qualton El Viejo y Mar, plus a series of condominiums, apartments, and villas (ext. 385 and 85). And there were six restaurants at press time, plus four bars, and the Discoteca Los Caneyes (ext. 7330), open 10 p.m.-4 a.m.

BY ORGANIZED TOURS

A wide range of organized tours to Cuba are offered from North America and Europe, and US citizens are well catered to (see below). Most such tours focus on the cultural and historical experience, with Havana as a focus, but there are plenty of sports-oriented tours and just plain ol' fun tours. Believe it or not, even US veterans are catered to.

Tours from the US

US citizens *can* legally travel to Cuba by qualifying for certain organized tours with nonprofit organizations and other entities that arrange trips with special government authorized licenses in hand. Almost any type of special interest activity is now catered to, although most programs are "study" tours that provide an immersion in particular aspects of Cuban life and issues. There's usually plenty of time for relaxation. Participants usually must demonstrate serious interest in the subject of study; in reality, this often proves a formality, especially in the realm of "arts," where Uncle Sam accepts that it is difficult for artists to make a living as professionals. Most US organizations that offer trips to Cuba are *not* accredited tour and travel operators, and do not offer consumer-protection programs.

Caribbean Music and Dance, 12545 Olive St. #241, St Louis, MO 63141, tel. (314) 542-3637 or toll free (877) 665-4321, fax (314) 469-2916, e-mail: caribmusic@igc.apc.org, website: www.caribmusic.com, offers a variety of music and dance study courses in Cuba under an OFAC license. For example, each February the organization offers a two-week Cuban Popular Music & Dance Workshop in association with the Havana Jazz Festival. Courses are taught at the prestigious Escuela Nacional de Arte (ENA). The dance workshops are open to everyone from beginners to professionals and include lively tuition in *danzón, son,* cha-cha-cha, mambo, rumba, salsa, *larueda,* and the hip-swiveling *despolote.* Chucho Valdés and Irakere, Juan Formell and Los Van Van, Changuito, and legendary flautist Richard Esqúes are among the faculty who provide one-on-one tuition. Imagine learning guitar from Eric Clapton, and you have the idea.

The **Center for Cuban Studies,** 124 W. 23rd St., New York, NY 10011, tel. (212) 242-0559, fax (212) 242-1937, e-mail: cubanctr@igc.apc.org, website: www.cubaupdate.org, offers an eclectic range of weeklong and longer trips focusing on education and health care, urban issues, welfare, African roots of Cuba Culture, sexual politics, architecture and preservation, and cultural events such as the Havana Film Festival. Most trips are a week to 10 days in duration and cost from US$900 to US$1,400, including roundtrip airfare from Miami or Nassau. The Center also offers an annual weeklong Jewish heritage tour in January (US$1,450), plus a one-week seminar on Cuban music in February in collaboration with the Cuban Music Institute and Music Museum (US$1,250, including airfare). Participation is limited to "researchers and journalists," including arrangements for individual travel.

Cuba Travel, Ave. Quintana Roo, Suite TIJ 1173, Zona Centro, Tijuana, Mexico 22000, tel (66) 865298 (Mexico), (310) 842-4148 (US answerphone), e-mail: info@cubatravel.com.mx website: www.cubatravel.com.mx, books air fares, makes hotel reservations, and offers package tours to Cuba, including scuba programs, architecture tours of Havana, bicycle tours, and

STUDY COURSES

Academic Exchanges

Wayne Smith, former chief of the US Interests Section in Havana (and an outspoken critic of US policy toward Cuba), heads the **Cuba Exchange Program** offered through the School of Advanced International Studies at Johns Hopkins University, 1740 Massachusetts Ave. NW, Washington, DC 20036, tel. (202) 663-5732, fax (202) 663-5737. Smith escorts scholars on learning programs. Also try **CamBas Association,** tel. (319) 354-3189, fax (319) 338-3320, associated with the University of Iowa.

Mercadu S.A., Calle 13 #951, Vedado, Havana, tel. (33) 3893, fax (33) 3028, arranges study visits for foreigners at centers of higher learning that span a wide range of academic subjects. It also arranges working holidays and runs a summer school at the University of Havana.

The Arts

The **Ballet Nacional de Cuba,** Calzada #510 e/ D y E, Vedado, Ciudad Habana, CP 10400, tel. (55) 2953, fax (33) 3117, offers three-week and month-long courses for intermediate- and advanced-level professionals and students (US$250 monthly).

The **Centro Nacional de Conservación, Restauració y Museologico,** Calle Cuba #610, e/ Sol y Luz, tel. (61) 3335, fax (33) 5696, offers residential courses for urban planners, conservationists, architects, etc., at the Convento de Santa Clara in Habana Vieja. Most are of 12 days' length (average cost is US$300).

The **Instituto Superior de Arte,** Calle 120 #11110, Playa, Havana, tel. (21) 6075, fax (33) 6633, e-mail isa@reduniv.edu.cu, offers courses spanning the gamut of the art world. Besides short-term courses, it also accepts foreigners for full-year study beginning in September (from US$2,000 for tuition).

The **Unión de Escritores y Artistas de Cuba,** Calle 17 #354 e/ G y H, Vedado, tel. (55) 3113, fax (33) 3158, e-mail: uneac@artsoft.cult.cu, offers a series of courses in the arts and Cuban culture, focusing on music.

In the US, **Caribbean Music & Dance,** 12545 Olive Rd. #241, St. Louis, MO 63141, tel. (314) 542-3637, fax (314) 469-2916, e-mail: caribmusic@igc.org, web site: www.caribmusic.com, offers a series of cultural workshops in Cuba, where tour participants can learn to dance like a real Cuban.

In Canada, **Eleggua Project,** 7171 Torbram Rd., Suite 51, Mississauga, ON L4T 3W4, tel. (800) 818-8840, fax (905) 678-1421, e-mail: cancuba@pathcom.com, website: www.pathcom.com/~cancuba, offers a series of study courses in Afro-Cuban culture, plus music, dance, etc.

Culture

In Cuba, **Paradiso: Promotora de Viajes Culturales,** Calle 19 #560 esq. C, Vedado, tel. (32) 6928, fax (33) 3921, arranges visits and participation in cultural courses and programs, such as children's book publishing, theater criticism, contemporary visual art, ballet, and modern dance, plus festivals such as the International Benny Moré Festival, the International Hemingway Colloquium, and the Artisans' Fair.

ewish heritage tours. It's US-run and its services are recommended by readers.

The **Cuban-Jewish Aid Society,** 44 Mercury ve., Colonia, NJ 07067, tel. (908) 499-9132, ffers annual Jewish heritage tours to Havana.

Global Exchange, 2017 Mission St. #303, San rancisco, CA 94110, tel. (415) 255-7296 or (800) 97-1994, fax (415) 255-7498, e-mail global-xch@igc.org, website: www.globalexchange. om, sponsors study tours to Cuba focusing on different aspects of Cuban life, including health care, rt, culture and education, religion, Afro-Cuban ulture, women's issues, and music and dance. lost trips are 10 days long and cost an average of US$1,300, including roundtrip airfare from Mexico or the Bahamas. The organization also has bicycle tours. It refuses to obtain an OFAC license on the grounds that to do so would acknowledge the legitimacy of the US embargo. (Global Exchange, in association with Jim Long, a Vietnam veteran, P.O. Box 40430, San Francisco, CA 94140, e-mail jimlong@sf.com, even offers an annual trip to Cuba for US veterans, though little time is spent in Havana.)

Last Frontier Expeditions, 4823 White Rock Circle, Suite H, Boulder, CO 80301-3260, tel. (303) 530-9275, fax (303) 530-9275, e-mail: CopaBob@aol.com, website: www.clubhavana.

The **Conjunto Folclórico Nacional** (National Folklore Dance Group) and **Danza Contemporánea de Cuba** offer twice-yearly, two-week courses in Afro-Cuban music and dance (contact **ARTEX,** Avenida 5ta #8010 esq. 82, Miramar, tel. (24) 2710, fax (24) 2033). ARTEX also sponsors other courses in the arts and literature, including seminars in *cutumba* (Franco-Haitian-Cuban song and dance), plus courses at the Cuban School of Ballet (La Escuela Cubana de Ballet), the Instituto Superior de Arte, and the National School of Art (Centro Nacional de Escuelas de Arte).

Spanish Language Courses

There's no shortage of Spanish language tuition in Cuba. Most courses offer options from beginner to advanced and include at least a modicum of workshops or lectures on Cuban culture. The norm is three to five hours of instruction daily, more in intensive courses. Classes are best arranged from abroad via one of the following organizations:

Cubamar Viajes, Calle 15 #752 esq. Paseo, Vedado, tel. (66) 2523, fax (33) 3111, e-mail: cubamar@cubamar.mit.cma.net, offers courses in Spanish at the **José Martí Language and Computer Center for Foreigners,** Calle 16 #109, Miramar. It offers four levels from basic to specialized, each either "intensive" (20-100 hours) or "regular" (120-160 hours).

Global Exchange, 2017 Mission St. #203, San Francisco, CA 94110, tel. (415) 255-7296 or (800) 497-1994, fax (415) 255-7498, e-mail: roberto@globalexchange.com, website: www.globalexchange.com, offers a Spanish language school with the University of Havana that includes private tutors and group classes plus cultural activities. Two-week (US$1,200 including airfare from Cancún) and month-long (US$1,750) courses are offered monthly.

The **Grupo de Turismo Científico Educacional,** Avenida 5ta #601, Miramar, tel. (24) 1567, offers intensive Spanish language courses at the José Martí Language Center.

You can also sign up for two-week to four-month Spanish language and Cuban culture courses offered by **Mercadu S.A.,** Calle 13 #951, Vedado, Havana, tel. (33) 3893, fax (33) 3028.

In the UK, the **School of Latin American Spanish,** Docklands Enterprise Centre, 11 Marshalsea Rd., London SE1 1EP, tel. (0171) 357-8793, offers seven-week regular and intensive summer language courses in Cuba.

Volunteer Programs

Volunteers for Peace, c/o International Work Camp, 43 Tiffany Rd., Belmont, VT 05730, tel. (802) 259-2759, fax (802) 259-2922, takes participants from around the world to work alongside Cubans and assist with community development. The three-week trips—US$1,200 (US$850 for non-US citizens, meeting in Havana)—are hosted by the Cuban Institute for Friendship with the People (ICAP) but coordinated by people in local communities.

Cross-Cultural Journeys, P.O. Box 1369, Sausalito, CA 94666-1369, tel. (800) 874-4221, also offers volunteer programs, while the **Venceremos Brigade,** P.O. Box 7071, Oakland, CA 94601-0071, tel. (415) 267-0606, offers "workcamp brigades" for committed leftists.

England's **Cuban Solidarity Campaign,** 44 Morat St., London SW9 ORR, tel. (0171) 820-9976, offers work brigades, including visits to hospitals and schools. Participants work in construction and agriculture.

com, an Aruba-based company, offers packages for cigar lovers, plus hosted sports-related events such as the Ernest Hemingway International Sports Classic 10K race, the Ernest Hemingway Sportfishing Tournament, the Havana Open Golf Tournament, hunting and fishing trips, and baseball fantasy camps. It also has a Classic Car Rally tour, programs for a male audience (including an "Old Havana Nostalgia Tour"), Caribbean cruises, plus motorcycle tours using BMWs.

In 1999, Last Frontier Expeditions joined forces with Club Havana (a Canadian cigar wholesaler) to form **Cuban Adventures**, tel. (877) 642-8262 (toll free) or (604) 542-0085, fax (604) 542-2251, offering cigar tours and other tours "that will appeal to the cigar aficionado and the seasoned traveler alike." A one-week "International Hemingway Centennial Tour," for example, costs US$2,198 from Cancún or US$2,398 from Toronto.

Marazul Tours, Tower Plaza Mall, 4100 Park Ave., Weehawken, NJ 07087, tel. (201) 319-9670 or (800) 223-5334, fax (201) 319-9009, e-mail: bguild@marazultours.com, website: www.marazultours.com, organizes special-interest tours and individual travel for those with OFAC licenses.

Wings of the World, 1200 William St. #706, Buffalo, NY 14240-0706; or 1636 3rd Ave. #232, New York, NY 10128, tel. (800) 465-8687, fax (416) 486-4001, actively—and legally—promotes its Cuban "cultural adventures" to *all* US citizens. Because the company's tours are "fully hosted and totally prepaid," including personal amenities, participants ostensibly "neither exchange nor spend money while in Cuba." Available are 10- and 12-day tours of Cuba, departing from Nassau (Bahamas) or Cancún (Mexico). Trips start at US$2,495, excluding airfare. The company also offers a wide range of special tours, including sports tours, a Hemingway tour to coincide with the annual Hemingway Colloquium in Havana, and monthly "Cuban cigar adventures." The company claims that "not one of our American travelers has had any problems with the State Department" as the company "abides by all the legal requirements."

Queers for Cuba, 3543 18th St. #33, San Francisco, CA 94110, tel. (415) 995-4678, operates an annual "solidarity and education delegation" to Havana each December. The trip focuses on expanding understanding and expressing solidarity with Cuba's gay and lesbian population.

Tours from Canada

Canadians primarily book inexpensive beach vacation packages, and most of the many travel and tour operators cater to this market. Havana based tours are few.

One of the leading Cuba specialist travel agencies is **Wings of the World**, 653 Mt. Pleasant Rd., Toronto, ON M4S 2N2, tel. (416) 482-1222 or (800) 465-8687, fax (416) 486-4011.

Friendship Tours, 12883-98th Ave., Surrey BC V3T 1B1, tel. (604) 581-4065, fax: (604) 581 0785, email: friendship@home.com, website members.home.net:80/friendship, offers a variety of Havana-based tours—including a two-week "Explore Havana Plus" trip, with one week each in Havana and Varadero (CAN$2,099 from Toronto; CAN$2,499 from Vancouver), and two- and four-week "Learn Spanish in Cuba" trips (CAN$1,499 and CAN$1,899)—primarily for people sympathetic to the goals of the Revolution.

Tours from the UK

Interchange, 27 Stafford Rd., Croydon, Surrey CR0 4NG, tel. (181) 681-3612, fax (181) 760 0031, represents Havanatur and offers special interest group tours, plus tailor-made itineraries for independent travelers. Likewise, contact **Cubanacán UK**, Skylines, Unit 49, Limehar bour, Docklands, London E14 9TS, tel. (0171) 537-7909.

Journey Latin America, 12 Heathfield Terr. London W4 4JE, tel. (0181) 747-3108, fax (0181) 742-1312, e-mail: flights@journeylatinameri ca.co.uk, website: www.journeylatinamerica.co.uk features Havana on its nine-day "Cuban Discovery" (from £499, including airfare) and two-week "Cubana Libre" trips (from £477). JLA also has an office at 2nd Floor Barton Arcade, 51-63 Deansgate, Manchester M3 2BH, tel. (0161) 832-1441 fax (44161) 832-1551, e-mail: man@journeylati namerica.co.uk.

Captivating Cuba, tel. (0181) 891-2909, is an independent tour operator, specializing exclusively in holidays to Cuba and offering a wide range of package holidays and individually tai

Colina Lenin

red trips. Its website—www.travelcoast.demon. o.uk—was not functioning at press time.

Regent Holidays, 15 John St., Bristol BS1 HR, tel. (0117) 921-1711, fax (0117) 925-4866, -mail: regent@regent-holidays.co.uk, special-es in customizing tours for independent travelers ut also has package tours that include a seven-ay "Pearl of the Caribbean" tour from £789.

Festival Tours International, 96 Providence n., Long Ashton, Bristol BS18 9DN, tel./fax 01275) 392-953, offers packages to Carnival nd the Havana Jazz and Film Festivals.

A score of other companies offer tours. Many dvertise in the travel sections of leading news-apers, plus *Time Out,* and *What's On* in London.

Also contact the **Britain-Cuba Dance Stu-dent Exchange,** Weekends Arts College, Inter-change Studios, Dalby St., London NW5 3NQ.

Tours from Europe

In Switzerland, try **Jelmoli Reisen,** tel. (1) 211-1357, and in France, **Havanatur,** tel. (1) 4742-5858.

Several Italian tour operators specialize in Cuba. **Sol y Med,** Via Boezio #2, 0-0192 Rome, tel. (06) 688-07252, fax (06) 636-700, e-mail: choa1@yahoo.com, specializes in medical tourism and special events. **Ostiensis Viaggi,** Viale dei Romagnoli, 760 Ostia Antica, 00119 Rome, tel. (06) 565-2473, fax (06) 565-2399, e-mail: ostiensisviaggigroup@micanet.it, also has Cuba programs.

GETTING AROUND

ON FOOT

Despite its seemingly overwhelming size, most of Havana's sightseeing highlights are concentrated in Habana Vieja. Thus, Havana is a walker's city par excellence, and one easily and best explored on foot. You'll probably want to restrict your walking to a single district, such as Habana Vieja—whose compact, narrow, warren-like lanes are no place for vehicular traffic—the Malecón, or Vedado. Only when traveling beyond and between these districts will you need transport.

Sidewalks are generally in reasonably good repair, but beware potholes and dog excrement underfoot.

BY BUS

Tourist Bus

Rumbos S.A., Casa Matriz, Linea and M, Vedado, tel. (66) 9713 or (24) 9626, operates a splendid minibus service for tourists. The **Vaivén Bus Turístico** makes a circuit of Havana on a continual basis (*vaivén* means "roundtrip" or "to go and return") between Club Habana and Marina Hemingway in the west and Parque Morro-Cabaña in the east (the route may be expanded east to Hotel Panamericano, in Ciudad Panamericano). Four separate buses operate 9 a.m.-9:40 p.m. every 40-50 minutes, and stop at 23 bus stops (*parradas*) at key locations along the route. A US$4 ticket is good all day for as many stops and times as you wish. Each bus has a guide.

You can pick up a map at the Rumbos headquarters in Casa Matriz. Use the published map with caution, however, as the route has already changed since the service was introduced in 1998.

Public Bus

Havana's public buses, or *guaguas* (WAH-wahs), are for stoics. Habaneros are inured and would rather take a bus than walk under almost all circumstances, even if this means traveling like sardines in a can. Note, however, that no buses operate within Habana Vieja except along th[e] major peripheral thoroughfares. Fares are ridiculously cheap, but most buses are usually packe[d] to the gills, especially during rush hours—7-1[0] a.m. and 3-6 p.m. Be wary of pickpockets o[n] crowded buses.

Prior to the Special Period, Havana boasted [a] fine bus system that served the entire city. The[n] as the gasoline shortage and lack of spare part[s] hit home, things ground to a virtual halt—wors[-]ened by a general lack of efficiency. In sprin[g] 1999, things were almost back to normal.

Bus service is the responsibility of three agen[-]cies: **Asociación de Transportes de Servicio[s] de Omnibus** (Astro), **Transmetro,** and **Omnibu[s] Metropolitano,** which has introduced some mod[-]ern Mercedes buses to its fleet. Most buses are ei[-]ther pass-me-down Yankee school buses (im[-]ported via Canada or Mexico); horribly uncom[-]

CAMELS IN CUBA?

Yes, camels roam the streets of Havana. These giant buses—*camellos*—were designed locally to save the day during the gasoline crisis, when ingenious engineers added bodies to articulated flatbed trucks. They're so named for the shape of the coach: sagging in between two humps like a bactrian camel.

About half of the one million trips that Habaneros make daily are aboard the rumbling behemoths, which carry the "M" designation (for Metro-bus) on bus routes. Designed to carry 220 people, they are usually stuffed with more than 300, so many that the true number can't be untangled. The "camel" is a warehouse on wheels: officially a *supertrenbus*.

About 220 camels roam the streets of Havana. More are being added each week, made in a factory in Havana for about US$30,000 apiece and weighing in at more than 20 tons. Of course, the Mack trucks that pull them weren't designed for stop and start work, so maintenance is an ongoing problem.

Most camels originate from Parque de la Fraternidad, but their routes span Havana and the most distant suburbs.

rtable Hungarian buses that belch out black mes; poorly made and equally uncomfy Cuban iróns; or *Tren Buses* (also called *camellos—* amels), which are lengthy, truck-pulled passen- er cars that sag in the middle, like the rolling ock on US railways. These ships of the desert e now the workhorses of the city bus system.

Two key "camel" routes to know are the M1 Parque de la Fraternidad to Habanas del Este) nd M2 (Parque de la Fraternidad to Santiago de s Vegas via the international airport).

Expect to wait in line for from 10 minutes to an our, depending on the route. Cuban lines (*colas*) e always fluid but tend to re-form when the us appears, so you should follow the Cubans' xample and identify the last person in line ahead you (ask *el último?*). Be prepared to push and stle if the line devolves into a skirmish. You'll un- ubtedly be the only foreigner aboard and may d yourself being ushered aboard and offered a eat as an honored guest.

Buses stop frequently, but when full, the driver ay stop only when requested to do so. Bus ops—*paradas*—are usually well marked; most ve shelter against rain. Shout *Pare!* (Stop!), or sh the box above the door in Cuban fashion. u'll need to elbow your way to the door well in dvance, however. Don't dally, as the bus driver is ely to hit the gas when you're only halfway out.

Schedules and Fares: Most *guaguas* run 24 urs, at least hourly during the day but on re- ced schedules 11 p.m.-5 a.m. The standard re is 10 centavos (exact change only), which u deposit in the box beside the driver. Fares to the suburbs range from 10 to 50 centavos. u'll also find lots of smaller, red-and-cream-col- ed buses called *omnibuses ruteros,* which arge 40 centavos and have the benefit of ing uncrowded.

Routes and Route Maps: Note that many ses follow a loop route, traveling to and from stinations along different streets. Most buses splay the bus number and destination above e front window. If in doubt, ask. Many buses ar- e and depart from Parque Central and Par- e de la Fraternidad in Habana Vieja and La ampa (Calle 23) in Vedado, especially at Calle nd at Calzada de Infanta.

Few maps show Havana's bus routes, most e out of date anyway (the best maps I know e shown in the booklet *La Habana Vieja: Guía rística,* published by the Instituto Cubano de Geodesia y Cartografía, but the latest edition— 1998—omitted the routes). Ostensibly, there's a *Rutas de Ómnibus* map, but I've never seen it— and, I suspect, neither will you.

BY TRAIN

Intracity service is provided to a limited number of suburban destinations on commuter trains from the following two stations.

Estación de 19 Noviembre

Local service aboard a two-car commuter train operates to ExpoCuba and the provincial town of San Antonio de los Baños from Estación de 19 Noviembre (also called Estación Tulipan) on Calle Tulipán and Hidalgo, 200 meters west of Avenida de la Independencia, south of Plaza de la Revolución, tel. (81) 4431.

Trains depart for San Antonio at 6:05 and 9:45 a.m., and 12:10, 3:50, 5:55, and 8:40 p.m. Departures from San Antonio are at 5:45, 7:35, and 11:50 a.m., and 2:45, 5:36, and 7:45 p.m.

The *Servicio ExpoCuba* departs Estación de 19 Noviembre at 9:20 a.m. via Vibora (50 minutes). Return trains depart ExpoCuba at 17:17 p.m.

Estación Cristina

This suburban station, at Cuatro Caminos in southwest Habana Vieja, tel. (78) 4971, serves Santiago de las Vegas, on the southern outskirts of Havana, and Batabanó on the south coast (the ferry and hydrofoils—*kometas*—to Isla de la Juventud depart from Batabanó). It has a snack bar. Trains also run from here to Parque Lenin and Playas del Este in summer only.

Trains depart for Santiago de las Vegas (40 centavos) at 6:05 and 10:40 a.m., and 2:50 and 7 p.m.; and for Batabanó (two pesos) at 7:45 a.m. and 12:25 p.m. Return trains depart Santi- ago de las Vegas for Cristina at 7:57 a.m. and 12:30, 4:54, and 8:40 p.m.; and Batabanó at 3:35 and 5:10 p.m.

TAXI

Havana has a superb taxi system. Hundreds of taxis serve both the tourist trade and the local population. If you use a tourist taxi four or five times a day, the cost may approach that of renting a car—especially if you're traveling between, say, Miramar and Habana Vieja.

True to international form, Havana's taxi drivers are more aggressive on the road than other Havana drivers and are known (as were their *coche*-driving forebears before the invention of the internal-combustion engine) for belting around the street like charioteers.

Dollar Taxis

Most licensed *turistaxis* are operated by state organizations, all of which charge in dollars.

The cheapest is **Panataxi,** tel. (55) 5555, fax (55) 5461, which provides efficient radio-dispatched taxi service using new Peugeots. It's used by Cubans and foreigners alike. It's rare to have to wait more than 15 minutes for a taxi to arrive. A ride from the Habana Libre in Vedado to Habana Vieja will cost about US$4 with Panataxi.

Taxis exclusively serving the tourist trade use modern Japanese cars (mostly Subarus and Hyundais), plus Peugeots and Mercedes. Prices vary slightly according to size: the larger, the more expensive. These hang around outside tourist hotels but can also be radio dispatched. The following companies operate tourist taxis: **Habanataxi,** tel. (41) 9600; **Taxis-OK,** tel. (24) 1446; **Taxi Transtur,** tel. (33) 5539 or (33) 6666, fax (33) 5535, e-mail: taxihab@transtur.com.cu, and (in Playas del Este) tel. (96) 3939; **Transgaviota,** tel. (20) 4650 or (33) 9780, fax (27) 1626 or (33) 0742, e-mail: dtor_tr@nwgaviot.gav.mca.net; and **Turistaxi,** tel. (33) 5539.

Micar, 1ra y Paseo, Vedado, tel. (55) 2444, fax (33) 6476, offers minibuses at hourly rates on a sliding scale (US$40 four hours, US$70 eight hours, US$90 10 hours) but charges US$85 cents per km for the first 50 km (US70 cents per km thereafter).

Tourist taxis are slightly more expensive than Panataxi cabs. Rates vary slightly depending on the size of the car. By international standards, however, Havana's taxis are relatively cheap, and you will rarely pay more than US$10 or so for any journey within town. Taxis are metered and strictly controlled; drivers are assiduous in using their meters, which begin at US$1. Expect to pay about US$5 from La Rampa to Habana Vieja, double that from Miramar. Nighttime fares cost about 20% more.

The taxi companies all offer special long-distance and hourly rates (the cost normally compares favorably to hiring a car for the day). Although relatively expensive, they are a value option for three or four passengers sharing the cost. If you want to get the price down, you might be able to strike a bargain with the driver. Here's the deal. Your driver will stop the meter at so many dollars, and you give him a slightly greater amount. Since his dispatcher records the destination, mile for mile, usually a dollar per mile, the taxi driver splits the excess with the dispatcher. Most taxi drivers are scrupulously honest with passengers. If you think you're being gouged, contest the fee.

Classic Cars: Fancy tootling around in an old Studebaker? You can rent classic cars for city tour through **Gran Car,** tel. (33) 5647 or (40) 1955, for US$15 per hour (20 km limit the first hour, with shorter limits per extra hour). Daily rates decline from US$90 for one day to US$7 daily for five days (120 km daily limit). Set prices apply for provincial touring. One or two such cars can usually be found outside the major hotels, notably the Hotels Inglaterra, Nacional, and Melía Cohiba.

Peso Taxis

Peso-only taxis—deprecatingly called *los in capturables* (the uncatchables)—serve Cubans and until recently were not supposed to give rides to foreigners, although many did so (especially for a dollar gratuity). In spring 1999, however, there seemed to be no restriction. They are radio dispatched, tel. (70) 1326 or (79) 0443, and charge in pesos at ludicrously low rates using Ladas, the Russian-made Fiat described as "tough as a Land Rover, with iron-hard upholstery and, judging by sensation, no springs." They're painted black-and-yellow (with a strange Hebrew-type logo on the sides); most also have meters. Drivers now require you to pay in dollars, in which case negotiate the price (expect to pay about half the fare you'd pay in a turistaxi). You find plenty around Coppelia in Vedado, and Parque Central and Parque de la Fraternidad in Habana Vieja. Look for a light lit up above the cab; it signifies if the taxi is *libre* (free). With luck, you might be able to pay in pesos (you should change dollars for pesos beforehand). The base fare is one peso. Each km costs 25 centavos (35 centavos at night).

The workhorses of the taxi system for Cubans are the *colectivos* (shared cabs that pick up any one who flags them down, often until they're packed to the gills), which generally run along fixed routes. Most are old Yankee jalopies. Ostensibly, they're not supposed to pick up foreigners, but I've rarely had a problem. Most *colectivos* have a taxi sign above the cab and markings on the side, but follow the local example—wave down any large Yankee behemoth coming your way. Avenida 5ta and the Malecón linking Miramar with Habana Vieja are favorite routes. The south side of Parque de la Fraternidad is their preferred gathering spot. They depart from here on set routes throughout the city.

"Gypsy" Cabs

Illegal "gypsy" cabs driven by freelance chauffeurs are everywhere, too. Most are beat-up Ladas or American jalopies. You'll find freelance driver-guides outside the largest tourist hotels—especially the Hotel Inglaterra on Parque Central, and the Hotel Habana Libre Tryp and, to a lesser degree, the Hotels Riviera and Melía Cohiba in Vedado—and outside discos late at night. Fares are negotiable, and you often can hire a car and driver for the whole day for, say, US$20. But you'll usually end up paying *more* than you would in a tourist taxi. Educate yourself about *turistaxi* fares to your destination beforehand, as many drivers attempt to gouge you. Beware scams.

The drivers are constantly wary of the police. *Jiniteros* work on commission and will approach you and whisper under their breath, "Hey, friend—taxi?"

Ciclotaxis

Hundreds of tricycle taxis—"rickshaws"—ply the streets of Habana Vieja and Vedado. They offer a relaxing (and cheap) way of sightseeing and getting around if you're in no hurry. You can go the full length of the Malecón, from Habana Vieja to Vedado, for US$3—not much less than a taxi ride, but would *you* want to pedal two passengers for less? You can hire them by the hour for about US$5.

Most have fashioned their seats from car seats and offer shade canopies.

Cocotaxis

It could be the strangest taxi you'll ever take in your life. These bright yellow motorized tricycles look like scooped-out Easter eggs on wheels, like something out of a children's pic-

ciclotaxis, *Havana*

turebook. Most depart from outside the Hotel Inglaterra on Parque Central. They charge US$5 per hour for up to three people.

Calezas (Horsedrawn Buggies)

Horsedrawn *calezas* (open-air coaches) offer a popular way of exploring the historic quarter of Old Havana, although the buggies are barred from entering the pedestrian-only quarter. They're operated by Agencia San Cristóba, Calle Oficios #110 e/ Lamparilla y Amargura, tel. (33) 9585, fax (33) 9586. Their official starting point is the junction of Empedrado and Tacón, but you can hail them wherever you see them. Others can be hailed outside the Hotel Inglaterra, on Parque Central. Expect to pay US$3 per person per hour in low season, US$5 in high season (Oct.-April).

BY RENTAL CAR

I recommend renting a car only if you anticipate exploring the suburbs or if you intend touring beyond Havana. Virtually every tourist hotel ei-

TWENTY-FOUR-HOUR GASOLINE STATIONS IN HAVANA

Cupet-Cimex has 24-hour service centers (dollars only) at:

Habana Vieja, Centro Habana, and Cerro
Vento y Santa Catalina

Vedado and Plaza de la Revolución
Avenida de la Independencia y Conill
Calle L y 17
Malecón y 11
Paseo y Malecón

Playa (Miramar and Beyond)
Avenida 5ta y Calle 112
Avenida 31 y Calle 38
Avenida 33 y Calle 70
Calle 41 y 72 (Marianao)

Suburbs
Autopista y 224
Avenida de la Independencia y 271
Ayesteran y Boyeros
Carretera Monumental (Habana del Este)
Carretera Via Blanca
Rotonda de Guanabo (Playas del Este)
Valle de Berroa (Habana del Este)

ther has a car rental desk or can arrange for a rental car to be delivered. The five state-owned car rental companies have main offices in addition to outlets in leading hotels.

Habaneros' standard of driving is, in general, admirable (certain taxi drivers excepted), although in recent years Cubans with newer cars have begun to drive faster and more aggressively than a few years ago. In Havana, there are no bottlenecks. Havana is probably the only Latin American city without rush-hour traffic. Traffic police do an efficient job. Traffic signage is very good, and most of the traffic lights work— and are even obeyed. Havana's streets show deterioration, but in general, the roads are superior to, or at least no worse, than those of most other Caribbean or Latin American cities.

Roads to Avoid: Two notable exceptions to the generally high standards are busy Vía Blanca, which (south of Havana harbor) is in terri-

ble shape and dangerous; and the dual carriageway **Autopista Circular,** or route Calle 100, which forms an almost continuous semicircle around the city, linking the arterial highways into Havana. The latter has little traffic and, frankly, it's too far out from the city to serve a useful function unless skirting the city entirely, when traveling, say, between Pinar del Río and Matanzas. Be careful! It has treacherous pot holes, and some are deathtraps—massive hollows invisible until you're upon them. They're usually at intersections.

Car Rental Companies: See the Getting Away section, below, for car rental companies plus further details on car rentals.

Parking

A capital city without parking meters? Imagine! Parking meters were detested during the Batista era, mostly because they were a source of *botellas* (skimming) for corrupt officials, despite their introduction as a policy to restrain excessive traffic in the city center. After the triumph of the Revolution, Habaneros rampaged through the city smashing the meters.

Finding parking is rarely a problem, except in Habana Vieja (you should avoid driving in Habana Vieja, anyway, east of Monserrate). No parking zones are well marked. Avoid these like the plague, especially if it's an officials-only zone, in which case a policeman will usually be on hand to blow his whistle. Havana has an efficient towing system for the recalcitrant. You can pay your parking ticket through your car rental agency (and be sure to do so before leaving the country).

Theft is a serious problem. As such, Habaneros prefer to park in *parqueos,* parking lots found throughout the city, with a *custodio* to guard against thieves 24 hours. Expect to pay US$1-2 overnight. In questionable areas, pay a kid some pocket change to keep an eye on your vehicle.

In central Vedado, the Hotel Habana Libre Tryp has an underground car park (US80 cents for one hour, US50 cents each additional hour, US$4 maximum for 24 hours).

Car Repairs

Your car rental company can arrange repairs. However, if you need emergency treatment, **Diplogarage** has centers open 24 hours at Aven

(continued on page 28.

HAVANA'S VINTAGE AMERICAN CARS

"Magnificent finned automobiles cruise grandly down the street like parade floats. I feel like we're back in time, in a kind of Cuban version of an earlier America."

—CRISTINA GARCÍA,
DREAMING IN CUBAN

Fifties nostalgia is alive and well on the streets of Havana. Stylish Chevrolets, Packards, and Cadillacs weave among the sober Russian-made Ladas and Moskovitches, their large engines guzzling precious gas at an astonishing rate. Automotive sentimentality is reason enough to visit Havana—the greatest living car museum in the world.

American cars flooded Havana for 50 years. During Batista's days, Cuba probably imported more Cadillacs, Buicks, and DeSotos than any other nation in the world. Then came the Cuban Revolution and the US trade embargo. In terms of American automobiles, time stopped when Castro took power.

Still, relics from Detroit's high-style heyday are everywhere, ubiquitous reminders of that period in the 1950s when American cars—high-finned, big-boned, with the come-hither allure of Marilyn Monroe—seemed tailor-made for the streets of prerevolutionary Havana.

Imagine. A '57 Packard gleams in the lyrical Cuban sunlight. Nearby, perhaps, sits a 1950 Chevy Deluxe, a '57 Chevrolet Bel Air hardtop, and an Oldsmobile Golden Rocket from the same year, inviting foreigners to admire the dashboard or run their fingers along a tail fin. More numerous are staid Chrysler New Yorker sedans, Ford Customlines, and Buick Centuries.

Lacking proper tools and replacement parts, Cubans constantly are adeptly cajoling one more kilometer out of their battered hulks. Their intestinally reconstituted engines are monuments to ingenuity and geopolitics—decades of improvised repairs have melded parts from Detroit and Moscow alike. (Russian Gaz jeeps are favorite targets for cannibalization, since their engines were cloned from a Detroit engine.)

One occasionally spots a shining example of museum quality. The majority, though, have long ago been touched up with house paint and decorated with flashy mirrors and metallic stars, as if to celebrate a religious holiday. Some are adorned with multicolored flags to invoke the protection of Changó or another *santería* god.

The mechanical dinosaurs are called *cacharros*. Normally, the word means a broken-down jalopy, but in the case of old Yankee classics, the word is "whispered softly, tenderly, like the name of a lost first love," says Cristina García in the introduction to *Cars of Cuba*, a beautiful little photo-essay book published by Harry N. Abrams (New York, 1995).

Last Frontier Expeditions, 4823 White Rock Circle, Suite H, Boulder, CO 80301-3260, tel. (303) 530-9275, fax (303) 530-9275, e-mail: CopaBob@aol.com, website: www.clubhavana.com, offers a classic car tour that includes a classic car rally. **Wings of the World,** 1200 William St. #706, Buffalo, NY 14240, tel. (800) 465-8687, occasionally offers a "Classic Car Adventure" in Cuba using chauffeur-driven vintage autos.

THE BICYCLE REVOLUTION

In 1991, when the first shipment of Flying Pigeon bicycles arrived from China, there were only an estimated 30,000 bicycles in Havana, a city of two million people. The visitor arriving in Havana today could be forgiven for imagining he or she had arrived in Ho Chi Minh City. Bicycles are everywhere, outnumbering cars, trucks, and buses 20 to one. The story is the same across the island.

Cynics have dubbed Cuba's wholesale switch to bicycles since the collapse of the Soviet bloc as a socialist failing, a symbol of the nation's backwardness. Others acclaim it an astounding achievement, a two-wheel triumph over an overnight loss of gasoline and adversity. *Granma,* the Cuban newspaper, christened it the "bicycle revolution."

American cars had flooded the island for half a century. Then came the US trade embargo. The 1960s saw the arrival of the first sober-looking Lada and Moskovitch sedans, imported in the ensuing decades by the tens of thousands from the Soviet Union, along with Hungarian and Czech buses, which provided an efficient transport network. The Eastern bloc buses were notorious for their lack of comfort, as were the stunted Girón buses that Cuba began producing in 1967. But they carried millions of Cubans for years despite their defects, most notably their low mileage.

Professor Maurice Halperin, who taught at the University of Havana, does not "recall seeing a single adult Cuban on a bicycle in Havana during the entire period of my residence in the city, from 1962 to 1968."

Goodbye to Gas

The collapse of the Soviet Union severed the nation's gasoline pipeline. Transportation virtually ground to a halt, along with the rest of the Cuban economy.

In November 1990, the Cuban government launched sweeping energy-saving measures that called for a "widespread substitution of oxen for farm machinery and hundreds of thousands of bicycles for gasoline-consuming vehicles." Cuba's program of massive importation, domestic production, and mass distribution was launched as a "militant and defensive campaign," symbolized on 1 May 1991 when the armed forces appeared on bicycles in the May Day parade.

The government contracted with China to purchase 1.2 million bicycles, and by the end of 1991, 530,000 single-gear Chinese bicycles were in use on the streets of Havana.

Cuba: Bicycle Capital of the Americas

Overnight, Cuba transformed itself into the bicycle capital of the Americas. "The comprehensiveness and speed of implementation of this program," said a 1994 World Bank report, "is unprecedented in the history of transportation." The report noted that about two million bicycles were in use islandwide.

"Today, we can say that the bicycle is as much a part of the Cuban scenario as the palm tree," says Narciso Hernández, director of Empresa Claudio Arugelles Fábrica de Bicicletas in Havana. Hernández's factory is one of five established in 1991 by the Cuban government to supplement the Chinese imports. The government's goal was to produce half

Ciclobuses *are specially appointed to carry bicycles*

a million domestic two-wheelers within five years. Each of the factories produces a different model. Cuba imports parts such as small bolts, chains, spindles, and brakes, but makes the frames, forks, and handlebars.

The bicycles are disbursed through MINCIN (Ministerio de Comercial Interior), which parcels them out to schools, factories, and workers' associations. Others are sold at special stores. Lucky recipients can purchase their bicycles outright or pay for them in monthly installments. Workers pay 125 pesos—equivalent to about half the average monthly salary—while students pay 65 pesos. Cuba still can't produce enough bicycles to satisfy the demand, and a thriving black market has arisen.

The Chinese bicycles were cumbersome, hard-to-pump beasts—true antediluvian pachyderms with only one gear. Worse, they weighed 48 pounds. The Cubans redesigned the chunky models with smaller frames, thereby lopping off 15 pounds. Other Cuban innovations include a tricycle for disabled people, and a "bicibus," a Dr. Seuss-worthy contraption made of two bicycles with rows of seats—and pedals—for 12 people in-between. "One day soon, Cuba hopes to begin exporting bikes," comments Hernández.

Cubans manage to coax great speed from their sturdy steeds. Young men zigzag through the streets, disdainful of all other traffic, while old men and women pedal painstakingly down the middle of the road with leisurely sovereignty, like holy cattle. During the early phase of the bicycle revolution,

hospital emergency rooms were flooded with victims. Most Cubans had never ridden bicycles before. They teetered en masse through the potholed streets, often with passengers, even whole families, hanging onto jury-rigged seats and rear-hub extenders. Due to the paucity of cars, cyclists rode the wrong way down major boulevards, which they crisscrossed at will. Few bicis had rear reflectors, and the brakes on the Chinese-made models barely worked. Handlebar warning bells chirp incessantly.

Cuban planners like Gina Rey, of the Group for the Integral Development of the Capital, were challenged to reorganize Havana's transportation network to prevent turmoil on the streets. The plan called for many colonial streets in Habana Vieja to be closed to motorized traffic. Bicycle lanes were created. The city government initiated classes in bicycle safety. Bicycle parking lots were cleared throughout the city. Ferry boats threading their way across Havana harbor were equipped for bicycles. And special buses (Ciclobuses) were detailed to carry cyclists through the tunnel beneath the bay.

"We've entered the bicycle era," Castro has noted. "But after this Special Period disappears we mustn't abandon this wonderful custom." Bicycles would solve many of the country's energy quandaries—and pollution and health problems, too. "With bicycles, we will improve the quality of life in our society," Castro claims. Anyone who has seen Hungarian buses coughing fitfully through the streets of Cuba, belching thick black clouds, would agree.

---

da 5ta esq. 120, Playa, tel. (33) 6159, and at Calle 2 esq. Avenida 7ma, tel. (23) 5588 or (33) 1906.

BY SCOOTER

Transtur Rent-a-Car, Calle 19 #210 esq. J, Vedado, tel. (33) 8384, fax (55) 3995, e-mail: webmaster@transtur.com.cu, rents Suzuki scooters for US$10 for one hour, US$15 for three hours, US$23 per day, or US$147 weekly.

BY BICYCLE

Habaneros do it—almost one million bicycles wheel through the streets of the Cuban capital—so why not you? Be careful—there are plenty of pot-

holes, and at night many of the streets are unlit. Cuban cyclists are notoriously lackadaisical on the roads, and an average of two cyclists are killed in traffic accidents in Havana every three days.

Cyclists are not allowed to ride through the tunnel beneath Havana harbor. The municipal government provides specially converted buses—the sky-blue **Ciclobus**—to ferry cyclists and their bicis through the tunnel (10 centavos). In summer 1999, buses departed from Parque de la Fraternidad, but location is subject to change (the ciclobus formerly departed from Avenida de los Estudiantes, at the base of La Rampa).

The only place that I'm aware of currently renting bicycles is at the Hotel Jardín del Eden in Marina Hemingway, tel. (24) 1150, ext. 371 (it charges US$1 per hour, or US$12 per day for mountain bikes).

In prior years, Panataxi has rented bicycles through a division called **Panaciclo,** Avenida Rancho Boyeros y Santa Ana, near the main bus station in Plaza de la Revolución, tel. (81) 4444 or (45) 3746. It has ceased doing so at press time.

BY FERRY

Tiny ferries (standing room only—no seats) bob across the harbor between the Havana waterfront and Regla (on the east side of the bay) and Casablanca (on the north side of the bay). The ferries leave on a constant yet irregular basis, 24 hours, from a wharf called Muelle Luz on Avenida San Pedro at the foot of Calle Santa Clara in Havana Vieja, tel. (97) 9130 (in Regla); 10 centavos; five minutes.

ORGANIZED EXCURSIONS

City Tours

A city tour is a great way to get an initial feel for Havana. All the hotel tour bureaus offer guided city tours through the major tour agencies aboard a/c buses. For example, **Tour & Travel,** Avenida 1ra e/ Calles 0 y 2, Miramar, Havana, tel. (24) 7541, fax (24) 2074, a division of Havanatur, offers a city tour (US$15), plus excursions to the botanical garden. It has an office in Vedado on La Rampa and Calle M, one block downhill from the Hotel Habana Libre Tryp.

Tropical Travel Agency, tel. (24) 9626, fax (24) 4520, a division of Rumbos, has a three-and-a-half-hour city tour departing daily at 9 a.m. and 2 p.m., including Habana Vieja, Vedado, and Miramar (US$10).

Agencia Vaijes San Cristóbal, Calles Oficios #110 e/ Lamparilla y Amargura, tel. (33) 9585, fax (33) 9586, offers guided walking tours of Habana Vieja and excursions farther afield, plus books festivals and makes other travel

arrangements. Open Mon.-Sat. 8:30 a.m.-6 p.m., Sunday 8:30 a.m.-4 p.m.

Amistur S.A., Calle Paseo #4606 e/ 17 y 19, Vedado, tel. (33) 4544, fax (33) 3515, website: www.igc.apc.org/cubasol/amistur.html, is a Cuban tour agency handling specialized tourism.

Private Guides: Hotel tour bureaus and tour agencies can arrange personal guided tours. **Cubatur,** Calle F #157, e/ Calzada y Calle 9ra, tel. (33) 4155, fax (33) 3104, offers guides for US$25 per day (up to 12 hours) in Havana, US$30 outside Havana. You can also hire a guide weekly (US$200). **Agencía San Cristóbal** (see above), also arranges guides.

A US resident student in Cuba, Olivia King Carter, Calle 35 #168 e/ 6 y Loma, tel. (66) 6471, e-mail: olivia@ip.etecsa.cu, has proved useful in pointing the way to guides, etc. She's a fountain of local knowledge. She welcomes your calls and will be happy to assist you.

Harbor Cruises

Marlin S.A., Calle 184 #123, Flores, Havana, tel. (33) 6675, offers a harbor cruise taking in the Morro headlands aboard *La Niña* from the wharf on Avenida Carlos M. Céspedes at the foot of O'Reilly, one block east of Plaza de Armas. The boat departs Mon.-Fri. at 1 p.m., plus Saturday at 10 a.m., 1 p.m., and 5 p.m. (US$2).

Marlin also offers a coastal cruise aboard the *XIV Festival* from the wharf on San Pedro at the foot of Luz, Tue.-Fri. at 10 a.m. and 4 p.m. (US$10). A kiddie's matinee cruise is hosted Sat.-Sun. at 10 a.m., noon, and 2 p.m. (US$2).

The *Gitana* (Gypsy) leaves Marina Hemingway. The boat was built in 1928 with art deco styling. It offers daily excursions along the coast to Playa El Salado, where guests are taken ashore in small boats for a buffet lunch and activities on the beach. Nocturnal cruises pass by Morro Castle.

You can make reservations for all three cruises at your hotel tour desk or via Puertosol, tel. (66) 7117 or (33) 2161, fax (66) 7716 or (33) 2877.

GETTING AWAY

DEPARTING CUBA

By Air

Those airlines serving Havana also, logically, depart Havana, usually on the same day.

The international airlines are linked by computer to their reservations headquarters abroad. However, the Cuban computers "go down" frequently, and confirming and changing reservations may be more time-consuming than you're probably used to. Don't leave things until the last minute. Reconfirm your flight at least 72 hours before departure. It's a good idea to check in any event because flight schedules change on a frequent basis.

Cubana, Calle 23 #64, tel. (33) 4949 or (33) 4446, has a fully computerized reservation system. You can pick up printed timetables of Cubana's domestic and international service at the information desk in the lobby of the Cubana office (open Mon.-Fri. 8:30 a.m.-4 p.m., Saturday 8 a.m.-1 p.m.). Double-check departure times, which change frequently and at short notice. Cubana is especially notorious for canceling the reservations of those who don't reconfirm on time. Cubana's office gets crowded, and you can often wait an hour or more before being attended. Allow plenty of time.

Tickets for Cubana **charter flights** must be purchased through Havanatur's **Tour & Travel,** at Calle 6 e/ Avenida 1ra y 3ra, Miramar, tel. (33) 2712, or below the Hotel Habana Libre Tryp on Calle L at the top of La Rampa, tel. (33) 4082. Don't expect to be able to purchase a ticket at the airport. You may be able to purchase tickets at the airport (you can use your credit card to get a cash advance from the Banco Nacional in the departure lounge), but don't count on it. If you miss your flight and want to buy another ticket, you will have to go to the Miramar or Vedado offices.

Airline Offices

The following have offices in the Hotel Habana Libre Tryp: **Aeropostal,** tel. (54) 4000, fax (55) 2148; **Air Europa,** tel. (66) 6918, open Mon.-Sat. 9 a.m.-6 p.m.; **AirEurope** (not to be confused with Air Europa), open Mon.-Fri. 9 a.m.-5 p.m., Saturday 9 a.m.-1 p.m.; **Air Jamaica,** tel. (66) 2447, fax (66) 2449; **Grupo Taca,** tel. (66) 2702, fax (33) 3728, open Mon.-Fri. 9 a.m.-4 p.m., Saturday 9 a.m.-1 p.m.

Air Europe also has an office in La Lonja del Comercio, on the west side of Plaza de San Francisco in Habana Vieja.

The following have offices at Calle 23 #64, at the base of La Rampa in Vedado, e/ Calles P y Infanta: **Aero Caribbean,** tel. (79) 7524 or (33) 3621, fax (33) 3871, open Mon.-Fri. 9 a.m.-5 p.m., Saturday 9 a.m.-1 p.m.; **Aeroflot,** tel. (33) 3200, fax (33) 3288, open Mon.-Fri. 8:30 a.m.-12:30 p.m. and 1:30-4 p.m.; **Air France,** tel. (66) 2642, fax (66) 2634, open Mon.-Fri. 8:30 am.-4:45 p.m.; **ALM Antillean Airlines,** tel. (33) 3730, fax (33) 3729; **AOM,** tel. (33) 4098 or (33) 39997, open Mon.-Fri. 9 a.m.-1 p.m. and 2:30-5 p.m.; **COPA,** tel. (33) 1758, fax (33) 3951; **Cubana,** tel. (33) 4446/7/8/9; open Mon.-Fri. 8:30 a.m.-4 p.m.; **Iberia,** tel. (33) 5041, fax (33) 5061; **LTU,** tel. (33) 3524, fax (33) 3590; **Martinair,** tel. (33) 4364, fax (33) 3729, open Mon.-Fri. 9 a.m.-4 p.m.; **Mexicana,** tel. (33) 3531 or (33) 3532, fax (33) 3077; **TAAG** of Angola, tel. (33) 3527; and **Tame,** tel. (33) 4949, fax (33) 4126, of Ecuador.

Aero Gaviota has its office at Calle 47 #2814, Reparto Kohly, tel. (81) 3068.

José Martí International Airport

The airport, 25 km southwest of downtown Havana, in the Rancho Boyeros district, is accessed by Avenida de la Independencia. A new freeway was under construction at press time paralleling Independencia about two miles west (the southernmost, six-mile-long section was complete; eventually it will be extended into the heart of Havana).

Remember that the airport has four terminals spaced well apart from each other and accessed by different roads (nor are they linked by a connecting bus service). *Make sure you arrive at the correct terminal for your departure.*

Terminal 1: This terminal, on the south side of the runway on Avenida Van Troi, off Avenida de la Independencia (Avenida Rancho Boyeros), in Reparto Rancho Boyero, tel. (33) 5177/78/79 or (79) 6081, handles Cubana's domestic flights. The terminal has a snack bar and restaurant, but the car rental companies have pulled out and relocated to the new international terminal.

Terminal 2: This terminal, also called Terminal Nacional, on the north side of the runway about one km east of the international terminal, handles Miami charter flights.

Terminal 3: All international flights (except Miami-bound charters) depart from this main terminal, tel. (45) 1424, fax (33) 9164.

The **departure tax** (US$20 at press time) must be paid at a separate counter after you've checked in with the airline. The foreign exchange bank refuses to accept Cuban pesos, so you should spend these in Havana (or give them to a needy Cuban) before leaving for the airport.

Listen carefully to the boarding annoucements; they are easy to miss, especially over the sound of the live band. Don't linger when your flight is called.

Terminal 4: This terminal, also called Terminal Caribbean, about 600 meters west of the international terminal, handles small-plane flights (mostly domestic) offered by Aero Caribbean, tel. (55) 8722. Flights to Cayo Largo also depart from here.

The following airlines have offices in the airport: **Aeroflot,** tel. (33) 5432; **Air France,** tel. (66) 9708; **Aero Caribbean,** tel. (33) 5958 or (45) 3013; **Grupo Taca** tel. (33) 0112, fax (33) 0113; **Iberia,** tel. (33) 5234; **LTU,** tel. (33) 5339; and **Mexicana,** (33) 5051.

Getting to the Airport: No buses serve the international terminals. Buses marked "Aeropuerto" operate to Terminal Nacional—the domestic terminal—from the east side of Parque Central in Habana Vieja (the *cola* begins near the José Martí statue). The journey costs one peso, takes about one hour, and is very unreliable. Allow plenty of time. You can also catch bus M-2 from the west side of Parque de la Fraternidad. It goes to Santiago de las Vegas via the domestic terminal. Make sure you wait in the line for people wanting seats *(sentados);* the other is for stoics willing to stand. Ask.

A licensed taxi to the airport will cost about US$13-16 from Havana (about US$10 for an unlicensed taxi). You can also arrange a shuttle through one of the tour agencies (US$10-15).

EXPLORING BEYOND HAVANA

Visitors can look forward to the fact that special bus and train services have been added for foreigners, with seat availability virtually guaranteed. All other public transport out of Havana to towns far afield is usually booked solid for weeks in advance: if you plan on traveling by air, bus, or train, make your reservations as far in advance as possible.

For details, see the *Cuba Handbook* (Avalon Travel Publishing, 1997), which offers complete information for exploring the island.

By Air

The fastest way to get around is to fly, although you'll miss out on the *real* fun of Cuba—exploring the countryside serendipitously. Most of Havana's main cities have an airport, and virtually every major tourism destination is within a two-hour drive of an airport. Domestic flights depart Terminal 1 at José Martí International Airport.

A good carrier is **Inter Grupo Taca,** Hotel Habana Libre Tryp, Calle L, Vedado, tel. (66) 2703, fax (33) 3728, the Central American carrier, which operates within Cuba using modern 14-passenger Cessna Gran Caravans. It flies to all major points of tourist interest. Flights depart from Terminal 1.

Several poorly managed Cuban carriers also offer service, but using less trustworthy aircraft. **Aero Caribbean,** Calle 23 #64, Vedado, tel. (33) 5343 or (79) 7524, operates charter flights from Havana to most of the popular tourist destinations, including Isla de la Juventud, Cayo Coco, Cayo Largo, and Santiago. **Aero Gaviota,** Avenida 47 #2814 e/ 28 y 34, Reparto Kohly, Playa, tel. (23) 0668, fax (24) 2621, offers charter flights in 30-passenger Yak-40s and 38-passenger Antonov-26s, as well as "executive" service in eight-seat helicopters. **AeroTaxi,** Calle 27 #102, e/ M y N, Vedado, Havana, tel. (32) 4460 or (33) 4064, utilizes 12-passenger biplanes, mostly for excursion flights. It has facilities at most airports. **Cubana,** Calle Infanta esq. Humbolt, Havana, tel. (33) 4949, the largest carrier, has service between all the major airports. Its fares are 25% cheaper if booked in conjunction with an international Cubana flight.

Reservations: Flights are frequently fully booked, especially in the Aug.-Dec. peak sea-on, when Cubans take their holidays. The most olidly booked routes are Havana-Santiago, Havana-Trinidad, Santa Lucía-Trinidad, and Varadero-Cayo Largo. Often you must make a eservation a week in advance. Fortunately, for-igners with dollars are usually given priority n waiting lists. Reservations usually must be aid in advance and are normally nonrefund-ble. Forego telephone reservations: make your ooking *in person* at the airline office or through ne of the major tour agencies. Better still, make eservations before arriving in Cuba (you'll be iven a voucher that you exchange for a ticket pon arrival in Cuba).

Be sure to arrive on time for check-in, other-vise your seat will likely be given away. If that appens, *don't expect a refund,* and bear in nind that you may not even be able to get a eat on the next plane out. Delays, flight can-ellations, and schedule changes are common. nd don't expect luxury—be happy if you get a Spam-and-cheese sandwich. More likely, since lights are short, you'll receive a boiled sweet.

By Bus

Tourist Buses: Vía Azul, tel. (81) 1413, fax (66) 092, operates bus services for foreigners to key places on the tourist circuit using modern a/c Volvo and Mercedes buses. Buses depart **Terminal Vía Azul** at the corner of Avenida 26 and Zoológico, opposite the entrance to the zoo in western Vedado. It has a small café and a/c waiting room, and offers free luggage storage. Children travel at half price.

You can also book yourself onto an excursion bus operated by one of the state-run tour agencies. Most agencies offer transfers. **Havanatur,** Calle 6 #117 e/ 1ra y 3ra, Miramar, Havana, tel. (33) 2712 or (33) 2090, fax (33) 2601, and other Cuban tour agencies offer seats on tour buses serving Varadero, Trinidad, and other key destinations. Take a sweater; some buses are overly air-conditioned.

Transmetro, tel. (81) 6089, offers buses and minibuses for rent to groups.

Public Buses: Public buses serve almost every nook and cranny of the island. Virtually the entire population relies on the bus system for travel within and between cities. Many Cubans say bus travel is more reliable and faster than train travel, although they sometimes must wait *weeks* to get a seat. The state agency **Empresa Ómnibus Nacionales,** Avenida Independencia #101, Havana, tel. (70) 6155, fax (33) 5908, operates all **interprovincial services.** Reservations are essential; do *not* expect to show up at the station and simply board a bus.

There are two classes of buses for long-distance travel: a/c *especiales* are faster, air-conditioned, and more comfortable than *regulares.* Long-distance travel is usually aboard noisy, rickety old Hungarian-made buses, with stuck windows, noxious exhaust fumes, and (often) bottom-numbing seats. Fortunately, upscale Mercedes and Volvo buses are gradually being added to the service.

Most buses to destinations outside metropolitan Havana leave from the **Ter-**

INTER GRUPO TACA FLIGHTS FROM HAVANA

TO	DEPART TIME	RETURN TIME	PRICE (ONE-WAY)
Cayo Coco	11:15 a.m.	1:45 p.m.	US$100
Cayo Largo	7:15 a.m.	9:10 a.m.	US$60
	11:45 a.m.	3 p.m.	
	12:30 p.m.	2:25 p.m.	
	4:15 p.m.	6:10 p.m.	
Nuevo Gerona	11:15 a.m.	12:15 p.m.	US$100
Siguanea	11:15 a.m.	12:15 p.m.	
Trinidad	7 a.m.	9:05 a.m.	US$60
	11:45 a.m.	1:55 p.m.	
	3:30 p.m.	5:35 p.m.	
Varadero	7 a.m.	10:15 a.m.	US$30
	7:15 a.m.	10:20 a.m.	
	11:15 a.m.	3:25 p.m.	
	12:30 p.m.	3:30 p.m.	
	3:30 p.m.	7:15 p.m.	
	4:15 p.m.	6:35 p.m.	

minal de Ómnibus Nacionales (also called Terminal de Ómnibus Interprovinciales) on Avenida Rancho Boyeros, two blocks north of Plaza de la Revolución at Calle 19 de Mayo, tel. (70) 3397. Buses leave from here for virtually every town throughout the country. The **information booth** for Cubans, tel. (70) 9401, is downstairs, but there is no posted bus schedule and the service is often surly. Facilities include a post office and snack bars. The terminal is served by local bus no. 47 from the Prado (at Calle Animas) in Habana Vieja; by bus no. 265 from the east side of Parque Central; and by buses no. 67 and 84 from La Rampa in Vedado.

Foreigners, however, now pay in dollars and receive preferential seating. The booking office for foreigners is to the right of the entrance and has an a/c lounge with TV.

For Cubans, demand so exceeds supply that there is often a waiting line in excess of one month for the most popular long-distance routes. Intercity buses rarely have a spare seat. Hence, Cuban bus stations have been called "citadels of desperation."

If you plan to travel like a Cuban, you should try to make your reservation as early as possible, either at the bus terminal or at the **Buro de Reservaciones** (also called the Oficina Reservaciones Pasajes), at Calles 21 y 4 in Vedado. Open Mon.-Fri. 7 a.m.-2 p.m., Saturday 7 a.m.-noon. If you don't get shooed away to the dollars-only counter expect a Kafkaesque experience. First, there's often a milling mob to contend with, with everyone clamoring to get his or her name on the list. Your name will be scrawled on a decrepit pile of parchment and added to the scores of names ahead of you. Ask to see the sheets for the destination you want so that you can gauge how many days delay is likely.

Only one-way tickets are available. Don't forget to book any return trip also as far in advance as possible. On the day of travel, arrive at the terminal at least one hour ahead of departure, otherwise your seat may be issued to people on the waiting list. You may be asked to reconfirm your booking.

If you don't have a reservation or miss your departure, you can try getting on the standby list—*Lista de Esperas*—at **Terminal La Coubre**, tel. (78) 2696, on Avenida del Puerto at the foot of Avenida de Bélgica (Egido) in southwest Habana Vieja. Interprovincial buses that have unfilled seats call in here after departing the Terminal de Ómnibus Nacionales to pick up folks on the standby list. The eastern end of the terminal is slated to provide train service; the bus service is at the western end.

Passengers are granted a 22 kg baggage limit (plus one piece of hand luggage), although it seems not to be strictly enforced. Some buses have room for storage below; others do not, in which case luggage space will be limited to overhead racks. *Travel light!* Consider leaving some luggage at your hotel in Havana.

If possible, sit toward the front. Conditions can get very cramped and—if the a/c isn't working—very hot; the back tends to get the hottest (and often smelliest—from exhaust fumes). You'll want some water to guard against de

---

VIA AZUL BUS SCHEDULE

Havana—Varadero; 8 a.m., 8:30 a.m., and 4 p.m. (2 hours 45 mins.); US$10

Varadero—Havana; 8 a.m., 4 p.m., and 6 p.m.

Havana—Viñales; 9 a.m. (3 hours 15 mins; alternate days only); US$12

Viñales—Havana; 1:30 p.m. (alternate days only)

Havana—Trinidad; 8:15 a.m. (5 hours 35 mins.); S$25

Trinidad—Havana; p.m.

Havana—Playa Girón (Bay of Pigs); 7:45 a.m. (3 hours 20 mins.; daily except Monday); US$15

Playa Girón—Havana; 4 p.m.

Havana—Santiago; 3 p.m. (13 hours 50 mins.; Tuesday and Friday only); US$51

Santiago—Havana; 5:30 p.m. (Monday and Thursday only)

The Havana-Trinidad bus stops in Cienfuegos (US$20).

The Havana-Santiago bus stops in Santa Clara (US$18), Sancti Spíritus (US$23), Ciego de Ávila (US$27), Camagüey (US$33), Las Tunas (US$39), Holguín (US$44), and Bayamo (US$44).

PUBLIC BUS SERVICE FROM HAVANA

Pinar del Río; 9 a.m. and 12:30, 2:20, and 5:30 p.m.; Regular; US$7

Viñales; 9:50 a.m.; Regular; US$8

Matanzas; 4:55 p.m.; Regular; US$4

Varadero; 2:45 p.m.; Regular; US$6

Cardenas; 8:45 a.m.; Regular; US$6

Playa Girón; 11:40 a.m. (Fri.-Sun. only); Regular; US$10.50

Santa Clara; 6:30 and 8:40 a.m.; Regular; US$12

Cienfuegos; 6:15 a.m. and 12:05, 4:15, and 7:30 p.m.; Regular; US$14

Trinidad; 5:45 a.m.; Especial; US$21

Sancti Spíritus; 4:40 a.m.; Regular; US$15.50 3:50 p.m. ; Especial; US$15.50

Camagüey; 9:20 a.m. and 7:45 p.m.; Especial; US$27

Ciego de Ávila; 12:25 p.m.; Especial; US$22.50

Morón; 9:50 a.m. (Fri.-Sun. only); Especial; US$24

Santiago de Cuba; 12:15 and 7:20 p.m.; Regular; US$35

Las Tunas; 8:45 p.m.; Regular; US$27

Holguín; 9:15 a.m. (Fri.-Sun. only) ; Regular; US$36 6:25 p.m. (daily); Especial; US$36

Bayamo; 9:45 p.m.; Regular; US$30

Manzanillo; 8:15 p.m.; Regular; US$32

Guantánamo; 3:15 p.m.; Regular; US$38

Baracoa; 10:45 a.m. (Fri.-Sun. only); Especial; US$43

---

hydration, but don't drink too much coffee or other liquids—toilet stops can be few and far between. *Bring plenty of snacks.* Long-distance buses make food stops, but often there isn't sufficient food for everyone. Likewise, Cubans will rush to the bathroom, where a long line may develop.

By Rail

Traveling from Havana by train is increasingly a viable option. One main rail axis spans the country connecting all the major cities, with major ports and secondary cities linked by branch lines. Rail services, which virtually ceased in 1990-91, continue to be restored to their pre-Special Period schedules as the restored flow of gasoline and diesel fuel again grease the wheels of the Cuban economy. Unfortunately, departure times change as often as you change your underwear (frequently, one hopes). The schedule is in no way firm, so double-check days and times given in this book. Also check the arrival time at your destination carefully and plan accordingly, as many trains arrive (and depart) in the wee hours of the morning. Few trains run on time.

Bicycles are allowed on most trains. You usually pay (in pesos) at the end of the journey.

There are four railway stations:

Estación Central de Ferrocarril: The most important station is the Central Railway Station at Avenida de Bélgica (Egido) and Arsenal, in Habana Vieja, tel. (57) 2041, (61) 2807, or (61) 8382. Trains depart here for most major cities, including Pinar del Río, Cienfuegos, Santa Clara, Sancti Spíritus, Ciego de Ávila, Camagüey, Las Tunas, Santiago and Guantánamo, and Bayamo and Manzanillo. Two services operate between Havana and Santiago de Cuba: the fast *especial,* which takes 16-20 hours for the 860-km journey, and the slow *regular.* The *especial* (which has a poorly stocked *cafetería* wagon, comfy seats, and bone-chilling a/c) stops at all the major cities en route but is not particularly good for sightseeing if you're bound for Santiago, as most of the journey takes place at night; the slower train (far less salubrious, but lazy and quite adequate) is colloquially called the *lechero*—the "milkman"—because it stops at virtually every village.

At press time, certain trains were scheduled to begin operating from the **Terminal La Coubre,** 100 meters south of the main railway station at the foot of Avenida de Bélgica (Egido). The terminal opened in March 1999, but repairs were still to be made to the tracks and the terminal was not yet functioning for train service, although the published timetable showed departures: for Cienfuegos at 1:25 p.m. (train #67; arrive 11:35 p.m.), and for Pinar del Río at 9:45 p.m. (train #313; arrive 3:26 a.m.).

Estación 19 de Noviembre: The railcar *(ferro-ómnibus)* to ExpoCuba and Santiago de las Vegas departs from the 19th of November Station (also called Tulipán), tel. (81) 4431, located southwest of the Plaza de la Revolución, at Calles Tulipán and Hidalgo.

THE HERSHEY TRAIN

Rail journeys hold a particular magic, none more so in Cuba than the Hershey Train, which runs lazily between Casablanca and Matanzas year-round, four times a day. The diminutive vermilion MU-train locomotive (Ferrocarril de Cuba #20803) looks as if it could have fallen from the pages of a story about Thomas, the little "live" engine.

This fascinating electric railway has its origin in a chocolate bar.

In its heyday, before the Revolution, the Hershey estates—belonging to the Pennsylvania-based chocolate company—occupied 69 square miles of lush canefields around a modern sugar-factory town (now called Camilo Cienfuegos). Milton Hershey built an electric railway to take tourists to visit the Hershey sugar mill in Matanzas province that produced sugar for his chocolate factory in Hershey, Pennsylvania. Hershey also built a model town next to the mill, with a baseball field, movie theater, and amusements, and a hotel and bungalows for rent.

At its peak, the estate had 19 steam locomotives. Their sparks, however, constituted a serious fire hazard, so they were replaced with seven 60-ton electric locomotives built especially for the Hershey-Cuban Railroad. Though it was primarily a sugar-cane-moving venture, the railroad provided three-car passenger train service between Havana and Matanzas every hour. Today's Hershey Train is the sole working survivor.

Estación Cristina: The Cristina Station, tel. (78) 4971, at Avenida de México and Arroyo, facing Cuatros Palmas, on the southwest side of Habana Vieja, serves outer Havana, including Parque Lenin and Playas del Este in midsummer only.

Estación Casablanca: An electric train—the famous **Hershey Train,** tel. (62) 4888, operates to Matanzas from a harborfront station at Casablanca, on the north side of Havana harbor. It's a splendid journey (three hours each way), which you can take either with the locals or on a tourist junket.

Purchasing Tickets: The state agency **Ladis** (formerly Ferrotur), tel. (62) 4259, handles ticket sales and reservations for all national train service. Foreigners must now pay in dollars, for which you get a guaranteed seat (for departures from Estación Cristina and Estación 19 de Noviembre, tickets can be bought on-site in pesos by foreigners). The Ladis office serving foreigners is at Calles Arsenal and Zulueta (open daily 8:30 a.m.-6 p.m.), on the north side of the main railway station in Habana Vieja. Tickets can be purchased up to 30 minutes prior to de-

A Sugar of a Journey

The train departs Casablanca on the north side of Havana harbor and stops at Guanabacoa and dozens of little way stations en route to Matanzas. Two minutes before departure, the conductor gives a toot on the horn and a mad rush ensues. The train shudders and begins to thread its way along the narrow main street that parallels the waterfront of Casablanca. The rattle of the rails soon gathers rhythm, with the doors remaining wide open, providing plenty of breeze.

The train winds in and out among the palm-studded hills, speeds along the coast within sight of the Atlantic, then slips between palms, past broad swathes of sugarcane, and through the Yumurí Valley, a region of such beauty that Humboldt, the explorer, called it "the loveliest valley in the world."

Two hours into the journey, you'll arrive at a blue station still bearing the Hershey sign. You are now in the heart of the old Hershey sugar factory, where the train pauses sufficiently for you to get down and capture the scene for posterity. Bring some snacks to share with locals, who willingly share from their meager packages unfolded on laps.

After a mesmerizing (albeit tiring) four-hour journey, you finally arrive at the sky-blue Matanzas station.

The train—which makes about 40 stops en route!—departs Casablanca station, tel. (62) 4888, at 4:10 and 8:32 a.m., and 12:30, 4:22, and 9 p.m., arriving at Matanzas three-and-a-half hours later. Tickets cost $2.80 to Matanzas (foreigners can pay in pesos) and go on sale one hour in advance. Kids ride half price. Passengers are assigned seat numbers—ask for a window seat. In 1998, the old, hard-on-the-bum, barebones carriages were replaced with a smart fleet of more comfortable Spanish cars.

Five of the spiffy-clean Spanish coaches are intended for tourist service, to be pulled by a second train—a Brill 3008—that ran for the first time in 1922. **Transnico** will market the Hershey tourist train.

---

parture, but you must purchase your ticket that day for a nighttime departure.

On the day of departure, get there early. The seating in the waiting room is comfortable. You'll need to listen attentively for departure announcements because the electronic information board is usually out of order.

Classes: Foreigners paying dollars are now expected to travel on the *especial,* which has reclining cushioned seats. Service in this "luxury class" includes a basic meal (usually fried chicken or beans and rice with soda to wash it down). Regardless, take snacks and drinks. Most branch line services are *clase segunda* (second class) only, which, though inexpensive, is arduous for long journeys and best suited to hardy travelers—the trains are typically dirty and overcrowded, with uncushioned wooden seats. *Clase primera* (first class) is marginally better, with padded seats, though still crowded and hardly comfortable. Some routes offer *clase primera especial,* which provides more comfort and, often, basic boxed meals.

Tourist Trains Transnico Train Tours, in the Lonja del Comercia, Plaza San Francisco de Asís, Habana Vieja, planned to introduce a luxury train journey in the style of the Orient Express, using original American coaches. For information and reservations in Canada, contact: Canadian Caboose Press, Box 844, Skookumchuck, BC V0B 2EO, Canada, cellular tel. (250) 342-1421, website: www.cal.shaw. wave.ca/~hfinklem/GoodMed.htm; in the UK, Rob Dickinson, 5, Ash Lane, Monmouth, NP5 4FJ, tel./fax (01600) 713-405, e-mail: steam@ dial.pipex.com; and in Belgium, Trannico, Avenue Montjoie, 114 -1180 Brussels, R.C. 579074, Belgium BE 447.460.901, tel. (322) 344-4690, fax (322) 346-5665, e-mail: transnico.international.group@skynet.be, website: users.skynet. be/transnico/index.html.

By Taxi

Touring far from Havana by taxi can be inordinately expensive. It's certainly a viable option, however, for places close at hand, such as Cojímar or even Playas del Este. Beyond that, you're probably better off renting a car or hiring a private freelance driver.

Taxi Transtur, Calle 19 #210 esq. J, Vedado, tel. (33) 6666, fax (33) 5535, e-mail: taxihab @transtur.com.cu, offers chauffeured Taxi Excursions by car or minivan. For example, an excursion to Viñales costs US$165/200 (car/minivan); to Varadero, US$120/150; and to Soroa, US$75/85.

TRAIN SCHEDULES AND FARES

NO.	DESTINATION	ORIGIN STATION	DEPART	ARRIVE
11	Santiago (Especial)	Estación Central	7:30 p.m.	9:10 a.m.
13	Santiago	Estación Central	4:40 p.m.	6:40 a.m.
15	Holguín	Estación Central	2:05 p.m.	4:05 a.m.
17	Bayamo	Estación Central	8:25 p.m.	10:20 a.m.
17	Manzanillo	Estación Central	8:25 p.m.	11:40 a.m.
19	Santiago	Estación Central	10:40 a.m.	10:30 p.m.
21	Morón	Estación Central	8:45 a.m.	3:06 p.m.
25	Sancti Spíritus	Estación Central	9:25 p.m.	5:40 a.m.
67	Cienfuegos	Estación Coubre	1:25 p.m.	11:35 p.m.
313	Pinar del Río	Estación Coubre	9:45 p.m.	3:26 a.m.
315	Güines Union	Estación Coubre	5:30 p.m.	9:25 p.m.

DESTINATION	FARE (REGULAR)	TRAIN NO.
Aguacate	US$2	15, 25
Artemisa	US$2.50	313
Cacocum (Holguín)	US$23.50	13
Camagüey	US$19.50	13, 15
Ciego de Ávila	US$15.50	13, 15, 21
Cienfuegos	US$9.50	67
Colón	US$6	15, 25
Florida	US$18	15
Guantánamo	US$33	13
Holguín	US$27	15
Jatibónico	US$14	15
Jovellanos	US$5	15, 25
Las Tunas	US$23.50	13, 15
Matanzas	US$3.50	13, 15, 21, 25
Morón	US$24	21
Pinar del Río	US$6.50	313
Placetas	US$11.50	15, 25
Sancti Spíritus	US$13.50	25
Santa Clara	US$10	13, 15, 21, 25
Santiago de Cuba	US$30.50	12
Zaza del Medio	US$13	25

DESTINATION (IN ORDER OF STOP)	FARE (ESPECIAL)	TRAIN NO.
Matanzas	US$10	11
Santa Clara	US$15	11
Ciego de Ávila	US$22	11
Camagüey	US$27	11
Las Tunas	US$37	11
Cacocum (Holguín)	US$37	11
Santiago de Cuba	US$43	11

DISTANCES FROM HAVANA
All figures represent kilometers.

Baracoa	1,069
Bayamo	842
Camagüey	570
Cárdenas	152
Ciego de Ávila	461
Cienfuegos	336
Guantánamo	971
Holguín	771
Isla de la Juventud	138
Las Tunas	694
Matanzas	101
Pinar del Río	176
Rancho Boyeros	17
Sancti Spíritus	386
Santa Clara	300
Santiago de Cuba	876
Soroa	95
Surgidero de Batabanó	56
Trinidad	454
Varadero	140
Viñales	188

Palcocar, tel. (33) 7235, fax (33) 7250, offers chauffeured excursions to places within a 50-mile radius of Havana. A trip to Varadero costs US$180; to Soroa, US$85; to the Bay of Pigs (Playa Girón), US$320; and to Viñales, US$252. Hourly rates for a chauffeured taxi are on a sliding scale, from US$15 the first hour (20-km limit) to US$80 for eight hours (125-km limit), with US70 cents per km for extra distance.

Freelance Cabs: Don't mind the possibility of breaking down in the boonies? Many Cubans with classic cars from the heyday of Detroit treat their prized possessions as exotic cash cows—they rent them out (mostly illegally) for guided tours. Says Cristina García, "Twenty dollars buys gas enough for a decent spin. Seventy dollars gets you a day in a top-of-the-line Cadillac convertible with fins so big they block the rear-view mirror. Forget about renting from Hertz or Avis ever again."

Your fare is negotiable, so ask around. Agree on the fare *before* getting in. Make sure you know whether this is one-way or roundtrip. Don't be afraid to bargain. You may get a better deal if you speak Spanish and know local customs. The driver will usually be amenable to any request you make. It's possible to hire a car and driver for as little as US$20 for a full day, plus gasoline (a common courtesy is also to buy your driver his or her lunch), but much depends on the quality of the car—and your negotiating skills.

Penny-pinchers might try finding a *colectivo* taxi at Parque de la Fraternidad or near the central railway station, where drivers are used to making long-distance runs to Playas del Este or even Pinar del Río and Viñales. You'll need to negotiate a price—be patient and firm. The days when *colectivo* drivers would take pesos from foreigners are over. With luck, however, you can still find someone who might run you to Playas del Este for as little as US$40-50.

Maquinas, the intercity taxis, are usually big Yankee cars that hang around outside railway and bus terminals. Often they won't depart until they fill up with passengers. Count on traveling about three km per peso.

By Rental Car
For lengthy exploring outside Havana, it's best to rent a car. It grants ease, freedom, and control (there are no restrictions on where you can go), plus you can cover a lot of turf without the time delays of public transport.

You'll want the 714-page *Cuba Handbook* (Avalon Travel Publishing, 1997), which has complete information for exploring Cuba, including comprehensive sections for drivers.

If you intend to explore Cuba far and wide, be sure to obtain a copy of *Guía de Carrateras,* a complete atlas in booklet form for drivers, published by Editorial Limusa, Balderas 95, Mexico DF, CP 06040, tel. (521) 2105, fax (512) 2903. It can be purchased in Cuba from tour desks and souvenir outlets.

To drive in Cuba, you must be 21 years or older and hold either an International Drivers' License (IDL) or a valid national driver's license. You must also have at least one year's driving experience. Traffic drives on the right, as in the US. The speed limit is 100 kph (62 mph) on freeways, 90 kph (56 mph) on highways, 60 kph (37 mph) on rural roads, 50 kph (31 mph) on urban roads, and 40 kph (25 mph) in children's zones. Speed limits are vigorously enforced by an efficient highway patrol. If you receive a traffic fine,

CAR RENTAL LOCATIONS

Cubacar
Main office: Avenida 5ta, e/ B y Miramar; tel. (24) 2718, fax (33) 7233
José Martí International Airport; tel. (33) 5546 (Terminal 2)
Avenida 1ra #16401, Miramar; tel. (24) 2277
Hotel Bellocaribe; tel. (33) 6032
Hotel Chateau Miramar; tel. (24) 0760
Hotel Comodoro; tel. (24) 1706
Hotel La Pradera; tel. (24) 7473
Hotel Meliá Cohiba; tel. (33) 4661
Hotel Meliá Habana; tel. (24) 8500
Hotel Parque Central; tel. (66) 6627
Marina Hemingway; tel. (24) 1707

Fenix
Main office: Calle Cuba #66, Habana Vieja; tel. (63) 9720, fax (66) 9546

Grancar (Autos Clasicos)
Main office: Via Blanca y Palatino, Cerro; tel. (33) 5647, fax (33) 5647

Havanautos
Reservations: tel. (24) 0647
Main office: Avenida 1ra, e/ 2 y 0, Miramar; tel. (23) 9658, fax (24) 0648
José Martí International Airport; tel. (33) 5197 (Terminal 2), tel. (33) 5215 (Terminal 1)
Apartotel Atlántico (Playas del Este); tel. (80) 2946
Calle 462 y 5ta (Playas del Este); tel. (80) 2946
Malecón y 11, Vedado; tel. (33) 4691
Hotel Habana Libre Tryp; tel. (33) 3484
Hotel Nacional; tel. (33) 3192
Hotel Neptuno/Tritón; tel. (24) 2921
Hotel Riviera; tel. (33) 3577
Hotel Sevilla; tel. (33) 8956
Hotel Tropicoco (Playas del Este); tel. (80) 2952
Villa Panamericana (Ciudad Panamericano); tel. (33) 8113

Micar (Cubalse)
Main Office: Calle 13 #562, Vedado; tel. (33) 6725
Calle O #306, Miramar; tel./fax (24) 2444

Panautos
Main office: Calle Linea y Malecón, Vedado; tel. (30) 4763, fax (55) 5657
Servicentro La Copa, Calle 42 esq. 3, Miramar; tel. (22) 7684
José Martí International Airport ; tel. (80) 3921 (Terminal 2)
Avenida Zoológico y 26, Vedado; tel. (66) 6226
Calle 42 esq. 3ra, Miramar; tel. (22) 7684

Rex
Main office: Avenida Rancho Boyeros y Calzada de Bejucal, Boyeros; tel. (33) 9160, fax (33) 9159
Linea y Malecón, Vedado; tel. (33) 7788, fax (33) 7789

Transauto
Main office: Calle 40-A esq. 3ra, Miramar; tel. (24) 5552
José Martí International Airport; tel. (33) 5765 (Terminal 3), tel. (33) 5764 (Terminal 2)
Avenida 3ra y Paseo, Vedado; tel. (33) 5763
Hotel Capri; tel. (33) 4038
Hotel Copacabana; tel. (24) 0621
Hotel Nacional; tel. (33) 5910
Hotel Neptuno/Tritón; tel. (24) 0951
Hotel Riviera ; tel. (33) 3056
Playas del Este; tel. (96) 2917
Villa Panamericano; tel. (33) 8802
Hotel Neptuno; tel. (29) 0881

Via Rent-a-Car
Main office: Edificio La Marina, Avenida del Puerto #102, Habana Vieja; tel. (33) 9781, fax (33) 9159

it will be deducted from the deposit for your rental (there's a space for fines provided on the rental-car papers).

Unfortunately, you can't book Avis or Hertz in Cuba and must make do with the badly managed Cuban car rental agencies. Most tourist hotels have a car rental bureau on site, but the main car rental agencies also have main offices. Demand sometimes exceeds supply, so you may need to hunt around, particularly for the smaller models or a 4WD jeep. You can also rent a car at the airport upon arrival. If you're red or jet-lagged, this is not a good idea: relax ɔr a day or two, then rent your car. The companies accept payment by Visa, MasterCard, Euɔcard, Banamex, Carnet, and JCB, as well as in ɔash and traveler's checks.

Be sure to book a current-year model only. Most Cuban car rental agencies fail to budget for ɔdequate maintenance and let their cars go to ɔuin quickly—often dangerously so! Don't acɔept a car without thoroughly inspecting it, inɔluding a test drive. Insist on this.

Rates: Expect to pay about US$45-100 per ɔay plus insurance, depending on the size of ɔe vehicle. You will normally be required to pay ɔ deposit of US$200-500. Most companies offer ɔ choice of Type A insurance (with a deductible ɔf US$250) or Type B (fully comprehensive, exɔept car radio and one tire). If you plan on doing ɔonsiderable mileage, take the unlimited mileage ɔption. (*Jiniteros* on Calle 23 and La Rampa will ɔffer to alter your odometer to avoid excess ɔileage charge. *¿Kilometraje?*)

Rental Companies: Havanautos, Edificio ɔierra Maestra, Calle 1ra and O, Miramar, tel. ɔ3) 9815, fax (24) 0648 (reservations: tel. (24) ɔ646, website: www.havanautos.cubaweb.cu), ɔffers a range of Japanese cars in all categories, ɔrom a small Daewoo Tico (US$50 per day with ɔnlimited mileage; less for seven days or more, ɔn a sliding scale) to a five-passenger Daewoo ɔeganza for US$77 daily, a Daihatsu Tenios ɔeep for US$70 daily, and a six-passenger Dodge ɔaravan for US$120 daily. "Special Weekend" ɔackage rates are offered, but they don't proɔide any extra savings. Insurance is additionɔl—US$9 per day with US$250 deductible, ɔS$15 with no deductible.

Micar, 1ra y Paseo, Vedado, tel. (55) 2444, ɔax (33) 6476, rents five models of Fiats. The ɔinquecento, Uno, Panda, and Punto are all ɔmall and perfect for nippy commuting in Haɔana or for two people for touring. Rates are ɔS$35-45 daily (with a 100-km limit; US20 cents ɔer extra km) or US$45-55 for unlimited mileage. ɔ larger Fiat Brava costs US$65 or US$77, reɔpectively. Micar has an office at the airport plus ɔhree offices in Havana and one in Boca Ciega in ɔlayas del Este, tel. (96) 2130.

Palcocar, tel. (33) 7235, fax (33) 7250, serves ɔhe convention business and rents Subaru Vivios ɔS$35 daily; US$45 with unlimited mileage)

and Mitsubishi Lancers (US$50 per day; US$65 with unlimited mileage).

Panautos, Linea y Malecón, Vedado, tel. (55) 3286, fax (55) 657, e-mail: panatrans@dpt. transnet.cu, specializes in diesel vehicles and rents seven-seat Mitsubishi jeeps (US$130) and Ssang Yong Musso jeeps (US$95), plus Citroën sedans (US$51-71). Prices include limited mileage. It has several offices in Vedado and Miramar.

Rex Limousine Service, Avenida de Rancho Boyeros and Calzada de Bejucal in Plaza de la Revolución, tel. (33) 9160, fax (33) 9159, and Linea and Malecón in Vedado, tel. (33) 7788, fax (33) 7789, rents Volvo sedans from US$150 per day, US$750 weekly plus insurance (US$25 daily), and Volvo limousines for US$325 daily, US$1,625 weekly, including insurance and chauffeur. Hourly rentals are available.

Via Rent-a-Car, Avenida del Puerto #102, between Obrapía and Justiz, tel. (33) 9781 or (66) 6777, fax (33) 2780, e-mail: dtor_rc@nwgaitov. gav.cm.net, a division of Gaviota, rents Peugeots (US$40-80 daily depending on model for 100 km, then US35 cents per km extra; US$48-92 unlimited mileage); Suzuki jeeps (US$38 daily for 1997 models, US$48 for 1999 models; US$46-60 unlimited mileage); and Ssangyong sedans. Each additional designated driver costs US$10 (US$15 if the driver is Cuban). Chauffeurs cost US$30 daily. It also has offices at the airport, and in the Hotels Bosque, Kohly, Habana Libre Tryp, and Tropicoco (in Playas del Este).

Other car rental agencies include **Cubacar,** Avenida 5ta y 84, Miramar, tel. (24) 2718, fax (33) 7233; **Fenix,** Calle Cuba #66, Habana Vieja, tel. (63) 9720, fax (66) 9546; and **Transauto,** Calle 3ra #2605, e/ 26 y 28, Miramar, tel. (24) 5532, fax (24) 4057.

Fly-Drive Packages: Viajes Horizontes, tel. (33) 4042, fax (33) 4361, e-mail: crh@s1.hor.cma. net, website: www.horizont.cu, part of the Hoteles Horizontes group, offers a "Flexi Fly & Drive" prepurchased package combining car rental and hotel vouchers that offers the freedom to follow your whims. You simply pick up your car at the international airport in Havana and hit the road armed with vouchers good at any of Horizontes' 70-plus hotels islandwide.

Campervans: Yes, campervans have come to Cuba courtesy of an Italian company—**Cuba-**

mar **Campertour,** Via Ghibellina 110, 1-50122 Firenze, Italy, tel. (055) 239-6293, fax (055) 238-2042, e-mail: lucia99@ats.it—working in association with Cubamar and using imported BRIG 670s, which sleep six people. The vehicles are powered by Mercedes turbodiesel engines and contain all the services of a small apartment: bathroom with flush toilet and shower, kitchen with fridge and three-burner stove, wardrobes, and even a security box. No prices had been established at press time.

Guides: You can request a personal guide from any of the Havanatur offices nationwide. Most are familiar with at least two languages. They're also extremely well versed in history. If you want to hire one, contact **Havanatur,** Avenida 5 #8409 e/ 84 y 86, Miramar, Havana, tel. (33) 2433 or (33) 2595, fax (33) 1760.

Countless *jineteros* will offer to be your guide. Few freelance guides are versed in history, etc. A good guide is José "Pepe" Alvarez, a bilingual chap who has been running a personal guide service for 10 years. Contact him at Lazada Norte I #182, Santa Catalina, Havana CP 13400, tel. (41) 1209, fax (33) 3921, e-mail: americacuba@yahoo.com, or visit his website at www.members.aol.com/_ht_a/cubatours.

By Whatever Moves!

Stoics among stoics can travel the Cuban way—hitchhiking. The Special Period has had such a traumatic effect on the transportation system that the populace now relies on anything that moves. In many areas, flatbed trucks have been converted and have basic wooden seats welded to the floor. Often there are no seats, and the local "bus" might be a converted cattle truck or a flatbed pulled by a tractor, with passengers crammed in and standing like cows. If you're hitchhiking, this is for you.

So many Cubans rely on hitching that the state has set up *botellas* (literally bottles, but colloquially used to signify hitchhiking posts) on the edge of towns. Here, officials of the Inspección Estatal, wearing mustard-colored uniforms (and therefore termed *coges amarillas,* or yellow jackets) are in charge. They wave down virtually anything that moves, and all state vehicles—those with red license plates—must stop to pick up hitchers. Many *botellas* even have rain shelters and steps to help you climb into trucks. Early morning is easiest for hitching, when there' more traffic.

A queue system prevails: first come, firs serve. The Cubans will be honored and delight ed by the presence of a foreigner and may ushe you to the front of the line.

Cuba is probably the safest place in the world t hitch. Sticking out your thumb won't do it. Do thing the Cuban way: try to wave down the vehicle—whether it be a tractor, a truck, or a motorcycle. I it moves in Cuba, it's fair game. Open-bed truck are the most common vehicles (no fun if it rains)

If you receive a ride in a private car, polite ness dictates that you offer to pay for your ride *"¿Cuando lo debo?"* after you're safely deliv ered. Even Cubans pay a few coins, and s should you. Expect to be asked for dollars as foreigner.

Botellas are located on all the major arteria highways out of town. Ask around.

Organized Tours and Excursions

This is one area where Cuba runs a top-class op eration. If your time is limited and you like th idea of a smooth-running itinerary, book an ex cursion with one of the national tour agencies Their guides are very good—usually friendly enthusiastic, well educated, and bilingual, al though the spiel is often quite naive. You car book excursions at the tour desk in the lobby o virtually any tourist hotel.

Popular one-day excursions (and typica prices) include to Cayo Coco (US$143), Cayc Largo (US$109), Soroa (US$29), the Valle d Yumurí (US$32), Varadero (US$35), and Vall de Viñales (US$44). Typical overnight trips in clude to Trinidad (US$195) and Viñales (US$79)

Cubanacán Viajes Tour, Calle 146 esq. 9na Playa, tel. (33) 9884, fax (33) 0107, offers a gamu of excursions and tours to destinations throughou Cuba, as well as multidestination excursions to Ja maica, the Dominican Republic, the Cayman Is lands, and Mexico. You can book most excur sions through the tour desk of major hotels.

Gaviota Tours, Avenida 49 esq. 36A, Repar to Kohly, tel. (24) 4781, fax (24) 9470, e-mail gavitour@gaitur.gav.cma.net, acts as a full-ser vice inbound tour operator and travel agency It offers a series of day excursions to Soroa anc Viñales in Pinar del Río, plus Trinidad and Cien fuegos, and Varadero.

The seat of a horse-drawn cab makes a nice vantage point for seeing the sights.

Rumbos S.A., Casa Matriz on Linea and M, tel. (66) 9713 or (24) 9626, offers one-day excursions to Pinar del Río (four hours) and to "dude ranches" near Playas del Este, as well as multiday tours to Viñales, Playa Girón, and Trinidad.

Sol y Son, on La Rampa #64, Vedado, tel. (33) 3162, fax (33) 5150, e-mail: solyson@ce-niai.inf.cu, is the tour operator of Cubana Aviación. It has offices at the airport and in the Hotel Neptuno/Triton, and offers a wide range of one-day and longer excursions.

Havanatur's **Tour & Travel,** Avenida 5ta e/ 84 y 86, Miramar, tel. (24) 9200 or (24) 9199, fax (24) 1547, has a wide range of excursions. It also has offices in the lobbies of leading hotels, plus outside the Hotel Habana Libre Tryp on La Rampa and Calle M, tel. (24) 7541, fax (24) 2074.

Paradiso: Promotora de Viajes Culturales, Calle 19 #560 esq. C, Vedado, tel. (32) 6928, fax (33) 3921, e-mail: paradis@turcult.get.cma, website: www.cult.cu\paradiso\index.html.

Cuba has been slow off the mark to develop ecotourism but is beginning to catch on. **Eco-Tur S.A.,** Avenida 5ra #9802 esq. 98, Playa, tel. (24) 5195, fax (24) 7520, offers a series of eco-oriented tours and excursions. The guides have very little knowledge of ecotourism, however, and the planning and execution of trips is a far cry from those of, say, Costa Rica. **Veracuba,** Casa Matriz, Calle 146 #1002, Miramar, Havana, tel. (33) 6619, fax (33) 6312, has 350 buses. **Transtur,** Avenida de Santa Catalina #360, Vibora, Havana, tel. (41) 3906, (40) 4754,

or (41) 8571, which has been around for more than 30 years, is the biggest transport provider specializing in ground transportation for tourists. **Tropical Travel Agency** offers a full-day guided excursion to Varadero Beach daily (US$27, US$37 with lunch). It has a similar full-day tour to Trinidad, including a visit to Playa Ancón (US$112, including breakfast and dinner). **Viajes Horizontes,** at Calle 21 e/ N y O, tel. (66) 2160, fax (33) 4585, is part of the Hoteles Horizontes chain and was created in 1997 to introduce ecotourism, trekking, bicycling, and more than 20 other types of travel programs. It also acts as a general travel agency for car, hotel, and tour bookings. Open Mon.-Fri. 8:30 a.m.-12:30 p.m. and 1:30-5:30 p.m., Saturday 8:30 a.m.-1 p.m.

Viñales Tours, Calle 1 #2210 between 22 y 24, Miramar, tel. (33) 1051, fax (33) 1054, specializes in tours to Pinar del Río province.

Foreign Pastures: Cuba is actively promoting multidestination travel, combining Cuba with a visit to one or more neighboring countries.

For example, **Havanatur,** Edificio Sierra Maestra, Avenida 1ra e/ 0 y 2, Miramar, tel. (24) 7417, promotes multidestination "Vacation Plus!" packages combining excursions in Cuba with a choice of Cancún, Mérida, Nassau, Jamaica, Costa Rica, Panama, Guatemala, and other destinations served by Cubana Aviación

Italturist, tel./fax (33) 3977 in Havana, tel. (02) 535-4949 and fax (02) 535-4901 in Milan, offers five-day eco-archeological excursions from Havana to Campeche.

GENERAL INFORMATION AND SERVICES

IMMIGRATION AND CUSTOMS

Visas
Tourist Visas: Tourists must enter Cuba on a tourist visa, issued by Cuba-based travel agents such as Havanatur and by non-US-based travel agents at the ticket counter of the airline providing travel to Cuba. In some cases, tourist visas are issued at an airport upon arrival within Cuba. Visas cost US$25, but commercial agencies generally charge US$35.

Your initial tourist visa is good for 30 days only, but you can request a single 30-day extension, or *prórroga* (US$25), from the immigration table to the right of the reception desk in the Hotel Habana Libre Tryp; open Mon.-Fri. 10 a.m.-1 p.m. and 2-3 p.m. Foreigners are limited to a 60-day stay. Extensions can also be obtained at Marina Hemingway for people arriving by private vessel.

Don't list your occupation as journalist, police, military personnel, or government employer, as the Cuban government is highly suspicious of anyone with these occupations. Listing yourself as such can cause problems. "Consultant" is a far safer gambit.

Non-Tourist Visas: Journalists are permitted a 90-day stay and must enter on a journalists' D-6 visa (US$60). These must be obtained in advance from Cuban embassies, and in the US from the Cuban Interests Section, 2630 16th St. NW, Washington, DC 20009, tel. (202) 797-8518, fax (202) 797-8521, e-mail: cubaseccion@igc.apc.com. If you enter on a tourist visa and intend to exercise your profession, you must register for a D-6 visa at the Centro de Prensa Internacional, on La Rampa between N and O, tel. (32) 0526, fax (33) 3836. The Accreditaciones de Prensa Extranjeras (Foreign Journalist's Accreditation) office is to the rear of the *telecorreos* to the right of the entrance. You can have **passport photos** taken at the Photo Service store adjacent to the International Press Center. You can also have photos for visas, passports, etc., taken at **Fotógrafa,** Calle Obispo #515, a tiny hole in the wall open 10 a.m.-4 p.m.

USEFUL TELEPHONE NUMBERS

EMERGENCY

Ambulance, tel. (40) 5093/4
Fire, tel. (81) 1115
Police, tel. (82) 0116

MEDICAL

Clínica Cira García (international clinic),
tel. (24) 0330
Farmácia Internacional (24-hour pharmacy),
tel. (24) 2051

EMBASSIES

Canada, tel. (24) 2516,
emergency tel. (24) 2516
France, tel. (24) 2143
Germany, tel. (33) 2460
Italy, tel. (33) 3378
Spain, tel. (33) 8025
United Kingdom, tel. (24) 1771
United States (Interest Office),
tel. (33) 3551 to (33) 3559

TRANSPORTATION

Cubana de Aviación Reservations (National),
tel. (55) 1022
Cubana de Aviación Reservations
(International), tel. (55) 1046
José Martí International Airport (information),
tel. (45) 3133
Estación Central de Ferrocarril (Central
railway station: information), tel. (57) 2014
Estación Central de Ferrocarril (Central
railway station: Ladis ticket office),
tel. (62) 4259
Estación 19 de Noviembre , tel. (81) 4431
Estación Cristina , tel. (78) 4971
Terminal de Ómnibus Nacionales (bus
terminal: information for Cubans),
tel. (79) 2456
Terminal de Ómnibus Nacionales (bus
terminal: information for foreigners),
tel. (70) 3397
Vía Azul Bus Terminal, tel. (81) 1413
Taxi (inexpensive), tel. (79) 2968
Panataxi, tel. (55) 5555
Taxis-OK, tel. (24) 1446

A commercial visa is required for individuals traveling to Cuba for business. These must also be obtained in advance from Cuban embassies, or the Cuban Interests Section in Washington, D.C. (see above). If you wish to enter using a tourist visa and then, while within Cuba, change your visa status, contact the Ministerio de Relaciones Exteriores (Ministry of Foreign Affairs), Calle Calzada No. 360 e/ G y H, Vedado, tel. (32) 190 or (30) 5031, fax (31) 2314, which handles immigration issues relating to foreigners.

Are US Citizens Welcome? The Cubans have no restrictions on US tourists. On the contrary; they welcome US visitors with open arms. The Cubans are savvy—they stamp your visa, not your passport.

Customs

All hand-carried baggage is X-rayed upon entry. Havana's airport has the international two-zone system: red for items to declare and green for nothing to declare. The Customs regulations are complicated and open to interpretation by individual Customs agents. Visitors to Cuba are permitted 20 kilos of personal effects plus "other articles and equipment depending on their profession," all of which must be re-exported. In addition, up to 10 kilos of medicines, 200 cigarettes, 50 cigars, 250 grams of pipe tobacco, and three liters of wine and alcohol, plus US$50 of additional goods are permitted tax-free. An additional US$200 of "objects and articles for noncommercial use" can be imported, subject to a tax equal to 100 percent of the declared value (you must fill out a Customs form and use the red zone), but this applies mostly to Cubans and returning foreign residents bringing in electrical goods, etc. Most electrical goods are banned, including videocassette recorders. "Obscene and pornographic" literature is also banned (the definition of "obscene" includes politically unacceptable tracts).

The main Customs office is on Avenida San Pedro, opposite the Iglesia San Francisco de Asís; it's upstairs, to the right.

Consulates

Most consulates and embassies are located in Miramar. The **US Interests Section,** the equivalent of an embassy but lacking an ambassador, faces the Malecón at Calzada (Calle 5ta) e/ L y

EMBASSIES AND CONSULATES IN HAVANA

The following nations have embassies/consulates in Havana (additional countries can be found in the local telephone directory under *Embajadas*). Phone numbers and addresses change frequently. Call to confirm address and hours of operation.

Argentina: Calle 36 #511 e/ 5ta y 7ma, Miramar, tel. (24) 2972, fax (24) 2140

Austria: Calle 4 #101 esq. 1ra, Miramar, tel. (24) 2394, fax (24) 1235

Belgium: Avenida 5ta # 7408 esq. 76, Miramar, tel. (24) 2410, fax (24) 1318

Brazil: Calle 16 #503e/ 5ta y 7ma, Miramar, tel. (24) 2139, fax (24) 2328

Canada: Calle 30 #518, esq. 7ma, Miramar, tel. (24) 2516, fax (24) 2044; emergency tel. (24) 2516; e-mail: havan@havan01.x400.gc.ca

Chile: Avenida 33 #1423, Miramar, tel. (24) 1222, fax (24) 1694

China, People's Republic of: Calle C #317 e/ 13 and 15, Vedado, tel. (33) 3005, fax (33) 3092

Colombia: Calle 14 #515 e/ 5ta y 7ma, Miramar, tel. (24) 1246, fax (24) 1249

Costa Rica: Calle 46 #306, Miramar, tel. (24) 6937

Czech Republic: Avenida Kohly #259, Nuevo Vedado, tel. (33) 3467, fax (33) 3596

Denmark: Paseo de Martí #20, Habana Vieja, tel. (33) 8128, fax (33) 8127

Ecuador: Avenida 5ta #4407 e/ 44 y 46, Miramar, tel. (24) 2034, fax (24) 2868

Finland: Calle 140 #3121 e/ 21 y 23, Miramar, tel./fax (24) 0793

France: Calle 14 #312 e/ 3ra y 5ta, Miramar, tel. (24) 2143, fax (24) 2317

Germany: Calle 13 #652, Vedado, tel. (33) 2460, fax (33) 1586

Greece: Avenida 5ta #7802 esq. 78, Miramar, tel. (24) 2995, fax (24) 1784

Hungary: Calle G #458, Vedado, tel. (33) 3365, fax (33) 3286

India: Calle 21 #202 esq. K, Vedado, tel. (33) 3169, fax (33) 3287

Italy: Paseo #606 e/ 25 y 27, Vedado, tel. (33) 3378; e-mail: ambitcub@ceniai.inf.cu

Jamaica: Avenida 5ta #3608 e/ 36 y 36A, Miramar, tel. (24) 2908

Japan: Calle N #62 esq. 15, Vedado, tel. (33) 3454, fax (33) 3172

Mexico: Calle 12 #518 e/ 5ta y 7ma, Miramar, tel. (24) 2909, fax (24) 2719

Netherlands: Calle 8 #307, e/ 5ta y 7ma, Miramar, tel. (24) 2511, fax (24) 2059

Nicaragua: Calle 20 #709, Miramar, tel. (24) 1025, fax (24) 6323

Norway: Paseo de Martí #20, Habana Vieja, tel. (33) 8128, fax (33) 8127

Panama: Calle 26 #109, Miramar, tel. (24) 1673, fax (24) 1674

Peru: Calle 36 #109 e/ 1ra y 3ra, Miramar, tel. (24) 2474, fax (24) 2636

Poland: Avenida 5ta #4407, Miramar, tel./fax (24) 1323

Portugal: Avenida 5ta #6604 e/ 66 y 68, Miramar, tel. (24) 2871, fax (24) 2593

Romania: Calle 21 #307, Vedado, tel. (33) 3325, fax (33) 3324

Russia: Avenida 5ta #6402 e/ 62 y 66, Miramar, tel. (24) 1749, fax (24) 1074

Spain: Calle Cárcel #51 esq. Agramonte (Zulueta), Habana Viejo, tel. (33) 8025, fax (33) 8006

Sweden: Avenida 31A #1411 e/ 14 y 18, Miramar, tel. (24) 2563, fax (24) 1194

Switzerland: Avenida 5ta #2005 e/ 20 y 22, Miramar, tel. (24) 2611, fax (24) 1148

Turkey: Calle 20 #301, Miramar, tel. (24) 2933, fax (24) 2899

Ukraine: Avenida 5ta #4405, Miramar, tel. (24) 2586, fax (24) 2341

United Kingdom: Calle 34 #708, Miramar, tel. (24) 1771, (24) 1049, fax (24) 1772

United States: (Interest Office) Calzada e/ L y M, Vedado, tel. (33) 3551 to (33) 3559, fax (33) 3700

Uruguay: Calle 14 #506 e/ 5ta y 7ma, Miramar, tel. (24) 2311, fax (24) 2246

Venezuela: Calle 36A #704 e/ 7ma y 42, Miramar, tel. (24) 2662, fax (24) 2773

Vietnam: Avenida 5ta #1802, Miramar, tel. (24) 1042, fax (24) 1041

Yugoslavia: Calle 42 #115, Miramar, tel. (24) 2982, fax (24) 2982

Zimbabwe: Avenida 3ra #1001, Miramar, tel. (24) 2137, fax (24) 2720

1 in Vedado, tel. (33) 3551 to (33) 3559, fax 3) 3700.

The **Canadian Embassy** is open weekdays 30 a.m.-5 p.m. except Wednesday, 8:30 a.m.- p.m.

xiting Cuba

ravelers exiting Cuba are charged US$20 de- arture tax on international flights. No charge pplies for travelers leaving by private boat. uba prohibits the export of valuable antiques nd art without a license, as well (ostensibly) as ndangered wildlife products.

You may not export more than US$5,000 in ash.

MONEY

urrency

ollars: In a word, Cuba wants *dollars! dollars! ollars!* All prices in this book are quoted in US ollars unless otherwise indicated.

Take as much as you want—there is no limit to e amount of convertible currency you can bring to Cuba (however, Cuba does not permit more an US$5,000 to be exported; an exception is if ou're bringing in more than that amount and nticipate leaving with more than US$5,000, in hich case you must declare it). All hotels, car ental agencies, resort facilities, restaurants, and her places dealing with international tourists ccept *only* foreign currency, notably US dol- rs (sometimes called *moneda efectiva* or *di- isa,* and colloquially known as *fula, guano, uaniquiqi, varo,* and *verde*). Most European rrencies are also accepted in a pinch, as are exican pesos and Canadian dollars, but having S dollars will make life considerably easier.

You can exchange your foreign currency for e necessary US dollars at banks or hotel cash esks (arriving, you can change money at the osé Martí International Airport). Note that Cuban anks buy foreign currency in exchange for US ollars, not for pesos.

Watch out! A large quantity of counterfeit S$100 bills are in circulation (printed in Colom- a, apparently), and Cubans are wary of these. ou'll usually have to supply your passport num- er or other ID number, which will be recorded hen paying with a US$100 bill (and sometimes with a US$50 bill). You'll usually be able to change a US$100 bill, even if someone has to make the rounds to find someone to break it down. Nonetheless, it's always best to have plenty of small bills, especially for the boonies. Supposedly, only post-1962 bills are now legal tender, but you'll find greenbacks going back to the 1930s still circulating.

Cuban Currency: The Cuban currency is the peso, which is designated *$* and should not be confused with the US *$* (to make matters worse, the dollar is sometimes colloquially called the peso). Cuban currency is often called *moneda nacional* (national money). Bills are issued in denominations of one (olive), three (red), five (green), 10 (brown), 20 (blue), and 50 (purple) pesos; a one-peso coin is also issued. The peso is divided into 100 *centavos,* issued in coin de- nominations of one, two, five, 10, and 20 cen- tavos (which is also called a peseta).

Very few state-run entities will accept pesos from foreigners. In reality, there is very little that most foreigners will need pesos for. Exceptions are if you want to travel on local trains and buses, and hang out at local bars and restaurants not normally frequented by tourists, or buy *refres- coes, batidos,* or other snacks on the street, and of course, for ice cream at Coppelia Park. Oth- erwise, spending pesos in Havana is nigh im- possible.

The Cuban peso is not traded on internation- al markets as a convertible currency. Nonethe- less, the Cuban government likes to pretend that its value is at parity with the US dollar. How- ever, the *unofficial* exchange rate—the black market rate—is used by almost everyone (in- cluding the government) to set the peso's true value, and that of goods and services. When possession and spending of dollars was legal- ized for Cubans in 1993, the value of the peso plunged to 150 to the dollar (by August 1995) before climbing back to 25 to one. The rate has remained relatively stable ever since and, in May 1999, stood at 21 pesos to one US dollar (it trades at about 10% higher outside Havana, however).

Exchanging Dollars for Pesos: Legally, for- eign currency can be changed for pesos only at an official *buro de cambio* (exchange bureau) operated by **Cadeca S.A.** (an acronym for *casa de cambio*). Cadeca operates exchange booths at key points throughout Havana. Notable for tourists are those on the north side of Plaza de San Francisco in Habana Vieja, tel. (66) 9628, open Mon.-Sat. 8 a.m.-7 p.m., Sunday 8 a.m.-1 p.m.; at Calle Obispo #360, next to the Infotur office, in Habana Vieja; and catercorner to the Hotel Habana Libre Tryp, outside the entrance to Coppelia, in Vedado—perfect for paying for Coppelia ice cream. Most are aimed at culling dollars from the local economy, rather than from tourists. Nonetheless, foreigners can exchange dollars for pesos here (you *cannot* change any unused pesos into dollars, however, even at the airport upon departure). Exchange only small amounts of dollars for pesos as pocket change for local buses, etc. And spend all your local currency before leaving.

The creation of Cadeca has taken the wind out of the sails of *jiniteros* who change cash illegally on the streets (and face heavy fines if caught). You'll be offered about the same deal as Cadeca offers. They're the guys making a strange "hands-on-the-steering-wheel-running-a-chicane" motion. If you change money illegally, be cautious of scams. Many tourists are ripped off during the deal, so due caution is urged. Even muggings have been reported. A few ripoff artists work as pairs. Always count your pesos before handing over your US dollars; otherwise, you could find yourself holding a bunch of newspaper clippings wrapped inside a wad of real notes. *It ain't worth it!*

Tourist Currency: Although they're now being taken out of circulation, you may occasionally be given rainbow-colored notes and flimsy coins that look like Monopoly money. They're called *pesos convertibles* (convertible pesos), or "B Certificates," and the flimsy coins are stamped "INTUR," valid in lieu of dollars for all transactions. This currency is widely accepted. Bills are issued in the following denominations: one, two, five, 10, 20, 50, and 100 pesos, on a par with US dollar denominations. You can use them as you would US dollar bills and can exchange them for hard currency at the airport on the day of departure.

Banks

The most important of the relatively few banks in Havana catering to foreigners is the autonomous, state-run **Banco Financiero Inter-nacional,** which offers a full range of banking services, including currency exchange services at free-market rates. The branches are all open Mon.-Sat. 8 a.m.-3 p.m., but 8 a.m.-noon only on the last working day of each month. Its main outlet is in the Hotel Habana Libre Tryp in Vedado, tel. (33) 4011, at the end of the corridor past the airline offices. This branch has a special cashiers" desk handling traveler's checks and credit card advances (Mon.-Sat. 9 a.m.-7 p.m., Sunday 9 a.m.-2 p.m.).

Other BFI branches are located at Calle Brasil and Oficios, Habana Vieja; Linea (Avenida 7ra) #1 and O, Vedado, tel. (33) 3003 or (33) 3148, fax (33) 3006; and in the forecourt of the Edificio Sierra Maestra, Avenida 1ra y 0, Miramar.

The state-controlled **Banco de Crédito y Comercio** (formerly the Banco Nacional de Cuba) is the main commercial bank with numerous outlets citywide. In Vedado, the branch at Calle M and Linea has a foreign-exchange desk (open Mon.-Fri. 8:30 a.m.-1 p.m.), as does the branch at the base of La Rampa, immediately west of the Malecón (open Mon.-Fri. 8:30 a.m.-3 p.m.).

The **Banco Internacional de Comercio** Avenida 20 de Mayo and Ayestarán, Habana 6, tel. (33) 5115, fax (33) 5112, open Mon.-Fri. 8 a.m.-1 p.m., caters primarily to foreign businesses, as does the Dutch-owned **Netherlands Caribbean Banking,** Avenida 5ta #6407 esq 76, Miramar, tel. (24) 0419, fax (24) 0472, open Mon.-Fri. 8 a.m.-5 p.m.

Credit Cards

Most hotels, car rental companies, and travel suppliers, as well as larger restaurants, will accept credit card payments as long as the cards are not issued by US banks (blame Uncle Sam; the US Treasury Department forbids US banks to process transactions involving Cuba). The following credit cards are honored: Access, Banamex, Bancomer, Carnet, Diners Club International, JCB, MasterCard, and VISA International

You can use your non-US credit card to obtain a cash advance up to US$5,000 (US$100 minimum) at the **Banco Financiero Internacional** in the Hotel Habana Libre Tryp in Vedado.

US citizens must travel on a cash-only basis However, in 1999, the **Bank of Nova Scotia** near the Hotel Ambos Mundos, in Habana Vieja began giving cash advances against *US-issued*

MasterCards (but not Visa). If you have a foreign bank account, you can try to obtain a credit card, which you can then use without restraint (aside from your credit limit). You'll still be breaking US laws, but the Cubans make no distinctions.

Don't rely entirely on credit cards, however, because often you may find that no vouchers are available to process transactions.

Traveler's Checks

Traveler's checks (unless issued by US banks) are accepted in most tourist restaurant and hotels, and in some foreign-goods stores, although with more hesitancy than credit cards. Traveler's checks can also be cashed at most hotel cashier desks, as well as at banks. They can be in any foreign currency, but non-US dollar denominations can cause problems. Thomas Cook traveler's checks are best. In past years, travelers could ostensibly get American Express traveler's checks cashed through **Asistur** offices. Just before press time, a reader reported that American Express traveler's checks were now being accepted at Cuban banks.

You should *not* enter the date or the place when signing your checks—a Cuban requirement.

Money Transfers

In June 1999, President Clinton granted permission for **Western Union,** tel. (800) 325-6000, website: www.westernunion.com, to handle wire transfers to Cuba, permitting anyone in the US to send up to US$300 every three months, but not to Cuban officials or government entities. Western Union's old office in Havana (still closed at press time) was at Calle Obispo #35.

Citizens of other countries can arrange a "wire transfer" through the Banco Financiero Internacional (see above). You'll need to telex your home bank. It's a good idea to carry full details of your home account with you in Cuba, including your bank's telex number. The process can take many days. **DHL** reputedly is trustworthy for sending money in the form of traveler's checks.

Quickcash, e-mail: paymaster@careebe-cons.com, website: quickcash.careebecons.com, lets you make money transfers from your Visa or MasterCard account online through the Internet. Deliveries are made in US dollar cash (or the currency of your choosing) in one to five days through banks in Havana, although the pro-cessing is via the Canadian banking system, and transfers are settled on your account in Canadian dollars. Each transaction is limited to a maximum of CAN$450, but you can make as many transactions as you wish. A posting on Cuba's own web page—www.cubaweb.cu—also lists information. (Additional online information is also available at www.duales.com.)

In Canada, **Antilles Express,** 9632 Charlton Ave., Montreal, PQ H2B 2C5, tel. (514) 385-9449, can also forward money to Havana in five days (longer elsewhere in Cuba) for a hefty commission.

In case of an emergency, you can also arrange money transfers or even a cash advance through **Asistur.**

Costs

The Cuban government—which enjoys a virtual monopoly on services—is guilty of gouging and in danger of overpricing itself in its greed to cull dollars at every turn. Without competition to regulate the market, the state has jacked up prices in recent years to ridiculous levels. Hotels and restaurants are, on average, at least 50% more expensive than they deserve to be, and often much more.

Still, Havana can be as expensive or inexpensive as you wish, depending on how you travel. If you get around on public transport, rent rooms with Cuban families, dine on the street at *paladares* and peso snack bars, and keep your entertainment to nontouristy venues, then the truly impecunious may be able to survive on as little as US$40 a day, with your room taking the lion's share. However, by being so frugal, you'll have to rough it and be prepared for a basic food regimen. If you want at least a modicum of comforts, then budget *at least* US$60 a day.

Accommodation in Havana costs US$25-200 per night. Meals average US$5-15 with a beer; although lunch or dinner at a *good* restaurant will usually cost upward of US$20 and can easily run to US$50 per person. Entrance to a cabaret or disco will cost US$5-25, plus drinks (a visit to Tropicana will set you back a minimum US$50). Day tours featuring sightseeing and meals average US$35-50. Taxis average about US$1.50 per mile.

Be prepared, too, for lots of extra expenses for minor services that are provided free of charge in North America and most European nations.

If you plan on touring, take enough cash to leave deposits for a rental car. Don't forget: if you run out of money, you may have difficulty getting more money forwarded quickly and easily. Bring items you think you'll need; you don't want to start shelling out for toiletries and the like. And don't forget that you'll want to buy some Cuban cigars, souvenirs, and artwork.

Discounts
Cuba is not in the business of offering discounts. Quite the opposite. However, **Interchange** (also known as Havanatur UK), Interchange House, 27 Stafford Rd., Croydon, Surrey, England RO 4NG, tel. (181) 681-3613, fax (181) 760-0031, offers a **Discount Card** good for a 10% discount on all optional tours, excursions, and meals at selected restaurants in Havana and elsewhere. Keep your eyes peeled while in Cuba for any similar cards.

COMMUNICATIONS

The **Ministry of Communications,** Avenida de Independencia and 19 de Mayo, Plaza de la Revolución, tel. (79) 8653, controls all communications, including mail, telephone, and online services (open Mon.-Fri. 8 a.m.-5 p.m.).

Postal Service
Correos de Cuba operates the Cuban postal service. There are *correos* (post offices) throughout Havana. However, Cuba's mail system is terminally slow, and delivery is never guaranteed (much mail is censored or for other reasons disappears en route; *never* send cash). Most mail in Havana is delivered to a street address. Virtually no one rents a mailbox.

International airmail (*correo aereo*) averages about one month each way (to save time, savvy Cubans usually hand their letters to foreigners to mail outside Cuba). Don't even think about sea-mail! When mailing from Cuba, it helps to write the country destination in Spanish: England is *Inglaterra* (use this for Wales and Scotland also, on the line below either country); France is *Francia;* Italy is *Italia;* Germany is *Alemania;* Spain is *España;* Switzerland is *Suiza;* and the US is *Estados Unidos*.

Most major tourist hotels have small post offices and philatelic bureaus, and will accept your mail for delivery. Havana is also well served by post offices, which are relatively efficient (to buy stamps, go to the *Sellos* counter; you'll need pesos). If you use those in residential districts, expect a long wait in line. Far quicker is to use the small post office inside the lobby of the Hotel Habana Libre Tryp in Vedado (open 24 hours). In Habana Vieja, try the post office on the northeast corner of the Plaza de la Catedral; the one on the west side of Plaza de San Francisco; the one at 518 Calle Obispo, tel. (63) 2560, open daily 9 a.m.-7 p.m. the one next to the Gran Teatro on Parque Central; or the one on the north side of the railway station on Avenida de Bélgica.

Most post offices are open weekdays 10 a.m.- 5 p.m. and Saturday 8 a.m.-3 p.m. You can send a fax, telex, or telegram at most post offices.

Rates: Within Cuba, rates are incredibly low letters cost from 15 centavos (20 grams or less) to 2.05 pesos (up to 500 grams); postcards cost 10 *centavos.* An international postcard costs US50 cents to all destinations; letters cost US75 cents.

Parcels: The Ministerio de Comunicaciones requires that parcels to be mailed from Cuba should be delivered to the post office *unwrapped* for inspection. It is far better to send packages through an express courier service. If mailing to the US, remember that Uncle Sam is ever-vigilant for parcels from Cuba. Don't try mailing Uncle Fred a box of Cohibas for Christmas. They'll go up in smoke all right—on the US Customs 24-hour funeral pyre!

Receiving Mail: Getting incoming mail is time consuming. You can receive mail in Havana by having letters and parcels addressed to you using your name as it appears on your passport or other ID for general delivery to: "c/o Espera [your name] Ministerio de Comunicaciones, Avenida Independencia y 19 de Mayo, Habana 6, Cuba." To collect mail *poste restante,* go to the **Ministry of Communications,** tel. (81) 8008 or (7)-4461, or

ie northeast corner of the Plaza de la Revolu-
ón. The names of people who have received
ail are posted. Keep incoming mail simple—
arcels are less likely to make it. It may be more
fficient to have incoming mail addressed "Es-
era" [your name] at your hotel or embassy.

**Express Mail Services: DHL Worldwide
xpress** is headquartered at Avenida 1ra y Calle
6, Miramar, tel. (24) 1578 or (24) 1876, fax (24)
999, open weekdays 8 a.m.-8 p.m., Saturday 8
.m.-4 p.m. DHL operates other offices—in the
lotel Yagrumas, tel. (650) 4460; at Calle 40
nd Avenida 1; and in the Hotel Habana Libre
ryp. DHL acts as Customs broker and offers
aily door-to-door pickup and delivery service
t no extra charge. It guarantees delivery in Ha-
ana in less than 24 hours. It offers four options:
xpress, for sending documents with no comercial value; International, for documents to
nywhere in the world; International Packages,
r commercial samples; and National (still in its
romotional stage), for sending documents and
ackages between towns throughout Cuba.

An express document to Canada, Mexico, or
e US costs US$20; to anywhere else, US$25.
one-kilo document package costs US$47 (or
JS$57); a five-kilo package costs US$111 (or
JS$121). Rates are slightly higher for commer-
ial packages. The minimum cost to send to
Cuba by DHL is US$60. Within Cuba, docu-
nents up to three kilos cost US$4 within Ha-
ana, and US50 cents more for each additional
ilo. (A similar package to Pinar del Río, Matan-
as, Villa Clara, or Cienfuegos province costs
JS$6; to Sancti Spíritus, Ciego de Ávila, Cam-
güey, Isla de la Juventud, or Cayo Largo, US$8;
nd to the provinces of Oriente, US$10.)

Cubapost, Calle 21 #10099, e/ 10 y 12, Veda-
lo, tel. (33) 0485, fax (33) 6097, offers an in-
ernational express mail service (EMS) to virtually
very country in the world except the US. Rates
egin at US$27 (0.5 kg) to Canada and Mexico,
nd US$34 for the rest of the world. Service
vithin Havana costs US$4 for the first five kg,
nd delivery is guaranteed within 24 hours. Do-
nestic service within Cuba costs US$5-9 (up to
ve kg) according to zone. Open Mon.-Fri. 8
.m.-5 p.m., Saturday 8 a.m.-noon.

Cubapacks, Calle 22 #4115, Miramar, tel. (24)
134 or (33) 2817, fax (24) 2226 (open Mon.-Fri.
:30 a.m.-noon and 1:30-5:30 p.m.), and **Cuba**

Express, Avenida 5ta #8210, e/ 82 y 84, Miramar,
tel. (24) 2331, fax (24) 2584 (open Mon.-Fri. 8
a.m.-5 p.m.), also offer express mail services.

US Restrictions: Uncle Sam restricts what
may be mailed to Cuba from the US. Letters
and literature can be mailed without restriction.
Gift parcels can be "sent or carried by an authorized traveler" to an individual or religious or
educational organization if the domestic retail
value does not exceed US$200. Only one parcel
per month is allowed. And contents are limited to
food, vitamins, seeds, medicines, medical supplies, clothing, personal hygiene items, and a
few other categories. All other parcels are subject
to seizure! Don't think you can skirt around this
by sending by DHL. Your package will either be
returned or seized.

Telephone Service

Cuba's telephone system is the responsibility
of the Empresa de Telecomunicaciones de Cuba
(ETECSA), headquartered in the Lonja del Comercio, Plaza de San Francisco, Habana Vieja.
ETECSA, set up in 1992, is a joint venture with
the Italian telecommunications company, ILTE,
and has the awesome task of upgrading Cuba's
inept and derelict phone system. Much of the
telephone network predates the Revolution (the
AT&T system, installed long before the Revolution, was replaced in the 1960s by "fraternal
Hungarian equipment"—Castro's words—and
it was downhill from there). Fortunately, ETECSA
has begun modernizing the phone system and
plans to replace Havana's analog system with a
digital system, and a fiber-optic network is being
installed. But they have a long way to go.

Telephone service has never been good, and
unless you're making a call from a modern international hotel, calling can be a wearying experience. Phones in international hotels and
centros telefónicos tend to be modern and up
to par; private phones, and those in most state-
run enterprises, are usually antiques and perform like something from a Hitchcock movie.
Getting a dial tone is the first obstacle. You may
get a busy signal (though this does not necessarily mean that the line is engaged) or a series
of squeaks and squawks. You just have to keep
trying. A telephone line that is working one
minute may simply go dead the next. Some days
are better than others.

Cubans usually answer the phone by saying either *"¡Oigo!"* (I'm listening!) or *"¡Dígame!"* (Speak to me!). It sounds abrupt, but they're not being rude.

Public Phone Booths: ETECSA operates modern, efficient, glass-enclosed telephone kiosks called *centros telefónicos* (*telecorreos* where they combine postal services) throughout the city. They utilize phone cards as well as coins. These telephone bureaus do not accept collect or incoming calls.

Key ETECSA kiosks in Habana Vieja are on the ground floor of La Lonja del Comercio, on Plaza de San Francisco; in Vedado at the base of La Rampa (Calle 23), on the north side of the street at P; at the top of La Rampa, facing Coppelia between K y L; in the Centro de Prensa Internacional, tel. (33) 0526/27/28, on La Rampa and Calle O; and outside the Hotel Melía Cohiba at the foot of Paseo.

There is also no shortage of stand-alone public phones throughout the city. Avoid these if possible; they tend to be on noisy street corners. Some are modern and take phonecards. Others are older and can only be used for local calls; they take five-centavo coins. When you hear the "time-up" signal (a short *blip*), you must *immediately* put in another coin to avoid being cut off. Newer public phones also take 20-centavo coins and can be used for long-distance calls (you get any change back when you hang up).

International Calls: When calling Cuba from abroad, dial 011 (the international dialing code), then 53 (the Cuba country code), followed by 7 (Havana's city code) and the number. For direct outbound international calls from Cuba, dial 119, then the country code (for example, 44 for the UK), followed by the area code and number. For the international operator, dial 0, wait 30 seconds for the tone, then dial 9. For operator-assisted calls from Havana to the US, dial 66-1212. (Using a Cuban telephone operator can be a Kafkaesque experience, as many do not speak English. In the US, AT&T has a "language line" that will connect you with an interpreter, tel. (800) 843-8420; US$3.50 per minute.)

Some of the large, upscale tourist hotels now have direct-dial telephones in guest rooms for international calls. Others will connect you via the hotel operator. Or you can call from ETECSA's *centros telefónicos*. The main international telephone exchange is in Vedado in the lobby of the Hotel Habana Libre Tryp; a receptionist links you with the international operator (it can take forever, so leave plenty of time).

Calls are charged per minute: US$2.45 to the United States and Canada, US$3.40 to Central America and Caribbean countries, US$4.45 to South America, and US$5.85 to Europe and the rest of the world. Operator-assisted calls cost more.

Domestic Calls: For local calls in Havana, simply dial the number you wish to reach. To dial a number outside Havana, dial 0, wait for a tone, then dial the local city code and the number you wish to reach. For the local operator, dial 0, wait for a tone, then dial 0. Rates range from 30 centavos to three pesos and 15 centavos for the first three minutes, depending on zone (tourist hotels and ETECSA booths charge in US dollar equivalent).

Prepaid Phonecards: All ETECSA *telecorreos* and an increasing number of streetside public phones take prepaid phonecards (you insert the card into the phone and it automatically deducts from the value of the card according to period of time of your conversation). You can buy phonecards at tourist hotels, ETECSA outlets, certain restaurants, and several dozen other outlets listed in the telephone directory, as well as from **Intertel**, Calle 33 #1427 e/ 14 y 18, Miramar, Havana, tel. (33) 2476, fax (33) 2504. Cards can be bought in denominations of US$10, US$25 or $US45. They can be used for domestic and international calls. You'll be able to see the diminishing value of the card displayed during your call (if it expires, you can replace it with a new one without interrupting your call by pushing button C and inserting a new card).

Cellular Phones: Cubacel (a joint agreement between Mexico's TIMSA and Emtelcuba) provides cellular phone service. Its main office is at Calle 28 #510, e/ 5 y 7, Miramar, tel. (33) 2222, fax (80) 0000 or (33) 1737, website www.cubacel.com; open Mon.-Fri. 8 a.m.-5 p.m., Saturday 8 a.m.-noon. It also has an office at José Martí International Airport, tel. (80) 0043, fax (80) 0400 (Terminal 2), and tel. (80) 0222, fax (80) 0445 (Terminal 3).

Cubacel rents cellular phones for US$7 daily (plus a US$3 one-time activation fee). You also have to pay a US$410 security deposit, plus

S$100 per day deposit for use. Air time costs S90 cents per minute in addition to relevant ng-distance charges. Long-term service costs S$40 monthly (plus US$120 activation and S30-40 cents per minute air time). Cubacel ells cellular phones at outrageous markup. Far etter is to bring your own cellular phone into he country; Cubacel will activate it and provide ou with a local line for US$12.

Telephone Directories: ETECSA publishes our comprehensive regional directories, including "Ciudad de la Habana," which can be obtained (US$10) from ETECSA headquarters in he Lonja del Comercio. A national directory osts US$25.

Unfortunately, telephone numbers in Havana hange with dizzying regularity as ETECSA tries o rationalize the old system. Even the 1998 elephone directory was out-of-date at press me, when the 1999 directory had not yet been rinted. Trying to determine a correct number an be problematic because many entities have everal numbers and rarely publish the same umber twice. For example, you may receive a ecorded message saying the number doesn't xist ("*Este numero no existe por ningún o ada*"), but keep trying.

The hotel switchboards can be helpful in finding telephone numbers, but it often requires time nd patience. Call 113 for directory inquiries.

Telex, Fax, and Telegram

Telex and Fax: You can send telexes and faxes rom most tourist hotels, usually for a fee slightly more than the comparable telephone charge. You can also transmit from most *telecorreos,* notably the main international telephone center n the Hotel Habana Libre Tryp. You can also send faxes or make a telex at the **Centro de Prensa Internacional** (International Press Center), on La Rampa and Calle O, Vedado, tel. 32) 0526/27/28; open 8:30 a.m.-5 p.m. A fax costs US$6.50 minimum plus $1 per minute to he US and Canada.

Telegrams: ETECSA offers 24-hour "telegram by telephone" service by calling (81) 8844 or going through its *telecorreo* offices. International telegraphic service is charged per word: 75 centavos to North America, 80 to Europe, 85 to he rest of world. Domestic rates are posted in *elecorreos.* In Havana, telegrams may also be

sent from **Cuba Transatlantic Radio Corporation (RCA),** Calle Obispo y Aguiar.

Online Service in Cuba

Cuba is amazingly advanced in its application of online services, and most state entities now have websites and e-mail connections. However, computer communications are tightly controlled by the government, and access for the average citizen is severely restricted. In any event, few individuals have access to a computer or modem.

You can send and receive e-mails at the **Infotur** office at Avenida 5ra and 112 in Miramar, tel. (24) 7036, fax (24) 3977, e-mail: infomire@ teleda.get.cma.net (US$1 per message). Similar service was to be extended to the other Infotur offices by 2000.

Most upscale tourist hotels now have business centers with online access for guests. A few, such as the Hotel Parque Central, also feature modem outlets in guest rooms. Tourists are permitted to bring laptop computers, which must be declared and may not be left behind in Cuba.

There are numerous computer clubs and formal classes in computer technology in Cuba, centered in the **Palacio Central de Computación y Electrónica,** tel. (63) 3349 or (61) 7555, in the old Sears building on 'Calle Reina No. 2 at Calle Amistad in Centro Havana, which also houses the popular e-mail network, *tinored.* The administrative contact is Pedro Espineira: peter%tinored@apc.org.

Foreign Newspapers and Magazines

Cuba imposes its own blockade—on information. No foreign radio or TV station is permitted to sully the airwaves. Foreign magazines of whatever shade are sold only in tourist hotel lobbies. Their availability is hit and miss. For example, in spring 1999 (during the Kosovo crisis, when Cuba's media were having a field day reporting on NATO's atrocities while portraying Slobodan Milosevic as a hero), there were *no* foreign newspapers for sale. But sometimes you can find a small selection of leading international newspapers and magazines (including *Newsweek, Time, USA Today, New York Times, Le Figaro,* and *Der Spiegel,* plus carefully selected consumer magazines such as *Scuba Times* and *Cigar Aficionado*). Most Cuban bookstores carry only a meager stock of foreign literature and other books.

A good source in Vedado is the **Hotel Victoria,** which caters mostly to a business clientele. Expect to pay up to three times what you'd pay at home.

Most foreign publications are distributed in Cuba through **World Services Publications,** Calle 33 #2003, e/ 20 y 22, Miramar, tel. (24) 3002, fax (24) 3066, which can steer you in the right direction.

Cuban Publications

The most important publication, and virtually the sole mouthpiece of international news, is *Granma,* the cheaply produced, badly inked official Communist Party propaganda piece published daily. It focuses heavily on profiling a daily succession of victories in the building of socialism; "lingo sludge" and "a degradation of the act of reading" are among the accusations hurled at it. It's essential reading if you want to get the Cuban take on international events (some of the unsigned editorials are written by Castro, whose colorful style, highlighted with subtle invective, is unmistakable), but its triumphalist tone is often a bit Alice-in-Wonderlandish, often inspired by *Granma's* determination to denigrate the US at every turn. Its international reporting, for example, makes heroes out of Yugoslavia's Slobodan Milosevic and Iraq's Saddam Hussein on the premise that the enemy of my enemy is my friend. A weekly edition is also published in Spanish, English, and French. You'll find it in the glove pocket of Cubana Airlines' flights, plus many hotel gift stores and at the editorial offices, at Avenida General Suárez y Calle Territorial, Plaza de la Revolución, Havana, tel. (81) 6265 or (70) 6521, fax (33) 5176, e-mail granmai@tinored.cu, website: www.cubaweb.cu/granma. You can buy *Granma* at streetside kiosks, but they rapidly run out (many Cubans make some extra money by reselling their newspapers once the last issue runs out; others—seriously—stand in line to take *Granma* home to use as toilet paper).

Juventud Rebelde, General Suárez e/ Ayesteran y Territorial, tel. (6) 9876, is the evening paper of the Communist Youth League. It echoes *Granma,* being little more than a propagandist piece delighting in pointing out Uncle Sam's faults. (The Communist Party also publishes the monthly *El Militante Communista.*). *Opciones* is a weekly serving the business, commercial, and tourist sectors, aimed at foreign businesspeople in Cuba.

Similar mouthpieces include the daily *Tribuna de la Habana; Trabajadores,* the newspaper of the trades unions; *Mujeres,* Av. Rancho Boyeros y San Pedro, Havana, tel. (70) 1000, a monthly magazine for women; and *Contactos,* published bimonthly by the Chamber of Commerce.

Cuba also produces some excellent magazines focusing on the arts and culture, such as *Habanera,* a monthly magazine about Havana, and *Prisma,* an English-language, bimonthly magazine covering politics, economics, travel, and general subjects on Cuba and the Americas published by Prensa Latina. In a similar vein is the weekly magazine *Bohemia,* while *Tropicana Internacional* is a bimonthly covering the Cuban music scene, *Mar y Pesca* is a monthly magazine on maritime issues, including watersports. And the Casa de las Américas publishes a splendid eponymous bimonthly about the arts (in Spanish only), as well as the *Conjunto: Revista de Teatro Latinamericano.*

Radio and Television

The state-owned **Instituto Cubano de Radio y Televisión,** tel. (32) 9544, controls all broadcast media. There are two national TV networks—**Canal 6: Cubavision** and **Canal 2: Tele Rebelde**—and one provincial station (in Oriente). Virtually every home has a TV, and Cubans are addicted to television, especially Brazilian *telenovelas* (soap operas).

Although illegal, a few jerrybuilt satellite dishes festoon Havana's rooftops, picking up CNN, the Discovery Channel, and other US stations. The Cuban government supposedly pirates foreign cable TV stations by stealing a signal captured by a government satellite dish mounted on the Hotel Habana Libre Tryp and retransmitted to other tourist hotels. Most tourist hotels have TVs that receive HBO, ESPN, Cinemax, CNN, VH1, and the international service of TV España.

The weekly tourist publication *Cartelera,* available free at hotel newsstands, lists television programming for the coming week. Tele Rebelde features national and international news at 12:30 and 8 p.m. Cubavision shows movies (usually recent Hollywood classics) every Saturday night.

Cuban television stations have some very intelligent programming, with a heavy emphasis on science and culture, sports, Hispanic soaps, and foreign movies. Cartoons are heavily moralistic and aim to teach Cuban youth proper behavior, and educational shows have a broadly internationalist focus (Uncle Sam is the most common villain). There is little of the mindless violence that seems to dominate contemporary American cartoons. Cuban television advertisements typically inveigh against abortions ("Aborción no es un metodo anticonceptivo"), exhort Cubans to work hard, or call for their participation in important festivals.

Cuba has five national radio stations: **Radio Liberación** offers mostly cultural programs; **Radio Musicál** airs classical music; **Radio Progreso** features light entertainment; **Radio Rebelde** and **Radio Reloj** both report news. There are also provincial and local stations, and in Havana, you can tune in to radio stations from southern Florida.

The *Christian Science Monitor* beams into Cuba with greater success, as does the *BBC World Service.*

For Tourists: Radio Taíno (AM 1160) is geared for tourists and airs in both English and Spanish daily 1-3 p.m. It promotes Cuban culture and plays middle-of-the-road music. **TV Taíno** is the television equivalent, aired 7-8 p.m. each Thursday. Watch, too, for screenings of *Walking in Havana* (a guided tour with City Historian Eusebio Leal).

TRAVEL AGENCIES

Most hotels have tour bureaus that can make reservations for excursions, car rental, and flights, as do the Cuban state tour companies. However, there are no independent travel agencies familiar to the rest of the world. For international airline reservations, contact the airlines directly.

TOURIST INFORMATION

Tourist Offices
Cuba's **Ministerio de Turismo,** Calle 19 #710, Vedado, Havana, tel. (33) 4202 or (33) 0545

(for international relations), is in charge of tourism. However, Cuba's tourist offices abroad are represented by other state tourism agencies, most notably **Cubatur,** but also by Havanatur and Cubanacán. There is no such office in the US; however, **Cubanacán,** 55 Queen St. E, Suite 705, Toronto, ON M5C 1R5, Canada, tel. (416) 362-0700, fax (416) 362-6799, e-mail: cuba.tbtor@sympatico.ca, will provide information and mail literature to US citizens.

The office of the Cuban tourism agency, **Cubatur,** at Calle F #157, e/ Calzada y Calle 9, Vedado, tel. (33) 4155, provides information and can make arrangements for independent travelers, as can the headquarters of **Havanatur,** in Edificio Sierra Maestra, Avenida 1ra, e/ 0 y 2, Miramar, tel. (23) 9879, fax (24) 9038, and Havanatur's **Tour & Travel,** (same address), tel. (24) 1549, fax (24) 2074, or at La Rampa and Calle P, tel. (70) 5284.

Publicitur, Calle 19 #60, e/ M and N, Vedado, tel. (55) 2826, fax (33) 3422, e-mail: public@public.mit.cma.net, is the agency responsible for publishing and disseminating tourism literature.

Information Bureaus
Infotur (Información Turística), the government tourist information bureau, has three information centers in Havana, including in the arrivals lounge at José Martí International Airport, tel. (66) 6112 or (45) 3542. The Habana Vieja office is on Calle Obispo #360, tel. (33) 3333. A third office is in west Miramar, on Avenida 5ra on the north side of the traffic circle at Calle 112, tel. (24) 7036, fax (24) 3977, e-mail: infomire@teleda.get.cma.net. The staff are friendly and can make reservations for car rentals, accommodations, and bus transfers, as well as selling prepaid telephone cards. However, they stock only a limited range of tourist literature and maps.

Virtually every hotel has a **buro de turismo** in the lobby. Most of the bureaus are geared to selling package excursions, but you'll usually find the staff willing and conscientious, if not always chock-full of information. The best ensemble of bureaus is undoubtedly that in the lobby of the Hotel Habana Libre Tryp, in Vedado.

In Habana Vieja, **Habaguanex,** Calle Oficios #110, on Plaza de San Francisco, tel. (33) 8693, fax (33) 8697, website: habaguanex.cubaweb.cu/habaguanex.html, can provide information

CUBAN TOURIST BUREAUS ABROAD

Argentina
Paraguay no. 631, Buenos Aires,
tel. (11) 4326-7810, fax (11) 4326-3325,
e-mail: oturcuar@tournet.com.ar

Brazil
Av. Sao Luis 50-39 Andar, CEP 01046 Sao Paulo SP,
tel. (11) 259-3044, fax (11) 258-8818

Canada
55 Queen St. E, Suite 705, Toronto, ON M5C 1R5, tel.
(416) 362-0700, fax (416) 362-6799, e-mail:
cuba.tbtor@sympatico.ca
440 Blvd. René Lévesque Quest, Bureau 1402,
Montreal, PQ H2Z 1V7,
tel. (514) 875-8004, fax (514) 875-8006,
e-mail: mintur@generation.net

France
24 rue du Quatre Septembre, 75002 Paris,
tel. (145) 389-010, fax (145) 389-930,
e-mail: ot.cuba@wanadoo.fr

Germany
Steinweg 2, 6000 Frankfurt Main 1,
tel. (069) 28-8322/23, fax (069) 29-6664,
e-mail: gocuba@compuserve.com

Italy
via General Fara 30, Terzo Piano, 20124 Milano,
tel. (02) 6698-1463,
fax (02) 6738-0725, e-mail:
ufficioturisticodicuba@interbusiness.it

Mexico
Insurgentes Sur no. 421, Complejo Aristo, Edif. B,
06100 México D.F., tel. (5) 255-5897,
fax (5) 255-5866,
e-mail: otcumex@mail.internet.cma.net

Russia
Hotel Belgrado, Moscow, tel./fax (095) 243-0383

Spain
Paseo de la Habana no. 28, 1ed 28036, Madrid, tel. (91)
411-3097, fax (91) 564-5804,
e-mail: otcuba@develnet.es

United Kingdom
161 High Holborn, London WC1V 6PA,
tel. (171) 836-3606, fax (171) 240-6655,
e-mail: cubatouristboard.london.@virgin.net

on hotels, restaurants, and other places under its umbrella.

Información Nacionál dispenses information about virtually every aspect of Cuba. Its main office is at Calle 23 #358, two blocks west of the Hotel Habana Libre Tryp, Vedado, Havana, tel. (32) 1269. The **Oficina Nacional de Estádisticas,** on Paseo, between 3ra and 5ra, one block south of the Melía Cohiba, can provide all manner of statistics on Cuba.

Olivia King Carter, Calle 35 #168 e/ 6 y Loma, tel. (66) 6471, e-mail: olivia@ip.etecsa.cu, a US student living in Havana, is a fountain of local knowledge. She welcomes calls.

Tourist Guides and Publications

Cartelera is a free weekly tourist publication for Havana that offers up-to-date listings of the forthcoming week's events, including TV programing, theater, music and dance, and other entertainment. You can pick up a copy at most tourist hotels or from the editorial office at Calle 15 #602 e/ B y C, Vedado, tel. (33) 3732.

Guía Cultural de la Habana is published monthly by Centro de Desarrollo y Comunicación Cultural (CREART) Calle 4 #205 e/ Linea y 11, Vedado tel. (32) 9691, fax (66) 2562, and provides a tremendous up-to-date resource for what's on at cinemas, theaters, etc. You'll find free copies at tou desks in leading hotels and at Palacios de Turismo.

Look, too, for Infotur's "touristic and commercial guide" called *La Habana* which lists the addresses and telephone numbers of hotels, restaurants, bars shopping centers, and a full range of services. It contains a fold-out map You can pick it up at any hotel or tou bureau.

La Habana Antigua is a pocket-siz guidebook to Habana Vieja published in Spanish and English by Ediciones Ge and available from souvenir stall throughout the city. It features detaile treet maps plus concise sightseeing information, and a modest listing of hotels, restaurants, and services.

Sol y Son, Graphic Publicidad, Calle 14 #113 / 1ra y 3ra, Miramar, Havana, tel. (24) 2245, ax (24) 2186, is the slick in-flight magazine of Cubana Airlines, published in English and Spanish. This sophisticated magazine provides profiles and news information on destinations, culture, and the arts.

The 300-page-plus *Directorio Turístico de Cuba* (Tourist Directory of Cuba, US$40) is published once per year as a venture between a Cuban and Mexican company. It includes names, addresses, telephone and fax numbers or ministries, hotels, airports, and airline offices, plus maps and other information. You can order it from the US-Cuba Trade & Economic Council, 0 Rockefeller Plaza New York, NY 10112-0002, el. (212) 246-1444, fax (212) 246-2345, website www.cubatrade.org.

Travel agents are also catered to by *Travel Trade Cuba,* Hotel Deauville, Hab. 207, Galiano Malecón, Centro Habana, tel. (33) 6268, fax 66) 2398, e-mail: ttccuba@ip.etecsa.cu, website: tc.cubaweb.cu., published in English and Spanish. Although useful, unlike international counterparts in the Italian-based Travel Trade Gazette group, this glossy publication is simply a public relations tool for Cuban travel companies.

US-Based Information Sources

The Center for Cuban Studies maintains the **Lourdes Casal Library,** 124 W. 23rd St., New York, NY 10011, tel. (212) 242-0559, fax (212) 242-1937, e-mail: cubanctr@igc.apc.org, website: www.cubaupdate.org. It has a collection of more than 5,000 books on Cuba, as well as subscriptions to *Granma, Bohemia,* and other Cuban journals. Open Mon.-Fri. 10 a.m.-6 p.m. and Saturday by appointment. The Cuban Art Space and Cuban Center Bookstore are also here.

Information Services Latin America (ISLA), 904 Franklin St. #900, Oakland, CA 94612, tel. 510) 835-4692, e-mail: isla@datacenter.org, website: www.igc.org/isla, maintains a superb clipping service of news regarding Cuba, emphasizing politics, the economy, culture, and foreign affairs.

Cuba: Consular Information Sheet is published on a regular updated basis by the US State Department's Bureau of Consular Affairs (D.O.S. Publication #9232, D.C.A.). It's available from the Superintendent of Documents, US Government Printing Office, Washington, DC 20402, tel. (202) 783-3283, and online at http://travel.state.gove/cuba.html.

Online Sources

There are dozens of Internet sites on Cuba. A key starting point should be the Republic of Cuba's Havana-based **CubaWeb,** website: www.cubaweb.cu, which carries information direct from Havana reflecting the views of the Cuban government. It has links to individual sites in the following categories: news, travel and tourism, politics and government, business and commerce, Internet and technology, health and science, culture and arts, and festivals and events.

The identically named **CubaWeb,** website: www.cubaweb.com, is a US-based site that acts as a clearinghouse for information on Cuba, but it is weak on up-to-date information.

Cubanacán maintains a website—www.cubanacan.cu—with information on all aspects of tourism, from auto rentals to marinas and health tourism, plus links to Cubana Aviación, the Buro de Convenciones, and more than a score of tourism-related sites. It includes "tourist bulletins."

Another starting point should be www.cubanet.org, which offers breaking news and news reports from the leading wire services. It's particularly good for hard-hitting info on Cuba's darker side (drug trafficking and the like).

The **Latin American Network Information Center,** website: www.lanic.utexas.edu, is a well-organized reference site with links to many Internet resources on Cuba, as well as a database of Castro's speeches.

California-based Boulevards News Media maintains a Havana site—www.lahabana.com—featuring updates on travel, arts, culture, and news. **USA*ENGAGE,** www.usaengage.org, offers a listing of feature articles and other news items on Cuba relating to economics and politics, and has a superb list of government and non-governmental agency links at www.usaengage.org/resources/links.

California-based Boulevards News Media maintains a Havana site—www.lahabana.com—featuring updates on travel, arts, culture, and related news.

A British firm, **Tour & Marketing,** e-mail: help@ gocuba.com, offers complete travel services at www.gocuba.com, plus broad-based information on arts, culture, sports, etc. at

www.cubavip.com. The Mexican company **Cuba Travel Service** maintains a useful list of Cuba links at www.cuba-travel.com.mx. Likewise, **Latin American Travel Consultants,** P.O. Box 17

KEY US ORGANIZATIONS TO KNOW

Center for Cuban Studies, 124 W. 23rd St., New York, NY 10011, tel. (212) 242-0559, fax (212) 242-1937, e-mail: cubanctr@igc.apc.org, website: www.cubaupdate.org. Supports educational forums on Cuba, publishes the splendid quarterly *Cuba Update,* organizes study tours, and distributes a wide range of books and videos on Cuba. It also has an art gallery and the largest research library on Cuba in North America.

Cuba Information Project, One Union Square West #211, New York, NY 10003, tel. (212) 366-6703, fax (212) 227-4859. Provides information on legislation and lobbying, and publishes the quarterly *Cuba Action.* Organizes monthly study tours on a variety of subjects and runs the **US+Cuba Medical Project,** which ships humanitarian aid to Cuba.

Cuban American Alliance Education Fund, 614 Maryland Ave. NE #2, Washington, DC 20002-5825, tel. (202) 543-6780, fax (202) 543-6434, e-mail: caaef@igc.org, website: www.cubamer. org. Represents moderate Cuban-Americans who wish for dialogue with Cuba. In particular, it sponsors efforts at family reunification and an end to travel restrictions imposed by Washington on Cuban-Americans wishing to visit Cuba. It also has a program to assist in the physical rehabilitation needs of children at the Julito Díaz Hospital (donations of medicines and medical equipment are needed).

Global Exchange, 2017 Mission St. #303, San Francisco, CA 94110, tel. (415) 255-7296, fax (415) 255-7498, e-mail: info@globalexchange. org, website: www.globalexchange.org. Organizes monthly study tours to Cuba on an eclectic range of themes. Global Exchange has launched a Campaign to End the Cold War Against Cuba, and the Campaign to Exempt Food and Medicines from the Embargo.Has also sponsored "Freedom to Travel Challenge" tours for those who want to challenge the legality of US travel restrictions.

IFCO/Pastors for Peace, 402 W. 145th St., New York, NY 10031, tel. (212) 926-5757, fax (212) 926-5842, email: ifco@igc.apc.org, website: www.ifconews.org. Organizes the US-Friendshipment Caravans to Cuba, challenging the embargo by traveling with vehicles filled with donations of humanitarian aid. Also has study tours and organizes work brigades to assist in community projects in Cuba. IFCO stands for Interreligious Foundation for Community Organization.

Peace for Cuba Task Force, P.O. Box 450, Santa Clara, CA 95052, tel. (408) 243-4359, fax (408) 243-1229, e-mail jreardon@igc.apc.org or dwald@igc.apc.org. Devoted to improving relations with Cuba. It sponsors speaking forums and accepts donations of medicines, foodstuffs, and educational materials for the US-Cuba Friendshipment Caravans. It also runs Project INFOMED to supply desperately needed computers to medical centers in Cuba. Donations of computers and peripherals are requested.

US-Cuba Medical Project, P.O. Box 206, 408 Thirteenth St., Oakland, CA 94612, tel. (510) 869-5655; and One Union Square West #211, New York, NY 10003, tel. (212) 227-5270, fax (212) 227-4859, e-mail: uscubamed@igc.apc.org. Provides medical and humanitarian aid to Cuba, working through the Cuban Red Cross. Leads caravans that deliver medical supplies to hospitals in Cuba.

US-Cuba Trade and Economic Council, 30 Rockefeller Plaza, New York, NY 10112, tel. (212) 246-1444, fax (212) 246-2345, e-mail council@cubatrade.org, website: www.cubatrade.org. A nonpartisan business organization that publishes the newsletter *Economic Eye on Cuba.* It claims not "to take positions with respect to US-Republic of Cuba political relations," but it favors trade.

17-908, Quito, Ecuador, fax (593) 2-562-566, e-mail: LATC@ pi.pro.ec, has a **Latin American Travel Resource Center** with a list of Cuba links at www.amerispan.com; it also publishes the *Latin American Travel Advisor* online at www.amerispan.com.

La Casa del Habano has www.cubamall.com, with links to numerous Cuba-related sites. For information on all things related to Afro-Cuban affairs, from music to conferences, check out **AfroCuba Web,** at www.afrocubaweb.com.

Uncle Sam has a website devoted to Cuba—www.state.gov/www/regions/wha/cuba/index—with information on such themes as human rights, people-to-people contacts, and travel. It's a none-too-flattering, highly biased picture.

General searches on Yahoo!, Excite, and other major search engines will pull up hundreds of other sites related to Havana and Cuba.

MAPS AND NAUTICAL CHARTS

Before You Go
The 1:250,000 topographical road maps produced by Kartografiai Vallalat, of Hungary, and the map by Freytag & Berndt both feature street maps of Havana. You can buy or order either from travel bookstores in North America and Europe.

SouthTrek, 1301 Oxford Ave., Austin, TX 78704, tel. (512) 440-7125, fax (512) 443-0973, e-mail sotrek@onr.com, specializes in maps of Latin America. It sells a 250:000 scale map of Cuba (US$9.95), including maps of Havana and five other cities. Send for a free catalog. Likewise, **Omni Resources,** P.O. Box 2096, Burlington, NC 72160, tel. (800) 742-2677, fax (910) 227-3748, website: www.omnimap.com, and **Treaty Oak,** P.O. Box 50295, Austin, TX 78763, tel. (512) 326-4141, fax (512) 443-0973, e-mail: maps@treatyoak.com, sell Cuba maps.

In Canada, **ITMB Publishing,** 736A Granville St., Vancouver, BC V6Z 1G3, tel. (604) 687-5925, is the best resource.

In the UK, try **Stanford's,** 12-14 Long Acre, London WC2E 9LP, tel. (171) 836-1321, fax (171) 836-0189, and the **Ordnance Survey International,** Romsey Rd., Maybush, Southampton SO9 4DH, tel. (0703) 792-000, fax (0703) 792-404.

In Australia, try **The Map Shop,** 16a Peel St.,

Adelaide, SA 5000, tel. (08) 231-2033; in New Zealand, try **Specialty Maps,** 58 Albert St., Auckland, tel. (09) 307-2217.

Needless to say, various US agencies have mapped Cuba to the inch.

In Havana
You'll find maps of Havana for sale at most Infotur offices and many hotel gift stores and souvenir stalls, as well as at various *telecorreos* (post offices and telephone exchanges).

However, the best source is **Tienda de las Navegantes,** Calle Mercaderes #115, e/ Obispo y Obrapía, Habana Vieja, tel. (61) 3625 or (66) 6763 (for boaters, VHF channel 16 CMYP3050), which has a wide range of tourist maps of Havana and provinces as well as specialized maps such as *Cementerio Colón: Map Turistico.* If you're planning on touring farther afield, you should definitely head here. Don't count on being able to buy maps covering your destination once you leave Havana.

Two of the best maps are *Mapa de La Habana Vieja: Patrimonio de la Humanidad* and *Ciudad de la Habana: Mapa Turística,* both produced by the Instituto Cubano de Geodesia y Cartografía. The road maps are very detailed. The map of Habana Vieja even includes pictures and details of most historic buildings of importance, plus other sites of interest. The Instituto also produces a road map *(mapa de carreteras)* to La Habana Province, as well as maps of individual tourist attractions such as Parque Lenin. The road map isn't very good.

Look for the excellent little booklet **La Habana Antigua** (also published by the Instistuto Cubano de Geodesia y Cartografía), which contains the most detailed maps of Habana Vieja available.

Detailed specialist maps are produced by the **Instituto de Planificación Física,** Laparilla 65, Habana Vieja, tel. (62) 9330, fax (61) 9533. They don't normally sell maps.

WHEN TO GO

Havana lies within the tropics, though its climate—generally hot and moist (average relative humidity is 78%)—is more properly semi- or subtropical.

HAVANA'S CLIMATE

AVERAGE TEMPERATURES (Temperatures are listed in degrees Celsius.)

Jan.	Feb.	March	April	May	June	July	Aug.	Sept.	Oct.	Nov.	Dec.
22	22.5	23	25	26	27	28	28	27.5	26	24	22.5

DAYS WITH RAINFALL

Jan.	Feb.	March	April	May	June	July	Aug.	Sept.	Oct.	Nov.	Dec.
6	4	4	4	7	10	9	10	11	11	7	6

Cuba has distinct summer and winter seasons despite its subtropical location. There are only two seasons: hot and wet (May-Oct.), and warm and dry (Nov.-April). Spring and autumn are preferable. The winter period, Nov.-April, is most pleasant, but this is also the busy season, and many hotels in Havana can be fully booked, especially during Christmas, New Year's, and Easter. Consider making advance reservations for the first few nights during these periods.

Most hotels charge lower rates in the summer low season, usually 20-40% below winter rates, and it's often easier to find rooms in the most popular hotels.

The newspaper *Granma* prints a weather forecast. *Cartelera,* the weekly tourist newspaper, also publishes a weather forecast on page two. Cuban TV newscasts feature weather forecasts (in Spanish).

Temperatures

Havana's mean annual temperature is 25.2° C (77° F), with an average of eight hours of sunshine per day throughout the year. There is little seasonal variation, with an *average* temperature in January of 22° C (67° F), rising (along with humidity) to an average of 27.2° C (81° F) in July. Midwinter temperatures can take a sharp dip, occasionally falling below 50° F when severe cold fronts sweep down into the Gulf of Mexico, and visitors to Havana will be glad for a sweater and jacket.

The island is influenced by the warm Gulf Stream currents and by the North Atlantic high-pressure zone that lies northeast of Cuba and gives rise to the near-constant *brisa,* the local name for the prevailing northeast trade winds that caress Havana year-round. Indeed, despite its more southerly latitude, Havana, wrote Ernest Hemingway, "is cooler than most northern cities in those months [July and August], because the northern trades get up about ten o'clock in the morning and blow until about five o'clock the next morning."

Rainfall

Some rain falls on Cuba an average of 85-100 days a year, totaling an annual average of 132 cm (52 inches). Almost two-thirds falls during the May-Oct. wet season, which can be astoundingly humid. Summer rain is most often a series of intermittent showers interspersed with sunshine, but lingering downpours and storms that last two or three days are common. When it rains hard, sheets of water collect in the streets, waves crash over the Malecón, power snaps off, telephone lines go down, and taxis are impossible to find.

Havana can experience a three- to five-month dry period known as *La Seca.* December, and February through April are the driest months, although heavy winter downpours can occur when cold fronts sweep south from North America.

Hurricanes

Cuba lies within the hurricane belt. Aug.-Oct. is hurricane season, but freak hurricane-force storms can hit Cuba in other months, too. Hurricane Lili battered the island in October 1996, destroying thousands of homes islandwide. In September 1998, Hurricane George ripped along the north shore and blasted Havana, causing extensive flooding. When there are no hurricanes, midsummer weather is the best of all the year.

The **National Weather Service,** 1325 East-West Hwy., Silver Spring, MD 20910, website:

www.nws.noaa.gov, provides updated weather forecasts and hurricane warnings.

WHAT TO TAKE

Pack light! A good rule of thumb is to lay out everything you wish to take—then cut it by half. Most often, I've regretted packing too much, not too little. Remember, you'll need some spare room, too, for any souvenirs you plan to bring home. Leave your jewelry at home—it invites theft. Try to limit yourself to *one* bag (preferably a sturdy duffel or garment bag with plenty of pockets), plus a small day pack or camera bag. If using public transport to travel beyond Havana, note that space on domestic buses and planes is limited. One of the best investments is a well-made duffel bag that doubles as a backpack and can be carried by hand or on the back.

Most important, don't forget your passport, airline tickets, traveler's checks, and other documentation. You'd be amazed how many folks get to the airport before discovering this "minor" oversight.

Many items are scarce in Cuba. You can usually find a full range of Western toiletries available in hotel stores and **Tiendas Panamericanos** (dollar stores stocking Western goods). However, don't depend on it. Take all the toiletries you think you'll need—including toilet paper. Don't forget a towel and face cloth—upscale hotels will provide them, but not less expensive hotels. Women should pack extra tampons (those you don't use will make good gifts for Cuban women).

Most Western medicines and pharmaceuticals can be purchased at special pharmacies and clinics for foreigners, but you should bring any specific medications you think you'll need. If you bring prescription drugs, be sure the druggist's identification label is on the container.

Writing materials are extremely hard to come by: take pens, pencils, and notepads (and lots of extras to give away to children). An English/Spanish dictionary is handy and makes a great parting gift.

Coping with the Climate

Cuba is mostly hot and humid, and you'll want light, loose-fitting shirts and pants. You'll sweat often. But it can occasionally get chilly in mid-winter, especially at night. It's always a good idea to pack a sweater and/or a warm windproof jacket. You'll need one to cope with the bone-chilling a/c in hotels and restaurants. Pack items that you can layer and which work in various combinations—preferably darker items that don't show the inevitable dirt and stains you'll quickly collect walking the streets of Havana. Note, though, that dark clothes tend to be hotter than light clothing, which reflects the sun's rays.

Some people recommend packing just two sets of clothes—one to wash and one to wear. Two sets of clothing seems ascetic. Three T-shirts, two dressier shirts, a couple of tank tops, a polo-neck, a sweatshirt, a polo shirt, a pair of Levi's, plus a pair of "cargo" pants and dress pants, two pairs of shorts, swimming trunks, and a sleeveless photographer's jacket with heaps of pockets suffice for me (and that's usually for a month or more). Women may wish to substitute blouses and skirts (the shorter the better—less is more for Cuban women). Be resigned in advance to the fact that the climate takes the wave out of your hair—get it cut short or simplify it before you leave home.

Denim jeans take forever to dry when wet. Light cotton-polyester safari-style pants are cooler, dry quickly, and have plenty of pockets. Ideally, everything should be drip-dry, wash-and-wear.

Pack plenty of socks and undergarments—you may need a daily change. Wash them frequently to help keep athlete's foot and other fungal growths at bay.

In the wet season, plan on rain. A small fold-up umbrella is best (they're in short supply in Havana, so bring one with you). Raincoats are heavy and tend to make you sweat. Breathable Gore-Tex rainproof jackets work fine. A hooded poncho is also good. Make sure it has slits down the side for your arms and that it is large enough to carry a small day pack underneath.

How Dressy?

Cubans do not stand on ceremony, and most travelers will not need dressy clothes. Habaneros dress informally but always very neatly (they rarely go out in the evening without first changing into fresh clothes). Even Cuban businesspeople and officials dress simply, usually with a *guayabara* shirt worn outside the trousers, even at official functions.

Still, pack a pair of slacks and a dressy shirt for discos or the fancier restaurants (some establishments have a dress code; T-shirts and shorts are not permissible). You may even wish to take a jacket and tie or cocktail dress for dinners in more expensive hotels and restaurants—or, for the lucky few, an impromptu meeting with Castro at other organized functions. (The past few years has seen a creeping trend toward business suits among fashion-conscious Cubans.).

Shorts are acceptable wear in Havana for men, but save shorter-style runner's shorts for the beach. Women can get away with just about any skimpy item, following in the footsteps of their Cuban counterparts, although you're sure to attract attention from males.

You'll need a comfortable pair of low-heeled walking shoes. A pair of lightweight sandals are de rigueur. Sneakers will do double-duty for most occasions. High heels for women? Sure, they're all the rage among Habaneras.

FILM AND PHOTOGRAPHY

Havana is a photographer's dream. John Kings, the photographer who accompanied James Michener to illustrate his book *Six Days in Havana,* called Havana "one of the most photogenic cities in the world. . . . It was captivating and challenging and for the next five days my finger barely left the shutter of my little German eye." You'll agree, so come prepared.

You are never denied access to anything you wish to photograph (except people in uniform).

Equipment and Film
A 35mm SLR camera is most versatile and will give top-notch results, but an instamatic is fine.

You're allowed to bring two cameras plus six rolls of film into Cuba (don't worry about the official film limit; I've never heard of it being enforced). Film is susceptible to damage by airport X-ray machines. Usually one or two passes through a machine won't harm it, but the effect is cumulative. You should *always* request that your film (including your loaded camera) be hand-checked by airport security.

Decide how much film you think you'll need to bring—then triple it. I recommend one roll per day as a minimum if you're even half-serious about your photography. Bring all the film you need with you. If you do need to buy film in Cuba, check the expiration date; it may be outdated. And the film may have been sitting in the sun—not good. If you want the best results, only buy film that is refrigerated or at least stored in an a/c room.

Film—limited throughout Havana to Kodak or Agfa—is sold at most tourist hotels and at **Photo Service** stores. Usually only print film is available. Very rarely will you find slide (transparency) film. At press time, film cost: Fujicolor 100 US$4.85, Ektachrome Elite 100 US$10, Kodacolor 100 US$5.45. Agfa has its headquarters at Avenida 9ta between Calles 20 and 22 in Miramar, tel. (24) 0744, fax (24) 1475, but even this office claims a minimal stock of film.

The main Photo Service office is inside the International Press Center at Calle 23 y O, Vedado, tel. (33) 5031, but there are other Photo Service outlets scattered about town.

Most Photo Service stores also sell a few Nikon, Minolta, and Canon instamatic cameras, as well as a meager stock of batteries. In spring 1999, SLRs had begun to appear, with the outlet in the Hotel Habana Libre Tryp selling Canon's new EOS models (US$548) and a few accompanying lenses. **Imágenes,** Calle 26 #120 esq. Avenida 3ra, Miramar, tel. (24) 2469, also rents and sells cameras and film. Open Mon.-Sat. 8 a.m.-9 p.m. *Take spare batteries* for light meters and flashes. You will *not* be able to buy filters in Cuba.

Keep your film out of the sun. If possible, refrigerate it. Color emulsions are particularly sensitive to tropical heat, and film rolls can also soften with the humidity so that they easily stretch and refuse to wind in your camera. Pack both your virgin and exposed film in a Ziploc plastic bag with silica gel inside to protect against moisture. Always put used film in a plastic film container—the felt edging attracts dirt, which can leave a nasty scratch along the *entire* film when unrolled.

Keep your lenses clean and dry when not in use. Silica gel packs are essential to help protect your camera gear from moisture; use them if you carry your camera equipment inside a plastic bag. Cameras are valuable goods. Never turn your back on your camera gear. Watch it at all times.

Film Processing

Photo Service offers a rapid development service at all its outlets (film processing US$2, slide processing US$5, slide framing US20 cents per slide) and passport photos (six for US$3). It also makes color prints and copies up to 50 by 60 inches and offers framing. However, Cuba faces a chemical shortage, and there is no guarantee that the processing chemicals are clean. For this reason, you should consider waiting until you get home (try to keep your film cool). You can also buy film with prepaid processing—each roll comes with a self-mailer and you can simply pop it in a mailbox; the prints or slides will then be mailed to your home. However, given the vicissitudes of the Cuban mail system, you're more likely to arrive home first (and your film may never show up).

Video Cameras

Cuban Customs states that video cameras may not be imported, but this seems to apply only to their being left in Cuba. If you bring one in, you may have to declare it and be sure to take it out with you. It's best to ensure that you have fresh batteries before arriving, although camcorder batteries can be found at Photo Service outlets in Havana. The same rule holds true for blank tapes, which are not always readily available outside major tourist locales.

Photo Etiquette

Cubans of every shade and stripe will ham for your camera and will generally cooperate willingly. However, never assume an automatic right to take a personal photograph. If you come across individuals who don't want to be photographed, honor their wishes. It's a common courtesy, too, to ask permission to photograph what might be considered private situations. Use your judgment and discretion. Don't attempt to photograph members of the police or military—they are under strict instructions not to allow themselves to be photographed.

Many children will request money for being photographed. So, too, will the mulattas dressed in traditional costume in Plaza de la Catedral. The latter are officially sanctioned to do so, but the government discourages other citizens from "begging." Whether you pay is a matter of conscience. If they insist on being paid and you don't want to pay, don't take the shot. It is considered a courtesy to buy a small trinket in markets from vendors you wish to photograph. Don't forget to send photographs to anyone you promise to send to.

Warning: Several foreigners have been arrested and deported in recent years for filming pornography. The Cuban government defines it fairly broadly—and keeps a strict watch for such illicit use of cameras.

MEDICAL SERVICES

Sanitary standards in Havana are very high, and the chances of succumbing to illness or serious disease are low. As long as you take appropriate precautions and use common sense, you're not likely to incur serious illness. If you do, you have the benefit of knowing that the nation has a healthcare system that guarantees treatment. Although Cuba's much-vaunted health system has been severely challenged since the collapse of the Soviet Bloc, foreigners get special treatment through **Servimed** (a Spanish acronym for Specialized Medical Services for Health Tourism), Calle 18 #4304 e/ 43 y 47, Miramar, tel. (24) 2658, fax (24) 2948. With a few exceptions, facilities and standards, however, are not up to those of North America (despite the fact that Cuba's health indices—which surpass those of the US in several regards—prove that socialized medicine *can* guarantee everyone good care).

The larger, upscale tourist hotels have nurses on duty. Other hotels will be able to request a doctor for in-house diagnosis and treatment for minor ailments.

US citizens should note that Uncle Sam's concern for your welfare is such that even if visiting Cuba legally, payment for "nonemergency medical services" is prohibited. Developing an in-grown toenail? Sorry, buddy—endure!

Hospitals

Tourists needing medical assistance are usually steered to the **Clínica Cira García,** Calle 20 #4101 and Avenida 41, Miramar, tel. (24) 2811, fax (24) 1633. The gleaming full-service hospital

HEALTH TOURISM

The need for foreign currency has resulted in some health-care resources being diverted to "health tourism" (originally developed for an Eastern bloc clientele), where foreign patients come to Cuba for advanced treatment.

Cuba's "sun and surgery" program is run by **Servimed,** Calle 18 #4304 e/ 43 y 47, Playa, tel. (24) 2023, fax (24) 1630, a division of Cubanacán, which offers everything from spas and health resorts offering "stress breaks" to advanced treatments such as eye, open-heart, and plastic surgery. It is acknowledged as a world leader in orthopedics, and the **Frank País Orthopedic Hospital** recently had to double the capacity of its 40-bed ward for foreigners to meet demand. Cuba has even established the **International Placental Histotherapy Center** for treating vitiligo. And the **International Neurological Restoration Center** is claimed to be the only center in the world devoted entirely to the field of "neuro-restoration" (it offers treatments for Parkinson's disease, Alzheimer's disease, multiple sclerosis, epilepsy, etc.). Treatment for stress, asthma, hypertension, obesity, and alcohol control are also provided. Even silicon breast implants are available (foreigners are charged about US$4,500 for implants).

is entirely dedicated to serving foreigners. It is staffed by English-speaking doctors and nurses. You pay in dollars—credit cards are acceptable unless they're issued on a US bank (in which case, greenbacks are required).

In Vedado, the **Centro Internacional Oftalmológica Camilo Cienfuegos,** on Calle L between Linea and 13, tel. (32) 5554, fax (33) 3536, e-mail cirpcc@infomed.sid.cu, specializes in eye disorders but also offers a range of medical services running from optometry to odontology. Similarly, the recently opened **Instituto Pedro Kouri,** in Marianao, is devoted to "international medical care," especially HIV/AIDS, hepatitis, and contagious and parasitic diseases.

Havana is blessed with dozens of other hospitals for Cubans, notably the 24-story, 1,000-bed **Hospital Hermanos Ameijeiras,** at the corner of Padre Varela and San Lazaro, in Centro Habana, tel. (70) 7721.

The Cuban state guarantees free treatment even to foreigners in the case of a dire emergency, such as may result from a car accident.

Pharmacies

There are local pharmacies everywhere, but they are meagerly stocked (*turnos regulares* are open 8 a.m.-5 p.m., *turnos permanentes* are open 24 hours). Fortunately, a number of international pharmacies (*farmacías internacionales*) cater to foreigners and supply a large range of Western drugs for not much more than the same price you'd pay in the US. (The service is for foreigners only, who pay in dollars. You may be approached by Cubans outside tendering dollars and begging you to purchase desperately needed medicines on their behalf.)

In Vedado, **Centro Internacional Oftalmológica Camilo Cienfuegos,** on Calle L between Linea and 13, tel. (32) 5554, fax (33) 3536, e-mail cirpcc@infomed.sid.cu, has a *farmacía internaciónal.* In Miramar, **Clínica Cira García** has a similar 24-hour pharmacy at the rear, tel. (24) 2811, ext. 14; and the **Farmacía Internacional,** across the street on Avenida 41, tel. (24) 2051, is also fully stocked with Western pharmaceuticals and toiletries. Open Mon.-Fri. 9 a.m.-5:45 p.m., Saturday 9 a.m.-noon. **Biotop,** Avenida 7 #2603, Miramar, tel. (24) 2377, fax (33) 2378, also contains a smaller international pharmacy, open 9 a.m.-6:30 p.m.

A licensed medicinal herbalist operates at Obrapía #212, Mon.-Sat. 9 a.m.-6 p.m.

Opticians

Óptima Miramar, Avenida 7ma and Calle 24, Miramar, tel. (24) 2990, fax (24) 2803, provides full-service optician and optometrist services, and sells imported products such as solutions for contact lenses. It also has an office on Neptuno, e/ San Nicolas and Manrique, in Centro Habana.

You'll find other opticians serving Cubans under *Ópticas* in the phone book. (I had my spectacles stolen in Cuba—remember to take a spare pair.)

Gyms and Massage

Need an invigorating massage or beauty treatment? Try **Biotop,** Avenida 7 #2603, Miramar, tel. (24) 2377, fax (33) 2378, which has a poorly equipped gym (US$5), a sauna (US$5), two outdoor jacuzzis (not in use during my visit), and salt and algae baths. It's run by Servimed. It offers health and beauty treatments, but the uninspired facility gets few visitors and looked a bit rundown in spring 1999. A massage costs US$10. Open 10 a.m.-8 p.m.

Spa La Pradera, Calle 230 e/ 15 y 17, Reparto Siboney, tel. (33) 7467, fax (33) 7198, e-mail: aloja@pradera.cha.cyt.cu, is a Cubanacán spa-hotel specializing in health treatments. It has a sauna, gym, hydro-massage, massages, paraffin and mud treatments, ozone therapy, and the like.

Most luxury hotels offer massages and have tiny gyms and/or spas. Most are a let-down, but those of the **Hotel Melía Cohiba,** at the base of Avenida Paseo, Vedado, tel. (33) 3636, and **Hotel Parque Central,** Neptuno e/ Prado y Agramonte, tel. (66) 6627, are well stocked with modern equipment and mirrored walls.

Specialized massages are also offered by Dulce María in the **Hostal Valencia,** on Calle Oficios in Habana Vieja, tel. (62) 3801. She offers acupressure and reflexology using both Japanese *yumeiho* and Chinese techniques. She also offers massages at her home on Calle San Ignacio #78, tel. (61) 0412. "After an hour of massage you will feel like a teddy bear," she says. María charges US$8 for 45 minutes.

Before You Go

Dental and medical checkups may be advisable before departing home, particularly if you intend to travel for a considerable time, partake in strenuous activities, or have an existing medical problem. Take along any medications, including prescriptions for eyewear; keep prescription drugs in their original bottles to avoid suspicion at Customs. If you suffer from a debilitating health problem, wear a medical alert bracelet. Pharmacies can prescribe drugs (be wary of expiration dates, as shelf life of drugs may be shortened under tropical conditions).

A basic health kit is a good idea. Pack the following (as a minimum) in a small plastic container: alcohol swabs and medicinal alcohol, antiseptic cream, Band-Aids, aspirin or painkillers, diarrhea medication, sunburn remedy, antifungal foot powder, calamine and/or antihistamine, water-purification tablets, surgical tape, bandages and gauze, and scissors. **Adventure**

Medical Kits, 5555 San Leandro, Oakland, CA 94624, tel. (510) 261-7414 or (800) 324-3517, fax (510) 261-7419, e-mail: amkusa@aol.cpm, website: www.adventuremedicalkits.com, has the most comprehensive range of travel medical kits, which come with handy medical booklets.

Information on health concerns can be answered by **Intermedic,** 777 3rd Ave., New York, NY 10017, tel. (212) 486-8974, and the **Department of State Citizens Emergency Center,** tel. (202) 647-5225. In the UK, you can get information, innoculations, and medical supplies from the **British Airways Travel Clinic,** tel. (171) 831-5333, which has branches nationwide, or the **Thomas Cook Vaccination Center,** 3-4 Wellington Terrace, Turnpike Lane, London N8 0PXX, tel. (181) 889-7014.

The **International Association for Medical Assistance to Travellers** (IAMAT), 417 Center St., Lewiston, NY 14092, tel. (716) 754-4883; in Canada, 40 Regal Rd., Guelph, ON N1K 1B5, tel. (519) 836-0102; in Europe, 57 Voirets, 1212 Grand-Lancy, Geneva, Switzerland, publishes helpful information, including a list of approved physicians and clinics. A useful pocket-size book is *Staying Healthy in Asia, Africa, and Latin America,* Avalon Travel Publishing, 5855 Beaudry St., Emeryville, CA 94608, tel. (510) 595-3664, website: www.moon.com, which is packed with first-aid and basic medical information.

Vaccinations

No vaccinations are required to enter Cuba unless visitors are arriving from areas of cholera and yellow fever infection (mostly Africa and South America), in which case they must have valid vaccinations. Epidemic diseases have mostly been eradicated throughout the country. Cuba's achievements in eliminating infectious disease are unrivaled in the world: it is the only country to have totally eliminated measles, for example.

Consult your physician for recommended vaccinations. At the least, you should consider vaccinations against tetanus and infectious hepatitis, although infectious hepatitis (hepatitis A) is reported only infrequently in Cuba. The main symptoms are stomach pains, loss of appetite, yellowing skin and eyes, and extreme tiredness. Hepatitis A is contracted through unhygienic foods or contaminated water (salads and unpeeled fruits are major culprits). A gamma globulin vaccination is recommended. The much rarer Hepatitis B is usually contracted through unclean needles, blood transfusions, or unsafe sex.

Health Problems

Infection: Regardless of Cuba's admirable health records, it *is* a tropical country, and Havana is a dirty city. Even the slightest scratch can fester quickly in the tropics. Treat promptly and regularly with antiseptic and keep the wound clean.

Intestinal Problems: Havana's tap water is questionable, especially after heavy storms, which may render water supplies unsafe. Play it safe and drink bottled mineral water *(agua mineral)*, which is widely available. Remember, ice cubes are water, too. Always wash your hands before eating, and don't brush your teeth using suspect water.

Food hygiene standards are very high. Milk is pasteurized, so you're not likely to encounter any problems normally associated with dairy products. However, the change in diet—which may alter the bacteria that are normal and necessary in the bowel—may briefly cause diarrhea or constipation (in case of the latter, eat lots of fruit). Fortunately, the stomach usually builds up a resistance to unaccustomed foods. Most cases of diarrhea are caused by microbial bowel infections resulting from contaminated food. Common-sense precautions include not eating uncooked fish or shellfish (which collect cholera bugs), uncooked vegetables, unwashed salads, or unpeeled fruit (peel the fruit *yourself*). And be fastidious with personal hygiene.

Diarrhea is usually temporary, and many doctors recommend letting it run its course. Personally, I prefer to medicate straight away with Lomotil or another antidiarrheal products. Treat diarrhea with rest and lots of liquid to replace the water and salts lost. Avoid alcohol and milk products. If conditions don't improve after three days, seek medical help.

Diarrhea accompanied by severe abdominal pain, blood in your stool, and fever is a sign of **dysentery.** Seek immediate medical diagnosis. Tetracycline or ampicillin is normally used to cure bacillary dysentery. More complex professional treatment is required for amoebic dysentery. The symptoms of both are similar. **Giardiasis,** acquired from infected water, is another intestinal complaint. It causes diarrhea, bloat-

ing, persistent indigestion, and weight loss. Again, seek medical advice. **Intestinal worms** can be contracted by walking barefoot on infested beaches, grass, or earth.

Sunburn and Skin Problems: Don't underestimate the tropical sun. It's intense and can fry you in minutes. It can even burn you through light clothing or while you're lying in the shade. The midday sun is especially potent. Even if you consider yourself nicely tanned already, use a suncream or sunblock of at least SPF 8. Zinc oxide provides almost 100% protection. Bring sun lotions with you; they're not always readily available in Havana, although most hotel stores sell them. If you're intent on a tan, have patience. Build up gradually, and use an aloe gel after sunbathing; it helps repair any skin damage. The tops of feet and backs of knees are particularly susceptible to burning when walking Havana's streets. Consider wearing a wide-brimmed hat, too. Calamine lotion and aloe gel will soothe light burns; for more serious burns, use steroid creams.

Sun glare can cause conjunctivitis. Sunglasses will protect against this. **Prickly heat** is an itchy rash, normally caused by clothing that is too tight or in need of washing. This, and **athlete's foot,** are best treated by airing out the body and washing your clothes.

Dehydration and Heat Problems: The tropical humidity and heat can sap your body fluids like blotting paper. You'll sweat profusely and steadily while exploring Havana. Leg cramps, exhaustion, dizziness, and headaches are possible signs of dehydration. Although your body may acclimatize to the heat gradually, at the same time, dehydration can develop slowly. Diarrhea will drain your body of fluids swiftly.

Drink regularly to avoid dehydration. Ideally, drink water, but *batidos* or *refrescoes* purchased at streetside stalls are a perfectly refreshing antidote to dehydration. Avoid alcohol, which processes water in the body; the more alcohol you drink, the more water you'll need, too.

Excessive exposure to too much heat can cause **heat stroke,** a potentially fatal result of a failure in the body's heat-regulation mechanisms. Excessive sweating, extreme headaches, and disorientation leading to possible convulsions and delirium are typical symptoms. Emergency medical care is essential! If hospitalization is not possible, place the victim in the shade, cover with a wet cloth, and fan continually to cool the person down.

Don't be alarmed if your ankles and legs get puffy. It's the tropical climate. When you rest, keep your feet higher than your head (a cold Epsom salts footbath also helps).

Many tourists come down with colds *(catarro Cubano),* often brought on by the debilitating effects of constantly shifting from icily air-conditioned restaurants and hotels to sultry outdoor heat. A more serious ailment is **bronchitis,** which should be treated with antibiotics.

Insects and Arachnids: The most common bugs you'll see will be cockroaches, which are found virtually everywhere and are harmless, although they carry disease (you don't want them crawling over your food).

Mosquitoes: Although breezes help keep them at bay, Havana has plenty of rapacious mosquitoes. The waterfront region of Miramar is particularly noted for mosquitoes. Their bites itch, sure, but you need have no fear of malaria—it's not present in Cuba. However, mosquitoes (particularly those active by day) *do* transmit **dengue fever,** which *is* present on the island, although extremely rare in Havana. The illness can be fatal (death usually results from internal hemorrhaging). Its symptoms are similar to those for malaria, with additional severe pain in the joints and bones, for which it is sometimes called "breaking bones disease." Other symptoms include severe headaches and high fever. Unlike malaria, it is not recurring. There is no cure. Dengue fever must run its course. In the unlikely event you contract it, have plenty of aspirin or other painkillers on hand. Drink lots of water.

To keep mosquitoes at bay, turn on your a/c or overhead 'fan as high as is comfortable. The best mosquito repellents contain DEET (diethylmetatoluamide). DEET is quite toxic; avoid using it on small children, and avoid getting it on plastic or lycra—which it will melt. A fan over your bed and mosquito coils *(espirales,* which are rarely sold in Cuba) that smolder for up to eight hours also help keep mosquitoes at bay. Citronella candles may help, too.

Bites can easily become infected in the tropics, so avoid scratching. Treat with antiseptics or antibiotics. A baking-soda bath can help relieve itching if you're badly bitten, as can antihistamine tablets, and hydrocortisone and calamine lotion.

Scabies: Many Habaneros live in poor hygienic conditions that are a perfect breeding ground for scabies (a microscopic mite) and lice. Infestation is possible if you're sleeping in similarly unhygienic conditions or engage in sex with people already infested. If you're unfortunate enough to contract scabies, you'll need to use a body shampoo containing gamma benzene hexachloride or one percent lindane solution (lindane is a highly toxic pesticide). At the same time, you must also wash all your clothing and bedding in very hot water—and throw out your underwear. Your sexual partner will need to do the same. The severe itching caused by scabies infestation appears after three or four weeks (it appears as little dots, often in lines and sometimes ending in blisters, especially around the genitals, elbows, wrists, lower abdomen, nipples, and on the head of the penis). A second bout of scabies usually shows itself within 48 hours of reinfestation. Treatment in the US is by prescription only. However, you can obtain *Scabisan* from the **Farmácia Internacional.**

Scorpions are present—I saw one scuttle across the floor of a *paladar*—but are rarely encountered. Still, it pays to be wary about putting your hands into crevices without first checking things out with a flashlight.

Rabies: Though rare in Cuba, rabies can be contracted through the bite of an infected dog or other animal. It's always fatal unless treated.

Gynecological Problems: Travel, hot climates, and a change of diet or health regime can play havoc with your body, leading to yeast and other infections. A douche of diluted vinegar or lemon juice can help alleviate yeast infections. Loose, cotton underwear may help prevent infections such as Candida, typified by itching and a white, cheesy discharge. A foul-smelling discharge accompanied by a burning sensation may indicate Trichomoniasis, usually caught through intercourse but also by contact with unclean towels, etc.

AIDS and Sexually Transmitted Diseases: The risk of contracting AIDS in Cuba is relatively minor. The rate of infection is among the world's lowest, and the Cuban government conducts an exemplary anti-AIDS campaign (Cuba even manufactures AIDS diagnostic kits as well as interferons for treatment). However, the incidence of AIDS is already showing signs of rapid increase, a situation likely to get worse in coming years due to the growing prevalence of sexual liaisons between Cubans and foreigners.

Gonorrhea, syphilis, and other sexually transmitted diseases are fairly common. Avoiding casual sexual contact is the best prevention. If you do succumb to the mating urge, use condoms *(preservativos)*, which can be purchased at dollar stores, although the selection is limited. You should purchase a supply before departing for Cuba. Practice safe sex!

SAFETY

Theft

All the negative media hype sponsored by Washington has left many people with a false impression that Havana is unsafe. Far from it. Few places in the world are as safe for visitors. The vast majority of Cubans are supremely honest and friendly people. Rape and other violent crime is virtually unknown. However, Havana's many charms can lull visitors into a false sense of security. The material hardships of Cubans have

---

BITE YOUR TONGUE!

M any foreigners are fearful because Cuba is a communist country. Fear not! It is disconcerting to see the degree to which "Big Brother" keeps a close eye on Cubans—who must account to the state for their every move. Even foreigners (excluding the average tourist) are not above surreptitious surveillance. But you're free to roam wherever you wish without hindrance or a need to look over your shoulder.

That said, you can be sure that nay-saying the Revolution in public can swiftly land you in trouble. Criticism of the government is defined as "anti-social behavior" and is punishable by law. Given four decades of US efforts to destabilize the Castro regime, Cuban authorities understandably do not look favorably on foreigners who become involved in political activity, especially with known dissidents. Avoid making inflammatory or derogatory comments; otherwise you could well find yourself on the next plane home.

Bite your tongue!

EMERGENCY TELEPHONE NUMBERS

Ambulance . . . . (40) 5093/94 or (40) 7173
Fire . . . . (81) 1115
Police . . . . (82) 0116

---

combined with the influx of wealthy tourists during the last decade to foster a breakdown of the old social order and sense of morals. Crime is resurgent.

A growing number of pickpockets (*carteristas*) and purse slashers work the streets of Havana. Theft from hotel rooms is a problem, including items of clothing. A spate of tourist muggings have been reported in recent years. Even corruption and drug use—until very recently virtually unknown in revolutionary Cuba—have reared their ugly heads again.

The situation deteriorated markedly during 1996-98 and threatened to get out of hand. In January 1999, hundreds of policeman took to the streets on a 24-hour basis and, by some accounts, as many as 7,000 *jiniteras* and *jiniteros* were arrested. Overnight, freelancers of every stripe disappeared, including most petty thieves and muggers.

Still, Havana is not entirely safe despite this remarkable policing. Most crime is opportunistic, and thieves seek easy targets. Crowded places are the happy hunting grounds of crafty crooks. If you sense yourself being squeezed or jostled, don't hold back—elbow your way out of there immediately. Better safe than sorry. Don't leave items unattended in restaurants and the like.

Walking Havana at night is, in general, safe. However, be wary of darker back streets at night (very few streets have lights). Note that some local bars can get rowdy after the *aguardente* (cheap rum) has been flowing a while. Drunkenness is not tolerated, although you'll occasionally see drunks.

Where to Avoid?

Several muggings and nonviolent robberies have occurred near key tourist sites. Particular spots to be wary are around the Capitolio and Parque Central, the Paseo de Martí, the Plaza de Armas, and Plaza 13 de Marzo in front of the Museo de

Capitolio, *Havana*

la Revolución, said to be a favorite spot for nocturnal muggings. Other areas that require special caution by night are the back streets of southern Habana Vieja, anywhere in the Cerro district, and the Cayo Hueso and neighboring areas of Centro Habana.

Traffic

Traffic is perhaps the greatest danger, despite a relative paucity of vehicles on the road. Be especially wary when crossing the streets in Havana. Stand well away from the curb—especially on corners, where buses often mount the sidewalk. Cyclists are everywhere, making insouciant turns and weaving with a lackadaisical disdain for safety. Sidewalks are full of gaping potholes and tilted curbstones. Watch your step!

Travel Insurance

Travel insurance is highly recommended. Travelers should check to see if their health insurance or other policies cover medical expenses while abroad—and specifically in Cuba. Traveler's in-

surance isn't cheap, but it can be a sound investment. Travel agencies can sell you traveler's health and baggage insurance, as well as insurance against cancellation of a prepaid tour.

International: If you're concerned about things going wrong, consider purchasing insurance through **Assist-Card,** an international company, 15 rue du Cendrier, 1201 Geneva, Switzerland, tel. (22) 738-5852, fax (22) 738-6305, website: www.assist-card.com, which offers travel assistance with everything from tracking lost luggage and finding medical, legal, and technical services to emergency transfers and repatriation, which you can request 24 hours a day. It has Regional Assistance Centers worldwide, including in Cuba (even for US citizens). Insurance premiums cost from US$40 for five days, US$70 for 10 days, US$80 for 16 days, and US$100 for 30 days (US$6 per day for additional days), and cover up to US$12,000 in medical costs plus other benefits. A "premium" package costs more. Assist-Card International has regional headquarters in the following locations: **Argentina:** Suipacha 1109, 1008 Buenos Aires, tel. (11) 4312-6801 or toll free (0800) 81981, fax (11) 4311-2971; **Spain:** Calle Silva 2, Madrid, tel. (01) 559-0500, fax (01) 542-4680; and the **United States:** 1001 South Bayshore Dr. #2302, Miami, FL 33131, tel. (305) 381-9959, fax (305) 375-8135. For assistance in Cuba, call Asistur (see below); if you have difficulty, you can call the regional office in Miami.

In the US: US citizens are in luck: some insurance programs guarantee coverage for Cuba. These include **American Express,** P.O. Box 919010, San Diego, CA 92190, tel. (800) 234-0375; **Travelers,** 1 Tower Square, Hartford, CT 06183, tel. (203) 277-0111 or (800) 243-3174; and **TravelGuard International,** 1145 Clark St., Stevens Point, WI 54481, tel. (715) 345-0505 or (800) 782-5151.

In the UK: The **Association of British Insurers,** 51 Gresham St., London BC2V 7HQ, tel. (171) 600-3333, and **Europe Assistance,** 252 High St., Croyden, Surrey CR0 1NF, tel. (181) 680-1234, can provide advice for obtaining travel insurance in Britain. Inexpensive travel insurance is offered through **Campus Travel,** tel. (0171) 730-8111; **Endsleigh Insurance,** tel. (0171) 436-4451; and **STA Travel,** tel. (0171) 361-6262.

In Cuba: You can obtain insurance once you

arrive in Cuba through **Asistur,** Paseo del Prado #254, Habana Vieja, tel. (33) 8920, (33) 8527, or (33) 8339, fax (33) 8087, e-mail: seguro@asist. sid.cu, in association with the Cuban insurance agency, **Aseguradora del Turismo La Isla S.A.,** Calle 14 #301 esq. Calle 3ra, Miramar, tel. (24) 7490, fax (24) 7494. The basic package covers up to US$400 of baggage, US$7,000 in medical expenses, US$5,000 for repatriation, plus additional coverage.

The Cuban agency **ESEN,** Avenida 5ta #306, Vedado, tel. (32) 2508, fax (33) 8717, also offers medical insurance for foreign travelers (US$10 per US$1,000 of treatment). Another Cuban company, **ESICUBA,** Seguros Internacionales de Cuba, Calle Cuba 314, e/ Obispo y Obrapía, tel. (57) 3231, fax (33) 8038, e-mail: esicuba@sic.get, offers travelers' insurance, although most of its policies are oriented toward the needs of companies, not individuals. ESICUBA insures all kinds of risks. Premiums are expensive and can be paid in any convertible foreign currency (indemnities are paid in the same currency). Open 8 a.m.-3 p.m. Both ESEN and ESICUBA are independent companies, although the Cuban government is the major shareholder. They're rated by Insurance Solvency International and reinsure through Lloyd's of London and other major insurers.

Common-Sense Precautions

Make photocopies of all important documents: your passport (showing photograph and visas, if applicable), airline ticket, credit cards, insurance policy, driver's license. Carry the photocopies with you, and leave the originals along with your other valuables in the hotel safe where possible. If this isn't possible, carry the originals with you in a secure inside pocket. Don't put all your eggs in one basket. Prepare an "emergency kit" that includes photocopies of your documents and an adequate sum of money to tide you over if your wallet gets stolen.

Never carry more cash than you need for the day. The rest should be kept in the hotel safe. If you don't trust the hotel or if it doesn't have a safe, try as best you can to hide your valuables and secure your room. The majority of your money should be in the form of traveler's checks, which can be refunded if lost or stolen.

Never carry your wallet in your back pocket. In-

stead, wear a secure money belt. Alternatively, you can carry your bills in your front pocket. Pack them beneath a handkerchief. Carry any other money in an inside pocket, a "secret" pocket sewn into your pants or jacket, or hidden in a body pouch or an elasticized wallet below the knee. Spread your money around your person.

Don't wear jewelry, chains, or expensive watches. Leave them with your ego at home. Wear an inexpensive digital watch. And be particularly wary after cashing money at a bank, or if doing a deal with a *jinitero*. For credit card security, insist that imprints are made in your presence. Make sure any imprints incorrectly completed are torn up. Don't take someone else's word that it will be done. Destroy the carbons yourself.

Never leave your purse, camera, or luggage unattended in public places. Always keep a wary eye on your luggage on public transportation, especially backpacks (sneak thieves love their zippered compartments). Don't carry more luggage than you can adequately manage. Limit your baggage to *one* suitcase or duffel. And have a lock for each luggage item. Purses should have a short strap (ideally, one with metal woven in) that fits tightly against the body and snaps closed or has a zipper. *Always* keep purses fully zipped and luggage locked.

Don't leave anything of value within reach of an open window. And don't leave anything of value in your car.

If Trouble Strikes

If things turn dire, you should contact **Asistur,** which exists to provide assistance to tourists in trouble. Its services include providing insurance, medical assistance, funeral repatriation, and legal and financial aid. Asistur also helps obtain new travel documents and locate lost luggage, and may even indemnify against loss (assuming you already have travelers' insurance). The main office is at Calle 4 #110 e/ 1ra y 3ra, Miramar, tel. (24) 8835, fax (24) 1613 or (33) 8088, e-mail: comercia@asistur.get.cma.net, website: www.asistur.cubaweb.cu. It has an **alarm center** at Prado #212 esq. Trocadero in Habana Vieja, tel. (33) 8920, fax (33) 8087, e-mail: asisten@asisten.get. cma.net, open 24 hours, 365 days a year.

You should also contact your embassy or consulate. Consulate officials can't get you out of jail, but they can help you locate a lawyer, alle-

DRUGS

Cuban law prohibits the possession, sale, or use of narcotic substances, including marijuana. Laws are strictly enforced, and Cuba vigorously prosecutes drug traffickers caught in Cuban territory. Whatever your personal beliefs on drug use, Cuba is no place to try to make a statement about rights. If you're caught, you will receive no special favors because you're foreign. A trial could take many months, in which case you'll be jailed on the premise that you're guilty until proven innocent. Be aware that if offered drugs on the street, you may be dealing with a plainclothes policeman.

Drug use has been increasing in recent years with the blossoming of tourism and as Colombian drug lords take advantage of Cuba's remote, scattered cays to make transshipments en route to the United States. Still, few countries are so drug-free, and use is negligible among the Cuban populace. You may, rarely, come across homegrown marijuana, but serious drug use is unknown.

---

viate unhealthy conditions, or arrange for funds to be wired if you run short of money. They may even be able to authorize a reimbursable loan while you arrange for cash to be forwarded, or even lend you money to get home (the US State Department hates to admit this).

If you're robbed, immediately file a police report. You'll need this to make an insurance claim. You'll receive a statement *(denuncio)* for insurance purposes (and to replace lost tourist cards, traveler's checks, etc.), which you should make sure is dated and stamped. (The Cuban police energetically investigate theft against foreigners, although there have been recent reports that this may not always be the case. At press time, there was no special unit responsible for pursuing thefts from tourists.)

US citizens shouldn't expect the **US Interests Section,** c/o Embassy of Switzerland, Calzada e/ L y M, Vedado, tel. (32) 0551 or (32) 9700, to bend over backward; it exists for political reasons, not to help citizens (nonetheless, depending on your predicament, your plight may be sufficient to ensure assistance). The *Handbook of Consular Services,* Public Affairs

Staff, Bureau of Consular Affairs, US Department of State, Washington, DC 20520, provides details of such assistance. Friends and family can also call the Department of State's **Overseas Citizen Service,** tel. (202) 647-5225, to check on you if things go awry. Remember, however, that the US does not have *full* diplomatic representation in Cuba, and its tapestry of pullable strings is understandably threadbare. If arrested, US citizens should ask Cuban authorities to notify the US Interests Section. A US consular officer will then try to arrange regular visits, at the discretion of the Cuban government. (Cuba does not recognize dual citizenship for Cuban citizens who are also US citizens; Cuban-born citizens are—according to the US State Department—thereby denied representation through the US Interests Section in the event of arrest).

Legal Assistance: Asistur (see above) provides legal assistance. The **Consultoría Jurídica Internacional** (International Judicial Consultative Bureau), Calle 18 #120, esq. Avenida 3, Miramar, Havana, tel. (24) 2490, fax (24) 2303; and Avenida 1 #2008, esq. Calle 21, Varadero, tel. (33) 7077, fax (33) 7080, also provides legal advice and services regarding all aspects of Cuban law—from marriages and notarization to advising on the constitutionality of business ventures. It can assist travelers, including those who lose their passports or have them stolen (for US citizens, Cuban officials can produce documents—US$175—that preclude needing to have a new US passport issued in the USA via the US Interests Section).

Medical Evacuation

Uncle Sam has deemed that even US emergency evacuation services cannot fly to Cuba to evacuate US citizens without a license from the Treasury Department. Of course, the rules keep changing, so it may be worth checking the latest situation with such companies as **Traveler's Emergency Network,** P.O. Box 238, Hyattsville, MD 20797, tel. (800) 275-4836, and **International SOS Assistance,** Box 11568, Philadelphia, PA 19116, tel. (215) 244-1500 or (800) 523-8930, fax (215) 244-0165, e-mail: individual@intsos.com, website: www.intsos.com, both of which provide worldwide ground and air evacuation as well as medical assistance.

EMERGENCY HELP FOR U.S. CITIZENS

In the event of an emergency, the following may be of help:

Citizen's Emergency Center, US State Department, tel. (202) 647-5225, fax (202) 647-3000.

International SOS Assistance, 8 Neshaminy Interplex, P.O. Box 11568, Philadelphia, PA 19116, tel. (215) 244-1500.

International Legal Defense Counsel, 11 S. 15th St., Packard Bldg., Philadelphia, PA 19102, tel. (215) 977-9982.

The insurance packages sold by **Aseguradora del Turismo La Isla S.A.,** Calle 14 #301 esq. Calle 3ra, Miramar, tel. (24) 7490, fax (24) 7494, include US$5,000 coverage for repatriation in the need of medical evacuation.

OTHER PRACTICALITIES

Weights and Measures

Cuba operates on the metric system. Liquids are sold in liters, fruits and vegetables by the kilo. Distances are given in meters and kilometers. See the chart at the back of the book for metric conversions.

Vestiges of the US system and old Spanish systems remain, however, such as the *pulgada* (2.54 cm, or one inch), *cordel* (20.35 meters, or 22.26 yards), or more commonly, the *caballeria* (about 324 square *cordeles,* deemed sufficient to support a mounted soldier and his family). Old units of weight still heard include the *onza* (about one ounce), *libra* (about one pound), *saco* (a measure of coffee), and *quintal.*

Time

Cuban time is equivalent to US eastern standard time: five hours behind Greenwich mean time, the same as New York and Miami, and three hours ahead of the US West Coast. There is little seasonal variation in dawn. Cuba has daylight saving time May-October.

Business Hours

Hours are flexible. Government offices usually open Mon.-Fri. 8:30 a.m.-12:30 p.m. and 1:30-5:30 p.m. and every second Saturday 8:30 a.m.-noon. Banks are usually open Mon.-Fri. 8:30 a.m.-noon and 1:30-3 p.m., Saturday 8:30-10:30 a.m. Post offices are usually open Mon.-Sat. 8 a.m.-10 p.m., Sunday 8 a.m.-6 p.m. Most shops are open Mon.-Sat. 8:30 a.m.-5:30 p.m., although many remain open later, including all day Sunday. Museum opening times vary widely (and change frequently), although most are closed on Monday. Most banks, businesses, and government offices close during national holidays.

Many Cubans still honor the *merienda,* coffee breaks taken usually at about 10 a.m. and 3 p.m.

Habaneros like to dine late. Hence, many restaurants are open until midnight, and some stay open 24 hours. However, local eateries

NATIONAL HOLIDAYS

1 January, Liberation Day (Día de la Liberación)

2 January, Victory Day (Día de la Victoria)

28 January, José Martí's birthday

24 February, Anniversary of the Second War of Independence

8 March, International Women's Day (Día de las Mujeres)

13 March, Anniversary of the students' attack on the presidential palace

19 April, Bay of Pigs Victory (Victoria del Playa Girón)

1 May, Labor Day (Día de las Trabajadores)

26 July, National Revolution Day (anniversary of the attack on the Moncada barracks)

30 July, Day of the Martyrs of the Revolution

8 October, Anniversary of Che Guevara's death

10 October, Anniversary of the First War of Independence

28 October, Memorial day to Camilio Cienfuegos

2 December, Anniversary of the landing of the *Granma*

7 December, Memorial day to Antonio Maceo

serving Cubans often run out of food by mid-evening—don't leave dining too late.

Electricity
Cuba operates on 110-volt AC (60-cycle) nationwide, although a few newer hotels operate on 220 volts. Most outlets use US plugs: flat, parallel two-pins, and three rectangular pins. A two-prong adapter is a good idea (take one with you; they're hard to come by in Cuba).

Although things have improved of late, Havana still suffers regular electricity blackouts (*apagones*). Take a flashlight and spare batteries. A couple of long-lasting candles are also a good idea. Don't forget the matches or a lighter. (Since blackouts strike different areas at different times, many Habaneros have managed to avoid the effects of the *apagones* by rigging *tendederas,* or extension wires, between two adjacent buildings that lie across the dividing lines of areas affected by *apagones*. Thus, neither house goes without electricity. Often, the *tendederas* extend for blocks around.)

Laundromats
The only "self-service" laundry is the ultramodern **Aster Lavandería,** on Calle 34 e/ 3 y 5, Miramar, tel. (24) 1622. You can leave your clothes here and pick them up the same day. It costs US$3 per load for wash-and-dry. Open Mon.-Sat. 8 a.m.-3 p.m. It also offers dry-cleaning (US$2 for pants, US$1.50 for shirts).

Most upscale hotels offer dry-cleaning and laundry service. It's expensive and usually takes two days, and the results are sometimes questionable. It's easy enough to find locals willing to wash your clothes for a few dollars. Ask around.

The telephone directory lists several dozen other laundries throughout Havana, including more than a dozen self-service *(auto servicio)* locales, most in outlying areas. Look under the heading "Tintorerías y Lavanderías."

Libraries
Havana has many libraries, although none come up to international standard, being poorly stocked and largely devoid of international texts. The main one is the **Biblioteca Nacional,** on the east side of Plaza de la Revolución, tel. (81) 8780, fax (35) 5442. Open Mon.-Sat. 8:30 a.m.-6:30 p.m. You can use the reference room.

The **Biblioteca Provincial de la Habana** opened in 1999 on the east side of Plaza de Armas, to much ballyhoo. However, it's a meagerly stocked affair (on a par with a rural village in the US or UK), with only a modest supply of mostly out-of-date encyclopedias and texts, mostly from the 1960s. I saw *no* book published later than the 1980s. It also has a small magazine room, plus a small musical library. Open Mon.-Fri. 8:10 a.m.-9 p.m., Saturday 9 a.m.-5:30 p.m., but closed the first Monday of each month.

There are several specialized libraries, too. The **Biblioteca del Instituto de Literatura y**

Calle San Ignacio

Linguística, on Avenida Salvador Allende #710 e/ Castillejo y Soledad, tel. (75) 405, for example, has a huge collection of novels and foreign-language texts (open Mon.-Fri. 8 a.m.-5 p.m., Saturday 8 a.m.-2 p.m.); and the **Biblioteca de Medicinas** on La Rampa at Calle N, tel. (32) 4317, offers medical texts (open Mon.-Sat. 7:45 a.m.-7:45 p.m.). The **Biblioteca Nacional de Ciencias y Tecnología,** in the Academy of Sciences at the Capitolio in Habana Vieja, tel. (60) 3411, ext. 1329, has books on sciences and technology. Open Mon.-Sat. 8 a.m.-5 p.m.

Toilets

Public toilets are as rare as four-leaf clovers. Exceptions are at Obispo #511, which costs US20 cents, and near the Capitolio at Dragones #57.

Most hotels and restaurants will let you use their facilities, but expect to have a security guard follow you in to check that you're not planting a bomb. Seriously! There's often an attendant sitting outside the door: note the bowl with a few coins meant to invite a tip.

Be sure to pack a roll of toilet paper. There is hardly any toilet paper available in Cuba, including in the dollar stores. Even hotel bathrooms often are without (the rolls get stolen by needy Cubans, who often resort to using soap and water after visiting the loo).

CUBAN SPANISH

Learning the basics of Spanish will aid your travels considerably. In key tourist destinations, however, you should be able to get along fine without it. Most Cubans are well educated, and English is widely spoken in Havana; the number of English speakers is growing rapidly. (For example, English is now required of all university students and hotel staff. Most larger hotels have bilingual desk staffs, and English is widely spoken by the staff of car rental agencies and tour companies.) Cubans are exceedingly keen to practice their English, and you will be approached often by such individuals. Many Cubans know at least the basics of one other European language (a surprising number are fluent in French and, of course, Russian). Away from the tourist path, far fewer people speak English.

Use that as an excuse to learn some Spanish. Cubans warm quickly to those who make an effort to speak their language. Don't be bashful. Use what Spanish you know, and you'll be surprised how quickly you become familiar with the language.

Several Spanish language courses are offered in Havana.

Pronunciation

Castilian Spanish, with its lisping "c"s and "z"s, is the Spanish of Spain, not Latin America (Cubans do not lisp their "c"s and "z"s; they pronounce the letters more like an "s," as do Andalusians and most other Latin Americans). In its literary form, Cuban Spanish is pure, classical Castilian. Unhappily, in its spoken form, Cuban Spanish is the most difficult to understand in all of Latin America. Cubans have lent their own renditions to the Spanish sound: like a zebra that is not quite a horse, Cuban Spanish is white but with black stripes.

Cubans speak far more briskly than other Latin Americans, blurring their rapid-fire words together. The diction of Cuba is lazy and unclear. The letter "s," for example, is usually swallowed altogether, especially in plurals. The swallowed "s"s are accumulated for use in restaurants, where they are released to get the server's attention—"S-s-s-s-s-st!" Because of this, a restaurant with bad service can sound like a pit of snakes. The final consonants of words are also often deleted, as are dipthongs such as "d" and, often, the entire last syllable of words ("If they dropped any more syllables, they would be speechless," suggests author Tom Miller). Regional variants exist, too. I find the Spanish of the Oriente a bit slower and less confusing. Around Baracoa, the idiom of the Indians endures.

Cubanisms to Know

Cubans are long-winded and full of flowery, passionate, rhetorical flourishes. Fidel Castro didn't inherit his penchant for long speeches from dour, taciturn Galicia—it's a purely Cuban characteristic. Cubans also spice up the language with little affectations and teasing endearments—*piropos*—given and taken among themselves without offense.

Many English (or "American") words have found their way into Cuban diction. Cubans go to *beisbol* and today eat *hamburgesas.* But like the English, Cubans are clever in their use of words, imbuing their language with double entendres and their own lexicon of similes. Cubans are also great cussers. The two most common cuss words littering the verbal landscape are *cojones* (balls) and *coño* (cunt).

Formal courtesies are rarely used when greeting someone. Since the Revolution, everyone is a *compañero* or *compañera,* although *señor* and *señora* (which were considered too bourgeois following the Revolution) are coming back into vogue. Cubans speak to each other directly, no holds barred. Even conversations with strangers are laced with *"¡Ay, muchacha!"* ("Hey, girl!"), *"¡Mira chica!"* ("Look, girl!"), and *"¡Hombre!"* ("Listen man!") when someone disagrees with the other.

Confusingly, ciao! (used as a long-term goodbye) is also used as a greeting in casual passing—the equivalent of "Hi!" You will also be asked *¿Como anda?* ("How goes it?").

A common courtesy when paying a call on someone, especially in the countryside, is to call out *"¡Upe!"* from outside the house to let him or her know you're there. As you enter, you should say *"Con permiso"* ("With your permission").

Ediciones Universal, P.O. Box 450353, Miami, FL 33145, publishes a *Diccionario de Cubanismos,* but in Spanish only.

APPENDIX: INTERNET ADDRESSES

Information Sources
CubaWeb Travel and Tourism:
www.cubaweb.cu
Cuba Turismo:
www2.ceniai.inf.cu/homepage/turismo.html
The Cuban Experience:
www.library.advanced.org/18355/
Havana supersite: www.lahabana.com
Cuban government (official site):
www.cubaweb.cu

Cuban Tour and Travel Operators
Aerostar Viajes a Cuba: www.aero-star.com
Cubana de Aviación: www.cuba.cu
Grupo Cubanacán: www.cubanacan.cu
Havanatur tour agency:
www.havanatur.cubaweb.cu
Havanautos car rental:
www.havanautos.cubaweb.cu
Horizontes Hoteles: www.horizontes.cu
Transtur: www.transtur.cubaweb.cu:

US and US-Related Tour Operators
Cuba Connection: www.cuba.tc
Cuba Travel: www.cubatravel.com.mx
Last Frontier Expeditions:
www.clubhavana.com
Marazul Tours: www.marazultours.com

News Organizations and Publications
Cubanet: www.cubanet.org
Bohemia:
www.2.cuba.cu/cultura/revistas/bohemia
Granma: www.granma.cu
Information Services Latin America (ISLA):
www.igc.org/isla
Juventud Rebelde: www.jreblede.cubaweb.cu
Latin American News Syndicate: www.latam-news.com

Prensa Latina: www.prensa-latina.org
Radio Rebelde: www.2.cuba.cu/RRebelde

Generic
Caribbean Super Site:
www.caribbeansupersite.com/cuba/index.htm
Center for Cuban Studies:
www.cubaupdate.com
Consultoria Juridica Internacional:
www.cji.cubaweb.cu
Cuba (culture): www.2.cuba.cu/cultura
Cuba (education): www.2.cuba.cu/education
Cuba (general): www.city.net/countries/cuba/
Cuba (weather report): www.intellicast.com
Cuba (people): www.cubaweb.cu/pueblo
Cuba (medical sciences): www.infomed.sld.cu
Cuba (museums): www.cubaweb.cu/museos
Cuba (science): www.2.cuba.cu/cienciacuba
Cuba (sports): www.2.cuba.cu/deportes
Cuba (websites):
www.smallshop.com/cubawebsites.htm
Cuban American Alliance Education Fund:
www.cubamer.org
Fidel Castro's speeches:
gopher://lanic.utexas.edu:70/00/
Havana weather report:
weather.yahoo.com/forecast/Havana

Government Organizations
US Government health advisories:
www.cdc.gov
US Government Cuba advisories:
www.travel.state.gov/cuba.html

Information on Moon Travel Handbooks and the Author
Moon Travel Handbooks: www.moon.com
Christopher P. Baker:
www.travelguidebooks.com

BOOKLIST

For a complete range of texts on Cuba, visit www.cubabooks.com, which also offers most of the books listed here available online at a discount.

BOOKS ABOUT HAVANA

Coffee Table

Aguilar Cabello, Juan Carlos (photography by Alberto Fernández Miranda. *Tropicana de Cuba*. Havana: Visual América, 1998. The story of Havana's showiest nightclub, from its beginnings in 1939 to the present day, lavishly illustrated in full color.

Barclay, Juliet (photographs by Martin Charles). *Havana: Portrait of a City*. London: Cassell, 1993. A well-researched and abundantly illustrated coffee-table volume especially emphasizing the city's history. Written in a lively, readable style.

Edinger, Claudio. *Old Havana*. New York: Distributed Art Publishers, 1998. Life in Habana Vieja is portrayed in evocative and dramatic fashion, with orange color throughout, as seen by this noted photographer. Introductions by Guillermo Cabrera Infante and Humbert Wernerck provide equally powerful statements.

Graetz, Rick. *Havana: The City, The People*. Helena, MT: American Geographic Publishing, 1991. A tribute to Havana in full-color photography that captures the spirit of the 500-year-old city. Minimal text.

Krantz, Jim. *Havana*. Poignant and provocative, this superb coffee-table book offers mostly black-and-white images that capture the tender side of a Havana in lamentable decline. The "good" and the "bad" in equal measure. The silently eloquent photos are supported by text by Christopher P. Baker.

Michener, James, and John Kings. *Six Days in Havana*. Austin, TX: University of Texas Press, 1989. A wonderful read regaling the noted novelist's brief but emotionally touching week in Havana. Beautifully illustrated.

Sapieha, Nicolas. *Old Havana, Cuba*. London: Tauris Parke Books, 1990. A small yet beautifully illustrated coffee-table book accompanied by lively text.

Stout, Nancy, and Jorge Rigau. *Havana*. New York: Rizzoli, 1994. A stunning coffee-table book that captures the mood of the city in color and black-and-white photography; superb text and essays add to the photographic perspectives on Havana's cultural and architectural history.

Walker, Evans. *Havana*. New York: Pantheon, 1989. A reissue of the classic collection of black-and-white photographs depicting life in Cuba in the 1930s, first published in 1933.

Fiction

Greene, Graham. *Our Man in Havana*. New York: Penguin, 1971. The story of Wormold, a conservative British vacuum-cleaner salesman in prerevolutionary Havana. Recruited by British intelligence, Wormold finds little information to pass on, and so invents it. Full of the sensuality of Havana and the tensions of Batista's last days.

Travel Guides

Segre, Roberto, Mario Coyula, and Joseph L. Scarpaci. *Havana: Two Faces of the Antillean Metropolis*. New York: John Wiley & Sons, 1997 Aimed at both the academic and lay reader, this informative and accessible volume (written by two architects and an urban geographer) profiles the urbanization of Havana over its 500-year history.

Travel Literature

Codrescu, Andrei. *Ay, Cuba!* New York: St. Martin's Press, 1999. A no-holds-barred barefist account of the Rumanian author's 12-day sojourn in Havana during the Pope's visit in January 1998. Combining trenchant, witty social criticism, Codrescu explores the sensual and engaging culture while skewering you-know-who at every turn.

Miller, John, and Susannah Clark, eds. *Chronicles Abroad: Havana.* San Francisco: Chronicle Books, 1996. Short essays and extracts on Havana (but also on other places in Cuba), by such authors as Richard Henry Dana, Graham Greene, Ernest Hemingway, Mario Puzo, and Fidel Castro. A marvelous read.

General

Schwartz, Rosalie. *Pleasure Island: Tourism & Temptation in Cuba.* Lincoln, NE: University of Nebraska Press, 1997. A brilliant review of tourism development in Cuba and how it has shaped the face of Havana for more than a century, including a fair-minded look at the economic prosperity and notable civic works of the Machado and Batista eras. The book is balanced, and the story is surprisingly lively and engagingly told.

BOOKS ABOUT CUBA

Coffee Table

Beytout, Olivier, and François Missen. *Memories of Cuba.* New York: Thunder's Mouth Press, 1997. Spanning the country, two French photographers capture the spirit and sadness and, above all, the surrealism of Cuba in this small book of images backed by snippets of text from well-known Cubans.

Carley, Rachel (photography by Andrea Brizzi). *Cuba: 400 Years of Architectural Heritage.* New York: Whitney Library of Design, 1997. A beautiful large-format work that spans the island and ages, tracing the evolution of architectural styles from the earliest colonial influences to the contemporary edifices and influences that are reshaping the face of the country.

Friedman, Marcia. *Cuba: The Special Period.* Madison, Samuel Book Publishers, 1998. Friedman's title is a weakly devised peg to hang generic photos of Havana and Santiago de Cuba. The effect is further diluted by too many snapshot quality images. Cuban exiles provide text.

García, Cristina, and Joshua Greene. *Cars of Cuba.* New York: Harry N. Abrams, 1995. A splendid book with color photographs of 53 lovingly maintained beauties from the heyday of Detroit. It also features a lively introduction.

Giovan, Tria. *Cuba: The Elusive Island.* New York: Abrams, 1996. More than 100 images capture the richness of Cuba in all its complex and enigmatic forms, with textual extracts from a wide range of contemporary and historical sources.

Graetz, Rick. *Cuba: The Land, The People.* Helena, MT: American Geographic Publishing, 1990. A slender coffee-table book that shows Cuba's diverse beauty with stunning visual imagery. Meager text.

Kohli, Eddy. *Cuba.* New York: Rizzoli, 1997. A luxurious large-format book in which the sharp-eyed photographer captures the spirit of the people and land in dreamy, impressionistic imagery. Compelling!

Kufeld, Adam. *Cuba.* New York: W.W. Norton, 1994. A stunning photographic portrait of Cuba depicting all aspects of life. The book is enhanced by Tom Miller's introduction ("Kufeld has achieved that rare perspective of looking at Cuba from the inside out, and in doing so he has given us a gentle look at a hard place").

Lewis, Barry, and Peter Marshall. *Into Cuba.* New York: Alfred Van Der Marck Editions, 1985. An evocative and richly illustrated coffee-table book widely available in Cuba.

Núñez Jiménez, Antonio. *The Journey of the Havana Cigar.* Havana: Empresa Cubana del Tabaco, 1995. A large-volume treatise on the history of Cuban cigars lavishly illustrated with glossy photos.

Smith, Wayne (photographs by Michael Reagan). *Portrait of Cuba.* Atlanta, GA: Turner

Publishing, 1991. A succinct, lucid, and entertaining profile on contemporary Cuba told by a noted expert. This splendid coffee-table book is superbly illustrated.

Stout, Nancy. *Habanos: The Story of the Havana Cigar*. New York: Rizzoli, 1997. Stout explores the history and culture of Cuba in-depth to tell the tale of the Havana cigar. The large-format book is lavishly illustrated with the author's own photography.

Williams, Stephen. *Cuba: The Land, The History, The People, The Culture*. Philadelphia, PA: Running Press Books, 1994. A richly evocative, lavishly illustrated coffee-table book with a concise and enlivened text.

Art and Culture

Behar, Ruth, ed. *Bridges to Cuba/Puentes á Cuba*. Ann Arbor, MI: University of Michigan Press, 1995. An evocative and sometimes moving anthology of essays, poetry, and fiction providing perspectives on contemporary Cuba from within Cuba and throughout the Cuban diaspora.

Camnitzer, Luís. *New Art of Cuba*. Austin, TX: University of Texas Press, 1994. Profiles the work of 40 young Cubans who formed part of the first generaton of postrevolutionary artists.

Geldof, Lynn. *Cubans: Voices of Change*. New York: St. Martin's Press, 1991. Interviews with Cubans representing the spectrum of viewpoints and backgrounds.

Lewis, Oscar, Ruth M. Lewis, and Susan M. Rigdon. *Four Men: Living the Revolution, An Oral History of Contemporary Cuba*. Urbana, IL: University of Illinois Press, 1977.

Montejo, Estebán. *The Autobiography of a Runaway Slave*. Newark, NJ: Pantheon, 1968 (edited by Miguel Barnet).

Moore, Carlos. *Castro, the Blacks, and Africa*. Los Angeles: Center for Afro-American Studies, University of California, 1988.

Stubbs, Jean, and Pedro Pérez Sarduy, eds. *AfroCuba: An Anthology of Cuban Writing on Race, Politics and Culture*. New York: Ocean Press/Center for Cuban Studies, 1993. An anthology of black Cuban writing on aspects of "Afrocuba," including essays, poetry, and extracts from novels.

Timerman, Jacobo. *Cuba: A Journey*. New York: Knopf, 1990. A passionate, provocative, and sometimes scathing report of a recent journey through Cuba by a man who suffered torture at the hands of right-wing Argentinian extremists and who formerly idealized Cuba as a model socialist state.

General

Calder, Simon, and Emily Hatchwell. *Cuba: A Guide to the People, Politics and Culture*. London: Latin America Bureau, 1995. A slender yet thoughtful and insightful overview of Cuba.

Halperin, Maurice. *Return to Havana*. Nashville, TN: Vanderbilt University Press, 1994. An engaging and scathing personal essay on contemporary Cuba by a professor who taught in Havana and worked for Cuba's Ministry of Foreign Trade in the 1960s.

Rudolf, James, ed. *Cuba: A Country Study*. Washington, D.C.: Government Printing Office (write to: Superintendent of Documents, Government Printing Office, Washington, DC 20402). Part of the US Government Area Handbook Studies. A surprisingly balanced general study of Cuba, with detailed sections on history, economics, and politics.

Fiction

Carpentier, Alejo. *Reasons of State*. Havana: Writers and Readers. A novelistic tour de force, alive with wit and erudition, about the despotic head of state of an unnamed Latin American country in the early days of the 20th century.

Cabrera Infante, Guillermo. *Three Trapped Tigers*. New York: Avon, 1985. A poignant and comic novel, described as "a vernacular, elegiac masterpiece," that captures the essence of life in Havana before the ascendance of Castro. Written by an "enemy of the state" who has lived in embittered exile since 1962.

García, Cristina. *Dreaming in Cuban.* New York: Ballantine Books, 1992. A brilliant, poignant, languid, and sensual tale of a family divided politically and geographically by the Cuban revolution and the generational fissures that open on each side: in Cuba, between an ardently pro-Castro grandmother and a daughter who retreats into *santería;* in America, between another, militantly anti-Castro daughter and her own rebellious punk-artist daughter, who mocks her obsession.

Hemingway, Ernest. *Islands in the Stream.* New York: Harper Collins, 1970. An exciting triptych. The second and third parts are set in Cuba during the war and draw heavily on the author's own experience hunting Nazi U-boats at sea. Havana features prominently.

Hemingway, Ernest. *The Old Man and the Sea.* New York: Scribner's, 1952. The simple yet profound story of an unlucky Cuban fisherman. The slim novel won the author the Nobel Prize for Literature.

Hemingway, Ernest. *To Have and Have Not.* New York: Macmillan Publishing, 1937. The dramatic, brutal tale of running contraband between Havana and Key West.

Iyer, Pico. *Cuba in the Night.* New York: Alfred A. Knopf, 1995. A slow-moving story of a love affair between a globetrotting photojournalist and a young Cuban woman. The spirit of José Martí hovers over the trysts and political musings. Set in Cuba during the Special Period, the author stresses the atmosphere of suspicion and negativity.

Leonard, Elmore. *Cuba Libre.* New York: Delacorte Press, 1998. Set on the eve of the Spanish-American War, this explosive mix of adventure and history makes exciting reading.

History and Politics

Aguila, Juan M. del. *Cuba: Dilemnas of a Revolution.* Boulder, CO: Westview Press, 1994. An up-to-date, well-balanced review of the history and contemporary reality of Cuba.

Benjamin, Jules R. *The United States and the Origins of the Cuban Revolution.* Princeton, NJ: Princeton University Press, 1990. A superb study explaining how Cuba and the United States arrived at the traumatic rupture in their relations.

Benjamin, Medea, ed. *Cuba: A Current Issues Reader.* San Francisco: Global Exchange, 1994. A compilation of recent articles on a wide range of Cuban topics.

Bonachea, Rolando, and Nelson Valdés. *Cuba in Revolution.* New York: Anchor Books, 1972. A collection of essays by noted academics, providing a comprehensive, many-sided overview of the Cuban Revolution and the issues it raises.

Eckstein, Susan. *Back from the Future: Cuba under Castro.* Princeton, NJ: Princeton University Press, 1994. A well-reasoned and balanced attempt to provide a broad overview of Castro's Cuba. Eckstein contends that Cuba is less rigidly Marxist than presented and that a revisionist view is needed.

Halebsky, Sandor, and John Kirk, eds. *Cuba in Transition: Crisis and Transformation.* Westview Press, 1992.

Johnson, Haynes. *The Bay of Pigs.* New York: Norton, 1964. Writing in collaboration with leaders of the Brigade, Haynes provides both perspectives in this masterful, encyclopedic work.

Kennedy, Robert F. *Thirteen Days: A Memoir of the Cuban Missile Crisis.* New York: Norton, 1969.

Martí, José. *Inside the Monster: Writings on the United States and American Imperialism.* New York: Monthly Review Press, 1975 (Phillip S. Fosner, ed.). Essential prose works of the late-19th-century activist, literary man, and national hero, who has exercised a lasting influence on the politics of 20th-century Cuba.

Mesa-Lago, Carmelo, ed. *Cuba After the Cold War*. Pittsburgh, PA: University of Pittsburgh, 1993.

Meyer, Karl E., and Tad Szulc. *The Cuban Invasion*. New York: Praeger, 1962. A shrewd and fascinating interpretation of the Bay of Pigs.

Ortíz, Fernando. *Cuban Counterpoint: Tobacco and Sugar*. New York: Alfred A. Knopf, 1947. A seminal work on the decisiveness of tobacco and sugar in Cuban history.

Patterson, Thomas G. *Contesting Castro: The United States and the Triumph of the Cuban Revolution*. New York: Oxford University Press, 1994.

Pérez, Louis A. *Cuba: Between Reform and Revolution*. New York: Oxford University Press, 1988.

Pérez-Stable, Marifeli. *The Cuban Revolution: Origins, Course, and Legacy*. New York: Oxford University Press, 1993. A negative review of the past four decades. It closes with a polemic offering a damning accusation of a revolution betrayed.

Schulz, Donald, ed. *Cuba and the Future*. Westport, CT: Greenwood Press, 1994. A series of essays analysizing Cuba's contemporary economic and political dilemnas.

Smith, Wayne. *The Closest of Enemies*. New York: W.W. Norton, 1987.

Stubbs, Jean. *Cuba: The Test of Time*. London: Latin American Bureau, 1989. A comprehensive overview of Cuban economics, politics, religion, and social structure.

Thomas, Hugh. *Cuba: The Pursuit of Freedom, 1726-1969*. New York: Harper & Row, 1971. A seminal work—called a "magisterial conspectus of Cuban history"—tracing the evolution of conditions that eventually engendered the Revolution.

Thomas, Hugh. *The Cuban Revolution*. London: Weidenfeld and Nicolson, 1986. The definitive work on the Revolution, offering a brilliant analysis of all aspects of the country's diverse and tragic history.

Wyden, Peter. *Bay of Pigs: The Untold Story*. New York: Simon and Schuster, 1979. An in-depth and riveting exposé of the CIA's ill-conceived mission to topple Castro.

Yglesias, José. *In the Fist of the Revolution*. New York: Pantheon, 1968.

Personalities

Anderson, John. *Che Guevara: A Revolutionary Life*. New York: Grove Press, 1997. The definitive and spellbinding biography on Guevara, revealing an astonishing profile of this fascinating, controversial, and charismatic figure.

Bonachea, Rolando, and Nelson Valdés. *Selected Works of Ernesto Guevara*. Cambridge, MA: M.I.T. Press, 1969.

Castro, Fidel. *Che: A Memoir by Fidel Castro*, Melbourne, Australia: Ocean Press, 1983. Fidel's candid account of his relationship with Che Guevara documents the man, the revolutionary, the thinker, and the Argentine-born doctor's extraordinary bond with Cuba.

Cruz, Mary. *Cuba and Hemingway on the Great Blue River*. Havana: Editorial José Martí, 1994. A splendid critical study of Hemingway's writings in which the author presents the theory that Hemingway's works reflect core tenets of Cuban ideology.

Franqui, Carlos. *Family Portrait with Fidel*. New York: Vintage Books, 1985. An insider's look at how the Sovietization of the Cuban Revolution occurred and precisely what goals Fidel Castro had in mind. The author debunks myths and provides startling revelations.

Fuentes, Norberto. *Hemingway in Cuba*. Secaucus, NY: Lyle Stuart, 1984. The seminal, lavishly illustrated study of the Nobel Prize winner's years in Cuba.

Geyer, Georgie Anne. *Guerrilla Prince: The Untold Story of Fidel Castro.* Boston: Little, Brown & Company, 1991. An extraordinary biography that reveals the Machiavellianism of Fidel Castro as the author attempts to explain the mysticism of the meticulously secretive Cuban leader. The result is at times astounding.

Gray, Richard Butler. *José Martí, Cuban Patriot.* Gainesville, FL: University of Florida Press, 1962.

Halperin, Maurice. *The Taming of Fidel Castro.* Berkeley, CA: University of California Press, 1981.

Hemingway, Gregory. *Papa, A Personal Memory.* New York: Pocket Books, 1976. A funny, serious, and touching account of the author's childhood, including a long period in Cuba with his father, Ernest Hemingway.

Kenner, Martin, and James Petras. *Fidel Castro Speaks.* New York: Penguin Books, 1969. A collection of 16 of Castro's most important speeches, made between his seizure of power in 1959 and 1968.

Lockwood, Lee. *Castro's Cuba, Cuba's Fidel.* Boulder, CO: Westview Press, 1990.

Oppenheimer, Andres. *Castro's Final Hour.* New York: Simon & Schuster, 1992. A sobering, in-depth expose of the darker side of both Fidel Castro and the state system, including controversial topics such as drug trading.

Quirk, Robert E. *Fidel Castro.* New York: W.W. Norton, 1993. A detailed, none-too-complimentary profile of the Cuban leader.

Szulc, Tad. *Fidel: A Critical Portrait.* New York: Morrow, 1986. A riveting profile of the astounding life of this larger-than-life figure. The book is full of never-before-revealed tidbits. A marvelous read and the best of the biographies on Castro.

Travel Literature

Baker, Christopher P. *Mi Moto Fidel: Motorcycling Through Castro's Cuba.* (forthcoming). Riveting and self-deprecating tales of the author's 11,000-km adventure by motorcycle through Cuba.

Gébler, Carlo. *Driving Through Cuba.* New York: Simon & Schuster, 1988. The tale of a three-month sojourn through Cuba by car. Full of wry, often acerbic, commentary. Strong historical analyses, but incomplete and at times naive interpretations of Cuban society.

Hazard, Samuel. *Cuba with Pen and Pencil.* Hartford, CT: Hartford Publishing, 1871.

Hungry Wolf, Adolf. *Letters from Cuba.* Skookumchuck, BC: Candian Caboose Press, 1996. A tender and sympathetic account of the author's journeys through Cuba in fulfillment of his passion for steam trains. This collection of "letters home" portrays the beauty of the island and its people in a compellingly sensitive tone.

Iyer, Pico. *Falling off the Map.* New York: Alfred A. Knopf, 1993. Presents a far rosier picture than the author's dour novel *Cuba in the Night*

Miller, Tom. *Trading with the Enemy: A Yankee Travels Through Castro's Cuba.* New York, Atheneum, 1992. A fabulous travelogue told by a famous author who lived in Cuba for almost a year. Thoughtful, engaging, insightful, compassionate, and told in rich narrative

Ryan, Alan, ed. *The Reader's Companion to Cuba.* New York: Harcourt Brace & Company, 1997. This anthology offers two-dozen eyewitness "reports" from visitors to Cuban shores spanning two centuries. It includes extracts ranging from mob-lawyer Frank Ragano's recollections of the Mafia in Havana to Tommy Lasorda's remembrances of his years playing in the Cuban leagues. Ryan provides his own astute interpretations.

Samuelson, Arnold. *With Hemingway: A Year in Key West and Cuba.* Maine: Thorndike Press, 1984. The true-life tale of a young Midwestern farm boy who wanted to become a writer and was hired to guard Hemingway's *Pilar.* For a year, he accompanied "E.H." on fishing excursions around Key West and Cuba, recording this diary, in which he captures Hemingway "off-guard and all-too-human."

Other

Agee, Philip. *Inside the Company: CIA Diary.* New York: Bantam Books, 1975. This sobering work details the mission to discredit Cuba, including dirty tricks—disinformation campaigns, bombings, political assassinations, etc.—employed by the CIA against Latin America leftists. Told by a CIA "deep-cover" agent who eventually resigned because he "finally understood how much suffering [the CIA] was causing."

Benjamin, Medea, and Peter Rosset. *The Greening of the Revolution.* Melbourne: Ocean Press, 1994. A detailed account of Cuba's turn to a system of organic agriculture told by two noted authorities on the subject.

Benjamin, Medea, Joseph Collins, and Michael Scott. *No Free Lunch: Food and Revolution in Cuba.* San Francisco: Institute for Food and Development Policy, 1984.

Cabrera Infante, Guillermo. *¡Mea Cuba!* New York: Farrar Straus Giroux, 1994. An acerbic, indignant, raw, wistful, and brilliant set of essays in which the author pours out his bile at the Castro regime.

Howard, Christopher. *Living and Investing in the New Cuba.* Miami: Costa Rica Books, 1999. The first and only guide to living, making money, and the good life in Cuba. Indispensable for anyone eyeing Cuba as an investment opportunity or a place to live.

LaFray, Joyce. *¡Cuba Cocina!* New York: Hearst Books, 1994. A sweeping compilation of Cuban recipes, both classic and *nuevo cubano,* from Floridian Cuban restaurants and such famous Havana restaurants as Bodeguita del Medio. Should be compulsory reading in Cuba.

Murray, Mary. *Cruel and Unusual Punishment: The US Blockade Against Cuba.* Melbourne:

Ocean Press, 1992. Details the US embargo from its inception in 1960 to today. Presents Cuba's perspectives.

Padula, Alfred, and Lois Smith. *Sex and Revolution: Women in Socialist Cuba.* New York: Oxford University Press, 1996. An examination of Cuba's attempt to conceptualize, prioritize, and implement sexual equality, offering an assessment of the successes, failures, and dilemmas of that process.

Randall, Margaret. *Women in Cuba: Twenty Years Later.* Union City, NY: Smyrna Press, 1981. An important book for an understanding of Cuban society and the goals of the Revolution, full of examples of how a society can marshal its resources to undermine centuries of female subjugation.

Rius. *Cuba for Beginners: An Illustrated Guide for Americans.* New York: Pathfinder Press, 1970. The Mexican leftist caricaturist presents the internationalist view of Cuba-US relations with comic inventiveness. Hilarious depictions of Uncle Sam's machinations and misadventures.

Senzel, Howard. *Baseball and the Cold War.* New York: Harcourt Brace Jovanovich, 1977.

Thurston, Charles W. *In From the Cold: How to Do Business with Cuba.* New York: Journal of Commerce, 1995. Detailed information on current opportunities in sectors ranging from agriculture to transportation. Lists of useful Cuban, US, and foreign private- and public-sector contacts.

Walker, Alice. *In Search of Our Mother's Gardens.* New York: Harcourt Books, 1983. This biography of experiences includes a chapter in which the noted novelist and activist explores her feelings about and recounts her experiences in Cuba.

VIDEOS

Cuba. An 80-minute video that looks at the lives of Cubans. US$25, plus US$2 shipping, from

John Holod, 140 Mullan Rd. W, Superior, MI 59872.

Cuba Va: The Challenge of the Next Generation. A fascinating 60-minute documentary released in 1993 captures the vigor and diversity of Cuban youth—the politically committed and the alienated—who express their divergent perspectives on the Revolution, the Special Period, and the future. Copies cost US$95 from Cuba Va Video Project, 12 Liberty St., San Francisco, CA 94110, tel. (415) 282-1812, fax (415) 282-1798.

Gay Cuba. This one-hour documentary takes a candid look at one of Cuba's most controversial human rights issues: the treatment of the gay and lesbian people in Cuba since the Revolution. Order from Frameline, 346 Ninth St., San Francisco, CA 94103, tel. (415) 703-8654, fax (415) 861-1404, e-mail: frameline@aol.com, website: www.frameline.org.

Havana Nagila: The Jews of Cuba. An hour-long look at the history of Jews in Cuba during five centuries. Copies can be ordered from Schnitzki & Stone, 819 W. Roseburg Ave. #240, Modesto, CA 95350, tel. (209) 575-1775, fax (209) 575-1404.

Workers Democracy in Cuba. This 30-minute video records the 17th National Congress of the Cuban Workers Federation, in April 1996. US$25, plus US$3 postage, from International Peace for Cuba Appeal, 2489 Mission St #28, San Francisco, CA 94110, tel. (415) 821-7575, fax (415) 821-5782.

ACCOMMODATIONS INDEX

FOOD INDEX

INDEX

ARCHITECTURE

Alamar: 161-163
Alameda de Paula: 99
Albear, General Francisco de: 16, 108
alcohol: general discussion 241-242; daiquiri 78; Museo de Ron 99, 209; shopping for 208-209; see also Bars/Nightclubs/Entertainment; rum; specific place
ALM Antillean Airlines: 289
Alonso, Alicia: 125-126
American-Joint Jewish Distribution Committee: 123
amusement parks: Jalisco Parque 200; Parque Lenin 200; Playas del Este 166; Tarará 164
anfiteatro: 147
Angulo, Gonzalo Pérez de: 7, 82
Antilles Express: 307
antiques: general discussion 201; automobiles 91, 150

AOM: 267, 289
aparthotels: 167, 220; see also Accommodations
aqua bikes: 140
aquariums: Acuario Nacional 138; National Aquarium 192; Parque Lenin 147
aqueducts: 7, 15, 19, 82, 126
Arab culture: Casa del Árabe 91, 192; food 247-248; Islam 91
arachnids: 325
Árbol de la Fraternidad Americana: 72
archaeological sites: city walls 100; Cortina de Valdés 80; Gabinete de la Arqueología 80; organized tours 301
Argentina: Cuban tourist bureau 314; embassies/consulates 304; food 257; travel insurance 327
Armada, Chago: 203

Armería 19 de Abril: 94
Arocha, Rene: 198
Arrojo, Rolando: 198
Arroyo Naranjo: 64, 146-151
Artesanías Para Turismo Taller: 96
ARTEX: 277
arts and crafts: Artesanías Para Turismo Taller 96; Cortina de Valdés 80; shopping for 201-206; see also Art Venues
Aseguradora del Turismo La Isla S.A.: 328, 330
Asamblea Provincial de Poder Popular: 77, 93
Asia: embassies/consulates 304; Museo de Asia 94; Oriental food 248, 251, 258-260; travel from 270-271
Asistur S.A.: 288, 307, 328
Asociación Cubana de Artesana Artistas: 205

ART VENUES

general discussion: 189-191, 201-206, 276
Art of Our Americas: 190
Asociación Cubana de Artesana Artistas: 205
Casa de África: 94-95
Casa de Benito Juárez: 94
Casa de las Américas: 125, 205
Casa de los Condes de Jaruco: 204
Casa Guayasamú: 95
Centro de Desarrollo de las Artes Visuales: 96, 189, 204-205
Centro Gráfico de Reproducciones Para el Turismo: 158
Centro Nacional de Escuelas de Arte: 169
Centro Wilfredo Lam: 83, 190-191, 205
Cuban Art Space: 189
Estudio Galerai Los Oficios: 93
Fondo Cubano de Bienes Culturales: 95, 202, 204
Galería de la Casona: 204-205
Galeria de la Plaza Vieja: 205

Galería del Arte Amelia Peláez: 146-147
Galeria del Arte galiano: 190
Galeria del Arte Latinoamericano: 190
Galería del Centro Gallego: 204
Galería Forma: 190, 205
Galeria Francisco Javier Baez: 190
Galeria Habana: 190
Galeria Haydee Santamaría: 125, 190
Galeria Horacio Ruíz: 190, 205
Galeria Kahlo: 114
Galería la Acacia: 190, 204
Galeria Mariano: 190, 205
Galeria Nelson Dominguez: 190
Galeria Pequeño Formato: 95
Galeria Plaza Vieja: 190
Galeria Roberto Diago: 190
Galeria UNEAC: 190
Galería Victor Manuel: 82, 190, 204
Galeria Villena: 88, 206
Havana Biennale: 172, 191
Iglesia de San Francisco de Paula: 99

Instituto Superior de Arte: 141, 202
Museo de Arte Colonial: 66, 82
Museo de Arte Religioso: 93
Museo de Artes Decorativas: 66, 124-125
Museo de Asia: 94
Museo de Simón Bolívar: 94
Museo Nacional de Bellas Artes: 67, 74-75
National Arts Museum: 191
Nelson Domínguez Experimental Graphics Art Gallery: 82
organized tours: 276
Palacio de Artesanía Cubana: 205
Taller de Pintura: 205
Taller de Seregráfia Rene Portocarrero: 190
Taller Experimental de la Gráfica: 82, 190, 204
Unión Nacional de Escritores y Artistes de Cuba: 124, 191-192

BARS/NIGHTCLUBS/ENTERTAINMENT

EVENTS

HOMES/MANSIONS/PALACES

KID STUFF

MUSEUMS

general discussion: 66-67, 189-191
Casa Abel Santamaría: 121-122
Casa de las Américas: 125
Casa Guayasamú: 95
Casa Natal de José Martí: 101
Castillo de San Carlos de la Cabaña: 106
Che Guevara Pioneer Palace: 147
ExpoCuba: 150
Finca Vigía: 151, 153
Granma Memorial: 64, 76
Instituto de la Historia de la Ciudad: 73
Monumento y Museo José Martí: 64-65, 133
Museo Antropológico Montane: 66, 123
Museo Carpentier: 84
Museo Casa Abel Santamaría: 66
Museo Casa Natal de José Martí: 66
Museo Che Guevara: 106
Museo de Arte Colonial: 66, 82
Museo de Arte Religioso: 93
Museo de Artes Decorativas: 66, 124-125
Museo de Asia: 94

Museo de Autos Antiguo: 91
Museo de Bomberos: 74
Museo de Ciencias Naturales: 88
Museo de Finanzas: 90
Museo de Fortificaciones y Armas: 106
Museo de História del Deportivo: 133
Museo de História Naturales Felipe Poey: 66, 123-124
Museo de la Alfabetización: 143
Museo de la Ciudad de la Habana: 66, 86
Museo de la Danza: 125
Museo de la Educación: 66, 90
Museo del Aire: 142
Museo de la Música: 77, 188
Museo de la Perfumeria: 66
Museo de la Revolución: 64, 76
Museo de Máximo Gómez: 126
Museo de Ministerio del Interior: 139-140
Museo de Plata: 88-89
Museo de Pueblo Combatiente: 67
Museo de Ron: 99
Museo de Simón Bolívar: 94
Museo Ernest Hemingway: 64, 66

Museo Histórico de Guanabacao: 157
Museo Histórico de las Ciencias Carlos Finlay: 66, 96
Museo Lezana Lima: 109
Museo Marcha del Pueblo Combatiente: 139
Museo Máximo Gómez: 67
Museo Municipal de Fegla: 67
Museo Municipal de Guanabacoa: 67
Museo Municipal de Regla: 156
Museo Nacional de Aire: 67
Museo Nacional de Bellas Artes: 67, 74-75
Museo Nacional de Cerámica: 67
Museo Nacional de Música: 67
Museo Napoleónico: 67, 124
Museo Navegación: 103
Museo Numismático: 67, 91
Museo Postal Cubano: 67, 133
Museo y Archivo de la Música: 66
Museo y Farmácia Tequechel: 90
Museo y Taller de Cerámica: 87
Museum of Fine Arts: 192
Museum of Tobacco: 93-94

Nelson Domínguez Experimental Graphics Art Gallery: 82
The Netherlands: embassies/consulates 304; KLM 267; Netherlands Caribbean Banking 306; travel from 267
newspapers/magazines: 133, 169-170, 311-312, 314-315
New Zealand: maps of Cuba 317; travel from 271
Nicaragua: embassies/consulates 304; travel from 270
Nina Cruise Lines: 272
Noche en la Plaza de la Catedral: 80, 171, 173
Norwegian embassies/consulates: 304

Nouvelle Frontieres: 272
Nuevo Vedado: 134-135

O
Ocampo, Sebastian de: 6
Oficina del Historidades de la Ciudad: 89
Oficina Nacional de Estádisticas: 314
Old Havana: *see* Habana Viejo
Old Man and the Sea Fishing Tournament: 163
olympics: Academía Gimnástico 71; baseball 198; International Conference on Olympic Style Boxing 200
Omnibus Metropolitano: 280
online service: general discussion

311; web sites/internet addresses 315-317, 334; *see also specific organization; place*
Opciones: 312
open-air markets: 203-204
Operation 40: 139-140
Operation Mongoose: 67, 139
opium dens: 112-113
opticians: 322
Óptima Miramar: 322
Orejón y Gastón, Don Francisco: 12
Organización de Pioneeros José Martí: 77
Oriental food: 248, 251, 258-260
Oriental Park: 20-21, 28
orishas: 60
O'Rourke, P.J.: 4, 132

SPORTFISHING

TRAVEL AGENTS/TOUR OPERATORS

ABOUT THE AUTHOR

Christopher P. Baker was born and raised in Yorkshire, England. After graduating with honors from University College, London, with a B.A. in Geography (including two Sahara research expeditions and an exchange program at Krakow University, Poland), he earned master's degrees in Latin American Studies from Liverpool University and Education from the Institute of Education, London University. He began his writing career in 1978 as Contributing Editor on Latin America for *Land & Liberty,* a London-based political journal. In 1980, he received a Scripps-Howard Foundation Scholarship in Journalism to attend the University of California, Berkeley. Since 1983, he has made his living as a professional travel and natural science writer. His work has appeared in more than 150 publications worldwide, including *Newsweek,* BBC's *World Magazine, National Wildlife, Islands, Elle, GEO,* and the *Los Angeles Times.*

For seven years, Baker was president of British Pride Tours, which he founded. He has escorted group tours to New Zealand, Hong Kong, Korea, England, and Cuba. He appears frequently on radio and television talk shows and as a guest-lecturer aboard cruise ships throughout the Caribbean and farther afield. His other books include Avalon Travel Publishing's *Cuba Handbook* and *Costa Rica Handbook, National Geographic Traveler's Costa Rica,* Lonely Planet's *Jamaica* and *Bahamas and Turks & Caicos,* the *Passport Illustrated Guide to Jamaica,* plus *Mi Moto Fidel: Motorcycling Through Castro's Cuba,* a literary travelogue to be published by National Geographic in October 2000. He also wrote the text for *Cuba: Within Sight, Beyond Reach,* a coffee-table book by photographer Jim Krantz, and has contributed chapters to Tehabi Books' *Voyages: The Romance of Cruising,* The Discovery Channel's *Rainforests,* Frommer's *America on Wheels: California & Nevada, Travelers' Tales: Food,* Nature Company's *World Travel: A Guide to International Ecojourneys, Writer's Digest Beginner's Guide to Getting Published,* and *I Should Have Stayed Home.*

Baker is a member of the Society of American Travel Writers and National Writers Union and has been honored with several awards for outstanding writing, among them the prestigious Lowell Thomas Travel Journalism Award (four times, including "Best Travel News Investigative Reporter") and the 1995 Benjamin Franklin "Best Travel Guide" award for *Costa Rica Handbook.* In 1998, the Caribbean Tourism Organization named him "Travel Journalist of the Year." He lives in California.

For more, visit the author's website: www.travelguidebooks.com.

LOSE YOURSELF IN THE EXPERIENCE, NOT THE CROWD

For more than 25 years, Moon Travel Handbooks have been the guidebooks of choice fc adventurous travelers. Our award-winning Handbook series provides focused, comprehensive coverage of distinct destinations all over the world. Each Handbook is like an entire bookcase cultural insight and introductory information in one portable volume. Our goal at Moon is to give trav elers all the background and practical information they'll need for an extraordinary travel experience

The following pages include a complete list of Handbooks, covering North America and Hawai Mexico, Latin America and the Caribbean, and Asia and the Pacific.To purchase Moon Trave Handbooks, check your local bookstore or check our Web site at **www.moon.com** for currer prices and editions.

"An in-depth dunk into the land, the people and their history, arts, and politics."
—*Student Travels*

"I consider these books to be superior to Lonely Planet. When Moon produces a book it is more humorous, incisive, and off-beat."
—*Toronto Sun*

"Outdoor enthusiasts gravitate to the well-written Moon Travel Handbooks. In addition to politically correct historic and cultural features, the series focuses on flora, fauna and outdoor recreation. Maps and meticulous directions also are a trademark of Moon guides."
—*Houston Chronicle*

"Moon [Travel Handbooks] . . . bring a healthy respect to the places they investigate. Best of all, they provide a host of odd nuggets that give a place texture and prod the wary traveler from the beaten path. The finest are written with such care and insight they deserve listing as literature."
—*American Geographical Society*

"Moon Travel Handbooks offer in-depth historical essays and useful maps, enhanced by a sense of humor and a neat, compact format."
—*Swing*

"Perfect for the more adventurous, these are long on history, sightseeing and nitty-gritty information and very price-specific."
—*Columbus Dispatch*

"Moon guides manage to be comprehensive and countercultural at the same time . . . Handbooks are packed with maps, photographs, drawings, and sidebars that constitute a college-level introduction to each country's history, culture, people, and crafts."
—*National Geographic Traveler*

"Few travel guides do a better job helping travelers create their own itineraries than the Moon Travel Handbook series. The authors have a knack for homing in on the essentials."
—**Colorado Springs** *Gazette Telegraph*

MEXICO

These books will delight the armchair traveler, aid the undecided person in selecting a destination, and guide the seasoned road warrior looking for lesser-known hideaways."

—*Mexican Meanderings* Newsletter

From tourist traps to off-the-beaten track hideaways, these guides offer consistent, accurate details without pretension."

—*Foreign Service Journal*

Archaeological Mexico	**$19.95**
Andrew Coe	420 pages, 27 maps
Baja Handbook	**$16.95**
Joe Cummings	540 pages, 46 maps
Cabo Handbook	**$14.95**
Joe Cummings	270 pages, 17 maps
Cancún Handbook	**$14.95**
Chicki Mallan	240 pages, 25 maps
Colonial Mexico	**$18.95**
Chicki Mallan	400 pages, 38 maps
Mexico Handbook	**$21.95**
Joe Cummings and Chicki Mallan	1,200 pages, 201 maps
Northern Mexico Handbook	**$17.95**
Joe Cummings	610 pages, 69 maps
Pacific Mexico Handbook	**$17.95**
Bruce Whipperman	580 pages, 68 maps
Puerto Vallarta Handbook	**$14.95**
Bruce Whipperman	330 pages, 36 maps
Yucatán Handbook	**$16.95**
Chicki Mallan	400 pages, 52 maps

Beyond question, the most comprehensive Mexican resources available for those who prefer deep travel to shallow tourism. But don't worry, the fiesta-fun stuff's all here too."

—*New York Daily News*

LATIN AMERICA
AND THE CARIBBEAN

"Solidly packed with practical information and full of significant cultural asides that will enlighten you on the whys and wherefores of things you might easily see but not easily grasp."

—Boston Glob

Belize Handbook	$15.9
Chicki Mallan and Patti Lange	390 pages, 45 map
Caribbean Vacations	$18.9
Karl Luntta	910 pages, 64 map
Costa Rica Handbook	$19.9
Christopher P. Baker	780 pages, 73 map
Cuba Handbook	$19.9
Christopher P. Baker	740 pages, 70 map
Dominican Republic Handbook	$15.9
Gaylord Dold	420 pages, 24 map
Ecuador Handbook	$16.9
Julian Smith	450 pages, 43 map
Honduras Handbook	$15.9
Chris Humphrey	330 pages, 40 map
Jamaica Handbook	$15.9
Karl Luntta	330 pages, 17 map
Virgin Islands Handbook	$13.9
Karl Luntta	220 pages, 19 map

NORTH AMERICA AND HAWAII

"These domestic guides convey the same sense of exoticism that their foreign counterparts do, making home-country travel seem like far-flung adventure."

—Sierra Magazin

Alaska-Yukon Handbook	$17.9
Deke Castleman and Don Pitcher	530 pages, 92 map
Alberta and the Northwest Territories Handbook	$18.9
Andrew Hempstead	520 pages, 79 map
Arizona Handbook	$18.9
Bill Weir	600 pages, 36 map
Atlantic Canada Handbook	$18.9
Mark Morris	490 pages, 60 map
Big Island of Hawaii Handbook	$15.9
J.D. Bisignani	390 pages, 25 map
Boston Handbook	$13.9
Jeff Perk	200 pages, 20 map
British Columbia Handbook	$16.9
Jane King and Andrew Hempstead	430 pages, 69 map

Canadian Rockies Handbook	**$14.95**
Andrew Hempstead	220 pages, 22 maps
Colorado Handbook	**$17.95**
Stephen Metzger	480 pages, 46 maps
Georgia Handbook	**$17.95**
Kap Stann	380 pages, 44 maps
Grand Canyon Handbook	**$14.95**
Bill Weir	220 pages, 10 maps
Hawaii Handbook	**$19.95**
J.D. Bisignani	1,030 pages, 88 maps
Honolulu-Waikiki Handbook	**$14.95**
J.D. Bisignani	360 pages, 20 maps
Idaho Handbook	**$18.95**
Don Root	610 pages, 42 maps
Kauai Handbook	**$15.95**
J.D. Bisignani	320 pages, 23 maps
Los Angeles Handbook	**$16.95**
Kim Weir	370 pages, 15 maps
Maine Handbook	**$18.95**
Kathleen M. Brandes	660 pages, 27 maps
Massachusetts Handbook	**$18.95**
Jeff Perk	600 pages, 23 maps
Maui Handbook	**$15.95**
J.D. Bisignani	450 pages, 37 maps
Michigan Handbook	**$15.95**
Tina Lassen	360 pages, 32 maps
Montana Handbook	**$17.95**
Judy Jewell and W.C. McRae	490 pages, 52 maps
Nevada Handbook	**$18.95**
Deke Castleman	530 pages, 40 maps
New Hampshire Handbook	**$18.95**
Steve Lantos	500 pages, 18 maps
New Mexico Handbook	**$15.95**
Stephen Metzger	360 pages, 47 maps
New York Handbook	**$19.95**
Christiane Bird	780 pages, 95 maps
New York City Handbook	**$13.95**
Christiane Bird	300 pages, 20 maps
North Carolina Handbook	**$14.95**
Rob Hirtz and Jenny Daughtry Hirtz	320 pages, 27 maps
Northern California Handbook	**$19.95**
Kim Weir	800 pages, 50 maps
Ohio Handbook	**$15.95**
David K. Wright	340 pages, 18 maps
Oregon Handbook	**$17.95**
Stuart Warren and Ted Long Ishikawa	590 pages, 34 maps

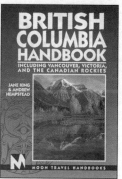

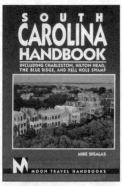

Pennsylvania Handbook	**$18.95**
Joanne Miller	448 pages, 40 maps
Road Trip USA	**$24.00**
Jamie Jensen	940 pages, 175 maps
Road Trip USA Getaways: Chicago	**$9.95**
	60 pages, 1 map
Road Trip USA Getaways: Seattle	**$9.95**
	60 pages, 1 map
Santa Fe-Taos Handbook	**$13.95**
Stephen Metzger	160 pages, 13 maps
South Carolina Handbook	**$16.95**
Mike Sigalas	400 pages, 20 maps
Southern California Handbook	**$19.95**
Kim Weir	720 pages, 26 maps
Tennessee Handbook	**$17.95**
Jeff Bradley	530 pages, 42 maps
Texas Handbook	**$18.95**
Joe Cummings	690 pages, 70 maps
Utah Handbook	**$17.95**
Bill Weir and W.C. McRae	490 pages, 40 maps
Virginia Handbook	**$15.95**
Julian Smith	410 pages, 37 maps
Washington Handbook	**$19.95**
Don Pitcher	840 pages, 111 maps
Wisconsin Handbook	**$18.95**
Thomas Huhti	590 pages, 69 maps
Wyoming Handbook	**$17.95**
Don Pitcher	610 pages, 80 maps

ASIA AND THE PACIFIC

"Scores of maps, detailed practical info down to business hours of small-town libraries. You can't beat the Asian titles for sheer heft. (The) series is sort of an American Lonely Planet, with better writing but fewer titles. (The) individual voice of researchers comes through."

—*Travel & Leisure*

Australia Handbook	**$21.95**
Marael Johnson, Andrew Hempstead,	
and Nadina Purdon	940 pages, 141 maps
Bali Handbook	**$19.95**
Bill Dalton	750 pages, 54 maps
Fiji Islands Handbook	**$14.95**
David Stanley	350 pages, 42 maps
Hong Kong Handbook	**$16.95**
Kerry Moran	378 pages, 49 maps

Indonesia Handbook	**$25.00**
Bill Dalton	1,380 pages, 249 maps
Micronesia Handbook	**$16.95**
Neil M. Levy	340 pages, 70 maps
Nepal Handbook	**$18.95**
Kerry Moran	490 pages, 51 maps
New Zealand Handbook	**$19.95**
Jane King	620 pages, 81 maps
Outback Australia Handbook	**$18.95**
Marael Johnson	450 pages, 57 maps
Philippines Handbook	**$17.95**
Peter Harper and Laurie Fullerton	670 pages, 116 maps
Singapore Handbook	**$15.95**
Carl Parkes	350 pages, 29 maps
South Korea Handbook	**$19.95**
Robert Nilsen	820 pages, 141 maps
South Pacific Handbook	**$24.00**
David Stanley	920 pages, 147 maps
Southeast Asia Handbook	**$21.95**
Carl Parkes	1,080 pages, 204 maps
Tahiti Handbook	**$15.95**
David Stanley	450 pages, 51 maps
Thailand Handbook	**$19.95**
Carl Parkes	860 pages, 142 maps
Vietnam, Cambodia & Laos Handbook	**$18.95**
Michael Buckley	760 pages, 116 maps

OTHER GREAT TITLES FROM MOON

"For hardy wanderers, few guides come more highly recommended than the Handbooks. They include good maps, steer clear of fluff and flackery, and offer plenty of money-saving tips. They also give you the kind of information that visitors to strange lands—on any budget— need to survive."

—*US News & World Report*

Moon Handbook	**$10.00**
Carl Koppeschaar	150 pages, 8 maps
The Practical Nomad: How to Travel Around the World	**$17.95**
Edward Hasbrouck	580 pages
Staying Healthy in Asia, Africa, and Latin America	**$11.95**
Dirk Schroeder	230 pages, 4 maps

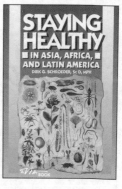

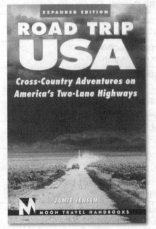

U.S.~METRIC CONVERSION

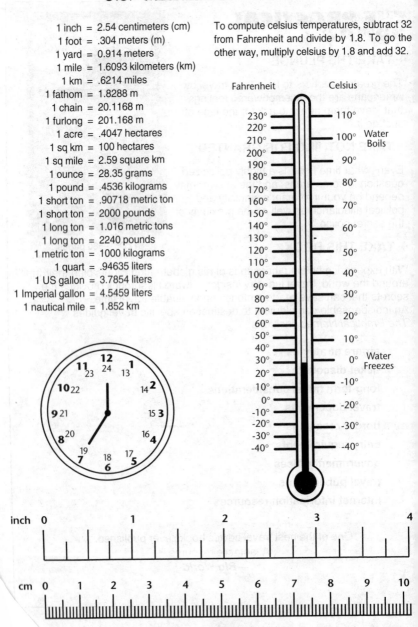

1 inch = 2.54 centimeters (cm)
1 foot = .304 meters (m)
1 yard = 0.914 meters
1 mile = 1.6093 kilometers (km)
1 km = .6214 miles
1 fathom = 1.8288 m
1 chain = 20.1168 m
1 furlong = 201.168 m
1 acre = .4047 hectares
1 sq km = 100 hectares
1 sq mile = 2.59 square km
1 ounce = 28.35 grams
1 pound = .4536 kilograms
1 short ton = .90718 metric ton
1 short ton = 2000 pounds
1 long ton = 1.016 metric tons
1 long ton = 2240 pounds
1 metric ton = 1000 kilograms
1 quart = .94635 liters
1 US gallon = 3.7854 liters
1 Imperial gallon = 4.5459 liters
1 nautical mile = 1.852 km

To compute celsius temperatures, subtract 32 from Fahrenheit and divide by 1.8. To go the other way, multiply celsius by 1.8 and add 32.